EYEWITNESS TRAVEL

FLORIDA

DK

LONDON, NEW YORK,
MELBOURNE, MUNICH AND DELHI
www.dk.com

Project Editor Emily Hatchwell

Art Editors Janice English, Robert Purnell

EDITORS Freddy Hamilton, Jane Oliver, Naomi Peck, Andrew Szudek

DESIGNERS Jill Andrews, Frank Cawley, Dawn Davies-Cook, Eli Estaugh,
Simon Oon, Edmund White

Contributors

Ruth and Eric Bailey, Richard Cawthorne, David Dick, Guy Mansell,
Fred Mawer, Emma Stanford, Phyllis Steinberg, Ian Williams

Photographers

Max Alexander, Dave King,
Stephen Whitehorne, Linda Whitwam

Illustrators

Richard Bonson, Richard Draper, Chris Orr & Assocs,
Pat Thorne, John Woodcock

Printed and bound by South China Printing Company Limited, China

First American Edition, 1997

14 15 16 17 10 9 8 7 6 5 4 3 2 1

Published in the United States by:
Dorling Kindersley Limited, 80 Strand, London WC2R 0RL, UK

**Reprinted with revisions 1999, 2000, 2001, 2002, 2004, 2005,
2006, 2008, 2010, 2012, 2014**

Copyright 1997, 2014 © Dorling Kindersley Limited, London

A Penguin Random House Company

ISSN 1542-1554

ISBN 978-1-46541-183-9

This book makes reference to various trademarks, marks, and registered marks
owned by the Disney Company and Disney Enterprises, Inc.

Throughout this book, floors are referred to in accordance with American usage,
ie the "first floor" is at ground level.

MIX
Paper from
responsible sources
FSC™ C018179

Front cover main image: Aerial view of Miami Beach, Florida

◀ Renovated Art Deco hotels on the Miami South Beach Strip.

Contents

A Tiffany window in
St Augustine *(see p217)*

Introducing
Florida

Rollerbladers, a common feature
of Florida's seaside resorts

Dolphins entertaining the crowds at Sea World *(see pp180–83)*

A woman taking in the view from a snow-white Florida beach

Tourists enjoying the traditional Key West sunset *(see p304)*

Villa Vizcaya, Miami

HOW TO USE THIS GUIDE

This guide helps you get the most from your visit to Florida. It provides expert recommendations as well as detailed practical information. *Introducing Florida* maps the whole state and sets Florida in its historical and cultural context. *Miami Area by Area* and the six regional chapters describe all the important sights, using maps, pictures, and illustrations. Features cover topics from architecture to food and sport. Hotel and restaurant recommendations can be found in *Travelers' Needs*, while the *Survival Guide* includes tips on everything from transportation to safety.

Miami Area by Area

Miami is divided into three sightseeing areas. Each has its own chapter, which opens with a list of the sights described. A fourth chapter, *Farther Afield*, covers outlying sights. All sights are numbered and plotted on an *Area Map*. Descriptions of each sight follow the map's numerical order, making sights easy to locate within the chapter.

Sights at a Glance lists the chapter's sights by category: Museums and Galleries, Streets and Neighborhoods, Historic Buildings, for example.

1 Area Map
For easy reference, the sights are numbered and located on a map. Sights are also shown on the Miami Street Finder on pages 100–105.

All pages relating to Miami have red thumb tabs.

A locator map shows where you are in relation to other areas of the city center.

2 Street-by-Street Map
This gives a bird's-eye view of the heart of each sightseeing area.

A suggested route for a walk is shown in red.

Stars indicate the sights that no visitor should miss.

3 Detailed information
All the sights in Miami are described individually, with addresses, opening hours, and other practical information. The key to the symbols used in the information block is found on the back flap.

Florida Area by Area

Apart from Miami, Florida has been divided into six regions, each of which has a separate chapter. The most interesting cities, towns, and places to visit in each area are numbered on a *Regional Map*.

1 Introduction
The landscape, history, and character of each region is described here, showing how the area has developed over the centuries and what it offers to the visitor today.

Each region of Florida can be quickly identified by its color coding, shown on the inside front cover.

2 Regional Map
This shows the main road network and gives an illustrated overview of the whole region. All entries are numbered, and there are also useful tips on getting around by car and public transportation.

3 Detailed information
All the important towns and other places to visit are described individually. They are listed in order, following the numbering given on the Regional Map. Within each town or city there is detailed information on important buildings and other sights.

The Visitors' Checklist provides all the practical information you will need to plan your visit to all the top sights.

4 Florida's top sights
These are given two or more full pages. Historic buildings are dissected to reveal their interiors; art galleries have color-coded floor plans to help you locate the best exhibits; theme parks are shown in a bird's-eye view, with the top attractions picked out.

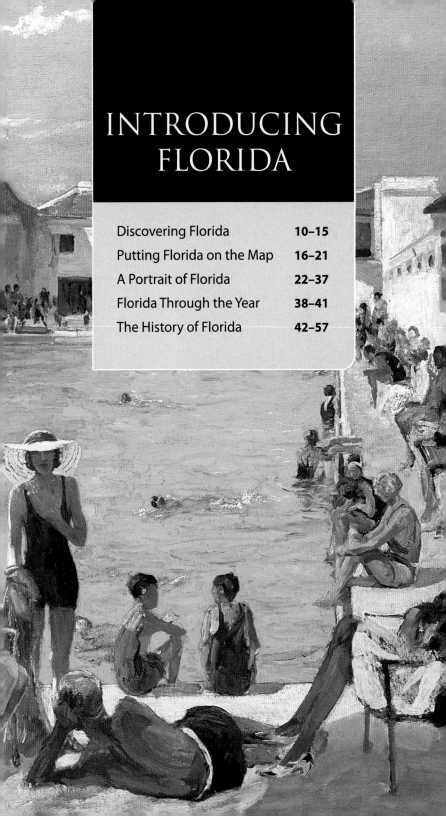

INTRODUCING
FLORIDA

DISCOVERING FLORIDA

Florida spans two time zones and it takes over twelve hours of driving to get from Key West to Pensacola. This state is packed with things to see and do, and these itineraries sample some of the best of what Florida has to offer. They focus on areas within an easy drive of the two major gateway cities for air travel, Miami and Orlando, keeping long drives between stops to a minimum. A two-day tour of Miami introduces you to this vibrant city, while a week-long tour encompassing Miami, the Florida Keys, and the Everglades immerses you in tropical Florida. A five-day tour in Orlando and the Space Coast is an easy add-on to a planned trip to the theme parks, or a new route to explore in a popular destination. A two-week tour sweeps through Central and North Florida, introducing you to natural and cultural attractions. Use these tours to inspire your next Florida adventure.

The Daytona International Speedway
This is an adrenalin-fueled day out, featuring exciting racing events from Superbike and Motocross to the fast and furious NASCAR races.

Two Weeks in Central and North Florida

- Savor the views from **Bok Tower Gardens** atop the highest accessible point in the Florida peninsula.
- Discover the impressive legacy of circus magnate John Ringling in **Sarasota**.
- Watch mermaids perform underwater acrobatics at **Weeki Wachee**.
- Splash in crystalline springs in the **Ocala National Forest**.
- Experience the world of racing at the **Daytona International Speedway**.
- See the remains of a 1790s Loyalist plantation on **Fort George Island**.

One Week in South Florida

- Wander shaded paths in **Miami's** tropical gardens.
- Drive America's most scenic highway, the Overseas Highway, to **Key West**.
- Snorkel or swim the coral reefs of the **Florida Keys**.
- Be amazed by the vast landscapes of the **Everglades** and **Big Cypress Swamp**.
- See Florida history through the eyes of the **Seminole** and **Miccosukee**.
- Walk among ancient cypress trees in **Corkscrew Swamp Sanctuary**.

0 kilometers 80
0 miles 40

Key

— Central and Northern Florida Tour
— Southern Florida Tour
— Orlando and Space Coast Tour

◄ Cars lining the main street and foreshore of the popular Daytona Beach in 1926

Fort George Island
Mayport
Jacksonville
St Johns
St Augustine
Anastasia Island
Fort Matanzas
National Monument
Marjorie
Kinnan Rawlings
Historic State Park
Flagler Beach
Bulow Plantation
Ruins State Park
Ormond Beach
Daytona Beach
Silver
Springs
Ocala National
Forest
Ponce de Leon
Inlet Lighthouse

Winter Park
Orlando
Pointe
Orlando
Arabian
Nights
Gatorland
Kissimmee
Lake
Toho
Merritt Island
National Wildlife
Refuge
Cocoa
Village
Cocoa
Beach
Banana River
Kennedy
Space
Center

0 miles 10
0 km 10

Orlando

Melbourne

Lake
Wales

Lake
Okeechobee

Corkscrew
Swamp
Sanctuary
Billie Swamp
Safari
Ah-Tah-Thi-Ki
Museum
Naples
Big Cypress Seminole
Reservation
Fakahatchee
Strand Preserve
State Park
Big Cypress
National
Preserve
Miccosukee
Indian Village
Ten
Thousand
Islands
Shark Valley
Miami
Coral Gables
Biscayne Bay
Florida City
Fairchild Tropical
Gardens
Everglades
National Park
**Key
Largo**
John Pennekamp
Coral Reef
State Park
Flamingo
National Key
Deer Refuge
Marathon
**Key
West**
Big Pine
Key

Five Days in Orlando and the Space Coast

- Visit **Cocoa Beach**, the heart of Florida's surf culture.

- Come nose-to-nose with a Space Shuttle at **Kennedy Space Center**.

- See the finest collection of Tiffany glass in the world in **Winter Park**.

- Discover Florida's largest rose garden in Orlando's **Leu Gardens**.

- Photograph colorful native birds nesting at **Gatorland**.

Key Largo
Take a boat trip and snorkel amidst the abundant underwater sealife and kaleidoscopic colours of Key Largo's coral reef.

Two Days in Miami

Florida's tightest ties to Latin America flow through this sprawling metropolis, which has a central core of vibrant culture.

- **Arriving** Miami International Airport is 12 miles (19 km) west of Miami Beach.
- **Transport** From the airport take a taxi or Metrobus 150 Airport Flyer express to Miami Beach.
- **Booking Ahead** It's always a smart idea to book hotel rooms ahead, especially in the Miami metro area.

Day 1
Morning Watch the sunrise across the ocean, when **Miami Beach** is at its quietest, before heading downtown to **Bayside Marketplace** (p78), the launch point for many **Biscayne Bay** boat trips (p79). A 90-minute cruise sees the mansions of the rich and famous, and the Miami skyline. The ten-minute loop around downtown on the MetroMover (p77) gives a good overview of architecture in the city center, or you can walk the streets and admire the buildings.

Afternoon Stop at the **Miami-Dade Cultural Center** (p78) for the history of how Miami has grown, then relax and people-watch on **South Beach** (p70) before trying

Atlantis Space Shuttle, now out of service, can be seen at Kennedy Space Center

out one of its famed clubs like the Marlin Hotel (p69) after hours.

Day 2
Morning Recharge on the beach, then wander down **Ocean Drive** (pp64–7), between 6th and 13th Streets, to view the most concentrated collection of tropical-motif Art Deco buildings in the world – the Miami Design Preservation League offers a walking tour (p68). Stroll the shops of the **Lincoln Road Mall** (p68) before settling in a sidewalk café.

Afternoon With more than 80,000 historic fine art objects on display, the **Wolfsonian Museum** (p71) will keep you busy for several hours. Miami has one of the largest populations of Holocaust survivors in the world, and the city's Jewish heritage is well-documented at the **Florida Jewish Museum** (p71) and **Holocaust Memorial** (p72).

Five Days in Orlando and the Space Coast

The Disney theme parks and Universal Studios bring people from far and wide to Orlando, but this exciting region has plenty more attractions to offer and activities to be enjoyed.

- **Arriving** Arrive and depart from Orlando International Airport.
- **Transport** A car is essential to explore Orlando and the Space Coast.

Day 1: Cocoa and Cocoa Beach
From Orlando, head to the pretty, historic community of **Cocoa Village** (p199). A ramble around the village finds many eclectic shops and historic sites, like the **Porcher House** (p199). Lunch in one of the little cafés before crossing the bridge to **Cocoa Beach** (p199), the heart of Florida's surf culture. Ron Jon's Surf Shop (p199) is a destination in itself, offering rentals and surfing classes. To end the day, relax on the beach: **Lori Wilson Park** is the nicest natural stretch.

Day 2: KSC and Merritt Island
The heart of America's connection to space is **Kennedy Space Center** (pp200–203). First, walk through Early Space Exploration (p203) for an overview of the technology used for space travel. The IMAX Theater (p202) and the Space Shuttle Atlantis (p201) are not to be missed; the Shuttle Launch Experience (p201) simulates the power of a Shuttle launch. After lunch with an astronaut (p200), take the KSC bus tour (p201) for an insight into the future of the US in space (pp208–9). To finish, follow the Black Point Wildlife Drive through **Merritt Island National Wildlife Refuge** (p198) for up-close encounters.

> **To extend your trip...**
> Spend a day in **New Smyrna Beach** enjoying the historic downtown and quiet shoreline parks.

Day 3: Orlando and Winter Park
Arrive early in **Winter Park** (p193) to see the finest Tiffany glass collection in the world at **Charles Hosmer Morse Museum of American Art** (p193). Lunch at a sidewalk café along trendy **Park Avenue** (p193), then seek out the Scenic Boat Ride (p193). End the day at **Cornell Fine Arts Museum** (p193) at Rollins College.

Day 4: Orlando and International Drive
Enjoy a morning walk through Florida's largest rose garden at **Harry P. Leu Gardens** (p188). Then explore **Orlando Science Center** (p193) before heading downtown to **Lake Eola** (p192) for a lunchtime stroll. Stop off at **Orange County Regional History Center** (p192) to see life-size dioramas recounting the area's history, and then finish the day at **Pointe Orlando** (p194) on International Drive for a choice of restaurants. For an evening of family fun, head to **Wonderworks** (p194).

> **To extend your trip...**
> spend two days roaming **Sea World** and **Aquatica** (pp180–82).

Coral Gables City Hall lit up in Miracle Mile

Day 5: Kissimmee
Alligators and crocs are the star attractions at **Gatorland** (p195), but there are also ziplines over the alligator ponds and a rookery of colorful wading birds. Next, head to **Lake Toho** (p196) to enjoy Kissimmee Lakefront Park shoreline. If there is time, a stop at **Old Town** (p195) is fun for the family. Top off your evening with a rousing spectacle of a dinner show at **Arabian Nights** (p195).

One Week in South Florida

- **Arriving** Arrive and depart from Miami International Airport.
- **Transport** A car is essential to explore this part of Florida.

Day 1: Tropical Miami-Dade
The tropical vibe of South Florida is easy to slip into as you head to **Coconut Grove** (p88), a leafy neighborhood fronting Biscayne Bay. A walk through **The Barnacle** (p88) will put you in touch with pioneer life inside a tropical forest. Continue south into **Coral Gables** (pp83–5) to spend the rest of the day amid the beautiful **Fairchild Tropical Gardens** (p96). Relax in Coconut Grove in the evening.

Day 2: Everglades Main Park Road
Enter **Everglades National Park** (pp290–95), laden with water, sunscreen, insect repellent, and a picnic lunch, via Main Park Road for a 39-mile (63-km) scenic drive. Stop at the **Ernest Coe Visitor Center** (p291) for an introduction to the Everglades and its unique habitats. At **Royal Palm Hammock** (p294), take a

walk along the short and wildlife-rich **Anhinga Trail** (p291). On the Pinelands Trail (p294), look out for colorful liguus tree snails. Stop off at **Pa-hay-okee Overlook** (p295) for a panoramic view of the vast "river of grass," and walk the tunnelling boardwalk through the mangrove forest at **West Lake** (p295). At **Flamingo** (p295), manatees and American crocs may be spotted near the marina. On your return trip, stroll down the **Mahogany Hammock Boardwalk** (p291) through one of the Everglades' tree islands.

Day 3: Key Largo, Big Pine Key, and Key West
Drive down the Overseas Highway (US 1) into the Florida Keys. At **Key Largo** (p296), head for **John Pennekamp Coral Reef State Park** (pp296–7) to arrange a boat tour (at least 3 hours) to the coral reef. After lunch, continue along US 1 towards Key West, taking a peek into the **National Key Deer Refuge** (p301) at Blue Hole, an excellent observation spot for deer. Then it's on to **Key West** (pp302–7) for a walk along Duval Street (p302) and sunset at Mallory Square (p304).

> **To extend your trip...**
> Spend two days in Key West (pp302–7) to explore the plethora of attractions the island has to offer.

Day 4: Key West, Marathon, and Key Largo
Tour **Fort Zachary Taylor Historic State Park** (p302) in the morning, then hop on the Conch Train (p304) for a narrated overview of the city. Stop at **Wrecker's Museum** (p306), which illustrates the

Keys' long maritime history. Driving back north along the Overseas Highway, take a break at **Crane Point Hammock** (p300) in Marathon, site of the oldest home in the Keys, to admire the views of Florida Bay. Spend the evening along **Key Largo's** (p296) beach.

Day 5: Everglades and Big Cypress
From Key Largo, continue north to the **Tamiami Trail** (p285) – the scenic highway across the Everglades. At **Shark Valley** (p291), hop on a tram, or cycle the 15-mile (24-km) paved loop, stopping at the tall observation tower. Try native favorites like fry bread at the adjacent **Miccosukee Indian Village** (p289). Back in the car, head to **Big Cypress National Preserve** (pp288–9), and stop at Oasis Visitor Center (p289) for an orientation to this unusual mosaic of ecosystems.

Day 6: Everglades, Big Cypress, and Naples
Take an early morning boat tour from the **Gulf Coast Visitor Center** (p291) to see the west side of Everglades National Park in the **Ten Thousand Islands** (p290). Head north and you'll pass through **Fakahatchee Strand Preserve State Park** (p289), one of Florida's high biodiversity areas, en route to **Corkscrew Swamp Sanctuary** (p289) – a virgin forest of ancient cypress trees. Finish the day with an evening in artsy **Naples** (p288).

> **To extend your trip...**
> Continue north on the Tamiami Trail, for two days in **Fort Myers** (pp280–81) and **Sanibel Island** (pp282–3).

Day 7: Naples, Big Cypress, and Coral Gables
Drive east across the Big Cypress Swamp on the Alligator Alley expressway (I-75). Exit at the **Big Cypress Seminole Reservation** (p289), home to the **Ah-Tah-Thi-Ki Museum** (p289) of Seminole culture. At **Billie Swamp Safari** (p289), take a swamp buggy or airboat ride. Finally finish your journey in cosmopolitan **Coral Gables** (p83–5).

Two Weeks in Central and North Florida

- **Arriving** Arrive and depart from Orlando International Airport.
- **Transport** A car is essential to explore Florida.

Day 1: Orlando to Bradenton

From Orlando, follow Scenic Highway 17 south to Lake Wales. Spend several hours savoring the views and beauty of **Bok Tower Gardens** (*p197*). Continue southwest across the state, visiting the antebellum **Gamble Plantation** (*p270*) en route to **Anna Maria Island** (*p271*).

> **To extend your trip...**
> Spend a day at **Legoland** (*p197*), which includes the botanical beauty of historic **Cypress Gardens**.

Day 2: Bradenton and Sarasota

Rise early for a walk at **De Soto National Memorial** (*p271*) before heading into Sarasota to spend most of your day on the expansive grounds of the **Ringling Museum** (*pp274–7*). Take in a spot of window shopping on Main Street in **downtown Sarasota** (*p272*) before crossing the bridge to **St. Armands Circle** (*p273*) for dinner.

Day 3: Tampa and Ybor City

The **Florida Aquarium** (*p266*) is one of America's largest, featuring a tropical atrium on top of the building and marine galleries on multiple floors below. It connects to historic **Ybor City** (*p264–5*) via the TECO Line Streetcar System (*p262*). Learn about the area's Cuban roots at the **Ybor City State Museum** (*p265*), and plan your dinner at one of Ybor City's restaurants.

> **To extend your trip...**
> Spend two days in Tampa to visit **Busch Gardens** (*pp268–9*) and the **Lowry Park Zoo** (*p266*).

Day 4: St. Petersburg and Clearwater Beach

A pleasant place to explore on foot, **St. Petersburg** (*p258*) is home to the **Salvador Dali Museum** (*pp260–61*) and the **Museum of Fine Arts** (*p259*) – notable cultural attractions in an its arts-focused downtown. For a taste of the tropics, wander through **Sunken Gardens** (*p259*) before working your way to the nearby coast for some beach time at **Sand Key Park** (*p257*). Spend the night at **Clearwater Beach** (*p256*), where there are many small motels on the bay side.

Day 5: Dunedin and Tarpon Springs

Founded by a Scotsman, **Dunedin** (*p255*) has a small-village feel and is a pleasant destination for antiques and art. It is bisected by the **Pinellas Trail** (*p255*). You can rent a bicycle to follow the trail north, or continue your drive to **Honeymoon Island State Park** (*p255*), one of the best places in Florida to see nesting ospreys. The Pinellas Trail also connects to **Tarpon Springs** (*p255*), your final destination for the day.

Day 6: The Nature Coast

Continue up the Gulf Coast on US 19 to **Weeki Wachee Springs** (*pp254–5*), the home of "real live mermaids". At **Homosassa Springs Wildlife State Park** (*p254*), you can get to know Florida's native wildlife, especially the manatee. Spend the evening in **Crystal River** (*p254*) enjoying

Flamingos at Homosassa Springs Wildlife State Park

one of the best sunsets in the region at the end of the Fort Island Trail – a driving route through the salt marsh, ending on an island on the Gulf of Mexico.

> **To extend your trip...**
> Go snorkeling with the manatees (in winter) at **Crystal River National Wildlife Refuge** (*p255*).

Day 7: Ocala

Best known for its horse farms – of which you'll see many if approaching via SR 40 – **Ocala** (*p226*) is also a hub for outdoor recreation. Visit **Silver Springs** (*p225*) and cruise down the crystalline river, surrounded by jungle-like floodplain forests, by boat, or paddle with a kayak if you're feeling energetic. The Black Bear Scenic Byway leads into the **Ocala National Forest** (*p225*), where Juniper Springs boasts a compelling pair of tributaries linked by glassy waterways.

The picture-perfect St. Petersburg skyline and marina

Day 8: Gainesville

Centered around the University of Florida, Gainesville is surrounded by natural and cultural attractions. At Cross Creek, **Marjorie Kinnan Rawlings Historic State Park** (*p226*) provides a peek into 1940s Florida life. From here, continue to **Micanopy** (*p226*) to explore this old trading post, established in 1821. Spend some time admiring the antiques and art that dominate the quaint downtown, then watch the wildlife at **Paynes Prairie Preserve State Park** (*p227*) for the rest of the day.

Day 9: Gainesville and the Suwannee River

Start your morning with a visit to the **Florida Museum of Natural History** (*p227*) for a deeper understanding of Florida's natural habitats. Take a gentle drive north via US 41 through small historic towns to White Springs, home of **Stephen Foster Folk Culture Center State Park** (*p248*), where Florida folkways are preserved in a beautiful setting along the Suwannee River.

> **To extend your trip…**
> Spend two days in the Florida Panhandle to visit the state capital of **Tallahassee** (*p246*), where the plantation home of Goodwood (*p247*) and the **Tallahassee Museum of History and Natural Science** (*p247*) interpret Florida's early history.

Day 10: Jacksonville

Along the St. Johns River waterfront, the **Cummer Museum of Art and Gardens** (*p213*) is a perfect blend of cultural and natural spaces. Follow Heckscher Drive to Fort George Island, home to the **Kingsley Plantation** (*p211*), the oldest plantation home in Florida. Use the Mayport Ferry to cross the St. Johns River to **Mayport** (*p213*) for a splash in the surf at **Kathryn Abbey Hanna Park** (*p213*) before dinner.

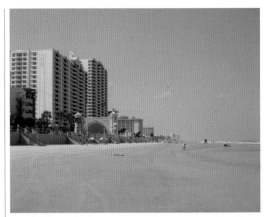

The expansive Daytona Beach

Day 11: St. Augustine

Take A1A south along the coast for a scenic approach to **St. Augustine** (*pp214–17*), and explore the **Fort Mose Historic State Park** (*p217*) – the site of the first free African settlement in North America. Continue into the hubbub of **St. Georges Street** (*pp216–17*) to start exploring on foot. Early life in the city is well illustrated at the **Colonial Spanish Quarter** (*p216*), and the **Lightner Museum** (*p217*) has many fasci-nating collections. Browse shops, galleries, and historic sites into the evening before taking on a pub crawl through the Old City.

Day 12: St. Augustine

Walk through the **Castillo de San Marcos** (*pp218–19*) before hopping in your car to cross the Bridge of Lions to Anastasia Island. The **St. Augustine Alligator Farm Zoological Park** (*p217*) is Florida's oldest zoo. Continue across the street to the **St. Augustine Lighthouse** (*p217*), the oldest brick structure in the city, and climb the 219 stairs to the top for the must-see view.

Day 13: Scenic A1A

Following Florida A1A south from St. Augustine, stop for a tour of **Fort Matanzas National Monument** (*p220*) – the site of a coquina fortress. At **Washington Oaks Gardens State Park** (*p220*), don't miss the unique coquina beach on the ocean side of the park. Continuing along the route, the quaint downtown of **Flagler Beach** (*p220*), perched on bluffs above the sea, is a delightful stop en route to **Bulow Plantation Ruins State Park** (*p220*). Return to A1A south on the very scenic "The Loop." End your day at **Ormond Beach** (*p220*).

Day 14: Daytona Beach

A visit to the **Daytona International Speedway** (*p222*), the home of racing, is a must, as is a visit to the **Museum of Arts and Sciences** (*p221*) for its extensive collection of Cuban art. Catch your last glimpse of the Florida coastline from the top of the **Ponce de Leon Inlet Lighthouse** (*p222*).

Formal gardens adorn the natural beauty of Washington Oaks Gardens State National Park

Putting Florida on the Map

Florida, with a population of about 18 million, is the southernmost state of the continental US, jutting down toward the Caribbean between the Atlantic Ocean and the Gulf of Mexico. The Florida peninsula measures about 430 miles (690 km) north to south, and the state as a whole covers an area of 58,560 sq miles (151,714 sq km) – roughly the same size as England. The state capital is Tallahassee, a comparatively small city in the Panhandle – the narrow strip of land extending west along the shore of the Gulf of Mexico. Florida's principal international gateways, however, are Miami and Orlando.

Lake Winnipeg

MANITOBA

Regina

Winnipeg

SASKATCHEWAN

NORTH DAKOTA

Bismarck

SOUTH DAKOTA

Rapid City

Casper

WYOMING

Sioux Falls

NEBRASKA

Salt Lake City

Salt Lake City

NEVADA

San Francisco

San Francisco

UTAH

Denver

Denver

COLORADO

KANSAS

CALIFORNIA

Las Vegas

McCarran

UNITED STATES OF AMERICA

Los Angeles

Los Angeles

ARIZONA

Amarillo

OKLAHOMA

Oklahoma City

San Diego

San Diego

Phoenix

Phoenix Sky Harbor

Albuquerque

Rio Grande

Tucson

NEW MEXICO

TEXAS

Dallas Fort Worth

Dallas

Ciudad Juarez

Colorado

SONORA

BAJA CALIFORNIA

CHIHUAHUA

Rio Grande

San Antonio

San Antonio

Chihuahua

COAHUILA

MEXICO

PACIFIC OCEAN

SINALOA

Culiacán

Torreón

Monterrey

NUEVO LEON

DURANGO

ZACATECAS

SAN LUIS POTOSÍ

TAMAULIPAS

Aguascalientes

San Luis Potosí

VERACRUZ

JALISCO

León

Guadalajara

HIDALGO

COLIMA

MICHOACAN

MEXICO

Colima

Mexico City

Veracruz

MICHOACAN

Balsas

PUEBLA

ORSACA

Acapulco

See inset map next page

Key

— Highway

— Railroad

— International border

--- State border

Road Map of Florida

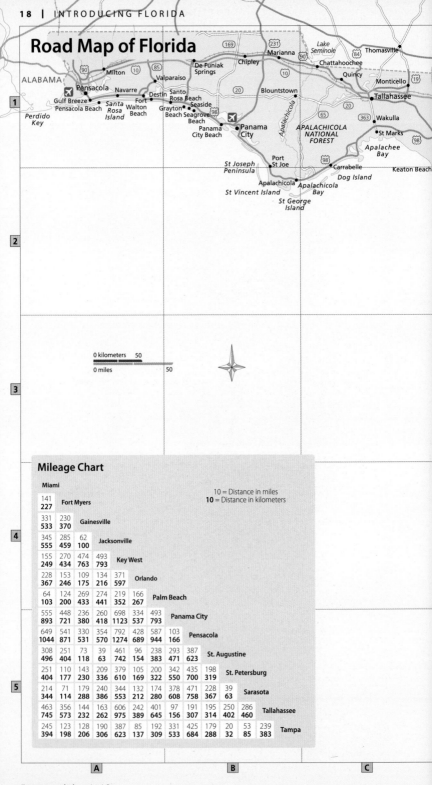

ALABAMA

Perdido Key · Gulf Breeze · Pensacola · Pensacola Beach · Santa Rosa Island · Navarre · Fort Walton Beach · Destin · Valparaiso · Milton · Santo Rosa Beach · Grayton Beach · Seaside · Seagrove Beach · Panama City Beach · Panama City · De Funiak Springs · Chipley · Marianna · Blountstown · Chattahoochee · Quincy · Monticello · Tallahassee · Wakulla · St Marks · Thomasville

Lake Seminole

APALACHICOLA NATIONAL FOREST

Apalachee Bay

St Joseph Peninsula · Port St Joe · Apalachicola · St Vincent Island · Apalachicola Bay · St George Island · Carrabelle · Dog Island · Keaton Beach

0 kilometers 50
0 miles 50

Mileage Chart

Miami

10 = Distance in miles
10 = Distance in kilometers

Miami												
141 **227**	Fort Myers											
331 **533**	230 **370**	Gainesville										
345 **555**	285 **459**	62 **100**	Jacksonville									
155 **249**	270 **434**	474 **763**	493 **793**	Key West								
228 **367**	153 **246**	109 **175**	134 **216**	371 **597**	Orlando							
64 **103**	124 **200**	269 **433**	274 **441**	219 **352**	166 **267**	Palm Beach						
555 **893**	448 **721**	236 **380**	260 **418**	698 **1123**	334 **537**	493 **793**	Panama City					
649 **1044**	541 **871**	330 **531**	354 **570**	792 **1274**	428 **689**	587 **944**	103 **166**	Pensacola				
308 **496**	251 **404**	73 **118**	39 **63**	461 **742**	96 **154**	238 **383**	293 **471**	387 **623**	St. Augustine			
251 **404**	110 **177**	143 **230**	209 **336**	379 **610**	105 **169**	200 **322**	342 **550**	435 **700**	198 **319**	St. Petersburg		
214 **344**	71 **114**	179 **288**	240 **386**	344 **553**	132 **212**	174 **280**	378 **608**	471 **758**	228 **367**	39 **63**	Sarasota	
463 **745**	356 **573**	144 **232**	163 **262**	606 **975**	242 **389**	401 **645**	97 **156**	191 **307**	195 **314**	250 **402**	286 **460**	Tallahassee
245 **394**	123 **198**	128 **206**	190 **306**	387 **623**	85 **137**	192 **309**	331 **533**	425 **684**	179 **288**	20 **32**	53 **85**	239 **383**	Tampa

GEORGIA

Valdosta

Live Oak

Lake City
Olustee

Steinhatchee
Cross City

Suwannee

Cedar Key

Gainesville

Micanopy

Cross Creek

OCALA NATIONAL FOREST

Palatka

Fernandina Beach

Amelia Island

Jacksonville

Neptune Beach
Jacksonville Beach
Ponte vedra Beach
Mandarin

St Augustine

Marineland

Flagler Beach

Ormond Beach

Crystal River

Homosassa Springs

Weeki Wachee

Tarpon Springs
Palm Harbor
Dunedin
Saftey Harbor
Clearwater

St Petersburg

St Petersburg Beach

Anna Maria Island
Longboat Key

Sarasota

Ocala

Silver Springs

De Land

Mount Dora

Sanford

Lake George

Withlacoochee

Daytona Beach
Ponce Inlet

New Smyrna Beach

Titusville

John F. Kennedy Space Center

Clermont

Dade City

Walt Disney World

Celebration

Winter Park

Orlando

Kissimmee

Cocoa

Cape Canaveral
Cocoa Beach

Indian River

Lakeland

Winter Haven

Bartow

Lake Wales

Gibsonton

Tampa Bay

Tampa

Bradenton

Melbourne

Sebastian Inlet

Sebastian

Vero Beach

Yeehaw Junction

Sebring

Myakka

Venice

Port Charlotte

Boca Grande

Cayo Costa

Captiva Island

Sanibel Island

Fort Myers

Fort Myers Beach

Bonita Springs

Immokalee

Naples

Marco Island

Ochopee

Everglades City

Arcadia

Okeechobee

Lake Okeechobee

Pahokee

Clewiston

Belle Glade

Caloosahatchee

Fort Pierce

Port St Lucie

Hutchinson Island

Jensen Beach
Stuart

St Lucie Canal

Hobe Sound
Jupiter Island
Jupiter
Singer Island

West Palm Beach
Palm Beach

Lake Worth

Delray Beach
Boca Raton
Deerfield Beach
Lauderdale-By-The-Sea
Fort Lauderdale

Pompano Beach

Davie
Dania
Hollywood

Ten Thousand Islands

THE EVERGLADES

ALLIGATOR ALLEY

Miami

Homestead

Florida City

Biscayne Bay

BISCAYNE NATIONAL PARK

Flamingo

Dry Tortugas

Key West

Big Pine Key
Little Torch Key

Bahia Honda
Marathon

Long Key

Islamorada

Tavernier

Key Largo

Florida Bay

FLORIDA KEYS

Key

— Expressway
— Major highway
═ Secondary route
— Rail line

Miami

The metropolis, often referred to simply as Miami, or Greater Miami, is more accurately called Miami-Dade County. It covers 2,000 sq miles (5,180 sq km) and incorporates many districts and several cities. In this book, Miami has been divided up into three sightseeing areas: Miami Beach, including the resort of South Beach; Downtown and Little Havana, more traditionally urban areas; and the leafy suburbs of Coral Gables and Coconut Grove.

Coral Gables: Miami's most desirable residential district, laid out around a series of canals

Miami Beach: a city in its own right, linked by causeways to the mainland

Downtown: the visual and commercial focus of the metropolis, with high-rises spanning the Miami River

A PORTRAIT OF FLORIDA

For the majority of Florida's 40 million-plus annual visitors, the typical travel poster images of Florida – sun, sea, sand, and Mickey Mouse – are reason enough to jump on the next plane. The Sunshine State deserves its reputation as the perfect family vacation spot, but Florida is much richer in its culture, landscape, and character than its stereotypical image suggests.

It is easy to turn a blind eye to what lies beyond the Florida coast, where the beaches are varied and abundant enough to satisfy every visitor – whether you want simply to relax beneath azure skies or make the most of the state's fine sports facilities. However, great rewards await those who put aside their suntan lotion and beach towels to explore.

The lush forests, the rolling hills of the north, the colorful displays of bougainvillea and azaleas in spring shatter the myth that Florida's landscape is totally dull and flat. Wherever you are, it is only a short trip from civilization to wild areas, such as the Everglades, which harbor an extraordinary diversity of plant and animal life, and where alli-gators and snakes are living reminders of the

inhospitable place that Florida was not much more than 100 years ago. By world standards the state was a late developer (most of its historic districts date only from the early 1900s), but Florida boasts the nation's oldest town: St. Augustine, where a rare wealth of well-preserved buildings provide a glimpse of life in the 18th century.

Both climatically and culturally, Florida is a state divided – a bridge between temperate North America and tropical Latin America and the Caribbean. In the north, roads are lined with stately live oak trees and people speak with a southern drawl, while, in the south, shade from the subtropical sun is cast by palm trees, and the inhabitants of Miami are as likely to speak Spanish as English.

The unspoiled, watery landscape near Flamingo in Everglades National Park

◀ An aerial view of the white, sandy beaches and warm, emerald waters of Panama City Beach

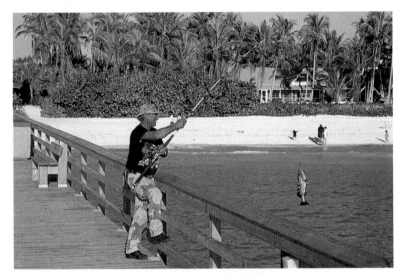

A local resident enjoying some leisurely fishing off Naples pier, on the shores of the Gulf of Mexico

People and Society

The state "where everyone is from somewhere else," Florida has always been a cultural hodgepodge. The Seminole Indians, who arrived in the 17th century, have been in Florida longer than any other group. They live mostly on reservations, but you see them by the roadside in some southern areas, selling their colorful, hand-made crafts. The best candidates for the title of "true Floridian" are the Cracker farmers, whose ancestors settled in the state in the 1800s; their name comes perhaps from the cracking of their cattle whips or the cracking of

A stand selling clothes made by Seminole Indians

corn to make grits. Unless you explore the interior, you probably won't meet a Cracker; along the affluent, heavily populated coast, you'll rub shoulders mainly with people whose roots lie in more northerly states.

North Americans have poured into Florida since World War II; the twentieth most populous state in the US in 1950, Florida is now ranked fourth.

Miami Cubans playing dominos

The largest single group to move south has been the retirees, for whom Florida's climate and lifestyle of leisure (plus its tax concessions) hold great appeal after a life of hard work. Retirees take full advantage of Florida's recreational and cultural opportunities. You'll see many seniors playing a round of golf, fishing, or browsing around one of Florida's state-of-the art shopping malls. While super-rich communities like Palm Beach fit the conservative and staid image that some people still have of Florida, the reality is very different. An increasing number of the new arrivals are young people, for whom Florida is a land of opportunity, a place to have fun and enjoy the good life. It is this younger generation that has helped turnMiami's South Beach, where beautiful bodies pose against a backdrop of Art Deco hotels, into one of the trendiest resorts in the US.

There has also been massive immigration from Latin America, and Miami has a large Cuban community. Here, salsa and merengue beats fill the air while exuberant festivals fill the calendar. The ethnic diversity is also celebrated in the local food: as well as genuine re-creations of Caribbean and other ethnic dishes, you can enjoy the exciting and innovative dishes that have emerged with the craze for cross-cultural cuisine.

A refreshing ride in one of Florida's popular water parks

Oranges, Florida's juiciest crop

Economics and Tourism

Economically, Florida is in relatively good shape comp-ared with other US states. For most of its history,

the state's main source of revenue has been agriculture: citrus fruits, vegetables, sugar, and cattle. Citrus grows mainly in southern central Florida, where fruit trees can stretch as far as the eye can see. High-tech industry is significant too, while the proximity of Miami to Latin America and the Carib-bean has made it the natural route for US trade with the region. Florida's warm climate has also generated high-profile moneyspinners: spring baseball training draws teams and lots of fans south, while the fashion trade brings models by the hundreds and plenty of glamour to Miami.

It is tourism that fills the state's coffers. The Walt Disney World* Resort may appear to dominate the industry, but Florida makes the most of all its assets: its superb beaches, its location near the Bahamas and the Caribbean (its cruise industry is flourishing), and its natural habitats. After decades of unbridled development, Florida has learned the importance of safeguarding its natural heritage. Vast areas of land have already disappeared beneath factories, condos, and sugarcane fields, but those involved in industry and agriculture are acting more responsibly, and water use is strictly monitored. Florida's natural treasures, from its swamps to its last remaining panthers, are now protected for posterity.

Flamingos, seen in some parks and a popular icon

The Landscape of Florida

Florida's landscape is relentlessly low-lying, the highest point in the state being just 345 ft (105 m) above sea level. The rare, rolling hills of the Panhandle provide some of the loveliest countryside in the state, whose flat peninsula is otherwise dominated by grassland and swamp, punctuated by forests and thousands of lakes. Great swathes of the natural landscape have had to surrender to the onslaught of urban development and agriculture – second only to tourism as the state's main economic resource. However, you can still find areas that are surprisingly wild and unpopulated.

Wetlands consist mainly of tree-covered swamps, like this cypress swamp, and more open, grassy marshes.

Pensacola

Tallahassee

Panama City

APALACHICOLA NATIONAL FOREST

Gainesville

Ocala

0 kilometers 50
0 miles 50

Sandy beaches account for over 1,000 miles (1,600 km) of Florida's coastline. In contrast to the coral sand on the Atlantic side, the fine quartz sand in the Panhandle is so white that legend has it that unscrupulous traders sold it as sugar during World War II.

Tampa

St Petersburg

Sarasota

Florida's Sinkholes

Many of Florida's 30,000 lakes and ponds started out as sinkholes, or "sinks." This curious phenomenon, which occurs mainly in northern and central Florida, is a result of the natural erosion of the limestone that forms the bedrock of much of the state. Most sinkholes form gradually, as the soil sinks slowly into a depression. Others appear more dramatically, often after heavy rain, when an underground cavern collapses beneath the weight of the ground above. The largest recorded sinkhole occurred in Winter Park in 1981. It swallowed six cars and a house, and formed a crater more than 300 ft (90 m) in diameter. There is no sure way to predict sinkhole development, and many homeowners take out sinkhole insurance.

City workers surveying a sinkhole in the middle of a road

Barrier islands, formed by the piling up of drifting sand, ring much of Florida's coast.

Key

- Main urban areas
- Main wetland areas
- Main wetland areas
- - - Main wetland areas
- Cattle
- Fish and seafood
- Citrus fruit
- Sugarcane
- Tobacco
- Peanuts

The Intracoastal Waterway is a natural but dredged channel, whose main section along the east coast is a continuation of a route that begins farther north in Maryland; some of the Florida sections were dredged back in the 1880s. It is a popular boating route *(see p364)*.

Cattle were shipped from Florida to market in Cuba under the Spanish. Today, Florida is second only to Kentucky in the raising of beef cattle in the southeastern states, its industry based largely on the Brahman, a hardy breed of cattle originally from India. The state's principal cattle ranching country lies along the Kissimmee River, and the town of Kissimmee is known as the "cow capital of Florida" *(see p195)*.

Forest, mostly pine, covers 50 percent of the state's land area, but more than half of this is grown for commercial use.

Florida's citrus industry produces over 70 percent of the citrus fruits consumed in the US. Oranges are grown mainly for their juice, for which the state is famous.

Sugarcane thrives on the rich soil south of Lake Okeechobee *(see p132)*. Once reliant on migrant laborers from the Caribbean, who cut the cane by machete, the industry is now largely mechanized.

Urban growth is the inevitable result of the constant influx of migrants from other US states and abroad, as well as of the general movement from rural to urban areas. The southeastern coast of Florida is almost completely built up – as seen at Delray Beach, which straddles the Intracoastal Waterway on the Gold Coast.

The Florida Keys are a chain of fossilized coral islands, many of which are tiny and uninhabited.

Jacksonville · St Johns · Daytona Beach · Orlando · OCALA NATIONAL FOREST · Kissimmee · Fort Pierce · Lake Okeechobee · Caloosahatchee · Fort Myers · Naples · Palm Beach · Miami Canal · Fort Lauderdale · MIAMI · Tamiami Canal · EVERGLADES · FLORIDA KEYS · Key West

Wildlife and Natural Habitats

Florida's great variety of habitats and wildlife is due in part to the meeting of temperate north Florida with the subtropical south. Other factors include the state's humidity, sandy soils, low elevation, and proximity to the water. Some plants and animals can live in several habitats, while others can survive only in one. The bird life in Florida is particularly rich in winter, when migratory birds arrive from the colder northern states.

A tropical hardwood hammock in southern Florida

Coastal Areas

Florida's coasts are rich in wildlife despite the often exposed conditions. Apart from wading birds, many animals remain hidden during the day. Some lie buried in the sand, while others leave the water only in darkness. Salt marshes and lagoons, protected from the ocean by dunes, are a particularly rich habitat.

Saltwater lagoons are fertile territory for fish and shellfish.

Horseshoe crabs emerge from the ocean in great hordes, usually in spring. They congregate on the beaches to breed.

Ocean

Shrubs on the dunes are "pruned" by the ocean's salty spray and bent by the wind.

Limestone bedrock

Clay, sand, and shells

The bald eagle, an endangered species found throughout the entire state, has a wingspan of 7 ft (2 m).

Dunes, shaped by the wind and waves, shift all the time but are stabilized by the roots of sea oats and other plants.

The sea grape, which grows on dunes mainly in southeast Florida, is named after the oval fruit that hangs in grapelike clusters.

Pine Flatwoods

These woods, where pines tower over an understory of plants and shrubs, cover about half of Florida and are often interspersed with swamps and other habitats. They thrive when swept by fire periodically, and the plants and animals that live here have adapted to survive the difficult conditions.

Saw palmetto, as well as shrubs such as wax myrtle, do well in the open woodlands.

Slash pine is the most common tree in the flatwoods.

Clay and sand

White-tailed deer are solitary creatures. Those in Florida are smaller than the white-tailed deer found in more northerly states of the US.

Sand

Pygmy rattlesnakes are well camouflaged to blend easily into a background of grass and scrub.

The red-bellied **woodpecker** nests in dead trees and may use the same nest in successive years.

Freshwater Swamps

Many swamps have been drained to make way for agriculture or development, but they are still found all over Florida. They are often dominated by cypress trees, which are well suited to the watery conditions, requiring little soil to grow. The dwarf cypress is the most common species, the larger giant or bald cypress tree being rare these days.

White ibis find ample food in freshwater marshes and swamps. They nest in large colonies in high trees or among reeds.

Peat

The bob- cat has a distinctive short tail, facial ruff, and spotted coat.

Cypress trees often form a "dome." The trees at the water's edge are shorter than those at the center.

Sawgrass

Cypress knees are special roots that supply oxygen to the tree, which would otherwise die in the wet soil.

Water and organic matter

Anole lizards are usually green but can change to dark brown, depending on body heat or levels of stress.

Water lilies are the most spectacular freshwater flowering plants. The large leaf is a common resting site for frogs.

Hardwood Forests

These are among the most verdant habitats in the state. Hardwood-dominated forests are called "hammocks." Unlike the tropical hardwood hammocks of southern Florida, those in the north are dominated by the splendid live oak tree, interspersed with other species such as hickory and magnolia.

Spanish moss, like other epiphytes or air plants, grows on (but does no harm to) its host tree.

Wild turkeys are easily recognized by their colored plumage and "beard."

Magnolia, one of the oldest known flowering plants, is characterized by its showy ornamental flowers and aromatic bark.

Cabbage or sabal palm

Live oak

Sand and clay

Hammocks occur mainly in patches or narrow bands along rivers.

Opossums are proficient climbers, with hands, feet, and tail well adapted to grasping thin branches.

Armadillos are mainly nocturnal. When threatened they roll into a ball, the hard armor protecting the soft body from predators such as bobcats.

Hurricanes in Florida

A hurricane is a tropical cyclone with wind speeds of at least 74 mph (119 km/h). One in ten of the hurricanes to occur in the North Atlantic hits Florida – which means an average of one of these big storms every two years. The hurricane season runs from June 1 to November 30, but the greatest threat is from August to October. The Saffir-Simpson Hurricane Scale, which measures the winds and ocean flooding expected, categorizes hurricanes from one to five; category five is the worst, with winds of over 155 mph (249 km/h).

Monument to the 1935 hurricane *(see p298)*

Hurricane names come from a recognized alphabetical list of names, which rotates every six years. Originally, only women's names were used, but since 1979 men's and women's names have been alternated.

The areas of Florida most likely to be hit by a hurricane are the south-east coast, including the Florida Keys, the west coast of the Everglades, and the western Panhandle.

The Life of a Hurricane

The development of a hurricane is influenced by several factors – primarily heat and wind. First the sun must warm the ocean's surface enough for water to evaporate. This rises and condenses into thunderclouds, which are sent spinning by the earth's rotation. The hurricane moves forward and can be tracked using satellite images like this one. On hitting land, the storm loses power because it is cut off from its source of energy – the warm ocean.

A boat lifted out of the water onto Miami's Rickenbacker Causeway by the force of the hurricane

An apartment building after its façade was ripped off by Andrew's ferocious winds

A tent camp, set up to house some of the 250,000 left temporarily homeless by Hurricane Andrew

Hurricane Andrew

On August 24, 1992 Hurricane Andrew devastated South Florida. It measured only "4" on the Saffir-Simpson Scale (less than the 1935 hurricane that hit the Florida Keys), but until Katrina in 2005 it was the country's costliest ever natural disaster, causing $35 billion worth of damage. Astonishingly, only 15 pseople died in Florida (23 in the whole country) from the direct effects of Hurricane Andrew.

The Eye
Encircled by the fastest winds, the "eye" at the heart of the storm is a calm area. Once the eye has passed by, the winds return to their full force.

Monitoring a Hurricane

Using satellites, computer models, and radar, the National Hurricane Center in Miami can detect a hurricane long before it reaches Florida. The most detailed information, however, is provided by pilots known as Hurricane Hunters, who fly in and out of the hurricane gathering data.

The damage from a hurricane is greatly reduced by preparedness: television and radio bulletins keep the public informed, and everyone is encouraged to plan the route of the storm on special hurricane tracking maps.

Trees bent by hurricane force winds

922 MB

A typical hurricane is 300 miles (480 km) wide and can rise 50,000–60,000 ft (15,250–18,300 m) above the ocean. It moves forward at a speed of 10–45 mph (15–70 km/h).

Many hurricanes, including Andrew, form off Africa and then move west across the Atlantic.

1 Hurricane Alerts The issuing of a Hurricane Watch is the first indication that a hurricane could hit Florida. This means that a storm may arrive within 36–48 hours. A Hurricane Warning heralds the storm's likely arrival within 24 hours. Airports are likely to close during these alerts.

Traditional hurricane alert flag

2 Evacuation Emergency management officials may issue evacuation orders via the local news media before a hurricane hits. People living in high-rise buildings, mobile homes, and low-lying areas are particularly vulnerable. Signs bearing the hurricane symbol direct people along safe routes. The Red Cross shelters those with nowhere else to go.

EVACUATION ROUTE

Evacuation sign

The Storm Surge

Most damage and deaths during a hurricane are a result not of wind and rain but of flooding from the storm surge. This wall of water is whipped up by fierce winds near the eye of the storm and then crashes onto the shore; it can span over 50 miles (80 km) and reach a height of 20 ft (6 m) or more.

17-ft (5-m) storm tide
15-ft (4.5-m) surge
2-ft (0.6-m) normal high tide
Mean sea level

3 The All Clear After a hurricane dissipates or moves on, the all clear is given for people to return home. However, safety is still a concern after the storm because of downed power lines, flooding, and cleanup-related accidents.

Shipwrecks and Salvage

The waters off Florida are littered with thousands of shipwrecks that have accumulated over hundreds of years. Many sank during storms at sea, while others were tossed onto the reefs off the Keys. The salvaged wrecks picked out on the map are those that have had a large amount of their cargo recovered. Spain's treasure ships are the greatest prize among salvagers, just as they were once the favored target of pirates. In museums all over Florida everyday objects and treasure offer an insight into the lives and riches of the Spanish.

Lighthouses
Since the 1800s, lighthouses like the one at Jupiter have helped ships stay on course.

The Atocha
Florida's best-known Spanish wreck, which sank in 1622, was located by Mel Fisher (see p118) in 1985 after a 16-year search. The treasure, worth an estimated $300 million, included coins, gold bars, and jewelry.

The Florida Keys
were ideal territory for "wreckers" (see p307), who rescued and then sold the cargo from ships that foundered on the nearby reef.

From Mexico

Salvaging Treasure
Salvaging has always required ingenuity. This manuscript from 1623 shows a Spanish technique invented to rescue sunken treasure in the Keys.

Havana

MEXICO

From South America

Havana, the Cuban capital, was the main assembly point for Spanish fleets en route home.

Spanish ships sailing from the New World would pick up the Gulf Stream and tradewinds near Florida to aid their journey back across the Atlantic.

Key

⚓ Salvaged wreck

⚓ Unsalvaged wreck

↗ Shipping route

Treasure Seekers

It took Mel Fisher more than 100 court hearings to establish his right to keep the treasures of the *Atocha*. Federal law states that wrecks located up to 3 miles (5 km) offshore belong to the state in whose waters they are found, but the law is unclear when it comes to ships lying outside that limit. Amateurs who find coins with metal detectors on land can keep what they find, but in Florida a license is required to remove anything from an offshore wreck within its jurisdiction.

A treasure hunter on the beach

Where to See Spanish Treasure in Florida

McLarty Treasure Museum
see p118
Mel Fisher Maritime Museum
see p306
Mel Fisher's Treasure Museum
see p118
Museum of Man in the Sea
see p242
St. Lucie County Historical Museum
see p119

A Spanish treasure fleet that sank here in 1715 *(see p118)* is still being salvaged. Amateurs scour nearby beaches for coins that are sometimes washed up after a storm.

To Spain

Spanish Ships
Caravels and galleons transported treasure back to Spain. These ships could carry a crew of about 200. The chests of gold and silver were usually kept under guard in a room on the lower deck.

Blackbeard
Notorious for his cruelty – and also for his habit of setting fire to hemp cords attached to his hat in order to intimidate his victims – Blackbeard preyed on Spanish ships in the early 18th century. He was killed by the British Navy in 1718.

BAHAMAS

CUBA

Hispaniola and nearby Tortuga were favorite haunts of French and English pirates, who would launch attacks on Spanish ships from here.

TORTUGA

CARIBBEAN SEA

HISPANIOLA

0 kilometres 200

0 miles 200

Florida's Architecture

Buildings in Florida are perhaps most interesting as a reflection of the way in which the state was settled. Early pioneers built simple homes, but aspirations grew from the railroad era onward. Entrepreneurs, eager to lure people south, imitated styles with which northerners would be familiar. This trend, plus the speed of settlement, meant that Florida never really developed an indigenous style. But the Sunshine State has some quirky and memorable architecture, often inspired by the need to adapt to the warm climate.

High-rise architecture in downtown Jacksonville

Florida's Vernacular Style

The early pioneers of the 1800s built houses whose design was dictated mainly by the climate and the location: the most identifiable common elements are the devices to maximize natural ventilation. Local materials, usually wood, were used. Original "Cracker" homes, so named after the people who built and lived in them (see p24), don't survive in great numbers, but the vernacular style has influenced Florida's architecture ever since.

A chickee, the traditional simple home of Florida's native Indians

The brick chimney replaced the original one, which was made of mud and sticks.

A dog trot, or open walk-through, was often added if, as here, the original house was extended.

The roof, here made of cypress shingle, was usually steeply pitched.

The McMullen Log House, a pine log cabin completed in 1852, is a typical Cracker dwelling. It is now preserved in Pinellas County Heritage Village. (See p256.)

Overhanging eaves shade both the porch and the windows.

The Gilded Age

From the 1880s on, the railroads and tourism brought new wealth and ideas from outside the state. The love affair with Mediterranean Revivalism began and can be seen in Flagler's brick hotels in St. Augustine. Wood was still the favored material, though, and was used more decoratively – most famously in Key West. Other concentrations of Victorian houses are found in Fernandina Beach (see p210) and Mount Dora (see p224).

Moorish tower, Tampa Bay Hotel

A tower fulfilled a decorative more than a practical purpose.

Gabled roofs were popular and could be high enough to fit in an attic.

Ventilation was still a primary concern, hence the generous number of windows.

Verandas that wrapped around the house were quite common.

The McCreary House, a Queen Anne home in Pensacola dated c.1900, shows the refinement of vernacular styles during the Victorian period (See p235).

The Fantasy of the Boom Years

The most notable buildings of the period 1920–50 set out to inspire romantic images of faraway places. Each new development had a theme, spawning islands of architectural styles from Moorish to Art Deco – the latter in Miami's South Beach district (*see pp64–9*). Mediterranean Revivalism dominated, however. Its chief exponents were Addison Mizner in Palm Beach (*see pp122–9*) and George Merrick in Coral Gables (*see pp84–7*).

The Art Deco Park Central Hotel on Miami's Ocean Drive

Terra-cotta tiles evoke the colors of the Mediterranean.

Ornamentation in stone, terra-cotta, or other materials is usually concentrated around doors and windows.

Balconies, turrets, and irregular roof levels are all recurrent features.

Palm Beach mansions are primarily Spanish Revival in style. This one on South Ocean Boulevard was built by Julius Jacobs, one of Mizner's chief designers, in *1929*.

Postwar Architecture

Many of Florida's most striking modern buildings are either shopping malls or public buildings, such as theaters or sports stadiums, which are often as impressive for their scale as for their design. More of a curiosity are the new towns of Seaside and Disney's Celebration (*see p158*), which have arisen out of nostalgia for small-town America and as a reaction to the impersonal nature of the modern city.

Van Wezel Performing Arts Hall in Sarasota (*see p272*)

Large sash windows allow abundant sun-light and sea breezes to enter the house.

Seaside, a piece of award-winning town planning in Florida's Panhandle, has houses with picket fences and other quaint pseudo-Victorian features. (*See p240.*)

A veranda on the second floor offers a shady place to sit or enjoy the ocean views.

Wood, characteristic of vernacular architecture in Florida, is the favored material in Seaside.

The Highway

Neon signs along International Drive, Orlando

In the 20th century, the flood of visitors and settlers speeding south along Florida's high-ways has spawned buildings unique to the road. Alongside the drive-in banks and restaurants are buildings shaped like ice-cream cones or alligators – designed to catch the eye of the motorist driving past at speed. Such outlandishness, aided too by colorful neon signs, breaks up the monotonous strips of motels and fast food outlets.

Spectator Sports in Florida

Florida offers a wide choice of sports entertainment. Thrilling and exciting events ranging from football, baseball, and basketball to horse, greyhound, and motor racing can be watched and enjoyed throughout the state. All of these sports plus jai alai are popular in Miami where a number of sporting events are held *(see p100)*. Florida's sunny climate makes participation sports such as tennis, golf, and watersports popular throughout the year *(see pp364–7)*. Football, basketball, and hockey are all winter sports.

College football game at EverBank Field stadium in Jacksonville

Football

Florida presently boasts three teams in the National Football League (NFL): the Miami Dolphins, the Tampa Bay Buccaneers, and the Jacksonville Jaguars. The Miami Dolphins, members of the NFL long before the Buccaneers and the Jaguars, have appeared in five Super Bowls, winning twice. The season runs from September to December *(see p100)*.

Among the college teams, the Seminoles of Tallahassee, the Hurricanes out of Miami, and the Gators from Gainesville often finish high in national football ratings; their rivalry is fierce. Florida holds more college bowl games than any other state.

Around New Year's Day there is a glut of important and popular college bowl games. The three favorites are the Citrus Bowl in Orlando, the Orange Bowl Classic in Miami, and the annual Gator Bowl clash in Jacksonville.

Baseball

Set up in 1993, the Florida Marlins was the state's first major league baseball team. Despite the relatively short time since joining the National League, the Marlins have won two World Series championships. The second Florida team to join the major leagues was the Tampa Bay Devil Rays based at St. Petersburg Tropicana Field stadium. The baseball season runs from April to October.

Sixteen major league baseball teams hold spring training in Florida. In March the teams play friendly games in many cities in the so-called **Grapefruit League**. These games, which take place throughout the week, attract large crowds, with fans often coming from outside the state. For dates and tickets contact the individual stadiums in advance. A more comprehensive list of the teams, cities and phone numbers is also available from the Florida Sports Foundation *(see p365)*.

Grapefruit League: Who Plays Where

Atlanta Braves
Walt Disney World.
Tel (407) 939-4263.

Baltimore Orioles
Sarasota. **Tel** (941) 954-4101,
(800) 745-3000.

Boston Red Sox
Fort Myers. **Tel** (617) 482-4769.

Houston Astros
Kissimmee.
Tel (321) 697-3200.

Minnesota Twins
Fort Myers.
Tel (800) 338-9467.

New York Yankees
Tampa.
Tel (813) 879-2244.

Philadelphia Phillies
Clearwater.
Tel (727) 467-4457.

St. Louis Cardinals
Jupiter.
Tel (561) 775-1818.

Tampa Bay Rays
Port Charlotte. **Tel** (727) 825-3250.
A complete list is available from the Florida Sports Foundation *(see p373)*.
ⓦ flasports.com

Horse Racing and Greyhound Racing

Florida boasts the country's second largest thoroughbred industry, centered on Ocala *(see p226)*. Gulfstream Park in Hallandale has racing from January through April. This is the home of the prestigious one million dollar Florida Derby

New York Yankees baseball team, at Tampa for spring training

which is run in March or in the first part of April. The famous Breeder's Cup is often held at Gulfstream. From May through December racing moves to Calder Race Course in Miami. The Summit of Speed in July and the Festival of the Sun in October are two days of stakes racing at Calder, each with purses totaling over one million dollars.

Thoroughbred racing also takes place at Tampa Bay Downs in Tampa from December to May. There is one harness racing track in Florida, Pompano Park in Pompano Beach. Here standardbreds race year-round.

Greyhound racing is popular in Florida and held at several tracks across the state.

Horse racing at Gulfstream Park, Florida's premier venue

Hockey

Although hockey is usually thought of as a cold weather sport, Florida has two teams in the National Hockey League. The Florida Panthers play at the BB&T Center in Sunrise, and the Tampa Bay Lightning, the 2004 Stanley Cup champions, play at the Tampa Bay Times Forum. Thousands of Floridians have taken to watching the sport. The season runs from October to April.

Jai Alai

Florida's game of jai alai, a kind of pelota that originated in Europe, is virtually unique in the US (see p141). Games take

Jai alai, claimed by its fans as the oldest and fastest game in the world

place on a three-walled court, where players use a curved wicker basket to catch and hurl the ball, generating speeds in excess of 150 mph (240 km/h). The back wall is made of granite to absorb the resultant force.

Games are usually played by eight teams of one or two players. After the first point the winners stay on to meet the next team. This goes on until one team has seven points. An evening usually consists of 14 such games.

Jai alai is played all year round in indoor stadiums known as frontons. One of the main attractions is the chance to gamble, and millions are wagered every year.

Motor Racing

Auto and motorcycle racing are big in Florida. The season starts in February at the Daytona International Speedway (see p222), one of the world's fastest tracks, with two very popular races. The Rolex 24, like its older brother at Le Mans, runs all day and all night, and the Daytona 500 is a season highlight for the

The Daytona 500, first held in 1959

National Association of Stock Car Auto Racing (NASCAR). Other big races take place in Homestead, Pensacola, and Sebring. Hot rods come to Gainesville in March for the Gatornationals, the top drag-racing event on the Atlantic seaboard. Motorcycles also race in the annual Daytona 200.

Basketball

Both professional and college basketball have a huge fan following in Florida. The Miami Heat, based at the American Airlines Arena, and the Orlando Magic, whose home court is the Amway Center, provide the best in exciting NBA action. The season runs from October to April.

Orlando in action

Golf and Tennis

Golf tournaments abound in Florida, birthplace of golf ace Jack Nicklaus. Top of the bill are the Bay Hill Invitational in Orlando and the PGA Tournament Players Championship in Ponte Vedra Beach near Jacksonville; both are held at the end of March.

Tennis is another big favorite. For example, Key Biscayne's Crandon Tennis Center is famous for its annual Sony Ericsson Open in March, which pulls huge crowds.

FLORIDA THROUGH THE YEAR

With its warm climate, Florida is a year-round destination, but the difference in the weather between north and south means it has two distinct tourist seasons. In south Florida (including Orlando) the busiest time is from October to April, when tourists come to enjoy the mild winters. Most will have left well before summer arrives, when it can be uncomfortably hot. Orlando's theme parks still attract families with kids on school vacations, but in summer the Panhandle sees some of the biggest crowds. Be warned that prices in the relevant tourist season can be double those charged during the rest of the year. Whatever time of year you visit, you are bound to encounter a festival of some kind, but apart from national holidays (see p41), few of these are Florida-wide. For a full list contact the local tourist office.

Spring

In late February, college students invade Florida for Spring Break, pouring in by the thousands. For the next six weeks Florida's coastal resorts are bursting, putting pressure on accommodations, particularly in Daytona Beach, Panama City Beach, Fort Lauderdale, and Miami.

Baseball training (see p36) is also a big attraction in the spring. In the north, feast your eyes on the blooming azaleas and dogwood trees.

Daytona Beach swarming with pleasure seekers on Spring Break

March
Sanibel Shell Fair (first week). Shell collectors and artists come to Sanibel Island (see pp282–3).
Florida Strawberry Festival (first week), Plant City near Tampa. Strawberry shortcake and country music.
Carnaval Miami (early Mar), Miami. Ten days of Latino Miami festivities with beauty pageants, sports, food, and concerts. The

Little Havana's Calle Ocho, hub of the party at Carnival Miami (see p40)

Calle Ocho street festival finale is the largest in the world.
Motorcycle Races "Bike Week" (early Mar), Daytona Beach (see pp222–3). Bikers converge from all over, on vintage and modern bikes.
Festival of the States (early Mar), St. Petersburg. Three weeks of parades, balls, jazz, and fireworks.
Winter Park Art Festival (mid-Mar). Greater Orlando's arts and fine crafts.
St. Augustine Arts and Crafts Festival (last weekend). Skilled craft artists offer their wares at the city's historical sites.
Antique Boat Festival (late Mar), Mount Dora (see p224). Antique boats race on the lake as visitors attend exhibitions in the pretty town.
Springtime Tallahassee (late Mar, early Apr). One of the South's biggest festivals, with parades, balloon races, great food, and plenty of live music.

April
Easter (Mar/Apr). Celebrate sunrise services at the Castillo de San Marcos (see pp218–9) and take carriage rides around St. Augustine.
Conch Republic Celebration (mid-Apr–early May), Key West. Party all week with parades, bed races, dancing – all in honor of the town's founding fathers.

May
SunFest (first week), West Palm Beach. Cultural and sports events.
Pensacola Crawfish Festival (first week). Enjoy boiled crawfish and fried 'gator to the music of Cajun bands.
Isle of Eight Flags Shrimp Festival (first weekend), Fernandina Beach. Shrimp and other seafood.
Florida Folk Festival (late May). A renowned three-day fiddle and food festival.
Jacksonville Jazz Festival (mid- to late May). Art and craft exhibitions mixed with three days of international jazz.

Emblem of the Conch Republic

Average Daily Hours of Sunshine

Hours

12

9

6

3

0

Jan Feb Mar Apr May Jun Jul Aug Sep Oct Nov Dec

Sunshine Chart
The chart gives figures for the entire state. The west coast near St. Petersburg, which boasts an average of 361 days of sunshine per year, enjoys more sun than elsewhere, but blue skies are a fairly consistent feature everywhere. Even in southern Florida's wetter summer months, the clouds generally disperse quickly.

Young boy in patriotic colors at a Fourth of July celebration

Orlando International Fringe Festival *(late May).* Ten days of comedy, drama, dance, mime, and musicals.

Summer

Temperatures and humidity rise as summer progresses, with only Atlantic breezes and almost daily afternoon storms to bring some relief. Florida's hurricane season *(see pp30–31)* is also underway. Travelers on a tight budget can make the most of the off-season hotel prices in the south.

The big summer holiday is Independence Day on July 4, celebrated with street pageants, fireworks, barbecues, picnics, and mass cooling off in the water.

June

Fiesta of Five Flags *(early Jun),* Pensacola. Two weeks of parades, marathons, fishing rodeos, plus the reenactment of Tristan de Luna's beach landing in 1559.
Monticello Watermelon Festival *(mid-Jun),* Monticello *(see p247).* The harvest is

celebrated in back-country style with barbecues and hoedowns.
Downtown Venice Street Craft Festival *(mid-Jun).* Quiet, romantic Venice spruces up its downtown streets for this very popular crafts bazaar.
Silver Spurs Rodeo *(Jun, Feb),* Osceola Heritage Park, Kissimmee *(see p195).* This is the state's oldest and wildest rodeo, now housed in an indoor air-conditioned arena.

July

America's Birthday Bash *(Jul 4),* Miami. Fireworks at mid-night are preceded by picnics and fun for all the family, in south Florida's biggest Independence Day celebration.
Hemingway Days Festival *(mid-Jul),* Key West. The city offers up a week of author signings, short story contests, theatrical productions, and a very entertaining Hemingway look-alike competition.

August

Goombay Festival *(early Aug),* Coconut Grove, Miami *(see p88).* A Bahamian party offering a parade, great food, and Caribbean music.
Key West Lobsterfest *(early Aug),* Key West. Live music, cold drinks, and fresh lobster at this end of summer party, complete with a sunset Duval Street Crawl.
Boca Festival Days *(all month),* Boca Raton. This celebration features an arts-and-craft fair, barbershop quartet performances, and a sand castle building contest.
Annual Wausau Possum Festival *(first Saturday),* Wausau. This town north of Panama City Beach honors the marsupial with activities such as greased-pole climbing and corn-bread baking, and offers the chance to sample possum-based dishes.

Bearded contenders at the Hemingway Days Festival look-alike contest

Average Monthly Rainfall

Rainfall Chart
The chart gives figures for the whole state. The north-south climatic divide means that, for example, October is the driest month in the Panhandle but the wettest in the Keys. The rule is that southern Florida is wetter than the north in summer (when short, sharp downpours are the norm), while in winter it's the reverse.

Fall (Autumn)

The temperatures begin to cool, and although storms are still a threat, the weather is pleasant. The fall months are a good time to visit as they are usually quiet: the beaches, attractions, and highways are all much less crowded.

Thanksgiving, on the fourth Thursday in November, is the highlight of fall for many, when families come together to eat turkey and pumpkin pie. It is followed by the biggest shopping day of the year, called Black Friday, which commercially launches the countdown to Christmas.

September

St. Augustine's Founding Anniversary *(Saturday nearest 8th)*. This period-dress reenactment of the Spanish landing in 1565 is held near the spot where the first settlers stepped off their ships.

Sleek craft on display at the Fort Lauderdale Boat Show

October

Carnival Miami *(second Sunday)*. A nine-day street party in Miami's Latin district *(see pp80–81)*.
Destin Fishing Rodeo *(all month)*. Hordes of competitive anglers show up for a frenzy of fishing that includes a two-day seafood festival in the first week.
Boggy Bayou Mullet Festival *(mid-Oct)*, Valparaiso and Niceville. These twin cities near Fort Walton Beach celebrate the local fish with fine food, arts, and entertainment.
Fort Lauderdale Boat Show *(late Oct)*. The largest in-water boat show in the world draws yachting enthusiasts to four separate city locations.
Fantasy Fest *(last week)*, Key West. This wild, week-long Halloween celebration features gay festivities, masked balls, a costume contest, and lively street processions.
Johns Pass Seafood Festival *(last weekend)*, Madeira Beach. This popular festival attracts seafood lovers to Johns Pass Village *(see p256)*.
Guavaween *(last Saturday)*, Tampa. This zany Halloween parade pokes fun at the life and history of the city, espe-cially at an early attempt to grow guavas in the area.

November

Florida Seafood Festival *(first weekend)*. The fishing fleet is blessed, net-making lessons are given, and oyster-shucking-and-eating contests are held in Apalachicola.
Orange Bowl Festival *(early Nov–late Feb)*, Miami. This youth festival presents over 20 sports and cultural events.
Festival of the Masters *(second weekend)*, Walt Disney World*. Artists from across the country show their work in Downtown Disney* *(see p176)*.
Miami Book Fair International *(mid-Nov)*. Publishers, authors, and bookworms congregate for this cultural highlight.
Medieval Fair *(last weekend Feb)*, Sarasota. Celebrate the Middle Ages with food and festivities.

Costumed revelers out on the streets for Key West's Fantasy Fest

Average Monthly Temperature

Temperature Chart
This chart gives the average temperature in Miami and Jacksonville, the higher level being the figure for Miami. In the north, even in winter, the evenings are only mildly chilly, and snow is very rare, although it's too cold for swimming. In southern Florida, the hot summer temperatures are exacerbated by the high humidity.

Winter

Winter months are full of excitement in anticipation of Christmas and New Year's. The flood of "snowbirds" from the north intensifies. The celebrities arrive too, some to relax, others to perform during the state's busiest entertainment season. The crowds multiply at Walt Disney World® and the Magic Kingdom® is at its most colorful.

December
Winterfest Boat Parade *(early Dec)*, Fort Lauderdale. Boats decked with lights cruise the Intracoastal Waterway in a magical night-time display.
St. Augustine Grand Illumination *(early Dec)*. Torch-light parade through the old town and a boat parade in front of the Castillo de San Marcos.

Santa on the Intracoastal Waterway for a sunny Florida Christmas

January
Las Olas Art Fair *(early Jan)*, Fort Lauderdale. Las Olas Boulevard is the main drag for this street fair offering art displays, tasty food, and music.
Orange Bowl *(New Year's Day)*, Miami. The big post-season football game *(see p100)*.
Greek Epiphany Day *(Jan 6)*, Tarpon Springs. Ceremonies, feasts, and music at the Greek

Pirates arriving for mock invasion at Tampa's annual Gasparilla Festival

Orthodox Cathedral *(see p255)*.
Art Deco Weekend *(mid-Jan)*, Miami Beach. A street party in the Art Deco area *(see pp64–72)*.
Winter Equestrian Festival *(Jan–Mar)*, Wellington. Seven major equestrian events.
Gasparilla Festival *(late Jan)*, Tampa. A boisterous party, with boat parades and locals in appropriate dress, in memory of the pirates who ravaged the coast *(see p267)*.

February
Speed Weeks *(first three weeks)*, Daytona Beach. These motor races build up to the famous Daytona 500 on the final Sunday *(see pp2223)*.
Coconut Grove Arts Festival *(mid-Feb)*, Miami. This avant-garde art show is one of the country's largest *(see p88)*.
Florida State Fair *(mid-Feb)*, Tampa. Carnival rides, big-name performers, and even alligator wrestling can be enjoyed at this big fair.

Miami Film Festival *(late Feb, early Mar)*. The Film Society of America hosts a broad array of films over ten days *(see p359)*.
Swamp Cabbage Festival *(last weekend)*, La Belle, east of Fort Myers. This celebration features rodeos and dancing, and you can sample delicacies made from the edible heart of the honored state tree.

Public Holidays

New Year's Day (Jan 1)
Martin Luther King Day (3rd Mon, Jan)
Presidents' Day (3rd Mon, Feb)
Memorial Day (last Mon, May)
Independence Day (Jul 4)
Labor Day (1st Mon, Sep)
Columbus Day (2nd Mon, Oct)
Election Day (1st Tue, Nov)
Veterans Day (Nov 11)
Thanksgiving (4th Thu, Nov)
Christmas Day (Dec 25)

THE HISTORY OF FLORIDA

At first glance, Florida appears to be a state with little history, but behind the state's modern veneer lies a long and rich past, molded by many different nationalities and cultures.

Until the 16th century, Florida supported a large indigenous pop- ulation. Many of its tribes had complex political and religious systems that demonstrated a high degree of social organization. However, after Ponce de León first sighted "La Florida" in 1513, Spanish colonization quickly decimated the Indians through warfare and disease.

French explorers troubled the Spanish initially, but a real threat to their control came only much later. In 1742 English colonists from Georgia defeated the Spanish, and thus acquired Florida through the Treaty of Paris in 1763. Florida was returned to Spain in 1783, but numerous boundary disputes and the War of 1812 soon followed; Andrew Jackson captured Pensacola from the British in 1819, and the official US occupation took place in 1821. American attempts to remove the

Seminoles from Florida led to conflicts that lasted for over 65 years. Soon after the Seminole Wars came the Civil War, by the end of which, in 1865, the state was in ruins. But Florida soon recovered. Entrepreneurs like Henry Flagler built a network of railroads and luxurious hotels that attracted wealthy tourists from the north. Tourism flourished during the early 20th century and by 1950 had become Florida's top industry.

As the state opened up, agriculture expanded and migrants flooded in. The recession of the 1920s and 1930s was only a short hiatus in the state's growth, and between 1940 and 1990 the population increased sixfold.

Today, Florida is home to a sizeable Hispanic community, with a strong Cuban presence as well as many other ethnic groups. Economic inequalities have led to social problems and the state's relentless urbanization has put a severe strain on the environment, but Florida is still booming.

Theodore de Brys' 16th-century map of Florida, one of the earliest in existence

◀ An early postcard from Florida, a popular vacation destination in the 1920s

Prehistoric Florida

Florida was once part of the volcanic chain that formed the Caribbean islands. This eroded over millions of years and was sub- merged. When the land finally reemerged, Florida was connected to North America. Humans first arrived in Florida after the last Ice Age and formed distinct tribes. Some developed from nomadic hunter-gatherer societies to ones with permanent settlements along Florida's bountiful rivers and rich seaboard. A high degree of religious and political organization was common to many groups by around AD 1000 and was manifested especially in the building of burial and temple mounds.

Early Tribal Contacts
— Areas in contact

Human Effigy Vessel
This painted ceramic burial urn dates from AD 400–600. Such vessels were often very ornate and usually depicted birds and animals. "Kill holes" were often made in the pots to allow the soul of the pottery to accompany that of the dead.

Pots were often incised. This added to the surface area of the vessel and increased its resistance to heat, as well as making it more aesthetically pleasing.

Copper headdress plates were made of hammered copper that came from as far away as the Great Lakes.

Florida's Prehistoric Tribes

Agriculture and burial mounds, traits shared with groups elsewhere in the southeast US, were associated with the Timucua and other tribes in north Florida. Southern tribes, such as the Calusa and Tequesta, left a legacy of wood carvings and midden mounds, which indicate a diet based on fish and shellfish.

Marco Island's Secret

In 1896, a unique discovery was made on Marco Island (see p288). Many ancient Calusa Indian artifacts of perishable organic material were found perfectly preserved in swampland. However, once out of the protective mangrove sludge the objects quickly crumbled away. Today, sadly, just one or two of these extraordinary pieces, which include ceremonial items such as carvings and masks, survive.

Calusa wood carving

Fired Bowl
Made c. AD 800, this ceramic bowl probably had a ceremonial use. Markings help archaeologists to identify the pot's makers.

c. 10,000 Palaeo-Indian stone tools are first made by Florida's earliest inhabitants

Atlatls *or throwing sticks, part of the tool-kit after 6000 BC*

10,000 BC	9000 BC	8000 BC	7000 BC	6000 BC	5000 BC

The skeleton of a mastodon, an Ice Age animal that once lived in Florida

c. 7500 The temperature rises and people start to hunt smaller animals like deer and include more plant foods in their diet

c. 5000 The first semipermanent settlements are built along the St. Johns River, creating large midden mounds

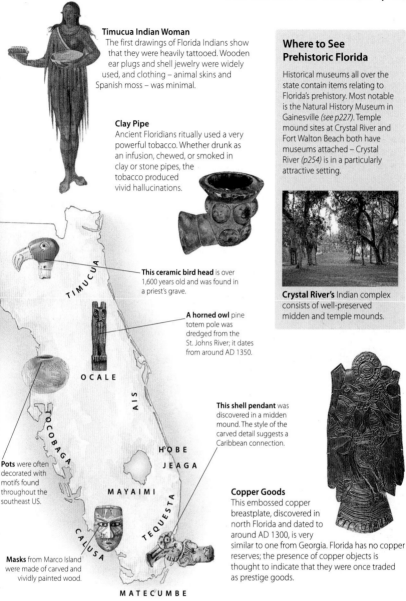

Timucua Indian Woman
The first drawings of Florida Indians show that they were heavily tattooed. Wooden ear plugs and shell jewelry were widely used, and clothing – animal skins and Spanish moss – was minimal.

Clay Pipe
Ancient Floridians ritually used a very powerful tobacco. Whether drunk as an infusion, chewed, or smoked in clay or stone pipes, the tobacco produced vivid hallucinations.

Where to See Prehistoric Florida

Historical museums all over the state contain items relating to Florida's prehistory. Most notable is the Natural History Museum in Gainesville *(see p227)*. Temple mound sites at Crystal River and Fort Walton Beach both have museums attached – Crystal River *(p254)* is in a particularly attractive setting.

Crystal River's Indian complex consists of well-preserved midden and temple mounds.

This ceramic bird head is over 1,600 years old and was found in a priest's grave.

A horned owl pine totem pole was dredged from the St. Johns River; it dates from around AD 1350.

This shell pendant was discovered in a midden mound. The style of the carved detail suggests a Caribbean connection.

TIMUCUA

OCALE

AIS

TOCOBAGA

HOBE

JEAGA

MAYAIMI

TEQUESTA

Pots were often decorated with motifs found throughout the southeast US.

Copper Goods
This embossed copper breastplate, discovered in north Florida and dated to around AD 1300, is very similar to one from Georgia. Florida has no copper reserves; the presence of copper objects is thought to indicate that they were once traded as prestige goods.

CALUSA

Masks from Marco Island were made of carved and vividly painted wood.

MATECUMBE

c. 1000 Northern Florida sees a shift from a basic hunter-gatherer economy to one of cultivation. The settled communities develop more complex societies, and the first burial mounds are built

c.1000 Political systems and religious practices develop, and temple mounds are built. Increased contact with tribal groups outside Florida

4000 BC	3000 BC	2000 BC	1000 BC	AD 1	AD 1000

c. 3000 From this time, Florida enjoys a climate that is similar to today's-

c. 2000 The first crude pottery appears in Florida

A temple structure, built on top of a burial mound

c. 800 First evidence of corn crops being grown in north Florida

Spanish Florida

After Juan Ponce de León first sighted Florida in 1513, several Spanish conquista- dors attempted unsuccessfully to find gold and colonize the region. The French were the first to establish a fort in 1564, but it was soon destroyed by the Spanish: the Gulf Stream carried Spanish treasure ships from other New World colonies past Florida's coast, and it was vital that "La Florida" did not fall into enemy hands. The Spanish introduced Christianity, horses, and cattle. European diseases, in addition to the brutality of the conquistadors, decimated local Indian populations. Britain, eager to expand her American colonies, led several raids into Florida in the 1700s, in an attempt to supplant Spanish rule.

Spanish Fleet Sea Routes
— Sea routes

Ribault's column, erected in 1562 *(see p211)*, marked the French claim to north Florida.

Juan Ponce de León
While searching for gold, Ponce de León found land that he named *Pascua Florida,* after the Feast of Flowers (Easter).

El Adelantado IUAN PONCE Des cubridor de la Florida .

Corn, native to Florida, was a staple crop for the Indians.

Fort Mose

Runaway slaves escaping the harsh conditions in the British Carolinas fled to Florida, where, as in other Spanish colonies, slaves enjoyed certain rights. The Spanish saw the advantage of helping Britain's enemies and in 1738 created Fort Mose, near the garrison town of St. Augustine *(see p216–17)*, for the runaways. This fort, with its own militia and businesses, is regarded as North America's first independent black community.

Black militiaman in the Spanish colonies

Florida's First Settlement

The Huguenot René de Laudonnière founded "La Caroline," Florida's first successful European settlement, in 1564. Another Frenchman, Le Moyne, painted the Indians greeting the colonizers.

1513 Ponce de León discovers Florida. He tries to establish a Spanish colony eight years later, but is unsuccessful

Hernando de Soto's signature

c.1609 *A History of the Conquest of Florida* is published by Garcilasso Inca del Vega

1622 The Spanish ships *Atocha* and *Santa Margarita* sink during a hurricane

| 1520 | 1540 | 1560 | 1580 | 1600 | 1620 |

1528 Pánfilo de Narváez lands in Tampa Bay in search of El Dorado, the land of gold

1539 Hernando de Soto arrives at Tampa Bay with 600 men, but he dies by the Mississippi River three years later

1566 The Jesuits arrive in Florida

1565 Pedro Menéndez de Avilés founds San Agustín (St. Augustine) after defeating the French

Cross-section of the Atocha

Hernando de Soto
De Soto was the most ruthless of the conquistadors. His search for gold led to the massacre of many Indians; only a third of his own party survived.

Silver and Gold Hair Ornament
Indian artifacts made of precious metals fueled the Spanish myth of El Dorado. In fact, the metals came from Spanish wrecks.

Where to See Spanish Florida

In St. Petersburg, the De Soto National Memorial marks the spot where de Soto landed *(see p271)*. A reconstruction of Fort Caroline *(p211)* lies just outside Jacksonville. However, the best place to see the Spanish legacy is in St. Augustine *(pp214–15)* and its imposing Castillo de San Marcos *(pp218–19)*.

Nuestra Senora de la Leche is a shrine in St. Augustine founded by de Avilés in 1565.

René de Laudonnière surveys the offerings of the Indians.

Sir Francis Drake
Spain's power in the New World colonies worried the British. Drake, an English buccaneer, burned down St. Augustine in 1586.

Athore, the chief of the Timucua, shows the French colonizers his tribe worshiping at Ribault's column.

Codice Osune
This 16th-century manuscript depicts members of Tristan de Luna's expedition to Florida. In 1559, a hurricane destroyed his camp at Pensacola Bay, defeating his attempts at colonization.

1670 The Treaty of Madrid defines the Spanish claim to the New World

The pirate Blackbeard's flag

1718 Blackbeard, who terrorized the east coast of Florida, is killed off North Carolina

1740 The British, based in Georgia, besiege the Castillo de San Marcos

1763 Under the Treaty of Paris, Britain gets Florida and returns recently captured Cuba to Spain

| 1640 | 1660 | 1680 | 1700 | 1720 | 1740 | 1760 |

1687 The first eight slaves fleeing the British plantations in the Carolinas arrive in Florida

1693 The Spanish establish Pensacola, which is permanently settled five years later

1702 The British raze St. Augustine

Castillo de San Marcos, St. Augustine

1756 Castillo de San Marcos is completed

The Fight for Florida

A plentiful supply of hides and furs, and the opportunity to expand the plantation system, attracted the British to Florida. After taking control in 1763, they divided the colony in two. Florida was subsidized by Britain and so stayed loyal during the American Revolution. However, Spain regained West Florida in 1781 and then East Florida was handed back two years later. American slaves fled to Florida creating antagonism between Spain and the US. This was exacerbated by Indian raids to the north and an Indian alliance with the runaway slaves. General Andrew Jackson invaded Spanish Florida, captured Pensacola, and even occupied West Florida, thus provoking the First Seminole War.

British Florida 1764–83
East Florida
West Florida

Fort George was the main British fortification at Pensacola.

A drummer kept the marching beat, and led soldiers into battle.

The Spanish Caste System
Few Spanish women came to the colonies, so Spanish men often took black or Indian wives. A hierarchical caste system emerged – with those of pure Spanish blood at the top.

Brazier
Used for warmth during northern Florida winters, a brasero could also smoke out mosquitos in summer.

The Capture of Pensacola
In 1781, after a month-long siege, the Spaniard Bernardo de Gálvez defeated the British and captured Pensacola for Spain. His victory undoubtedly helped the bid for independence made by the American colonies.

1776 American Revolution leaves Britain's reserves heavily depleted, and British loyalists begin to abandon Florida

1783 Under the Second Treaty of Paris, Britain recognizes American independence, gains the Bahamas and Gibraltar, and returns Florida to the Spanish, who start to colonize it in earnest

1785–1821 Several Spanish-American border disputes occur

| 1765 | 1770 | 1775 | 1780 | 1785 | 17 |

British soldier in the American Revolution

1781 Under de Gálvez, the Spanish land at Pensacola and capture West Florida

1782 US Congress chooses the bald eagle as the emblem of the new republic

National emblem

General Jackson
An ambitious soldier, Andrew Jackson led many raids into Florida and eventually conquered it. His successes made him the ideal candidate to become Florida's first American governor in 1821 and, later, the seventh US president.

Where to See the Fight for Florida

The Kingsley Plantation (see p211) near Jacksonville is the state's oldest surviving plantation house. Pensacola's historic Seville District (p234) was laid out by the British during their occupation, and St. Augustine (pp214–17) contains several buildings dating from this era; they include the British Government House, and the Ximenez-Fatio house, from the second period of Spanish rule.

Kingsley Plantation occupies a lovely setting at the mouth of the St. Johns River.

William Bartram's Illustrations
In 1765, William Bartram was appointed the royal botanist in America. He documented Florida's wildlife and her indigenous peoples.

Bernardo de Gálvez,
the 27-year-old Spanish governor of Louisiana, was wounded in action in the battle for Pensacola.

Political Cartoon
This cartoon shows the horse America throwing his master. British loyalists in East Florida were dismayed by the loss of the Colonies after 1783, and soon chose to leave Florida.

The Slave Trade
Slavery fueled the plantation system. The journey from Africa to America could take months, and slaves were so tightly packed on board ship that many died en route.

1803 The US buys Louisiana and pushes east, creating Florida's present western boundary. The US claims West Florida

1800 Spain cedes West Florida's Louisiana territories to the French

1808 A law banning the slave trade is enacted by the US Congress, but it is widely ignored

Slave manacles

1817 First Seminole War begins

| 1795 | 1800 | 1805 | 1810 | 1815 |

1795 Spain cedes territory north of the 31st parallel to the US

The Patriots of East Florida's flag

1812 American patriots capture Amelia Island, demanding that the US annex East Florida from the Spanish. Their attempt fails but instills the feeling that Florida should belong to America

1819 To settle Spain's $5-million debt to the US, all Spanish territories east of the Mississippi (including Florida) are ceded to the US.

Antebellum Florida

After Florida became part of the US in 1821, American settlement proceeded apace, and the plantation system was firmly established in north Florida. The settlers wanted good land, so the Federal government tried to remove all Indians to west of the Mississippi; resulting conflicts developed into the Second and Third Seminole Wars. After Abraham Lincoln, an opponent of slavery, was elected president in 1860, Florida became the third state to secede from the Union. During the ensuing Civil War it saw little action; Florida's chief role was to supply food to the Confederates, especially beef and salt.

Indian Lands 1823–32
 Indian reservation land

Slave cabins were often log huts, built away from the main residence.

Overseer's cabin

Barn and stables

Well

Osceola
The influential Indian leader Osceola refused to move from Florida with his tribe. In 1835 he started the Second Seminole War, during which many plantations were destroyed.

Uncle Tom's Cabin

In 1852, Harriet Beecher Stowe, a religious northerner who spent her later years in Florida, published a novel that helped to change the face of America. *Uncle Tom's Cabin* is a tale about a slave who, having rescued a white child, is sold to a sadistic master and is eventually flogged to death. It was hugely successful and furthered the cause of the antislavery lobby. During the Civil War, President Lincoln joked that Mrs. Stowe was the "little woman who started this big war."

Poster for *Uncle Tom's Cabin*

Cotton
The principal cash crop on plantations was cotton. It required intensive labor and the work was grueling – especially picking the cotton off the spiny bushes.

1821 Jackson becomes governor of the territory of Florida

1823 Treaty of Moultrie Creek requires the Seminoles to move from north to central Florida

1832 Under the Treaty of Payne's Creek, 15 Seminole chiefs cede their land in Florida to the US and agree to move west

1835 Second Seminole War begins

Early horse-drawn train

1820   **1825**   **1830**   **1835**   **1840**

Osceola refusing to sign 1832 treaty

c.1824 The Indian village of Talasi is chosen as the site of the new state capital and is renamed Tallahassee

1832 JJ Audubon, the naturalist, visits Key West

1829 General Jackson becomes President of the US

1842 Second Seminole War ends

1836 The first railroads in Florida begin operating

Paddlesteamer
During the Seminole and Civil Wars, steamboats were used to transport troops and supplies to the interior.

Chief Billy Bowlegs
In 1855, a group of surveyors pillaged Indian land. Chief Billy Bowlegs retaliated, starting the Third Seminole War. He surrendered in 1858; however, other Seminoles retreated into the Everglades.

Goodwood House was built in a grand style that befitted its wealth and importance within the local community.

Where to See Antebellum Florida

Gamble Plantation *(see p270)* sheds light on the lifestyle of a wealthy plantation owner, while at Bulow Plantation *(p220)* and Indian Key *(p298)* you can see the ruins of communities destroyed by the Seminoles. The Museum of Science and History *(p212)* in Jacksonville contains Civil War artifacts, including some from the US army steamboat *Maple Leaf*. Key West's East Martello Tower *(p304)* and Fort Zachary *(p306)*, and Fort Clinch *(p210)*, in the north-east, are fine examples of 19th-century forts.

The East Martello Tower was built by Union forces to defend Key West's Atlantic coast.

Laundry

Privy

Guest House

Spring House

The kitchen was in a separate building because of the risk of fire.

Battle of Olustee
In February 1864, Union forces, including two Negro regiments, were defeated by Confederate troops in the northeast. Some 10,000 men fought in the six-hour battle; 2,000 were injured and 300 died.

Plantation Life

Antebellum plantations such as Goodwood (see p247), reconstructed here, were almost self-sufficient. They had their own laws, and some housed over 200 slaves who tended cotton, corn, and other crops.

1845 On July 4 Florida becomes the 27th state to join the United States of America. The Capitol building in Tallahassee is completed

1848 John Gorrie invents an ice-making machine

1855 Third Seminole War begins; three years later 163 Indians surrender (including Billy Bowlegs) and are forcibly removed from Florida

1861 Civil War begins

1865 The northern army is defeated at the Battle of Natural Bridge. The Civil War ends in the same year

1845	1850	1855	1860	1865

STATE OF FLORIDA

Florida's first state seal

1852 Harriet Beecher Stowe publishes the antislavery epic, *Uncle Tom's Cabin*

1860s Scottish merchants found Dunedin on Florida's west coast

Civil War bond

STATE OF FLORIDA

Florida's Golden Age

After the Civil War Florida's economy was devastated, but its fine climate and small population meant it was a land ripe for investment. The railroad barons Henry Flagler and Henry Plant forged their lines down the east and west coasts of Florida during the late 1880s and 1890s, and tourists followed in increasing numbers, stimulating the economy. A diverse agricultural base also sheltered Florida from the depression of the 1890s that ravaged other cotton-producing states. Fortunes were made and fine mansions were built. Blacks were less fortunate; most lost the right to vote, Ku Klux Klan violence grew, and segregation was the norm.

Growth of the Railroads
— Railroads by 1860
— Railroads by 1890
— Overseas Railroad by 1912

Steamboat Tourism
Before the advent of the railroads, tourists explored Florida's interior by paddlesteamer. Steamboats plied scenic rivers such as the Oklawaha and the St. Johns.

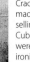

Jacob Summerlin
After the Civil War, Jacob Summerlin, the "King of the Crackers" (see p24), made his fortune by selling beef to Spanish Cuba. His wild cattle were descended, ironically, from animals that had been introduced to Florida by the conquistadors.

Cigar labels were miniature works of art, and the design would often depict a topographical scene. The cigar industry took off in Florida in the late 1800s.

Grand Hotels
Both Plant and Flagler built opulent palaces for rich tourists who used the railroads to escape the northern winters; these "snowbirds" would spend the winter season in style, in towns like Tampa and St. Augustine.

1869 The first black Cabinet member is appointed as Secretary of State in Florida

A Ringling Brothers' circus act

1885 Vincente Ybor transfers his cigar industry to Tampa

1870s More than 100 blacks are killed by the Ku Klux Klan in Jackson County

1892 In the election, only 11 percent of blacks remain eligible to vote

1870	1875	1880	1885	1890

1870 Steamboats start to take tourists, as well as goods, into the interior of Florida

1884 Ringling brothers set up their traveling circus

1891 The Cuban, José Martí, makes a speech in Tampa to drum up support for his independence movement

1886 Flagler starts construction of the Florida East Coast Railroad

1868 Vote granted to all male American citizens aged 21 and over, including blacks

Rail Travel
Many rich tourists had private railroad cars. Today Henry Flagler's is at his former Palm Beach home (see p128).

Spanish-American War
When America joined Cuba's fight against Spain in 1898, Florida boomed. Thousands of troops converged on Tampa, Miami, and Key West, and money from the nation's coffers poured in to support the war effort.

Where to see The Golden Age

St. Augustine (see pp214–17) boasts several of Flagler's buildings, including what is today the Lightner Museum. The Tampa Bay Hotel is now the Henry B. Plant Museum (p262), and Fernandina has some fine examples of steam-boat architecture (p210). On Pigeon Key (p300) you'll find Flagler's Overseas Railroad construction camp.

Flagler College in St. Augustine was once Henry Flagler's magnificent Ponce de Leon Hotel.

The Tampa Bay Hotel, built by Henry Plant in 1891, operated as a hotel until 1932. It had 511 rooms, and during the Spanish-American War served as the officers' quarters.

Gilded Rocking Chair
Representative of the decorative excesses of the 19th century, this rocking chair from the Lightner Museum (see p216) is elaborately embellished with scrolls and swans.

The Hillsborough River and nearby Tampa Bay helped turn Tampa into one of the three largest Gulf ports by 1900.

The Birth of a Nation
On its release in 1915, this epic film provoked a resurgence of violence by the Ku Klux Klan in Florida.

1895 Blossoming citrus groves are hit by the "Great Freeze." Julia Tuttle sends some orange blossoms to Flagler in Palm Beach to persuade him to continue his railroad to Miami

1905 The University of Florida is established at Gainesville

Driving on the sand at Daytona Beach

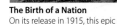

1918 Prohibition starts in Florida

| 1895 | 1900 | 1905 | 1910 | 1915 |

Orange blossom

1898 Teddy Roosevelt and his Rough Riders arrive in Tampa en route to fight in the Spanish-American War in Cuba

1903 Alexander Winton sets a 68-mph (109-km/h) land speed record on the hard sand at Daytona Beach

1912 Flagler steams into Key West

1915 Dredging doubles the size of Miami Beach

1916 Florida's cotton crop is wiped out by the boll weevil

Boom, Bust, and Recovery

Like the rest of the US, Florida saw times of both rapid growth and depression during the first half of the 20th century. Excited by the rampant development during the 1920s land boom, northerners poured in, many as "Tin Can Tourists" in their Model T Fords. Then, in 1926, three years before the Wall Street Crash, a real estate slump ruined many in the state. But economic recovery came earlier than in the rest of the US, with the the growth of tourism and the introduction of federal schemes; many unemployed fled to Florida from the north looking for work. During and after World War II, the state continued to prosper; in the 1950s it was boosted by the launch of the NASA space program.

Population Figures
☐ 1920   ☐ 1950

Land Boom
At the height of the boom, prime land could fetch $26,000 per acre. A great many northerners were bankrupted after unwittingly investing in swampland far from the waterfront.

Hurricane of 1926
On September 18 a hurricane hit South Florida, destroying 5,000 homes. Locals said the winds "blowed a crooked road straight."

The American Dream in Florida
Florida's warm winter climate and economic upswing attracted floods of northerners. Many who first came as visitors returned to settle, and foreign immigrants also favored the state. It was a land of opportunity with rapid urban growth and industries that provided good jobs – even the young could expect a good standard of living.

1928 The Tamiami Trail between Tampa and Miami is officially opened

1929 The first commercial flight between Miami to Havana is made by Pan American World Airways

1931 Ernest Hemingway buys a house in Key West

1935 Hurricane destroys Flagler's Overseas Railroad

| 1920 | 1925 | 1930 | 1935 | 1940 |

1926 Florida land prices crash, two banks collapse, and a hurricane hits the southeast and the Everglades, devastating Miami

1931 Hialeah Park race track opens after pari-mutuel betting (*see p141*) is legalized

Horse race at Hialeah Park

1939 Gangster Al Capone retires to an estate on Palm Island in Miami

Tin Can Tourists
Each winter, this new breed of tourist loaded up their cars and headed south. They stayed en masse in trailer parks, sharing their canned food and enjoying the Florida sun.

Where to See Boomtime Florida

The Wolfsonian Foundation *(see p71)* and Miami Beach's Art Deco buildings *(pp64–70)* shouldn't be missed. Mizner's whimsical Palm Beach legacy *(pp122–7)* is also worth visiting. Frank Lloyd Wright's college in Lakeland *(p270)* is very impressive; Henry Ford's winter home in Fort Myers *(p280)* is more modest.

Miami Beach contains a striking assortment of restored Art Deco buildings.

Zora Neale Hurston
Zora wrote about the lives of rural blacks. Her best known novel, *Their Eyes Were Watching God*, was written in 1937.

Roosevelt's New Deal
The president's New Deal, which allowed farmers to borrow money, helped Florida to recover from the Great Depression. Writers and photographers documented the policy's effects.

World War II
Florida was a training ground for many thousands of troops from 1941 to 1945. War reduced tourism, but the camps helped the economy.

Citrus Industry
Florida became the largest citrus producer in the country, helping it to survive the Depression of the 1930s.

1947 President Truman opens Everglades National Park

Racing car in the Daytona 200

1954 The first span of the Sunshine Skyway bridge over Tampa Bay opens

1959 Lee Perry wins the first Daytona 200 race at the Daytona Speedway

1945	1950	1955	1960

1945 On December 5, the disappearance of Flight 19 starts the myth of the Bermuda Triangle

1942 In February, German U-boats torpedo a tanker just off the coast of Florida, in full view of bathers

1958 The first Earth satellite, *Explorer I*, is launched from Florida after NASA chooses Cape Canaveral as the site of its satellite and rocket programs

NASA logo

The Sixties and Beyond

Since 1960, Florida has flourished. Tourism has expanded at an unprecedented rate, and countless hotels have been built to cater to all budgets. Theme parks like Walt Disney World® and the Kennedy Space Center, home to NASA's space program, have brought both worldwide fame and crowds of visitors to the Sunshine State. The population has also grown rapidly, through migration from within the US and from abroad; modern Florida is home to many ethnic groups. The rapidly growing Hispanic community includes the largest Cuban population outside of Cuba. Florida is also home to a large Asian community. The negative effects of development have led to increased steps to protect natural resources: conservation has become a major issue.

State Population Figures

☐ 1960   ☐ 2010

The Cuban Exodus
Over 300,000 Cubans have fled to Florida since Castro took over Cuba in 1959. Early arrivals came on "freedom flights," but later refugees had to make the perilous trip by sea on flimsy rafts.

Martin Luther King
The Civil Rights movement reached Florida in the 1960s. Martin Luther King Jr., the movement's most prominent leader, was arrested while on a march in St. Augustine in 1964.

SpaceX Dragon
In 2012, Space X became the world's first commercial space company to deliver cargo to the International Space Station. Under an agreement with NASA, SpaceX is developing the vessel to fly crew for manned flights.

1964 Martin Luther King Jr. is arrested and imprisoned in St. Augustine

1969 Apollo II is launched from Cape Canaveral. Buzz Aldrin and Neil Armstrong are the first men to walk on the moon

1973 Dade County is officially bilingual, and English-Spanish road signs are erected

1980 125,000 Cubans arrive in Florida in the Mariel boatlift, which is begun by Fidel Castro and lasts for five months

1986 The space shuttle *Challenger* explodes, killing all seven crew membe[r]s

1970

1980

1

1962 Cuban missile crisis

1961 Alan Shepherd becomes the first US man in space

Alan Shepherd, NASA astronaut

1971 The Magic Kingdom®, Walt Disney's first venture in Florida, opens in Orlando at a cost of $700 million

1977 Snow falls on Miami in January

1981 Maiden voyage of the Space Shuttle

1982 Key West declares itself the "Conch Republic" for just one week

1990 General Noriega, the former ruler of Panama, faces drugs charges in Miami

Conservation
One way Floridians can support the conservation movement is by buying a special license plate. Money raised goes to the cause depicted.

Miami on TV
Miami has a reputation for crime and violence, graphically portrayed in the 1980s' TV show, *Miami Vice*, and nowadays in *CSI: Miami*.

Where to See Modern Florida

Florida has plenty of fine modern architecture, from the skyscrapers in downtown Miami (*see pp74–9*) and Jacksonville (*see p212*) to the Florida Aquarium in Tampa (*see p266*). To see a more nostalgic approach to modern architecture, visit Seaside in the Panhandle (*see p240*).

Naturalization
Becoming a US citizen is the dream of many immigrants. Mass ceremonies see thousands pledge an oath of allegiance together.

Downtown Miami's modern skyscrapers create a distinctive and impressive city skyline.

SpaceX Falcon 9 rocket launches the Dragon capsule into orbit from Cape Canaveral.

Florida's Elderly
Just under 20 percent of Florida's population is over 65 years old. Many retirees are attracted to the state by its low taxes and easy, outdoors lifestyle.

Caribbean Cruises
Tourism is big business in Florida, and cruises in state-of-the-art ships are an increasingly popular vacation choice.

1992 Hurricane Andrew wreaks havoc in south Florida

1993 The Task Force on Tourist Safety is created

2002 Jimmy Carter becomes the first US President to visit Cuba since the embargo began

2003 Space shuttle *Columbia* explodes on re-entry into Earth's atmosphere, killing all its crew

2011 After operating for 30 years, NASA's Space Shuttle program ends with its final mission, *Atlantis*

2000 | **2010** | **2020**

1994 Another influx of Cubans arrives in Florida

2000 George Bush wins controversial presidential elections

George W. Bush

2004 One of the deadliest hurricane seasons in history inflicts over $40 billion in damage

2012 The first commercial space company, SpaceX, delivers cargo to the International Space Station, carried on the Dragon spacecraft.

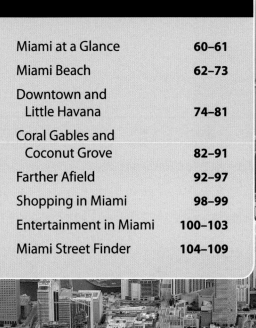

MIAMI AREA BY AREA

Miami at a Glance

Miami has been called the Magic City because what was merely a trading outpost a century ago now sprawls for 2,000 sq miles (5,200 sq km) and boasts a population of two million. Visitors are most likely to remember Miami for its fun-filled South Beach, for its lustrous beaches, and for the Latin and Caribbean culture that permeates daily life. Greater Miami is home to more than two million residents, and it draws close to nine million visitors each year. As in any urban area, safety guidelines are important.

Little Havana, the original heart of the city's Cuban community, is Miami's most welcoming neighborhood. Life in the streets is fun, with domino games and buzzing cafés (see pp80–81).

The Biltmore Hotel epitomizes Coral Gables, the exclusive minicity developed during the 1920s real estate boom. Tales of celebrity guests and Mafia murders add to the mystique of the luxurious hotel (see pp84–7).

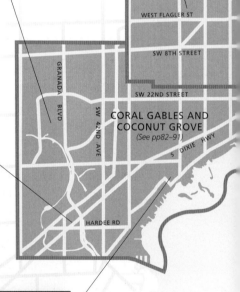

WEST FLAGLER ST

SW 8TH STREET

GRANADA BLVD

SW 42ND AVE

SW 22ND STREET

CORAL GABLES AND COCONUT GROVE
(See pp82–91)

S DIXIE HWY

HARDEE RD

The "International Villages" are clusters of ethnic architecture, from French to Chinese, hidden away along the shady streets of Coral Gables. A tour of them will provide a taste of Miami's loveliest suburb (see pp84–5).

Coconut Grove Village is a small, friendly area where the focus is on entertainment. Enjoy a relaxing amble or shop in the daytime, before heading for the restaurants and bars, which come to life in the evening (see p88).

◀ Aerial view of Downtown Miami

Downtown Miami is the commercial hub of the city. Its appeal lies in its eyecatching high-rise architecture, such as the Southeast Financial Center, pictured here, and in the Hispanic bustle on the streets *(see pp76–9).*

W 41ST ST

MIAMI BEACH
(See pp62–73)

ALTON RD

W 8TH STREET

OWNTOWN AND
TTLE HAVANA
(See pp74–81)

The Art Deco District of South Beach boasts many dazzling 1930s buildings, with decorative features unique to Florida *(see pp64–71).*

0 kilometers   2

0 miles   1

South Beach is for watching or taking part in the fun and games of the resort. During the daytime you can take it easy on the fabulous sandy beach *(see pp68–70).*

Vizcaya is Miami's top single sight. The early 20th-century Italianate mansion has rooms decorated in all imaginable styles, while the gardens are dotted with statues, and picturesque buildings, such as this romantic tea house *(see pp90–91).*

MIAMI BEACH

Now often referred to as the American Riviera, Miami Beach was a sandbar accessible only by boat a century ago. It was the building of a bridge to the mainland in 1913 that enabled real estate investors like millionaire Carl Fisher to begin developing the island. The resort they created from nothing took off in the 1920s, becoming a spectacular winter playground. The devastating hurricane of 1926 and the 1929 Wall Street Crash signaled the end of the boom, but Miami Beach bounced back in the 1930s with the erection of hundreds of Art Deco buildings, only to decline again after World War II. In another metamorphosis, Miami Beach rose once again. As a result of a spirited preservation campaign, South Beach (the southern part of Miami Beach) has been given a new lease of life. It boasts the world's largest concentration of Art Deco buildings, whose funky colors are no less arresting than the local population of body builders, fashion models, and drag queens. Anything goes in South Beach, where the mood veers between the chic and the bohemian, hence its nickname SoBe – after New York's hip SoHo district. The Art Deco hotels along Ocean Drive are everyone's favorite haunt but there are other diversions, from trendy shops to higher-brow art museums. The district north of SoBe tempts few people, but what the two areas do share is a superb sandy beach, unbroken mile after mile.

Sights at a Glance

Museums and Galleries

3 Jewish Museum of Florida
5 The Wolfsonian Museum-FIU
9 Bass Museum of Art

Streets and Neighborhoods

1 Ocean Drive
4 Collins and Washington Avenues
6 Española Way
7 Lincoln Road Mall
10 Central Miami Beach

Beaches

2 The Beach

Monuments

8 Holocaust Memorial

0 meters   1,000
0 yards   1,000

See also Street Finder map 2

◄ Miami's famous Art Deco Colony Theater

For map symbols *see back flap*

Ocean Drive: Deco Style

The cream of South Beach's Art Deco District, which consists of some 800 preserved buildings, is found on Ocean Drive. Its splendid array of buildings illustrates Miami's unique interpretation of the Art Deco style, which took the world by storm in the 1920s and '30s. Florida's version, often called Tropical Deco, is fun and jaunty. Motifs such as flamingos and sunbursts are common, and South Beach's seaside location inspired features more befitting an ocean liner than a building. Using inexpensive materials, architects managed to create an impression of stylishness for what were, in fact, very modest hotels. The best of the buildings along Ocean Drive are illustrated here and on pages 66–7.

Ocean Drive: 6th to 9th Streets

White, blue, and green were popular colors in the 1930s and '40s; they echo Miami's tropical vegetation and the ocean.

Windows are often continuous around corners.

View along Ocean Drive

① **Park Central** (1937) Henry Hohauser, the most famous architect to work in Miami, designed this hotel. It has fine etched windows.

Angular edges exemplify the influence of Cubism.

Bands of windows give plenty of light and, when open, encourage the circulation of cooling sea breezes.

A flamingo is etched into glass doors in the Beacon's lobby.

④ **Avalon** (1941) The Avalon is a fine example of Streamline Moderne. The lack of ornamentation and the asymmetrical design are typical, as is the emphasis on horizontal as opposed to vertical lines.

⑤ **Beacon** (1936) The traditional abstract decoration above the ground floor windows of the Beacon has been brightened by a contemporary color scheme, an example of Leonard Horowitz's Deco Dazzle (*see p71*).

Art Deco: from Paris to Miami

The Art Deco style emerged following the 1925 Exposition Internationale des Arts Décoratifs et Industriels Modernes in Paris. Traditional Art Deco combined all kinds of influences, from Art Nouveau's flowery forms and Egyptian imagery to the geometric patterns of Cubism. In 1930s America, Art Deco buildings reflected the belief that technology was the way forward, absorbing features that embodied the Machine Age and the fantasies of science fiction. Art Deco evolved into a style called Stream-line Moderne, which dominates along Ocean Drive. Few buildings in South Beach stick to just one style. Indeed it is the creative mix of classic Art Deco details with streamlining and tropical motifs that has made the architecture along Ocean Drive unique.

Deco-style postcard of the Avalon Hotel

The Berkeley Shore, behind Ocean Drive on Collins Avenue, has classic Streamline Moderne features such as this stepped parapet.

Color has been used to give the idea of vertical fluting.

Circles, as decoration or as windows, were inspired by the portholes used in ship design.

The lobby of the Majestic has splendid brass elevator doors.

Bas-relief friezes are a recurrent decorative element on Ocean Drive façades.

② **Imperial** (1939) The design of the Imperial echoes that of the earlier Park Central next door.

③ **Majestic** (1940) This hotel was the work of Albert Anis, the architect also responsible for the nearby Avalon and Waldorf hotels.

Racing stripes are typical of Streamline Moderne.

"Eyebrows" – flat overhangs above the windows – are ideal for providing shade against the unrelenting Miami sun.

This ornamental lighthouse is one of the most evocative examples of Ocean Drive's "architecture for the seashore."

Neon lighting was frequently used to highlight hotel signs and architectural features, so that they could be enjoyed after dark.

Porthole windows

⑥ **Colony** (1935) One of Henry Hohauser's finest hotels, the Colony has Ocean Drive's most famous neon sign and an interesting mural in the lobby.

⑦ **Waldorf Towers** (1937) The maritime influence on the design of the Waldorf and some other hotels led to the coining of the phrase "Nautical Moderne."

Ocean Drive: Deco Style

Three principal Art Deco styles exist in South Beach: traditional Art Deco, the more futuristic Streamline Moderne, and Mediterranean Revival, which is derivative of French, Italian, and Spanish architecture. The unusual injection of Mediterranean Revival influences along Ocean Drive is noticeable mainly between 9th and 13th streets. Here too you will find some of South Beach's most classic Art Deco buildings.

Ocean Drive: 9th to 13th Streets

Colored strips, or "racing stripes," give a feeling of speed and motion.

The central tower recalls both a ship's funnel and the totems of American Indian culture.

The railings edging the roof imitate those on a ship's deck.

The window arches and columned porch are evocative of Mediterranean architecture.

⑧ **Breakwater** (1939)
The Breakwater, by Anton Skislewicz, is a classic Streamline Moderne hotel with its racing stripes and a striking central tower. A multimillion-dollar renovation has seen the hotel restored to its original splendor.

⑨ **Edison** (1935) Hohauser (see p64) experimented here with Mediterranean Revivalism, although he was preceded by the architect of the nearby Adrian.

The sign for the Leslie hotel is simple, like the building – in contrast with the more exuberant Carlyle next door.

Corner windows

Flat roofs are the norm along Ocean Drive, but these are often broken by a tower or other vertical projection.

⑫ **Leslie** (1937)
This classic Art Deco hotel's coat of bright yellow paint stands out against the paler shades now popular on South Beach.

⑬ **Carlyle** (1941)
With its three stories and three vertical columns, the Carlyle makes use of the classic Deco divisions, sometimes known as the "holy three." Most hotels along Ocean Drive have three floors.

A salamander in stucco over the front entrance to the Abbey Hotel, on 21st Street, adds a colorful and play-ful touch to the building's façade.

Preserving South Beach

The campaign to save the Art Deco architecture of South Beach began in 1976, when Barbara Capitman (1920–90) set up the Miami Design Preservation League – at a time when much of the area was destined to disappear under a sea of high-rises. Three years later, one square mile (2.5 sq km) of South Beach became the first 20th-century district in the country's National Register of Historic Places. Battles still raged against developers throughout the 1980s and '90s, when candlelit vigils helped save some buildings.

Barbara Capitman in 1981

Vertical fluting occurs frequently along Ocean Drive.

"Eyebrow" overhangs shade the windows.

⑩ Clevelander (1938)
This hotel's architect, Albert Anis, used classic Deco materials – such as glass blocks in the hotel's bar, now a top South Beach nightspot.

Terra-cotta tiles

Reinforced concrete was the most common building material used along Ocean Drive, with walls generally covered in stucco.

A veranda is a prerequisite for most Ocean Drive hotels.

⑪ Adrian (1934)
With its subdued colors and chiefly Mediterranean inspiration, the Adrian stands out among neighboring buildings.

The corners of the building are beautifully rounded.

The terrazzo floor in the bar is a mix of stone chips and mortar – a cheap version of marble that brought style at minimal cost.

The frieze recalls the abstract designs of the Aztecs.

⑭ Cardozo (1939)
A late Hohauser work and Barbara Capitman's favorite hotel, this is a Streamline masterpiece, in which the detail of traditional Art Deco is replaced with curved sides and other expressions of the modern age.

⑮ Cavalier (1936)
With its sharp edges, this traditional Art Deco hotel provides quite a contrast to the later Cardozo next door.

Street-by-Street: South Beach

The Art Deco district of South Beach, which runs from 6th to 23rd streets between Lenox Avenue and Ocean Drive, has attracted more and more visitors since the 1980s. Helped by the interest shown by celebrities such as Gloria Estefan and Michael Caine, the area has been transformed into one of the trendiest places in the States. For many visitors the Deco buildings serve merely as a backdrop for a hedonistic playground, where days are for sleeping, lying on the beach, or long workouts at the gym, evenings for dancing into the early hours. But whether your passions are social or architectural, the route shown can be enjoyed both during the day and at night – when a sea of neon enhances the party atmosphere.

The Old City Hall, a 1920s Mediterranean-style building, ended its service as city hall in 1977, but it remains a distinctive South Beach landmark, towering over the surrounding streets.

⑤ Wolfsonian Museum-FIU
The Wolfsonian, with a striking Spanish Baroque-style relief around its main entrance, houses an excellent collection of fine and decorative arts.

11th Street Diner
(see p329)

The Essex House Hotel, by Henry Hohauser *(see p64)*, has typical Deco features such as the rounded corner entry. Its lobby is also well worth a look.

The News Café is a favorite South Beach haunt *(see p329)*, open 24 hours a day and always buzzing. The sidewalk tables make it a prime spot for people-watching.

ART DECO TOURS

The Miami Design Preservation League offers 90-minute guided walking tours from the Art Deco Welcome Center (1001 Ocean Drive) Mon, Tue, Wed, Fri, Sat, Sun 10:30am, Thu 6:30pm; audio tours daily; also the Art Deco Weekend (see p37). For infor-mation call the Art Deco Welcome Center at (305) 763-8026. 🖼
Ⓦ mdpl.org

0 meters 75
0 yards 75

Key

— Suggested route

11TH STREET

WASHINGTON AVENUE

9TH STREET

10TH STREET

COLLINS AVENUE

Beach Patrol Station

Art Deco Welcome Center

★ South Beach Bars and Clubs
A visit to South Beach is not complete unless you experience one of its trendy bars or clubs, such as the Marlin Hotel on Collins Avenue.

MIAMI BEACH

Locator Map
See Street Finder map 2

❶ ★ Ocean Drive
Ocean Drive is the star attraction of South Beach – for its many stylish hotels and the colorful parade of rollerbladers and other people out being seen.

14TH STREET

DREXEL AVENUE

WASHINGTON AVENUE

COLLINS AVENUE

13TH STREET

12TH STREET

OCEAN DRIVE

The Netherland Hotel *(1935)*, at the quiet end of Ocean Drive, boasts colorful stucco decoration. It is now a condominium.

The Cardozo Hotel, among the cream of Ocean Drive's Deco buildings, marked the start of a new era of restoration in South Beach when it reopened in 1982. It is now owned by Gloria Estefan.

The Amsterdam Palace, now known as Casa Casuarina, is a rare private residence on Ocean Drive *(see p70)*.

Lummus Park

❷ ★ The Beach
Sand extends for 10 miles (16 km) up the coast. The beach changes atmosphere depending on where you are, being at its broadest and liveliest in South Beach.

South Beach

Ocean Drive has the best known Deco buildings in South Beach. There are wonderful discoveries to be made on Collins and Washington Avenues too, as well as farther west in quieter residential streets, such as Lenox Avenue, where you'll find doors etched with flamingos and other Deco features.

South Beach, or SoBe, is best explored on foot since parking is difficult. If you don't wish to walk, join the locals on rollerblades or bicycles, both of which can be rented locally.

The Amsterdam Palace, one of Ocean Drive's few non-Deco buildings

❶ Ocean Drive

Map 2 F3, F4. 🚌 150 Miami Beach Airport Flyer, M (113), S (119), C (103), 120 Beach MAX. 🛈 1001 Ocean Drive, (305) 672-2014; Art Deco Welcome Center, (305) 763-8026.
W mdpl.org

Spending time at one of the bars or cafés on the waterfront is arguably the best way to experience Ocean Drive. It is effectively a catwalk for a constant procession of well-toned flesh and avant-garde outfits; even the street cleaners look cool in their pith helmets and white uniforms, while police officers in skintight shorts cruise past on mountain bikes. A more active exploration, however, needn't involve much more than a stroll.

At No. 1114 is the 1930 Mediterranean Revival Amsterdam Palace, also known as Casa Casuarina, which the late designer Gianni Versace purchased in 1993 for $3.7 million. This is now a luxury boutique hotel. Nearby, behind the Art Deco Welcome Center, the Beach Patrol Station is a classic Nautical Moderne building *(see p65)*, with ship's railings along the top and port-hole windows; it still functions as the base for local lifeguards.

There is little to lure you south of 6th Street, but from the tip of South Pointe Park you can watch cruise liners entering Government Cut *(see p79)*.

❷ The Beach

Map 2. 🚌 M (113), S (119), C (103), 120 Beach MAX, 150 Miami Beach Airport Flyer, A (101).

Much of the sand flanking Miami Beach was imported a few decades ago, and it continues to be replenished to counter coastal erosion. The vast stretches of sand are still impressive and people flock to them.

Up to 5th Street the beach is popular with surfers. The immense beach beyond is an extension of SoBe's persona, with colorful lifeguard huts and hordes of posing bathers. Alongside runs Lummus Park, where you still find Jewish folk chatting in Yiddish – evidence of the district's pre-gentrification era. Around 12th Street the clientele on the beach is predominantly gay.

Lifeguard huts in South Beach, with the colors and style to match Ocean Drive

For hotels and restaurants in this area see pp314–25 and pp329–49

❸ Jewish Museum of Florida

301 Washington Ave. **Map** 2 E4.
Tel (305) 672-5044. 🚌 C (103),
120 Beach MAX, 150 Miami Beach
Airport Flyer, 123 South Beach Local,
M (113). **Open** 10am–5pm Tue–Sun.
Closed Jewish and national hols. 🅿
♿ 🎥 🅦 jewishmuseum.com

This museum occupies the first synagogue built in Miami Beach, in 1936. When large numbers of Jews arrived in the 1930s, they often faced fierce anti-Semitism – local hotels carried such signs as "No Jews or Dogs." Today, Jews are a vital, if aging, part of Miami Beach's community.

The once dilapidated synagogue reopened in 1995 as a museum and research center of Jewish life in Florida. The building boasts colorful stained-glass windows and other Art Deco features, making it almost as memorable as the exhibitions that are staged here.

The unmistakable tower of the Delano Hotel on Collins Avenue

❹ Collins and Washington Avenues

Map 2. 🚌 C (103), M (113), S (119), 120 Beach MAX, 123 South Beach Local.
ℹ 1920 Meridian Avenue (Miami Beach Visitor Center), (305) 672-1270.
🅦 miami beachchamber.com

These streets are not as well-kept as Ocean Drive: stores sell kinky clothes or tattoos, and

Changing Colors in South Beach

Art Deco buildings were originally very plain, typically in white with only the trim in bright colors; the paint never extended to the backs of the buildings since money was too tight in the 1930s to allow anything more than a jazzy façade. In the 1980s, designer Leonard Horowitz created the "Deco dazzle" by smothering some 150 buildings in color. Purists express dismay at this reinvention of the look of South Beach, but advocates argue that the Deco details are better highlighted than ever.

Touching up the color on the Cardozo Hotel on Ocean Drive

there is a more Hispanic flavor. Some of South Beach's top clubs are here *(see p101)*, and there is an abundance of modest Art Deco buildings worth seeing. The Marlin Hotel, at 1200 Collins Avenue, is one of the district's best-known and finest Streamline buildings. It used to be owned by Christopher Blackwell, founder of Island Records. Behind, at 1300 Washington Avenue, Miami Beach Post Office is one of SoBe's starker Deco creations; a mural inside shows the arrival of Ponce de León *(see p46)* and his battle with the native Indians.

North up Collins Avenue past Lincoln Road the buildings are interesting rather than beautiful. High-rise 1940s hotels such as the Delano and Ritz Plaza still bear Deco traits, particularly in their towers inspired by the futuristic fantasies of comic strips such as *Buck Rogers* and *Flash Gordon*. The strikingly non-Deco interior of the luxury Delano Hotel on South Beach *(see p315)* is well worth seeing, with its billowing

Electric kettle (1909) in the Wolfsonian

white drapes and original works by Gaudí, Dalí, and Man Ray.

❺ The Wolfsonian Museum – Florida International University

1001 Washington Ave. **Map** 2 E3.
Tel (305) 531-1001. 🚌 C (103), 120 Beach MAX, 150 Miami Beach Airport Flyer, 123 South Beach Local.
Open noon–6pm Thu–Tue. 🅿 🚫
♿ 🎥 🅦 wolfsonian.org

This sturdy 1920s building *(see p68)* used to be the Washington Storage Company, where Miami's wealthy stored their valuables while traveling north. Now it holds a collection of decorative and fine arts from the period 1885–1945, primarily from North America and Europe. The museum's collection of 80,000 objects include books, posters, furniture, and sculpture, and focus on the aesthetic, political, and social significance of design throughout the turn of the century.

Española Way, a leafy Mediterranean-style shopping street

❻ Española Way

Map 2 E2. 🚌 C (103), 123 South Beach Local.

Between Washington and Drexel Avenues, Española Way is a tiny, tree-lined enclave of Mediterranean Revival buildings, where ornate arches, capitals, and balconies adorn salmon-colored, stuccoed frontages. Built from 1922–5, it is said to have been the inspiration for Addison Mizner's Worth Avenue in Palm Beach (see pp122–3).

Española Way was meant to be an artists' colony but instead became an infamous red-light district. Over the last couple of decades, however, its intended use has been resurrected in its dozen or more boutiques and offbeat art galleries (see p99).

❼ Lincoln Road Mall

Map 2 E2. 🚌 A (101), 120 Beach MAX, 150 Miami Beach Airport Flyer, 123 South Beach Local, S (119), M (113), L (112), C (103). **Tel** (305) 538-7887. **Open** 11am–10pm Mon–Wed, 11am–11pm Thu–Sun. **Closed** Jan 1, Thanksgiving, Dec 25. ♿

One of the up-and-coming cultural corners of South Beach has had a roller-coaster history. Developer Carl Fisher (see p63) envisaged it as the "Fifth Avenue of the South" when it was planned in the 1920s, and its stores did indeed become the height of fashion. Four decades later, Morris Lapidus (designer of the Fontainebleau Hotel) turned the street into one of the country's first pedestrian malls,

but this did not prevent Lincoln Road's decline in the 1970s; the concrete pavilions that Lapidus introduced may not have helped.

The street's revival was initiated by the setting up of the ArtCenter South Florida here in 1984. Between Lenox and Meridian Avenues there are three exhibition areas and some dozen studios, as well as other independent galleries (see p99). Education programs are also on offer. The art may be too experimental for most living rooms.

The galleries are usually open in the evenings. This is when the mall comes alive, as theater-goers frequent the restored Art Deco Lincoln and Colony theaters (see p100). Those searching for a less intense alternative to Ocean Drive hang out at voguish restaurants and cafés, such as the Van Dyke at No. 846 – Lincoln Road's answer to the News Café (see p68). At night, the Streamline Moderne Sterling Building at No. 927 looks terrific, its glass blocks emanating a blue glow.

❾ Holocaust Memorial

1933–45 Meridian Ave. **Map** 2 E1. **Tel** (305) 538-1663. 🚌 A (101), L (112), M (113), S (119), 123 South Beach Local. **Open** 9am–9pm daily. ♿

Miami Beach has one of the largest populations of Holocaust survivors in the world, hence the great appropriateness of Kenneth Treister's gut-wrenching memorial, finished in 1990. The centerpiece is an enormous bronze arm and hand stretching skyward, representing the final grasp of a dying person. It is stamped with a number from Auschwitz and covered with nearly 100 life-size bronze statues of men, women, and children in the throes of unbearable grief. Around this central plaza is a tunnel lined with the names of Europe's concentration camps, a graphic pictorial history of the Holocaust, and a granite wall inscribed with the names of thousands of victims.

The Holocaust Memorial

Winers and diners outside the Van Dyke Café, Lincoln Road Mall

Coronation of the Virgin (c.1492) by Domenico Ghirlandaio

❾ Bass Museum of Art

2121 Park Ave. **Map** 2 F1. **Tel** (305) 673-7530. 🚌 C (103), S (119), L (112), M (113), 120 Beach MAX, 150 Miami Beach Airport Flyer, 123 South Beach Local. **Open** noon–5pm Wed–Sun. **Closed** Mon, Tue & public hols. ♿ 🅿 ♿
W bassmuseum.org

This Mayan-influenced Deco building was erected in 1930 as the city's library and art center. As a museum it came of age in 1964 when philanthropists John and Johanna Bass donated their own art collection, made up mainly of European paintings, sculpture, and textiles from the 15th to 17th centuries.

Gallery space is divided between permanent and temporary exhibitions, the former displaying more than 2,800 pieces of sculpture, graphic art and photography. Highlights include a few Renaissance works, paintings from the northern European schools and giant 16th-century Flemish tapestries. There are also exhibits on contemporary architecture.

Shooting Fashion in Miami Beach

Thanks to its combination of Art Deco buildings, palm trees, beach, and warm climate, South Beach is one of the world's most popular places for fashion shoots. About 1,500 models live here, but this doesn't include the thousands of young hopefuls who flock here uninvited during the season and stroll about looking cool in the bars and on the beach. The season runs from October through to March, when the weather in Europe and northern America is too cold for outdoor shoots.

Stroll around SoBe in the early morning and you cannot fail to spot the teams of directors, photographers, make-up artists, and their assistants as well as, of course, the models themselves. Ocean Drive is the top spot for shoots, but you can surprise a team at work even in the quieter back streets.

Photographer and crew shooting a model in Miami Beach

❿ Central Miami Beach

Map 2 F1. 🚌 C (103), M (113), S (119), J (110), L (112), 120 Beach MAX, 150 Miami Beach Airport Flyer.

Miami Beach north of 23rd Street, sometimes called Central Miami Beach, is a largely unprepossessing sight, with endless 1950s and 1960s high-rise apartments separating the Atlantic from busy Collins Avenue. A boardwalk running all the way from 23rd to 46th Street overlooks a narrow beach, frequented primarily by families.

The most eye-catching sight in the area is the **Fontainebleau Hotel** (pronounced "Fountain-blue" locally).

Completed in 1954, the curvaceous Fontainebleau is apparently the nearest the architect Morris Lapidus (b.1903) could get to his client's wishes for a modern French château style. The hotel's dated grandeur still impresses, particularly the pool with waterfall and the lobby with Lapidus's signature bow ties on the tiles. The hotel was an ideal setting for the James Bond film *Goldfinger* in the 1960s.

Star guests have included Frank Sinatra, Elvis Presley, Bob Hope, Sammy Davis Jr., and Lucille Ball. Today the lobby is still one of the best places to spot celebrities in Central Miami Beach.

From the Bayside Marketplace (see p78) you can take a tour on any of several cruise boats available. The tours provide a more leisurely view of many of the millionaires' mansions of Biscayne Bay (see p77). There are, however, no water taxis in Miami or Miami Beach.

Poolside view of the Fontainebleau Hotel, Central Miami Beach

DOWNTOWN AND LITTLE HAVANA

When the development of Miami took off with the arrival of the Florida East Coast Railroad in 1896, the early city focused on one square mile (2.5 sq km) on the banks of the Miami River, site of the present downtown area. Wealthy industrialists from the northern US set up banks and other institutions and built winter estates along Brickell Avenue. This is now the hub of Miami's financial district that was spawned by a banking boom in the 1980s. Downtown's futuristic skyscrapers, bathed nightly in neon, demonstrate the city's status as a major financial and trade center.

Even after World War II, Miami was still little more than a resort. It was largely the arrival of Cuban exiles from 1959 onward *(see p56)* that turned Miami into a metropolis. The effect of this Cuban influx is visible most clearly on the streets both Downtown and just across the river in Little Havana. The chatter, faces, shop signs, and food make both districts feel more like an Hispanic city with an American flavor than the other way around.

Downtown and Little Havana are enjoyable as much for their atmosphere as for their sights. Downtown has the Miami-Dade Cultural Center, with one of Florida's best historical museums, and the Perez Art Museum Miami on Biscayne Bay, but tourists are catered to primarily at the shopping and entertainment mall of Bayside Marketplace – a starting point for relaxing boat trips around Biscayne Bay.

Sights at a Glance

Museums and Galleries
1 Miami-Dade Cultural Center
3 Perez Art Museum Miami

Historic Buildings
2 US Federal Courthouse

Modern Architecture
6 Brickell Avenue

Neighborhoods
7 Little Havana

Shops and Restaurants
4 Bayside Marketplace

Boat Trips
5 Port Miami Boat Trips

See also Street Finder maps 2, 3

◄ Downtown Miami's Bayside Marketplace at night

For map symbols *see back flap*

Street-by-Street: Downtown

Downtown's skyline is sublime. It undoubtedly looks best from a distance, particularly at night, but the architecture can also be enjoyed close-up. The raised track of the Metromover gives a good overall view; or you can explore at ground level, allowing you to investigate the handsome interiors of some of Downtown's public buildings.

The commercial district that lurks beneath the flash high-rises is surprisingly downscale, full of cut-price jewelry and electronics stores, but the Latin street life is vibrant: cafés specialize in Cuban coffee and street vendors sell freshly peeled oranges, Caribbean-style. Flagler Street, Downtown's main thoroughfare, is the best place to get the Hispanic buzz. While the area has a vibrant scene and is home to an increasing number of shops, restaurants and condos, it is still important to be aware of your surroundings at all times.

The Downtown Skyline is a monument to the banking boom of the 1980s. There is an excellent view of it from the MacArthur Causeway.

❶ US Federal Courthouse
This detail from the mural inside the courtroom depicts Miami's transformation from a wilderness to a modern city.

Dade County Courthouse has an impressive lobby, with ceiling mosaics that feature this copy of the earliest version of Florida's state seal, complete with mountains.

| 0 meters | 150 |
| 0 yards | 150 |

Key

— Suggested route

❷ ★ Miami-Dade Cultural Center
This large complex, with a Mediterranean-style central courtyard and fountains, contains the only museum in downtown Miami.

For hotels and restaurants in this area see pp314–25 and pp329–49

Gesu Church, home to Miami's oldest Catholic parish, was built in 1922. It is most noted for its stained-glass windows, which were made in Munich, Germany.

To Freedom Tower

The Alfred I. DuPont Building (1938), home of the Florida National Bank, retains many original fittings, including beautiful brass elevator doors decorated with palm trees and flamingos.

To Bayside Marketplace

Locator Map
See Street Finder map 4

DOWNTOWN AND LITTLE HAVANA

CORAL GABLES AND COCONUT GROVE

The Ingraham Building (1927) is a Neo-Classical-*cum*-Renaissance Revival work. The lobby has a lavish ceiling decorated in gold leaf and features the building's insignia etched in brass.

Southeast Financial Center

NE 2ND AVE
NE 2ND ST
NE 1ST ST
NE 3RD AVE
NE 1ST AVE
E FLAGLER ST
SE 3RD AVE
SE 1ST ST
SE 2ND ST
SE 2ND AVE

★ Bank of America Tower
The city's most striking skyscraper is famous for its changing nighttime illuminations. Built in 1983, the office block was known first as Centrust Tower but is now named after its current main tenant.

The Metromover, launched in 1986, is a driver-less shuttle that makes a clockwise 4.4-mile (7-km) loop around downtown Miami (*see p386*). The free ride takes about ten minutes, and provides a swift but worthwhile overview of the area.

Downtown

Downtown's grand early 20th-century buildings, scattered among modern high-rises, are very evocative of the confidence of those boom years. The Mediterranean Revival and Neo-Classical styles were both popular. A fine example of the latter is Freedom Tower (1925) on Biscayne Boulevard, modeled very loosely on the Giralda in Seville. At first home to the now-defunct *Miami News*, its role and name changed in the 1960s when it became the reception center for Cubans fleeing from Castro *(see p56)*. Downtown has a few Deco buildings, such as Macy's (formerly Burdines) on Flagler Street *(see p98)*.

❶ Miami-Dade Cultural Center

101 West Flagler St. **Map** 4 E1. 🚉 Metrorail (Government Center). 🚌 2, 3, 66, 77, all buses to Government Center. **Tel** (305) 375-1492. **Open** 10am–5pm Mon–Wed, Fri, Sat, noon–5pm Sun. 🅿 🅱 🆆 **historymiami.org**

Designed by the celebrated American architect Philip Johnson in 1982, the Miami-Dade Cultural Center is an art gallery, museum, and library.

HistoryMiami concentrates on pre-1945 Miami. There are informative displays on the Spanish colonization and Seminole culture among other topics, but it is the old photographs that really bring Miami's history to life: from the hardships endured by the early pioneers to the fun and games of the Roaring Twenties.

❷ US Federal Courthouse

301 N Miami Ave. **Map** 4 E1. **Tel** (305) 523-5100. 🅼 Wilkie D. Ferguson. 🚉 Metrorail (Historic Overtown/Lyric Theatre). 🚌 6, all downtown routes. **Open** 8am–5pm Mon–Fri. **Closed** public hols. 🅱

This imposing Neo-Classical building, finished in 1931, has hosted a number of high-profile trials, including that of José Padilla, who, in 2007, was found guilty of supporting terrorism. It has a pleasant, thoroughly Mediterr-anean courtyard, but the main attraction (for the casual visitor at least) is the mural entitled *Law Guides Florida's Progress (see p76)* on the second floor; this was designed by Denman Fink, famous for his work in Coral Gables *(see p86)*. Public access to the courthouse is often restricted, especially during important cases.

❸ Pérez Art Museum Miami

1075 Biscayne Blvd. **Map** 4 F1. **Tel** (305) 375-3000. 🅼 College/Bayside. **Open** 10am–5pm Tue–Sun. **Closed** Thanksgiving, Dec 25. 🅱 🆆 **pamm.org**

A modern and contemporary art museum displaying 20th- and 21st-century international art, the Pérez Art Museum Miami (PAMM) opened in December 2013 after the Miami Art Museum outgrew the Miami-Dade Cultural Center. Located in an impressive building designed by Swiss architects Herzog and de Meuron, and overlooking Biscayne Bay, the museum is named after its benefactor, real-estate developer Jorge Pérez.

Hew Locke's striking *For Those in Peril on the Sea* is a permanent installation that features a vast array of sea vessels hanging from the ceiling, and signifies Miami's history as the site for numerous waves of immigration.

❹ Bayside Marketplace

401 Biscayne Blvd. **Map** 4 F1. **Tel** (305) 577-3344. 🅼 College/Bayside. 🚌 3, 11, C (103), S (119), 95, 93 Biscayne MAX, 120 Beach MAX. **Open** 10am–10pm Mon–Thu, 10am–11pm Fri & Sat, 11am–9pm Sun. **Closed** Thanksgiving, Dec 25. 🅱

By far the most popular spot among tourists Downtown (as well as the best place to park in the area), Bayside Marketplace is an undeniably fun complex. It curves around Miamarina, where a plethora of boats, some private, some offering trips around Biscayne Bay, lie docked.

With its numerous bars and restaurants – among them a remarkable-looking Hard Rock Café complete with a guitar erupting from its roof – Bayside is a good place to eat as well as shop. The food court on the first floor does not serve *haute cuisine* but is fine for a fast-food meal. Bands often play in the waterfront esplanade.

The nearby Bayfront Park is austere by comparison. At its center the Torch of Friend-ship commemorates President John F. Kennedy, surrounded by the coats of arms of Central and South American countries; a plaque from the city's exiled Cuban community thanks the US for allowing them to settle here.

Boats moored in Miamarina in front of Bayside Marketplace

For hotels and restaurants in this area see pp314–25 and pp329–49

❺ Port Miami Boat Trips

Bayside Marketplace. **Map** 4 F1.
Ⓜ College/Bayside. 🚌 3, 16, A (101),
C (103), S (119), 11, 120 Beach MAX, 93
Biscayne MAX. **Island Queen Cruises:**
(305) 379-5119. **Duck Tours:** (786)
673-2217. **Bayside Marketplace tour
boats:** (305) 577-3344.

The world's busiest cruise port
and a sprinkling of exclusive
private island communities
occupy Biscayne Bay between
Downtown and Miami Beach.
Since racing along MacArthur
Causeway in a car provides only
a brief glimpse of this area,
cruises from Bayside Marketplace offer a better, more
leisurely view. "Estates of the
Rich and Famous" tours run by
Island Queen Cruises and other
companies leave regularly and
last about 90 minutes.

The stunningly modern exterior of Pérez Art Museum Miami

Tours begin
by sailing past
the port,
situated on

ISLAND QUEEN

Port Miami
tour boat sign

Dodge and Lummus
islands. The port
contributes more than $18
billion a year to the local
economy, handling over four
million cruise passengers
annually. The mammoth ships
make an impressive sight when
they're in dock or heading to or
from port (usually on weekends).
    Near the eastern end of
MacArthur Causeway you pass
the US Coastguard's fleet of high-
speed craft. Opposite lies
unbridged Fisher Island,
separated from South Beach by
Government Cut, a deep water
channel dredged in 1905. A
beach for Blacks in the 1920s,
Fisher Island has ironically
become a highly exclusive

residential enclave, with homes
rarely costing less than $500,000.
The tour continues north around
Star, Palm, and Hibiscus islands,
which were all man-made
in the second
decade of the
20th century,
when real estate
lots were sometimes
sold "by the gallon."
Mansions in every possible
architectural style lurk beneath
the tropical foliage, among
them the former homes of Frank
Sinatra and Al Capone, as well
as the present abodes of celebrities such as Gloria Estefan
and Julio Iglesias.
    Other boat trips from Bayside
Marketplace include nighttime
cruises, deep-sea fishing
excursions, and even a tall ship
cruise. A particularly good tour is
run by Duck Tours who have an
amphi- bious vehicle that
departs several times a day from
South Beach and splashes down
in Biscayne Bay for a closer look
at the many mansions.

❻ Brickell Avenue

Map 4 E2–E4. Ⓜ various stations.
🚆 Metrorail (Brickell & Government
Center). 🚌 6, 8, 48, B (102), 207, 208,
95, 500 Midnight Owl. ℹ️ Greater
Miami Beaches Convention and
Visitors Bureau, 701 Brickell Ave, Suite
2700, (305) 539-3000.
🆆 miamiandbeaches.com

In the early 20th century, the
building of palatial mansions
along Brickell Avenue earned it the
name Millionaires' Row. Today, its
northern section is Miami's palm-
lined version of New York's Wall
Street – its international banks
enclosed in modern, glass blocks
reflecting each other and the sky.
South of the bend at Southwest
15th Road is a series of startling
apartment houses glimpsed in
the opening credits of TV series
Miami Vice. Created in the early
1980s by an iconoclastic firm of
Postmodernist architects called
Arquitectonica, the buildings, now
condos, still manage to impress.
    The most memorable is the
Atlantis (at No. 2025), for its
"skycourt" – a hole high up in its
façade containing a palm tree
and Jacuzzi. The punched-out
hole reappears as an identically
sized cube in the grounds below.
Arquitectonica also designed the
Palace, at No. 1541, and the
Imperial, at No. 1627. Described
as "architecture for 55 mph" (that
is, best seen when passing in a
car), these exclusive residences
and high-rise office buildings
were designed to be admired
from a distance.

One of the lavish mansions seen during a Port Miami boat tour

❼ Little Havana

Map 3 C2. 🚌 207 and 208 Little Havana Connections. **El Titan de Bronze Cigar Mfg.:** 1071 W. 8th St. **Tel** (305) 860-1412. **Open** 9am–5pm Mon–Fri, 8am–4pm Sat. **Closed** Sun, public hols. **El Aguila Vidente (The Seeing Eagle):** 1122 SW 8th St. **Map** 3 C2. **Tel** (305) 854-4086. **Open** 10:30am–5:30pm Mon–Sat. **Closed** Sun, public hols.

Cubans live all over Greater Miami, but it is the 3.5 sq miles (9 sq km) making up Little Havana that, as its name suggests, have been their surrogate homeland since they first started fleeing Cuba in the 1960s (see p56). Other Hispanic groups have now settled here too.

Your time in Little Havana is best spent out in the streets, where the bustling workday atmosphere is vibrant. A salsa beat emanates from every other shop; *bodegas* (canteens) sell Cuban specialties such as *moros y cristianos*, while elderly men knock back thimblefuls of *café cubano*.

Little Havana's principal commercial thoroughfare and sentimental heart is Southwest 8th Street, better known as **Calle Ocho.** Its liveliest stretch, between 11th and 17th Avenues, is best enjoyed on foot, but other points of interest are more easily explored by car.

Recalling the spirit of Havana cigar factories, **El Titan de Bronze**, on Calle Ocho, is family owned and all the cigars are made by "Level 9" masters. You are welcome to watch the handful of cigar rollers at work. The leaves are grown in Nicaragua – reputedly from Cuban tobacco seeds, the world's best. Local smokers, mainly non-Cuban, come to buy boxes of the wide range of cigars on sale (see p99).

Also found on 8th Street are several *botánicas*, and spiritual stores dedicated to the practice of the Afro-Cuban religion Santeria. The merchandise includes herbs, potions, and ceramic figures of saints.

Southwest 13th Avenue, south from Calle Ocho, is known as **Cuban Memorial Boulevard** and is the district's nationalistic focal point. The eternal flame of the Brigade 2506 Memorial remembers the Cubans who died in the Bay of Pigs invasion of Cuba in 1961. Every year people gather here on April 17 to remember the disastrous attempt to overthrow Fidel Castro's regime. Beyond, other memorials pay tribute to Cuban heroes Antonio Maceo and José Martí, who fought against Cuba's Spanish colonialists in the 1800s (see pp52–3). At intervals along Calle Ocho between 12th and 17th Avenues, more recent Latin celebrities such as Julio Iglesias and Gloria Estefan are honored with stars on the pavement in Little

Waitress at the Versailles

The eternal flame commemorating the Bay of Pigs invasion

Havana's version of Hollywood's Walk of Fame.

At the corner of 15th Avenue, older male Cubans match their wits over dominoes in tiny **Máximo Gómez Park** – also known as Domino Park. According to a list of rules, players can be banned from the park for foul language, spitting, or shouting.

North of Calle Ocho at West Flagler Street and Southwest 17th Avenue, **Plaza de la Cubanidad** has a map of Cuba sculpted in bronze; José Martí's enigmatic words alongside translate as "the palm trees are sweethearts that wait." Behind, a flourish of flags and banners advertises the headquarters of Alpha 66, Miami's most hard-line grouping of anti-Castro Cubans, whose supporters once trained in the Everglades.

Much farther west, at 3260 Calle Ocho, lies **Woodlawn Cemetery**. You can ask for directions to the memorials to the unknown Cuban freedom fighter in plot 31, with Cuban and US flags flying alongside, or to the tomb of Gerardo Machado, an infamous Cuban dictator of the 1930s.

Finish off a tour of Little Havana with a snack or full meal at the nearby **Versailles** restaurant (see p331); this is a cultural and culinary bastion of Miami's Cuban community that has served nostalgic exiles, as well as tourists, since 1971.

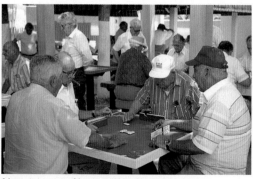
Cubans enjoying a game of dominoes in Máximo Gómez Park

Miami's Cuban Community

The Cuban community in Miami is unusually cohesive, thanks to a shared passion for its home-land and a common hatred for Fidel Castro and his dictatorship. The exiles, as they often call themselves, come from all walks of life. Early immigrants were largely wealthy white (and right-wing) professionals, who now sit on the boards of some of Miami's biggest companies and live in the city's stylish and upscale suburbs. The "Marielitos", who came in 1980 *(see p56)*, were mostly working class, like many of those who have arrived since. Some second-generation Cubans, such as pop star Gloria Estefan, now have very successful careers. Nowadays these professionals are often dubbed "yucas," or Young, Up-and-coming Cuban-Americans.The Cuban presence is felt in every layer of Miami society – seen in everything from the food to the Spanish spoken on the street, and visible everywhere from Little Havana to elite Coral Gables.

Images of Old Cuba
Murals, such as this one of the Cuban resort of Varadero, symbolize the nostalgia and love for the homeland felt by Cubans of all generations. Many hope to return to the island one day.

Political Action
Cubans in Miami eagerly follow events in Cuba. They often take to the streets to wave the Cuban flag and protest against the Castro regime or the US government's Cuban policy.

Salsa music, recorded by Cubans in Miami and popular in the city

Cuban Culture in Miami

The Cubans have brought their music, their religion, their whole way of life to Miami. They are nominally Catholic, but many Cubans adhere to Santería, an unusual blend of Catholic beliefs and the animist cults taken to Cuba by African slaves during the colonial period.

A Cuban-style hole in the wall café, where coffee, snacks, and conversation are enjoyed

A religious shop or *botánica* in Little Havana selling the paraphernalia of Santería

CORAL GABLES AND COCONUT GROVE

Coral Gables, one of the country's richest neighborhoods, is a separate city within Greater Miami, and feels it. Aptly named the City Beautiful, its elegant homes line winding avenues shaded by banyans and live oaks; backing up to hidden canals, many have their own jetties. Regulations ensure that new buildings use the same architectural vocabulary advocated by George Merrick when he planned Coral Gables in the 1920s (see p86). As well as exploring Merrick's legacy, you can peer into some of Miami's most stylish shops. Coconut Grove is Miami's

oldest community. Wreckers (see p307) lived here from the mid-1800s, but the area attracted few people until the 1880s, when Ralph Monroe (see p88) persuaded some friends to open a hotel. It was staffed by Bahamians and frequented by Monroe's intellectual friends. Ever since, the area has had a mixed flavor, with posh homes just a stone's throw from the blighted, so-called Black Coconut Grove. Affordable restaurants and shops draw weekend and evening crowds, making Coconut Grove the liveliest district in Miami after South Beach.

Sights at a Glance

Museums and Galleries
- ⑥ Lowe Art Museum
- ⑪ Miami Museum of Science and Planetarium

Streets and Neighborhoods
- ① Miracle Mile
- ⑦ Coconut Grove Village

Historic Buildings
- ② Coral Gables City Hall
- ③ Coral Gables Merrick House

- ④ Venetian Pool
- ⑤ Biltmore Hotel
- ⑧ The Barnacle
- ⑫ Vizcaya Museum and Gardens pp86–7

Churches
- ⑩ Ermita de la Caridad

Marinas
- ⑨ Dinner Key

See also Driving tour map pp84–5

◄ The historic Biltmore Hotel in Coral Gables

For map symbols see back flap

Coral Gables Driving Tour

This driving tour wends its way along Coral Gables' lush and peaceful lanes connecting the major landmarks of George Merrick's 1920s planned city *(see pp86–7)*. As well as much-admired public buildings like the Biltmore Hotel, it takes in two of the original four grand entrances and six of Merrick's Disneyesque international "villages."

It is quite possible to visit all the sights on the tour in one busy day. Allow time to get lost; Coral Gables is very confusing for a planned city. Signs for streets, named after Spanish places that Merrick allegedly pulled out of a dictionary, are often hard to spot, lurking on white stone blocks in the grass.

③ Alhambra Water Tower
This folly, built in 1925, was the work of Denman Fink *(see p86)*.

⑥ Venetian Pool is a beautiful public swimming pool embellished with Venetian-style buildings.

⑦ Coral Gables Congregational Church
Coral Gables' first church, built by Merrick in Spanish Baroque style, has an elaborate bell tower and portal.

⑩ The Lowe Art Museum boasts an excellent collection, including some fine European and Native American art.

⑧ Biltmore Hotel
One of the most stunning hotels in the country, the Biltmore has been beautifully restored to its 1920s grandeur.

⑪ French City Village
This is one of seven international villages that were built to add variety to the mostly Mediterranean-style city.

0 meters   500
0 yards   500

① **The Granada Entrance** is a copy of the gate to Granada in Spain.

② **The Country Club Prado Entrance**, complete with ornamental pillars, is the most elegant of the grand entrances.

DOWNTOWN AND LITTLE HAVANA

CORAL GABLES AND COCONUT GROVE

Locator Map
See Street Finder map 5

④ **Coral Way**
Live oaks and Spanish-style houses line one of Coral Gables' loveliest and oldest streets.

⑤ **Coral Gables Merrick House** was once the home of George Merrick and is now a museum.

⑯ **Coral Gables City Hall** has a decorative interior, featuring murals painted in the 1920s and '50s.

LISTER JEWELERS

⑰ **Miracle Mile**
Conservative bridal, fashion, and jewelry stores set the tone along the district's most important shopping street.

Key

═══ Expressway

▬▬▬ Tour route

─── Metrorail line

═══ Other Road

Tips for Drivers

Tour length: 14 miles (23 km).
Starting point: Anywhere, but the route is best done in a counterclockwise direction.
Stopping-off points: There are some highly rated restaurants off Miracle Mile, and you can enjoy an English-style tea at the Biltmore if you book 24 hours in advance. Or, you can take a dip at the Venetian Pool.
When to go: Wednesdays and Sundays are the best days to visit because of the hours of the Coral Gables Merrick House, Lowe Art Museum, and the Biltmore tours *(see pp86–7)*. Avoid the rush hours (7–9:30am, 4:30–6:30pm).

A private boat moored on one of Coral Gables' canals

Finding the Sights

① Granada Entrance
② Country Club Prado Entrance
③ Alhambra Water Tower
④ Coral Way
⑤ Coral Gables Merrick House
⑥ Venetian Pool
⑦ Coral Gables Congregational Church
⑧ Biltmore Hotel
⑨ Colonial Village
⑩ Lowe Art Museum
⑪ French City Village
⑫ Dutch South African Village
⑬ French Country Village
⑭ Chinese Village
⑮ French Normandy Village
⑯ Coral Gables City Hall
⑰ Miracle Mile

Galleried rotunda inside the Colonnade Building on Miracle Mile

❶ Miracle Mile

Coral Way between Douglas and Le Jeune roads. **Map** 5 C1. 🚇 Metrorail (Douglas Rd, Vizcaya). 🚌 37, 42 (both from Douglas Rd), 24 (from Vizcaya).

In 1940, a developer hyped Coral Gables' main shopping street by naming it Miracle Mile (the walk along one side and down the other equating a mile). Colorful canopies adorn shops as prim and proper as their clientele *(see p98)*. High prices and competition from out-of-town malls mean the street is rarely busy.

The Colonnade Building, at No. 169, was built in 1926 by George Merrick as the sales headquarters for his real estate business. Its superb rotunda is now a lobby for the deceptively modern and very impressive Colonnade Hotel. Caffe Abbracci *(see p332)* offers Italian food and celebrity-viewing opportunities. Nearby, at Salzedo Street and Aragon Avenue, the Old Police and Fire Station Building, built in 1939, features a fine pair of sculpted firemen.

❷ Coral Gables City Hall

405 Biltmore Way. **Map** 5 C1. **Tel** (305) 446-6800. 🚇 Metrorail (Douglas Rd). 🚌 24, 42, 56. **Open** 8am–5pm Mon–Fri. **Closed** public hols. ♿
🌐 coralgables.com

Built in 1928, Coral Gables City Hall epitomizes the Spanish Renaissance style favored by Merrick and his colleagues. Its semicircular façade even has a Spanish-style coat of arms, which was designed for the new city of Coral Gables by Denman Fink, George Merrick's uncle. Fink was also responsible for the mural of the four seasons that decorates the dome of the bell tower: Winter is represented as an old man, the other seasons as young women. Above the stairs, a mural that illustrates Coral Gables' early days, *Landmarks of the Twenties*, was the work of John St. John in the 1950s; he artificially aged it by chain-smoking and exhaling onto the paint as it dried.

Coat of arms on Coral Gables City Hall

❸ Coral Gables Merrick House

907 Coral Way. **Map** 5 B1. **Tel** (305) 460-5361. 🚌 24, 42. **Open** 1–4pm Wed & Sun. 📷 ♿ 🚻

Make the effort to visit the Merrick family home to appreciate the comparatively modest background of Coral Gables' creator. However, its opening hours are limited.

When Reverend Solomon Merrick brought his family to Florida from New England in 1899, they settled in a wooden cabin south of the growing city of Miami. They later added a much larger extension and named the house Coral Gables, thinking the local oolitic limestone used to build it was coral because of the fossilized marine life it contained. Now a museum, the emphasis is on the family, particularly Solomon's famous son, George. Some of the furniture was owned by the Merricks, and there are family portraits and paintings by George's mother and his uncle. The grounds have been reduced in size, but the small garden is awash with tropical trees and plants.

George Merrick's Dream City

The dream of George Merrick was to build a new city. With the help of Denman Fink as artistic advisor, Frank Button as landscaper, and Phineas Paist as architectural director, he conjured up a wholly planned aesthetic wonderland. Its architecture was to be part-Spanish, part-Italian – in Merrick's words "a combination of what seemed best in each, with an added touch of gaiety to suit the Florida mood." The dream spawned the biggest real estate venture of the 1920s, costing around $100 million. Some $3 million a year was spent on advertising alone, with posters promoting idyllic canal scenes while they were still on the drawing board. The 1926 hurricane *(see p54)* and the Wall Street crash left Merrick's city incomplete, but what remains together with subsequent imitations is a great testament to his imagination.

Portrait of George Merrick, on display in his family home

Venetian Pool, ingeniously created in the 1920s out of an old coral rock quarry

❹ Venetian Pool

2701 De Soto Blvd. **Map** 5 B2. **Tel** (305) 460-5306. 🚊 Metrorail (Douglas Rd, Vizcaya). 🚌 42 (from Douglas Rd), 24 (from Vizcaya). **Open** Apr–May & Sep–Oct: 11am–5:30pm Tue–Thu; mid-Jun–mid-Aug: 11am–7:30pm Mon–Fri; Nov–Mar: 10am–4:30pm Tue–Thu; all year: 10am–4:30pm Sat & Sun. **Closed** Jan 1, Thanksgiving, Dec 24–25. 🅿️ ♿ W **coralgablesvenetianpool.com**

This may be the most beautiful swimming pool in the world. It was fashioned from a coral rock quarry in 1923 by Denman Fink and Phineas Paist. Pink stucco towers and loggias, candy-cane Venetian poles, a cobblestone bridge, caves, and waterfalls surround the clear, spring-fed waters. The pool was originally one of the most fashionable social spots in Coral Gables: see the photographs in the lobby of beauty pageants staged here during the 1920s.

❺ Biltmore Hotel

1200 Anastasia Ave. **Map** 5 A2. **Tel** (305) 445-1926. 🚊 Metrorail (Douglas Rd). 🚌 40 (from Douglas Rd), 24, 57. ♿ 📷 Sun only. W **biltmorehotel.com**

Coral Gables' outstanding single building was completed in 1926. In its heyday, when it hosted celebrities such as Al Capone (who had a speakeasy here), Judy Garland, and the Duke and Duchess of Windsor, guests hunted fox in the vast grounds

(now a golf course) and were punted along canals in gondolas. The Biltmore served as a military hospital during World War II, when its marble floors were covered in linoleum, and it remained a veterans' hospital until 1968. Following a $55-million restoration in 1986 the hotel went bankrupt in 1990, but then opened its doors again two years later.

A 315-ft (96-m) near replica of Seville Cathedral's Giralda tower, which was also the model for Miami's Freedom Tower *(see p78)*, rises from the hotel's imposing façade. Inside, Herculean pillars line the grand lobby, while from the terrace behind you can survey the largest hotel swimming pool in the US. The Biltmore's famous swimming instructor, Johnny Weismuller, known for his role as Tarzan, set a world record here in the 1930s.

Weekly tours of the hotel depart from the desk.

Han dynasty horse, Lowe Art Museum

❻ Lowe Art Museum

1301 Stanford Drive. **Map** 5 A5. **Tel** (305) 284-3535. 🚊 Metrorail (University). 🚌 48, 56. **Open** 10am–4pm Tue–Sat, noon–4pm Sun. **Closed** Mon, public holidays. 📷 ♿ W **lowemuseum.org**

This museum is located in the middle of the campus of the University of Miami, founded in 1925 thanks to a $5-million donation from George Merrick. Among the 8,000 permanent exhibits are impressive Renais-sance and Baroque works, and an excellent collection of Native American art. There is also an Egyptian collection, some fine works in the 17th-century and contemporary European and American collections, Afro-Cuban lore, and historical memorabilia. Ancient art from Latin America and Asia, and 20th-century photography are also well represented.

South view of the Biltmore Hotel, Coral Gables' most famous landmark

❼ Coconut Grove Village

Map 6 E4, F4. 🚇 Metrorail (Coconut Grove, Douglas Rd). 🚌 48, 249 Coconut Grove Circulator.

A fabled hippy hangout in the 1960s, these days the focal point of Coconut Grove cultivates a more salubrious air. Well-groomed young couples wining and dining beneath old-fashioned streetlamps now typify what is often known simply as "the village." Only the odd snake charmer and neck masseur, plus a few New Age shops, offer glimpses of alternative lifestyles. Come at night or on the weekend to see the Grove at its best.

The village's nerve center is at the intersection of Grand Avenue, McFarlane Avenue, and Main Highway, where you'll find Johnny Rockets, a great 1950s-style burger bar, and the hyped-up **CocoWalk**. This outdoor mall (see p98) is Coconut Grove's busiest spot. Its courtyard is full of cafés and souvenir stands, while on upper floors a band often plays. There are also family restaurants (see pp329–49), a movie theater, and nightclub.

A short distance east along Grand Avenue, a stylish mall called the **Streets of Mayfair** (see p98) is worth visiting as much for its striking ensemble of Spanish tiles, waterfalls, and

CocoWalk open-air mall in Coconut Grove Village

foliage as for its shops. But in order to better appreciate Coconut Grove's relaxed café lifestyle, head along the side-streets of Commodore Plaza and Fuller Street.

For a different atmosphere, browse among the food stands of the colorful **Farmers' Market**, held on Saturdays at McDonald Street and Grand Avenue. Farther along Grand Avenue are the simple homes of the local Bahamian community. This neighborhood comes alive during Coconut Grove's exuberant Goombay Festival during the first weekend in June (see p39).

A five-minute stroll south along Main Highway takes you through a shady, affluent neighborhood where palms, bougainvillea, and hibiscus conceal handsome clapboard

villas. At 3400 Devon Road is the picturesque **Plymouth Congregational Church**, which appears to have been built a lot longer ago than 1916. It is usually locked, but the ivy-covered façade and setting are the main attraction.

Monroe, designer of the Barnacle, painted by Lewis Benton in 1931

❽ The Barnacle

3485 Main Highway, Coconut Grove. **Map** 6 E4. **Tel** (305) 442-6866. 🚌 37 (with a short walk), 48, 249 Coconut Grove Circulator. **Open** 9am–5pm Fri–Mon. **Closed** Tue, Jan 1, Thanksgiving, Dec 25. 🅿️ 📷 🆆 **floridastateparks. org/thebarnacle**

Hidden from Main Highway by tropical hardwood trees, the Barnacle is Dade County's oldest home. It was designed and occupied by Ralph Monroe, a Renaissance man who made his living from boat building and wrecking (see p307). A botanist and photographer, he was also an avid environmentalist with a strong belief in the importance of self-sufficiency.

Miami: Fact Meets Fiction

In the 1980s, the public perception of Miami was as the drug and crime capital of the entire country. Ironically, the popular TV series *Miami Vice (see p57)* played on this reputation, glamorizing both the city and the violence. The best novels about Miami in the 1990s have also emanated from its seedier side. Its two most renowned crime writers are Edna Buchanan, winner of a Pulitzer prize for news reporting on the *Miami Herald*, and Carl Hiaasen, a columnist for the same newspaper. However fanciful his plots might seem (building inspectors practicing voodoo or talk-show hosts having plastic surgery on the air), Carl Hiaasen claims the ideas come straight from the *Herald's* news pages. *Striptease* was the first of his novels to be made into a movie.

Hiaasen's bestsellers

When first constructed in 1891 the house was a bungalow, built of wood salvaged from wrecks and laid out to allow air to circulate (essential in those pre-air-conditioning times). Then, in 1908, Monroe jacked the building up and added a new ground floor to accommodate his family.

Inside the two-story house visitors can explore rooms stuffed with old family heirlooms and wonderful, dated practical appliances, such as an early refrigerator. The hour-long tours of the property also take in Monroe's clapboard boathouse, full of his tools and workbenches. Alongside, you can see the rail track that Monroe used to winch boats out of the bay.

The Planetarium, venue for star and laser showsz

❾ Dinner Key

S Bayshore Drive. **Map** 6 F4. 🚇 Metrorail (Coconut Grove). 🚌 22, 249 Coconut Grove Circulator (both from Coconut Grove), 48.

In the 1930s, Pan American Airways transformed Dinner Key into the busiest seaplane base in the US. It was also the point of departure for Amelia Earhart's doomed round-the-world flight in 1937. You can still see the airline's sleek Streamline Moderne-style *(see p65)* terminal, which houses Miami City Hall; the hangars where seaplanes were once

harbored are now boatyards. To see how some people enjoy their leisure time, walk among the yachts berthed in Miami's most prestigious marina.

❿ Ermita de la Caridad

3609 S Miami Ave. **Map** 3 C5. **Tel** (305) 854-2404. 🚇 Metrorail (Vizcaya). 🚌 12, 48. **Open** noon–8pm, Spanish mass daily, 3pm Sun vigil. ♿

Deco detail on Miami City Hall façade, Dinner Key

This peculiar conical church, erected in 1966, is a very holy place for Miami's Cuban exiles – a shrine to their patron saint, the Virgin of Charity. A mural above the altar (which faces Cuba rather than being oriented eastward) illustrates the history of the Catholic church in Cuba, showing the Virgin and her shrine on the island. (The church is hard to find: take the first turn north of the Mercy Hospital.)

⓫ Miami Museum of Science and Planetarium

3280 S Miami Ave. **Map** 3 C5. **Tel** (305) 646-4200. 🚇 Metrorail (Vizcaya). 🚌 12, 17, 24 (all from Vizcaya), 48, 500 Midnight Owl. **Open** 10am–6pm daily. **Closed** Thanksgiving, Dec 25. 📷 **W** miamisci.org

The complex is filled with interactive permanent and traveling science exhibits designed to educate people of all ages in topics ranging from astronomy to zoology.

The Wildlife Center houses live animals and reptiles and is home to the Falcon Batchelor Bird of Prey Center, a facility dedicated to the rescue, rehabilitation, and release of injured birds of prey. The Planetarium features laser light shows every first Friday of the month, plus informative multimedia programing showcasing the wonders of the night sky.

Another complex being built in downtown's Museum Park is scheduled to open in 2015.

The Ermita de la Caridad, right on the edge of Biscayne Bay, which attracts many Cuban worshipers

⑫ Vizcaya Museum and Gardens

Florida's grandest residence was completed in 1916 as the winter retreat for millionaire industrialist James Deering. His vision was to replicate a 16th-century Italian estate, but one that had been altered by succeeding generations. Hence, Vizcaya and its opulent rooms come in a blend of styles from Renaissance to Neo-Classical, furnished with the fruits of Deering's shopping sprees around Europe. The formal gardens combine the features of Italian and French gardens with Florida's tropical foliage.

Deering would constantly enquire of his ambitious architect: "Must we be so grand?" fearing that Vizcaya would be too costly to support. After his death in 1925, it proved to be so until 1952, when it was bought by Miami-Dade County. The house and gardens were opened to the public soon after.

★ **Deering Bathroom**
Deering's elaborate bathroom has marble walls, silver plaques, and a canopied ceiling reminiscent of a Napoleonic campaign tent.

Pulcinella
The 18th-century English statue of Pulcinella, in the intimate Theater Garden, is one of many European sculptures in the grounds of the villa.

KEY

① **The East Loggia**, used for informal entertaining, contains a model caravel, a favorite Deering motif.

② **The Dining Room** resembles a Renaissance banquet hall, complete with tapestries and a 16th-century refectory table.

③ **Seahorse weathervane**

④ **The courtyard**, now protected by glass, was once open to the sky.

⑤ **The roof** is covered with barrel tiles taken from buildings in Cuba.

⑥ **The Living Room**, is a grand Renaissance hall with the curious addition of an organ, made especially for Vizcaya.

⑦ **The Swimming Pool** extends under the house and was accessible via an interior staircase.

★ **Music Room**
This Rococo room is arguably the loveliest in the house. It is lit by a striking chandelier of multicolored glass flowers.

★ **Gardens**
Formal gardens like those at Vizcaya are a rarity in Florida. The Mound provides a lovely view down the symmetrical Center Island to the South Terrace of the villa.

VISITORS' CHECKLIST

Practical Information
3251 S Miami Ave. **Map**: 3 C5.
Tel (305) 250-9133. **Open** 9:30am–4:30pm Mon, Wed–Sun. **Closed** Tue, Thanksgiving, Dec 25. 🅿️ 🎫 ♿ limited. 📷 📁 🛍️
Ⓦ **vizcayamuseum.org**

Transport
🚇 Metrorail (Vizcaya) 🚌 12, 17, 18, 24 (all from Vizcaya), 48 (from Coconut Grove).

Entrance

⑤

④

⑥

⑦

Cathay Bedroom
Overwhelmed by the luxurious canopied bed, the Cathay Bedroom is decorated with chinoiserie, which was immensely popular in Europe in the 18th century.

Deering Sitting Room
The ceiling decoration of this Neo-Classical room features a seahorse, one of Vizcaya's recurrent motifs.

Villa and Gardens

Parking

Ticket booth

Center Island

Entrance

Café and shop

The Mount

Villa

Theater Garden

Tea House

South Terrace

FARTHER AFIELD

The areas north of Miami Beach and Downtown and south of Coral Gables are seldom very scenic, but they are well worth exploring for the great beaches and fun family attractions, as well as some really bizarre sights.

Much of northern Miami has a reputation for poverty and danger, in particular Liberty City and Overtown. Avoid these areas, and follow the safety tips on page 372. Be careful, too, when driving through Hialeah or visiting Opa-Locka or Little Haiti – atmospheric neighborhoods but ones that are likely to appeal mainly to the more adventurous sightseers.

Southern Miami's dull, non-descript suburbs eventually give way to mile after mile of citrus orchards and nurseries. These flatlands were at the epicenter of Hurricane Andrew in 1992 (see p30), and the natural landscape still shows some scars. Many of this area's attractions, which consist primarily of zoos, parks, and gardens, give visitors a glimpse of tropical flora and fauna, as well as a chance to enjoy the area's abundant marine life.

Sights at a Glance

Historic Buildings

❷ Ancient Spanish Monastery
⓮ Coral Castle

Museums and Galleries

❿ Wings Over Miami
⓫ Gold Coast Railroad Museum

Parks, Gardens, and Zoos

❺ Miami Seaquarium
❼ Fairchild Tropical Botanic Garden
❽ Charles Deering Estate
❾ Jungle Island
⓬ Zoo Miami
⓭ Monkey Jungle

Beaches

❶ North Beaches
❻ Key Biscayne

Neighborhoods

❸ Opa-Locka
❹ Little Haiti

0 kilometers   10
0 miles   10

Key

▨ Main sightseeing areas
▧ Urban area
═══ Expressway
▬▬ Major highway
═ Secondary route
— Rail line

◀ Palm trees and blue skies at Crandon Park Beach, Key Biscayne   **For map symbols** see back flap

❶ North Beaches

Collins Avenue. ⬜ G (107), H (108),
E (105), S (119), 120 Beach MAX.

The barrier islands north of
Miami Beach are occupied
mainly by exclusively posh
residential areas and unlovely
resorts, strung out along
Collins Avenue. Package
tourists often get stuck here
when many would probably
prefer South Beach. Still, there
are lots of inexpensive
accommodations and a long
sandy beach.

A peaceful strip of sand
between 79th and 87th Streets
separates Miami Beach from

Beach at Haulover Park, under the protective eye of a lifeguard

Surfside, a simple community
very popular with French
Canadians. At 96th Street
Surfside merges with **Bal
Harbour**, a stylish enclave
known for some flashy hotels

and one of the swankiest malls
around (see p98). Northward is
the pleasant **Haulover Park**,
with a marina on the creek
side and dune-backed sands
facing the ocean.

❷ Ancient Spanish Monastery

16711 W Dixie Hwy, N Miami Beach.
Tel (305) 945-1462. ⬜ 3 (from
downtown Miami), 93, E (105), H (108).
Open 10am–4pm Mon–Sat,
11am–4pm Sun. **Closed** some
weekends (call to check), public hols.
🖼 🔧 🌐 spanishmonastery.com

These monastery cloisters have
an unusual history. Built in
1133–41 in Spain, in 1925 they
were bought by newspaper
tycoon William Randolph
Hearst, who had their
35,000 stones packed
into crates. An outbreak
of foot-and-mouth

disease led to the crates being
opened (for the packing straw
to be checked), and the stones
were repacked incorrectly.
Once in New York, they
remained there until
1952, when it was
decided to

piece together "the world's
largest and most expensive
jigsaw puzzle." The cloisters
resemble the original version,
but there is still a pile of
unidentified stones in one
corner of the gardens.

Chapterhouse

The Chapel, at
one time the
dining hall, is
still used for
worship.

Statue of Alphonso VII,
patron of the
monastery

**The cloister
entrance** is a
carved, early
Gothic arch.

The bell outside the
chapel door

**The quiet
gardens** are a
popular spot for
wedding photos.

❸ Opa-Locka

Junction of NW 27th Ave & NW 135th St, 10 miles (16 km) NW of Downtown. 27, 32, 42, 135, 297 Orange MAX.

Nicknamed the "Baghdad of Dade County," Opa-Locka was the brain-child of aviator Glenn Curtiss. Taking his ins-piration from the tales of *The Arabian Nights*, he created his own fantasy city, financing the construction of more than 90 Moorish buildings in the 1920s boom *(see pp54–55)*.

Nowadays, Opa-Locka is a depressed area; it would not be wise to stray far from the City Hall (at Opa-Locka and Sharasad boulevards). All in pink with minarets, domes, and keyhole arches, this is the best example of the remaining Moorish-style architecture. Otherwise, Opa-Locka's fantasy lives on mainly in hotels, restaurants, and shops with names such as Ali Baba Appliances and streets called Caliph or Sultan.

Arabian-style dome of the City Hall in Opa-Locka

❹ Little Haiti

46th to 79th Streets, E of I-95. 2 & 202 Little Haiti Connection.

Ever since the 1980s, many Haitian refugees have settled in this part of Miami. It is a visibly impoverished but colorful community, and fairly safe if you stick to the main streets, 54th Street and NE 2nd Avenue.

The **Caribbean Market-place**, at NE 2nd Avenue and 60th Street, has a few craft stalls, but more interesting are the surrounding shops painted in

Mural advertising a religious shop *(botánica)* in Little Haiti

dazzling colors. High-decibel Haitian music blares out of some; others are *botánicas* stocking herbal potions and saints' ephemera *(see p81)*; more sell "Caribbean-style" chicken and plantains.

❺ Miami Seaquarium

4400 Rickenbacker Cswy, Virginia Key. **Tel** (305) 361–5705. Metrorail (Brickell). B from Brickell station. **Open** 9:30am–6pm daily. **W** miamiseaquarium.com

If you're visiting Orlando's SeaWorld® *(see pp180–81)*, you may not want to bother with the 35-acre Miami Seaquarium, but the sea lion, dolphin, and killer whale shows are surefire crowd pleasers. The "Swim with the Dolphins" program draws the largest crowds twice daily; but all participants who are going into the water must be able to read and understand English. Other attractions include sharks, viewing areas for manatees, a mangrove swamp full of pelicans, and a tropical fish aquarium with coral, fish, and other marine life.

❻ Key Biscayne

7 miles (11 km) SE of Downtown. B (102). Bill Baggs Cape Florida State Park: **Tel** (305) 361–5811. **Open** daily. **W** floridastateparks.org

The view of Downtown from Rickenbacker Causeway, connecting the mainland to Virginia Key and Key Biscayne, is one of Miami's best. Views aside,

Key Biscayne has some of the city's top beaches. Most impressive is the beach in **Crandon Park** in the upper half of the key, which is 3 miles (5 km) long and with palm trees and offshore sandbar. There is also a fenced beachfront picnic area which can accommodate up to 2,000 people. At the key's southern end, the **Bill Baggs Cape Florida State Park** has a shorter beach joined to more picnic areas by boardwalks across dunes. The lighthouse near the tip, built in 1825, is the oldest building in South Florida.

A mix of mini-malls and oceanfront apartments line Crandon Boulevard between the two parks, as well as a golf course and tennis center, which is open to the public.

Atlantic bottlenose dolphins – the stars at Miami Seaquarium

❼ Fairchild Tropical Botanic Garden

10901 Old Cutler Rd. **Tel** (305) 667-1651. 🚌 57, 136 (both require a walk). **Open** sunrise–sunset (office: 8am–5pm). **Closed** Dec 25. 🎫 📷 ♿ 🅦 **fairchildgarden.org**

Mattheson Hammock Park: **Tel** (305) 665-5475. **Open** 6am–sunset daily. 🅦 **miamidade.gov/parks**

This huge and dizzyingly beautiful tropical garden, established in 1938, doubles as a major botanical research institution. Around a series of man-made lakes stands one of the largest collections of palm trees in the world (550 of the 2,500 known species) as well as an impressive array of cycads – relatives of palms and ferns that bear unusual giant red cones. There are countless other wonderful trees and plants, including a comical-looking sausage tree.

During 40-minute tram tours, guides describe how plants are used in the manufacture of medicines and perfumes (the flowers of the ylang-ylang tree, for example, are used in Chanel No. 5). Allow another two hours to explore on your own.

Next to the Fairchild Tropical Botanic Garden is the waterfront Mattheson Hammock Park. There are walking and cycling trails through mangrove swamps, but most visitors head for the Atoll Pool, an artificial salt-water swimming pool encircled by sand and palm trees alongside Biscayne Bay. There is also a marina with a sailing school, and a first-rate beachfront restaurant.

❽ Charles Deering Estate

16701 SW 72nd Ave. **Tel** (305) 235-1668. **Open** 10am–5pm daily. 🎫 📷 ♿ **Closed** Thanksgiving, Dec 25. 🅦 **miamidade.gov/parks**

While his brother James enjoyed the splendor of Vizcaya *(see pp90–91)*, Charles Deering had his own stylish winter retreat on Biscayne Bay, which he used regularly between 1916 and 1927. His 400-acre (162-ha) estate, including a Mediterranean Revival mansion, was acquired by the state in 1985, and offers public access to Biscayne Bay.

The estate's buildings include the main house and a 19th-century inn called Richmond Cottage, which, when it was built, was the southernmost hotel on the US mainland .

The grounds are the main attraction, with mangrove and rockland pine forests, a salt marsh, and what is apparently the largest virgin coastal tropical hardwood hammock on the US mainland. There is an extensive fossil site on the grounds and youth camps, conservation programs, and canoe tours at the weekend.

The Charles Deering Estate offers ecotours and access to Biscayne Bay.

❾ Jungle Island

1111 Parrot Jungle Trail, Watson Island. **Tel** (305) 400-7000. 🚌 C (103), M (113), S (119), 120 Beach MAX. **Open** 10am–6pm daily. 🎫 ♿ 🅦 **jungleisland.com**

More than 1,100 birds populate this beautifully maintained tropical garden. Some birds are caged, some roam wild, others perform tricks such as riding roller skates in the ever-popular Trained Bird Show. In other shows you can feed fish and flamingos, and see snakes close-up.

There is also an Education Center, which provides activities for children and adults alike, as well as a range of summer camps and field trips.

The tranquil, palm-fringed lakes of the Fairchild Tropical Garden

A Bengal tiger in front of a mock Khmer temple at Zoo Miami

❿ Wings Over Miami

14710 SW 128th St, adjacent to Tamiami Airport. **Tel** (305) 233-5197. 🚌 136, 137 (both require a walk). **Open** 10am–5pm Wed–Sun. **Closed** public holidays. 🅿️ ♿ 🆆 wingsovermiami.com

This museum is dedicated to the preservation of old aircraft. Its hangars contain a superb collection of finely preserved examples of operating aircraft, including a 1943 AT6D Texan "Old Timer," a Douglas B-23 Dragon, and a British Provost jet, as well as other exhibits such as a machine-gun turret.

All these planes take to the sky during the Memorial Day weekend celebration. In January or February they are joined by B-17 and B-24 bombers in the Wings of Freedom event.

⓫ Gold Coast Railroad Museum

12450 SW 152nd St, Miami. **Tel** (305) 253-0063. 🚇 Metrorail (Dadeland North) then Zoo Bus. 🚌 252. **Open** 10am–4pm Mon–Fri, 11am–4pm Sat–Sun. 🅿️ ♿ 🆆 gcrm.org

Located next to the Zoo Miami, this unusual museum is a must-see for railroad enthusiasts. Highlights include the presidential railroad car "Ferdinand Magellan," two California Zephyr cars, and three old Florida East Coast Railway steam locomotives. There is even a two-foot gauge railroad for children to ride on weekends.

⓬ Zoo Miami

12400 SW 152nd St, Miami. **Tel** (305) 251-0400. 🚇 Metrorail (Dadeland North) then Zoo Bus. **Open** 9:30am–5:30pm daily. 🅿️ ♿ 🆆 miamimetrozoo.com

This giant zoo is one of the country's best. Animals are kept in spacious landscaped habitats, separated from humans by moats. Highlights include lowland gorillas, Malayan sun bears, and white Bengal tigers. The Petting Zoo is a hit with the kids, and the Wildlife Show demonstrates the agility of big cats.

Take the 20-minute ride on the monorail for an overview, and then visit what you like; or take the monorail to Station 4 and then walk back.

⓭ Monkey Jungle

14805 SW 216th St, Miami. **Tel** (305) 235-1611. 🚇 Metrorail (Dadeland South) then bus 31, 38 (or Busway flyer during peak hours) to Cutler Ridge Mall, then taxi. **Open** 9:30am–5pm daily. 🅿️ ♿ 🆆 monkeyjungle.com

A macaque, one of the most active primates at Monkey Jungle

Still run by the family that founded it back in 1933, Monkey Jungle's best selling point is that human visitors are caged while the animals roam free. You walk through a caged area with Java macaques clambering above you, or you can observe South American monkeys at close quarters in a simulated rainforest. Other primates, including gorillas and gibbons, are kept conventionally in cages.

Demonstrations showing the various capabilities of macaques, chimpanzees, and other species take place regularly throughout the day.

Crescent moon sculpted from rock at Coral Castle

⓮ Coral Castle

28655 S Dixie Hwy, Homestead. **Tel** (305) 248-6345. 🚇 Metrorail (Dadeland South) then bus Busway Max. 🚌 38, 70. **Open** 7am–8pm daily. **Closed** Dec 25. 🅿️ ♿ 🆆 coralcastle.com

From 1920 to 1940, a Latvian named Edward Leedskalnin single-handedly built this series of giant castle-like sculptures out of coral rock, using tools assembled from automobile parts. He sculpted most of the stones 10 miles (16 km) away in Florida City, moving them again on his own to their present site. Some, such as a working telescope, represent their creator's great passion for astrology. Others, such as the heart-shaped table, remember a Latvian girl who refused to marry him.

SHOPPING IN MIAMI

Miami's shops range from the ultra chic to the quirky and colorful, reflecting the nature of the city. Being made up of neighborhoods, Miami offers a choice of districts to shop in. Serious shoppers will probably gravitate toward the malls, which attract visitors from all over Latin America and the Caribbean. Some of these double as entertainment centers (see p348), often staying open until 11pm, but most of the stores tend to keep normal hours.

If your shopping tastes are more offbeat, head for Coconut Grove or South Beach, where shops are aimed at a totally different market. Here, wild leather gear, motorized skateboards, cardboard art, and the like are offered, and you can pick up fun souvenirs too. Most stores in Coconut Grove stay open late, especially on weekends. Stores in South Beach keep irregular hours, with most opening up late in the day; some don't get going until 11am or noon.

Where to Shop

South Beach is a fun place to shop, but the most relaxed shopping area is Coconut Grove. It has numerous boutiques concentrated in a small area and boasts two malls (see p88): CocoWalk, whose two dozen jewelry, gift, and clothing stores play second fiddle to cafés and restaurants, and the **Streets of Mayfair** – where pricey boutiques are suitable mainly for window-shopping.

Bayside Marketplace (see p78) has a wide range of stores, with all kinds of gift emporia and fashion stores. Otherwise, Downtown offers cut-price electronics and jewelry, although **Macy's** department store, founded in 1898, is of more general interest.

Entirely different in tone is Coral Gables, with its demure stores along Miracle Mile (see p86) and its posh art galleries. The **Village of Merrick Park** offers an added dimension to Coral Gables with its luxury retail stores complete with concierge services.

Dedicated shoppers head for Miami's famous malls. **Bal Harbour Shops** is an alluring up-market mall in a tropical garden setting where the increasing number of retail shops provide luxury goods to the rich and famous. **Aventura Mall**, also in North Miami, boasts over 200 shops including four department stores, one of which is **Macy's**.

Typical window-dressing in a South Beach boutique

Fashion and Jewelry

Miami has everything, from top designer to discount clothes. In Bal Harbour Shops, jewelers and fashion stores with names such as Tiffany & Co., Gucci, and Cartier stand alongside shops like J. W. Cooper, specializing in Western gear. By contrast, **Loehmann's**, in nearby Aventura, deals in cut-rate designer clothes. More good

deals can be had in the 100 odd discount stores of Downtown's Fashion District – on 5th Avenue between 24th and 29th Streets. The **Seybold Building**, also Downtown, is famous for its cut-rate gold, diamonds, and watches.

In South Beach, stores on Lincoln Road and Washington Avenue deal primarily in leather and "disco dolly" outfits, but there are more chic stores too. The boutiques along Miracle Mile in Coral Gables are more consistently up-scale: **J. Bolado**, for made-to-measure clothes, is typical.

Gifts and Souvenirs

Bayside marketplace is reliable gift-buying territory, with shops such as the **Caribbean Life** store and the **Disney Store**, and a gaggle of pushcarts laden with espadrilles, ties, and other items. In Coconut Grove, alongside numerous shops

CocoWalk mall in Coconut Grove

Cigarmaker in action

selling T-shirts and sunglasses are shops specializing in anything from oriental crafts to condoms. In North Miami visit **Edwin Watts Golf Shop**; this is the place to go for everything golf, including discounts on greens fees.

Macy's is not a classic hunting-ground for souvenirs, but you can sometimes pick up unusual items, such as genuine artifacts from the wreck of the *Atocha* salvaged by Mel Fisher *(see p32).*

Intermix is an upscale, pricey boutique and epitomizes all that is sexy about Miami Beach.

South Beach is probably the best place for fun mementos and gifts. The **Art Deco Welcome Center** on Ocean Drive has a small but good choice, including T-shirts,

posters, and models of Ocean Drive buildings, in addition to a few genuine Art Deco antiques. The shop also maintains an impressive selection of pertinent books. A mix of tourists and locals come to buy handmade cigars at the well-known **El Titan de Bronze** in Little Havana *(see p80).* A favorite brand among locals is La Palina, which celebrates the role of women in the cigar industry. **Macabi Cigars** and **El Credito Cigar Factory** also have an excellent selection.

A good shop for edible souvenirs, such as Florida jellies and sauces, is **Epicure** in South Beach, although tourists are not targeted by this gourmet supermarket.

Craft stalls are set up in Española Way *(see p72)* on weekends, but Miami is generally not a good place to buy locally made crafts. Fine art is a much easier proposition. Española Way itself has a few avant-garde galleries, but a greater

concentration of better quality fine art is found along Lincoln Road. Most of the galleries, including the South Florida Art Center *(see p72),* feature contemporary paintings, sculpture, ceramics, and furniture in provocative or Pop Art style. The art in Coral Gables' galleries is more traditional.

Books and Music

Books & Books in Coral Gables is everyone's favorite bookshop, with shelves from floor to ceiling and a good selection of travel and arts titles. For books about Florida, don't fail to visit the Indies Company gift shop in the Historical Museum of Southern Florida *(see p78),* whose stock of books covers every imaginable subject relating to the state. You'll find branches of chain bookstores, such as Barnes & Noble, in many shopping malls.

Uncle Sam's Music is an independent music store in Miami Beach, which has been offering the latest sounds since 1984.

A ceramic Art Deco hotel

DIRECTORY

ENTERTAINMENT IN MIAMI

A fleet of stretch limos parked outside the hottest nightclubs attests to the fact that South Beach (SoBe) is one of the trendiest places on the planet. For many people, the chance to party in style is one of the city's chief attractions. Most visitors make for the nightclubs, which are surprisingly laid-back, and these are also good spots for live music. For anyone not into celebrity-spotting or dancing, Miami offers a wide range of cultural and sports events. The city used to be thought of as something of a cultural desert, but its performing arts scene is now buoyant. The winter season is the busiest, when Miami attracts many internationally renowned artists. If you are lucky, your visit may coincide with one of the city's colorful and large-scale festivals. The easiest way to purchase tickets for most cultural or sports events is to call Ticketmaster *(see p361)*. Otherwise, contact the stadium or theater direct.

Information

Two essential sources of information are the weekend section of Friday's edition of the *Miami Herald*, and the free and more comprehensive *New Times*, which comes out every Wednesday.

For hot tips about the latest and most happening spots in the city, check out the **Night Guide Miami** website. The vibrant gay nightlife of South Beach is covered in detail in several free and widely available magazines.

Performing Arts

Major touring companies usually perform at **Adrienne Arsht Center for the Performing Arts**, consisting of the Ziff Ballet Opera House and the Knight Concert Hall; the **Miami/Dade County Auditorium**; the **Jackie Gleason Theater** in South Beach; and Downtown's **Gusman Center for the Performing Arts**, a fabulous 1920s theater with an ornate Moorish interior. The Broadway Series (November to April) in the Ziff Ballet Opera House leads Miami's drama scene. More intimate spots include the **MTCplayground** theater in Miami Shores, and **Gable Stage** and the **Actors' Playhouse** in Coral Gables for new shows and old favorites.

Miami City Ballet performs classical and contemporary work, often at the Jackie Gleason Theater, and you can sometimes see dancers rehearse at the company's base on Liberty Avenue. Also in South Beach, the Ballet Flamenco La Rosa, part of the **Performing Arts Network** group of dance companies, is well worth seeing; they often appear at the **Colony Theatre**.

Miami's most acclaimed classical orchestra is Michael Tilson Thomas's New World Symphony, which comprises some of the most stellar musicians in the country. The orchestra performs at the **New World Symphony Theater**, from October to May. The Concert Association of Florida *(see p359)* organizes most of Miami's top concerts.

A crowd of spectators at the Gulfstream Park Racetrack

Spectator Sports

Miami boasts a wide variety of spectator sports. The Miami Dolphins football team competes at the **Sun Life Stadium**, while the Florida Marlins play at the **Marlins Stadium**, under a retractable roof. The Hurricanes from the University of Miami are one of Florida's top college football squads, and attract large crowds. The popular Miami Heat basketball team plays at **American Airlines Arena.**

For some Hispanic flair, catch a game of jai alai *(see p37)*. A primary venue for this uniquely Floridian version of pelota is the **Miami Jai Alai Fronton**. Betting is *de rigueur* here, just as it is at **Gulfstream Park Racetrack**, **Calder Race Course**, and **Flagler Dog Track**.

Latin Sounds

Mango's Tropical Café on Ocean Drive in South Beach specializes in loud, brassy Latin music, and it is routine for

Adrienne Arsht Center for the Performing Arts

Interior of the 2,400-seat Ziff Ballet Opera House

female as well as male staff to dance upon the bar tops. Very touristy, but also a lot of fun. Also in the South Beach area, **Tapas & Tintos** is a great place for a few drinks and a light bite to eat on a Saturday, while watching live Flamenco.

Hoy Como Ayer offers energetic and smoky cabaret right on Calle Ocho, in the heart of Little Havana. Brimming with an array of Cuban memorabilia, this popular nightclub promises late-night dancing to Cuban musicians playing mambo, rumba, cha-cha-cha, and son. Live bands play some nights, while DJs spin Afro Cuban, funk, Latin, and jazz on others.

If in doubt about your dancing skills, take a free lesson from some of Miami's best. Instructors are on hand on Thursdays at **Café Mystique**, and on Fridays and Saturdays at **Bongo's Cuban Café**, at the American Airlines Arena.

Live Music

Most of the bars on Ocean Drive offer live music, which is typically Latin, jazz, reggae, or salsa. A few blocks away, **Jazid** hosts live jazz, blues, and funk, with Latin bands on the lower level, and a DJ spinning fusion and trance upstairs. In Lincoln Road Mall, you'll find **Upstairs at the Van Dyke Café**. Local jazz musicians perform at this venue which resembles a classic speakeasy.

Just south of the Downtown area is **Tobacco Road**, Miami's oldest club, which presents anything from rock to Latin jazz nightly. The house band, Iko Iko, has a bayou-inspired sound that has landed them a deal with Jimmy Buffet's record label.

Coral Gables is where you will find **The Globe Café & Bar**, which features live jazz every Saturday night.

Bars

For that extra special touch of sophistication, head to the Tides Hotel's **The Bar at 1220**. Try a popsicle martini in the late afternoon during happy hour. If you like to shoot a little eight-ball, try **Felt** in SoBe, which has drink specials nightly. Nearby, enjoy a drink and a range of musical styles at swanky **Marlin Bar**. A celebrity favorite, **Skybar** features three distinct areas on the rooftop, and is one of SoBe's most happening and glamorous hangout zones.

Closer to ground, the glitzy **Rose Bar** pours out top-dollar martinis, while **Raleigh Hotel's** pool bar has a legendary soiree on Sunday. At the other end of the spectrum, the pool area bars at **The Clevelander** embody a party atmosphere similar to that experienced during the infamous spring break season.

Outside SoBe, try upscale **Noir Bar**. The bar's Friday cocktail hours of 6–9pm offer great drink specials. Enjoy tasty hors d'oeuvres and the lovely view.

One of the four bars at The Clevelander on Ocean Drive

The swanky Mansion nightclub in South Beach's Opium Garden Complex *(see p102)*

Nightclubs

Miami has long been reputed as a hardcore party town, and with good reason. Most of the city's hottest venues have long queues of would-be party goers waiting at the entrances. To get in, tip the scales in your favor by dressing to impress. Groups of men hoping to make it past the door person stand a better chance of gaining entry if they invite some female friends to accompany them. Most clubs prefer to keep the customer ratio heavily skewed towards the feminine. You have been warned!

Greater Miami boasts three areas that really liven up after dark: the exceedingly trendy South Beach; Downtown, which is undergoing a Renaissance of sorts; and the more understated Coconut Grove, which offers the best wining and dining options.

In SoBe, the bars along Ocean Drive and nearby streets are busy all day, but the nightclubs only really get going after midnight. It is not uncommon to see people winding their way out as the sun rises the next day. The supremely hip **Penrod's Complex** houses Nikki Beach and Pearl, a restaurant and lounge, which is a regular haunt of supermodels and celebrities. Try one of their Sunday parties, which start at noon and carry on into the early hours of the morning. A block away, **Opium Group** encompasses Cameo, Louis Bar, and the cavernous **Mansion Nightclub**, attracting a regular rotation of A-list celebrities. It is almost impossible to get in on Fridays and Saturdays, but if you do, you'll find yourself among the who's who of South Beach.

A few blocks farther up the street, **SoBe Live** rocks with hip hop, R&B, and reggae, and offers the opportunity to rub shoulders with celebrities. If you seek Latin rhythms, Mango's Tropical Café has live bands and DJs playing high-energy salsa, merengue, and popular songs in several dance rooms. Live entertainment also includes male and female dancers performing Latin dance routines on the bar.

Club Deep on Washington Avenue caters more to the hip hop crowd than to club kids, and brings in a lot of rappers to host special events. Further up, near the Delano, you will find **Mynt Lounge**, which bills itself as the hottest club in SoBe. It is known for its exclusivity, and gaining entry can be rather difficult.

Sophisticated cocktails and DJs are the draw at the Shore Club's **Skybar** nightclub areas: The Red Room, with its rich scarlet and gold decor; the Moroccan-themed garden area; and the Sand Bar on the beach. A short trek south on Collins brings you to **The Florida Room** at the Delano South Beach, where a modern-day piano lounge, featuring a Lucite grand piano, offers classic South Florida glamor.

Rivaling SoBe, Downtown Miami is fast evolving into a hot clubbing area where you'll find the newly-opened, $12 million club **Nocturnal**. The three-clubs-in-one concept applies here, with each floor in the building housing a very different club vibe.

Three blocks away, **Area 51** boasts five different nightclubs in one building. It claims to be the largest nightclub compound in the world. As well as Area 51 itself which is the largest and main live performance area here with live bands and top DJs, the other clubs are Allure (formerly The Nile), with a decidedly Egyptian theme, Discotekka, a gay-oriented club, and Whiskey, with a large lounge area and probably the most laid-back of all the clubs here. Finally, there is Adrenalin, definitely the most raucous scene in the entire complex. It tends to attract a younger college crowd and features a glass-enclosed shower which guests can use.

The Area 51 complex is open Thursday through Sunday, and patrons should always be able to find a sound to fit their mood. Each club alternates between live music and DJs. A single cover charge allows you entrance to the entire complex.

Over in the more refined area of Coconut Grove, the reigning hotspot is **Oxygen Lounge**, which functions as a restaurant by day and a club-lounge by night – restaurants that turn into lounges after 10pm are becoming increasingly popular in SoBe, too. **B.E.D. Miami** is a decadent affair, with beds in place of sofas. Befitting the luxuriously lazy surroundings, nightly events tend to be laid back and relaxing. Unsurprisingly, it is necessary to make reservations at this chic dining club.

Tantra is a popular upscale restaurant and club with a Middle-Eastern theme and a natural grass floor. Three blocks away at **Sushi Samba**, Wasabi Tuesdays are a must for lovers of sushi, sake, and karaoke.

Many clubs have a gay night, while others categorically advertise themselves as exclusively gay. However, most venues seem to draw a mixed crowd. **Twist**, with a Key West-style terrace, is a very popular gay bar and also sports a dance floor. Saturday nights at **Club Space** draw a massive gay crowd into its cavernous building, though you'll find that Friday night brings in a wide cross-section of club goers.

Festivals

If you are lucky, your visit may coincide with one of the city's colorful and large-scale festivals (see pp38–41).

Two of the largest and best known festivals are very different but equally popular: the Winter Music Festival in March, when thousands of DJs and club kids flood South Beach, and the South Beach Food & Wine Festival in May, which offers opportunities to meet celebrity chefs.

Both festivals bring in a lot of visitors to the packed SoBe area, so the downside is that the already-crowded clubs are that much harder to get into. However, celebrity-spotters can have a real field day at these festivals.

DIRECTORY

Information

Night Guide Miami
w miami.nightguide.com

Performing Arts

Actors' Playhouse
280 Miracle Mile.
Map 5 C1.
Tel (305) 444-9293.

Adrienne Arsht Center for the Performing Arts
1300 Biscayne Blvd.
Map 4 F1.
Tel (305) 949-6722.

Colony Theatre
1040 Lincoln Rd.
Map 2 D2.
Tel (305) 674-1026.

Gable Stage
1200 Anastasia Ave,
Coral Gables.
Map 5 A2.
Tel (305) 445-1119.

Gusman Center for the Performing Arts
174 E Flagler St.
Map 4 E1.
Tel (305) 374-2444.

Jackie Gleason Theater
1700 Washington Ave.
Map 2 E2.
Tel (305) 673-7300.

Miami City Ballet
2200 Liberty Ave.
Map 2 E2.
Tel (305) 929-7010.

Miami/Dade County Auditorium
2901 W Flagler St.
Tel (305) 547-5414.

MTCplayground
9806 NE 2nd Ave.
Map 4 E1.
Tel (305) 751-9550.

New World Symphony Theater
541 Lincoln Rd.
Map 2 E2.
Tel (305) 673-3330.

Performing Arts Network
555 17th St.
Map 2 E2.
Tel (305) 899-7730.

Spectator Sports

American Airlines Arena
721 NW 1st Ave.
Tel (786) 777-1000.

Calder Race Course
21001 NW 27th Ave.
Tel (305) 625-1311.

Flagler Dog Track
1401 NW 38th Court.
Tel (305) 649-3000.

Gulfstream Park Racetrack
901 S Federal Hwy.
Tel (954) 454-7000.

Marlins Stadium
1400 NW 4th St.
Tel (305) 626-7378.

Miami Jai Alai Fronton
3500 NW 37th Ave.
Tel (305) 633-6400.

Sun Life Stadium
2269 NW Dan Marino Blvd.
Tel (305) 623-6100.

Latin Sounds

Bongo's Cuban Café
601 Biscayne Blvd.
Tel (786) 777-2100.

Café Mystique
7250 NW 11th St.
Tel (305) 262-9500.

Hoy Como Ayer
2212 SW 8th St.
Tel (305) 541-2631

Mango's Tropical Café
900 Ocean Drive.
Map 2 E5.
Tel (305) 673-4422.

Tapas & Tintos
448 Española Way.
Map 2 E2.
Tel (305) 538-8272.

Live Music

The Globe Café & Bar
377 Alhambra Circle,
Coral Gables.
Map 5 C1.
Tel (305) 445-3555.

Jazid
1342 Washington Ave.
Map 2 E2.
Tel (305) 673-9372.

Tobacco Road
626 S Miami Ave.
Map 4 E2.
Tel (305) 374-1198.

Upstairs at the Van Dyke Café
846 Lincoln Rd.
Map 2 E2.
Tel (305) 534-3600.

Bars

The Bar at 1220
The Tides Hotel, 1220 Ocean Drive.
Map 2 F3.
Tel (305) 604-5070.

The Clevelander
1020 Ocean Drive.
Map 2 F3.
Tel (786) 276-1414.

Felt
1242 Washington Ave.
Map 2 E3.
Tel (305) 531-2114.

Marlin Bar
1200 Collins Ave.
Map 2 E3.
Tel (305) 604-3595.

Noir Bar
Conrad Miami Hotel,
1395 Brickell Ave.
Map 4 E2.
Tel (305) 503-6560.

Raleigh Hotel
1775 Collins Ave.
Map 2 F1.
Tel (305) 534-6300.

Rose Bar
The Delano Hotel,
1685 Collins Ave.
Map 2 F1.
Tel (305) 672-2000.

Skybar
The Shore Club Hotel,
1901 Collins Ave.
Map 2 F1.
Tel (305) 695-3100.

Nightclubs

Area 51
950 NE 2nd Ave.
Tel (305) 358-5655.

B.E.D. Miami
929 Washington Ave.
Map 2 E3.
Tel (305) 532-9070.

Club Deep
621 Washington Ave.
Map 2 E4.
Tel (305) 532-1509.

Club Space
142 NE 11th St.
Tel (305) 375-0001.

The Florida Room
Delano South Beach,
1685 Collins Ave.
Map 2 E2.
Tel (305) 674-6152.

Mansion Nightclub
1235 Washington Ave.
Map 2 E3.
Tel (305) 695-8411.

Mynt Lounge
1921 Collins Ave.
Map 2 F1.
Tel (786) 276-6132.

Nocturnal
50 NE 11th St.
Tel (305) 576-6996.

Opium Group
136 Collins Ave.
Map 2 E5.
Tel (305) 531-7181.

Oxygen Lounge
2911 Grand Ave,
Coconut Grove.
Map 6 F4.
Tel (305) 476-0202.

Penrod's Complex
1 Ocean Drive.
Map 2 E5.
Tel (305) 538-1111.

Skybar
The Shore Club Hotel,
1901 Collins Ave.
Map 2 F1.
Tel (305) 695-3100.

SoBe Live
1203 Washington Ave.
Map 2 E3.
Tel (305) 695-2820.

Sushi Samba
600 Lincoln Rd.
Map 2 E2.
Tel (305) 673-5337.

Tantra
1445 Pennsylvania Ave.
Map 2 E3.
Tel (305) 672-4765.

Twist
1057 Washington Ave.
Map 2 E3.
Tel (305) 538-9478.

MIAMI STREET FINDER

The map references given with all sights, shops, and entertainment venues described in the Miami chapter refer to the five pages of maps in this section. The key map below shows the area of the city that is covered, with the three major sightseeing districts color-coded pink. All the principal sights mentioned in the text are marked, as well as useful information, such as transit stops, tourist offices, and post offices; a full list is given in the key. Map references are also given for Miami's hotels *(see pp314–25)*, restaurants *(see pp329–49)*, and bars and cafés *(see p348–9)* included in the Travelers' Needs section.

Key

■	Major sight	🕆	Church
■	Place of interest	✡	Synagogue
🅡	Metrorail station	☪	Mosque
🅜	Metromover station	⛳	Golf course
🚤	Boat trip boarding point	=	Metrorail line
🅸	Tourist information		Expressway
✚	Hospital with emergency room		Pedestrian street
🚓	Police station		

Scale of Map Pages

0 meters   500
0 yards   500

FLORIDA AREA BY AREA

Florida at a Glance

Walt Disney World aside, Florida is best known for its beaches; there are so many of these that everyone should be able to find one to suit his taste. Most tourist attractions, from state-of-the-art museums to historic towns, are also found along the coast. The joy of Florida, however, is that inland destinations are within easy reach. It is well worth venturing away from the hubbub of the coast to explore some of the state's richest natural landscapes and get the full flavor of Florida.

Canoeing is very popular in the Panhandle, where rivers such as the Suwannee are frequently flanked by lush vegetation (see p248).

De Funiak Springs

Milton

Pensacola

THE PANHANDLE
(See pp228–249)

Tallahassee

Panama City

Suwannee

Carrabelle

Steinhatchee

Gainesvil

Beaches in the Panhandle boast the finest sand in Florida, washed by the warm waters of the Gulf of Mexico. Resorts like Panama City Beach throng with people in the summer (see pp240–41).

Homosassa Springs

Weeki Wachee

Tam

St Petersburg

Sarasota

Busch Gardens, which combines a wildlife park with roller coasters and other rides, is the top large-scale family attraction outside Orlando (see pp268–9).

The Ringling Museum of Art boasts one of the state's top art collections and has a handsome courtyard filled with copies of Classical statuary, including this *Lygia and the Bull* (see pp274–7).

0 kilometers   75

0 miles   75

◀ Dawn at Long Pine Key Lake in Everglades National Park

Castillo de San Marcos is a 17th-century Spanish fort in Florida's oldest town, St. Augustine. Its well-preserved state is due to both its design and its 18-ft (6-m) thick walls *(see pp218–19).*

Orlando's theme parks are Florida's principal attraction away from the coast. Here, you can escape into a man-made fantasy world, where an extraordinary array of shows and rides provide the entertainment. Most famous is Walt Disney World *(see pp146–61),* but Universal Studios *(see pp184–9),* pictured here, and SeaWorld *(see pp180–81)* draw their own vast crowds.

ksonville

St Augustine

THE NORTHEAST
(See pp206–227)

Ocala

Daytona Beach
(see pp221–3)

Daytona Beach

Kennedy Space Center *(see pp200–205)*

Orlando

ORLANDO AND THE SPACE COAST
(See pp142–205)

Melbourne

Yeehaw Junction

Vero Beach

THE GULF COAST
(pp250–283)

THE GOLD AND TREASURE COASTS
(See pp114–141)

Fort Pierce

Jupiter

Lake Okeechobee

Port Charlotte

Fort Myers

Palm Beach

Boca Raton

Naples

Fort Lauderdale

THE EVERGLADES AND THE KEYS
(See pp284–307)

Miami

Florida City

John Pennekamp Coral Reef State Park *(see pp296–7)*

Islamorada

Marathon

Key West

The Gold Coast is full of luxurious homes. In Palm Beach you can visit the 1920s home of Henry Flagler, and marvel at the mansions and yachts along the Intracoastal Waterway *(see pp122–9).*

Everglades National Park, a vast expanse of prairie, swamp, and mangrove that teems with wildlife, is as wild as Florida gets. It is just a short drive from Miami (See pp290–91).

THE GOLD AND TREASURE COASTS

Named after booty found in Spanish galleons wrecked along their shores, the Gold and Treasure coasts today are two of the state's wealthiest regions. The promise of winter sunshine once lured just the well-to-do but now entices millions of vacationers.

Vacations center on the pencil-thin barrier islands that extend right along the coast, squeezed between prime beaches and the Intracoastal Waterway *(see p27)*. The Treasure Coast, stretching from Sebastian Inlet down to Jupiter Inlet, is relatively undeveloped, with great sweeps of wild, sandy beaches and affluent but unshowy communities.

Wedged between the Atlantic and the Everglades, the 60-mile (97-km) Gold Coast extends from just north of West Palm Beach down to Miami. Before being opened up by Flagler's East Coast Railroad in the late 19th century, this part of Florida was a wilderness populated only by Indians and the occasional settler. Today, except for golf courses and scattered

parks, it is unremittingly built up. The Gold Coast divides into two counties. In Palm Beach County, rich northerners, most of whom have made their fortunes elsewhere, flaunt their privileged lifestyle in million-dollar homes and on croquet lawns and polo fields. The winter resorts of Palm Beach and Boca Raton offer the most memorable glimpses of how affluent Americans spend their time and money. Broward County, synonymous with Greater Fort Lauderdale, is one huge metropolis. Its relentless urbanization is relieved by waterways and beaches: including in Fort Lauderdale itself, one of several local resorts that let their hair down more than their stuffy Palm Beach County counterparts.

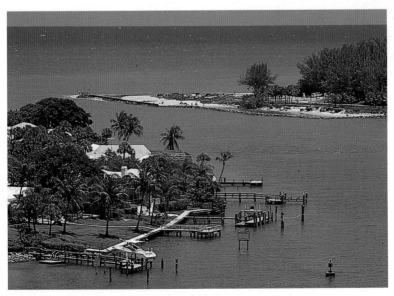

Looking out toward the Atlantic Ocean from the top of Jupiter Inlet Lighthouse

◀ Aerial view of Fort Lauderdale

Exploring the Gold and Treasure Coasts

Most visitors come here for a stay-put beach vacation. North of Palm Beach you can expect an unspoiled, uncrowded littoral, while to the south you'll find condos, sunbeds, and lots of company. Coastal parks rich in bird life provide reminders of how the land looked in its virgin state. Cultural sightseeing comes fairly low on the agenda, but West Palm Beach's superb Norton Museum of Art and the exclusive town of Palm Beach should not be missed. The more active can play golf, shop, and fish – the main reason to head inland is for the excellent fishing on Lake Okeechobee. All along the coast, hotel rooms are hard to come by and twice the price from December to April; in summer visitors take advantage of lower (bargain) rates.

Boca Raton's Old Town Hall, the work of Addison Mizner (see p124)

Sights at a Glance

1. Sebastian Inlet
2. Mel Fisher's Treasure Museum
3. Vero Beach
4. Fort Pierce
5. Hutchinson Island
6. Stuart
7. Jupiter Island
8. Jupiter
9. Juno Beach
10. *Palm Beach pp122–9*
11. West Palm Beach
12. Lion Country Safari
13. Lake Okeechobee
14. Lake Worth
15. Delray Beach
16. Loxahatchee Wildlife Refuge
17. Morikami Museum and Japanese Gardens
18. Butterfly World
19. Boca Raton
20. *Fort Lauderdale pp136–9*
21. Dania
22. Hollywood
23. Davie
24. Flamingo Gardens

0 kilometers 20
0 miles 20

Key

══ Highway
══ Major road
── Secondary road
┈┈ Minor road
── Scenic route
╍╍ Main railway

Designer shops and cars in exclusive Palm Beach

Getting Around

A car is absolutely essential, as public transportation is either limited or nonexistent. Amtrak basically offers ways to get to (rather than around) the area, but Tri-Rail (*see p384*) has services stopping at towns and airports between Miami and West Palm Beach. Three main highways run the length of the coast. Use the fast-moving, multilaned I-95 to travel any distance. Avoid US 1 where possible: it trawls slowly through the unscenic center of every significant urban area. Route A1A can be slower still but is normally far less congested and often delivers picturesque views. Avoid traveling on major roads anywhere along the Gold Coast and around the Treasure Coast's main centers during rush hours (weekdays 7:30–9:30am and 4:30–7pm).

Fort Lauderdale's popular beach, offering a wealth of water sports

For additional map symbols *see back flap*

❶ Sebastian Inlet

Road Map: F3. Indian River Co.
Sebastian. 🅸 700 Main St, (772) 589-5969. 🅆 sebastianchamber.com

At Sebastian Inlet, the Atlantic Ocean mingles with the brackish waters of the Indian River section of the Intra-coastal Waterway *(see p27)*. The **Sebastian Inlet State Park** spans this channel and, with its 3 miles (5 km) of pristine beaches, is one of the most popular state parks in Florida.

A tranquil cove on the northern side of the inlet is an ideal place to swim – avoiding the waves that make the southern shores (on Orchid Island) one of the best surfing spots on Florida's east coast. Competitions take place on many weekends, and there are boards for rent. The park is famous for its fishing too, and the inlet's mouth is invariably very crowded with fishing boats. The two jetties jutting out into the Atlantic Ocean on either side are also crammed with anglers, while more lines dangle in the limpid waters of the Indian River.

At the southern end of the park, the **McLarty Treasure Museum** takes an in-depth look at the history surrounding the loss of a Spanish Plate Fleet in 1715. On July 31 a hurricane wrecked 11 galleons on the shallow reefs off the coast between Sebastian Inlet and Fort Pierce. The ships were en route from Havana back to Spain, riding the waters of the warm Gulf Stream, and laden with booty

Spanish plate, McLarty Museum

from Spain's New World colonies. About a third of the 2,100 sailors lost their lives, while the survivors set up a camp where the McLarty Treasure Museum now stands.

Immediately following this tragedy, some 80 percent of the cargo was salvaged by the survivors, helped by local Ais Indians. The fleet then lay undisturbed until 1928, when one of the wrecks was rediscovered. Salvaging resumed in the early 1960s; since then, millions of dollars worth of treasures have been recovered. Finds on display include gold and silver coins but feature mostly domestic items.

🅼 **Sebastian Inlet State Park**
9700 S A1A, Melbourne Beach.
Tel (321) 984-4852. **Open** daily.
🅆 floridastateparks.com

🏛 **McLarty Treasure Museum**
13180 N Highway A1A. **Tel** (772) 589-2147. **Open** 10am–4pm daily

❷ Mel Fisher's Treasure Museum

Road Map: F3. Indian River Co.
Tel (772) 589-9875. Sebastian.
Open 10am–5pm Mon–Sat (from noon Sun). **Closed** Jan 1, Easter, Sep, Thanksgiving, Dec 25.
🅆 melfisher.com

One of the great rags-to-riches stories is presented at this amazing museum. Billed as "The World's Greatest Treasure Hunter," Mel Fisher died in

The late Mel Fisher, treasure hunter and founder of the Museum

1998, but his treasure-hunting team of divers lives on.

The museum contains treasures from different wrecks, including the 1715 fleet (which his team has been salvaging for decades), and the Atocha *(see p33)*. There are jewels, a gold bar and more everyday items. In the Bounty Room, you can buy original Spanish reales or copies of historic jewelry. See also The Mel Fisher Maritime Museum on p306.

❸ Vero Beach

Road Map: F3. Indian River Co.
18,000. 🅸 1216 21st St, (772) 567-3491. 🅆 indianriverchamber.com

The main town of Indian River County, Vero Beach, and in particular its resort community on Orchid Island, is a seductive, well-heeled place. Mature live oaks line the residential streets, and buildings are restricted to no more than four stories. Pretty clapboard houses along Ocean Drive contain galleries, boutiques, and antique shops.

The **Vero Beach Museum of Art** in Riverside Park on Orchid Island puts on high-profile exhibitions, but the town is most famous for its beaches and two hotels. The Driftwood Resort, in the heart of oceanfront Vero Beach, began life in 1935 as a beach house. It was created out of reclaimed wood and driftwood by a local eccentric and filled with an amazing array of bric-a-brac, still present today. Seven miles (11 km) north at Wabasso Beach, one of the best of the superb shell-strewn sands

Catching the waves at the Gold Coast's Sebastian Inlet

on Orchid Island, is the Vero Beach Resort. Disney's first Florida hotel outside Orlando. A model of measured elegance.

The **Indian River Citrus Museum**, on the mainland, is dedicated to the area's chief crop. All kinds of items to do with the citrus industry are displayed, including some old photographs, harvesting equipment, and brand labels.

🏛 **Vero Beach Museum of Art**
3001 Riverside Park Drive.
Tel (772) 231-0707. **Closed** Jan 1, Thanksgiving, Dec 25. ♿
W verobeachmuseum.com

🏛 **Indian River Citrus Museum**
2140 14th Ave. **Tel** (772) 770-2263.
Open 10am–4pm Tue–Fri.
Closed public hols. ♿
W veroheritage.com

❹ Fort Pierce

Road Map: F3. St. Lucie Co. 🅰 39,500.
✈ 🚌 🅸 2300 Virginia Ave, (772) 462-1535. W visitstluciefla.com

Named after a military post built during the Second Seminole War *(see pp50–51)*, Fort Pierce is not considered a tourist mecca. The town's biggest draw is its barrier islands, reached by way of two causeways that sweep across the Intracoastal Waterway.

Take the North Beach Causeway to reach North Hutchinson Island. Its southern tip is occupied by the **Fort Pierce Inlet State Park**, which includes the town's best beach, backed by dunes and popular with surfers. Just to the north,

Vero Beach's Driftwood Resort, built of reclaimed wood

on the site of a World War II training school, is the **UDT-SEAL Museum**. From 1943 to 1946, more than 3,000 US Navy frogmen of the Underwater Demolition Teams (UDTs) trained here, learning how to disarm sea mines and beach defenses. By the '60s, they had become an elite advance fighting force known as SEALs (Sea, Air, Land commandos). The museum explains the frogmen's roles in World War II, Korea, Vietnam, and in the present. Outside are several SEAL delivery vehicles, which are torpedo-like submarines used to carry people but not bombs and explosives.

Half a mile (0.8 km) away is Jack Island – actually a peninsula on the Indian River. This mangrove-covered preserve teems with bird life and is crossed by a short trail leading to an observation tower. Situated on the southern

causeway linking Fort Pierce to Hutchinson Island is the **St. Lucie County Historical Museum**. This has an enjoy-able array of displays, which include finds from the 1715 wrecks in the Galleon Room and reconstructions of a Seminole camp and an early 20th-century general store. You can also look around the adjacent "cracker" home *(see p34)*.

🏕 **Fort Pierce Inlet State Park**
905 Shorewinds Drive, N Hutchinson Island. **Tel** (772) 468-3985. ♿ limited.

🏛 **UDT-SEAL Museum**
3300 N Highway A1A. **Tel** (772) 595-5845. **Open** Jan–Apr: daily; May– Dec: Tue–Sun. **Closed** public hols. ♿
W navysealmuseum.com

🏛 **St. Lucie County Historical Museum**
414 Seaway Drive. **Tel** (772) 462-1795.
Open 10am–4pm Tue–Sat (from noon Sun). **Closed** public hols. ♿ limited. W stlucieco.gov

---

A 1937 brand label from central Florida using the Indian River name

Indian River's Citrus Industry

Citrus fruits were brought to Florida by the Spanish in the 16th century: each ship was purportedly required to leave Spain with 100 citrus seeds for planting in the new colonies. Conditions in Florida proved ideal, and the fruit trees flourished, particularly along the Indian River between Daytona and West Palm Beach, which became the state's most important citrus-growing region. In 1931, local farmers created the Indian River Citrus League to stop growers outside the area from describing their fruit as "Indian River." One third of Florida's citrus crop and 75 percent of its grapefruit yield is produced here. The majority of the oranges are used to make juice; the oranges are especially sweet and juicy because of the warm climate, soil conditions, and rainfall.

Gilbert's Bar House of Refuge Museum, on the Atlantic shore of Hutchinson Island

❺ Hutchinson Island

Road Map: F3. St. Lucie Co/Martin Co.
🏠 5,000. ℹ️ 1900 Ricou Jensen Beach, (772) 334-3444.
🌐 **jensenbeachchamber.org**

Extending more than 20 miles (32 km), this barrier island is most memorable for its breathtaking beaches. In the south, sun-worshipers head for Sea Turtle Beach and the adjacent Jensen Beach Park, close to the junction of routes 707 and A1A. Stuart Beach, at the head of the causeway across the Indian River to Stuart, is well frequented too.

By Stuart Beach is the **Elliott Museum**, created in 1961 in honor of inventor Sterling Elliott, some of whose quirky contraptions are on show. Focusing on art, history, technology, and innovation, the museum was completely rebuilt in 2013.

Continuing south for about a mile (1.6 km), you reach **Gilbert's Bar House of Refuge Museum**. Erected in 1875, it is one of ten such shelters along the east coast, established by the Lifesaving Service (predecessors of the US Coast Guard) for shipwreck victims. The stark rooms in the charming clapboard house show how hard life was for the early caretakers, who often stayed only a year. A replica of an 1840s "surf boat" used on rescue missions sits outside. Beyond the refuge is **Bathtub Beach,** the best on the island. The natural pool formed by a sandstone reef offshore forms a safe, popular swimming spot.

🏛 Elliott Museum
825 NE Ocean Blvd. **Tel** (772) 225-1961.
Open 10am–5pm daily. **Closed** Jan 1, Easter, Jul 4, Thanksgiving, Dec 25.
🅿️ ♿

🏛 Gilbert's Bar House of Refuge Museum
301 SE MacArthur Blvd. **Tel** (772) 225-1875.
Open 10am–4pm Mon–Sat (from 1pm Sun). **Closed** Jan 1, Easter, Thanksgiving, Dec 25. 🅿️ ♿

❻ Stuart

Road Map: F3. Martin Co. 🏠 17,000.
ℹ️ 1650 S Kanner Highway, (772) 287-1088. 🌐 **goodnature.org**

The magnificent causeway across the island-speckled Indian River from Hutchinson Island offers a fine approach to Martin County's main town. Ringed by affluent waterfront enclaves and residential golf developments, Stuart has a fetching, rejuvenated downtown area, which is by-passed by the busy coastal highways. South of Roosevelt Bridge, along Flagler Avenue and Osceola Street, is a short riverside boardwalk, a smattering of 1920s brick and stucco buildings, and a number of art galleries. In the evenings, live music emanates from buzzing restaurants and bars.

The Florida scrub jay, a resident of Jupiter Island's sand pine scrub

❼ Jupiter Island

Road Map: F4. Martin Co. 🏠 200.
ℹ️ 800 N US 1, (561) 746-7111.
🌐 **townofjupiterisland.com**

Much of this long, thin island is a well-to-do residential neighborhood, but there are also several excellent public beaches.

Toward Jupiter Island's northern end, **Hobe Sound National Wildlife Refuge** beckons with more than 3 miles (5 km) of beach, mangroves, and magnificent unspoiled dunes. The other half of the refuge, a strip of pine scrub flanking the Intracoastal Waterway, is a haven for birds, including the Florida scrub jay. There is a nature center by the junction of US 1 and A1A.

Blowing Rocks Preserve, a short distance south, has a fine beach. During storms, holes in the shoreline's limestone escarpment shoot water skyward – hence the name.

🏞 Hobe Sound National Wildlife Refuge
13640 SE Federal Hwy. **Tel** (772) 546-6141. 🅿️ to the beach. Beach: **Open** daily. Nature Center: **Tel** (772) 546-2067. **Open** Mon–Fri. **Closed** public hols.

The brightly painted Riverwalk Café, St. Lucie Street, downtown Stuart

For hotels and restaurants in this region see pp314–25 and pp329–49

Environs

Named after a man who was shipwrecked nearby in 1696, **Jonathan Dickinson State Park** comprises habitats as diverse as mangrove swamps, pine flatwoods, and a cypress-canopied stretch of the Loxahatchee River. As well as walking and horse-back riding trails, there are canoes for rent and boat trips along the river; manatees, alligators, ospreys, and herons are often sighted along the way.

Jupiter Inlet Lighthouse as seen from Jupiter Beach Park

Jonathan Dickinson State Park
16450 SE Federal Hwy. **Tel** (772) 546-2771. **Open** daily. limited.

❽ Jupiter

Road Map: F4. Palm Beach Co.
35,000. 800 N US 1, (561) 746-7111. townofjupiterisland.com

This small town is best known for its fine beaches and spring-training camps of the Miami Marlins and the St. Louis Cardinals. The **John D. MacArthur Beach** on Singer Island is one of the state's best *(see p131)*. The **Loxahatchee River Historical Society and Museum** has exhibits relating to the area's original inhabitants, the Hobe Indians, and the English settlers of the 18th century.

Loxahatchee River Historical Society and Museum
805 N US 1. **Tel** (561) 747-6639. **Open** 10am–5pm Tue–Fri, noon–5pm Sat & Sun. **Closed** public hols.

John D. MacArthur State Park
Singer Island (cross the Intracoastal Waterway on Blue Heron Blvd, turn north on Ocean Blvd). **Open** daily.

Environs

Close by, on the south side of Jupiter Inlet, is a beautiful county park, **Jupiter Beach Park**. It is easily accessible and has a superb beach of chocolate-colored sand, complete with lifeguards; it is also a mecca for anglers and pelicans. There are picnic pavilions, tables, a children's play area, rest rooms, and a fishing jetty. There is a good view across to scenic **Jupiter Inlet Lighthouse**, dating from 1860 and the oldest structure in the county, which you can climb for a wider perspective. The old oil house at its base is now a small museum. In addition to the Lighthouse, there is an added bonus for Sunday visitors: the 1896 Dubois House Museum, operated by the

Loxahatchee Historical Society and furnished in turn-of-the-century pioneer style, offers free tours. Nearby is the huge **Carlin Park,** operated by the Parks and Recreation Department of Palm Beach County. It offers playing fields, picnic areas, tennis courts, rest rooms, and a guarded beach.

Jupiter Inlet Lighthouse
Beach Rd at US 1. **Tel** (561) 747-8380. **Open** 10am–4pm Sat–Wed. **Closed** public hols. jupiterlighthouse.org

Carlin Park
400 South State Road A1A. **Tel** (561) 966-6600. **Open** daily. Lifeguards on duty from 9am to 5:20pm.

❾ Juno Beach

Road map: F4. Palm Beach Co.
2,700. **Open** 1555 Palm Beach Lakes Blvd, Suite 800, (561) 471-3995.

The pristine sands by Juno Beach, a small community that stretches north to Jupiter Inlet, are one of the world's most productive nesting sites for loggerhead turtles. In Loggerhead Park, nestled between US 1 and Route A1A, the fascinating **Loggerhead Marinelife Center** is an eco-science center and nature trail. Injured turtles, perhaps cut by boat propellers or snagged on fishing lines, recuperate in tanks. A path leads to the beach where turtles nest during the summer. Advance reservations are a must.

Loggerhead Marinelife Center
14200 US 1. **Tel** (561) 627-8280. **Open** 10am–4pm Mon–Sat, noon–3pm Sun. **Closed** Dec 25. marinelife.org

---

Florida's Sea Turtles

Florida's central east coast is the top sea turtle nesting area in the US. From May to September female turtles lumber up the beaches at night to lay about 100 eggs in the sand. Two months later the hatchlings emerge and dash for the ocean, again under the cover of darkness. Sea turtles, including Florida's most common species, the loggerhead, are threatened partly because hatchlings are disoriented by lights from buildings.

The approved way to see a turtle laying eggs is to join an organized turtle watch. These nocturnal expeditions are popular all along the coast: call local chambers of commerce, such as the one in Juno Beach, for details.

A loggerhead hatchling's first encounter with the sea

⑩ Palm Beach

Literally and metaphorically insular, Palm Beach has long provided an eye-opener on serious American wealth. Henry Flagler, pioneer developer of South Florida (see p129), created this winter playground for the rich at the end of the 19th century. In the 1920s, the architect Addison Mizner (see p124) gave the resort a further boost and transformed the look of Palm Beach by building lavish Spanish-style mansions for its seasonal residents. In the 1960s, the town virtually closed down in summer – even traffic lights were dismantled. Nowadays, Palm Beach stays open all year, but it is still essentially a winter resort. In purportedly the richest town in the US, visitors can observe members of the *beau monde* as they idle away the hours in some of the state's most stylish shops and restaurants or make their way to private clubs and glamorous charity balls.

Via Roma's grand entrance belies the charming alleyway beyond

Stylish Worth Avenue, shopping mecca for the very rich

Worth Avenue

For an insight into the Palm Beach lifestyle, Worth Avenue is compulsory viewing. While their employers toy over an Armani dress or an antique Russian icon, chauffeurs keep the air conditioning turning over in the Rolls Royces outside. Stretching four fabulous blocks from Lake Worth to the Atlantic Ocean, it is the town's best known thoroughfare.

Worth Avenue, as well as the architecture of Addison Mizner, first became fashionable with the construction of the exclusive Everglades Club, at the western end, in 1918. This was the result of the collaboration between Mizner and Paris Singer, the heir to the sewing machine fortune, who had first invited the architect down to Florida. Originally intended as a hospital for officers shellshocked during World War I, it never housed a single patient, and instead became the town's social hub. Today, the building's loggias and Spanish-style courtyards are still a very upscale, members-only enclave.

Across the street, and in stark contrast to the club's rather plain exterior, are Via Mizner and Via Parigi, lined with colorful shops and restaurants. These interlinking pedestrian alleys were created by Mizner in the 1920s, and are Worth Avenue's aesthetic highlights. Inspired by the backstreets of Spanish villages,

Water fountain, Via Mizner

the lanes are a riot of arches, tiled and twisting flights of steps, bougainvillea, fountains, and pretty courtyards. Overlooking the alleys' entrances are the office tower and villa that Mizner designed for himself. The tower's first floor originally housed display space for his ceramics business and was the avenue's first commercial unit. Connecting the two buildings is a walkway that forms the entrance to Via Mizner's shopping area. The other vias off Worth Avenue are more modern but, built in the same style and decorated with flowers and attractive window displays, they are nonetheless charming. Don't miss Via Roma or the courtyards joining Via de Lela and Via Flora.

Worth Avenue in 1939, captured by society photographer Bert Morgan

Shopping on Worth Avenue

The epitome of Palm Beach, Worth Avenue and the alleyways that connect with it contain some 250 exquisitely designed clothing boutiques, art galleries, and antique shops. The shop fronts, ranging in style from Mizner's signature Spanish look to Art Deco, form an eclectic and pleasing mix. The artful window displays of Florida's most famous shopping street look their best when brightly lit up at night. Some windows flaunt wonderfully ironic symbols of wealth, such as fake caviar on toast or a life-sized model of a butler. In 1979, a Rolls Royce fitted with a bulldozer blade symbolically broke the ground for 150 Worth, an open-air mall at the Avenue's eastern end. It is this sort of showy display that typifies Worth Avenue and distinguishes it from other prestigious shopping areas.

Worth Avenue's Exclusive Shops

Worth Avenue boasts a spectacular mix of glitzy shops. Jewelry stores abound, including those specializing in high quality imitations, and you'll also find elegant ready-to-wear houses, fancy gift shops, designer boutiques, and luxury department stores.

Cartier has the ultimate in gifts and souvenirs. Choose from gold jewelry, pens, and, of course, their signature watches.

Tiffany & Co. is one of the most famous names on Worth Avenue. Best known for its jewelry (including exclusive designs by Paloma Picasso) and silverware, it also sells perfume and leather goods.

Saks Fifth Avenue, located in the elegant Esplanade mall, has two floors of luxury apparel from lingerie to designer menswear.

Betteridge, Greenleaf, and Crosby, specialist jewelers, in Palm Beach since 1896.

Giorgio's boutique offers luxury, hand-made clothing, plus bags, shoes, and accessories made of alligator and ostrich leather, and executive furniture fashioned from alligator leather and wood.

Richter's of Palm Beach are specialists in rare estate jewelry, and purveyors of one-of-a-kind gems.

Exploring Palm Beach

The spirit and imagination of Addison Mizner infuses the whole of Palm Beach. As well as those buildings he designed himself, he influenced the look of countless others. Mizner's architecture, described by a biographer as a "Bastard-Spanish-Moorish-Romanesque-Gothic-Renaissance-Bull-Market-Damn-the-Expense Style," gave his contemporaries plenty of ideas to work from. Palm Beach is full of the splendid creations of men such as Marion Wyeth, Maurice Fatio, and Howard Major, all active in the 1920s, as well as more recent imitations. Gazing at the luxurious mansions of the rich and famous in the exclusive "suburbs" is an essential activity in Palm Beach.

A panel, representing drama, of the mural in the Four Arts Library

Exploring Palm Beach

After the opulence of Worth Avenue, the atmosphere along the mainly residential streets to the north is more restrained. Leafy Cocoanut Row features some luxurious private homes, but along South County Road, which runs parallel, Mizner's influence is more in evidence – in the street's eclectic architecture, such as the immaculately restored Town Hall, built in 1926. Nearby is the attractive Mizner Memorial Park, where the centerpiece is a fountain and narrow pool flanked by palm trees, and Phipps Plaza – a quiet, shady close containing some delightful buildings with tiled windowsills and flower-decked gates. Mizner himself designed the fine coral

Mizner Memorial Fountain

house at No. 264. Also memorable is Howard Major's tropical cottage (1939), which features delicate Chinese influences.

If you have time to spare, it's worth strolling along some of the streets to the west of South County Road, where you'll find a mix of Mizneresque houses and early 20th-century bungalows set in shady gardens. In contrast, the most imposing street in this area is Royal Palm Way. Its rank of palm trees makes a fine approach to Royal Palm Bridge, which is an excellent platform for gawking at the luxury yachts on Lake Worth. This is particularly worthwhile in December, when they are decked out in colored lights for the annual boat parade.

🎭 Society of the Four Arts

2 Four Arts Plaza. **Tel** (561) 655-7226. Gallery: **Open** Dec–Apr: 10am–5pm Mon–Sat, 2–5pm Sun. **Closed** Sun (May–Oct), public hols. Gardens: **Open** 10am–5pm Mon–Sun. Library: **Open** 10am–4:45pm Mon–Fri, 10am–12:45pm Sat. **Closed** Sat (May–Oct), Sun, public hols. ♿

Founded in 1936, the Society of the Four Arts incorporates two libraries, exhibition space, and an auditorium for lectures, concerts, and films.

The gallery and auditorium were originally part of a private club designed by Mizner, but Maurice Fatio's Italianate Four Arts Library building is far more striking. The murals in its loggia represent art, music, drama, and literature. The grounds include modern sculptures.

Mizner's Spanish Fantasy

Addison Mizner (1872–1933) came to Palm Beach from New York in 1918 to convalesce after an accident. An architect by profession, he soon began to design houses, and in the process changed the face of Palm Beach and, essentially, Florida (see p35). By adapting the design of old Spanish buildings to suit his environment, Mizner created a new style of architecture. He incorporated features such as loggias and external staircases to accommodate the region's high temperatures, and his workmen covered walls in condensed milk and rubbed them with steel wool to fake centuries-old dirt.

Addison Mizner became a multimillionaire, successful because of both his architectural vision and his ability to ingratiate himself into his prospective clients' milieu. He later turned his attention to Boca Raton (see pp134–5), but the collapse of the Florida land boom at the end of the 1920s hit him heavily, and by the end of his life Mizner had to rely on friends to pay his bills.

Addison Mizner in the mid-1920s

Via Mizner (see p122), a classic example of Mizner's work

🏛 Hibel Museum of Art

5353 Parkside Drive, Jupiter. **Tel** (561) 622-5560. **Open** 11am–4pm Tue–Fri (call first). **Closed** public hols. ♿
w hibelmuseum.org

Typical works of Edna Hibel, born in Boston in 1917 and still a resident of neighboring Singer Island *(see p131)*, are idealized, sugary portraits of mothers and children from around the world. She paints on all kinds of surfaces, ranging from wood and silk to crystal and porcelain.

The museum, founded in 1977, holds over 1,500 of the artist's creations.

Brittany and Child (1994) by Edna Hibel (oil, gesso, and gold on silk)

🏛 The Breakers

1 South County Rd. **Tel** (561) 655-6611. 📷 Wed pm. ♿
w breakers.com

Rising above Florida's oldest golf course, this mammoth Italian Renaissance structure is the third hotel on the site: the first Breakers, built in 1896, burned down in 1903. Its replacement went the same route in 1925, destroyed by a fire supposedly started by a guest's curling iron. Miraculously, the present Breakers was built in less than a year. The hotel has always been a focal point for the town's social life, hosting numerous galas in its magnificent ballrooms.

Palm Beach's grandest hotel is refreshingly welcoming to nonresidents: feel free to watch a game of croquet, have a milkshake in its old-fashioned soda shop, or nose around the lobby (with its hand-painted ceiling) and the palatial public rooms.

For a more in-depth look, take the weekly guided tour with the

The façade of the Breakers Hotel, designed by New York firm Schultze and Weaver

"resident historian." South of the hotel are three 19th-century wooden mansions, all that remain of **Breakers Row.** These were originally rented out to Palm Beach's wealthier visitors for the winter season.

🏛 Palm Beach suburbs

Palm Beach's high society normally hides away behind appropriately high hedges in multimillion-dollar mansions. Some of these were built by Addison Mizner and his imitators in the 1920s, but since then hundreds of others have proliferated, in all kinds of architectural styles, from Neo-Classical to Art Deco.

The most easily visible accommodations can be seen sitting on a ridge along South Ocean Boulevard, nicknamed "Mansion Row." At the top end, the Georgian residence at No. 126 belongs to Estée Lauder. No. 720, built by Mizner for himself in 1919, was for a time owned by John Lennon. Eight blocks beyond, Mar-a-Lago (No. 1100) is Palm Beach's

grandest residence, with 58 bedrooms, 33 bathrooms, and three bomb shelters. Built by Joseph Urban and Marion Wyeth in 1927, it was bought in 1985 by millionaire Donald Trump, who converted it into an expensive private club.

The homes in the northern suburbs are more secluded. North County Road passes Palm Beach's biggest domestic property at No. 513. Beyond, No. 1095 North Ocean Boulevard was used as a winter retreat by the Kennedy family until 1995.

Glimpsing how the other half lives is discouraged by a minimum speed limit of 25 mph (40 km/h). This makes cycling an attractive option. Bikes are easy to rent *(see p127)*, and there are various bicycle routes. The most scenic of these is the 3-mile (5-km) Lake Trail, which doubles as an exercise track for the locals. It runs from Worth Avenue virtually to the island's northern tip, hugging Lake Worth and skirting the backs of mansions; its prettiest section is north of Dunbar Road.

Mar-a-Lago, the most extravagant home in the Palm Beach suburbs

A Tour of Palm Beach

Circled by the main thoroughfares of South County Road and Cocoanut Row, this tour links up all the major sights of central Palm Beach, including Henry Flagler's impressive home, Whitehall. The section of the tour along Lake Drive South forms part of the scenic Palm Beach bicycle trail, which flanks Lake Worth and extends into the suburbs *(see p121)*. Although intended to be followed by car, parts (or all) could equally be done by bicycle, on foot, or even on skates. These alternatives get around the problem of Palm Beach's zealous traffic cops who patrol the streets in motorized golf carts.

① Flagler Museum
Formerly Flagler's private winter residence, "Whitehall" opened to the public in 1959. Beautifully restored, most of its furniture is original.

② Sea Gull Cottage
Built in 1886, this is Palm Beach's oldest building. It was Flagler's first winter home.

③ Royal Poinciana Chapel was built by Flagler for his guests in 1896.

LAKE WORTH

Royal Park Bridge

⑤ Casa de Leoni
No. 450 Worth Avenue is one of Mizner's most enchanting buildings. It set a trend for the Venetian Gothic style.

| 0 meters | 250 |
| 0 yards | 250 |

Key

▬▬ Route of tour

⑦ Public Beach
Despite the town's name, its public beach is perhaps surprisingly unspectacular, but it is free and open to all.

⑧ Town Hall was designed in 1926 and is a well-known Palm Beach landmark.

*Map labels: WHITEHALL, PRIMAVERA AVE, ANTIGUA LN, CLARKE, SEABRE, SEASPRAY, SEAVIEW, ROYAL PALM WAY, LAKE TRAIL, LAKE TRAIL CIRCLE, FOUR ARTS PLAZA, LAKE DRIVE SOUTH, COCOANUT ROW, MAJOR ALLEY, BRAZILIAN, AUSTRALIAN, CHILIAN, PERUVIAN, HIBISCUS, WORTH, EVERGLADES CLUB GOLF LINKS, SOUTH COUNTY ROAD, AVENUE, GOLF ROAD, HAMMON AVENUE, GULFSTREAM RD, ⑩, ⑨, ⑧*

⑬ **Green's Pharmacy**, open since 1937, is a drugstore with a diner attached. People come for the great breakfasts, the traditional ice-cream sodas, and terrific burgers – all served in a lively atmosphere.

LAKE TRAIL
Flagler Memorial Bridge
PARK AVENUE
SUNRISE
⑯
SUNSET
⑭
GRACE TERRACE
⑬
NORTH DR
SOUTH DR
ROYAL POINCIANA WAY
AVENUE
⑮
-NUT ROW
AVENUE
THE BREAKERS GOLF COURSE
MAIN STREET
AVENUE
COUNTY ROAD
-OANUT WALK
-E WALK
BREAKERS ROW
⑫
⑪
VIA BETHESDA
AVENUE
DRIVE
AVENUE
FLAGLER
-NUE
BOULEVARD
OCEAN
ATLANTIC OCEAN

⑫ **The Breakers**, originally called the Palm Beach Inn, was the fourth of Henry Flagler's impressive east coast hotels.

⑪ **Bethesda-by-the-Sea Church** is Gothic Revival in style, and has a cloistered court-yard and pleasant, quiet gardens to the rear.

⑩ **Phipps Plaza** contains some attractive buildings in fanciful designs, including Mediterranean and Southwest Spanish styles.

VISITORS' CHECKLIST

Practical Information
Road Map: F4. Palm Beach Co.
🏙 10,000 ℹ️ 45 Cocoanut Row, (561) 655-3282. 🎭 Artigras (Feb).

Transport
✈️ 3 miles (5 km) W. 🚆 Amtrak and Tri-Rail, 201 S Tamarind Ave, West Palm Beach, (800) 872-7245. 🚌 201 S Tamarind Ave, West Palm Beach, (800) 231-2222. 🚌 41, 42 from West Palm Beach.

⑮ **The Hotel Royal Poinciana** This lavish 2,000-room, wooden hotel was a winter retreat for the very rich. It burned down in 1935; today only the green house cupola survives.

⑭ **St. Edward's Church** Completed in 1927, St. Edward's was built in a Spanish Revival style and features a decorative, cast stone Baroque bell tower and entrance.

Tips for Drivers

Tour length: 4.5 miles (7 km).
Starting point: Anywhere. The tour is best followed in a clockwise direction since Worth Avenue is one way, running from east to west. The Palm Beach Bicycle Trail Shop, 223 Sunrise Ave, tel (561) 659-4583 (open daily), is a good starting point if you want to rent a bicycle, tandem, or skates.
Parking: Stock up on quarters (25c) for parking meters. There are also lots of spaces to park free for an hour, but remember not to overstay.

⑨ The Memorial Park fountain in downtown Palm Beach

Finding the Sights

① Flagler Museum (see pp124–5)
② Sea Gull Cottage
③ Royal Poinciana Chapel
④ Society of Four Arts (see p120)
⑤ Casa de Leoni
⑥ Worth Avenue (see pp118–19)
⑦ Public Beach
⑧ Town Hall (see p120)
⑨ Memorial Park (see p120)
⑩ Phipps Plaza (see p120)
⑪ Bethesda-by-the-Sea Church
⑫ The Breakers (see p121)
⑬ Green's Pharmacy
⑭ St. Edward's Church
⑮ The Hotel Royal Poinciana
⑯ Hibel Museum of Art (see p121)

Flagler Museum

This mansion, known as Whitehall, was "more wonderful than any palace in Europe" after it was built in 1902 by Henry Flagler. He gave the home to his wife, Mary Lily Kenan, as a wedding present. It was intended only as a winter residence; the Flaglers traveled down every year in one of their private railroad cars *(see p53)*. Railcar No. 91 is now on display in the Flagler Kenan Pavilion, which was constructed to resemble a Gilded Age railway palace, at the southern end of the grounds.

In 1925, 12 years after Flagler's death, a ten-story tower was added to the rear and Whitehall became a hotel. Jean Flagler Matthews bought her grandfather's mansion in 1959 and, after costly restoration, turned it into a museum.

Grand Ballroom
Of all the balls held in this sumptuous room, the *Bal Poudré* in 1903 was the most lavish.

Flagler ← Kenan Pavilion

★ Master Bathroom
Apart from a tub, a toilet, and a wonderful separate shower unit, the Flaglers' private bathroom boasts this gorgeous double washstand made of onyx.

KEY

① **The master bedroom is** furnished in yellow silk damask, a faithful copy of the original Rococo-style fabric.

② **Billiard room**

③ **The Yellow Roses Room** had matching wallpaper and furnishings – an innovation for its time.

④ **The east portico** is supported by massive fluted columns. Outsized urns are placed on the steps in front.

⑤ **Drawing room**

⑥ **The grand staircase** leads off the grand hall and is itself constructed of different marbles and decorated with intricate bronze railings.

Library
Lined with leather-bound books and filled with objects and ornate detailing, this red, wood-paneled room has a somewhat intimate feel.

Drawing Room
This ornate Louis XVI-style drawing room boasts a piano and French Gray walls – a popular decor color in the19th century.

VISITORS' CHECKLIST

Practical Information
Cocoanut Row & Whitehall Way.
Tel (561) 655-2833. **Open** 10am–5pm Tue–Sat, noon–5pm Sun. **Closed** Thanksgiving, Dec 25, Jan 1. 🚻 ♿ 🎧 normally available. 🅿 📷

★ **Grand Hall**
This grand marble entrance hall has a painted ceiling and contains gilded chairs and paintings, including this formal portrait of Jean Flagler Matthews.

★ **Colonial Chamber**
The early 1900s saw a steady flow of guests to Whitehall. The rich and famous stayed in this inviting room, decorated in a color scheme of cream and *Rose de Barry* red.

Main entrance

Flagler's Palm Beach

After the Spanish ship *Providencia* was wrecked in 1878, its cargo of coconuts was strewn along the beach near Lake Worth and soon took root. Henry Flagler, busy with his plans to develop Florida's east coast (*see pp52–3*), spotted the lovely palm-fringed beach around 1890. He was smitten with the area's beauty and immediately bought up land. In 1894, he opened the Hotel Royal Poinciana (*see p132*) and in so doing set the course for the growth of the exclusive resort of Palm Beach.

Henry Flagler and his third wife, Mary Lily, in 1910

High-rises towering over the still waters of Lake Worth in West Palm Beach

⓫ West Palm Beach

Road Map: F4. Palm Beach Co.
🚉 78,000. ✈ 🚆 Amtrak & Tri-Rail.
🚌 ℹ 1555 Palm Beach Lakes Blvd,
(561) 233-3000. 🔲 **palmbeachfl.com**

At the end of the 19th century, Henry Flagler *(see p129)* decided to move the unsightly homes of Palm Beach's workers and service businesses to the mainland, out of sight of the tourists. He thus created West Palm Beach, which has been the commercial center of Palm Beach County ever since.

The city has succeeded in forging a stronger identity for itself over the years, but it still plays second fiddle to its infinitely more glamorous (and considerably smaller) neighbor.

The Downtown Waterfront Commons on Clematis Street is alive with visitors enjoying the picturesque Lake Worth, and is home to an extensive calendar of events. Northwood Village is also worth a visit, boasting ethnic restaurants, antique and vintage shops, and funky boutiques. This eclectic, hip neighborhood, just north of Downtown West Palm Beach, is rich with cultural history.

West Palm Beach may not be the place to spend your entire holiday, but it enjoys a fine setting by Lake Worth, and its few attractions are well worth a visit – in particular the excellent Norton Museum of Art, rated the top museum in the southeastern US by *The New York Times*.

Polo and Equestrian Season

The Palm Beaches' west-central community of Wellington is one of the top three places for polo and equestrian activities in the world. The International Polo Club Palm Beach features the world's top Polo players, and is the epicenter of social activity among Palm Beaches' elite from January to April. It also has a Polo School for both children and adults.

The Palm Beach International Equestrian Center hosts equestrian competitions, attracting thousands of visitors, followed by an energetic nightlife scene. For information about dates call the clubs at Wellington, (561) 204-5687; Boca Raton, (561) 994-1876; or Lake Worth, (561) 965-2057.

Close quarters polo action, popular entertainment in Palm Beach County

🏛 South Florida Science Museum

4801 Dreher Trail N. **Tel** (561) 832-1988. **Open** daily, Sun pm.
Closed Thanks-giving, Dec 25. 🅿 ♿ 🔲 **sfsm.org**

This science museum, like many in Florida, is aimed at children. There are plenty of hands-on exhibits to teach visitors about subjects such as light, sound, color, and the weather. You can have a go at creating your own clouds and even touch a mini-tornado. The best time to visit is on a Friday evening, when you can also look through a giant telescope in its observatory and watch laser light shows in the Aldrin planetarium.

🏛 Norton Museum of Art

1451 South Olive Ave. **Tel** (561) 832-5196. **Open** 10am–5pm Tue–Sat (9pm Thu), 11am–5pm Sun. **Closed** Mon, public hols. 🅿 ♿ 🔲 **norton.org**

This art museum, the largest in Florida, has possibly the finest art collection in the state; it also attracts traveling exhibitions. The museum was established in 1941 with about 100 canvases belonging to Ralph Norton, a Chicago steel magnate who had retired to West Palm Beach. He and his wife had wide-ranging tastes, which is reflected in the art on display.

The collection falls into three main fields. First among these are the French Impressionist and Post-Impressionist art, which include paintings by Cézanne, Braque, Picasso, Matisse, and Gauguin, whose moving work *Agony in the Garden* is the most famous painting in the museum. *Night Mist* (1945) by Jackson Pollock is another proud possession, forming part of the Norton's impressive store of 20th-century American art; this gallery also features some fine works by Winslow Homer, Georgia O'Keeffe, Edward Hopper, and Andy Warhol.

Agony in the Garden by Paul Gauguin (1889)

The third principal collection comprises an outstanding array of artifacts from China, including tomb jades dating from about 1500 BC and ceramic figures of animals and courtiers from the T'ang Dynasty (4th–11th centuries AD). There is also much fine Buddhist carving, in addition to more modern sculptures by Brancusi, Degas, and Rodin.

A rare Florida panther at the Palm Beach Zoo

🏛 Palm Beach Zoo at Dreher Park

1301 Summit Blvd. **Tel** (561) 547-9453. **Open** daily. **Closed** Thanksgiving. 🅿️ 🚻 🌐 palmbeachzoo.org

This little zoo is as appealing to youngsters as the nearby South Florida Science Museum. Of the 100 or more species represented, most interesting are the endangered Florida panther and the giant tortoises, which can live for up to 200 years. At the re-created South American plain you can see llamas, rheas, and tapirs from an observation deck, follow a boardwalk trail through exotic foliage, or cruise around a lake alive with a huge population of pelicans.

Environs

A more pleasant alternative to staying in West Palm Beach (and a considerably cheaper option than Palm Beach) is to find accommodations north across the inlet at **Singer Island or Palm Beach Shores**. These are relaxing, slow-paced communities, and the wide beach is splendid, but marred by a skyline of apartment buildings.

Boating and fishing are popular activities here. Palm Beach Shores has sport-fishing boats for charter, as well as boats offering cruises around Lake Worth. The Manatee Queen is a catamaran *(see p360)* offering tours of the mansions along the Intracoastal Waterway.

At the north end of Singer Island is **John D. MacArthur Beach State Park**. Here, a dramatic boardwalk bridge meanders across a mangrove-lined inlet of Lake Worth to a hardwood hammock and a lovely beach. Brochures from the Nature Center pick out plants and wading birds, and in the summer guided night-time walks show you nesting loggerhead turtles *(see p121)*.

The Gardens mall, 2 miles (3 km) inland in Palm Beach Gardens has fragrant walkways and glass elevators that link the nearly 200 shops.

🏛 John D. MacArthur Beach State Park

A1A, 2 miles (3 km) N of Riviera Bridge. **Tel** (561) 624-6950. **Open** daily; Nature Center: 🚻 🚻 🅿️ 🌐 macarthurbeach.org

The Gardens Mall

3101 PGA Blvd. **Tel** (561) 622-2115. **Open** daily. **Closed** Easter Sun, Thanksgiving, Dec 25. 🚻

⑫ Lion Country Safari

Road Map: F4. Palm Beach Co. 2003 Lion Country Safari Rd, Loxahatchee. **Tel** (561) 793-1084. 🚉 West Palm Beach. 🚌 West Palm Beach. **Open** daily. 🅿️ 🚻 🌐 lioncountrysafari.com

Twenty miles (32 km) inland from West Palm Beach, off US 441, this park is the area's big family attraction.

There are two parts: First, you can drive through a 500-acre (200-ha) enclosure and observe lions, giraffes, rhinos, and other wildlife at close quarters. (If you have a convertible car you can rent a vehicle with a hard roof.) Second, there's a zoo and amusement park. Along with aviaries, petting areas, and islands inhabited by monkeys, there are fairground rides, boat tours, and a park populated by plastic dinosaurs. A camping area is also available. All parts of this park get very busy on weekends.

Antelope resting in the shade at Lion Country Safari

A fisherman enjoying early evening angling on Lake Okeechobee

⑬ Lake Okeechobee

Road Map: E4, F4. ▣ Palm Trans bus to Pahokee, (561) 841-4200. ▯ 115 E Main St, Pahokee, (561) 924-5579. W **pahokee.com** Roland Martin: 920 E Del Monte Ave, Clewiston. **Tel** (800) 473-6766. W **rolandmartinmarina.com**

Meaning "big water" in the Seminole language, Okeechobee is the second largest freshwater lake in the US, covering 750 sq miles (1,942 sq km). The "Big O," as the lake is often called, is famous for its abundance of fish, particularly largemouth bass. Roland Martin or any of the many marinas will rent you a boat, tackle, bait, picnic food, or a guide and chartered boat. Nearby **Clewiston** offers the best facilities, with three marinas and a choice of decent motels.

If you're not an angler, your time in Florida is better spent elsewhere. The bird life is rich along the shore, but the lake is too big to be scenic, and a high encircling dike, which protects the countryside from floods, prevents views from the road. **Pahokee** is one of the few places to offer easy lakeside access, and it boasts possibly the best sunsets in Florida, after the Gulf Coast.

The grim and hardworking communities at the lake's southern end are dependent on sugar for their prosperity. Half the sugarcane in the country is grown in the plains around Belle Glade and

A Lake Okeechobee sugar town proclaims its wealth

Clewiston ("America's Sweetest Town"), where the rich soil is darker than chocolate.

The federal government plans to return 100,000 acres (40,500 ha) of sugarcane land south of Lake Okeechobee to marshland, in order to cleanse and increase the water available to the Everglades. This is not popular with the locals.

⑭ Lake Worth

Road Map: F4. Palm Beach Co. ▥ 30,000. ▯ 807 Lucerne Ave, (561) 582-4401. W **lwchamber.com**

Lake Worth is a civilized, unpretentious community. On its barrier island side there is normally a jolly, public beach scene; on the mainland, a dozen or more antique shops set the tone along Lake and Lucerne Avenues, the heart of Lake Worth's low-key downtown area. Here, you'll find an Art Deco movie theater converted into an exciting space for art exhibitions, live music clubs, coffee houses, art galleries, antique malls, retail stores, and restaurants. The

community has gone to great lengths to retain its old Florida flavor, with rules in place that protect the town from insensitive development. Recreation includes boating in fresh and saltwater, a golf course, fishing pier, a waterfront amphitheater, parks, and athletic facilities.

⑮ Delray Beach

Road Map: F4. Palm Beach Co. ▥ 50,000. ▣ Amtrak and Tri-Rail. ▯ 64 SE 5th Ave, (561) 278-0424. Pilgrim Belle: **Tel** (561) 243-0686. W **delraybeach.com**

The most welcoming place between Palm Beach and Boca Raton, Delray Beach has an upscale but friendly air. The town is proud of the national awards for "civic-mindness" and being the "Most Fun Small Town in America" it has consistently received in recent decades.

The long stretch of sedate beach, with direct access and good facilities, is magnificent, and between November and April Pilgrim Belle Cruises run daily paddleboat trips along the Intracoastal Waterway. Drift fishing boats also offer rides.

Delray's heart lies inland, along Atlantic Avenue – an inviting street softly lit at night by old-fashioned lamps and lined with palm trees, chic cafés, antique shops, and art galleries. Alongside lies Old School Square, with a cluster of handsome 1920s buildings. Nearby, snug **Cason Cottage** has been meticulously restored to the way it might have looked originally, around 1915.

▦ **Cason Cottage** 5 NE 1st St. **Tel** (561) 274-9578. ☑ by appt. **Closed** public hols. ♿

A peaceful springtime scene by the ocean at Delray Beach

⑯ Loxahatchee National Wildlife Refuge

Road Map: F4. Palm Beach Co. 10216 Lee Rd. **Tel** (561) 732-3684. 🚌 Boynton Beach. 🚌 Delray Beach. Refuge: **Open** daily. **Closed** Dec 25. ♿ 🅿 📷 Visitor Center: **Open** Nov–Apr: daily; May–Oct: Wed–Sun. **Closed** Dec 25. 🅦 fws.gov/loxahatchee

This 221-sq mile (572-sq km) refuge, which contains the most northerly remaining part of the Everglades, has superb and abundant wildlife. The best time to visit is early or late in the day, and ideally in winter, when many migrating birds make temporary homes here.

The visitor center, off Route 441 on the refuge's eastern side, 10 miles (16 km) west of Delray Beach, has a good information center explaining the Everglades' ecology; it is also the starting point for two memorable trails. The half-mile (1-km) Cypress Swamp Boardwalk enters a magical natural world, with guava and wax myrtle trees and many epiphytes *(see p294)* grow-ing beneath the canopy. The longer Marsh Trail passes by marshland, whose water levels are manipulated to produce the best possible environment for waders and waterfowl. On a winter's evening it's a bird-watcher's paradise, with a cacophony of sound from herons,

A blue heron standing alert in the wildlife refuge at Loxahatchee

A schoolboy's bedroom, Japanese style, at the Morikami Museum

grebe, ibis, anhingas, and other birds. You may also spot turtles and alligators.

Those with their own canoes can embark on the 5.5-mile (9-km) canoe trail. There is also an extensive program of guided nature walks.

⑰ Morikami Museum and Japanese Gardens

Road Map: F4. Palm Beach Co. 4000 Morikami Park Rd. **Tel** (561) 495-0233. 🚌 Delray Beach. 🚌 Delray Beach. **Open** 10am–5pm Tue–Sun. **Closed** public hols. ♿ 🅿 🅦 morikami.org

The country's only museum devoted exclusively to Japanese culture is located on land donated by a farmer named George Morikami; he was one of a group of Japanese pioneers who established the Yamato Colony (named after ancient Japan) on the northern edge of Boca Raton in 1905. With the help of money from a development company owned by Henry Flagler *(see pp128–9)*, they hoped to grow rice, tea, and silk. The project never took off, however, and the colony gradually petered out in the 1920s.

Displays in the Yamato-kan villa, on a small island in a lake, tell the settlers' story and also delve into past and present Japanese culture. There are interesting reconstructions of a

bathroom, a schoolboy's bedroom, and eel-and-sake restaurants. Six historic garden sites surround the villa, and paths lead into serene pinewoods.

A building across the lake holds exhibitions on all matters Japanese, a café serving Japanese food, and a traditional tea house where tea ceremonies are performed once a month. Also, origami workshops are offered.

⑱ Butterfly World

Road Map: F4. Broward Co. 3600 W Sample Rd, Coconut Creek. **Tel** (954) 977-4400. 🚌 Deerfield Beach (Amtrak & Tri-Rail). 🚌 Pompano Beach. **Open** daily. **Closed** Easter, Thanksgiving, Dec 25. ♿ 🅿 🅦 butterflyworld.com

Within giant walk-through aviaries brimming with tropical flowers, thousands of dazzling butterflies from all over the world flit about, often landing on visitors' shoulders. Since they're effectively solar powered, the butterflies are most active on warm, sunny days, so plan your visit accordingly. There are also cabinets of emerging pupae and a fascinating collection of mounted insects – including morpho butterflies, with their incredible metallic blue wings, and beetles and grasshoppers the size of an adult hand. Outside, you can wander around the extensive gardens.

A blue morpho at Butterfly World

⑲ Boca Raton

In 1925, an advertisement for Boca Raton announced: "I am the greatest resort in the world." Although the city imagined by the architect Addison Mizner (*see p124*) did not materialize in his lifetime, Boca Raton has today become one of Florida's most affluent cities. Corporate headquarters and high-tech companies are located here, and executives in a national survey have judged it Florida's most enticing place to live. What must attract them are the country clubs, plush shopping malls, and gorgeous beachfront parks, not to mention desirable homes inspired, if not built, by Mizner.

Young musician performing at the Lynn University Conservatory

Peach-pink Mizner Park, one of Boca's shopping malls

Exploring Boca Raton

After initiating the development of Palm Beach, Addison Mizner turned his attention to a sleepy pineapple-growing settlement to the south. However, instead of his envisaged masterpiece of city planning, only a handful of buildings were completed by the time Florida's property bubble burst in 1926 (*see p54*). Boca, as it is often called today, remained little more than a hamlet until the late 1940s.

The nucleus of Mizner's vision was the ultra-luxurious Cloister Inn, finished in 1926 with his trademark Spanish details. It stands off the eastern end of Camino Real, which was intended as the city's main thoroughfare, complete with a central canal for gondolas. The hotel is now part of the greatly expanded and exclusive **Boca Raton Resort and Club** (*see p316*). Nonresidents can visit only on a weekly tour arranged by the Boca Raton Historical

Society, which is based at the **Town Hall** on Palmetto Park Road. A few rooms here have simple displays concerning local history.

Just opposite, built in a style that apes Mizner's work, is the open-air **Mizner Park**. This is perhaps the most impressive of Boca's dazzling malls that provide the best illustrations of the city's rarefied lifestyle. Even more Mizneresque is the nearby **Royal Palm Place**, with chic boutiques tucked away in hidden courtyards.

The verdant and historic **Old Floresta** district, about a mile (1.6 km) west of the town hall, contains 29 Mediterranean-style homes built by Mizner for his company directors. It is a pleasant area to explore.

🏛 Boca Raton Museum of Art

501 Plaza Real, Mizner Park.
Tel (561) 392-2500. **Open** Tue–Sun.
Closed public hols. 🎨 ♿
W bocamuseum.org

Located in a spectacular setting within beautiful Mizner Park in downtown Boca Raton, this museum contains 44,000 sq ft (4,088 sq m) of space for world class exhibitions and an impressive display of contemporary art.

🏛 Lynn University Conservatory of Music

3601 N Military Trail. **Tel** (561) 237-9000. **W** lynn.edu/music

The Conservatory of Music at Lynn University admits a highly select group of gifted music students from all over the world to train for a career in solo, chamber, and orchestral music performance, many achieving worldwide acclaim. As a center for the celebration of music, the Conservatory attracts thousands of music lovers who attend around one hundred student, faculty and guest artist performances, as well as master classes and lectures each year.

🏛 Sports Immortals Museum

6830 N Federal Hwy. **Tel** (561) 997-2575. **Open** 10am–6pm Mon–Sat.
Closed Sun, Jan 1, Dec 25. 🎨 ♿
W sportsimmortals.com

Among the 10,000 sports mementos at this museum are Babe Ruth's baseball bat and Muhammad Ali's boxing robes. The most prized item is a rare cigarette card worth an astonishing $1,000,000: the card was

Boca's attractive town hall, designed by Addison Mizner and built in 1927

Deerfield Beach, a quiet coastal resort within easy reach of Boca Raton

VISITORS' CHECKLIST

Practical Information
Road Map: F4. Palm Beach Co.
🚗 80,000. ℹ️ 1555 Palm Beach
Lakes Blvd, (561) 233-3000. Boca
Raton Historical Society: **Tel** (561)
395 6766 for tours. 🎭 Meet Me
Downtown (Mar); Boca Festival
(Aug); Holiday Boat Parade (Dec).

Transport
🚆 Tri-Rail, Yamato Rd, (800) 874-
7245. 🚌 1300 W. Hillsboro Blvd,
Deerfield Beach (800) 872-7245.

withdrawn when the baseball player depicted objected to any association with tobacco.

🏟 The Beaches
North of Boca Raton's inlet stretches a seductively long, undeveloped, dune-backed beach, reached via beachside parks. The most northerly of these, **Spanish River Park**, is also the most attractive, with pleasant picnic areas shaded by pines and palm trees. Its loveliest spot is a lagoon on the Intracoastal Waterway next to an observation tower. At **Red Reef Park** you can stroll along the boardwalk on top of the dunes and snorkel around an artificial reef *(see p364)* just offshore. Maybe because of the exorbitant parking fees, the sands are usually uncrowded.

🐢 Gumbo Limbo Nature Center
1801 North Ocean Blvd.
Tel (561) 338-1473.
Open daily. **Closed** Dec 25. 🚻
🌐 **gumbolimbo.org**
This first-rate, highly informative center lies next to the Intracoastal, within Red Reef Park. The boardwalk winds through mangroves and a tropical hardwood hammock to a tower, which offers sensational panoramic views.

Environs
High-rise development continues unabated south along Route A1A. Slow-paced **Deerfield Beach** is the area's most inviting community, thanks to its fishing pier and its fine, shell-flecked beach, backed by a palm-lined promenade. Five miles (8 km) south, **Pompano** is forever tied to its status as "swordfish capital of the world," corroborated by photos of giant catches displayed on its pier.

Boca Raton City Center

① Old Floresta
② Boca Raton Museum of Art
③ Town Hall
④ Lynn University Conservatory of Music
⑤ Mizner Park
⑥ Boca Raton Resort and Club
⑦ Red Reef Park
⑧ Gumbo Limbo Nature Center
⑨ Spanish River Park

0 meters 1,000
0 yards 1,000

Key to symbols *see back flap*

⓴ Fort Lauderdale

During the second Seminole War *(see p50)*, Fort Lauderdale consisted of little more than three forts. By 1900, it had become a busy trading post on the New River, which meanders through what has become a sprawling city.

Today, Greater Fort Lauderdale wears many hats: it is an important business and cultural center, a popular beach resort, and a giant cruise port. But it is still the city's waterways *(see p139)* that define its unique character.

Appel's *Big Bird with Child*, Museum of Art

Exploring Downtown Fort Lauderdale

Downtown Fort Lauderdale, with its modern, sleek, glass-sided office buildings, presents the city's business face. The **Riverwalk** follows a 1.5-mile (2.4-km) stretch of the New River's north bank and links most of the city's historical landmarks and cultural institutions. This promenade starts near Stranahan House, built on the site of the city's first trading post, through a strip of parkland to end up by the Broward Center for the Performing Arts *(see p358)*.

Old Fort Lauderdale extends along Southwest 2nd Avenue. It is made up of an attractive group of early 1900s' buildings administered by the Fort Lauderdale Historical Society, which is based at the Fort Lauderdale Historical Museum. The King-Cromartie House, built in 1907 on the south bank of the river, was transported by barge to its present site in 1971. Its modest furnishings reflect the basic living conditions of Florida's early settlers. Behind the home is a replica of the city's first schoolhouse, which opened in 1899. The clutch of cafés and restaurants in old brick buildings along adjacent Southwest 2nd Street are buzzing at lunchtime and in the early evening.

A hop-on hop-off trolley tour is an easy way to get to know the heart of the city. The tour links Fort Lauderdale's downtown area and the beach, taking in all the principal sights.

🏛 Fort Lauderdale History Center

231 SW 2nd Ave.
Tel (954) 463-4431.
Open Tue–Sun.
Closed Jan 1, Jul 4, Dec 25. 🎫 ♿

The New River Inn in Old Fort Lauderdale was built of concrete in 1905. Now a museum, it contains various fascinating exhibits that chart the area's history and the growth of the city up to the 1940s. A small theater shows amusing silent films that were made during the 1920s heyday of south Florida's film industry.

[Map of downtown Fort Lauderdale showing streets including NE 11TH, SUNRISE BOULEVARD, FLAGLER DRIVE, NORTH ANDREWS AVE, NORTH FEDERAL HIGHWAY, NE 6TH STREET, NE 5TH ST, NE 3RD ST, WEST BROWARD BLVD, EAST BROWARD BLVD, SE 2ND ST, S ANDREWS AVE, S 3RD AVE, SOUTH FEDERAL HIGHWAY, S MIAMI ROAD, SE 7TH ST, SE 9TH ST, SE 15TH ST, 17TH STREET. Landmarks marked: Amtrak & Tri-Rail Stations 3.5 km (2 miles), Greyhound Station, Museum of Discovery & Science ①, Broward Center for the Performing Arts ②, Fort Lauderdale History Center ③, Museum of Art ④, Stranahan House ⑤. Fort Lauderdale Hollywood International Airport 5 km (3 miles) MIAMI]

The shady Riverwalk, winding along the north bank of the New River

Sights at a Glance

① Museum of Discovery and Science
② Broward Center for the Performing Arts
③ Fort Lauderdale History Center
④ Museum of Art
⑤ Stranahan House
⑥ International Swimming Hall of Fame
⑦ Bonnet House
⑧ Hugh Taylor Birch State Park

🏛 Museum of Art

1 E Las Olas Blvd. **Tel** (954) 525-5500.
Open 11am–6pm Tue–Sun. **Closed**
Mon, public hols. 🏛 ♿ 🅦 **moafl.org**

This fine art museum, housed in
an impressive postmodern
building, is best known for its
large assemblage of works of
CoBrA art. The name CoBrA
derives from the initial letters
of Copenhagen, Brussels, and
Amsterdam, the capitals of the
home countries of a group of
Expressionist painters who
worked from 1948–51. The
museum displays works by
Karel Appel, Pierre Alechinsky,
and Asger Jorn, the movement's
leading exponents. The William
Glackens Wing features
this American
Impressionist's work.

🏛 Museum of Discovery and Science

401 SW 2nd St. **Tel** (954)
467- 6637. **Open** daily
year-round. 🏛 ♿
🅦 **mods.org**

This is one of the largest
and best museums of its
kind in Florida. Here, all
kinds of creatures,
including alligators, turtles,
snakes, and bats, appear
in re-created Florida
"ecoscapes." You can even
take a simulated ride to
Mars. In the AutoNation®
IMAX® theater, films are
projected on to a huge
60-ft (18-m) high screen.
This is also one of the few
places in the world to show
3-D IMAX films where the
audience uses special glasses
and personal headsets for
360-degree sound. The
EcoDiscovery Center, the latest
addition to the museum, offers
a vast array of interactive exhibits,
including an outdoor otter habitat.

🏠 Stranahan House

335 SE 6th Ave. **Tel** (954) 524-4736.
Open Wed–Sun. **Closed** public hols;
Jul–Aug: hours vary. 🏛 🅿 ♿ limited.
🅦 **stranahanhouse.org**

The oldest surviving house in
the city is a handsome pine and
oak building, built by the
pioneer Frank Stranahan in

1901. It became the center of
Fort Lauderdale's community,
serving as a trading post, meeting hall, post office, and bank.
Even more evocative of the
early days than the furnishings
inside are the old photos of
Stranahan trading with the local
Seminoles (see p289). Goods
such as alligator hides, otter
pelts, and egret plumes – used
in the fashions of the day – were
brought by the Seminoles from
the nearby Everglades in their
dugout canoes.

Las Olas Boulevard

Despite a constant stream of
traffic, the section of Las Olas
Boulevard between 6th and 11th
Avenues is Fort Lauderdale's most
picturesque and busiest street –
although a new crossing system
has made it more pedestrian
friendly. A winning mix of formal,
casual, and chic boutiques and
eateries line this thoroughfare,
where you can pick up anything
from a fur coat to Haitian art.

If you're not a serious shopper,
visit in the evenings when the
sidewalks overflow with drinkers
and diners, and the palm trees
are outlined with twinkling lights.

Heading toward the beach, the
boulevard crosses islands where
you can get a closer look at a
more lavish Fort Lauderdale
lifestyle (see p139).

VISITORS' CHECKLIST

Practical Information
Road Map: F4. Broward Co.
🏙 150,000. 🛈 100 East Broward
Blvd, (954) 765-4466. Trolley
charters: **Tel** (954) 429-3100.
🛥 Winter Fest Boat Parade (Dec).

Transport
✈ 5 miles (8 km) S. 🚃 200 SW
21st Terrace, (800) 872-7245.
🚌 515 NE 3rd St, (800) 231-2222.
🚌 1850 Eller Dr., (954) 523-3404.

Stranahan House on the New River, Broward County's oldest residence

Exploring Fort Lauderdale: Beyond Downtown

Even if you miss the signs proclaiming "Welcome to Fort Lauderdale – Yachting Capital of the World," it won't take you long to recognize the real focus of the city. For tourists and residents alike, the appeal of Fort Lauderdale lies, above all, in its attractive and buzzing beaches and in the waterways that branch from the city's historical lifeblood – the New River.

Cyclists and pedestrians enjoying the shady beachfront promenade

The Beach

Until the mid-1980s, when the local authorities began to discourage them, students by the thousand would descend on Fort Lauderdale for the Spring Break. Today, the city's image has been restored; its excellent beach is still the liveliest along the Gold Coast – especially at the end of Las Olas Boulevard, where in-line skaters cruise past a few unsophisticated bars and souvenir shops, faint recollections of more decadent days along "The Strip."

Elsewhere, beachside Fort Lauderdale is more like the family resort it's promoted to be; South Beach Park has the most pleasant strip of sand.

A break in training at the pool, at the Swimming Hall of Fame

🏛 International Swimming Hall of Fame

1 Hall of Fame Drive. **Tel** (954) 462-6536. **Open** daily. ♿ ♿

If you ever wanted to know about the history of Oman's aquatic sports or the evolution of diving positions, this is the place to come. This detailed museum displays an odd mix of exhibits, from ancient wooly swimsuits to amusing mannequins of stars, such as Johnny "Tarzan" Weismuller, holder of 57 world swimming records.

🏛 Bonnet House Museum and Gardens

900 N Birch Rd. **Tel** (954) 563-5393. 📷 compulsory, 10am–4pm Tue–Sat (from 11am Sun). **Closed** public hols. ♿ 🌐 bonnethouse.org

This oddly furnished house, close to the waterfront, is by far the most enjoyable piece of old Fort Lauderdale. It stands amid idyllic tropical grounds, where the bonnet water lily, from which the house took its name, once grew. Artist Frederic Bartlett built this cozy, plantation-style winter home himself in 1920, and examples of his work, especially murals, are everywhere. Swans and monkeys inhabit the grounds, which are also home to one of the largest orchid collections in the southeast US.

🛍 Sawgrass Mills Mall

12801 W Sunrise Blvd. **Tel** (954) 846-2300. **Open** 10am–9:30pm Mon–Sat, 11am–8pm Sun. **Closed** Dec 25. ♿ 🌐 sawgrassmillsmall.com

The largest outlet mall in Florida and one of the state's largest tourist attractions after Orlando's Disneyworld. There are some 300 stores, plus cinemas, restaurants, and a life-size Barbie house – the Barbie Dream House Experience .

🌳 Hugh Taylor Birch State Park

3109 E Sunrise Blvd. **Tel** (954) 564-4521. **Open** daily. 🚲 ♿

These 180 acres (73 ha), part of 3 miles (5 km) of barrier island that Chicago lawyer Hugh Taylor Birch bought in 1894, amount to one of the Gold Coast's few undeveloped oases of greenery. Visitors come to rent canoes on the lagoon, wander along a trail through a tropical hammock, and, above all, to exercise along a scenic circular road.

Jewelry stalls and neon lights at the Swap Shop of Fort Lauderdale

Environs

Bargain-hunters will love the **Swap Shop of Fort Lauderdale**, covering an incredible 75 acres (30 ha). This place is an American version of an oriental bazaar, with whole rows devoted to jewelry, sunglasses, and other trinkets. Many of the 12 million annual visitors are lured by the fresh produce and nursery selling indoor and outdoor plants. The parking lot becomes a huge drive-in movie theater in the evenings.

🛍 Swap Shop of Fort Lauderdale

3291 W Sunrise Blvd. **Tel** (954) 791-7927. **Open** daily. ♿

The Jungle Queen, Fort Lauderdale's most famous cruise boat

The Waterways

Around the mouth of the New River lie dozens of parallel, arrow-straight canals. The area is known as **The Isles**, after the rows of slender peninsulas created from mud when the canals were dug in the 1920s. This is the most desirable place to live in the city: looming behind lush foliage and luxurious yachts are ostentatious mansions worth millions of dollars. Their residents, such as Wayne Huizenga, former owner of the Blockbuster Video empire and present owner of the Miami Dolphins football team, are chiefly rich businesspeople.

The islands flank the Intracoastal Waterway, which also crosses **Port Everglades**. This is the world's second-largest cruise port after Miami, as well as a destination for container ships, oil tankers, destroyers, and submarines.

The best way to view the Intracoastal waterway is from a boat ride, as the mansions, yachts, and port can really only be properly viewed from the water. You can take your pick from all the different kinds of boat trips that are on offer. The **Jungle Queen** is a wonderful old-fashioned riverboat that chugs up the New River to a private island styled as an Indian village; there are day-time trips, that take three hours, and evening cruises, which include a vaudeville show and barbecue dinner.

A water taxi on the New River

Alternatively, 90-minute **Carrie B** riverboat tours depart from the Riverwalk, pass various mansions, browse around the port, and then visit the warm waters of a power plant discharge where large numbers of manatees (see p254) gather.

Water Taxis, operating like shared land taxis, go up New River to Downtown and anywhere from the port north to Oakland Park Boulevard. The taxis are on an hourly schedule for one flat-rate all-day pass. You can rent boats from the Bahia Mar Yachting Center and Pier 66 Marina.

Finally, a high-speed catamaran-styled ferry called **Bahamas Express**, run by the Spanish maritime group Baleària, sails daily at a speed of 32 knots between Port Everglades and the Bahamas (Bimini and Grand Bahama Island).

Useful Addresses

Carrie B
Las Olas Boulevard at SE 5th Avenue.
Tel (954) 768-9920.

Bahamas Express
Port Everglades Terminal 1.
Tel (954) 278-3791.
W **ferryexpress.com**

Jungle Queen
Bahia Mar Yachting Center, A1A, Fort Lauderdale Beach.
Tel (954) 462-5596.

Water Taxi
413 SW 3rd Ave.
Tel (954) 467-6677.
W **watertaxi.com**

Panoramic view over Fort Lauderdale's scenic waterways, with its luxurious yachts and mansion-lined canals

Swordfish statue outside the IGFA Fishing Hall of Fame and Museum

㉑ Dania

Road Map: F4. Broward Co. 🚗
13,000. 🚉 Hollywood. 🚌 Hollywood.
ℹ️ Dania, (954) 926-2323.
🌐 greaterdania.org

Dania blends seamlessly into the coastal conurbation. Some locals visit the town only to watch a game of jai alai, but the other main attraction is the **John U. Lloyd Beach State Park**, a chunk of virgin barrier island that contrasts acutely with nearby Port Everglades (see p139). From the park's northern tip, you can watch ships come and go; to the south stretches one of the Gold Coast's loveliest beaches: more than 2 miles (3 km) in length and backed by pine trees. You can rent canoes to explore the scenic, mangrove-lined creek that runs through the heart of the park.

The **IGFA (International Game Fishing Association) Fishing Hall of Fame and Museum** appeals to all ages and has seven different galleries highlighting the creatures of the sea, a discovery room for children, a virtual fishing exhibit, and a wetland area.

Along the northern part of US 1 are some 150 antique shops. Despite their poor location, alongside the traffic-ridden road, they make entertaining browsing.

🏞️ **John U. Lloyd Beach State Park**
6503 N Ocean Drive. **Tel** (954) 923-2833. **Open** daily. 🚗 ♿

🏛️ **IGFA Fishing Hall of Fame and Museum**
300 Gulf Stream Way, Dania Beach. **Tel** (954) 927-2628. **Open** 10am–6pm daily. **Closed** Thanksgiving, Dec 25. 🚗 ♿ 🌐 igfa.org

㉒ Hollywood

Road Map: F4. Broward Co. 🚗 126,000. 🚉 Amtrak and Tri-Rail. 🚌 ℹ️ 330 N Federal Hwy, (954) 923-4000. 🌐 hollywoodchamber.org

Founded by a Californian in the 1920s, this sizeable and unpretentious resort is the destination for the majority of the 300,000 French Canadians who migrate to Greater Fort Lauderdale every winter.

The development in Hollywood has since been concentrated in the historic downtown arts district around Young Circle. The area has many restaurants and the **Art and Culture Center of Hollywood**, which holds art exhibitions, theater, music, and dance performances. The **Anne Kolb Nature Center** includes a five-level observation fishing pier, two nature trails, outdoor amphitheater, and exhibit hall.

🏛️ **Art and Culture Center of Hollywood**
1650 Harrison Street. **Tel** (954) 921-3274. **Open** 10am–5pm Mon–Sat, noon–4pm Sun.
🌐 artandculturecenter.org

🏛️ **Anne Kolb Nature Center**
751 Sheridian. **Tel** (954) 926-2480.
🌐 broward.org/Parks/
WestLakePark/Pages/
AnneKolbNatureCenter.aspx

Environs
At the crossroads of State Road 7/441 and Route 848/Stirling Road, on the western edge of Hollywood resort, is the **Seminole Indian Hollywood Reservation**. Covering 480 acres (194 ha), it is Florida's smallest Indian reservation. Like other reservations in the state it is largely autonomous (see p289), and billboards advertising cut-price tobacco along the roadside are grim clues to its exemption from state cigarette taxes.

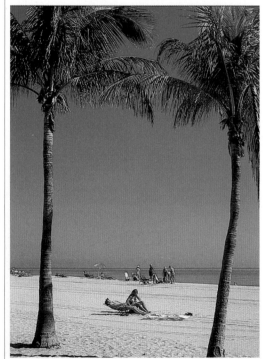

Sun worshipers enjoying the pristine sands of Hollywood Beach

Inside the huge Seminole Hard Rock Hotel and Casino

The Seminole Okalee Village offers alligator wrestling, guided tours, and demonstra-tions of Seminole crafts and ways of living. Across the street is the 24-hour **Seminole Casino in Hollywood**. Reservations are exempt from state gambling laws, and in the cavernous bingo hall as many as 1,400 players compete for five-figure cash prizes. The main attraction is the **Seminole Hard Rock Hotel and Casino**. This resort and hotel features a huge casino, tropical pool area, Hard Rock Live, and Seminole Paradise.

🏠 **Seminole Okalee Indian Village**
3551 N State Rd 7. **Tel** (954) 797-5551.
Open daily. **Closed** Dec 25. 🧿 🔥

🏠 **Seminole Casino in Hollywood**
4150 N State Rd 7. **Tel** (954) 961-3220.
Open 24 hours. **Closed** Dec 25. 🔥
�w semtribe.com

🏠 **Seminole Hard Rock Hotel and Casino**
1 Seminole Way. **Tel** (866) 502-7529, (924) 327-7625. **Open** 24 hours. 🔥
�w seminolehardrockhollywood.com

㉓ Davie

Road Map: F4. Broward Co. 🏠 70,000.
🚊 Fort Lauderdale. 🚌 Fort Lauderdale. 🛈 4185 Davie Rd, (954) 581-0790. �w davie-coopercity.org

Centered on Orange Drive and Davie Road, and surrounded by paddocks and stables, the bizarre town of Davie adheres to a strictly Old West theme. Cacti grow outside the town hall's wooden huts, and the local McDonald's even has a corral at the back. Drop in on Grif's Western Wear, a cowboy supermarket at 6211 South West 45th Street, to stock up on saddles, cowboy hats, and boots. The only way to sample the town's real flavor, however, is to see bronco busting, bull riding, and steer wrestling in a rodeo at the **Bergeron Rodeo Grounds**, home to the Davie

Stetsons for sale at Grif's Western Wear shop in Davie

Rodeo Association. In addition to the many rodeo events, the arena hosts a diverse program of concerts and circuses, plus monster truck and airboat shows.

Bergeron Rodeo Grounds
6591 Orange Drive. **Tel** (954) 475-9787. 🔥 �w davie-fl.gov

㉔ Flamingo Gardens

Road Map: F4. Broward Co. 3750 South Flamingo Rd, Davie. **Tel** (954) 473-2955. 🚊 Fort Lauderdale. 🚌 Fort Lauderdale. **Open** daily. **Closed** Mon (Jun–Oct), Thanksgiving, Dec 25.
🧿 🧿 🔥 �w flamingogardens.org

These beautiful gardens started out in 1927 as a weekend retreat for the Wrays, a citrus-farming family. You can tour their lovely 1930s home, furnished in period style, but the gardens are the attraction here. Tram tours pass groves of lemon and kumquat trees, live oaks, banyan trees, and other exotic vegetation.

The gardens are home to many Florida birds, including the rare bald eagle *(see p28)* and flamingos. Many species of ducks, gulls, doves, and waders – including the roseate spoonbill *(see p293)* – inhabit a walk-through aviary split into habitats such as cypress forest and mangrove swamp. Wildlife Encounter shows are held here in the afternoons.

Jai Alai – a Merry Sport

This curious game originated some 300 years ago in the Basque Country (jai alai means "merry festival" in Basque) and was brought to the US in the early 1900s via Cuba. Florida has eight of the country's ten arenas, or "frontons."

Watching a game of jai alai makes for a cheap night out (if you don't bet). The program explains both the scoring and the intricacies of pari-mutuel betting, where those who bet on the winners share in the total amount wagered. People yell and cheer loudly during the points, since many will have put money on the outcome. Games take place in Dania five times a week: call (954) 927-2841 for details. The rules of the game are explained on page 37.

Jai alai player poised for a hit

ORLANDO AND THE SPACE COAST

With everything from roller coasters to performing killer whales and a well-known mouse with very big ears, Orlando is a family-oriented fantasyland and the undisputed theme park capital of the world, attracting over 34 million visitors every year.

Orlando started out as an army post, Fort Gatlin, which was established during the Seminole Wars *(see pp50–51)*. The story goes that the fort was later renamed after a soldier called Orlando Reeves, who was hit by a Seminole arrow in 1835. A town developed, but even through the first half of the 20th century Orlando and neighboring towns like Kissimmee were only small, sleepy places dependent on cattle and the citrus crop.

Everything changed in the 1960s. First of all came the job opportunities associated with the space program at Cape Canaveral. Then Walt Disney World® started to take shape: its first theme park, the Magic Kingdom®, opened in 1971. Since then, Disney claims that over 500 million visitors have made the pilgrimage to what it modestly calls the world's most popular vacation destination. Its success has generated a booming entertainment industry in Greater Orlando, as more and more attractions appear on the scene, all eager to cash in on the captive market. Scenically, aside from dozens of lakes, the region is rather dull, with Greater Orlando sprawling gracelessly among the flat agricultural lands. Along the Space Coast, the communities on the mainland shore hold little appeal. However, the barrier islands across the broad Indian River boast 72 miles (116 km) of stunning sandy beaches, and there are two enormous nature preserves rich in bird life. Amid all this, set in a preserved marshy vastness beneath giant skies, in surprising harmony with nature, is the Kennedy Space Center, from where rockets were launched to the the Moon, and shuttles to orbit Earth.

The expansive and unspoiled watery landscape of Merritt Island on the Space Coast

◄ Guests enjoying the Astro Orbiter ride at Tomorrowland in Walt Disney World®

Exploring Orlando and the Space Coast

The reason so many vacationers come to Orlando is to experience the big theme parks, especially Walt Disney World®, SeaWorld®, and Universal Studios®. In and around the theme parks, International Drive, and in Kissimmee, there are over 115,000 hotel rooms, more than in the whole of New York. If you have time to spare, visit the serene Bok Tower Gardens or just up the road, the fun LEGOLAND®. At night, experience the razzmatazz at the fantastic entertainment complex of Universal's CityWalk®. The quaint boutiques and sidewalk cafés of Orlando's upscale neighbor, Winter Park, appeal to those seeking more sophisticated fare. Just 50 miles (80 km) away, the Space Coast is an easy day trip from Orlando. Here, beaches range from empty, wild sands to the buzzing surfing mecca of brash Cocoa Beach.

Daytona Beach
Lake Monroe
Sanford
Lake Mary
Lake Mary
Winter Spring
Ocala
Altamonte Springs
Ovie
Lake Apopka
Maitland
Minneola
Winter Garden
6 WINTER PAR
5 ORLANDO
Clermont
Conway
UNIVERSAL STUDIOS® ORLANDO 3
4 WET 'N WILD®
INTERNATIONAL DRIVE 7
BEACHL
WALT DISNEY 1
WORLD® RESORT
2 SEAWORLD AND DISCOVERY COVE
8 GATORLAND
9 KISSIMMEE
Campbell
Saint Cloud
FANTASY OF FLIGHT
12
10 LAKE TOHO
Davenport
Tampa Lake Alfred
Haines City
11 DISNEY WILDERNESS PRESERVE
Lakeland
Inwood
Winter Haven
Eagle Lake
13 LEGOLAND®
Highland City
BOK TOWER GARDENS
Lake Kissimmee
Bartow
14
Lake Wales
Crooked Lake Park
Lake Weohyakapka
Indian Lake Estates
Fort Meade
Frostproof
Avon Park Bombing Range
Bowling Green
Avon Park
Sebring

Key
— Highway
— Major road
— Secondary road
— Minor road
— Scenic route
⋯ Main railway

A performing orca, a star attraction at SeaWorld®

For additional map symbols *see back flap*

Rockets from the early days of space exploration, at the Kennedy Space Center

Getting Around

If you are exploring beyond the theme parks, rent a car. With an extensive network of divided highways, driving is relaxing and fast: from Walt Disney World®, downtown Orlando is half an hour's drive north and LEGOLAND® an hour south. If you are spending your whole vacation on Disney property, see page 147 for transit options. Many hotels offer free shuttle bus services to the theme parks, and Lynx buses *(see p387)* serve most tourist destinations in Greater Orlando. The Space Coast is an hour east from Orlando on Route 528 (Beachline Expressway). I-95 is the main north-south route along the coast; Route A1A connects the beaches on the barrier islands.

Sights at a Glance

1. *Walt Disney World® Resort pp146–79*
2. *SeaWorld® and Discovery Cove® pp180–83*
3. *Universal Orlando® pp184–9*
4. *Wet 'n Wild® pp190–91*
5. Orlando
6. Winter Park
7. International Drive
8. Gatorland
9. Kissimmee
10. Lake Toho
11. Disney Wilderness Preserve
12. Fantasy of Flight
13. LEGOLAND®
14. Bok Tower Gardens
15. Yeehaw Junction
16. American Police Hall of Fame
17. Merritt Island Wildlife Refuge
18. *Kennedy Space Center pp200–205*
19. US Astronaut Hall of Fame
20. Valiant Air Command Warbird Air Museum
21. Cocoa
22. Cocoa Beach

For hotels and restaurants in this region see pp314–25 and pp329–49

❶ Walt Disney World® Resort

Let your imagination take flight at this world-class entertainment center, where there is something for everyone, regardless of age. Plan to spend at least a day in each of Disney's "big four" – Magic Kingdom®, Epcot®, Disney's Hollywood Studios®, and Disney's Animal Kingdom®. Don't miss a chance to cool off at the two water parks – Blizzard Beach and Typhoon Lagoon. Or you might choose to let off steam at Disney's Wide World of Sports complex; golf courses; hiking and riding trails; and pools and lakes for swimming, boating, waterskiing and much more. With more than 30 resorts on the premises, you can go back to your hotel to rest before returning to one of the parks for the fireworks finale or checking out a show at Downtown Disney®.

Magic Kingdom®
Seven Lands of fantasy and adventure encircle the stunningly beautiful Cinderella's Castle.

Sights at a Glance

① Magic Kingdom® pp150–51
② Epcot® pp156–61
③ Disney's Hollywood Studios® pp166–9
④ Disney's Animal Kingdom® pp170–71
⑤ Blizzard Beach p172
⑥ Typhoon Lagoon p173
⑦ Fort Wilderness Resort & Campground p175
⑧ Downtown Disney® pp176–7

Disney's Animal Kingdom®
Experience the thrill of the wild through encounters with animals, as well as the pure fun of African safaris, river rafting, treks, and some enjoyable rides.

```
0 meters    500
0 yards     500
```

Key

— Monorail

▬ Interstate highway

Blizzard Beach
Thrilling rides and exhilarating water slides are on offer at this cleverly designed and delightful 66-acre (27-ha) water theme park.

For hotels and restaurants in this region see pp314–25 and pp329–49

Epcot®
Travel across continents, blast into space on a rocket to Mars, embark on an underwater adventure, and take a peek into the future with remarkable discoveries and inventions.

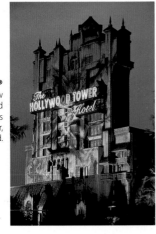

Disney's Hollywood Studios®
There's no business like show business at Disney's Hollywood Studios®, where guests of all ages are immersed in the glitz, glamor, and magic of Hollywood.

Getting Around

An extensive, efficient transportation system handles an average of 200,000 guests each day. The transportation hub of Walt Disney World® is the Ticket and Transportation Center (TTC). Monorails, ferryboats, and motorcoach shuttle services operate daily. Additionally, hotels outside the resort area offer free shuttle services to the parks. For further details, *see page 178.*

Downtown Disney®
Themed celebrity restaurants, nightclubs, shows, and the largest outlet for Disney merchandise – all this and much more are on offer at this exciting entertainment and shopping complex.

Key

Main sites

For additional map symbols *see back flap*

The Magic Kingdom®

Reappearing in similar form in California, Japan, and France, the Magic Kingdom® is the essential Disney theme park. Cartoon characters and nostalgic visions of how the world (and particularly America) once was and how it might be again fill its relentlessly cheerful 107 acres. The park is made up of seven "lands" evoking a particular theme or era, such as the Wild West, Colonial America, and the future. Binding the park together are stunning parades, musical street performers and three-dimensional Disney characters ready to greet their guests.

Fantasyland®'s landmark castle

Tackling the Park

Disney hotel guests can take advantage of Extra Magic Hours, which offer time in the park before and after regular opening hours.

If you are a Disney resort guest, plan to reach the entrance turnstiles one and a half hours before the official opening time. This will allow you to enjoy Fantasyland® and Tomorrowland® for an hour before the rest of the park opens. On arrival you will be given a map showing the lands

Tips

- If you're an early entry guest, plan to wait at the rope barrier next to Peter Pan and "it's a small world" about 15–20 minutes before the official opening time.
- If you want to visit Splash Mountain® first, board the train at Main Street® before the park has opened. On opening time, the train will pull out and stop in Frontierland® about 7 minutes later. The station is next to Splash Mountain® and Big Thunder.
- In order to reduce the number of guests in the attractions prior to closing, much of the internal queuing area is roped off so the lines of waiting guests still appear long from the outside.
- The best place to see all the parades is Frontierland®, although during peak periods you will still have to find a spot about 45 minutes before the parade.
- Daytime parades run from Splash Mountain® area to Town Square and the night-time parades in the opposite direction.

and rides and listing show and parade times. A notice board at the top of Main Street® also shows this and gives a list of waiting times at various attractions. It's best to get your FASTPASS tickets early for the major attractions. Insert your admission ticket into the FASTPASS machine and it will generate a FASTPASS ticket for you with a return time. Getting around the Park is relatively easy as the lands radiate from the central hub, in front of Cinderella's Castle.

The major attractions are at opposite sides of the park, so you will have to walk a fair way to avoid long waits in line. There are also more novel forms of transport. Main Street® has vehicles which, true to the Disney story-telling ideal, tell the story of transport from the horse-drawn tram to the motor car. A steam train circles the park, calling at Main Street®, Fantasyland, and Frontierland®.

Eating and Drinking

Food is mostly fast. For a reasonable meal, however, try Be Our Guest, inside the Beast's enchanted castle, for a quick-service lunch or sit-down dinner, or The Liberty Tree Tavern or the Crystal Palace for quieter dining. Cinderella's Royal Table in the castle has a regal ambience and the food is not too bad.

Main Street, USA®

This is a Disney fantasy of a small-town, Victorian America that never was. As you enter Main Street®, you pass beneath Main Street Station from where you can ride the train around the park. Trains run every ten minutes. Beneath the station are

lockers where, for a small fee, you can store valuables and bags. As you enter the town square, City Hall lies to your left and is the place to visit first for any information, such as which shows are running and what special events might be happening. Main Street® itself is a magnificent melange of color, shapes, and music, all in astonishing detail. Town Square Exposition Hall, to the right as you enter the square, can sort out any film problems you have but the main shops are, as you would expect, along Main Street®.

At night, this area assumes a magical ambience as thousands of lights bring a warm glow to the spotlessly clean paving. It's also an excellent place to see the Main Street Electrical Parade, a shimm-ering fantasy of music, live action and floats.

Adventureland®

Lush foliage, evocative drumbeats and colonial buildings combine to conjure images of Africa and the Caribbean. Crossing a wooden bridge from the central hub, Adventureland® is an exciting and entertaining fusion of the exotic and the tropical.

The Jungle Cruise boat ride, which takes guests around a variety of animatronically animated settings of deepest Africa, India, and South America is very popular due, in most part, to the great entertainment value of the "boatman" whose often wacky and infectious humor can't fail to amuse.

◄ Guests riding the Magic Carpets of Aladdin, Adventureland

1 Day Itinerary

If you really want to cover the Magic Kingdom® in one day, be warned, it's a daunting task, particularly in the summer. Begin early and follow these tips to ensure you get the most out of the inevitable busy schedule.

1. After leaving the turnstiles, head immediately for the central hub. If the entire park is open turn right and head for **Space Mountain®**. If there are ropes across areas at the hub, wait at the rope entrance to Tomorrowland® then head for Space Mountain® at rope drop. Those who like thrills should ride whilst others can head for **Buzz Lightyear's Space Ranger Spin**.
2. After Space Mountain head for **Fantasyland®** through Tomorrowland® (keep the speedway on your right and turn left at the Mad Hatter's Teacups) and ride the many **Adventures of Winnie the Pooh**.
3. After Winnie, turn left and head towards **Peter Pan's Flight** and also ride **"it's a small world"**.
4. Exit left, head to Liberty Square and visit **Haunted Mansion®** on the right.
5. Exit Haunted Mansion® to the right and continue to **Splash Mountain®**. If the wait is in excess of half an hour, get a FASTPASS, turn right and cross to **Big Thunder Mountain Railroad**.
6. Take the exit from Big Thunder and cross the bridge bearing right to **Pirates of the Caribbean®**. Ride.
7. Return to Splash Mountain® and ride, backtrack to the **Jungle Cruise**. If the time slot is right, ride, otherwise see the **Enchanted Tiki Room**.
8. Good time for lunch. Eat light at a fast food restaurant.
9. Walk off lunch at the **Swiss Family Treehouse** in Adventureland®.
10. Cross the central hub to Tomorrowland® and obtain a FASTPASS ticket for **Buzz Lightyear**.
11. Visit the **Monsters, Inc. Laugh Floor Comedy Club** *and choose between* **Astro Orbiter** and the **Carousel of Progress**.
12. Return to ride Buzz Lightyear.
13. Cross central hub to **Frontierland®**, and find a spot to stake out for the **afternoon parade**.
14. You will now have ridden and seen the top attractions in the Magic Kingdom®. This is a good time to rest before the **Main Street Electrical Parade**. If the park is closing early, view the parade from the Town Square. If it's open late it's a good idea to see the parade from Main Street® on the Tomorrowland® side so that, when the parade has passed, you can return to the attractions in Tomorrowland® and Fantasyland®.
15. Finally, stake out a bench in the park to see the **fireworks** in comfort.

The **Enchanted Tiki Room** is an amusing and cleverly animated attraction, and is a pleasant way to spend twenty minutes or so if you want to get out of the heat. Featuring characters from *Aladdin* and *The Lion King*, it's certainly worth a visit, just to see the walls change shape.

The **Pirates of the Caribbean®** is an extremely entertaining and remarkably detailed voyage where you cruise through crumbling, underground prisons, past fighting galleons of the 16th century, and past scenes of debauchery and mayhem. It used to be said that the version in Disneyland Paris was better, but it has now been upgraded, and the Audioanimatronic® effects are extremely well done. The ride is certainly a firm favorite with park visitors.

At the exit, there is one of the most interesting stores in the park, which sells a fantastic range of all the most essential Disneyland accessories.

Frontierland®

Set in Hollywood-inspired Wild West, this land abounds with raised walkways and trading posts. **The Frontierland Shootin' Arcade** is reminiscent of both the Wild West and of Country Fairs gone by, while the **Country Bear Jamboree** provides a completely audio animatronic animal show, much liked by all youngsters and a welcome respite from a hot summer's day.

Opposite Big Thunder Mountain is the landing stage where a raft can be taken to Tom Sawyer's Island. Complete with a fort, swinging bridges, waterfalls and tunnels, it's a child's dream adventure playground.

A stunningly conceived and superbly executed journey through America's Wild West on an out of control mine train, **Big Thunder Mountain Railroad** remains one of the Park's enduring attractions. In roller coaster terms, it's a relatively gentle experience, although the rear cars provide a wilder ride than the front. It also acquires large lines of people from early in the day, so this is a ride to be enjoyed sooner, rather than later.

Shows and Parades

Don't miss seeing at least one of each of these events. The shows – Mickey's PhilharMagic Orchestra, a 3-D animated film, and The Enchanted Tiki Room – are superb in their own right but the parades are unique. Floats of towering proportions surrounded by a multitude of actors and dancers travel on a set route between Frontierland® and the Town Square in Main Street®. There is always an afternoon parade and during the peak holiday season two evening parades called the Main Street Electrical Parade, usually at 8:30pm and 10:30pm. The evening also features Wishes – a Tinkerbell-led extravaganza of fireworks and music in which Cinderella's Castle is bathed in ever-changing lights.

For hotels and restaurants in this region see pp314–25 and pp329–49

An outstanding attraction which threatens to get you far wetter than it actually does is **Splash Mountain®**. This is the epitome of what Disney does best, with a seamless integration of music, special effects and beautifully crafted creatures. This, combined with a multitude of small drops prior to the big one make this one of the finest flume rides in the world. Absolutely guaranteed to make you want to do it again, this ride develops long queues early on and remains that way until closing.

Liberty Square

The smallest of all the lands, Liberty Square is set in post-colonial America and hosts the **Liberty Square Riverboat**, **Hall of Presidents** and **The Haunted Mansion®**. Entertaining rather than scary, except perhaps for very small children, The Haunted Mansion® rarely has long lines and provides a cool respite, particularly in the middle of a hot summer day. The ride travels through a graveyard into the namesake mansion, where walls and floors are not what they seem, and gravestones sing jolly songs as you pass. Watch out, because when your ghostly transport leaves the mansion behind, a transparent hitchhiker will be sitting right next to you.

For a dose of reality, board the Liberty Square Riverboat, a mock paddle steamer, and take a slow journey around Tom Sawyer's Island, looking out for real tropical birds along the way. The steamer gently cruises through America's 19th-century past whilst you listen to a recorded narration delivered in the voice of Mark Twain.

Refuge from the crowds and heat can be found in the nearby Hall of Presidents, an audio animatronic presentation featuring all 44 US presidents, including President Barack Obama. Before the presidents are introduced, an interesting film is shown that explores the history of America.

Shopping

There are shops everywhere in the Magic Kingdom® and they sell just about every type of clothing, confectionery (except chewing gum!) and badged merchandise imaginable. All Lands have their own shops selling items based on the theme of the Land and of the nearest ride (much piratical memorabilia can be purchased near Pirates of the Caribbean®, for instance) However, some of the best shopping is in Downtown Disney® where you can browse through the largest Disney store in the world.

Fantasyland®

Dominated by the soaring spires of Cinderella's Castle, this Land forms the core of the Magic Kingdom®. A major expansion that doubled the size of Fantasyland® added two new castles to the skyline: Beast's Castle and Prince Eric's castle. The circus area evokes Disney's classic film, *Dumbo*, with a big top and attractions such as **The Barnstormer**, where the Great Goofini performs daredevil acrobatics. But the big attraction of new Fantasyland® is the **Seven Dwarves Mine** roller coaster ride.

The delightfully designed attractions engender a feeling of amazement in even the most cynical and this land is usually the first destination for kids. **Prince Charming Regal Carousel** (a genuine 1917 restoration) seems to entice both old and young onto its gallopers. **Peter Pan's Flight** is deservedly popular combining the feeling of flying with the delight of perfectly matched music and movement.

Opposite is **"it's a small world"**, a water borne journey through a series of animated tableaux accompanied by a rather persistent melody which, if you're not careful, you'll find hard to get out of your head for the rest of the day. Lines are long here, so use a FASTPASS if possible. **The Many Adventures of Winnie the Pooh** incorporates the latest in ride vehicle technology, lighting and multi-channel sound effects, producing an attraction which deserves its FASTPASS status. The play-ground across from the ride, "Pooh's Thoughtful Spot" is a good place to take a

break. **Mickey's PhilharMagic** is an excellent 3-D animated film and is one of the newest attractions in Fantasyland®.

In the summer heat, the long lines for some of the short, child-friendly rides can be a strain on all concerned. Try alternating between outdoor rides, such as Dumbo and the carousel, and indoor attractions like "it's a small world", and Mickey's Philhar-Magic, which has an indoor line, giving a chance to cool down.

Tomorrowland®

Some years ago Disney revamped the facades and added new attractions to revitalise Tomorrowland®. Whether it has been entirely successful is largely a matter of opinion, but there's still plenty here to enjoy. **Space Mountain®** is the fastest ride where you shoot through tight bends and sharp drops in stygian blackness against projections of asteroids and the like. The effects of traveling through space are excellent, but the ride, though wilder than Big Thunder Mountain, may seem tame for seasoned thrillseekers.

Weary adults and kids will find unexpected fun at **Cosmic Ray's Starlight Café**. A giant alien, "Sonny Eclipse," holds court at a piano bar, and live dancers lead audience participation. It's also a great place to escape the heat or rain. There are three food areas with different menus at each.

Handling large crowds with ease, **Walt Disney's Carousel of Progress** is a sit down attraction where the auditorium rotates around a central stage. It examines domestic life through the ages and, although rather quaint, is a firm favourite, particularly late in the evening.

At **Monsters, Inc. Laugh Floor Comedy Club** you'll discover the power of laughter in an interactive adventure, as you match your wits with the one- eyed hero Mike Wazowski and his two comedian wannabee friends.

The Tomorrowland® Transit Authority is a serene, quiet and interesting ten-minute ride which uses linear induction drives. This journey through Tomorrowland® affords some of the best views in the park and an opportunity to relax after a great deal of walking. Almost never busy, it travels through Space Mountain® and offers views inside several other attractions as well.

One of Tomorrowland®'s greatest innovations is **Buzz Lightyear's Space Ranger Spin**. A superb and highly addictive journey through *Toy Story* adventures sets you in a two seater car, fitted with laser cannons, electronic scoreboards and a control which allows you to rotate the car rapidly for a better aim. A very fast loader, it's one of the best rides in the park.

Shooting at the targets with a red laser beam which evokes bangs, crashes, pings and rapid increases in your scores. This has become one of the few rides that children tear their parents away from, such is its popularity.

Tips

- Lines at attractions are shorter during parade times.
- Watch the fireworks from the top of Main Street® (near the hub), then enjoy the rides until the later evening parade, which is always less crowded.
- Ride the train around Magic Kingdom® for an overview of what is there.
- Grab a seat on the terrace at Cosmic Ray's for a perfect view of the fireworks and Cinderella Castle projection show.
- If you are staying on site, take the kids back to the hotel for lunch and a swim during the heat of the day .
- If you have young children, rent a stroller when you enter the park.

Rides and Shows Checklist

This chart is designed to help you plan what to visit the Magic Kingdom®. The rides and shows are listed in no particular order within each Land.

		WAITING TIME	HEIGHT / AGE RESTRICTION	BUSIEST TIME TO RIDE	FASTPASS	LOADING SPEED	MAY CAUSE MOTION SICKNESS	RATING OVERALL
ADVENTURELAND®								
R	Jungle Cruise	●		11am–5pm	➡	❷		▼
R	Pirates of the Carribbean®	○		noon–4pm		❶		◆
S	Enchanted Tiki Room	○				❶		▼
R	Magic Carpet of Aladdin	○				❶		▼
FRONTIERLAND®								
R	Big Thunder Mountain Railroad	●	1.02m	10am–7pm	➡	❶	✔	★
R	Splash Mountain®	●	1.02m	10am–7pm	➡	❶		★
S	Country Bear Jamboree	○				❶		▼
S	Frontierland Shootin' Arcade	◗				❶		◆
LIBERTY SQUARE								
R	Hall of Presidents	○				❶		▼
R	Haunted Mansion®	◗				❶		◆
R	Liberty Square Riverboat	○				❶		▼
FANTASYLAND®								
R	Dumbo the Flying Elephant	◗		9am–7pm		❸		▼
R	It's a Small World	○				❶		▼
R	The Many Adventures of Winnie the Pooh	●		10am–6pm	➡	❸		★
R	Peter Pan's Flight	●		9am–9pm	➡	❸		★
R	The Barnstormer	◗	89cm	9am–7pm		❷		▼
R	Mad Tea Party	○				❶	✔	▼
TOMORROWLAND®								
R	Buzz Lightyear's Space Ranger Spin	◗		10am–6pm	➡	❶		◆
R	Space Mountain®	●	1.2m	9am–7pm	➡	❷		★
S	Cosmic Ray's Starlight Café	○						▼
S	Monsters, Inc. Laugh Floor Comedy Club	◗						▼
R	Tomorrowland® Transit Authority	○				❶		▼

Key: Ride – R Show – S; Waiting Time Good – ○ Average – ◗ Bad – ●; Overall Rating Good – ▼ Excellent – ◆ Outstanding – ★ Loading Speed Fast – ❶ Leisurely – ❷ Slow – ❸

Epcot®

Epcot®, an acronym for the Experimental Prototype Community of Tomorrow, was Walt Disney's dream of a technologically replete, living community. It was intended to represent a utopian vision of the future but upon its opening in 1982 several changes had been made to the original dream and Epcot® opened as an educational center and permanent world's fair.

The 250-acre park is divided into two distinct halves: Future World with an emphasis on entertainment and education and World Showcase which represents the art, culture, and culinary expertise of different countries around the globe.

The France Pavillion in World Showcase

Tackling the Park

Epcot® is two and a half times the size of the Magic Kingdom® which means that at least two days are needed to see the Park in its entirety. World Showcase is not normally open until 11am so the early-morning crowds fill Future World. The "back gate" or International Gateway entrance opens at 9am, and visitors can enter World Showcase and eat breakfast at Les Halles Boulangerie and Patisserie in the French Pavilion. Arriving early is the key to a successful visit. If you are entitled to early entry privileges, arrive 1 hour and 40 minutes before the official opening time.

Although there are really only a small number of rides in Future World, two of these, Test Track and Mission: SPACE® are besieged from the outset. To reach them, bear left through the huge Innoventions East building. It sometimes helps to think of Future World as a clock face; if the turnstiles are at 6 o'clock then Mission: SPACE® is at 9 o'clock and Test Track is at 11 o'clock –

the equivalent of walking from the entrance to Magic Kingdom® and through to Splash Mountain®.

After leaving the Mission: SPACE®/Test Track area, retrace your steps back through Innoventions East and cross through Innoventions West, emerging to see the Soarin' and The Seas with Nemo & Friends. If you are most interested in seeing the world architecture and eating at one of the many restaurants in Epcot®, a more pleasant way to enter the park is through the International Gateway. Park at Disney's Boardwalk and walk, or take the boat and disembark at the entrance between France and England.

World Showcase holds far more interest for adults than children, but Kidcot Fun Spots offer free interactive and educational activities in several pavilions, and the diversionary tactic of buying each child a "Passport" to have stamped can prove a blessing. There are minor rides (usually boat rides) in some pavilions and several show films. The dining at some is

Illuminations: Reflections of Earth

The one Epcot® show that you mustn't miss is the nightly IllumiNations. Presented near closing time around World Showcase Lagoon, it is a rousing *son et lumière* show on an unbelievably extravagant scale with lasers, fire- and waterworks and a symphonic soundtrack that highlight the 11 featured nations. Best viewing spots are a seat on the veranda at the Cantina de San Angel in Mexico, the outside restaurant balcony in Japan, and the International Gateway bridge near the United Kingdom.

◀ The out-of-this-world entrance to the motion-simulator Mission: SPACE® ride at Epcot®

excellent and can be booked through your hotel. Transport is not very efficient (you'll always get there faster by walking) so good, comfortable shoes are essential. There is also not much shade so be sure to wear a hat.

Future World

The first area to be encountered by guests arriving at the main turnstiles, Future World comprises a series of huge, modernistic buildings around the outside, the access to which is through Innoventions East and West. Some buildings house a single ride attraction while others afford the opportunity to browse various exhibits – usually hands-on – and enjoy smaller rides within the main pavilion. Most of the attractions here are sponsored by major manufacturers, which will be evident from the signs.

Pin Trading

This answer to many a parent's prayer was introduced when Disney noticed that lapel pins it had produced for special events were re-selling at several times the market value. In a flash of inspiration, they created Pin Stations – small booths in every park selling only the hundreds of different pins that Disney produces. They usually cost $6–15 each. Following this up with a stroke of

genius, they also created Pin Traders – cast members who could be persuaded to swap pins with guests and cemented the whole idea with a set of very simple trading rules, which cast members could break in favour of the guest. This has captured the imagination of children and teenagers who happily spend hours tracking down the pin they don't have and swapping another for it. The concept has been so successful with guests and cast members that Disney have no plans to end it. Depending on the type of hotel package you have booked, you may be presented with a set of pins on arrival to start the ball rolling.

Spaceship Earth

Housed in an enormous 7,500-ton geodesic sphere, this continuously loading ride conveys visitors gently past superbly crafted tableaux and animatronic scenes portraying mankind's progress in the field of technology. This incredible story of development, narrated by actress Dame Judi Dench, travels through time beginning with prehistoric man's first words and finishing with the cyber age of the 21st century. Almost as interesting as the ride itself is the fascinating dome which cunningly re-circulates rainwater into the World Showcase Lagoon.

TOP 10 ATTRACTIONS

① **Test Track**

② **Mission: Space®**

③ **Rock 'n' Roller Coaster® Starring Aerosmith**

④ **The Seas with Nemo**

⑤ **Soarin'**

⑥ **Ellen's Energy Adventure**

⑦ **Maelstrom**

⑧ **Reflections of China**

⑨ **Impressions De France**

⑩ **Illuminations**

Innoventions

Both buildings of the Innoventions attraction, East and West, form a hands-on exhibition of products of the close future which, through ties to consumer electronics manufacturers, is constantly updated. However, time is needed to make the most of Innoventions and many of the games have now moved to Downtown Disney®, with the result that the theme has become more adult.

Ariel view of World Showcase Epcot®

For hotels and restaurants in this region see pp314–25 and pp329–49

Epcot®: Mission: SPACE®

The most impressive thrill ride at Epcot®, Mission: SPACE® takes guests on a journey to the heavens that culminates with a crash landing on Mars. This extremely popular attraction is the ultimate in simulator thrill rides, combining high-speed spinning – to simulate g-forces – with a simulator and a 3-D visual interactive storyline. The result is a completely mesmer-izing and convincing rocket launch and high-speed trip to Mars, which also involves a ride around the moon. Particularly impressive are the wholly realistic re-creations of a liftoff into space and a problem-fraught landing. The most technologically advanced of Disney's attractions, the ride is a creation of Disney imagination, but is based on scientific fact and theory provided by astronauts, scientists, and engineers.

International Space Training Center

The story is set at the International Space Training Center (ISTC) in the year 2036. In this future time of space exploration, many countries have joined together to train a new generation of space explorers. Mission: SPACE® participants become astronaut candidates on their first training mission.

The ISTC building is a gleaming, metallic affair, complete with curved walls and a state-of-the-art, Space Age look. The curvy steel exterior surrounds the courtyard, called **Planetary Plaza** – from the moment visitors step into this courtyard, they are taken straight into a futuristic world.Huge replicas of Earth, Jupiter, and the moon fill Planetary Plaza, and its walls feature quotations from historical figures about space travel and exploration.

The moon model displays brass plaques indicating the location of every US and Soviet manned and unmanned touchdown during the 1960s and 70s. The interior of the ISTC is compartmentalized into various areas for different levels of training. There are four ride bays, with ten capsules in each bay; each capsule can hold four guests.

Training

Before embarking on their flight, the explorers must follow a series of procedures in order to prepare for their "mission." These training and briefing sessions also go a long way in making the wait times for the show seem shorter, as they keep the crowds entertained prior to the actual ride portion of the show:

the ambience is well-executed and slightly militaristic – a rare feature at Disney parks. At the **ISTC Astronaut Recruiting Center**, explorers learn about training and view a model of the X-2 Trainer, the futuristic spacecraft they will board for their journey into space.

The second station of the mission is the **Space Simulation Lab**, a slowly spinning 35-ft (10-m) high gravity wheel containing work quarters, exercise rooms, sleeping cubicles, and dining areas for space teams.One of the highlights of the lab is an authentic Apollo-era Lunar Rover display unit on loan from the Smithsonian National Air and Space Museum, which describes mankind's first exploration of the moon.

Participants then enter the **Training Operations Room**, which bustles with the activity of various training sessions in progress. Several large monitors show live video feeds of ongoing ISTC training sessions. In **Team Dispatch**, a dispatch officer meets participants. Here, participants are split into teams of four people and sent to the **Ready Room**. This is the point at which each team member accepts an assignment: commander, pilot, navigator, or engineer.Each member is supposed to carry out the tasks associated with his or her assigned role during the flight. It is here that the explorers meet Capcom – the

Replicas of planets standing out dramatically against the metallic façade of the Mission: SPACE® building

capsule communicator – who will act as the astronauts' guide through the flight. In the **Pre-flight Corridor**, explorers receive their final instructions for the mission. A uniformed flight crew member then escorts the team to a capsule – the X-2 Space Shuttle.

Flight & Landing

The team members board the X-2 training capsule and are securely strapped in, with individual "windows" just inches away. The countdown begins and then there is a pulse-racing liftoff: the roar of engines, the clouds of exhaust, and the motion of the capsule all combine to generate in the participants sensations similar to those that astronauts feel during actual liftoff.

The cabin's windows are actually state-of-the-art video flat screens that use a combination of LCD glass and electronic video cards to present an ultra-sharp full-motion video based on actual data taken from Mars-orbiting

Top Tips

- This is the first ride created with Disney's Fastpass system in mind. Avoid a lengthy wait at this popular attraction by using the Fastpass, which is available at the entrance to Mission: SPACE®. Two times will be posted. If the wait is too long, guests can obtain a Fastpass ticket with an assigned return time.
- Read all the warning signs at the entrance to Mission: SPACE® and take the ride only if you are sure you'll be able to handle it.
- The ride has a minimum guest height requirement of 3 ft 8 in (1.1 m).
- The entire Mission: SPACE® experience, from pre-show to the Advance Training Lab, can last from 45 minutes to more than an hour. The ride to Mars lasts approximately four minutes from capsule door closing to it reopening.

satellites. The spectacular views of planets Earth and Mars that participants glimpse through the capsule windows, reinforce their illusion of traveling through space.

The members of the space team must work in unison, performing the roles of pilot, commander, navigator, and engineer in order to successfully face challenges and accomplish their mission to Mars. Throughout the flight, crew members receive instructions from Capcom regarding their duties, which consists of pressing buttons; the capsule obeys the commands very convincingly. Unexpected twists and turns keep participants on the edge of their seats, and call for tricky maneuvers with joysticks. Apart from the exhilarating "slingshot" around the moon, other thrills include a brief experience of "weightlessness" and dodging asteroids on the way to Mars.

The four-minute ride comes to a crashing finale with the Mars landing, complemented by superb sound effects that are achieved by the use of a stereo woofer built right into the back of the space capsules. Pioneering astronauts such as Buzz Aldrin and Rhea Seddon have taken their turn on the ride, comparing it favorably to actual space travel.

The g-forces that come into play during Mission: SPACE® are, in fact, of lower intensity than in a typical roller coaster but they are of much greater duration.

Advance Training Lab

After the ride, guests can go around the Advance Training Lab, a colorful interactive play area where they can test their skills in space-related games for people of all ages. You can explore this area even if you choose not to go on the ride itself. There is no minimum height requirement here.

In **Space Race**, two teams are involved in a race to be the first to complete a successful

mission from Mars back to Earth. The teams are composed of up to 60 guests, who are required to work together to overcome numerous challenges and setbacks in their mission. **Expedition: Mars** is another fun endeavor at the Advance Traning Lab. In this sophisticated video game, the player's mission is to locate four astronauts stranded on Mars. **Space Base** is targeted at junior astronauts. It is an excellent interactive play area where kids can climb, slide, crawl, explore, and get rid of excess energy. You can also send **Postcards from Space** at a kiosk in the Advanced Training Lab. Here, guests make a video of themselves in one of several space-related backdrops to create a fine memento of their Mission: SPACE® experience, and can email the result to friends and family.

Beyond the Advance Training Lab is the **Mission: SPACE® Cargo Bay**, a shopping area spreading over 1,500 sq ft (139 sq m). A 4-ft (1.2-m) high 3-D figure of Mickey Mouse dressed as an astronaut greets visitors, and the area is dominated by a 12-ft (3.6-m) mural depicting various Disney characters in space gear on the surface of Mars. Here, visitors can purchase a large variety of souvenirs, from inexpensive to costly, as a remembrance of their "space experience."

Future World Cont...

Ellen's Energy Adventure

A passably entertaining film is enlivened by some fascinating technology and host Ellen DeGeneres. The entire theatre rotates before breaking into self powered, moving sections, each seating more than 100 people which then proceed to take you through a prehistoric landscape, inhabited by some fairly convincing antediluvians.

The Seas with Nemo & Friends

The technology behind this attraction is quite stunning in its own right, but most people come here to visit Sea Base Alpha, Epcot®'s most ambitious research project. A pre-show presentation prepares you for your journey to the bottom of the ocean, after which you take the "clamobiles" to ride through a stunning coral reef setting. Picking up where the motion picture left off, you get to meet familiar characters like Dory, Bruce, Marlin, and Squirt, who inhabit a huge aquarium containing more than 65 species of marine life. **Turtle Talk with Crush** is a break-through exper-ience into real-time animation with many interactive components.

Visitors can take several behind-the-scenes tours of the saltwater tank at The Seas. Dolphins in Depth gives visitors an opportunity to see the dolphin trainers and feeders at work. It culminates in an up-close encounter with one of several dolphins in the giant aquarium. Other tours include Epcot Dive Quest, which takes guests underwater to see some of the aquarium's 6,000 sea creatures, including sea turtles, angelfish, eagle rays, and sharks, and the Seas Aqua Tour, that allows guests to snorkel on the surface.

Test Track

One of the most popular rides in Epcot®, long lines form quickly at park opening time and increase rapidly. Test Track uses the most sophis-ticated ride vehicle technology available placing you in a simulator that moves on tracks at high speed. Essentially, you are the passengers in a six seater prototype sports car being tested prior to going into production. Although the ride puts you through brake tests, hill climbs, sharp turns, near crashes and paint spraying bays, the climax is the outside lap of the ride where the vehicle exceeds 66 mph on a raised roadway around the outside of the Test Track building. So advanced is the technology that the ride is kept running 24 hours a day, as the start up procedure is so lengthy. However, the system has frequent stops – usually because the advanced safety systems have cut in and halted the entire run. While this is obviously reassuring in some ways, the lines continue to grow until, by the evening, you can expect a wait of between 90 minutes and two hours for this 4 minute ride. The ride itself, however, is so good you will want to ride it again

and again. The FastPass machines outside the entrance have normally exhausted their allocation by lunchtime.

The Imagination! Pavilion

The Imaginaton! Pavilion houses the Journey into Your Imagination with Figment ride, and an Imageworks Lab.

Phineas and Ferb: Agent P's World Showcase Adventure is an interactive game, based on the animated Disney series, that sends visitors around World Showcase seeking clues in each of the world pavilions to help thwart Doofenshmirtz's evil plot. The **Journey into Imagination with Figment** ride is a very upbeat and light-hearted trip in search of ideas in the arts and sciences. However, it is rather over complicated and also overlong.

Top Tips

- Test Track is exceptionally popular but unreliable. To avoid the long lines, try to ride this first. On leaving, take a Fastpass ticket for another ride later.
- If a breakdown occurs during your ride, after disembarking ask the cast member if you can ride again, immediately.
- Because Test Track runs continuously – even when the park is closed – you can jump back on it for a repeat ride in the last minutes before park closing.
- Ellen's Energy Adventure show is exceptionally long (45 minutes). Take it in for a break from the heat or while you wait for a FastPass ride window to become available.
- Although the lines for Ellen's Energy Adventure are long, it takes 600 guests every 17 minutes, so you won't have long to wait.
- The Land is an agriculturist's dream pavilion. It contains the thrill ride Soarin', which will appeal to all except the very young. A better bet for them is The Seas with Nemo & Friends, featuring characters from the movie Finding Nemo, along with over 6,000 sea creatures in the aquarium.

Celebration Florida

Materializing out of former swampland adjacent to Walt Disney World®, Celebration is a new town with old values. Inspired partly by the romantic streets of Charleston in South Carolina, Disney is attempting to re-create the wholesome small-town atmosphere that many middle-aged Americans remember and miss. The residents will experience a cookie-jar world of friendly neighbors and corner grocery stores.

People began moving here in 1996, the first of an expec-ted total of 20,000 inhabitants. Now, more than 11,000 residents enjoy the pedestrian-friendly streets, the nostalgic architecture (designed by some respected architects), and the hospital that treats both "wellness" and illness. The residents aren't daunted by Celebration's strict rules, which set out, for example, that visible curtains must be white or off-white and that streetside shrubbery must be approved by Disney. In some ways, however, Celebration is like any other town: the public is free to visit and look around.

The **Imageworks Lab** is an interactive playground of audio-visual sensory games and demonstrations.

The Land

Ecology and conservation form the main themes and permeate the three attractions housed around the fast food restaurant. These consequently are much busier during lunch times. Lion King characters lead **The Circle of Life**, a hymn to conservation expressed through film and anim-ation, while **Living with the Land** is a cruise through the past, present, and future of US farming, showing off Disney's famed hydroponic gardens, which supply onsite restaurants with fresh produce. However, the greatest attraction here has got to be the thrill ride **Soarin'**, where passengers are lifted off the ground in a simulated hang glider to experience the sensation of flying over California's breath-taking scenery such as Golden Gate Bridge and Yosemite national park.

One-day Itinerary

1 Arrive 1 hour 40 minutes before the official opening time on an early entry day or an hour before on a normal day.

2 Head straight towards Test Track and Mission: SPACE®, ride, collect FastPass tickets for later then backtrack to the opposite side of Future World for Journey into Imagination with Figment, or Imageworks.

3 Leave and head back towards the entrance and ride Spaceship Earth.

4 From there, head to The Land Pavilion and collect FastPass tickets for Soarin'.

5 Head to Ellen's Energy Adventure.

6 Head towards World Showcase.

7 Head to the left around the lagoon and visit Mexico. Ride Gran Fiesta Tour.

8 Continue to the left around the lagoon and go to Norway. Ride The Maelstrom.

9 Time to eat, then visit China (movie), France (movie) and Canada (movie).

10 Return to Future World and visit The Land pavilion. Experience the attractions there.

11 Leave the Land pavilion to the left and head for The Seas with Nemo & Friends. Experience both attractions there.

12 Exit Living Seas to the right, pass through both Innoventions East and West.

It's now a good time to head back to your hotel and return by 7pm to book a good spot to see IllumiNations.

Rides and Shows Checklist

This chart is designed to help you plan what to visit at Epcot. The rides and shows are listed in no particular order within Future World and World Showcase.

		WAITING TIME	HEIGHT / AGE RESTRICTION	BUSIEST TIME TO RIDE	FASTPASS	MAY CAUSE MOTION SICKNESS	RATING OVERALL
FUTURE WORLD							
S	The Circle of Life	○		noon–2pm			▼
R	Soarin'	●	1.02m	All day	➡	✔	★
S	Living with the Land	●		noon–2pm			◆
R	Mission: Space®	●	1.3m	9am–5pm	➡	✔	◆
R	Spaceship Earth	◗		9am–noon			★
R	Test Track	●	1.1m	All day	➡	✔	★
S	Ellen's Energy Adventure	◗		10am–1pm			◆
S	The Seas with Nemo & Friends / Turtle Talk with Crush	○		11am–3pm			◆
S	Phineas and Ferb: Agent P's World Showcase Adventure	○					▼
S	Journey into Imagination with Figment	◗					▼
WORLD SHOWCASE							
R	Gran Fiesta Tour	○		noon–3pm			▼
S	Impressions De France	○					▼
R	Maelstrom	●		11am–5pm			▼
S	The American Adventure	○					◆
S	O Canada	○					◆
S	Reflections of China	○					★
S	Japan Drummers						▼
S	Germany Biergarten Oompah Band						▼

Key: Ride – R Show – S; Waiting Times Good – ○ Average – ◗ Bad – ●
Overall Rating Good – ▼ Excellent – ◆ Outstanding – ★

World Showcase

The temples, churches, town halls, and castles of these 11 pavilions or countries are sometimes replicas of genuine buildings, sometimes merely in vernacular style. But World Showcase is much more than just a series of architectural set pieces. Every pavilion is staffed by people from the country it represents, selling high-quality local products as well as surprisingly good ethnic cuisine.

At set times (which are given on the guidemap) native performers stage live shows in the forecourts of each country: the best are the excellent acrobats at China and the bizarre and comic Living Statues at Italy. Only a couple of pavilions include rides, while a number have stunning giant-screen introductions to their country's history, culture, and landscapes. A few even have art galleries, though these often go unnoticed.

There are ferries across World Showcase Lagoon, linking Canada to Morocco and Mexico to Germany, but it is also relatively quick and easy to get around World Showcase on foot.

Mexico

A Mayan pyramid hides the most remarkable interior at World Showcase. Stalls selling sombreros, ponchos, and papier-mâché animals (*piñatas*), and musicians fill a plaza bathed in a purple twilight. The backdrop to this is a rumbling volcano. The **Gran**

Fiesta Tour boat ride tells the story of the Three Caballeros, passing through Audio-Animatronics and cinematic scenes of Mexico past and present while the fast-food restaurant outside the pavilion offers the best viewing spot for IllumiNations later on.

Norway

The architecture here includes replicas of a stave church (a medieval wooden church) and Akershus Castle (a 14th-century fortress above Oslo harbor), arranged attractively around a cobblestone square.

You can buy trolls and sweaters and other native crafts, but the essential element here is **Maelstrom**, a short but exhilarating journey down fjords in a longboat, into troll country, and across an oil rig-flecked North Sea – before docking at a fishing port. The ride is followed by a short film about Norway.

China

In this pavilion the *pièce de résistance* is the half-size replica of Beijing's well-known landmark, the Temple of Heaven. The peaceful scene here contrasts with the more rowdy atmosphere in some of the nearby pavilions.

For entertainment, there is **Reflections of China**, a Circle-Vision film (shown on nine screens all around the audience simultaneously), which makes the most of the country's fabulous, little-seen ancient sites and scenery. Note that you must stand throughout

the film. The pavilion's extensive shopping emporium sells everything from Chinese lanterns and painted screens to tea bags. .

Germany

The happiest country in World Showcase is a mixture of gabled and spired buildings gathered around a central square, St. Georgsplatz. They are based on real buildings from all over Germany, including a merchants' hall in Freiburg and a Rhine castle. If you have children, try to time your visit so that it coincides with the hourly chime of the glockenspiel in the square.

An accordionist sometimes plays, and the shops are full of quirky or clever gifts such as beautifully crafted wooden dolls. However, you really need to dine here to get the full flavor of Germany.

Italy

The bulk of Italy's relatively small pavilion represents Venice: from gondolas moored alongside candycane poles in the lagoon to the tremendous versions of the towering redbrick campanile and the 14th-century Doge's Palace of St. Mark's Square; even the fake marble looks authentic. The courtyard buildings behind are Veronese and Florentine in style, and the Neptune statue is a copy of a Bernini work.

The architecture is the big attraction, but you should also stop off to eat in one of the restaurants or browse around the shops where you can pick up pasta, amaretti, wine, and so forth.

The American Adventure

The American pavilion is the centerpiece of World Showcase, but it lacks the charm found in most of the other countries. However, Americans usually find **The American Adventure** show, which takes place inside the vast Georgian-style building, very moving. For others it will provide an interesting insight into the American psyche. The show is an

World Showcase: Behind the Scenes

If you'd like more than just a superficial view of Walt Disney World®, its behind-the-scenes tours may appeal. In World Showcase, two-hour Hidden Treasures tours provide a closer look at the architecture and traditions of the countries featured in the park, while in the Gardens of the World tours the creation of the World Showcase gardens is explained; you are even given tips on how to create a bit of Disney magic back home. These tours cost around $60–$95 per person. If you have $249 and seven hours to spare, you might want to sign up for the Backstage Magic tour, which includes all three theme parks. One of the highlights is the visit to the famous tunnel network beneath the Magic Kingdom®. For information on all Disney tours call (407) WDW-TOUR/(407) 939-8687.

openly patriotic yet thought-provoking romp through the history of the United States up to the present day. It incorporates tableaus on screen and some excellent Audio-Animatronics® figures, particularly of the author Mark Twain and the great 18th-century statesman, Benjamin Franklin.

Japan

This restrained, formal place has a traditional Japanese garden, a Samurai castle, and a pagoda where musicians play huge ceremonial drums several times a day; it is modeled on a seventh-century temple in Nara whose five levels represent earth, water, fire, wind, and sky.

The Mitsukoshi department store, a copy of the Imperial Palace's ceremonial hall in Kyoto, offers kimonos, bonsai trees, wind chimes, and the chance to pick a pearl from an oyster. Japan really only comes to life in its restaurants.

Morocco

Morocco's appeal lies in its enameled tiles, its keyhole-shaped doors, its ruddy fortress walls, and the twisting alleys of its *medina* (old city), which is reached via a reproduction of a gate into the city of Fez. The use of native artists gives the show a greater sense of authenticity.

Morocco offers some of the best handmade crafts in World Showcase. The alleys of the old city lead you to a bustling market of little stores selling carpets, brassware, leather-ware, and shawls, with belly dancing and couscous in the Restaurant Marrakesh.

France

A Gallic flair infuses everything in the France pavilion from its architecture (including a one-tenth scale replica of the Eiffel Tower, Parisian Belle Epoque mansions, and a rustic village main street) to its upscale stores (perfume, wine, and berets). French food can be sampled in a couple of restaurants and a patisserie selling croissants and cakes.

A film entitled **Impressions de France** is the main entertainment. The film, shown on five adjacent screens and set to the sounds of French classical music, offers a whirlwind tour through the country's most beautiful regions.

United Kingdom

The Rose and Crown Pub is the focal point in the this pavilion. It serves traditional English fare such as Cornish pasties, fish and chips, and even draft bitter – chilled to suit American tastes. Pleasant gardens surround the pub, as well as a medley of buildings of various historic architectural styles. These include a castle based on Hampton Court, an imitation Regency terrace, and a thatched cottage.

There is not much to do here in this pavilion other than browse around the shops, which sell everything from quality tea and china to sweaters, tartan ties, teddy bears, and toy soldiers. The terrace in the Rose and Crown, however, offers good views of IllumiNations.

Canada

A log cabin, 30-ft (9-m) high totem poles, a replica of Ottawa's Victorian-style Château Laurier Hotel, a rocky chasm, and ornamental gardens make up the large but rather staid Canadian pavilion.

The country in all its diversity, and particularly its grand scenery, comes to life much better in the Circle-Vision film **O Canada!** (though China's Circle-Vision film is even better). The audience stands in the middle of the theater and turns around to follow the film as it unfolds on no fewer than nine screens.

Shops at Canada sell a range of Indian and Inuit crafts, as well as various edible specialties, including wine.

Eating and Drinking

Dining well is fundamental to visiting Epcot® and particularly World Showcase. Some of the latter's pavilions have decent fast-food places, but the best restaurants (including those listed below unless otherwise stated) require reservations. Call (407) 939-3463 as soon as you know when you'll be at Epcot®. Book early in the day. Most restaurants serve lunch and dinner; try unpopular hours such as 11am or 4pm if other times are unavailable. Lunch is usually about two-thirds of the price of dinner, and children's menus are available at even the most upscale restaurants.

Recommended in World Showcase are:
Mexico: the San Angel Inn serves interesting but pricey Mexican cuisine. It is the most romantic place to dine at Epcot.
Norway: Restaurant Akershus offers a good-value *koldtbord* (buffet) of Norwegian dishes in a castle setting.
Germany: the Biergarten has a beer hall atmosphere, with a cheap and plentiful buffet and hearty oompah-pah music.
Italy: L'Originale Alfredo di Roma Ristorante is enormously popular and engagingly chaotic, with sophisticated dishes.
Japan: you can eat communally, either in the Teppan Yaki Dining Rooms around a grilling, stir-frying chef, or at the bar of Tempura Kiku for sushi and tempura (no reservations).
France: there are three top-notch restaurants here: the upscale Bistro de Paris (dinner only); Les Chefs de France, the most elegant restaurant in Epcot, with *haute cuisine* by acclaimed French chefs; and the terraced Chefs de France Steakhouse (no reservations) for steaks, escargots, and crêpes.
Canada: Le Cellier Steakhouse is excellent. Advance reservations are required.

Recommended in Future World are:
The Land: the revolving Garden Grill passes a re-created rainforest, prairie, and desert while Disney characters entertain.
The Seas with Nemo & Friends: at the expensive Coral Reef, both eat and watch fish through a clear, underwater wall.

Disney's Hollywood Studios®

Disney's Hollywood Studios® was launched in 1989 as a working film and TV production facility. In 2004, however, the animation department was shut down and the production facility was almost completely abandoned. Regardless of these changes, the park remains a famed tourist destination, with top-notch shows and rides based on Disney and Metro-Goldwyn-Mayer films and TV shows, offering a tribute to Hollywood. Popular rides like the Tower of Terror and Star Tours, and shows such as "Fantasmic!" and "Voyage of The Little Mermaid" have taken the park's popularity to new heights, and its educational yet highly entertaining interactive experiences are geared toward adults and teenagers.

The Sorcerer's Hat at Disney's Hollywood Studios®

Tackling the Park

This park is not laid out in the same way as the other theme parks, although Hollywood Boulevard acts as a sort of "Main Street USA" with the purpose of funnelling guests towards the attractions. Over the past few years, Disney has expanded the breadth and scope of the attractions here, building some of the finest in Orlando. The entertainment schedule changes frequently and streets can be closed off during the visit of a celebrity or a live filming session. Although most of this happens in winter, it's a good idea to find out times, locations, and events as soon as you enter the park from Guest Services, on the left of the main entrance.

As with the other theme parks, arriving early is the key to avoid waiting a long time in line. It's also worth bearing in mind that some attractions are particularly intense and can frighten young children.

At about 3:30pm, there is an afternoon parade. The open plan of the park means that guests may get hot while waiting for the parade, which is always based on one of the recent animated movies from Disney.

At night, **Fantasmic!** takes place. This superb event is held once a night during the slow season and twice during peak periods. Seating 10,000 people at a time, you will need to turn up at least two hours before, however, to get a good seat!

Hollywood Boulevard

Delightful Art Deco styled buildings vie with a replica of Grauman's Chinese Theater to present an image of Hollywood that never was. It's here that your picture will be taken and you might well see some of the cast members acting as reporters or police, chasing celebrities. More importantly, it is on the Boulevard that the cast members will try to direct you to the Indiana Jones™ Epic Stunt Spectacular – a live action show using many of the stunts from the Indiana Jones films. However, the top attractions are in the opposite direction.

Halfway up the boulevard, Sunset Boulevard breaks to the right, leading to the two most popular rides in the Park, The Twilight Zone Tower of Terror™ and the Rock 'n' Roller Coaster® Starring Aerosmith.

At the junction between Hollywood and Sunset Boulevards lies one of the ubiquitous pin stations where budding traders can ambush cast members and swap badges. At the top of Hollywood Boulevard lies the Central Plaza, dominated by the replica of Grauman's Chinese Theater and an enormous canopy shaped like Mickey's hat from The Sorcerer's Apprentice, where you can experience **The Great Movie Ride**. This is one of the few attractions where the queuing is almost as good as the ride itself. Here, huge ride

vehicles carrying 60 guests apiece track silently past the largest movie sets ever built for a Disney ride. As always, the most realistic sets imaginable are combined with real live action sequences to make this an enjoyable ride which ends on a very upbeat and optimistic note.

Sunset Boulevard

Like Hollywood Boulevard, Sunset Boulevard is a rose-tinted evocation of the famous Hollywood street in the 1940s. Theaters and storefronts (some real, some fake) have been re-created with characteristic

Tips

- The most popular rides here are the Twilight Zone Tower of Terror™ and the Rock 'n' Roller Coaster® so visit these early to avoid the queues.
- The best place to watch the afternoon parade is on the bench nearest the popcorn and drinks stand opposite "Sounds Dangerous". You still, however, have to get there first.
- During the parades, most of the other attractions are quiet, but almost impossible to reach if you're not on the correct side.
- In the boiler room of the Twilight Zone Tower of Terror™, take any open gateway to the lifts – don't worry if others are not. You'll get a better seat and a better view.

TOP 10 ATTRACTIONS

① Fantasmic!

② Twilight Zone Tower of Terror™

③ Rock 'n' Roller Coaster® Starring Aerosmith

④ Muppet Vision 3-D

⑤ Star Tours

⑥ Great Movie RidE

⑦ Voyage of the Little Mermaid

⑧ Indiana Jones™ Epic Stunt Spectacular

⑨ Studios Backlot Tour

⑩ The Magic of Disney Animation

attention to detail, and is dominated at one end by the Hollywood Tower Hotel. This lightning-ravaged, decrepit Hotel is the spot for Orlando's scariest ride – **The Twilight Zone Tower of Terror™** – in which you're strapped into the service elevator for a voyage inspired by the 1950s TV show *The Twilight Zone™*. The pre-show area is a library into which you are ushered by a melancholic bell cap. From here you enter what appears to be the boiler room of the hotel and you walk through to the lifts – apparently freight elevators fitted with plank seats. The elevator doors sometimes open to allow glimpses of ghostly corridors, but it's hard to concentrate on anything other than the ghastly 13-story plunge that everyone knows will

come – but not exactly when. When you arrive on the 13th floor the elevator actually trundles horizontally across the hotel.Once you are in the drop shaft you get dropped no fewer than seven times.

This is a masterpiece of ride technology and imagination. The original single drop has been expanded to seven and, during the first drop, enormously powerful engines actually pull you down faster than free fall.

You can also enjoy the fleeting view of the whole park and indeed outside the park (a break with Disney tradition) before you begin the terrifying descent. This ride is not to everyone's taste, but die-hard enthusiasts and novices alike pack this ride from the outset.

A triumph of noise over everything else, the **Rock 'n' Roller Coaster® Starring Aerosmith** accelerates you to nearly 60mph in 2.8 seconds in the dark and pulls 5G in the first corkscrew, of which there are several. The pre-show, a rather lame affair, links a recording session of the band Aerosmith to the ride. From here you queue up at two

doors. For those that like the front seats, you can get to these via the lower ramp. Replete with loops, corkscrews and steep drops, the Rock 'n' Roller Coaster® also employs a fully synchronised and very loud soundtrack as it hurls you towards the neon-lit equivalent of oblivion.

Sunset Boulevard houses the entrance to the **Theater of the Stars**, which shows a live stage show at indicated times and combines live action with animation and a great musical score. The shows change periodically. *Beauty and the Beast – Live on Stage* has been showing at this theater for the past several years. Sunset Boulevard is also where you will find the entrance to the outstanding **Fantasmic!** show.

Fantasmic!

This evening show tends to exhaust superlatives. It is, quite simply, the finest event of its kind in Florida. Combining music, lasers, fan fountain projection, animation and a cast of more than a hundred actors and dancers, Fantasmic! manages to choreograph the entire event with split second accuracy to music, fireworks and lighting. Set on an island in a lagoon, the story concerns the ongoing battle between good and evil. Illuminated boats, flying floats and a lake which bursts into flames are but some features of this enchanting event which plays to audiences of 10,000 per showing.

To get a good seat you'll have to be there at least two hours before it starts (alternatively, some restaurants offer a dinner package which includes reserved seating). Even in the quietest time of the off peak season, all 10,000 places are taken up to 30 minutes before the show starts. However, this truly is one event you will never forgive yourself for missing.

The Rock 'n' Roller Coaster® Starring Aerosmith, Sunset Boulevard

Animation Courtyard

The original idea behind Animation Courtyard was not just to give visitors an inside look into the history and process of animation, but also a glimpse at all forthcoming Disney animated films as they were being made. With the shutting down of Disney's animation unit in January 2004, this area of the park is now less popular, but still has features worth visiting.

The **Magic of Disney Animation** is a guided visit with a sole Disney artist and some films exploring Disney's rich history in animated films. The artist does live sketches and the "tour" concludes with the audience – mostly children – sitting at tables and working with the artist to create their own Disney character.

The **Voyage of The Little Mermaid** show is enacted by cartoon, live and Audio-Animatronic® characters. Lasers and water effects are used to create the feel of an underwater grotto. The show remains one of the most popular in the park, appealing to all ages, but young children sometimes find the lightning storm scary. **Disney Junior – Live on Stage!** is also aimed at youngsters and features singing and dancing Disney Junior characters.

Mickey Avenue

Mickey Avenue connects Animation Courtyard to the Disney's Hollywood Studios Backlot tour. The sound stages line the avenue and currently are the premises for **Journey into Narnia: Prince Caspian**. Here, you can step inside the epic Narnia films, with a 15-minute walking tour. Also, look out for Mickey Mouse who may be signing autographs here.

Next door is **Walt Disney: One Man's Dream**. This could be dismissed as propaganda, but it is difficult not to admire Walt's great vision and risk-taking. He would probably be shocked at the size of the company these days, having humbly said: "Never forget, it started because of a mouse."

Although it never fails to be entertaining, the half-hour **Disney's Hollywood Studios® Backlot Tour** best comes to life when a film is actually being shot. A tram ride takes you for a peek at the wardrobe, camera, props, and lighting departments as well as the suburban homes used as outdoor sets for TV shows. The most memorable part is Catastrophe Canyon, where the tram ends up in the midst of a flood and explosions.

The walking part of the tour is more informative. With audience participation, it demonstrates some of the special effects used in making films; battle scenes at sea are re-created using models in a water tank. You also get to look in on three sound stages, where, if you're lucky, a TV show, commercial, or movie might be being filmed.

Streets of America

In this area the streets of New York, San Francisco, Chicago, and other cities are recreated by movie sets, the buildings' façades simply propped up with girders. Washing on the line outside a brownstone, a Chinese laundry, and the Empire State Building (painted in forced perspective to make it appear tall) add authenticity to the city. The streets were once closed to visitors, but you can now wander around freely – even though the set is still used for filming.

Toy Story Pizza Planet is a trumped up arcade made to resemble Andy's favorite hangout. It is packed full of video games and fast food.

If you've got young children, don't miss the imaginative **Honey, I Shrunk the Kids Movie Set Adventure** playground with 30-ft (9-m) high blades of grass, a slide made from a roll of film, and an ant the size of a pony. The tunnels, slides, and other props keep children amused for hours. Being small, the play area can get very crowded, so it's best to go early.

In **Muppet™ Vision 3-D**, a highly enjoyable, slapstick 3-D movie (starring the Muppets), trombones, cars, and rocks launch themselves at you out of the screen; they are so realistic that children often grasp the air expecting to touch something.

Audio-Animatronics characters and special effects, such as a cannon blowing holes in the walls of the theater, provide the fourth dimension.

Eating and Drinking

It is definitely worth going to the trouble of making a reservation at three of the full-service restaurants at Disney's Hollywood Studios®, though more for their atmosphere than their food. You can reserve a table by calling (407) 939-3463/WDW-DINE, or by going directly to the Dining Reservation Booth, at the crossroads of Hollywood and Sunset boulevards, or to the restaurants themselves.

The civilized, costly Hollywood Brown Derby replicates the Original Brown Derby in Hollywood, where the stars met in the 1930s – right down to the celebrities' caricatures on the walls and the house specialties of Cobb Salad and grapefruit cake. Kids usually prefer the Sci-Fi Dine-In Theater Restaurant, a 1950s drive-in where customers sit in mini-Cadillacs under a starry sky to watch old science-fiction movies, while munching on popcorn and burgers. In the '50's Prime Time Café you are served by maternal waitresses in 1950s kitchens with the TV tuned to period sitcoms; the food, such as meatloaf and pot roast, is homey.

The best place to eat without a reservation is the self-service Art Deco-themed cafeteria Hollywood & Vine, where you can choose from a varied buffet that includes pasta, salads, seafood, ribs, and steaks.

For hotels and restaurants in this region see pp314–25 and pp329–49

Echo Lake

The interest here focuses on three shows and one thrill ride, Star Tours, but children also enjoy the sight of a great green dinosaur. The shows reveal tricks of the trade used in making movies and TV shows.

Selected members of the audience act as audio artists or "Foley" artists (Foley is the name of the sound effects system used in Hollywood) in **Sounds Dangerous Starring Drew Carey**. They add thunder, lightning, and other sounds to a short film, which is then played back to the audience. The show is narrated by popular comedic actor Drew Carey who stars as a police detective who goes undercover. The **American Idol Experience** allows visitors to participate in a simulated television show.

Nearby is the **Academy of Television, Arts, and Sciences Hall of Fame**. It features the likenesses of many television legends, who are honored for their outstanding achievements

either in front of or behind the camera. Surrounding Echo Lake are many eating spots that have been designed to look like sets from films.

The storyline of the sensational ride **Star Tours** is based on the *Star Wars* films. Your spaceship, a flight simulator similar to those used to train astronauts, takes a wrong turn and has to evade meteors and cope in an intergalactic battle. What you see on screen seems unbelievably real since your craft jolts in synchronicity with

the action. The large-scale show **Indiana Jones™ Epic Stunt Spectacular!** re-creates well-known scenes from the Indiana Jones movies to deliver lots of big bangs and daredevil feats to thrill the audience. Death-defying stuntmen leap between buildings as they avoid sniper fire and sudden explosions. As an educational sideline, the stunt director and real stunt doubles demonstrate how some of the action sequences are realized. Try to arrive early if you want to take part as an extra in the show.

Shopping

Most of the best shops are on Hollywood Boulevard, which stays open half an hour after the rest of the theme park has closed. Mickey's of Hollywood is the big emporium for general Disney merchandise. Celebrity 5 & 10 has a range of affordable movie souvenirs, such as clapper boards and Oscars®, as well as books and posters. Much pricier is Sid Cahuenga's One-Of-A-Kind, where you can buy rare film and TV memorabilia such as genuine autographed photos (of Boris Karloff and Greta Garbo, for example), or famous actors' clothes. Limited-edition "cels" in Animation Gallery in Animation Courtyard will make an even bigger dent in your wallet; the same shop sells good Disney posters and books too.

Rides, Shows, and Tours Checklist

This chart is designed to help you plan what to visit at Disney's Hollywood Studios®. The rides, shows, and tours are listed in no particular order within each area.

	WAITING TIME	HEIGHT / AGE RESTRICTION	BUSIEST TIME TO RIDE/ATTEND	FASTPASS	MAY CAUSE MOTION SICKNESS	RATING OVERALL
HOLLYWOOD BOULEVARD						
R Great Movie Ride	○		Any			★
SUNSET BOULEVARD						
S Fantasmic	●		Any			◆
R Rock 'n' Roller Coaster® Starring Aerosmith	●	1.2m	➤11	➡	✔	◆
R Twilight Zone Tower of Terror™	●	1.1m	➤11	➡	✔	★
ANIMATION COURTYARD						
T Magic of Disney Animation	◗		Any			◆
S Disney Junior – Live on Stage!	◗		Any			▼
S Voyage of the Little Mermaid	●		Any	➡		◆
MICKEY AVENUE						
T Disney's Hollywood Studios Backlot Tour	◗		Any			★
T Journey into Narnia: Prince Caspian	◗		Any	➡		▼
STREETS OF AMERICA						
S Muppet™ Vision 3-D	●		Any			★
ECHO LAKE						
S Indiana Jones™ Epic Stunt Spectacular!	●		Any			◆
S Sounds Dangerous Starring Drew Carey	◗		Any			▼
R Star Tours	◗	1.1m	➤11	➡	✔	★

Key: Ride – R Show – S Tour – T; Waiting Times Good – ○ Average – ◗ Bad – ●; Overall Rating Good – ▼ Excellent – ◆ Outstanding – ★ Time to Ride: Anytime – Any Before 11am – ➤11

Disney's Animal Kingdom®

The largest of the theme parks, Disney's Animal Kingdom® is five times the size of the Magic Kingdom®. It is rather unique in that it is home to more than 1,700 animals of 250 species, and consequently every visit is likely to be different. The park is loosely based on the real, the mythical, and the extinct and some areas are accessible only through safari-type tours.

Tackling the Park

The park is divided into seven lands: The Oasis, Discovery Island®, Dinoland USA®, Camp Minnie-Mickey, Africa, Asia, and Rafiki's Planet Watch®. Navigation within the park is also quite different from other parks. When you first pass through the turnstiles, you enter **The Oasis** – a foliage festooned area offering several routes to the park's central hub, Safari Village. The Oasis contains many little surprises, most of which are missed by visitors who race through to reach the attractions. Time spent waiting quietly at the various habitats will be well rewarded. For thrill-ride seekers, the park offers few traditional thrills, however, the "rides" they do have are outstanding and get very crowded.

Discovery Island

As you emerge into the open space of the village, the **Tree of Life** looms – this is a massive, 14-story structure that is the signature landmark of the park. It holds sway over a pageant of brightly colored shop fronts and a multitude of pools and gardens, each holding a variety of wildlife. The

Colorful camouflage at Animal Kingdom

main shops, baby care and first aid post all face the Tree of Life.

Under its branches lie the bridges that cross to the other lands and within the trunk itself is the **It's Tough to be a Bug®** show. This 3D theatre presentation is really outstanding and not to be missed.

Camp Minnie-Mickey

Designed primarily for guests to meet Disney characters, this land has some of the park's live stage productions. Lines for the **Camp Minnie-Mickey Greeting Trails** (at the end of which the youngsters can go and meet with the characters) can, predictably, become very long and sometimes become entwined with the lines waiting for the stage shows.

A very popular show, the **Festival of the Lion King** encourages cheering and singing like no other. The show is exceptionally well-choreographed and costumed, and is now housed in an air-conditioned auditorium, a welcome relief in summer. A daily parade that winds through the park, **Mickey's Jammin' Jungle Parade** brings a menagerie of abstract animal images to life in the form of towering animal puppets in fun costumes. Elaborate rickshaw taxis put selected guests in the middle of the parade, while party patrols of "animals" interact with guests and invite them to sing along with the music.

Africa

Entered through the village of Harambe, Africa is the largest of the lands. The architecture is closely modelled on a Kenyan village and conceals Disney cleanliness behind a façade of simple, run-down buildings and wobbly telegraph poles.

The **Kilimanjaro Safaris®** is the park's busiest attraction, though it gets quieter in the afternoon. Guests board open sided trucks driven into an astonishing replica of the East African landscape. During this 20-minute drive over mud holes and creaking bridges you have the opportunity to see many African animals including hippos, rhinos, lions, and elephants, all roaming apparently free and undisturbed. It isn't unusual for a white rhino to get close enough to sniff the truck! Affording an excellent opportunity to see gorillas close up, the **Pangani Forest Exploration Trail®** leads visitors into a world of streams and waterfalls. It can get rather congested with guests exiting the Safaris. It gets less busy in the late afternoon and you can actually spend some time

Animal roaming freely on the Kilimanjaro Safaris®

watching the animals. There are different vantage points to observe families of lowland gorillas foraging through trees and bushes. The pleasant Wildlife Express train ride takes you to **Rafiki's Planet Watch®**, featuring Conservation Station® and Habitat Habit, both educational programs, and Affection Section, a shaded petting yard.

Asia

This land features gibbons, exotic birds, and tigers set in a re-creation of post-colonial Indian ruins. **Kali River Rapids®** offers you a chance to get completely drenched. This short ride presents some of the most striking and detailed surroundings in the park, which you may miss as yet another wave saturates the parts still merely damp.

Tapirs, Komodo dragons and giant fruit bats can be found on the **Maharaja Jungle Trek®**, the climax of which is undoubtedly the magnificent Bengal tigers roaming the palace ruins. Through glazed walled sections of the palace, you can get within arm's length of the tigers.

At the **Flights of Wonder** birds perform fascinating and complex manoeuvres demonstrating the natural survival techniques used by the birds in the wild.

Expedition Everest – Legend of the Forbidden Mountain™ takes passengers on a high-speed train adventure across the rugged terrain and icy slopes of the Himalayas.

Dinoland USA®

This land gives you the chance to witness dinosaurs live and die. On the popular ride **DINOSAUR**, guests board a mobile motion simulator which bucks and weaves trying to ensnare and avoid carnivorous dinosaurs. This is a pretty wild ride, and mostly in the dark – best liked by older children. For family entertainment try **Finding Nemo – The Musical** at the Theater in the Wild, **Primeval Whirl®** or **TriceraTop Spin**, a rollercoaster with spinning cars. There is also **The Boneyard®**, where young children can dig for dinosaur bones.

TOP 10 ATTRACTIONS

① Kilimanjaro Safaris*

② Festival of the Lion King

③ It's Tough to Be a Bug*

④ Kali River Rapids*

⑤ Dinosaur

⑥ Finding Nemo – the Musical

⑦ Flights of Wonder

⑧ Primeval Whirl*

⑨ Triceratop Spin

⑩ Expedition Everest – Legend of the Forbidden Mountain™

Rides, Shows, and Tours Checklist — This chart is designed to help you plan what to visit at Animal Kingdom. The major rides, shows, and tours are listed in no particular order within each area.	WAITING TIME	HEIGHT/AGE RESTRICTION	BUSIEST TIME TO RIDE/ATTEND	FASTPASS	MAY CAUSE MOTION SICKNESS	RATING OVERALL
DISCOVERY ISLAND®						
S It's Tough to Be a Bug®	○		Any	➼		◆
DINOLAND USA®						
R Dinosaur	◗	3 ft 4 in	Any	➼	✔	▼
R Primeval Whirl®	●	4 ft	➤11	➼	✔	◆
R Triceratop Spin	●		➤11		✔	★
S Finding Nemo – the Musical	◗		Any			◆
AFRICA						
R Kilimanjaro Safaris®	●		Any	➼	✔	★
T Pangani Forest Exploration Trail®	●		Any			◆
ASIA						
R Kali River Rapids®	◗	3 ft 2 in	Any	➼	✔	★
S Flights of Wonder	◗		Any			★
T Expedition Everest – Legend of the Forbidden Mountain™	●	3 ft 8 in	➤11	➼	✔	▼
CAMP MINNIE-MICKEY						
S Camp Minnie-mickey Greeting Trails	●		Any			◆
S Festival of the Lion King	◗		Any			★
S Mickey's Jammin' Jungle Parade	○		pm			▼

Key: Ride – R Show – S Tour – T; Waiting Time Good – ○ Average – ◗ Bad – ●; Time to Ride: Anytime – Any Before 11am –➤11; Overall Rating Good – ▼ Excellent – ◆ Outstanding – ★

Water Parks

Walt Disney World® features two of the best water parks in the world, including the second-largest on record. A third water park, River Country – the first to be built in Walt Disney World® – is now closed. While playing second fiddle to the major theme parks of the resort, the water parks manage to attract huge numbers of visitors, particularly during the hot summer months.

Typhoon Lagoon bears only a pretense of a theme, a whimsical pirate/nautical motif that features everything from thrilling slides to winding rapids to gentle rivers. Apart from the chance to snorkel with real sharks and other fish, it's a normal water park, only Disney-fied. On the other hand, Disney's Blizzard Beach is a won-derful working "flooded ski resort" that throws visitors into a "failed" winter wonderland and substitutes flumes and slides for skis and toboggans. This truly clever idea keeps the area covered in "snow" but with nice warm water almost all year round.

Sliding down Mount Gushmore at Blizzard Beach

Blizzard Beach

During a "freak" winter storm – or so the legend goes – an entire section of the Disney property was buried under a pile of powdery snow. Disney Imagineers quickly set to work, building Florida's first ski resort, complete with ski lifts, toboggan runs, and a breathtaking ski slope. How-ever, the snow started to melt quickly, and the Disney people thought all was lost until they spotted an alligator snow-boarding himself down the mountainside. In a flash, they reinvented the ski resort as a water/ski park, Blizzard Beach; they turned luge runs into slides and the mountain into the world's longest and highest flume, and created creeks for inner-tube enthusiasts to paddle around in.

The centerpiece of Blizzard Beach is the 120-ft (36-m) high **Summit Plummet**, which rockets particularly brave visitors at speeds of over 60 mph (96 km/h). Incredibly popular with teenagers, it's a bit too intense for younger children – you must be at least 4 ft (1.2 m) tall to ride it.The Slusher Gusher and Toboggan Racer are similar, but less frightening, water slides. There's also the Snow Stormers flumes and Downhill Double Dipper racing slides, a favorite with families. The Downhill Double Dipper pits two racers against each other in an inner-tube waterslide for big kids, teens, and adults. Race down the parallel flumes to the bottom of Mount Gushmore.

The thrills continue with the **Teamboat Springs** whitewater raft ride, a rollicking race through choppy waters that lasts far longer than you'd expect but leaves you wanting more anyway. The Runoff Rapids is another speedy trip through harrowing water-ways, this time in an inner tube.

For those with a more relaxed agenda, there is the lovely chair lift to carry you up the side of **Mount Gushmore**, where you can go rock-climbing or hiking. Or you may choose to lazily float around the entire park by tubing down Cross Country Creek, or take a slide down the mild Cool Runners. The one-acre pool called Melt-Away Bay is no ordinary swimming hole, as it has waves big enough to ride, and a large, sandy beach with chairs for those who choose to relax and enjoy the sun.

Kids' areas include the Blizzard Beach Ski Patrol Training Camp, aimed at older children, and Tike's Peak for the little ones, which has scaled down versions of the more intense attractions.

Top Tips

- Blizzard Beach and Typhoon Lagoon have their own, free, parking lots; Winter Summerland shares the Blizzard Beach lot. You don't need to wait for Disney transportation if you've got a vehicle – you can drive to the water parks and park right there.

Swimmers head almost straight down Summit Plummet

Typhoon Lagoon

This water park offers less in the way of man-made thrills and more natural excitement, though it features some traditional water park favorites also. Where Blizzard Beach trades on its novelty, Typhoon Lagoon revels in natural beauty and sealife encounters, and boasts a surf pool that is the world's largest, at 650,000 cu ft (18,406 cu m). The park's motif is that of a ship-wreck – the "Miss Tilly" which got caught in a storm so severe it landed on the peak of **Mount Mayday** – in a tropical paradise.

At the top of Mount Mayday, visitors will find three whitewater raft rides of varying intensity – the thrilling Gang Plank Falls, the incredibly high and wild Mayday Falls, or the relatively tame Keelhaul Falls.

Also on Mount Mayday are the body-slide rides known collectively as Humunga-Kowabunga. Great fun but highly intimidating, these rides involve falls of roughly 50 ft (15 m) at speeds of 30 mph (48 km/h). Visitors must be at least 4 ft (1.2 m) tall to ride these. The Storm Slides offer three flumes that go twisting and turning inside the mountain itself; these rides are less intense. Crush 'n' Gusher has torrents of gushing water taking the most daring of raft riders on a gravity-defying

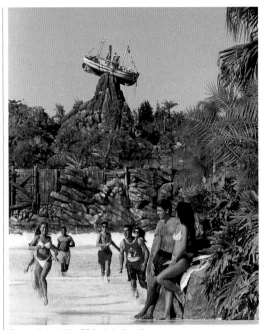

The Wave Pool, with "Miss Tilly" in the backgound

adventure through twisting caverns. More relaxing is the powerful **Wave Pool** which offers 6-ft (1.8-m) high waves alternating with gentler periods. The other peaceful attraction in Typhoon Lagoon is the high-light of the park for adults – the meandering, relaxing, and stunningly beautiful **Castaway Creek**, where you can inner-tube your troubles away through waterfalls, grottoes and rain

forests. Children can enjoy the aquatic playground, Ketchakiddee Creek, and the smaller wave pools. Of special note is the **Shark Reef**, which offers visitors the chance to either observe tropical fish and live, small sharks from the safety of a "overturned freighter" or to grab a snorkel and mask and go one-on-one with them.It's very safe and offers lovely views of the colorful sealife.

Getting up close and personal with sealife at Shark Reef

Winter Summerland

Although Fantasia Gardens, on Buena Vista Drive, was the first themed mini-golf park on Disney property, Winter Summerland is unique in that it continues the motifs of the neighboring water parks, Blizzard Beach and Typhoon Lagoon, but adds a Christmas twist, with two elaborately-designed 18-hole courses – the Winter and Summer courses.The two courses were supposedly built by St.Nick's elves, who were divided into two camps – those who missed the North Pole and those who preferred the Florida heat.

Both courses feature plenty of interactive elements, and are surprisingly challenging. Generally the most popular, the Winter Course is widely perceived as being slightly easier, with "snow" and holiday elements abounding. A few of the holes on each course are identical except for the substitution of sand for snow on the Summer holes. The Summer Course features surfboards, water sprays, and other tropical obstacles, including a sand-buried snoozing Santa. The two courses converge for the final two holes in a log cabin-style lodge.

For hotels and restaurants in this region see pp314–25 and pp329–49

Disney Cruise Line®

With a cruise line that offers four gorgeous, larger-than-average ships, private destinations, and an all-inclusive fare, Walt Disney World® has extended its reach to the high seas of the Caribbean, Mediterranean, Pacific, and Transatlantic cruises. In addition to the popular three- and four-night trips, there are extended itineraries available to passengers, which offer more island ports and longer duration cruises. Disney's Cruise Line® has a pair of powerful incentives no other cruise line can match: apart from its outstanding reputation for quality and comfort, it offers vacations that include stays at Walt Disney World® as part of the total package.

A Disney Cruise Line® ship docked at a pier

A Disney Cruise Line® ship at Castaway Cay

The Ships & the Destination

The four Disney cruise ships, the **Disney Magic®**, the **Disney Wonder®**, the **Disney Dream®** and the **Disney Fantasy®** have staterooms that are around 25 percent larger than those of most other cruise ships. The interiors reflect the stately elegance of European vessels of old, with an Art Deco theme for the Magic and Art Nouveau for the Wonder, and classic early 20th-century design for both the Dream® and the Fantasy®. All ships offer theater, restaurants, spas, and fitness centers among several other amenities.

Castaway Cay, Disney's own private island, is the end point of the Caribbean Disney cruise, and is very much a tropical extension of Walt Disney World®'s hotels and resorts. There are uncrowded beaches, snorkeling, bicycling, glass-bottom boat tours, watersports, and much more on offer. In addition, there is always plenty to do for children on board and off – so much so that you may see very little of them during your trip.

The Short (Three–Four-night) Cruises

The itinerary on the shorter cruises is the same – after arriving at Port Canaveral by charter bus and checking in, you cast off and arrive in Nassau in the Bahamas the next day. The following day you arrive at Castaway Cay, and leave there in the evening to return to Canaveral at 9am the following

morning. The four-night cruise adds a day at sea with the occasional stop in Freeport before returning to Port Canaveral.

The Long (Seven–Fourteen-Night) Cruises

As well as Eastern Caribbean and Western Caribbean cruises, Disney offers European cruises. These take you to seven ports of call across Italy, France, Spain, Tunisia, Malta, and Corsica, or you can see the Northern European capitals on a twelve-night cruise. There are also fourteen-night east and west-bound transatlantic journeys that begin or end in the Bahamas or the Mediterranean.

Tips for Cruisers

- Keep in mind that the all-inclusive fare does not include things such as tips for servers, stateroom hostess, assistant server, and head server. Other additional charges are for soft drinks at the pool, and alcoholic beverages. There is a $10 per person charge for eating in the adults-only specialty restaurant. Shore excursions are also extra significant charges – port charges as well as government taxes are added to the fee.

- It is a good idea to plan ahead for shore excursions to avoid waiting in a line to sign up for them once on the ship and taking a chance. You can log on to the website (see p179) to sign up for shore excursions.

Dining in style at Palo restaurant aboard a Disney ship

Fort Wilderness Resort & Campground

A campground would seem to be at odds with the provide-every-luxury mentality of most Walt Disney World® accommodations, but Fort Wilderness, which opened in 1971, still represents one of Walt Disney's aims – to foster an appreciation of nature and the outdoors. Located on Bay Lake in the Magic Kingdom® resort area, it has more than 750 shaded campsites and over 400 cabins to provide various levels of "roughing it." While wildlife is fairly sparse in this area, amenities and even entertainment are plentiful. The center of Fort Wilderness is Pioneer Hall, home to several restaurants and the hugely popular dinner show, Hoop-De-Do Musical Revue (see p177). There is convenient boat transportation to Magic Kingdom® and motorcoach conveyance to all theme parks.

Riders enjoying a stroll at Fort Wilderness Resort & Campground

A caravan at Disney's Fort Wilderness Resort & Campground

Accommodations & Community Areas

The campsites at Fort Wilderness are small but reasonably secluded, with electric and water "hookups" at all locations. All the cabins offer house-like comfort in confined quarters.

There are 15 air-conditioned "comfort stations" all around the campground, with facilities such as laundries, showers, telephones, and even ice machines, open 24 hours a day. Two "trading posts" offer groceries and rent out recreational equipment.

Recreation

There is plenty to keep visitors happily occupied at Fort Wilderness Resort. The **Tri-Circle D Ranch** has two heated pools, guided horseback tours, and pony rides. Other recreational facilities include tennis, volleyball, and basketball courts, bike and boat rentals, fishing, an exercise trail, nightly wagon rides, horseshoes and shuffleboard, carriage rides, a petting zoo, and video arcades. You can also opt for skiing, parasailing, and wakeboarding. Equipment is usually available for rental. Reservations are required for the guided tours on horse-back or for fishing.

In addition, Fort Wilderness offers a **Campfire** program with singalongs and outdoor movies. Available to all Disney guests – and not just Fort Wilderness residents – the program features an hour of singalongs complete with toasted marshmallows and the American delicacy "s'mores" – melted marshmallow and chocolate on graham crackers. Hosted in part by the Disney chipmunks Chip 'n' Dale, the singalong leads into the screening of a Disney animated feature. An additional attraction is the nighttime **Electrical Water Pageant** (see p177), which goes by Fort Wilderness Resort at 9:45pm. There is a nice all-you-can-eat breakfast buffet at Pioneer Hall.

Sports at Walt Disney World®

Besides Fort Wilderness, all Disney resorts have sports and fitness facilities, though available only for residents. In 1997, **Disney's Wide World of Sports®** complex was opened, primarily as a training camp and athletic haven for exhibition games, Olympic training, and other recreational activities. While the DWWS experience is largely passive, the same cannot be said for what is Disney's most "hands-on" experience to date: **The Richard Petty Driving Experience**, where visitors can train and become NASCAR-style race car drivers, actually driving real race cars at speeds in excess of 100 mph (161 km/h) around a race track. Unlike most Disney experiences, you are in full control of the vehicle. These cars boast over 600 horsepower engines so the thrill is most decidedly real. As might be expected, safety instruction takes top billing for this sport.

Downtown Disney®

Shopping, fine dining, exciting shows, and concerts are on offer at Downtown Disney®, giving visitors plenty to do at Walt Disney World® Resort after the theme parks have closed. Downtown Disney® includes the Marketplace, a lovely outdoor mall with stores and restaurants and West Side, featuring stores, eateries, and concert venues. Pleasure Island was originally the ultimate party zone based around several themed nightclubs and shows, but is being transformed into a family-friendly shopping and dining experience. Downtown Disney® offers free parking and free admission, though some venues, such as DisneyQuest®, a five-story "indoor interactive theme park," charge separate admission, unless you have the Ultimate Park Hopper and Premium Annual passes (see p178). Buses run continually to the on-property resort hotels. Downtown Disney® now has its own iconic attraction, a giant tethered balloon that takes guests 400 ft (122 m) into the air to view the amazing scenery of Walt Disney World® Resort and surrounding Orlando beyond.

is no chance of floating away. Passengers spend approximately 10 minutes enjoying breathtaking 360-degree views of Walt Disney World® Resort and, depending on the weather, there are views of up to 10 miles (16 km) away. The balloon is the world's largest tethered gas balloon, and is attached to a gondola that can hold up to 29 guests and a pilot. Weather permitting, flights operate daily from 9am until midnight and are wheelchair accessible. Flights cost $16 per adult and $10 per child (aged 3–9 years).

West Side

Each store, restaurant, or business on Downtown Disney®'s West Side has a unique feel to it, making for a splendid evening's exploring. Among the do-not-miss shops are the popular **Candy Cauldron** where sweets are made on the spot, the **Dino Store**, where visitors can assemble a plush pet dino at the Build-A-Dino® Workshop®, and the **Ghirardello Ice Cream Shop** from where the famous San-Francisco chocolatier delivers treats galore. There's also the state-of-the-art stadium-seating **AMC 24 Theatres**.

Full-service restaurants here include the popular Cuban and Latin fare of **Bongos Cuban Café** (which features a band and dancing), the gourmet entrées of the upstairs **Wolfgang Puck's Café**, the Southern US cuisine of the **House of Blues** restaurant, and the American food of

Harley-Davidson store at Pleasure Island, Downtown Disney®

Pleasure Island

For more than 20 years Pleasure Island was centered around live entertainment and nightly firework displays. Today, it is filled with shops and eateries while undergoing a facelift scheduled to finish in 2016. **Fuego by Sosa Cigars** combines an upscale lounge with a retail store for cigars and smoking accessories. The **Orlando Harley-Davidson** store offers a huge selection of men's, women's, and children's apparel, gifts, and collectibles. There are two Harley-Davidson motorcycles for guests to sit on, and you can even buy a Harley-Davidson cookbook. **Curl** is a high-end surf shop that offers

surfers a selection of fashionable surfwear clothing and accessories, plus skateboards and surfboards, and there are many other stores besides.

Dining experiences range from the energetic **Raglan Road Irish Pub** or kid-friendly **T Rex Café**, to fine dining at **Fulton's Crab House** or casual Italian at **Portobello**.

Characters in Flight

Visitors can take to the skies from Downtown Disney® in an illuminated balloon with handpainted silhouettes of a dozen of Disney's famous "flying characters" such as Mary Poppins, Aladdin, and Dumbo. The giant balloon, operated by **Aérophile**, is tethered so there

Downtown Disney® West Side glittering in the evening

Pirates of the Caribbean: Battle for Buccaneer Gold at DisneyQuest®

movie-memorabilia-studded **Planet Hollywood**. Quick bites can be obtained from **Wetzel's Pretzels**, featuring hot pretzels and cold Häagen-Dazs ice cream, and the lower level of Wolfgang Puck's Café, which serves brick-oven pizzas and salads. The West Side has three special attractions that require separate admissions: the House of Blues concert hall (part of the national chain, which attracts major music acts), the breathtaking **Cirque du Soleil®** show **La Nouba**TM, and the electronic funhouse called **DisneyQuest®**.

La Nouba™ show at Cirque du Soleil®

In addition to regular shows by national artists, with a side stage for smaller acts, the House of Blues offers a Sunday Gospel Brunch that features live gospel performers showing off their uniquely American religious singing. The Cirque du Soleil® show, which is a theatrical production based on a circus, is so popular that it is always sold out. This fabulous show has 64 performers on stage at the same time, performing a variety of gymnastic feats. Reservations are a must. DisneyQuest® is extremely popular with teens and younger kids and features state-of-the-art video arcades, virtual reality experiences, and other computer-driven and 3-D "interactivities" along with an assortment of traditional arcade games such as Skee-ball, Mario Kart, and Pac-Man. Among the best of the various "zone" offerings are the virtual reality "rides" for which you wear a special helmet with glasses, such as **Aladdin's Magic Carpet Ride**, **Ride the Comix**, and **Invasion!**, along with the two-man shooter rides such as **Pirates of the Caribbean: Battle for Buccaneer Gold**.

Marketplace

An open-air mall with some excellent shops and a good variety of restaurants, the Marketplace makes for a relaxing walk when you're not pressed for time. Among the highlights, especially for children, is the **LEGO Imagination Center**, which features photo-op displays of wonderful LEGO constructions, from a spaceship to a dragon in the pond next to the store. Also of interest to kids will be the **Once Upon a Toy** and **Disney's Days of Christmas** stores. Kids and adults alike will be awed by the sheer size of the **World of Disney** emporium, the largest Disney memorabilia store in the world and the "mother lode" for all Disney souvenirs. Restaurants include the colorful **Rainforest Café**, **Fulton's Crab House** with its superb seafood and riverboat ambience, and **Ghirardelli's Soda Fountain & Chocolate Shop** with its malt-shop atmosphere. Quick bites can be found at **Cap'n Jack's** floating restaurant and the **McDonald's**, **Wolfgang Puck Express**, and **Earl of Sandwich** chain eateries.

After Dark Events

Apart from the Downtown Disney® attractions, other prime after-dark entertainment includes **dinner shows** and the **Electrical Water Pageant**. A floating parade that wanders around park resorts such as Polynesian and Contemporary, the Electrical Water Pageant is best viewed from the unobstructed beach in Fort Wilderness. This kids' favorite showcases 20 minutes of dazzling electrical animation – dolphins jumping out of the water, whales swimming by, even a fire-breathing dragon. Around since 1971, it often serves as an opening act or postscript for the Magic Kingdom® and Epcot® fireworks. Disney's two long-running dinner shows, Hoop-Dee-Doo Musical Revue and Disney's Spirit of Aloha, should not tempt visitors to leave the theme parks early but they are still enjoyable. The first is a popular Western comedy show at Fort Wilderness' Pioneer Hall; the second features authentic Polynesian music, dance, and food. Another show, Mickey's Backyard BBQ, provides country 'n' western fun.

The superbly constructed LEGO dragon at the Marketplace

Essential Information

Spread over a large area of 47 sq miles (121 sq km) and brimming with attractions, Walt Disney World® Resort can provide entertainment for the whole family for at least a week. Guests who do not have much holiday time need to plan carefully to make the most of their visit to this dream vacationland. The information here is geared toward aiding them in this task.

When to Visit

The busiest times of the year are Christmas, the last week of February until Easter, and June to August. At these times, the parks begin to approach capacity – some 90,000 people a day in Magic Kingdom® alone. All the rides will be operating and the parks are open for longer periods. During off-season, 10,000 guests a day might visit the Magic Kingdom®, only one water park may be operating, and certain attractions may be closed for maintenance. The weather is also a factor – in July and August, hot and humid afternoons are regularly punctuated by torrential thunderstorms. Between October and March, however, the temperatures and humidity are both much more comfortable and permit a more energetic touring schedule.

Busiest Days

Each of the theme parks is packed on certain days. The busiest days are as follows: Magic Kingdom®: Monday, Thursday, and Saturday. Epcot®: Tuesday, Friday, and Saturday. Disney's Hollywood Studios®: Wednes-day and Sunday. Note, however, that after a thunderstorm, the water parks are often almost empty – even at the peak times of the year.

Opening Hours

When the theme parks are busiest, opening hours are the longest, typically 9am to 10–11pm or midnight. In less busy periods, hours are usually 9am to 6–8pm. Call to check. The parks open at least 30 minutes early for pass holders and guests at any of the WDW hotels and resorts.

Length of Visit

To enjoy Walt Disney World® to the full, you may want to give Magic Kingdom® and Epcot® two full days – or one and half days, with half a day at a water park – each, leaving a day for Disney's Hollywood Studios® and Animal Kingdom®. Set aside three nights to see Fantasmic!, IllumiNations, and Wishes firework displays.

The Ideal Schedule

To avoid the worst of the crowds and the heat:
• Arrive as early as possible and visit the most popular attractions first.
• Take a break in the early afternoon, when it's hottest and the parks are full.
• Return to the parks in the cool of the evening to see parades and fireworks.

Tickets & Types of Passes

There are several customized package plans available. Start with a base ticket, called **Magic Your Way**. This gives each member of your travel party entry to one theme park every ticketed day. The longer you stay, the less you pay per day. You can then add on up to three options. The **Park Hopper®** lets you come and go through multiple parks and gives you extra visitor hours. **Water Park Fun & More** includes your choice of two water parks, Disney-Quest® Indoor Interactive Theme Park, Disney's Wide World of Sports® Complex, or a round of golf at Disney's Oak Trail Golf Course. The **No Expiration** option allows you to return in the future to take advantage of unused days, whereas the Magic Your Way base tickets expire in 14 days. See http://disneyworld.disney.

go.com/tickets-passes for options and pricing. Non-Disney guests visiting for more than ten days should consider the **Annual Pass** or the **Premium Annual Pass**, which costs little more than a seven-day Park Hopper. Separate Annual Passes are offered by the water parks and DisneyQuest®. Child ticket pricing applies to ages three through nine.

Passes are available at Disney stores, the airport, the Tourist Information Center on I-Drive, and the official Disney website. In addition, passes are sometimes included in package deals.

Getting Around

An extensive, efficient transportation system handles an average of 200,000 guests each day. Even if you stay outside Walt Disney World® Resort, many nearby hotels offer free shuttle services to and from the theme parks, but you can check this when you make your reservation.

The transportation hub of Walt Disney World® is the **Ticket and Transportation Center (TTC)**. Connecting it to the Magic Kingdom® are two monorail services. A third monorail links the TTC to Epcot®. Ferries run from the TTC to the Magic Kingdom® across the Seven Seas Lagoon.

Ferries connect the Magic Kingdom® and Epcot® with the resorts in their respective areas, while buses link everything in Walt Disney World®, including direct links to the Magic Kingdom®. All ticket holders can use the entire transportation system for free.

Although Disney transportation is efficient, you may wish to rent a car if you want to enjoy the entire area without inconvenience. The theme parks are spread out and, especially for visits to swimming attractions such as Blizzard Beach and Typhoon Lagoon, Disney transportation is not always the best option for children. Young children who are wet and tired from swimming will not welcome waiting for the Disney bus.

Coping with Lines

Lines tend to be shortest at the beginning and end of the day, and during parade and meal times. Lines for the rides move slowly, but the wait for a show is rarely longer than the show itself. The **Fastpass** allows visitors to reserve time at 25 of the most popular attractions rather than wait in long lines. Disney parks fill rapidly after the first hour of opening. Until then, you can usually just walk onto rides for which you'll have to line up later.

Disabled Travelers

Wheelchairs can be borrowed at the park entrance and special bypass entrances allow disabled guests and carers to board rides without waiting in line. Staff, however, are not allowed to lift guests or assist with lifting for safety reasons.

Very Young Children

As Walt Disney World® can be physically and emotionally tiring for children, try to adapt your schedule accordingly. If you've come with pre-school-age kids, focus on Magic Kingdom®.

The waiting and walking involved in a theme park visit can exhaust young children quickly so it's a good idea to rent a stroller, available at every park entrance. Each stroller is personalized when you rent it, but if it should go missing when you leave a ride, you can get a replacement with your rental receipt. Baby Care Centers for changing and feeding are located all around the parks.

In a system called "switching off," parents can enjoy a ride one at a time while the other parent stays with the child – without having to line up twice.

Meeting Mickey

For many youngsters, the most exciting moment at WDW Resort is meeting the Disney characters. You will spot them in all the theme parks, but you can have more relaxed encounters in a number of restaurants, usually at breakfast. Each theme park and many of the resorts also offer "character dining," though you must call well ahead of time to make a reservation.

Safety

The resort's excellent safety record and first rate security force mean problems are rare and dealt with promptly. Cast members watch out for young unaccompanied children and escort them to lost children centers. Bags of all visitors are checked.

Staying & Dining

Lodging in the Disney-run hotels and villa complexes is of a very high standard. However, even the lowest-priced places are more expensive than many hotels outside Walt Disney World®. But do keep in mind that, apart from Disney quality, your money also buys:
• Early entry into the theme parks (up to 60 minutes).
• Guaranteed admission to the theme parks even when the parks are otherwise full.
• The delivery of shopping purchases made anywhere in Walt Disney World® Resort.

For dining at any full-service restaurant in Walt Disney World®, especially in Epcot®, book a Priority Seating – the table booking equivalent of the Fastpass.

For more information, see pages 144–51 and 154–61.

Parking

Visitors to Magic Kingdom® must park at the TTC and make their way by tram or foot; Epcot®, Disney's Hollywood Studios®, and Animal Kingdom® have their own parking lots. Parking is free for Disney resort residents – others must pay, but only once a day no matter how many times they move their vehicle. The lots are very large, so it's important to remember the character name and row of the section where you are parked.

DIRECTORY

General

Accommodation Information/ Reservation
Tel (407) 939-6244.

Dining Reservations (including Dinner Shows)
Tel (407) 939-3463. Operational 7am–11pm Sat–Sun.

Disney Tours
Tel (407) 939-8687.

Golf Reservations
Tel (407) 939-4653.

General Information
Tel (407) 939-6244.
W disneyworld. disney.go. com/wdw

Theme Parks & Attractions

Blizzard Beach
Tel (407) 560-3400.

Disney Cruise Line®
Tel (800) 939-2784.
W disneytravelagents.com

Disney's Animal Kingdom®
Tel (407) 938-3000.

Disney's Hollywood Studios®
Tel (407) 824-4321.

Disney's Wide World of Sports®
Tel (407) 939-4263.

Downtown Disney®
Tel (407) 828-3800.

Epcot®
Tel (407) 934-7639.

Fort Wilderness Resort & Campground
Tel (407) 824-2900.

Magic Kingdom®
Tel (407) 934-7639.

The Richard Petty Driving Experience
Tel (407) 939-0130.

Typhoon Lagoon
Tel (407) 939-6244.

❷ SeaWorld® and Discovery Cove®

In scale and sophistication, the world's most popular marine-life adventure park, opened in 1973. While eager to promote its educational, research, and conservation programs, the park delivers out-and-out entertainment too. SeaWorld®'s answer to the Disney mouse is Shamu, actually several orcas. This unique water park combines refreshing lagoons, waterfalls, beaches, and lush, tropical land-scapes with extreme, high-speed thrill slides. Discovery Cove®, an all-inclusive park, gives guests the opportunity to swim with dolphins, rays, and other fascinating sea animals. Following an unfortunate accident, SeaWorld® has recently faced controversy over its display of the giant killer whales with their trainers.

Thrillseekers hanging onto Kraken, an award-winning rollercoaster ride at SeaWorld*

Tackling the Park

SeaWorld® is usually less crowded than Orlando's other theme parks. Most of the presentations are walk through exhibits or sit down stadium shows. The stadiums seat so many that finding a good spot is seldom a problem and you will normally get a good seat by arriving 15 minutes before the show starts. Bear in mind that if you sit near the front you may get wet. SeaWorld®'s more gentle pace means that visiting after 3pm affords a cooler and less crowded experience. It is also worth noting that the shows are timed so that it's all but impossible to leave one show just in time for another. This is done to reduce crowding but it is possible to get a seat in the Clyde and Seamore (Sea Lion and Otter) show by leaving from the Shamu stadium four minutes early (while the performers are taking their bows.) At peak times, find a seat early for the Sea Lion and Otter show, performed in a small stadium, and see Wild Arctic, Shark Encounter, Journey to Atlantis and Kraken early in the day as they get very crowded later on.

Young children enjoy meeting the actors in furry suits who play the parts of Shamu and Crew – a killer whale accompanied by a penguin, pelican, dolphin, and an otter. You can normally find them near SeaWorld®'s exit at around closing time. For an overview of the park and a great view, take the six-minute ride up the 400-ft (122-m) Sky Tower.

Shamu, the park's official mascot

If you have any problems or queries, go to Guest Relations, situated near the exit gate.

Attractions

Three meticulously landscaped outdoor habitats, including two that allow you to feed and pet the marine life, are incorporated in **Key West at SeaWorld®**. Dolphin Cove, a wave pool in the style of a Caribbean beach, offers underwater viewing of Bottlenose dolphins and the chance to pat and even feed them. You can also touch magnificent stingrays, of which there are around 200 in Stingray Lagoon; stroking them is more enjoyable than it sounds. Turtle Point is home to rescued loggerhead, hawksbill, and green sea turtles, which are too injured to survive on their own in the wild.

TOP 10 ATTRACTIONS

① Kraken

② Shark Encounter

③ Journey to Atlantis

④ Wild Arctic

⑤ Antarctica: Empire of the Penguin

⑥ One Ocean

⑦ Clyde and Seamore Take Pirate Island

⑧ Key West at Seaworld

⑨ Blue Horizons

⑩ Manta

A close encounter at Key West at SeaWorld®

For hotels and restaurants in this region see pp314–25 and pp329–49

Pacific Point Preserve
re-creates the rugged north Pacific coast in the form of a large, rocky pool. Here, you can watch harbor seals, South American fur seals, and Californian sea lions (the ones making the noise) basking on the rocks and gliding elegantly through the water.

Most of the other wildlife at SeaWorld is viewed through glass. **Manatee Rescue**, which was named best zoological exhibit in the country by The American Zoological Association, offers a splendid underwater view of these ungainly, doleful

A'Lure, the Call of the Ocean

A'Lure, The Call of the Ocean is a popular addition to SeaWorld"'s impressive collection of water-themed shows. The stuff of legend is combined with spectacular special effects to tell the tale of the mysterious sea sirens, who for centuries have lured fishermen into their underwater lairs with their hypnotic powers and extraordinary beauty. Athletic performers and gravity-defying acrobatics add a touch of breathtaking magic to this captivating mariner's story.

and irresistibly appealing herbi-vores *(see p254)*. The exhibit is strongly educational and includes a film show.

In the altogether more upbeat **Antarctica: Empire of the Penguin**, audience members enter mobile simulators offering two levels of exploration – Wild Expedition or Mild Expedition – for different degrees of ride intensity, and follow the fictional adventures of Penguin Puck before emerging into an icy colony of 250 Adelie, Gentoo, King, and Rockhopper penguins.

Billed as the world's largest collection of dangerous sea creatures, **Shark Encounter** is understandably popular. Moray eels, barracuda, and pufferfish are the hors d'oeuvre, but the main attraction is the large quantity of sharks. You can either view them underwater by walking through a long acrylic tunnel inside their aquarium or up-close in the interactive program **Sharks Deep Dive**. Visitors can either snorkel or scuba dive in a protective shark-cage, which is immersed underwater, with over 50 different species of

Amazing dolphins are put through their paces

sharks, including sand tigers, sand bars, Atlantic and Pacific black tips. A wetsuit is provided and participants must be over ten years old.

Aquatica successfully captures the essence of an aquatic paradise, with over 3 million gallons of water in lagoons, rivers, and racing rides. Vibrant flora represents exotic destinations from all around the world.

Wild Arctic is a high-tech ride simulating a helicopter flight through blizzards and avalanches with real walruses, beluga whales, and polar bears.

Top Tips

- SeaWorld® allows guests to feed many of the animals, but restrict both the type and amount of food, which has to be purchased from them. If this is something you would like to do, check with guest services as soon as you enter the park for feeding times and food availability.
- Build your schedule around the four main presentations: One Ocean, A'Lure, Sea Lion and Otter, and Blue Horizons show.
- Bring a waterproof plastic bag for your camera as – especially during the One Ocean and Blue Horizons shows – people on the first 12 rows can get splashed by corrosive salt water.
- Journey to Atlantis is guaranteed to get you wet, so reserve this particular visit for the hottest part of the day.

Seaworld®'s Serious Side

The buzzwords at the nonprofit Hubbs SeaWorld® Research Institute are Research, Rescue, and Rehabilitation – the "three Rs." Florida's SeaWorld® has helped thousands of whales, dolphins, turtles, and manatees in difficulty. The animals are nursed and, if necessary, operated on in the park's rehabilitation center. Those that recover sufficiently are released back into the wild. SeaWorld® runs several popular tours, which offer a glimpse of this work. The Sharks! tour, for example, takes you behind the scenes at Shark Encounter. Inquire at Guest Relations when you enter the park.

A green turtle, one of the animals rehabilitated at SeaWorld®

VISITORS' CHECKLIST

Practical Information
Road map E2. Orange Co. 7007 SeaWorld Drive, intersection of I-4 and Bee Line Expressway.
Tel (407) 351-3600. 🅿️ ♿ 🚻
📷 🅦 sea world.com

Transport
🚌 8, 42 from Orlando.
Open 9am–7pm daily; until 11pm in summer.

Dolphin Cove®, where everyone can touch and feed the dolphins

You arrive at Base Station Wild Arctic, created around an old expedition ship, and encounter the animals that live there: polar bears, walruses, harbor seals, and beluga whales. SeaWorld®'s **Journey to Atlantis**, a water coaster with a mytho-logical twist, and **Kraken**, a winner of the annual Orlando roller-coaster competition, are hot tickets, as is **Manta**, another roller-coaster ride.

Discovery Cove®, adjacent to SeaWorld® and separately ticketed, is a reservations-only park (see p183) and worth a one-day visit of its own.

Shows and Tours

One Ocean is a production that features SeaWorld®'s entire family of majestic killer whales performing awe-inspiring choreography to music from a state-of-the-art sound system. The elaborate three-story set features an immense, iconic whale tail, panoramic LED screens, and hundreds of surround-sound speakers. The whales interact with trainers and their audience amid fountains, underwater imagery, and colored lights – a truly sensational spectacle that will delight viewers of all ages. If you don't mind getting wet, sit in the soak zone for the closest view of the whales.

This multi-sensory celebration of life under the sea, which lasts just over 20 minutes, is performed to an original contemporary orchestral score, consisting of three different songs.

Blue Horizons is a theatrical spectacular that showcases graceful dolphins and false killer whales, a rainbow of exotic birds, and an entire cast of world-class divers and aerialists wearing elaborate costumes. The vivid imagination of a young girl sets the stage for an emotional adventure to experience both the power of the sea and the elegance of flight. The show is filled with action both above and below water, as the cast members plunge off the set with amazing aerial artistry.

The **Clyde and Seamore Take Pirate Island** show, held in the Sea Lion and Otter Stadium, features two sea lions (Clyde and Seamore), otters, and walrus in a swash-buckling adventure of lost loot, pirate ships, and hilarity on the high seas.

Odyssea is a non-traditional circus that combines high-flying acrobatic performances, delightful comedy, and fantastic special effects within a spectacular set themed as an underwater fantasy world. Over a half-hour period you are transported from the surface of the sea to the depths of the ocean. On the way you encounter an Antarctic landscape with penguin characters, a contortionist inside a giant seashell, and enormous worms performing rhythmic dance. This show promises to enchant, and delight guests of all ages. **Pets Ahoy** features talented cats, birds, dogs, and pigs, most of which have been rescued from animal shelters.

The **Adventure Express Tour** offers exclusive guided park tours, reserved seats, feeding opportunities, and back-door access to rides.

Sea lions basking on the rocks at Pacific Point Preserve

Eating, Drinking, and Shopping

The Waterfront at SeaWorld™ is a world-class dining, entertainment, and shopping area spread over 5 acres (2 ha). Guests may choose from nine restaurants, ranging from full-service to cafeteria-style. They include The Seafire Inn, which offers stir-fried dishes and hosts the Makahiki Luau show; the Sandbar pub, which serves sushi and martinis; and the Spice Mill, which features international cuisine. The Dine with Shamu restaurant, located at Shamu Stadium, allows guests to eat alongside killer whales, while at Sharks Underwater Grill, guests eat just inches away from sharks. The shops at The Waterfront include Allura's Treasure Trove, where kids design their own porcelain dolls, and Under The Sun, which offers knick-knacks and several collectibles.

For hotels and restaurants in this region see pp314–25 and pp329–49

Exploring Discovery Cove®

Just across the road from its big sister, SeaWorld®, Discovery Cove® is a quiet revolution in terms of Florida's Theme parks. With a capacity of only 1,000 guests a day (the car park is limited to only 500 cars) and an entry price that makes all but lottery winners blink, the park offers some unforgettable experiences, the most vaunted of which is an opportunity to swim with Atlantic Bottlenose dolphins. Although expensive, forgoing the Dolphin experience can reduce the cost of a visit by half. However, Discovery Cove® represents many people's lifelong dreams and is extremely popular. Another popular attraction is an underwater walking tour around the Coral Reef, among schools of fish and rays. It is advisable to book tickets well in advance.

Top Tips

- Don't put any sunscreen on before you visit as the price includes Discovery Cove®'s own "fish friendly" screen, the only sun screen allowed.
- You don't need to be an expert swimmer for the Dolphin experience – just comfortable in the water. You will be given a flotation jacket which you must wear in any case.
- The Dolphin pool is cooler than the rest so a wet suit is provided if you are too cold.
- Make sure at least one person in your group has a watch on at all times as it is otherwise easy to forget your Dolphin time slot.
- It's a good idea to split your group into two in order to be able to take your own photographs and avoid the high charges of the resident photographers.

Swimming with dolphins, the highlight of a visit to Discovery Cove®

Tackling the Park

Discovery Cove® abounds with lush vegetation, thatched beach huts, and waterfalls. Intimate and beautifully constructed, you may be forgiven for thinking that the park is your own private island. The level of service here also reflects that of any good hotel.

The package prices ($289 plus tax per person, no child reductions) include the Dolphin experience (children below 6 are not allowed to participate), parking, all equipment, a free snorkel, one main meal and 14 days unlimited admission to Sea World or Busch Gardens Tampa Bay. Reservations are required and entry to the park is through a "hotel" reception where you are greeted by a personal guide, given a photo ID card and taken on a familiarisation tour. There are free lockers and towels and an almost concierge-like feel to the service.

Attractions

Inside the park there are five main areas: Coral Reef, the Aviary, Ray Lagoon, the Tropical River and Dolphin Lagoon. Coral Reef abounds with grottos and a ship wreck, as well as affording the opportunity to swim alongside threateningly large sharks separated from you by a substantial transparent plexiglass wall. In the park's encircling 'river', guests enter an aviary and can feed the birds with food provided by the staff whilst in Ray Lagoon guests can snorkel quietly over large rays, which can grow up to 5 ft (1.5 m) long. At the Dolphin Lagoon, 15-minute orientation is followed by 30 minutes wading and swimming with these magnificent and highly intelligent mammals. Although cameras are not allowed here it is worth considering splitting your party for the Dolphin experience as that will enable you to take photos of each other from the shore. There are waterfalls, bathing pools and little niches throughout the park connected by beaches. There is only one restaurant, which is self service, but the food standard is high. Cameras are welcome but guests are asked to remove jewelry and other impedimenta so as to avoid distracting the sea life. Guests with disabilities are welcome and specially-made outdoor wheelchairs with oversized tires for easy maneuvering on the beach are also offered.

Aerial view of Discovery Cove®

❸ Universal Orlando®

Once a single movie park, competing with the other area attractions, Universal Orlando® now boasts two major theme parks, a village and entertainment complex, and four resorts. Together, Universal Studios Florida®, Universal's Islands of Adventure®, and Universal CityWalk® present a formidable reason to spend at least some time away from Disney. Situated off exits 75A or B from I4, Universal's car parking takes the multi-storey approach, bringing guests through Universal CityWalk® on a series of moving walkways to a fork where they choose between the two parks.

Universal Globe marking the entrance to Universal Studios Park®

Tackling the Parks

The busiest times of the year at Universal Studios Orlando® are the same as at Walt Disney World® *(see p178)*.

When the parks are open until late, two full days are just about long enough to see everything at the two parks. When the parks close early – the only disadvantage of visiting in off season – you really need three or four days. Those staying for longer can opt for one of Universal's multi-day packages, which offer cost-effective admission to the parks and CityWalk® as well as several discounts.

Lines at Universal can be even longer and slower moving than at Walt Disney World®, especially since the opening of the Harry Potter section at the Islands of Adventure®. You may have to wait for up to two hours for the best rides. At peak times, combat lines by arriving early (the gates open an hour before the official opening time) and do as many of the popular rides *(see p185)* as possible before it gets too busy. You won't be able to do them all early, so ride the others just before the park closes. You are unlikely to have to wait

very long for shows but you should arrive 15 minutes early in tourist season to make sure of getting a seat. Those shows with no displayed schedule run continuously and you will rarely have to wait longer than the show's duration. Note that lines for rides near the big shows grow considerably when the performances end. Another way of combating the lines is by purchasing the Universal Express Pass, which allows visitors to make a reservation at an attraction and skip the line.

Most rides are likely to be too intense for very young children and of course some have minimum height restrictions; the exception to this is ET Adventure®. The attractions designed to appeal to youngsters are Despicable Me Minion Mayhem, Flight of the Hippogriff, E.T. Adventure, Pteranodon Flyers, Woody Woodpecker's Nuthouse Coaster®, Animal Actors on LocationSM, and Seuss and Jurassic Park Islands in Islands of Adventure®.

On a very busy day, you might like to indulge in one of the VIP Tours, which can last up to eight hours. This provides priority admission to at least one of the parks, as well as a walk around backstage areas and access to production facilities and sound stages.

If you stay at one of Universal's resorts, you can use your room key for more than just accessing your room. It is an express pass, giving priority seating at many attractions and can be used like a credit card throughout the park.

Live Filming

While there is no guarantee that you will be able to see live filming on the day that you visit Universal Studios Florida®, there is a chance that cameras may be rolling on the backlot (within the theme park itself).

It is more probable, especially from September to December, that you could be in the audience for the taping of a TV show. It is possible to call ahead to check which shows are being filmed during your visit: call (407) 224-4233. Tickets for shows are issued on a first come first served basis (on the day of filming) at the Studio Audience Center located near Guest Services. It's wise to go there as soon as you enter the park to be sure of getting tickets.

Board showing the shooting schedule

The imposing entrance archway to Universal Studios Florida®

Despicable Me characters pose for photos outside the Minion Mayhem attraction

Universal Studios Florida®

The entrance to Universal Studios Florida® is known as **Front Lot** because it is made to look like the front lot of a working Hollywood film studio from the 1940s. The shooting schedule notice board near the turnstiles, with details of shows being filmed, is real enough, however.

Immediately inside the park, the palm-lined Plaza of the Stars has several shops *(see p187)*, but do not linger here on arrival: instead you should head off immediately to the main attractions before the lines reach their peak.

Production Central is the least aesthetic section of the park. Maps show the studios' main sound stages here, but these are actually off limits to those not on a VIP Tour.

Despicable Me takes visitors into the high-tech empire of Gru, one of the great super-villains of animation. After being transformed into mischievous Minions, guests set out on a 3-D

Poster showing Shrek 4-D™ mesmerizing its audience

VISITORS' CHECKLIST

Practical Information
Road map E2. Orange Co. 1000 Universal Studios Plaza, exits 29 or 30B on I-4. **Tel** (407) 363-8000.
Open minimum opening hours 9am–6pm daily; extended evening opening in summer and on public hols. 🅰 🅑 🅒 🅓
Ⓦ **universalorlando.com**

Transport
🚌 21, 37, 40 from Orlando.

digital adventure with characters from the film – Gru and his adopted daughters Agnes, Edith, and Margo – and descend into Gru's secret lab. There, guests join a Minion-inspired, interactive dance party.

Shrek 4-D™ is a fun-packed ride which includes a 13- minute 3D movie starring the voices of Cameron Diaz, Eddie Murphy, John Lithgow, and Mike Myers. "OgreVision" glasses enable you to see, hear, and almost feel the action right in your seat.

Production Central also houses shops and restaurants, including the Universal Studios® Store.

New York

This area has more than 60 façades, some of which replicate real buildings, others which reproduce those that have appeared only on screen. There are cut-outs of the Guggenheim Museum and New York Public Library, cleverly creating an illusion of depth and distance. Macy's, the famous department store, is there, as is Louie's Italian Restaurant, where a shootout took place in the original

Godfather movie. The storefronts, warehouses, and even the cobblestones have been painted to appear old in a process called "distressing."

Head down to Delancey Street where Jake and Elwood perform a medley of their biggest hits in **The Blues Brothers**, a 20-minute live music stage show.

Another reality ride at New York is the state-of-the-art **Revenge of The Mummy – The Ride®**. The thrill ride is based on the phenomenally popular *Mummy* films and uses high-speed roller coaster engineering and space age robotics to propel riders through Egyptian sets, passageways and catacombs. The attraction includes an animated figure of the fearsome Mummy that thrills and frightens with its life-like movements.

Twister…Ride It Out® puts visitors right inside the action movie about storm chasers hunting a destructive tornado. It pits you against the ferocious winds, deafening roar, and heart-stopping intensity of Mother Nature at her wildest. Inside a huge compound, the special effects masters of Universal have con-structed a simulated tornado that consumes everything in its path. Watch it shatter windows, crush enormous signs, and hurl trucks as if they were toys, while you stand within 20 ft (6 m) of the five-story-high funnel of wind.

Braving the force of a simulated tornado in Twister…Ride It Out®

Hollywood Boulevard, a fine example of the park's superbly created sets

Hollywood

Hollywood Boulevard and Rodeo Drive are the most attractive streets in Universal Studios. While ignoring actual geography, these sets pay tribute to Hollywood's golden age from the 1920s to the 1950s.

The Brown Derby was a restaurant shaped like a hat where the film glitterati once congregated; Universal's own version is a fun hat shop. Schwab's Pharmacy, where hopefuls hung out sipping sodas and waiting to be discovered, is brought back to life as an old-fashioned ice-cream parlor. Notice, too, the Hollywood Walk of Fame, with the names of stars embedded in the sidewalk, just as in the real Hollywood Boulevard.

Transformers™: The Ride-3-D is the ultimate next-generation ride for thrill-seekers. It uses 1460-ft (18-m) custom-built screens to take the 3-D-glasses-wearing audience into the Decepticon-versus-humanity war, as they hurtle along a 2,000-ft (610-m) long track.

The top attraction in Hollywood is **Terminator 2®: 3-D**. This exciting ride also uses the latest in 3-D film technology and robotics, together with explosive live stunts, to catapult the audience into the action alongside the star of the *Terminator* films, Arnold Schwarzenegger.

Men in Black™ – Alien Attack™

Lucy – A Tribute^{SM} displays memorabilia of the Queen of Comedy, Lucille Ball, one of the world's favorite stage and television stars. This tribute includes the "I Love Lucy" set and the den of her Beverly Hills home, which have been meticulously re-created. There are scripts, clips, and costumes from the hit TV show, and there's even an interactive game for any trivia buffs so that they can test their Lucy knowledge.

Universal Horror Make-Up Show offers a fascinating, behind-the-scenes look at the skill of the make-up artist, and how the movie industry uses incredible make-up to create the most amazing scary monsters and creepy effects.

Woody Woodpecker's Kid Zone

Everyone should ride the enchanting, if rather tame, **ET Adventure®** based on Steven Spielberg's 1982 movie. You are off to ET's home planet on a flying bicycle, soaring over a twinkling cityscape.

In **Animal Actors on Location**^{SM}, animal look-alikes take the parts of canine superstars such as Lassie and Beethoven.

A Day in the Park with Barney™ appeals only to young children. Set in a magical park, it features a lovable Tyrannosaurus Rex called Barney from the top pre-school age TV show.

Fievel's Playland^{SM} is inspired by the popular animated films *An American Tail* and *An American Tail: Fievel Goes West*. Fievel is a mouse, and the playground's props, such as a cowboy hat, boots, glasses, and a tea cup, are oversized – just as they would seem to the film's star.

Woody Woodpecker's Nuthouse Coaster® is a gentle, child-friendly introduction to the world of amusement rides and is fun for younger kids.

Curious George Goes to Town^{SM} has lots of water to splash in and hundreds of foam balls.

Universal's Transformers™: The Ride-3-D, a state-of-the-art attraction

World Expo

The inspiration behind World Expo's architecture is the Los Angeles 1984 Olympic Games and Expo '86 in Vancouver. The focus here is on the rides and shows.

Men In Black™ – Alien Attack™ is an addictive ride in which you join Will Smith in a four-person simulator battling aliens using laser weapons and smoke bombs. Each person has their own cannon, and the scores reflect the team's ability to destroy aliens on a massive scale.

The Simpsons Ride™ transports visitors into the middle of Springfield, the Simpsons' hometown. The ride is the main attraction in a new area of World Expo, where guests can enjoy a drink at Moe's, grab a sandwich at Krusty Burger, or drop in for doughnuts at Lard Lad. The popular duo of aliens, Kang and Kodos, have their own, aptly named Kang and Kodos' Twirl 'n' Hurl ride, which sends visitors into an intergalactic spin.

San Francisco

Most of this area is based on San Francisco, notably the city's Fisherman's Wharf district. Chez Alcatraz, for instance, is a snack bar closely modeled on the ticket booths for tours to Alcatraz island.

San Francisco's big draw is **Disaster!℠ A Major Motion Picture Ride... Starring You**. Guests are asked to assist a studio that is going bankrupt by acting as extras for key insert scenes, thus becoming part of the production of a major motion picture, *Mutha Nature*. This ride features high-tech virtual imagery technology along with a special appearance by actor Dwayne Johnson, "The Rock", who has appeared in blockbusters such *The Mummy Returns*. The big finale sequence involves an updated version of an earthquake simulator. Also in this area, **Beetlejuice Graveyard Revue™** is a live mega-monster rock show.

Beetlejuice show's sign

The Wizarding World of Harry Potter™ – Diagon Alley™ brings Harry Potter's London to Universal Studios. Connected to the Hogsmeade™ all-wizarding village and Hogwarts™ School of Witchcraft and Wizardry in the Islands of Adventure® zone by the Hogwarts Express™ train, Diagon Alley™ shops and eateries can be enjoyed by visitors, along with the centerpiece Gringotts bank ride. A very popular attraction is **Fear Factor Live**, the first theme park experience based on a reality-TV show. Casting takes place 75 minutes before the show.

Transformers™ Optimus Prime at the Universal Orlando Resort

Eating, Drinking, and Shopping

The food at Universal Orlando's theme parks is generally good. The Hard Rock Café is the largest in the world but there are plenty of other options. Advance reservations are advisable for Lombard's Seafood Grille, which specializes in fish dishes and has a good-value buffet. Mel's Drive-In is definitely the place to go for fast food and shakes; the wonderful 1950s diner is straight out of the 1973 movie American Graffiti.

Most of the shops stay open after official closing times, and you can buy a full range of themed souvenirs from them. In the Front Lot you will find Universal Studios Store, which sells everything from fake Oscars to oven mitts bearing the Universal logo, and On Location, where a signed photo of your favourite movie star can set you back hundreds of dollars. Most of the attractions have their own store.

Meeting the Stars

Actors in wonderful costumes wander the streets playing the likes of Ghostbusters, Jake and Elwood from *The Blues Brothers*, Shrek, Scooby Doo, characters from *Madagascar*, *Dora the Explorer*, and *The Simpsons*, and legends of the silver screen such as Marilyn Monroe.

You can eat with the stars at a Character Breakfast in the park an hour prior to the scheduled opening time. Reservations are required: call (407) 224-4012 to reserve.

Actress playing screen star Marilyn Monroe

Exploring the Islands of Adventure®

One of the world's most technologically advanced theme parks, Islands of Adventure® demands a day's visit of its own. The themed islands include Jurassic Park, with an educational, interactive Discovery Center®, The Wizarding World of Harry Potter™ with the Dragon Challenge Coaster™, and the park's most popular ride: Harry Potter and the Forbidden Journey™. Marvel Super Hero Island® features Spiderman, the Incredible Hulk, Captain America, and Dr. Doom. Seuss Landing Island™ caters for young visitors, while Popeye, Bluto, and Olive Oyl are the comic strip stars of Toon Lagoon Island.

TOP 5 RIDES

① **Harry Potter and the Forbidden Journey™**

② **The Amazing Adventures of Spiderman®**

③ **The Incredible Hulk Coaster®**

④ **Popeye and Bluto's Bilge-rat Barges®**

⑤ **The Jurassic Park River Adventure®**

The river ride in Jurassic Park River Adventure®

Tackling the Park

There is no transport system within the park other than small boats which criss-cross the lake. A day will suffice to experience all the attractions, provided that you arrive at opening time. As with any theme park, a clearly organised schedule is essential if you are to make the most out of your visit.

The Islands

The entrance to the park is marked by the Pharos Light-house which sounds a bell every few minutes. The first island you encounter moving clockwise is the **Marvel Super Hero Island®** where the theme draws from the Marvel Comics' Super Hero stable of characters. The Incredible Hulk Coaster®, probably the best coaster in Florida, is a green leviathan that accelerates you to over 40mph in two seconds before inverting you at 110 ft

(33.5 m) above the ground as a prelude to diving into several watery looking holes in the ground.

Storm Force Accelatron® is just a faster and more intense version of Disney's Mad Hatter's Tea Party ride, and is incredibly fast-spinning and might induce motion sickness. Dr Doom's Fearfall®, although somewhat daunting to watch, is actually a remarkably pleasant ride in which you are strapped into seats surrounding a pillar and then catapulted into the air before plunging down a 150-ft (46-m) fall. Next to Dr Doom is The Amazing Adventures of Spiderman®, a complex ride which achieves a stunning integration of 3D film technology together with motion simulation as well live special effects.

Toon Lagoon, where cartoons transmute into reality, hosts two wet rides and scheduled performances of the riotous Toon Lagoon Beach Bash. Opposite is Popeye and Bluto's Bilge-Rat Barges®, a white-water raft ride that includes an encounter with a giant octopus. Me Ship, the Olive℠, a play area for young children overlooks the raft ride and provides water canons to soak riders on the rafts below.

Dudley Do-Right's Ripsaw Falls®, the adjacent flume ride, is loosely based on the Rocky and Bullwinkle™ cartoons. It combines a pleasant cruise with an excellent final drop in which you appear to submerge.

Jurassic Park®, based on the films of the same name, boasts exotic vegetation and offers some shade. The Jurassic Park River Adventure® is an exquisitely crafted cruise through the Jurassic Park® compound where you encounter Hadrosaurs, Stegosaurs and others before "accidentally" being diverted as a consequence of a "raptor" breakout. The ride ends with an 85-ft (26-m) drop into a lagoon which doesn't get you too wet. Camp Jurassic® is a playground area for pre-teenage children. Here, smaller children can explore amber mines, climb dinosaur nets, and explore the prehistoric playground to their heart's content. Situated near the Pteranodon Flyers, this ride flies pairs of riders over Jurassic Park® Island on an 80 second journey. The Discovery Center® is an interactive natural history exhibit where guests can view the results of mixing DNA from various species, including themselves.

The Wizarding World of Harry Potter™ transports visitors to the iconic locations of Hogwarts™ and Hogsmeade™, and is home to the park's two most popular rides: Harry Potter and the

Forbidden Journey™, a magical tour beginning at Hogwarts™ and finishing with a thrilling aerial adventure, and Dragon Challenge™, a pair of dueling high-speed roller coasters. The third ride, Flight of the Hippogriff™, is more family-friendly as it weaves its way through the pumpkin patch and Hagrid's hut.

Stage shows include The Eighth Voyage of Sinbad® Stunt Show, where stunts, flames and explosions never fail to amuse fans of television's Xena: Warrior Princess and Hercules. Poseidon's Fury is an equally stunning show where the battle between Poseidon and Zeus is superbly executed through a myriad of extraordinary special effects. **Seuss Landing™** is based on the fantastic Seuss children's books, and appeals mainly to the youngest and those familiar with the popular Seuss books. If I Ran The Zoo™ is another youngsters'

Harry Potter™ Flight of the Hippogriff roller coaster ride

playground. Discover some of the world's strangest creatures in this interactive play area for Dr Seuss fans of all ages. Caro-Suessel™ is an extraordinary merry-go-round with several popular Dr Seuss characters as the horses. On the ride One Fish Two Fish Red Fish Blue Fish™, you have the added excitement of attempting to catch fish while avoiding water jets. For those people who have had no previous experience of Seuss, The Cat in the Hat™ is a somewhat bewildering journey through a manic display of cat-like characters on a whirling couch.

Universal CityWalk®

A 30-acre (12-ha) entertainment complex of restaurants, night clubs, shops and cinemas, Universal CityWalk® offers the visitor the opportunity to continue their Universal experience long after the parks have closed. The gateway to all of Universal's entertainment offerings, CityWalk®'s design was inspired by many of popular culture's innovators, such as Bob Marley, Thelonius Monk and Motown.

The Complex

The appeal of CityWalk® is primarily to adults, and popular music and dance lovers are extremely well catered for. The complex is open 11am–2am and while there is no entrance fee, each club makes a small cover charge. An All-Club pass can be purchased which may also include a movie.

CityWalk® offers a dazzling array of restaurants that range from Emeril's® Restaurant Orlando (a top TV chef) to the famous Hard Rock Café® Orlando. For sports fans, the NASCAR Sports Grille℠ and NBA City Restaurant provide athletic offerings and the Bubba Gump Shrimp Co.™ the nostalgia. Bob Marley – A Tribute to Freedom is an exact replica of this famous musician's home. The complex

is also home to several night-clubs, including the groove℠ dance club with live music from today's finest performers.

CityWalk® boasts specialty shops and state-of-the-art cinemas and its outdoor stages and common areas are the setting for live concerts, art festivals, cooking demonstrations, celebrity personal appearances and street performances. A sparkling lagoon running through the complex provides visitors with a picturesque location to relax while sipping a cool drink in the late-afternoon sun or taking a romantic moonlight stroll.

The Hard Rock Café and music venue, Universal CityWalk®

❹ Wet 'n Wild®

One of Central Florida's top attractions, Wet 'n Wild® offers more themed thrill rides than most other water parks. It boasts an awesome collection of high-velocity rides – multi-passenger as well as solo, on toboggans, rafts, or inner tubes, down slides and chutes or through tubes. There are activities for smaller kids as well, with miniature versions of the park's popular adult attractions on offer at Kids' Park. A range of family activities during the summer add to Wet 'n Wild®'s appeal. Several outlets offer fast food; visitors can also bring in their own picnic hamper.

Wakezone
Ride a surfboard on your knees on this cable-operated, half-mile (0.8-km) course on the park's lake. You can also wakeskate at the lake.

Black Hole™: The Next Generation
Experience pulsating lights and dynamic effects as your two-person raft is propelled forward.

Beach Club
Surge Landing Picnic Area
Lakeside Terrace
Wild Tiki Lounge
The Sundeck
Mach 5 Pavilion
The Blast Pavilion
①
The Blast
Kids Park

The Flyer
Four-seater toboggans descend from a height of 40 ft (12 m), plowing through 450 ft (137 m) of banked curves and racing straight runs in this exhilarating watery ride.

Mach 5
Riders navigate this solo flume ride on a foam mat. On tight turns, ride the flowing water as far up the wall as possible. You can choose from three different twisting-and-turning flumes.

KEY

① **Surf Lagoon,** a 17,000-sq ft (1,580-sq m) wave pool, features 4-ft (1.2-m) high waves and a waterfall.

② **Lazy River®,** a mile-long (1.6-km) circular waterway, lets you swim or float gently past swaying palms, orange groves, and waterfalls a lovely re-creation of Old Florida.

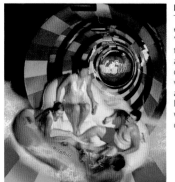

Brain Wash™

This is one of the most extreme rides at Wet 'n Wild®. Travel high through a dark tunnel and then straight down a six-story vertical drop into a funnel filled with lights and sounds, which shoots you out at the bottom.

Bomb Bay

A six-story plunge down a nearly vertical slide from a bomb-like capsule, this is one of Wet 'n Wild®'s most sensational rides. Der Stuka is a slightly less scary version.

Top Tips

- Steps to the rides and asphalt walkways can get very hot. Wear non-slip footwear as protection.
- High-speed rides can leave you uncovered.
- Rides have a 36-inch (91-cm) minimum height requirement for kids riding solo.
- The Florida sun can be very strong, so use sunscreen and make sure children are protected.

Cabanas

Relax with a drink in a comfortable cabana, set in a lush, tropical oasis on an island surrounded by a Lazy River®.

Knee Ski Dock

Bubba Tub Pavilion

Riverside BBQ

②

International Pavilion

Bubba Tub®

A raft large enough to hold five is the just the thing for watery splashes and fun for the family as it hurtles down a six-story slide with three big drops.

The Storm

Plummet down a chute with mist, thunder, and – at night – lightning effects, then drop into a huge open bowl, to swirl out with a splash into a lower pool in this exciting ride.

Downtown Orlando, dominated by the SunTrust Center

❺ Orlando

Road map E2. Orange Co. 🚉 200,000.
✈ 🚌 🚆 ℹ 6700 Forum Drive,
(407) 363-5800. **W** orlando.org

Until the 1950s, Orlando was not much more than a sleepy provincial town. Its proximity to Cape Canaveral and the theme parks, however, helped change all that.

Downtown Orlando, where glass-sided high-rises mark a burgeoning business district, beckons only at night, when tourists and locals flock to the many bars and restaurants around Orange Avenue, Orlando's main street.

During the daytime, take a stroll in the park around **Lake Eola**, three blocks east of Orange Avenue. Here, you'll get a taste of Orlando's (comparatively) early history. Overlooking the lake are a

mix of high-rise condos and a few older homes. Alternatively, visit the **Orange County Regional History Center** on Central Blvd.

In the quieter residential areas just north of Downtown, there are parks and museums. If you are short of time, Winter Park should be your priority.

🏛 Orange County Regional History Center

65 E Central Blvd. **Tel** (407) 836-8500.
Open daily. **Closed** public hols.
W thehistorycenter.org

Housed in the 1927 courthouse in central Downtown, the Center crams 12,000 years of Central Florida's past into three floors. Do not miss the diorama of the sink-hole that swallowed buildings and cars in Winter Park in the 1980s.

🏛 Loch Haven Park

N Mills Ave at Rollins St. Orlando Museum of Art: **Tel** (407) 896-4231.
Open 10am–4pm Tue–Fri, noon–4pm Sat & Sun. **Closed** public hols. 🚻 🚻
W omart.org Orlando Shakespeare Theater: **Tel** (407) 447-1700.

Loch Haven Park, 2 miles (3 km) north of Downtown, has a trio of small museums. The most highly regarded is the **Orlando Museum of Art**, which has three permanent collections: pre-Columbian artifacts, with figurines from Nazca in Peru; African art; and American paintings of the 19th and 20th centuries. The Park is home to the **Orlando Shakespeare Theater**, which includes the 350-seat Margeson Theater and

the smaller Goldman Theater. The Center produces the classics throughout the year (www.orlandoshakes.org).

🌿 Harry P. Leu Gardens

1920 N Forest Ave. **Tel** (407) 246-2620.
Open daily. **Closed** Dec 25. 🚻 🚻
W leugardens.org

The Harry P. Leu Gardens offer 50 acres of serenely beautiful gardens. Elements such as Florida's largest rose garden are formal, while elsewhere you find mature woods of spectacular live oaks, maples, and cypresses, festooned with Spanish moss; in winter, seek out the camellias. The pretty Floral Clock lawn was inspired by a similar one in Edinburgh, Scotland. You can also tour the early 20th-century **Leu House**, which businessman Harry P. Leu donated to the city of Orlando in 1961.

🏛 Enzian Theater

1300 S Orlando Ave, Maitland.
Tel (407) 629-0054 (showtime hotline).
Open daily. 🚻 🚻 **W** enzian.org

Home of the nationally recognized Florida Film Festival, this nonprofit, alternative cinema is one of the least mainstream attractions in Orlando. Set among weeping oaks with a distinctive wrap-around porch, the Enzian Theater has earned a reputation for promoting independent and foreign films, and also for devoting rare space to self-distributed films.

🏛 Maitland Art Center

231 W Packwood Ave, 6 miles (9 km) N of Downtown. **Tel** (407) 539-2181.
Open daily. **Closed** public hols. Voluntary donations. 🚻 (limited access). **W** maitlandartcenter.org

This art center located in the leafy suburb of Maitland occupies studios and living quarters which were designed in the 1930s by artist André Smith as a winter retreat for fellow artists. Set around courtyards and gardens, the buildings are delightful, with abundant use made of Mayan and Aztec motifs. The studios are still used, and there are exhibitions of contemporary American arts and crafts.

Fountain at the center of the rose garden, Harry P. Leu Gardens

▥ Orlando Science Center

777 East Princeton St. **Tel** (407) 514-2000 or (888) OSC 4FUN. **Open** 10am–5pm Sun–Fri, 10am–10pm Sat. 🅿 ▢ 🏛 ♿ 🆆 **osc.org**

The aim of this center is to provide a stimulating environ-ment for experiential science learning, which it achieves by providing a huge range of exciting, state-of-the-art interactive exhibits. Covering 207,000 square feet (19,200 sq m) of floor space, there are many fascinating attractions, including the Dr. Phillips CineDome, which surrounds people with amazing images and films as well as functioning as a planetarium. The DinoDigs exhibit with its collection of dinosaur fossils is very popular with children, as is the ShowBiz Science exhibit, which reveals some of the effects and tricks used in the movie business, while the Body Zone allows you to explore the intimate workings of the human body.

The original museum was opened in 1960 at Loch Haven Park and was called the Central Florida Museum. It wasn't until 1984 that it was renamed the Orlando Science Center. The present building, six times larger than its previous home, was completed and opened in February 1997.

Detail from Tiffany's Four Seasons *window*

❻ Winter Park

Road map: E2. Orange Co. ▦ 25,000. 🚋 🚌 **i** 150 N New York Ave, (407) 644-8281. Scenic Boat Tour: **Tel** (407) 644-4056. 🅿 🆆 **winterpark.org**

Bordering greater Orlando, this refined town took off in the 1880s, when wealthy northerners came south and began to build winter retreats here. The aroma of expensive perfume and coffee emanates from classy stores and cafés along its main street, Park Avenue, while at the country club up the road members all in white enjoy a game of croquet. At the northern end of Park Avenue, the **Charles Hosmer Morse Museum of American Art** holds probably the finest collection of works by Louis Comfort Tiffany (1848–1933) in the world. Magnificently displayed are superb examples of his Art Nouveau creations: jewelry, table lamps, and a large number of his windows, including the *Four Seasons* (1899). This is a staggering fusion of glass, gold leaf, lead, enamel, paint, and copper. The Tiffany Chapel is also stunning. Tiffany designed it for the 1893 World's Columbian Exposition in Chicago. For almost a century it was not seen by the general public. The galleries also exhibit pieces from the

Main door of Knowles Memorial Chapel, Rollins College

same period by luminaries such as Frank Lloyd Wright.

At the southern end of Park Avenue is **Rollins College**, with a delightful arboreal campus dotted with Spanish-style buildings erected in the 1930s. Noteworthy is the Knowles Memorial Chapel, whose main entrance features a relief of a meeting between the Seminoles and the Spanish conquistadors. The college's **Cornell Fine Arts Museum** has over 6,000 works of art, including an impressive collection of Italian Renais-sance paintings, and is the oldest collection in Florida.

To see where the wealthy Winter Park residents live, take the narrated **Scenic Boat Tour**. Between 10am and 4pm, boats depart hourly from the east end of Morse Boulevard and chug around nearby lakes and along interconnecting canals overhung with hibiscus, bamboo, and papaya. The lakes are surrounded by magnificent live oaks, cypress trees, and huge mansions with green, sweeping lawns.

▥ Charles Hosmer Morse Museum of American Art

445 Park Ave N. **Tel** (407) 645- 5311. **Open** Tue–Sun. **Closed** public hols. 🅿 ♿ 🆆 **morsemuseum.org**

▥ Cornell Fine Arts Museum

1000 Holt Ave. **Tel** (407) 646-2526. **Open** 10am–4pm Tue–Fri, noon–5pm Sat & Sun ♿ 🆆 **rollins.edu/cfam**

Potthast's *The Conference*, Orlando Museum of Art, Loch Haven Park

One of the gentler rides at Wet'n Wild® on International Drive

❶ International Drive

Road map: E2. Orange Co. 🚌 Orlando. 🚏 Orlando. ℹ️ Visitor Center, 8723 International Drive. **Tel** (407) 363-5872. **W** orlandoinfo.com

Only a stone's throw from Walt Disney World®, and anchored by Universal Studios® and SeaWorld® at either end, International Drive is here solely because of the theme parks. "I Drive," as everyone knows it, is a tawdry 3-mile (5-km) ribbon of restaurants, hotels, shops, and theaters. After dark, however, it becomes a lively neon strip with everything open until late.

I Drive's biggest and most popular attraction is **Wet 'n Wild®** *(see pp190–91)*, billed as the world's first water park when it opened in 1977. Unlike Disney's water parks *(see pp172–3)*, which better serve families with young children, Wet 'n Wild® excels in its fantastic big-thrill rides, which are not always suitable for the whole family, though there are tamer rides for the more faint-hearted visitors. Filled with fantastic objects, illusions, and film footage of strange feats, **Ripley's Believe It or Not!** is I Drive's other quality attraction. It is one of a world-wide chain of museums that was born out of the 1933 Chicago World Fair's so-called Odditorium – the creation of a famous American broad-caster and

cartoonist, Robert Ripley, who traveled the globe in search of the weird and wonderful. You can't miss Orlando's Ripley's Believe It or Not! – it is housed in a building that appears to be falling into one of Florida's infamous sinkholes *(see p26)*. **Wonder Works** offers interactive family fun with a simulated earthquake and lazer tag games. **Pointe Orlando** is an ultra-modern, outdoor shopping mall with upscale eateries, nightclubs, and shops, along with attractions such as an IMAX® movie theater, B.B. King's Blues Club, and an Improv Comedy Club.

Titanic – The Experience, the world's first permanent Titanic attraction, with artifacts, movie memorabilia, and full-scale recreations of the ship's rooms and grand staircase. Orlando's excellent Official Visitor Information Center, which has coupons for many of

Orlando and the surrounding area's most popular attractions, hotels, and restaurants, is well worth a visit, as you can save yourself a lot of money *(see p370)*.

🎢 **Wet 'n Wild®**
6200 I-Drive. **Tel** (407) 351-9453.
Open daily. ♿ ♿
W wetnwildorlando.com

🏬 **Pointe Orlando**
9101 I-Drive. **Tel** (407) 248-2838.
Open noon–10pm Mon–Sat, noon–8pm Sun. ♿ **W** pointeorlando.com

🏛 **Ripley's Believe It or Not!**
8201 I-Drive. **Tel** (407) 363-4418.
Open daily. ♿ ♿
W ripleysorlando.com

Wonder Works
9067 I-Drive. **Tel** (407) 351-8800.
Open daily. ♿ ♿
W wonderworksonline.com

❽ Gatorland

Road map: E3. Orange Co. 14501 S Orange Blossom Trail, Orlando.
Tel (407) 855-5496. 🚌 Orlando. 🚏 Orlando. **Open** daily. ♿ ♿
W gatorland.com

This giant working farm, open since the 1950s, has a license to raise alligators for their hides and meat. Its breeding pens, nurseries, and rearing ponds hold thousands of alligators, from infants that would fit into the palm of your hand to 12-ft (4-m) monsters. The alligators can be observed from a board-walk and tower as they bask in the shallows of a cypress swamp. The shows include alligator wrestling and the Gator Jumparoo, in which the

On sale at Gatorland

The unmistakable sinking home of Ripley's Believe It or Not!

The gaping jaws of an alligator marking the entrance to Gatorland

animals leap out of the water to grab chunks of chicken from the hands of trainers; there are also handling demonstrations of Florida's poisonous snakes.

The park's other highlights include an aviary, a zip line, and a petting zoo.

One of the typically offbeat shops in Kissimmee's Old Town

❾ Kissimmee

Road map: E3. Osceola Co. 🚗 41,000. 🚌 🚆 ℹ️ 1925 E Irlo Bronson Memorial Hwy. **Tel** (407) 847-5000. Old Town: 5770 W Irlo Bronson Mem. Hwy. **Tel** (407) 396-4888.
Ⓦ floridakiss.com

In the early 1900s, cows freely roamed the streets of this cattle boom town. Now, the only livestock you are likely to see are those that appear in the twice-yearly rodeo at Kissimmee's **Silver Spurs Arena** *(see p39)*. Kissimmee means "Heaven's Place" in the language of the Calusa Indians *(see pp44–5)*, but the reason most people visit is to make use of the glut of cheap motels close to Walt Disney World®. They are strung out along the traffic-ridden US 192, amid chain restaurants and billboards advertising the latest attractions, shopping malls, and dinner shows. The latter are the chief appeal of Kissimmee after dark.

After a day in a theme park, however, you might prefer to visit Kissimmee's **Old Town**. This re-created pedestrian street of early 20th-century buildings has eccentric shops offering psychic readings, tattoos, Irish linen, candles, and so forth. There is also a moderately entertaining haunted house and a small fairground with antique equipment.

Warbird Adventures, by the Kissimmee municipal airport, gives visitors the unforgettable opportunity to fly in an original World War II Advanced T-6 Navy Trainer or, alternatively, a classic MASH helicopter.

Whether you want a thrilling acrobatic adventure or a smooth sightseeing flight, you will be allowed to take the controls and learn about flying one of these historical aircraft from an experienced instructor.

Silver Spurs Arena
Osceola Heritage Park. **Tel** (321) 697-3495. **Open** for shows. 🅿️ ♿
Ⓦ silverspursrodeo.com

🏛️ **Warbird Adventures**
N. Hoagland Blvd. **Tel** (407) 870-7366. **Open** Mon–Sat. **Closed** Dec 25. 🅿️
♿ Ⓦ warbirdadventures.com

Dinner Shows

For great family fun, consider going to a dinner show *(see p359)*. Orlando boasts around a dozen – not including Disney's two shows *(see p177)* – strung along I Drive or off US 192 near Kissimmee. Tickets cost $40–50 for an adult and $20–25 for children, but discounts are available with coupons from the Orlando Visitor Center. The following are the best:

Capone's Dinner Show:
A 1931 Chicago speakeasy offers mobsters and Italian food.
Tel (407) 397-2378.
Ⓦ alcapones.com

Arabian Nights: A gaudy equestrian extravaganza in a giant indoor arena.
Tel (407) 239-9223.
Ⓦ arabian-nights.com

Pirate's Dinner Adventure: A lavish show set around a pirates' ship, with boat races, acrobatics, and a tour of the studios beforehand. **Tel** (407) 248-0590.
Ⓦ piratesdinneradventure. com

Sleuth's Mystery Dinner:
Eight different shows, all with a suspicious death with lots of twists. **Tel** (407) 363-1985.
Ⓦ sleuths.com

Medieval Times: Jousting knights get top billing at this colorful and dramatic show.
Tel (407) 396-1518.
Ⓦ medievaltimes.com

Outta Control Magic Comedy Dinner Show: A high-energy comedy magic show accompanied by unlimited dishes.
Tel (407) 351-8800.

A Knight preparing for battle on his horse in Medieval Times

❿ Lake Toho

Road map: E3. Osceola Co. 3 miles (5 km) S of Kissimmee. 🚇 Kissimmee. 🚌 Kissimmee. ⛴ from Big Toho Marina on Lakeshore Blvd, downtown Kissimmee.

At the headwaters of the Florida Everglades, and approximately 20 miles (32 km) from downtown Orlando, Lake Tohopekaliga (or Toho, as the locals call it) is famous for its wide variety of exotic wildlife. Makinson Island, in the middle of the lake, is a private nature preserve for animals including emus and llamas. There are several eagles nesting on the lake, as well as other birds such as ospreys, herons, and egrets. Approximately one third of the 22,700-acre lake is made up of maidencane grass and bullrush reeds. Anglers come from all over the world to compete in three-day events at Lake Toho, which is one of the best places in Florida for catching trophy bass.

If organized events aren't your thing, why not go fishing with a local guide, take a boat trip around the lake and the Kissimmee River, or simply spend a quiet afternoon with a picnic lunch.

The reflection of the setting sun on Lake Tohopekaliga

⓫ Disney Wilderness Preserve

Road map: E3. 2700 Scrub Jay Trail, 12 miles (18 km) SW of Kissimmee. **Tel** (407) 935-0002. 🚇 Kissimmee. 🚌 Kissimmee. **Open** 9am–5pm daily. **Closed** Sat & Sun Jun–Sep. 🎥 📷 Sun 1:30pm. 🌐 tnc.org

Orlando's best maintained wilderness preserve is a wonderfully peaceful place, where you can get away from the crowds. Opened to the public in 1992, the 12,000-acre preserve consists of tranquil lakes and swamps that are a haven for native plants and animals. The preserve is bordered by one of the last remaining undeveloped lakes in Florida.

More than 160 different species of wildlife live here, including Florida scrub-jays, Florida sandhill cranes, and Sherman's fox squirrels.

Unlike the other Disney attractions, there are no thrills or rides here, but there is still plenty to do. You can follow one of the three hiking trails that lead to the shores of Lake Russell. The shortest walk is the interpretive trail, a pleasant 0.8 miles (1.2 km), where you can learn first-hand about nature along the way. The longer trails are partially unshaded, so ensure you bring plenty of water and sunscreen during the hotter months.

You can also take an off-road buggy tour, which starts with a 20-minute introductory video about the preserve, before a guide takes you through the swampland.

⓬ Fantasy of Flight

Road: Map E3. Polk Co. 1400 Broadway Blvd SE, Polk City. **Tel** (863) 984-3500. 🚇 Winter Haven. 🚌 Winter Haven. **Open** daily. **Closed** Thanksgiving, Dec 25. 🎥 ♿ 🌐 fantasyofflight.com

Where Fantasy of Flight may have the edge over Florida's

Amateur pilot in simulated combat at Fantasy of Flight

many other aviation attractions is that it provides the very sensations of flying. A series of vivid walk-through exhibits takes you into a World War II B-17 Flying Fortress during a bombing mission and into World War I trenches in the middle of an air raid.

For an extra fee you can ride a World War II fighter aircraft simulator in a dogfight over the Pacific. In the cockpit, you will be given a preflight briefing and receive advice from the control tower about takeoff, landing, and the presence of enemy aircraft. A hangar full of the world's greatest collect- ion of mint antique airplanes contains the first widely used airliner in the US, the 1929 Ford Tri-Motor, which appeared in the film *Indiana Jones and the Temple of Doom*, and the Roadair 1, a combined plane and car that flew just once, in 1959.

Several tours are available, including a look behind the scenes at the huge storage bays, or a visit to the Restoration

Lake Russell, one of the many lakes at The Disney Wilderness Preserve

Shop where you'll meet expert craftsmen who rebuild the engines. You can also watch a pilot fly one of the aircraft in a private air show – or take to the skies.

The Dragon, a ride that enters the Enchanted Castle, LEGOLAND®

⑬ LEGOLAND®

Road map: E3. One Legoland Way, Winter Haven. **Tel** (877) 350-5346. �892 Winter Haven. **Open** 10am–5pm daily. **Closed** Tue & Wed during slow periods. 🎟️ ♿
Ⓦ florida.legoland.com

Enjoy an action-packed day of adventure and education in this beautiful setting on the shores of Lake Eloise. LEGOLAND® Florida, the fifth of its kind and the largest of the LEGOLAND® parks, is another of Florida's impressive family-friendly theme parks. It is conveniently located just 45 minutes from both Walt Disney World® and Tampa, in the city of Winter Haven. Built on the site of the former Cypress Gardens, the native plants and exotic species, including the original Banyan tree, planted when the gardens opened in 1939, have been carefully preserved.

The park contains ten different zones, ensuring an exciting experience for every family member. **The Beginning** features a 100-ft (30-m) high rotating platform offering a 360° view of the whole park, closely followed by **Fun Town**, with a two-story carousel and 4D movie theater. **Castle Hill** brings medieval times to life and

Miniland USA presents eight miniature replicas of famous American landmarks. **Land of Adventure** will delight thrill-seekers with its life-sized LEGO® dinosaur and dramatic roller coasters, while **XTreme** caters for more courageous visitors with its LEGO Technic® Test Track Coaster, and Aquazone® Wave Racers. **LEGO® City** and **Imagination Zone** offer an entire scaled-down town and hands-on models, and younger visitors will enjoy **DUPLO® Village** and **Pirate's Cove**.

⑭ Bok Tower Gardens

Road map: E3. Polk Co. 1151 Tower Blvd, Lake Wales. **Tel** (863) 676-1408. �892 Winter Haven. 🚌 Lake Wales. **Open** daily. 🎟️ ♿
Ⓦ boktowergardens.org

Edward W. Bok arrived in the US from Holland in 1870 at the age of six, and subsequently became an influential publisher. Shortly before his death in 1930, he presented 128 acres of beautiful woodland gardens to the American public "for the success they had given him."

The sanctuary now encompasses 250 acres (100 ha) at the highest spot in peninsular Florida – a dizzying 298 ft (91 m) above sea level – they center on the Singing Tower, which shelters Bok's grave at its base. You cannot climb the tower, but try to attend its 45-minute live carillon concert, rung daily at 3pm.

The striking, pink marble Singing Tower at Historic Bok Sanctuary

⑮ Yeehaw Junction

Road map: E3. Osceola Co. Desert Inn, 5570 South Kenansville Road, Yeehaw Junction 34972. **Tel** (407) 436-1054. **Open** daily. Ⓦ desertinnrestaurant.com

Yeehaw Junction was once known only as a watering hole for lumbermen and cowboys driving herds of cattle from the center of the state to the reservations and plantations of the coast. Located at the crossroads of Florida's Turnpike and the scenic Highway 441, the **Desert Inn** is a good place to stop. The restaurant serves gator- and turtle-burgers, and there is a gift shop and a large outdoor area for festivals and barbeques.

The 1880s building, which is listed on the National Registry of Historical Places, offers a fascinating look into the history of Cracker Country for busloads of tourists and bluegrass festival aficionados.

1930s police car, American Police Hall of Fame

⑯ American Police Hall of Fame

6350 Horizon Drive, Titusville. **Tel** (321) 264-0911. �892 Titusville. **Open** 10am–6pm daily. **Closed** Thanksgiving, Dec 25. 🎟️ ♿ Ⓦ aphf.org

Few visitors are unmoved by the Hall of Fame's vast marble memorial, engraved with the names of over 5,000 American police officers who have died in the line of duty. Yet some of the exhibits, while fascinating, are gory and sensationalist. The *RoboCop* mannequin, brass knuckles, and weapons disguised as lipstick and an umbrella are innocuous enough. Some visitors, however, may find the prospect of strapping themselves into an electric chair or inspecting the gas chamber harder to stomach.

⑰ Canaveral National Seashore and Merritt Island

Road map: F2. Brevard Co.
🚌 Titusville. 🇼 nps.gov/cana

These adjacent preserves on the Space Coast share an astounding variety of fauna and a wide range of habitats, including saltwater estuaries, marshes, pine flatwoods, and hardwood hammocks, all due to the meeting of temperate and subtropical climates here. You can often see alligators, as well as endangered species such as manatees, but the bird life makes the greatest visual impact.

Many visitors simply head straight for the beach. The **Canaveral National Seashore** incorporates Florida's largest undeveloped barrier island beach – a magnificent 24-mile (39-km) strip of sand backed by dunes strewn with sea oats and sea grapes. Apollo Beach, at the northern end, is accessible along Route A1A, while Playalinda Beach is reached from the south, along Route 402; no road connects the two. The beaches are fine for sunbathing, but swimming conditions can be hazardous, and there are no lifeguards.

Behind Apollo Beach, Turtle Mound is a 40-ft (12-m) high rubbish dump of oyster shells created by Timucua Indians *(see pp44–5)* between AD 800 and 1400. Climb the board-walk to the top for a view over Mosquito

Space Coast Bird Life

The magnificent and abundant bird life of the Space Coast is best viewed early in the morning or shortly before dusk. Between November and March, in particular, the marshes and lagoons teem with migratory ducks and waders, as up to 100,000 arrive from colder northern climes.

Sandhill crane

Brown pelican

Royal tern

Black skimmer

Lagoon, flecked with a myriad mangrove islets.

Route 402 to Playalinda Beach provides memorable views, too – of the Kennedy Space Center's shuttle launch pads, rising eerily out of the watery vastness. This route also crosses **Merritt Island National Wild-life Refuge**, which covers an area of 220 sq miles (570 sq km). Most of the refuge lies within Kennedy Space Center and is out of bounds.

By far the best way to experience the local wildlife at first hand is to follow the 6-mile (10-km) Black Point Wildlife Drive. An excellent leaflet, available at the track's start near the junction of

An alligator in the wild

routes 402 and 406, explains such matters as how dikes control local mosquito populations (although you should still come armed with insect repellent in summer). Halfway along the drive you can stretch your legs by following the 5-mile (8-km) Cruickshank Trail, which starts nearby and has an observation tower.

East along Route 402 towards Playalinda, the Merritt Island Visitor Information Center has excellent displays on the habitats and unique flora and forna within the refuge. A mile (1.5 km) farther east, the Oak Hammock and Palm Hammock trails have short board-walks across the marshland for bird watching and photography.

🗺 **Canaveral National Seashore**
Route A1A, 20 miles (32 km) N of Titusville or Route 402, 10 miles (16 km) E of Titusville. **Tel** (321) 267-1110. **Open** daily. ♿

🗺 **Merritt Island National Wildlife Refuge**
Route 406, 4 miles (6.5 km) E of Titusville. **Tel** (321) 861-0667. **Open** daily. 🇼 merrittisland.fws.gov

⑱ Kennedy Space Center

See pp200–205.

View from Black Point Drive, Merritt Island National Wildlife Refuge

⓳ US Astronaut Hall of Fame

Road map: E2. Brevard Co. Junction of Route 405 and US 1. **Tel** (866) 737-5235. 🚌 Titusville. **Open** noon–6:30pm daily. **Closed** Dec 25. 🅿 ♿
W kennedyspacecenter.com

Part of the Kennedy Space Center Visitor Complex, this Hall of Fame commemorates the astronauts of Mercury, Gemini, Apollo, and the Space Shuttle programs, and has many of their personal items on display plus artifacts, journals, and countdown recordings. There is also a 3-D journey around the world and the Solar System. Camp Kennedy Space Center, on the same site, runs courses for youngsters, with such activities as trying out weightlessness.

"Tico Belle," the prize exhibit at the Warbird Air Museum

⓴ Valiant Air Command Warbird Air Museum

Road map: E2. Brevard Co. 6600 Tico Road, Titusville. **Tel** (321) 268-1941. 🚌 Titusville. **Open** 10am–6pm daily. **Closed** Thanksgiving, Dec 25. 🅿 ♿
W vacwarbirds.org

At this museum an enormous hangar houses military planes from World War II and later, all

Porcher House, on the edge of Cocoa's leafy historic district

lovingly restored to flying condition. The pride of the collection is a working Douglas C-47 called Tico Belle: the aircraft saw service during World War II before becoming the official carrier for the Danish royal family.

Every March there is an air show, with mock dogfights.

㉑ Cocoa

Road map: E3. Brevard Co. Cocoa Beach Chamber of Commerce. 🄐 20,000. 🚌 ℹ 400 Fortenberry Rd, Merritt Island, (321) 459-2200.
W cocoabeachchamber.com

Cocoa is the most appealing community among the sprawling conurbations along the Space Coast mainland. Its historic district, near where Route 520 crosses the Indian River to Cocoa Beach, is an attractive enclave known as Cocoa Village – with buildings dating from the 1880s (some of which house unpretentious boutiques), replica gas street-lamps, and brick sidewalks.

In Delannoy Avenue, on the eastern edge of the village, is the Classical Revival Porcher

House, built of coquina stone *(see p219)* in 1916. Note the spade, heart, diamond, and club carvings on its portico wall: Mrs. Porcher was an extremely avid bridge player.

㉒ Cocoa Beach

Road map: F3. Brevard Co. 🄐 14,000. 🚌 Merritt Island. ℹ 400 Fortenberry Rd, (321) 459-2200.

The Space Coast's big, no-frills resort calls itself the east coast's surfing capital. Surfing festivals and bikini contests set the tone, along with win-your-weight-in-beer competitions on the pier. Motels, chain restaurants, and the odd strip joint characterize the main thoroughfare.

These are all eclipsed by the **Ron Jon Surf Shop**. This neon palace has surf boards galore (for sale and for rent) and a huge T-shirt collection. In front of its flashing towers, beach bum sports figures are frozen in modern sculpture.

🏠 **Ron Jon Surf Shop**
4151 N Atlantic Ave. **Tel** (321) 799-8888. **Open** daily: 24 hours. ♿

The Ron Jon Surf Shop in Cocoa Beach, with everything for the surfing or beach enthusiast

⑱ Kennedy Space Center

Situated on Merritt Island Wildlife Refuge just an hour's drive east of Orlando, the Kennedy Space Center has captured the world's attention. It was from here, with the launch of Apollo 11 in July 1969, that President Kennedy's dream of landing a man on the moon was realized. The center is one of the homes of NASA (National Aeronautics and Space Administration), and was the preparation and launch facility for the manned Space Shuttle *(see p204)*. The Kennedy Space Center Visitor Complex has events, attractions, and interactive programs to inform and entertain throughout the year.

★ **Apollo/Saturn V Center**
A Saturn V rocket, of the kind used by the Apollo missions, is the showpiece here. There is also a reconstructed control room where visitors experience a simulated launch *(see p203)*.

Lunch with an Astronaut
These sessions offer a one-of-a-kind opportunity to meet a veteran NASA astronaut.

★ **Rocket Garden**
You can walk through a group of towering rockets, each of which represents a different period of space flight's history.

Entrance

KEY

① Astronaut Encounter
② Children's Play Dome
③ Astronaut Memorial
④ Space shop
⑤ Shuttle Atlantis Experience
⑥ Departure point for bus tours
⑦ Robot Scouts
⑧ Information Central

Visitor Complex

Each year, more than 1.5 million visitors from around the world experience their very own space adventure. Built in 1967, the Visitor Complex is one of Central Florida's most popular tourist destinations.

★ KSC Bus Tour
See the historic launch pads of the Apollo and space shuttle programs, and look into the future of spaceflight as NASA prepares for its next generation of spacecraft.

VISITORS' CHECKLIST

Practical Information
Road map: F2. Brevard Co. Off Route 405, 6 miles (9.5 km) E of Titusville. **Tel** (877) 313-2610. **Open** 9am daily. Closing times vary by season 🅿️ ♿ all the exhibits are accessible; wheelchairs and strollers are available at Information Central. 🚻 📷 🌐 **kennedyspacecenter.com**

Transport
🚌 Titusville.

★ IMAX® Theater
The IMAX® theater runs films about space exploration. Float through the cosmos or visit the International Space Station with a 3D space movie *(see p202)*.

Shuttle Atlantis Experience
Strap in and get vertical for an all-too-real simulation of a space shuttle launch.

Kennedy Space Center

Launch Pad LC-39 B
Launch Pad LC-39 A
Apollo Saturn V Center
Vehicle Assembly Building
LC-39 Observation Gantry
INDIAN RIVER
MERRITT ISLAND
Visitor Complex
US Astronaut Hall of Fame
Air Force Space & Missile Museum
PORT CANAVERAL

0 kilometers 10
0 miles 5

0 meters 25
0 yards 25

Exploring the Kennedy Space Visitor Complex

Built in 1967 for astronauts and their families to view space center operations, today the Visitor Complex is host to more than 1.5 million tourists each year. The 131-sq mile (340-sq km) facility offers guests a full-day, comprehensive space experience, including the Space Shuttle Atlantis, excellent IMAX® films, live-action shows, astronaut encounters, and the Apollo/Saturn V Center – the climax of the narrated, video-enhanced bus tour. The go-at-your-own pace tour enables visitors to stop and explore the Apollo/Saturn V Center. One all-inclusive admission ticket takes visitors on the KSC Tour, both IMAX® space films, the U.S. Astronaut Hall of Fame, and all exhibits.

Kids enjoy the Robot Scouts at the IMAX® Theater

Visitor Complex

The place where everyone heads first is the **IMAX® Theater**, where two back-to-back theaters put on stunning films on screens more than five stories high. For some people this is the highlight of their visit.

Top of the bill is *Hubble 3D*, an IMAX® film narrated by Leonardo DiCaprio, which offers an inspiring look into the legacy of the Hubble Space Telescope, launched into space in 1990 aboard the Space Shuttle Discovery. The film illustrates the impact the telescope has had on the way we view the universe. Featuring footage from the final Hubble repair mission, this IMAX® 3D film takes audiences through a space-shuttle launch sequence, and allows them to float next to space-walking astronauts as they gaze into the vast reaches of the universe. Another film on offer at the IMAX® is *Space Station 3D*, which shows astronauts from Europe and America on board a space station. It provides great footage of those amazing views that only astronauts get to see. IMAX® films are included in the general admission ticket.

The 300-seat Astronaut Encounter Theater at the Visitor Complex offers visitors an opportunity to meet veteran astronauts and learn about their experiences.

The **NASA Art Gallery**, inside the IMAX® Theater, offers more than 200 artworks by some famous artists, including Andy Warhol, Robert Rauschenberg, and Annie Leibovitz. Kids will probably prefer the latest planetary explorer robots revealed in **Robot Scouts** or coming face-to-face with a real astronaut in the **Astronaut Encounter** show.

In Shuttle Plaza you can climb aboard and enjoy a close-up view of **Explorer** – a life-size replica of the Space Shuttle. The **Mission Status Center** alongside is where briefings are held thoughout the day that provide the latest mission details. Nearby, a "Space Mirror" tracks the movement of the sun, reflecting its light onto the names inscribed on the **Astronaut Memorial**. This honors the 16 astronauts, from the Apollo 1 to the Space Shuttle Challenger missions, who have given their lives in the service of space exploration.

Space Shuttle *Atlantis*

1958 First American satellite, the *Explorer 1*, is launched (Jan 31)	**1962** John Glenn orbits the earth in *Mercury* spacecraft	**1966** *Gemini 8* makes first space docking (Mar 16)	**1968** *Apollo 8* orbits the moon (Dec 24)	**1977** The Space Shuttle *Enterprise* is tested aboard a Boeing 747 (Feb 18)	**1983** The first American woman goes into space, aboard Space Shuttle *Challenger* (Jun 18)	

1955	1960	1965	1970	1975	1980	1

1961 On May 5, Alan Shepherd becomes the first American in space. Kennedy commits nation to moon landing	**1965** Edward White is the first American to walk in space (Jun 3)	**1969** Neil Armstrong and Buzz Aldrin (*Apollo 11*) walk on the moon (Jul 24)	**1975** American *Apollo* and Russian *Soyuz* vehicles dock in orbit (Jul 17)	**1981** *Columbia* is the first shuttle in space (Apr 12) **1982** The space shuttle program begins	**1986** Th *Challenge* explodes, killin all its crew (Jan 28	

KSC Exhibits and Bus Tour

The entrance gate leads guests to a grand plaza and fountain where ticket stations and self-service kiosks can be found along with information stations, a retail store, and a restaurant. A fascinating walk-through exhibit shows visitors a comprehensive history of the major missions that provided the foundation for the space program. The all-glass rotunda leads to **Early Space Exploration**, which showcases key figures from the early days of rocketry. In the **Mercury Mission Control Room**, visitors view from an observation deck the actual components and consoles from which the first eight manned missions were monitored. Footage and interviews with some of the personnel are highlights of this area. Next are displays of the authentic Mercury and Gemini spacecraft so visitors can relive some of the excitement and intensity of early space

The Vehicle Assembly Building, which dominates the flat landscape

exploration. KSC Tour buses leave every few minutes from the Visitor Complex and offer an exceptional tour of the space center's major facilities. The tour includes the Apollo/Saturn V Center. The tour takes guests into secured areas, where guides explain the inner workings of each of the facilities. Visitors can take as long as they wish to explore each sight.

There are two additional special-interest tours: **Cape Canaveral: Then & Now Tour**, which is an historic tour of the Mercury, Gemini, and Apollo launch pads as well as the Air Force Space and Missile Museum; and the **KSC Up-Close Tours**, which provide an insider's view of the entire space program. Tours may vary, as there are three available: The Vehicle Assembly Building, Launch Pad, and Launch Control Center. Tours sell out daily, so should be reserved in advance and taken on separate days, as they cover vast areas in great detail.

Rockets on display at the Cape Canaveral Air Station

Space Complex Tour

For each self-guided tour it can take between two and three hours to fully explore the facilities featured on the KSC Tour. The tours are fascinating and well worth the time it takes get around.

The **Apollo/Saturn V Center** features an actual 363-ft (110-m) Saturn V moon rocket. You'll see the historic launch of Apollo 8, the first manned mission to the moon in the Firing Room Theater, followed by a film at the Lunar Theater, which shows actual footage of the moon landing. The **Apollo Treasures Gallery** is a celebration of 40 years of Apollo. Here visitors can see the actual Apollo 14 Command Module, as well as various pieces of rare equipment and spacesuits from the original moon missions. The only place in the world where guests can dine next to a genuine moon rock is also here, at the atmospheric Moon Rock Café.

The Space Shuttle

By the late 1970s, the cost of sending astronauts into space had become too much for the American space budget; hundreds of millions of dollars were spent lifting the Apollo missions into space, with little more than a scorched command module ever returning to Earth. The time had come to develop reusable spacecraft made for years of service. The answer was the Space Shuttle Columbia, which was launched into space on April 12, 1981 *(see pp56–7)*. The shuttle's large cargo capacity allowed it to take all kinds of satellites and probes into space, and it was used to lift materials for the construction of the International Space Station. The Space Shuttle program officially ended in 2011.

The service tower gave access for fueling and cargo installation.

The access arm was the corridor through which the astronauts would board the shuttle.

Orbiter

Solid Rocket Booster

The flame trench channeled burning gases away from the vehicle.

Flight Deck
The shuttle was built like an aircraft, but its flight deck was even more complex. You can get some idea of how it was navigated at the Launch Status Center *(see p201)*.

Tracks enabled the tower to be moved away before lift off.

Crawlerway
This double pathway, 180 ft (55 m) wide, was specially designed to withstand the weight of the shuttle as it was taken to the launch pad by gigantic crawlers. The rock surface overlies a layer of asphalt and a 7 ft (2 m) bed of crushed stone.

The Crawler backed away once the shuttle was in place.

Vent for spent gases

Steel pedestals

The Shuttle Launches

Since the shuttle made its maiden voyage in 1981, there were many missions shared between the *Columbia, Challenger, Discovery, Atlantis,* and *Endeavour* vehicles. The program was severely crippled when *Challenger* exploded shortly after lift off in 1986, and again when *Columbia* disintegrated on re-entry in 2003. The safety of the other shuttles was later assured and so regular launches were planned until 2011, when the program was retired. The launch of *Atlantis* on July 8, 2011 marked the final mission of this inspirational era of space exploration. Shuttle Atlantis can be seen at its permanent home at the Kennedy Space Center.

Shuttle clearing the launch tower

Beyond the Shuttle Program

The future of space lies in the hands of private entrepreneurs – a band of billionaires made wealthy by various industries. Their companies, which include SpaceX, Virgin Galactic, and Blue Origin, have begun to take over the work traditionally done by NASA, and NASA shares its Kennedy Space Center launch pads and resources with them. Rockets designed by these companies launch from the Space Center regularly (launch schedules are available online), and visitors can see them during tours of the space center, or from across the lagoon.

SpaceX Falcon 9 rocket launcher with the Dragon spacecraft

Space Privateers

Defense contractors and private companies have been developing launch systems and sending commercial communications satellites into space from KSC and Cape Canaveral for more than a decade. But nothing set fire to the world's imagination as much as the efforts of high-tech entrepreneurs Elon Musk, Richard Branson, Jeff Bezos, Paul Allen, and others, who have turned their energies and wealth to space exploration.

SpaceX

Founded in 2002 by PayPal co-founder Elon Musk, SpaceX made history in 2012 when its Dragon spacecraft became the first private spacecraft to launch from Cape Canaveral, deliver cargo to the International Space Station, and return safely to Earth. Since then Dragon has continued to carry cargo to and from the Space Station, and has many more launches scheduled from Cape Canaveral, some from famed Launch Pad 39B. Musk's future plans include taking astronauts into space.

Blue Origin

Amazon owner Jeff Bezos founded Blue Origin more than a decade ago, to develop safe, reliable, cost-effective human access to space. Working in partnership with NASA, the company has successfully tested an innovative launch-pad escape system, and launched sub-orbital rockets. Blue Origin's future looks to take tourists into space, and deliver astronauts into orbit.

United Launch Alliance

Owned by Lockheed Martin and The Boeing Company, ULA is made up of two of the launch industry's most experienced teams – Atlas and Delta – which have been involved in America's presence in space since 1960s. Formed in December 2006, ULA regularly launches from Cape Canaveral Air Force Station, and continues its relationship with NASA, such as supplying rockets to launch spacecraft into orbit.

Orion

Not all space exploration has moved to the private sector. Current NASA missions include the unmanned Exploration Flight Test-1 mission (EFT-1), which will test its Orion crew module systems for the beginning of human journeys toward deep space, asteroids, and Mars. Visitors to Kennedy Space Center can find out more about this flight test, launched atop a mammoth Delta 4 Heavy Booster, as well as updated details of the ambitious mission.

Where to Watch the Launches

- Titusville, across the lagoon from KSC
- Marina Park: 501 Marina Road
- Sand Point Park: 101 N. Washington Ave (US 1)
- Space View Park: 8 Broad Street
- Manzo Park: 3335 S. Washington Ave (US 1)
- Rotary Riverfront Park: 4141 S. Washington Ave (US 1)
- Kennedy Point Park: 4915 S. Washington Ave (US 1)
- Westbound SR 528 Causeway over the Banana River
- Cocoa Beach
- Jetty Park: East end of Port Canaveral off George King Blvd.
- Cocoa Beach Pier: 401 Meade Ave
- Alan Shepard Park: East end of SR 520
- Fischer Park: East side of SR A1A 1/2 mile south of SR 520
- Lori Wilson Park: 1500 N. Atlantic Ave

The Dragon spacecraft berths at the Space Station with help from Canadarm2

THE NORTHEAST

The charms of the Northeast are more discreet than the glitz of Miami or the thrills of Orlando. Just a few miles from busy interstate highways, salty fishing villages, overgrown plantations, and quaint country towns recall old-time Florida. Fabulous beaches lure sun-worshipers, while the historic town of St. Augustine can claim to be the longest inhabited European settlement in the US.

The state's recorded history begins in the Northeast, on the aptly named First Coast. Juan Ponce de León first stepped ashore here in 1513 *(see p46)* and Spanish colonists established St. Augustine, now a well-preserved town guarded by the mighty San Marcos fortress – one of the region's highlights.

The Northeast also saw the first influx of pioneers and tourists during the 19th-century steamboat era *(see p52)*. At this time, Jacksonville was the gateway to Florida, with steam- boats plying the broad St. Johns River and its tributaries. In the 1880s, Henry Flagler's railroad opened up the east coast, and wealthy visitors flocked to his grand hotels in St. Augustine and Ormond Beach. Those in search of the

winter sun headed farther south, too. Broad sandy beaches flank the popular resort of Daytona, which has been synonymous with car racing ever since the likes of Henry Ford and Louis Chevrolet raced automobiles on the beach during their winter vacations. Daytona is also a popular place for students to spend the spring break: this is as lively as it gets in the Northeast.

Venturing inland, west of the St. Johns, is the wooded expanse of the Ocala National Forest; the woods then thin out to reveal the rolling pastures of Marion County's billion-dollar thoroughbred horse industry. Nearby, charming country towns and villages such as Micanopy have been virtually bypassed by the 20th century.

St. Augustine's splendid Lightner Museum, occupying the former exclusive Alcazar Hotel

◀ Dusk at Castillo de San Marcos, St. Augustine

Exploring the Northeast

The first coast is a well-traveled route, unfurling along the Atlantic shore in a 120-mile (193-km) string of beaches and resorts, interrupted by dunes and marshland popular with bird-watchers. Resorts run the gamut from decorous Fernandina Beach to action-packed Daytona Beach. Between these two extremes lies the historic jewel of St. Augustine. Strike inland, and the Ocala National Forest offers dozens of hiking trails, boating, and fishing on spring-fed lakes. Snorkeling and diving are also popular pursuits in crystal-clear springs. Many of the region's Victorian homes are now bed-and-breakfast inns, which make a pleasant change from hotels and provide a more homey base for exploring.

Sights at a Glance

1. Fernandina Beach
2. Little Talbot Island State Park
3. Kingsley Plantation
4. Fort Caroline National Memorial
5. *Jacksonville pp212–13*
6. Jacksonville Beaches
7. *St. Augustine pp214–19*
8. Fort Matanzas National Monument
9. Marineland Dolphin Conservation Center
10. Washington Oaks Gardens State Park
11. Bulow Plantation Ruins Historic State Park
12. Ormond Beach
13. Daytona Beach
14. Daytona International Speedway
15. Ponce de Leon Inlet Lighthouse
16. Blue Spring State Park
17. Sanford
18. Mount Dora
19. Ocala National Forest
20. Silver Springs
21. Ocala
22. Marjorie Kinnan Rawlings Historic State Park
23. Micanopy
24. Gainesville

Traditional American trailer, Ocala National Forest

For additional map symbols *see back flap*

St. Augustine, viewed from across the Intracoastal Waterway

1 FERNANDINA BEACH
Amelia Island
Yulee
American Beach
Nassau Sound

2 LITTLE TALBOT ISLAND STATE PARK
3 KINGSLEY PLANTATION
Maryport
4 FORT CAROLINE NATIONAL MEMORIAL
5 JACKSONVILLE
6 JACKSONVILLE BEACHES
Ponte Vedra Beach
Palm Valley
Orange Park
Fruit Grove
Durbin
Green Cove Springs
Araquey
Usinas Beach
7 SAINT AUGUSTINE
Saint Augustine Beach
Anastasia Island
Armstrong
8 FORT MATANZAS NATIONAL MONUMENT
Summer Haven
9 MARINELAND DOLPHIN CONSERVATION CENTER
10 WASHINGTON OAKS GARDENS STATE PARK
Palm Coast
11 BULOW PLANTATION RUINS HISTORIC STATE PARK
Ormond-by-the-Sea
12 ORMOND BEACH
13 DAYTONA BEACH
14 DAYTONA INTERNATIONAL SPEEDWAY
Port Orange
Wilbur-by-the-sea
15 PONCE DE LEON INLET LIGHTHOUSE
New Smyrna Beach
Edgewater
De Land
16 BLUE SPRING STATE PARK
Orange City
Deltona
DeBary
17 SANFORD
Lake Mary
Winter Springs
18 MOUNT DORA
Orlando

Getting Around

Jacksonville is the main transportation hub for the region: it lies at the intersection of I-10 from the Panhandle and the main north-south arteries I–95 and US 1, which run parallel to the coast. The scenic A1A, which is better for touring, runs along the shore linking the various resorts. To avoid Jacksonville, you can use the inexpensive Mayport ferry, which crosses the mouth of the St. Johns River. Several east-west routes link the coast and I-75, crossing the St. Johns at Palatka or south of Lake George. Jacksonville and Daytona Beach both have international airports. Amtrak trains stop at Jacksonville and then sweep inland to Ocala and Sanford – the terminus of the Auto Train *(see p384)* – but a car is essential to venture beyond the main cities.

Key
— Highway
— Major road
— Secondary road
— Minor road
— Scenic route
— Main railway
— State border

Chinese Chippendale architecture in Fernandina

● Fernandina Beach

Road map: E1. Nassau Co. 🚗 10,000.
🚂 Jacksonville 🚌 Jacksonville.
ℹ️ 961687 Gateway Blvd, (904) 261-3248. 🌐 islandchamber.com

The town of Fernandina Beach on Amelia Island, just across the St. Marys River from Georgia, was renowned as a pirates' den until the early 1800s. Its deep-water harbor attracted a motley crew of foreign armies and adventurers, whose various allegiances earned Amelia Island its soubriquet, the Isle of Eight Flags. Today, Fernandina is better known as a charming Victorian resort and Florida's primary source of sweet Atlantic white shrimp: more than two million pounds (900,000 kilos) are caught by the shrimping fleet each year.

The original Spanish settlement was established at Old Fernandina, a sleepy backwater just north of the present town. In the 1850s the whole town moved south to the eastern terminus of Senator David Yulee's cross-Florida railroad. The move, coupled with the dawn of Florida tourism in the 1870s *(see pp52–3)*, prompted the building boom that created the much-admired heart of today's Fernandina, the 50-block **Historic District**.

The legacy of Fernandina's golden age is best seen in the Silk Stocking District, which occupies more than half of the Historic District and is so-named

for the affluence of its original residents. Sea captains and timber barons built homes here in a variety of styles: Queen Anne houses decorated with fancy gingerbread detailing and turrets jostle graceful Italianate residences and fine examples of Chinese Chippendale.

Watching the shrimp boats put into harbor at sunset is a local ritual; the fleet is commemorated by a monument at the foot of downtown Centre Street, where chandleries and naval stores once held sway. These weathered brick buildings now house antique shops and upscale gift shops. The 1878 Palace Saloon still serves a wicked Pirate's Punch at the long mahogany bar adorned with hand-carved caryatids.

Down on 3rd Street, the 1857 Florida House Inn is the state's oldest tourist hotel, and a

Amelia Island's Atlantic shore, in easy reach of Fernandina Beach

couple of blocks farther south, the **Amelia Island Museum of History** occupies the former jail. Guided, 90-minute tours cover the island's turbulent past – from the time of the first Indian inhabitants to the early 1900s. Guided tours of the town are also offered (book ahead).

🏛️ **Amelia Island Museum of History**
233 S 3rd St. **Tel** (904) 261-7378.
Open daily. **Closed** public hols. 🅿️
♿ limited. 📷 compulsory; two tours daily. 🌐 ameliamuseum.org

Environs
Thirteen miles (21 km) long and only 2 miles (3 km) wide at its broadest point, **Amelia Island** was first settled by the Timucua tribe in the second century BC. The rich fishing grounds and abundant hunting suggest that the island may have supported around 30,000 Indians, although few signs remain of their presence. There's still excellent fishing, and the island also offers five golf courses and one of Florida's rare opportunities to ride horses along the beach. The splendid sands are backed by dunes that can reach 40 ft (12 m) high in places.

Peg Leg, of Fernandina Beach

The northern tip of the island is occupied by the 1,121-acre (453-ha) **Fort Clinch State Park**, with trails, beaches, and campsites, as well as a 19th-century fort built to guard the Cumberland Sound at the mouth of the St. Marys River. Construction of the fort, an irregular brick pentagon with massive earthworks, 4.5-ft (1.5-m) thick walls, and a battery of Civil War cannons, took from 1847 until the 1860s.

Park rangers wear Civil War uniforms. They are joined by volunteers on the first full weekend of each month in re-enactments, when a variety of duties are re-created; candlelit tours are given on the Saturday.

🏰 **Fort Clinch State Park**
2601 Atlantic Ave Tel: (904) 277-7274.
Open daily. 🅿️ ♿ limited ⚠️
🌐 floridastateparks.org

❷ Little Talbot Island State Park

Road map: E1. Duval Co. 12157 Heckscher Drive, Jacksonville. **Tel** (904) 251-2320. 🚗 Jacksonville. 🚌 Jacksonville. **Open** daily. 🚻 ♿ limited. ⛺ 🌐 floridastateparks.org

Much of Amelia Island and the neighboring islands of Big Talbot, Little Talbot, and Fort George to the south remains undeveloped and a natural haven for wildlife.

Little Talbot Island State Park has a good family campground, trails through coastal hammocks and marshlands, and great fishing. There are otters, marsh rabbits, fiddler crabs, herons, and laughing gulls. Bobcats hide out in the woods, manatees bob about in the Intracoastal waters, and in summer turtles lay their eggs on the beach *(see p121)*. In autumn, whales travel here to calve offshore.

View along a trail through marshland on Little Talbot Island

❸ Kingsley Plantation

Road map: E1. Duval Co. 11676 Palmetto Ave, Fort George. **Tel** (904) 251-3537. 🚗 Jacksonville. 🚌 Jacksonville. **Open** call first. ♿ 🌐 nps.gov

Located in the Timucuan Ecological and Historic Preserve, Kingsley Plantation is the oldest plantation house in Florida. Built in 1798 at the northern end of Fort George Island, it takes its name from Zephaniah Kingsley, who moved here in 1814. He amassed 32,000 acres

Ruins of the original slave cabins unique to the Kingsley Plantation

(12,950 ha) of land, stretching from Lake George near the Ocala National Forest north to the St. Marys River. This area used to encompass four major plantations; the Kingsley plantation itself had as many as 100 slaves working in its fields of cotton, sugarcane, and corn.

Kingsley was a rather liberal thinker for his time, supporting slavery while also advocating a more lenient "task-system" for his slaves. He married a slave, Anna Jai, and later freed her. They lived in the clapboard plantation house *(see p49)* until 1839.

Described at the time as "a very nice commodious house," Kingsley's relatively simple home is closed for restoration. The building is topped by a small rooftop parapet called a "widow's walk," once used to survey the surrounding fields. Nearby are the barn and separate kitchen house, but the plantation is best known for the 23 slave cabins located in woods near the entrance gate. Built of durable tabby *(see p300)*, these basic dwellings have survived the years, and one is now restored.

Fort Caroline in 1564 by Theodore de Bry

❹ Fort Caroline National Memorial

Road map: E1. Duval Co. 12713 Fort Caroline Rd, Jacksonville. **Tel** (904) 641-7155. 🚗 Jacksonville. 🚌 Jacksonville. **Open** daily. **Closed** Thanksgiving, Dec 25, Jan 1. ♿ 🌐 nps.gov/foca

The actual site of Fort Caroline was washed away when the St. Johns River was dredged in the 1880s. At Fort Caroline National Memorial, a reconstruction of the original 16th-century defenses clearly illustrates the style of the first European forts in the New World. Information panels around the site explain the fort's violent history, which began shortly after French settlers arrived in June 1564.

In the attempt to stake a claim to North America, three small French vessels carrying 300 men sailed up the St. Johns and made camp 5 miles (8 km) inland. René de Goulaine de Laudonnière led the French, who were helped by local Timucua Indians to build a triangular wooden fort, named La Caroline in honor of Charles IX of France *(see p46)*. A year later, with the settlers close to starvation, reinforcements under Jean Ribault arrived. The Spanish, however, took the fort.

In the park is a replica of the stone column erected by Jean Ribault.

The glass and steel skyline that dominates Jacksonville's north bank

❺ Jacksonville

Road map: E1. Duval Co. 🚗
1,201,984. ✈ 🚌 🚍 𝓲 550 Water
St, (904) 798-9111.
W visitjacksonville.com

Jacksonville, the capital of the First Coast of Florida, was founded in 1822. Named after General Andrew Jackson (see p49), the town boomed as a port and rail terminus in the late 1800s. Today, financial businesses fuel the impressive downtown commercial district, which you can view from the Skyway or ASE (see p387).

This, Florida's largest city in area, spans the St. Johns River, which provides a focus for visitors. Most people head for the pedestrian areas that flank the riverbanks and are con-nected by water taxi services (see p387).

The **Jacksonville Landing** shopping and dining complex and the Museum of Contemporary Art Jacksonville are located on the north side of the St. Johns. Riverside, a large residential area, is home to the Cummer Museum of Art. The pleasant 1.2-mile (2-km) long **Riverwalk** along the south

bank includes the impressive Museum of Science and History.

🏛 Museum of Science and History
1025 Museum Circle. **Tel** (904) 396-6674. **Open** daily. 🚗 ♿
W themosh.org

This ever-expanding museum houses an eclectic collection of exhibits and provides a user-friendly guide to local history. The 12,000-year-old culture of the local Timucua Indians (see pp44–5) and their predecessors is illustrated with tools, arrowheads, pottery, and other archaeological finds.

There are sections dealing with the ecology and history of the St. Johns River and the Maple Leaf, a Civil War steamship that sank in 1864. The Bryan Gooding Planetarium runs 3-D laser shows on Fridays and Saturdays.

🏛 Museum of Contemporary Art Jacksonville
333 North Laura Street. **Tel** (904) 366-6911. **Open** varies. **Closed** Mon. 🚗
W mocajacksonville.org

Jacksonville City Center

① Jacksonville Landing
② Jacksonville Maritime Heritage Center
③ Riverwalk
④ Museum of Science and History
⑤ Cummer Museum of Art and Gardens
⑥ Museum of Contemporary Art Jacksonville

Key to Symbols see back flap

For hotels and restaurants in this region see pp314–25 and pp329–49

Located in the heart of Jacksonville, this spacious museum of five galleries is home to the largest collection of modern and contemporary art in the Southeast.

🏛 Jacksonville Maritime Heritage Center

Jacksonville Landing. **Tel** (904) 355-9011. **Open** daily. **Closed** Mon, public hols. ♿
w jacksonvillemaritimeheritage center.org

This modest museum features a dozen replicas of famous vessels. The highlight is the USS Saratoga, which was supposedly sunk by a German submarine. The Germans and the US Navy both deny this, despite hundreds of witnesses.

Rare white rhinos at the famous Jacksonville Zoo

🐾 Jacksonville Zoo & Gardens

870 Zoo Parkway. **Tel** (904) 757-4463. **Open** daily. **Closed** Dec 25. ♿
w jacksonvillezoo.org

Opened in 1914, Jacksonville Zoo lies north of the city, off I-95. Some 1,800 animals, from anteaters to zebras, are on view in their natural habitats. Lions, elephants, and kudu roam the African veldt, while diminutive dik-dik deer, African crocodiles, and porcu-pines can be found along the zoo's Okavango Trail. Other attractions include the largest collection of jaguars in the US, an aviary, and a Magellanic penguin area.

For a broader picture, take the 15-minute miniature train journey that loops around half of the 89-acre site.

🏛 Cummer Museum of Art and Gardens

829 Riverside Ave. **Tel** (904) 356-6857. **Open** Tue–Sun. **Closed** public hols. ♿
w cummer.org

This excellent museum stands in exquisite formal gardens that lead down to the St. Johns River. With a permanent collection of 4,000 objects, the twelve galleries exhibit a small but satisfying selection of both decorative and fine arts. These range from Classical and pre-Columbian sculpture and ceramics through Renaissance paintings to the Wark Collection of jewel-like early Meissen porcelain.

Other notable pieces include the tiny *Entombment of Christ* (c.1605) by Rubens, and a striking collection of Japanese netsuke. There's also work by American Impressionists and such 19th- and 20th-century artists as John James Audubon.

⑥ Jacksonville Beaches

Road map: E1. Duval Co, St. Johns Co. 🚉 Jacksonville. 🚌 Jacksonville BH1, BH2, BH3. 🛈 325 Jacksonville Dr, (904) 249-3868.
w jacksonvillebeach.org

Some 12 miles (19 km) east of downtown Jacksonville, half a dozen beaches stretch 28 miles (45 km) north and south along the Atlantic shore. In the south, Ponte Vedra Beach is known for its sports facilities, particularly golf. Jacksonville Beach is the busiest spot, and is home to

Swimmers enjoying the freshwater lakes of Kathryn Abbey Hanna Park

Adventure Landing, a year-round entertainment complex and summer season water park. Heading north, Neptune Beach and Atlantic Beach are both quieter and are popular with families.

By far the nicest spot is the **Kathryn Abbey Hanna Park**, with its fine white sand beach, woodland trails, freshwater lake fishing, swimming, and camping areas. The park lies just south of **Mayport**, one of the oldest fishing villages in the US, still with its own shrimping fleet and home to a US Navy aircraft carrier.

🎢 Adventure Landing

1944 Beach Blvd. **Tel** (904) 246-4386. **Open** daily, weather permitting. ♿
w adventurelanding.com

🏞 Kathryn Abbey Hanna Park

500 Wonderwood Drive. **Tel** (904) 249-4700. **Open** daily. ♿
w coj.net

Shrimp boats moored at the picturesque docks of Mayport on the St. Johns

❼ Street-by-Street: St. Augustine

America's oldest continuously occupied European settlement was founded by Pedro Menéndez de Avilés *(see p46)* on the feast day of St. Augustine in 1565. The town burned down in 1702 but was soon rebuilt in the lee of the mighty Castillo de San Marcos; many of the picturesque, narrow streets of the old town, lined by attractive buildings made of indigenous coquina rock, date from this early period.

When Henry Flagler *(see p129)* honeymooned in St. Augustine in 1883, he was so taken by the place that he later returned to found the Ponce de Leon Hotel, now Flagler College, and soon the gentle trickle of visitors became a flood. St. Augustine has been a major stop on the tourist trail ever since. Today, it has many attractions for the modern tourist, not least its 43 miles of beaches and the fact that it is within easy reach of several golf courses and marinas.

★ Flagler College
Tiles and other Spanish touches were used in the architecture of this former Flagler hotel.

★ Lightner Museum
Cleopatra (c.1890) by Romanelli is one of the exhibits from Florida's Gilded Age on display here.

Casa Monica
became Flagler's third hotel in town in 1888.

Prince Murat House
Prince Achille Murat, nephew of Napoleon, resided in this house in 1824.

Government House
This imposing building houses the University of Florida's Museum of History and Archaeology. The exhibit "First Colony: Our Spanish Origins" tells the story of the founding of St. Augustine.

To Oldest House

★ Ximenez-Fatio House
This was built as a private house in 1797. Later, a second floor with an airy veranda was added and in the mid-19th century it became a boarding house.

For hotels and restaurants in this region see pp314–25 and pp329–49

Plaza de la Constitución
The heart of the Spanish settlement is this leafy square, which is host to a program of concerts, and flanked by Government House and the Cathedral Basilica.

VISITORS' CHECKLIST

Practical Information
Road map: E1. St. Johns Co.
16,000. 10 Castillo Drive, (904) 825-1000. Arts & Crafts Spring Festival (Apr).
FloridasHistoricCoast.com

Transport
1711A Dobbs Road, (904) 827-9273.

To City Gate

SPANISH STREET

ST GEORGE STREET

TREASURY STREET

CATHEDRAL PLACE

CHARLOTTE STREET

AVENIDA MENENDEZ

KING STREET

City Gate
Dating from the 18th century, this city entrance leads to the Old Town via historic St. George Street.

The Peña-Peck House, dating from the 1740s, is the finest First Spanish Period home in the city.

Bridge of Lions
Marble lions guard the bridge opened across Matanzas Bay in 1927.

| 0 meters | 50 |
| 0 yards | 50 |

Key

— Suggested route

Spanish Military Hospital
This reconstruction of a ward re-creates the spartan hospital conditions available to Spanish settlers in the late 18th century.

Exploring St. Augustine

The historic heart of St. Augustine is compact and easy to explore on foot. Part of the fun is escaping off the busy main streets and wandering down shady side turnings, peering into courtyards, and discovering quiet corners where cats bask in the sunshine and ancient live oaks trail curtains of gray-green Spanish moss. Horsedrawn carriage tours are a popular way to get around and depart from Avenida Menendez, north of the Bridge of Lions. Tourist trains and trolleys follow a more extensive route around the main sights while their drivers narrate an anecdotal history of St. Augustine.

St. George Street, the historic district's main thoroughfare, lit up at night

A Tour of St. Augustine

Pedestrian St. George Street is the focus of the historic district, with shops and some of St. Augustine's main attractions, including the excellent Colonial Quarter Museum. The street leads from the old City Gate to the town square, the Plaza de la Constitucion. Attractive, brick-paved Aviles Street runs south from this square and has several interesting colonial buildings.

King Street, west of the plaza, has a very different feel, with the Lightner Museum and Flagler College housed in hotels built by Henry Flagler (see pp52–3) in the late 19th century.

🏛 The Oldest Wooden Schoolhouse

14 St. George St. **Tel** (888) 653-7245. **Open** 9am–5pm daily. **Closed** Dec 25. 🅿🕭

Built some time before 1788, this is purportedly America's oldest wooden schoolhouse. Walls of cypress and red cedar are held together by wooden pins and cast-iron spikes, and a massive chain anchors it in high winds.

🏛 Colonial Quarter

33 St. George St. **Tel** (904) 342-2857. **Open** 9am–8pm daily. **Closed** Dec 25, for special events. 🆆 ColonialQuarter.com

Experience life in 16th–18th-century St. Augustine, and learn about the cultures that left their mark on it – from Minorcans and Native Americans to the Spanish, British, and African-Americans – on this two-acre plot in the downtown historic district. Guided tours operate several times a day, and interactive events, such as musket drills in the 17th-century fortified town, are fun for all ages.

The Colonial Quarter also showcases archaeological evidence of one of the town's first wooden forts, plus 16th-century boat-building and blacksmith skills. Climb the watchtower for views of the Castillo de San Marcos and the bay.

🏛 Peña-Peck House

143 St. George St. **Tel** (904) 829-5064. **Open** Mon–Sat. 🅿 🕭 limited.

This restored house was built in the 1740s for the Spanish Royal Treasurer, Juan de Peña. In 1837 it became the home and office of

Dr. Seth Peck, and the Peck family lived here for almost 100 years. It is furnished in mid-19th century style, and many of the objects displayed are family heirlooms.

🏛 Museum of History and Archaeology at the Government House

48 King St. **Tel** (904) 825-5079. **Open** daily. **Closed** Dec 25. 🅿 🕭 🆆 historicstaugustine.com

Government House, adorned with Spanish-style loggias copied from a 17th-century painting, overlooks the Plaza de la Constitucion, and houses the restored museum, managed by the University of Florida. The museum focuses on the founding of St. Augustine, and one exhibit tells the Hispanic story of American history.

🏛 Spanish Military Hospital

3 Aviles St. **Tel** (904) 827-0807. **Open** daily. **Closed** Dec 25. 🆆 ancientcitytours.net

Offering a rare glimpse into the care afforded soldiers in the late 1700s, the hospital rooms include an apothecary and cot-lined ward. On display is a list of hospital rules and gory medical practices.

🏛 Prince Murat House

246 St. George St. **Tel** (904) 823-9722. **Open** 9am-5pm daily. 🅿 🆆 DowMuseum.com

Part of the Dow Museum of Historic Homes, this house was once home to Prince Murat, nephew to Napoleon Bonaparte. The house is one of nine historic homes offering interactive experiences, exhibitions, and objects that tell the story of Florida's historical and cultural development.

The Oldest Wooden Schoolhouse, built in the 1700s

🏠 Ximenez-Fatio House

20 Aviles St. **Tel** (904) 829-3575. **Open** Tue–Sat. **Closed** public hols. 🏛 ♿ limited. W **ximenezfatiohouse.org**

This lovely house was built in 1797 as the home and store of a Spanish merchant. Today, run by the National Society of Colonial Dames, it is a museum that re-creates the genteel boarding house it became in the 1830s, decorated with period artworks and furnishings, when invalids, developers, and adventurers escaped to Florida from the harsh northern winters.

🏠 Oldest House

14 St. Francis St. **Tel** (904) 824-2872. **Open** daily. **Closed** Easter, Thanksgiving, Dec 25. 🏛 ♿ limited. W **oldesthouse.org**

Also known as the Gonzalez-Alvarez house, this building can be traced through almost 300 years. There is even evidence that the site was first occupied in the early 1600s, though the existing structure postdates the English raid of 1702 *(see p47)*.

The coquina walls *(see p219)* were part of the original one-story home of a Spanish artilleryman, Tomas Gonzalez. A second story was added during the English occupation of 1763–83. Each room is furnished in a style relevant to the different periods of the house's history.

🏛 Lightner Museum

75 King St. **Tel** (904) 824-2874. **Open** 9am–5pm daily. **Closed** Dec 25. 🏛 ♿ W **lightnermuseum.org**

Formerly the Alcazar Hotel, set up by Henry Flagler, this three-story Hispano-Moorish building is now, aptly, a museum devoted to the Gilded Age. It was selected by Chicago publisher Otto C. Lightner, who transferred his collections of Victorian arts to St. Augustine in 1948. There's a glittering display of superb glass (including work by Louis Tiffany), furnishings, sculpture, paintings, plus mechanical musical instruments and toys. The Grand Ballroom houses an exhibit of "American Castle" furniture.

The Gonzalez Room, named after the first residents of the Oldest House

🏛 Flagler College

King St at Cordova St. **Tel** (904) 829-6481. **Open** daily. 🎥 ♿ W **flagler.edu**

Starting out as the Ponce de Leon Hotel, another of Flagler's splendid endeavors, this building opened in 1888, heralded as "the world's finest hotel." A statue of Flagler greets visitors, but only the college dining room and marble-clad foyer in the rotunda are open to the public. Here, the cupola's symbolic motifs represent Spain and Florida: notably the golden mask of the Timucuan *(see pp44–5)* sun god. You can also visit the Flagler Room with its c. 1887 illusionary paintings.

Tiffany stained-glass window

🏛 Fort Mose Historic State Park

15 Fort Mose Trail. **Tel** (904) 823-2232. **Open** 9am–5pm daily. **Closed** Tue. 🏛 W **floridastateparks.org**

In 1738, this site became America's first legal free African settlement, for those fleeing slavery from the colonies in the Carolinas. In 1994 the site became a National Historic Landmark, and in 2009, a precursor site on the National Underground Railroad Network to Freedom. Visitors can explore the land, visitor center, and museum.

🏛 St. Augustine Lighthouse

81 Lighthouse Ave. **Tel** (904) 829-0745. **Open** 9am–6pm daily. 🏛 W **staugustinelighthouse.com**

This working historical lighthouse offers lofty views of St. Augustine, and visitors can learn about the changing coastline, the origins of the shrimping industry, and

traditional wooden boat-building (call for times). There are activities aplenty for children, from the walk-in kaleidoscope to tying sailors' knots and a play shipyard.

🐊 St. Augustine Alligator Farm Zoological Park

999 Anastasia Blvd. **Tel** (904) 824-3337. **Open** 9am–5pm daily. 🏛 W **alligatorfarm.com**

Opened in the late 19th century, this farm of Florida reptiles was a quintessential Florida attraction. Today it is a zoo with educational shows and exhibits, plus research and worldwide conservation efforts. Dare-devil visitors can zip-line across the alligator lagoon.

🏛 Villa Zorayda

83 King St. **Open** 10am–5pm Mon–Sat, 11am–4pm Sun. **Closed** Easter, Thanksgiving. W **villazorayda.com**

This is a one-tenth scale replica of part of the Alhambra palace in Granada, Spain. Built in 1883 with 40 windows differing in size, shape, and color, it contains valuable art and artifacts from the Middle East. Visitors can take self-guided audio tours in English or Spanish.

Moorish tracery and Arabic motifs decorating the Villa Zorayda

Castillo de San Marcos

Despite its role as protector of the Spanish fleets en route back to Europe, St. Augustine was guarded for over a century only by a succession of wooden forts. After suffering a century of attacks, including one by Sir Frances Drake *(see p47)* and many more by pirates, the Spanish colonizers began to build a stone fortification in 1672.

The resulting Castillo de San Marcos, which took 23 years to finish, is the largest and most complete Spanish fort in the US. Constructed of coquina, it is a textbook example of 17th-century military architecture, with layers of outer defenses and walls up to 18 ft (6 m) thick.

After the US gained Florida in 1821, the castillo was renamed Fort Marion. It was used chiefly as a military prison and storage depot for the rest of the 19th century.

Mortars
Often highly decorated and bearing the royal coat of arms, these short-barreled weapons fired large, heavy projectiles on a curved trajectory. Bombs could thus clear obstacles or land on ships' decks.

★ **Guard Rooms**
No Spanish soldiers actually lived in the fort. During guard duty (usually 24-hour shifts), they would cook, eat, and shelter in these reinforced vaults.

★ **Glacis and Covered Way**
Across the moat, a walled area known as the "covered way" shielded soldiers firing on the enemy. Leading up to the wall, a slope (the "glacis") protected the fort from cannon fire.

Coquina

This sedimentary limestone rock, formed by billions of compacted seashells and corals, had the consistency of hard cheese when waterlogged and was easy to quarry. It hardened as it dried but could still absorb the impact of a cannonball without shattering. During the siege of 1740, the English attackers fired projectiles that buried themselves in the fort's coquina walls. Legend has it that they were then dug out and fired back.

The thick coquina walls of the powder magazine

VISITORS' CHECKLIST

Practical Information
1 South Castillo Drive, St. Augustine. **Tel** (904) 829-6506. **Open** 8:45am–4:45pm daily. **Closed** Dec 25. 🅿 ♿ limited. 📷 call ahead for details. 🅦 **nps.gov/casa/**

★ Gun Deck
From here, cannons could reach targets up to 3 miles (5 km) away. Strategic positioning made a deadly crossfire.

KEY

① **The inner drawbridge and portcullis,** built of ironclad pine beams, were the fort's final defenses.

② **The ravelin** guarded the entrance from enemy attack.

③ **The moat,** which once encircled the entire fort, was usually kept dry. During sieges livestock was kept there.

④ **The Plaza de Armas** is ringed by rooms that were used to contain stockpiles of food and weapons.

⑤ **British room**

⑥ **Chapel**

⑦ **Watchtower** the fort's northeast bastion, this tower would have been manned day and night to look out for enemy ships.

⑧ **Powder magazine**

⑨ **Water battery**

⑩ **Sea wall**

⑪ **The shot furnace,** built in 1844 by the US Army, was designed to heat up cannon balls. The red-hot "shot" could set enemy ships on fire.

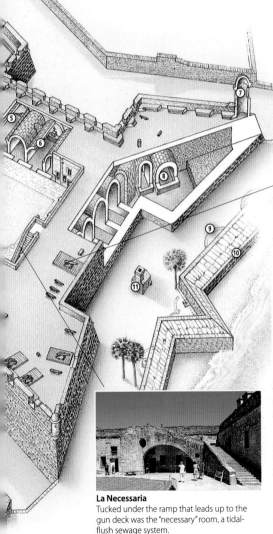

La Necessaria
Tucked under the ramp that leads up to the gun deck was the "necessary" room, a tidal-flush sewage system.

❽ Fort Matanzas National Park

Road map: E2. 8635 A1A South, St. Augustine. **Open** 9am–5:30pm daily. **Closed** Dec 25.

This Spanish outpost fort was built 1740–1742 to guard the Matanzas Inlet, and to warn St. Augustine of enemies, such as the British, advancing from the south. Today, Fort Matanzas is a historical reminder of Spain's early empire in the New World.

The park is situated on barrier islands along the Atlantic shores and Matanzas estuary, providing salt marshes, scrub, and maritime hammock to attract and protect endangered species.

❾ Marineland Dolphin Conservation Center

Road map: E2. Flagler Co. 9600 Ocean Shore Blvd, Marineland. **Tel** (904) 471-1111. Town St. Augustine. **Open** 8:30am–4:30pm daily. 🅿 ♿ **W** marineland.net

The center began in 1938 as Marine Studios, a film set location for many movies, including *Tarzan*. It now puts dolphins at center stage, and visitors can swim with these gentle creatures, touch and feed them, or learn to be a trainer with one- or three-day trainer camp programs. The dolphins live in a habitat of 1.3 million gallons, ensuring their well-being. The center's aim is to foster the preservation of marine life.

❿ Washington Oaks Gardens State Park

Road map: E2. Flagler Co. 6400 N Ocean Shore Blvd, 2 miles (3 km) S of Marineland. **Tel** (386) 446-6780. Town St. Augustine. **Open** daily. 🅿 ♿ **W** floridastateparks.org

Beneath a canopy of oaks and palms, 400 acres (162 ha) of former plantation land have been transformed into lovely gardens of hydrangeas, azaleas, and ferns, plus a rose garden and trails through a coastal hammock to

Ruins of the 19th-century sugar mill at Bulow Plantation

the Matanzas River. Across the A1A a boardwalk leads to the beach, strewn with coquina boulders *(see p215)*, and tidal pools eroded from the soft stone.

⓫ Bulow Plantation Ruins Historic State Park

Road map: E2. Flagler Co. Old Kings Rd, 3 miles (5 km) S of SR 100. **Tel**: (386) 517-2084. Town Daytona Beach. **Open** daily. 🅿 ♿ **W** floridastateparks.org

Somewhat off the beaten track, the ruins of this 19th-century plantation stand in a dense hammock where sugar cane once grew. The site is part of the 4,675 acres (1,890 ha) of land adjacent to a creek that Major Charles Bulow bought in 1821. His slaves cleared half this area and planted rice, cotton, and sugar cane. The plantation, known as Bulowville, was abandoned after Indian attacks during the Seminole Wars *(see pp50–51)*. Today, Bulow Creek is a state canoe trail, and you can rent canoes to explore this lovely backwater. On its

banks are the foundations of the plantation house, a ten-minute stroll takes you to the ruins of the old sugar mill, which resemble the remains of some ancient South American temple.

Environs

About 10 miles (16 km) north of Bulow Plantation is historic **Flagler Beach**, a charming old-worldy town with a fishing pier, quaint museum, and ocean-front eateries.

🏠 **Flagler Beach**
S Ocean Shore Blvd. **Tel**: (386) 517-2000. **W** cityofflaglerbeach.com

⓬ Ormond Beach

Road map: E2. Volusia Co. 🔼 38,000. Town Daytona Beach. 🛈 126 E Orange Ave, Daytona Beach (386) 255-0415. **W** daytonabeach.com

Ormond Beach was one of the earliest winter resorts on Henry Flagler's railroad *(see pp52–3)*. No longer standing, his fashionable Ormond Hotel boasted a star-studded guest list including Henry Ford and John D. Rockefeller.

The Rockefeller Room in The Casements, Ormond Beach

Rockefeller bought a house just across the street in 1918 – prompted by overhearing that another guest was paying less; despite his immense wealth, the millionaire chief of Standard Oil guarded his nickels and dimes closely. His winter home, **The Casements**, has been restored and is today a museum and cultural center, housing Rockefeller-era memorabilia such as the great man's high-sided wicker beach chair. There's also a period-style room and a rather incongruous Hungarian arts and crafts display.

A short walk from The Casements, the **Ormond Memorial Art Museum** is set in a small but charming tropical garden. Shady paths wind around lily ponds inhabited by basking turtles. The museum hosts changing exhibitions of works by contemporary Florida artists.

Old Flagler engine, Ormond Beach

🚇 The Casements
25 Riverside Drive. **Tel** (386) 676-3216. **Open** Mon–Sat. **Closed** public hols. ♿ limited. 📷 Mon–Fri.

🏛 Ormond Memorial Art Museum
78 E Granada Blvd. **Tel** (386) 676-3347. **Open** daily. **Closed** public hols. 📷 ♿ �W ormondartmuseum.org

⑬ Daytona Beach
Road map: E2. Volusia Co. 🚹 61,000. ✈ 🚌 ℹ 126 E Orange Ave, (386) 255-0415. �W daytonabeach.com

Extending south from Ormond Beach is brash and boisterous Daytona Beach. As many as 200,000 students descend on the resort for the Spring Break *(see p38)*, even though Daytona has tried to discourage them. Its famous 23-mile (37-km) beach is one of the few in Florida where cars are allowed on the sands, a hangover from the days when motor enthusiasts raced on the beaches *(see p223)*.

Daytona is still a mecca for motorsports fans. The nearby speedway *(see p222)* draws huge crowds, especially during the Speedweek in February and the Motorcycle Weeks in March and October. Downtown Daytona, known simply as "Mainland," lies across the Halifax River from the beach. Most of the action, though, takes place on the beach, which is lined with hotels. The Boardwalk still retains some of its arcades and carnival-style atmosphere, but the area has been regenerated and offers updated rides, including a roller coaster. The Daytona Lagoon waterpark and the bandstand still draw crowds. Down on the beach, jet skis, windsurf boards, buggies, and bicycles can be rented.

Across the Halifax River, in the restored downtown area, the **Halifax Historical Society Museum** occupies a 1910 bank building. Local history displays include a model of the Boardwalk in about 1938, with chicken-feather palm trees and a Ferris wheel.

West of downtown is the excellent **Museum of Arts and Sciences**. The Florida prehistory exhibit is dominated by the 13-ft (4-m) skeleton of a giant sloth, while Arts in America features arts from 1640–1920. There are also notable Cuban and African collections, and a planetarium.

Miss Perkins (c.1840) by J Whiting Stock, Museum of Arts and Sciences

Gamble Place is run by the same museum. Built in 1907 for James N. Gamble, of Procter & Gamble, this hunting lodge, surrounded by open porches, sits on a bluff above Spruce Creek. The furnishings are all period pieces. Tours are by reservation through the museum and take in the Snow White House – an exact copy of the one in Disney's 1937 classic – built in 1938 for Gamble's great-grandchildren.

🏛 Halifax Historical Museum
252 S Beach St. **Tel** (386) 255-6976. **Open** Tue–Sat. **Closed** public hols. 📷 ♿ �W halifaxhistorical.org

🏛 Museum of Arts & Sciences
1040 Museum Blvd. **Tel** (386) 255-0285. **Open** Tue–Sun. **Closed** Thanksgiving, Dec 24, Dec 25. 📷 ♿ **Gamble Place** 📷 �W moas.org

Cars cruising the hard-packed sands of Daytona Beach

⓭ Daytona International Speedway

Road map: E2. Volusia Co. 1801 W International Speedway Blvd. **Tel** (866) 761-7223. 🚍 Daytona. 🚍 9 from bus terminal at 209 Bethune Blvd. **Open** daily. **Closed** Dec 25. 🅰 ♿ ⓦ daytonainternational speedway.com

Daytona's very own "World Center of Racing," the Daytona International Speedway, attracts thousands of race fans and visitors every year. People come from around the world to attend the eight major racing weekends held annually at the track – which can hold about 160,000 spectators.

The Speedway is host to NASCAR (National Association for Stock Car Auto Racing) meets – the Daytona 500 being the most famous – and sports car, motorcycle, and karting races.

Visitors can experience the excitement of participating in the Daytona 500 at the Daytona 500 Experience. There are a number of high-energy thrills on offer, including two different motion simulators and performing a pitstop in an actual Sprint Cup Series race

The Daytona 500, held each February at Daytona International Speedway

car. This attraction is also home to the winning Daytona 500 car, complete with the confetti, tire marks, dents, and signatures of the winning team. The Coca-Cola 3-D IMAX® Theater shows *NASCAR 3D: The IMAX® Experience*, which gives an inside look at the world of NASCAR's elite team and drivers.

1953 red Corvette, a classic sports car

From April to October, you can participate in the Richard Petty Driving Experience, where guests can ride or drive around the historic high banks of the Speedway in an authentic stock car.

A half-hour tram tour around the speedway track is available on days when no races take place.

⓮ Ponce de Leon Inlet Lighthouse

Road map: E2. Volusia Co. 4931 S Peninsula Drive. **Tel** (386) 761-1821. **Open** daily. **Closed** Dec 25. 🅰 ♿ limited. ⓦ ponceinlet.org

This imposing red brick lighthouse dates from 1887 and guards the entrance to a hazardous inlet at the tip of the Daytona peninsula. The lighthouse tapers skyward for 175 ft (53 m), its beacon is visible 19 miles (30 km) out to sea, and there are far-reaching views from the windswept observation deck reached by a 203-step spiral staircase. One of the former keepers' cottages at its base has been restored to its 1890s appearance, another holds the small Museum of the Sea, and a third contains a magnificent 17-ft (5-m) high Fresnel lens.

Daytona International Speedway

Key
▢ Visitor center
▢ Track
▨ Grandstand
▩ Sprint tower

0 meters 500
0 yards 500

The striking Ponce de Leon Inlet lighthouse south of Daytona Beach

For hotels and restaurants in this region see pp314–25 and pp329–49

The Birthplace of Speed

Daytona's love affair with the car started in 1903, when the first timed automobile runs took place on the sands at Ormond Beach, the official "Birthplace of Speed." That year, Alexander Winton achieved a land speed record of 68 mph (109 km/h). The speed trials were enormously popular and attracted large crowds. Wealthy motor enthusiasts gathered at Henry Flagler's Ormond Hotel *(see p220)*, and included the likes of Harvey Firestone and Henry Ford. Speed trials continued until 1935, when Malcolm Campbell set the last world record on the beach. Stock cars began racing at Ormond Beach in 1936, and the first Daytona 200 motorcycle race took place there the following year. Development forced the racetrack to be moved in 1948; in 1959 Daytona International Speedway opened and racing on the beach was abandoned altogether.

Racing on the Beach

In 1902, a guest at the Ormond Hotel noticed just how easy it was to drive his car on the hard sandy beach. He organized the first speed trials, which continued for the next 32 years.

Ransom E. Olds' Pirate was the first car to race on Ormond Beach in 1902. The first official race was held in 1903, when Olds challenged Alexander Winton and Oscar Hedstrom on a motorcycle. Winton won in his car, *Bullet No 1.*

The *Bluebird Streamliner* was driven to a new world record for the measured mile by Malcolm Campbell at Ormond Beach in 1935. Powered by a Rolls-Royce engine, the car reached speeds of just over 276 mph (444 km/h).

The "World Center of Racing"

In 1953 Bill France, who had entered the inaugural stock car race, saw that the growth of Daytona Beach would soon put an end to the beach races. He proposed the construction of Daytona International Speedway, today one of the world's leading race tracks.

Go-karts look like the fun machines that you can race on vacation, but the karts that compete at Daytona manage speeds of over 81 mph (130 km/h).

Lee Petty won the first Daytona 500 at Daytona International Speedway in 1959, beating Johnny Beauchamp, his fellow competitor, by a mere 2 ft (50 cm). The 500-mile (800-km) competition was watched by a crowd of 41,000 and involved 59 cars.

⓯ Blue Spring State Park

Road map: E2. Volusia Co. 2100 W French Ave, Orange City. **Tel** (386) 775–3663. **Open** daily. 🏊 ♿
W floridastateparks.org

One of the country's largest first-magnitude artesian springs, Blue Spring pours out around 100 million gal (450 million liters) of water a day. The temperature of the water is at a constant 68° F (20° C), and consequently the park is a favorite winter refuge for manatees (see p254). Between the months of November and March, when the manatees escape the cooler waters of the St. Johns River, you can see them from the park's elevated boardwalks. Snorkeling or scuba diving are available in the turquoise waters of the spring head, as is canoeing on the St. Johns. **Thursby House**, atop one of the park's ancient shell mounds, was built in the late 19th century.

Environs

About 2 miles (3 km) north as the crow flies is wooded **Hontoon Island State Park**. Reached by a free passenger ferry from Hontoon Landing, the island has an 80-ft (24-m) observation tower, camping and picnic areas, and a nature trail. Canoes and fishing skiffs can also be rented.

In 1955 a rare wooden owl totem made by the ancient local Timucua Indians (see pp44–5) was found here.

🏕 **Hontoon Island State Park**
2309 River Ridge Rd, De Land. **Tel** (386) 736–5309. **Open** daily. 🏊 W floridastateparks.org

Children playing in front of Thursby House, Blue Spring State Park

Florida's Bubbling Springs

Most of Florida's 320 known springs are located in the upper half of the state. The majority are artesian springs, formed by waters forced up deep fissures from underground aquifers (rock deposits containing water). Those that gush over 100 cu ft (3 cu m) per second are known as first-magnitude springs.

Filtered through the rock, the water is extremely pure and sometimes high in salts and minerals. These properties, plus the sheer beauty of the springs, have long attracted visitors for recreational and health purposes.

Juniper Springs in Ocala National Forest, adapted for swimmers in the 1930s

⓰ Sanford

Road map: E2. Seminole Co. 🏙 50,000. 🛈 400 E 1st St, (407) 322–2212. 🚂 inc Auto Train. 🚌 Lynx buses from Orlando (see p387). W sanfordchamber.com

Built during the Seminole Wars (see pp48–51), Fort Mellon was the first permanent settlement on Lake Monroe. Sanford was founded nearby in the 1870s. It became a major inland port thanks to the commercial steamboat services, which eventually brought Florida's early tourists (see p52).

Restored downtown Sanford dates from the 1880s, the height of this Steamboat era. Several of the old red brick buildings (a rarity in Florida) house antique shops, and the area can easily be explored on foot in a couple of hours. Today's visitors are more

Sanford town sign

likely to arrive on the Auto Train (see p384) than by river, but short pleasure cruises are still available.

⓱ Mount Dora

Road map: E2. Lake Co. 🏙 13,000. 🚂 Sanford. 🛈 341 N Alexander St, (352) 383–2165. W mountdora.com

Set among the citrus groves of Lake County, this town is one of the prettiest Victorian settlements left in the state. Its name comes from both the relatively high local elevation of 184 ft (56 m) and the small lake on which it sits. The town was originally known as Royellou, after Roy, Ella, and Louis, the children of the first postmaster.

Mount Dora's attractive tree-lined streets are laid out on a bluff above the lakeshore, and a 3-mile (5-km) historic tour map is available from the chamber of commerce. The tour takes a scenic route around quiet neighborhoods of late 19th-century clapboard homes and the restored downtown historic district, with its stores and antique shops.

On Donnelly Street, the splendid Donnelly House, now a Masonic Hall, is a notable example of ornate Steamboat

Shingles and gingerbread decoration on Donnelly House, Mount Dora

architecture, adorned with pinnacles and a cupola. Nearby, the small Mount Dora History Museum depicts local history in the old fire station, which later became the jail. Down on Lake Dora, fishing and water sports are available.

Mount Dora History Museum
450 Royellou Lane. **Tel** (352) 383-0006. **Open** Tue–Sun. **Closed** Jan 1, Thanksgiving, Dec 25. limited.

⑱ Ocala National Forest

Road map: E2. Lake Co/Marion Co. **Open** daily. to camp site & swimming areas. Visitor Center: 3199 NE Co. Rd. **Tel** (352) 236–0288. Juniper Springs canoe rental: (352) 625-2808. **fs.usda.gov**

Between Ocala and the St. Johns River, the world's largest sand pine forest covers 366,000 acres (148,000 ha), crisscrossed by spring-fed rivers and numerous hiking trails. It is one of the last refuges of the endangered Florida black bear and also home to many more common animals such as deer and otter. Birds, including bald eagles, ospreys, barred owls, the non-native wild turkey, and many species of waders (which frequent the river swamp areas), can all be spotted here.

Dozens of hiking trails vary in length from boardwalks and short loop trails of under a mile (1.5 km) to a 66-mile (106-km) stretch of the cross-state National Scenic Trail *(see p367)*. Bass-fishing is popular on the many lakes scattered through the forest, and there are swimming holes, picnic areas, and camp grounds at recreation areas such as Salt Springs, Alexander Springs, and Fore Lake.

Canoe rental is widely available; the 7-mile (11-km) canoe run down Juniper Creek from the Juniper Springs Recreation Area is one of the finest in the state, but book in advance. Bird-watching is particularly good along the Salt Springs Trail, and wood ducks congregate on Lake Dorr.

You can pick up information and guides at the main visitor center on the western edge of the forest, or at the smaller centers at Salt Springs and Lake Dorr, both on Route 19.

⑲ Silver Springs

Road map: E2. Marion Co. 5656 E Silver Springs Blvd. **Tel** (352) 236-7148. **Open** daily. limited. **floridastateparks.org**

Glass-bottomed boat trips at Silver Springs have been revealing the natural wonders of the world's largest artesian spring since 1878.

Once Florida's oldest commercial tourist attraction, Silver Springs became a state park in 2013 after undergoing a $4-million makeover, which included removing exotic animals and amusement rides. The boat trips offer visitors a glimpse of the Florida outback, where the early Tarzan movies starring Johnny Weismuller were filmed.

Environs
On a quieter note, at **Silver River State Park**, 2 miles (3 km) southeast, you can take a lovely 15-minute walk along a trail through a hardwood hammock and a cypress swamp area, leading to a swimming hole in a bend of the crystal clear river.

Silver River State Park
1425 NE 58th Ave, Ocala. **Tel** (352) 236-7148. **Open** daily. **floridastateparks.org**

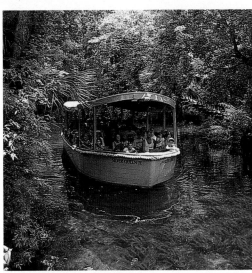

Boats cruise the Silver River from Silver Springs

The Young Shepherdess (1868) by Bougereau, Appleton Museum

⑳ Ocala

Road map: D2. Marion Co. 🅰 58,000. 🚃 🚌 **ⓘ** Chamber of Commerce, 110 E Silver Springs Blvd, (352) 629-8051. **W** ocalacc.com

Surrounded by undulating pastures neatly edged by mile upon mile of white wooden fences, Ocala is the seat of Marion County and center of Florida's thoroughbred horse industry. The grass hereabouts is enriched by the subterranean limestone aquifer *(see p224)*, and the calcium-rich grazing helps to contribute to the light, strong bones of championship horses. Florida's equine industry has produced more than 37 champions, including five Kentucky Derby winners.

There are over 400 thoroughbred farms and specialized breeding centers around Ocala. Many are open for visits, which are usually free of charge. Expect to see Arabians, Paso Finos, and miniature ponies on the farms; contact the Ocala Chamber of Commerce for up-to-date information regarding farm visits.

The other reason to stop off in this area is to visit the **Appleton Museum of Art**, east of Ocala. Built in 1984 of Italian marble by the industrialist and horsebreeder Arthur I. Appleton, the museum houses stunning art from around the world. His eclectic collection includes pre-Columbian and European antiquities, Oriental and African pieces, and Meissen porcelain and is known for its strong core of mainstream 19th-century European art.

🏛 **Appleton Museum of Art**
4333 NE Silver Springs Blvd.
Tel (352) 291-4455. **Open** Tue–Sun. **Closed** Dec 25, Jan 1. ♿ ⬇

㉑ Marjorie Kinnan Rawlings Historic State Park

Road map: D2. Alachua Co. S CR 325, Cross Creek. **Tel** (352) 466-3672. 🚌 Ocala. **Open** grounds daily; house Thu–Sun. **Closed** Aug–Sep. ♿ ⬇
📷 **W** floridastateparks.org

The author Marjorie Kinnan Rawlings arrived in the tiny settlement of Cross Creek, which she was later to describe fondly as "a bend in a country road," in 1928. Her rambling farmhouse remains largely unchanged, nestling in a well-tended citrus grove where ducks waddle up from the banks of Orange Lake.

The writer remained here through the 1930s and then visited on and off until her death in 1953. The local scenery and characters fill her autobiographical novel,

Herlong Inn, stick collection

Cross Creek (1942), while the big scrub country to the south inspired her Pulitzer prize-winning novel *The Yearling* (1938), a coming-of-age story about a boy and his fawn.

Guided tours around the site explore the Cracker-style homestead, built in the 1880s, which has been imaginatively preserved and contains original Rawlings' furnishings: bookcases full of contemporary writings by authors such as John Steinbeck and Ernest Hemingway, a secret liquor cabinet, a typewriter, and a sunhat on the veranda. Lived-in touches like fresh flowers make it look as though the owner has just popped out for a stroll around the garden.

㉒ Micanopy

Road map: D2. Alachua Co. 🅰 650. **ⓘ** 30 East University Ave, Gainesville, (352) 374-5260. **W** micanopytown.com

Established in 1821, Florida's second oldest permanent white settlement was a trading post on Indian lands, originally known as Wanton. Renamed Micanopy in 1826, after an Indian chief, this time-warp village is now as decorous as they come and a haven for filmmakers and antique lovers. Planted with live oaks trailing Spanish moss, the main street, Cholokka Boulevard, is lined with Victorian homes and a strip of historic, brick-fronted shops stuffed with bric-a-brac and craft galleries. Here, too, is the grandest building in Micanopy, the imposing red-brick antebellum **Herlong Mansion**, supported by four massive Corinthian columns. Built by a 19th-century lumber baron, today it serves as a bed and breakfast.

Micanopy's picturesque cemetery, established in 1825, is located on a canopied street off Seminary Road, en route to I-75. It is shaded by spreading live oaks and majestic cedars, and covered with velvety moss.

The airy porch where author Marjorie Kinnan Rawlings once wrote

Lichen-stained gravestones in Micanopy's atmospheric cemetery

Environs

During the 17th century one of the largest and most successful Spanish cattle ranches in Florida was located to the north of present-day Micanopy. Cattle, horses, and hogs once grazed on the lush grass of **Payne's Prairie State Preserve**, where a small herd of wild American bison can sometimes be seen, as well as more than 200 species of local and migratory birds.

Passing through the preserve is the pleasant 17-mile (27-km) **Gainesville-Hawthorne State Trail**, a rail trail used by hikers, riders, and cyclists.

🎣 **Paynes Prairie State Park**
100 Savannah Blvd, US 441, 1 mile (0.5 km) N of Micanopy. **Tel** (352) 466-3397. **Open** daily. 🅿️ 🅰️ 🆆 **floridastateparks.org**

㉓ Gainesville

Road map: D2. Alachua Co.
🏠 125,000 ✈️ 🚌 ℹ️ 300 East University Avenue, (352) 334-7100.
🆆 **gainesvillechamber.com**

A university town, the cultural capital of north central Florida and home of the Gators football team, Gainesville is a comfortable blend of town and gown. In the restored downtown historic district are brick buildings that date from the 1880s to the 1920s, several of which house cafés and restaurants. The campus is dotted with fraternity houses and two important museums.

Leave plenty of time for the first of these, the excellent **Florida Museum of Natural History**. The natural science collections contain over 10 million fossil specimens, plus superb butterfly and shell collections. There are displays dedicated to the various Florida environments and an anthropological journey through the state's history up to the 19th century. The striking **Samuel P. Harn Museum of Art** is one of the largest and best-equipped university art museums in the country. Its permanent collection of fine art and crafts includes Asian ceramics,

African ceremonial objects, Japanese woodcuts, and European and American paintings.

🏛️ **Florida Museum of Natural History**
Hull Rd at SW 34th St. **Tel** (352) 846-2000. **Open** daily.
Closed Thanksgiving, Dec 25.
🅰️ 🆆 **flmnh.ufl.edu**

🏛️ **Samuel P. Harn Museum of Art**
Hull Road (off SW 34th St).
Tel (352) 392-9826. **Open** Tue–Sun.
Closed public hols. 🅰️
🆆 **harn.ufl.edu**

Environs

Just southwest of town, the lovely **Kanapaha Botanical Gardens** are at the height of their beauty from June to September, although visitors in springtime are rewarded by masses of azaleas in bloom. A trail circles the sloping 62-acre site, whose beauty was first noted by the naturalist William Bartram (see p49) in the late 1800s. The paths meander beneath vine-covered arches and through bamboo groves. Other distinct areas include a desert garden, a lakeside bog garden, and a colorful hummingbird garden.

Gainesville's soft drink

🌺 **Kanapaha Botanical Gardens**
4700 SW 58th Drive (off Route 24).
Tel (352) 372-4981. **Open** Fri–Wed.
Closed Dec 25. 🅿️ 🅰️
🆆 **kanapaha.org**

Giant Amazonian water lilies, the late-summer highlight of the bog garden in Kanapaha Botanical Gardens

THE PANHANDLE

There is a saying in Florida that "the farther north you go, the farther south you get." Certainly, the Panhandle has a history and sensibility closer to that of the Deep South than to the lower part of the state. Not only geography and history but climate and even time (the western Panhandle is one hour behind the rest of the state) distinguish this intriguing region from other parts of Florida.

The Panhandle was the site of the first attempt by the Spanish at colonizing Florida and much subsequent fighting by colonial powers. A community was set up near present-day Pensacola in 1559, predating St. Augustine, but was abandoned after a hurricane. It later re-emerged and was the main settlement in the region until the 1820s, when Tallahassee was chosen as the capital of the new Territory of Florida *(see p52)*. The site of the new city, equidistant from St. Augustine and Pensacola, was a compromise – the precise location reputedly being the meeting point of two scouts sent out on horseback from the two cities. Today, Tallahassee is a dignified state capital with elegant architecture but a small-town air. Thanks to the lumber and cotton trade, the 1800s saw spells of prosperity, but the region was bypassed by the influx of wealth that came to other parts of Florida with the laying of the railroads. Tourism in the Panhandle is a more modern development, even though its fine white-sand beaches are unparalleled in the state. This stretch of coast has become increasingly popular with vacationers from the Deep South, but it is still often overlooked by overseas visitors. At the eastern end of the Panhandle, in the area known as the "Big Bend," the family resorts give way to quaint historic coastal towns like Cedar Key, a laid-back fishing village reminiscent of old-time Key West. Inland, large preserves and parks incorporating forests, springs, and navigable rivers provide the main attraction.

One of the Panhandle's many dazzling quartz sand beaches, near Pensacola

◄ The iconic Florida State Capitol building, Tallahassee

Exploring the Panhandle

Most visitors to the Panhandle head straight for the famous beach resorts that stretch in an arc between Pensacola and Panama City Beach. Ideal for family vacations, resorts such as Fort Walton Beach and Destin offer all kinds of accommodations as well as activities ranging from water sports and deep-sea fishing to golf and tennis. While most attention is focused on the coast, the rest of the Panhandle should not be ignored – the resorts can be used as a good base for forays into the hilly, pine-forested interior, where it is possible to escape the crowds. Excellent canoeing can be enjoyed on the Blackwater and the Suwannee rivers, while near Tallahassee you will find some of Florida's prettiest countryside, crossed by unspoiled canopied roads.

Quietwater Beach, near Pensacola on Santa Rosa Island

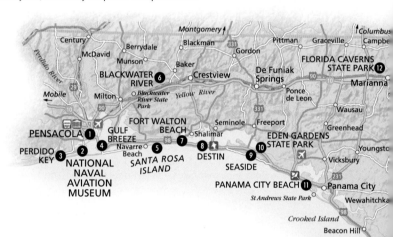

Sights at a Glance

1. Pensacola pp232–5
2. National Naval Aviation Museum pp236–7
3. Perdido Key
4. Gulf Breeze
5. Santa Rosa Island
6. Blackwater River
7. Fort Walton Beach
8. Destin
9. Seaside
10. Eden Gardens State Park
11. Panama City Beach
12. Florida Caverns State Park
13. Torreya State Park
14. St. Joseph Peninsula State Park
15. Apalachicola
16. St. Vincent, St. George, and Dog Islands
17. Wakulla Springs State Park
18. Tallahassee pp246–7
19. AB Maclay Gardens State Park
20. Monticello

22. Suwannee River State Park
23. Steinhatchee
24. Cedar Key

Tours

21. Cotton Trail pp248–9

Elegant, plantation-style mansion at Eden Gardens State Park

For hotels and restaurants in this region see pp314–25 and pp329–49

Getting Around

Although the Amtrak line ran through the region, following the line of I-10, passenger service was halted in 2005, when Hurricane Katrina damaged the lines, so a car is essential for exploring the Panhandle. There are two main driving routes: the fast but dull I-10, which streaks from Pensacola to Tallahassee and then on to the Atlantic Coast; and US 98, which parallels the coast all the way from Pensacola to the so-called "Big Bend," where it links up with the main north-south Gulf Coast highway, US 19. Country roads in the Panhandle are generally quiet, but be on the alert for logging trucks pulling out of concealed forest exits.

Waterfront buildings at the popular harbor of Destin

0 kilometers 30

0 miles 30

Key

= Highway

= Major road

= Secondary road

= Minor road

— Scenic route

–•– Main railway

= State border

Pelicans enjoying the peace and quiet of Apalachicola

For additional map symbols *see back flap*

❶ Street-by-Street: Pensacola

The city's first settlers were a party of Spanish colonists, led by Don Tristan de Luna, who sailed into Pensacola Bay in 1559. Their settlement survived only two years before being wiped out by a hurricane. The Spanish returned, but Pensacola changed hands frequently: in the space of just over 300 years the Spanish, French, English, Confederate, and US flags all flew over the city. Pensacola took off in the 1880s, when much of the present downtown district was built. This area features a variety of architectural styles, ranging from quaint colonial cottages to elegant Classical-Revival homes built during the late 19th-century timber boom. The route shown here focuses on the area known as Historic Pensacola Village *(see p234)*.

Lavalle House
The simple plan and bright color scheme of this early 19th-century two-room cottage was designed to appeal to its French Creole immigrant tenants.

The Museum of Industry
Recalls Pensacola's timber and maritime trades using a reconstructed sawmill ship's chandlery and a replica logging train.

Pensacola Historical Museum Exhibits here focus on the history of the Pensacola area. There is a great wealth of material and artifacts which is available to the public.

★ **TT Wentworth, Jr. Museum**
A broad collection of Florida memorabilia, such as this 1870s bed, fill this unusual museum.

A British officers' compound has been excavated in this parking lot. The exposed foundations form part of the city's Colonial Archaeological Trail *(see p234)*.

Pensacola Museum of Art
The old city jail, dating from 1908, was converted into a museum in the 1950s. This William Nell landscape is among the broad array of art exhibited.

For hotels and restaurants in this region see pp314–25 and pp329–49

Steamboat House
Dating from the mid-19th-century steamboat era *(see p52)*, this delightful house echoes the shape of a riverboat. It comes complete with veranda "decks."

VISITORS' CHECKLIST

Practical Information
Road map: A1. Escambia Co.
🚇 294,400. 🛈 1401 E Gregory St, (850) 434-1234. 🎭 Fiesta of Five Flags (Jun).
🆆 visitpensacola.com

Transport
✈ 5 miles (8 km) N. 🚌 980 E Heinburg St, (850) 433-4966. 🚏 505 W Burgess Rd, (850) 476-4800.

★ Seville Square
Shaded by live oaks and magnolia trees, Seville Square lies at the heart of the Seville District, which was laid out by the British in the 1770s.

GOVERNMENT STREET

ALCANIZ STREET

ADAMS STREET

ZARRAGOSSA ST.

BAYFRONT PARKWAY

Fountain Square
centers around a fountain decorated with plaques showing local features.

Dorr House, a fine Greek-Revival mansion, is the last of its kind in western Florida.

★ Museum of Commerce
A fully equipped print workshop is one of the many interesting exhibits in the museum's cleverly constructed late-Victorian streetscape.

0 meters	200
0 yards	200

Key

— Suggested route

Exploring Pensacola

Several historic districts provide the most interesting areas to explore in Pensacola. Foremost is the old downtown district, Historic Pensacola Village, which is centered on pretty Zarragossa Street. Farther north, in the North Hill Preservation District, you can stroll past the homes built by prominent local professionals and merchants during the 19th-century timber boom. Between the two, Palafox Place is a busy commercial district with a number of distinctive buildings and quaint shops.

Downtown Pensacola is linked by two bridges to its barrier island resort satellite, Pensacola Beach *(see p240)*. While sightseeing is focused on the mainland, visitors often stay in hotels by the beach.

Cell doors now standing open, Pensacola Museum of Art

Guides in 19th-century costume in Historic Pensacola Village

🏘 Historic Pensacola Village

Tivoli House, 205 E Zarragossa St. **Tel** (850) 595-5985. **Open** Tue–Sat. **Closed** public hols. 🎫 ♿ 📷
🌐 historicpensacola.org

This collection of museums and historic houses is located in Pensacola's oldest quarter, called the Historic Pensacola Village. You can enjoy an unhurried stroll through the village's streets, which offer a taste of the city as it was in the 19th century.

For a more in-depth look, you should take one of the guided tours that depart twice daily from Tivoli House on Zarragossa Street; in tourist season, tour guides liven up the proceedings by dressing in period costume. The tours visit the simply furnished French Creole Lavalle House (1805) and the gracious Dorr House (1871). Other properties, while not included on the tour, are open to visitors. A single ticket, available from Tivoli House, covers the tour and entrance to all village properties over two days. You will need this ticket to visit the

Museum of Industry and Museum of Commerce. Housed in a late 19th-century warehouse, the Museum of Industry on Church Street provides an informative introduction to Pensacola's early development. Exhibits cover brick-making, fishing, transportation, and the lumber trade.

Forming a backdrop to Zarragossa Street's Museum of Commerce is a Victorian street scene complete with reconstructed stores including a printer's shop with a working press, a pharmacy, a saddlery, and an old-time music store.

Overlooking leafy Seville Square is Old Christ Church, built in 1832 and one of the oldest churches in Florida still standing on its original site.

🏛 TT Wentworth, Jr., Florida State Museum

330 S Jefferson St. **Tel** (850) 595-5990. **Open** Tue–Sat. **Closed** public hols. ♿
This museum is laid out in the former City Hall, an imposing Spanish Renaissance Revival building. The founder's eclectic collections include West Florida memorabilia, artifacts from Spanish shipwrecks, and weird

and wonderful oddities from all over the world. These run the gamut from arrowheads and a shrunken head from pre-Columbian times to a 1930s telephone exchange and old Coca-Cola bottles.

The museum contains well thought-out historical displays and dioramas illustrating points along Pensacola's Colonial Archaeological Trail, which links remains of fortifications dating from 1752–1821. One of the exhibits chronicles over 450 years of Pensacola history.

🏛 Pensacola Museum of Art

407 S Jefferson St. **Tel** (850) 432-6247. **Open** Tue–Sat. **Closed** Jul 4, Thanksgiving, Dec 25, Jan 1. 🎫 except Tue. ♿
🌐 pensacolamuseumofart.org

The cells of the old city jail, complete with steel-barred doors, have taken on a new life as whitewashed galleries for this Museum. Frequently changing exhibitions draw on the museum's broad-based collections, which include pre-Columbian pottery, 19th-century satinware glass, and Roy Lichtenstein's Pop Art.

The Spanish Renaissance-style home of the TT Wentworth, Jr. Museum

🏛 Pensacola Children's Museum

115 E Zarragossa St. **Tel** (850) 595-1559. **Open** 10am–4pm Tue–Sat. **Closed** Sun, public hols. 🅿 🅰
W historicpensacola.org

Housed in an 1885 building first known as the Gulf Saloon, the museum, run by the West Florida Historic Preservation, Inc., offers an interactive learning experience of Pensacola history, showcasing military and multicultural histories plus the maritime and lumber industries. Child-friendly exhibits include the Panton Trading Post, Lavalle Cottage, the Fort, Native American Village, and Kiddie Corral. The second floor houses artifacts geared for older children and adults, but also offers a train set, building blocks, and dress-up clothes for younger kids.

🏛 North Hill Preservation District

This historic district (stretching for about ten blocks from Wright Street, north of Pensacola Historic Village) features

McCreary House in the North Hill Preservation District

The extensive, unspoiled sands at Johnson Beach on Perdido Key

elegant late 19th- and early 20th-century houses. They were built on the site of former British and Spanish forts, and even now cannon balls are occasionally dug up in their tree-shaded gardens. All the houses are privately owned. Among the most striking is the veranda-fronted McCreary House (see p34) on North Baylen Street, close to the intersection with De Soto Street.

❷ National Naval Aviation Museum

See pp236–7.

❸ Perdido Key

Road map: A1. Escambia Co. Route 292, 12 miles (19 km) W of Pensacola. 🚌 Pensacola. 🚐 Pensacola. 🛈 15500 Perdido Key Dr, Pensacola, (850) 492-4600. **W** perdidochamber.com

A 30-minute drive southwest from Pensacola are the pristine shores of Perdido Key, which regularly features in the list of the top 20 US beaches. There are bars and restaurants and facilities for water sports, fishing, and diving, or you can simply swim or soak up the sun.

The whole eastern end of the island is accessible only by foot. The road runs as far as the **Johnson Beach Day Use Area**, just east of the bridge from the mainland. The sands extend for some 6 miles (10 km) on both gulf and bay sides, and there are facilities for visitors and a ranger station.

On the mainland opposite Perdido Key, **Big Lagoon State Park** combines sandy beach with salt-marsh areas offering excellent bird-watching and hiking. Enjoy sweeping views from the observation tower.

🚻 Johnson Beach Day Use Area
13300 Johnson Beach Rd, off Route 292. **Tel** Federal Govt Office of National Seashore (850) 934-2600. **Open** daily. **Closed** Dec 25. 🅿 🅰

🏕 Big Lagoon State Park
12301 Gulf B each Highway. **Tel** (850) 492-1595. **Open** daily. 🅿 🅰

Florida's Lumber Boom

In the 19th century, the demand for lumber and naval stores including tar and turpentine played an important part in northern Florida's development. Its vast stands of live oaks were particularly popular with shipbuilders for their disease- and decay-resistant wood. Flourishing lumber towns such as Cedar Key *(see p249)* were established, and the fortunes made during the lumber boom of the 1870s–80s were transformed into Pensacola's elegant homes, including Eden Mansion *(see p241)*.

By the 1930s, most of Florida's mature hardwood forest had been destroyed, and other building materials and forms of fuel had begun to replace wood. The lumber mills closed, leaving thousands unemployed.

Loggers in the 19th century, who worked long hours of hard manual labor

❷ National Naval Aviation Museum

Opened in 1963, this free museum has grown over the years to more than 350,000 sq ft (32,500 sq m) of exhibit space, making it the world's largest Naval Aviation museum. More than 150 aircraft and spacecraft, as well as models, artifacts, and technological displays, don the decks aboard Naval Air Station Pensacola, attracting nearly a million visitors annually. Representing Navy, Marine Corps, and Coast Guard aviation, the museum offers tours by volunteers, many of whom are military veterans.

Hangar Bay One
The museum's Hangar Bay One exhibit displays aircraft of the post-World War II era, including a Marine One presidential helicopter and a replica of the Apollo 17 lunar module.

Flying Tigers
The painted jaws of these World War II fighters were the trademark of the Volunteer Flying Tiger pilots who fought in the skies over China and Burma.

The USS *Cabot* Flight Deck is a life-sized reproduction of a World War II aircraft carrier deck, complete with fighter planes.

Sunken Treasures displays two aircraft recovered from Lake Michigan, where they sank during training in World War II.

Spirit of Naval Aviation Monument

F-14 Tomcat

Entrance

The IMAX® theater shows four different features seven times daily.

Gallery Guide

The museum occupies two floors, or "decks," which are divided into two wings joined by an atrium. The west wing is devoted almost entirely to World War II carrier aircraft, while the south wing is more broadly historical. More aircraft can be found in Hangar Bay One, to the rear of the museum.

Biplane
Early aircraft include World War I training planes and biplanes once favored by circus barnstormers.

K47 Airship
America's "K"-type airships performed vital maritime patrol duties during World War II.

VISITORS' CHECKLIST

Practical Information
Road map: 1A. 1750 Radford Blvd, NAS Pensacola. **Tel** (850) 453-2389 🚂 Pensacola. 🚌 Pensacola. **Open** 9am–5pm Mon–Fri, 10am–5pm Sat–Sun. **Closed** Jan 1, Thanksgiving, Dec 25. 🐾 🅿 📷 ♿
W navalaviationmuseum.org

The Space Capsule Display features a Skylab Command Module, Mercury Capsule, Moon Rover Vehicle, astronaut suits, space films, and memorabilia.

★ MaxFlight Simulators
Visitors can experience mid-air combat and stunt flying in scenarios with dozens of different aircraft.

Cockpit trainers show actual layouts of various Naval Aviation aircraft.

★ Blue Angels
Four former Blue Angels A-4 Sky-hawks are suspended in a dramatic diamond formation from the ceiling of the seven-story glass atrium.

Fort Barrancas

Enclosed by water on three sides, the strategic Naval Air Station site was fortified by Spanish colonists in 1698. The original ram-parts, built on a bluff (*barranca* in Spanish) overlooking Pensacola Bay, were replaced by a more substantial fort in 1781, and major additions were made by the US Army in the 1840s. The remains of the Spanish and US forts, concealed behind formidable defensive earthworks, are linked by a tunnel. The fort is a few minutes' walk from the museum, where you can arrange to go on a guided tour of the area.

View of the earthworks surrounding Fort Barrancas

Key

⬜ WWII/Korean War aircraft
⬜ Early aircraft
⬜ Modern aircraft
⬜ Theater
⬜ Interactive exhibits
⬜ Displays
⬜ Art gallery
⬜ Hangar Bay One
⬜ Nonexhibition space

➍ Gulf Breeze

Road map: A1. Santa Rosa Co.
🏠 6,600. 🚊 Pensacola. 🚌 Pensacola.
ℹ 409 Gulf Breeze Parkway, (850) 932-7888. 🌐 gulfbreezechamber.com

The affluent community of Gulf Breeze lies at the western end of a promontory reaching out into Pensacola Bay. The area east of the town is heavily wooded and once formed part of the huge swathes of southern woodlands that were earmarked in the 1820s to provide lumber for shipbuilding (see p235).

The **Naval Live Oaks Reservation**, off US 98, was originally a government-owned tree farm and now protects some of the remaining woodland. Visitors can follow trails through 1,300 acres (500 ha) of oak hammock woodlands, sandhill areas, and wetlands, where wading birds feast off an abundance of marine life. A visitor center dispenses maps and information on local flora and fauna.

Ten miles (16 km) east of Gulf Breeze, **The Zoo** is a favorite family excursion, with more than 700 animals in residence. You can take a ride on the Safari Line train through 30 acres (12 ha) of land where animals roam freely, catch a show by Ellie the elephant, or stroll through the botanical

The Safari Line train, on its tour around The Zoo, Gulf Breeze

gardens. You can even look a giraffe in the eye from the feeding platform.

🎫 Naval Live Oaks Reservation
1801 Gulf Breeze Parkway. **Tel** (850) 934-2600. **Open** daily. **Closed** Dec 25.
🚻 limited. 🌐 nps.gov/guis

🎫 The Zoo
5701 Gulf Breeze Parkway. **Tel** (850) 932-2229. **Open** daily. **Closed** Thanksgiving, Dec 25. 🅿 🚻

➎ Santa Rosa Island

Road map: A1. Escambia Co, Okaloosa Co, Santa Rosa Co.
🚊 Pensacola. 🚌 Pensacola or Fort Walton Beach. ℹ 8543 Navarre Parkway, Navarre, (850) 939-2691.
🌐 floridabeachestorivers.com

A long, thin streak of sand, Santa Rosa stretches all the way from Pensacola Bay to Fort Walton Beach, a distance of 45 miles (70 km). At its western tip **Fort Pickens**, completed in 1834, is the largest of four US forts constructed in the early 19th century to defend Pensacola Bay.

The Apache chieftain Geronimo was imprisoned here from 1886–8, during which time people came from far and wide to see him; the authorities supposedly encouraged his transformation into a tourist attraction. The fort remained in use by the US Army until 1947. Now, you are free to explore the brick fort's dark passageways and small museum.

The nature trail, Naval Live Oaks Reservation

Santa Rosa has several fine white beaches. Pensacola Beach and Navarre Beach are both popular, each with a fishing pier and plenty of water sports activities. Between them is a beautiful, undeveloped stretch of sand where you can relax away from the crowds. There is a campground at the western end of the island, near Fort Pickens.

🏰 Fort Pickens
1400 Fort Pickens Rd (Route 399).
Tel (850) 934-2621. **Open** daily. 🅿
🚻 limited. 🏕 🌐 nps.gov/guis

Boardwalk leading onto Pensacola Beach on Santa Rosa Island

➏ Blackwater River

Road map: A1. Santa Rosa Co.
🚊 Pensacola. 🚌 Pensacola. ℹ 5247 Stewart St, Milton, (850) 623-2339.
🌐 santarosachamber.com

The Blackwater River starts in Alabama and flows for 60 miles (95 km) south to the Gulf of Mexico. One of the purest sand-bottomed rivers in the world, its dark, tannin-stained waters meander prettily through the forest, creating oxbow lakes and sand beaches.

The river's big attraction is its canoeing: one of the state's finest canoe trails runs for 31 miles (50 km) along its course. Canoe and kayak trips can be arranged through several operators in Milton, the self-styled "Canoeing Capital of Florida." These trips range from half-day paddles to three-day marathons, with the option of

The Blackwater River, well known for its canoeing trail

tackling the more challenging Sweetwater and Juniper creeks to the north.

The small **Blackwater River State Park**, located at the end of the canoe trail, offers swimming, picnicking areas, and the Chain of Lakes Trail. This 1-mile (1.5-km) nature trail runs through woodlands thick with oak, hickory, southern magnolia, and red maple trees.

Blackwater River State Park
Off US 90, 15 miles (24 km) NE of Milton. **Tel** (850) 983-5363. **Open** daily. limited. **W** floridastateparks.org

Fort Walton Beach

Road map: A1. Okaloosa Co. 18,500. Crestview. 34 Miracle Strip Parkway SE, (850) 244-8191, (800) 322-3319.
W fwbchamber.org

Fort Walton Beach lies at the western tip of the so-called Emerald Coast, a 24-mile (40-km) strip of dazzling beach stretching east to Destin and beyond.

Diving shops and marinas line US 98, which skirts the coast and links Fort Walton to Santa Rosa Island. Known locally as Okaloosa Island, this is where most local people and visitors go. There is superb swimming as well as pier and deep-sea fishing, and this is a prime location for water sports too.

You can also swim or go sailing or windsurfing off the island's north shore, on sheltered Chocta-whatchee Bay. Boat trips can be arranged at the numerous marinas. For those who prefer dry land, the Emerald Coast boasts a dozen golf courses.

Performing dolphins and sea lions star in daily shows at the popular **Gulfarium** marine park. The glass walls of the Living Sea aquarium reveal sharks, rays, and huge sea turtles. There are also seal and otter enclosures, as well as alligators and exotic birds. There's not a great deal to lure you downtown except for the

informative **Indian Temple Mound Museum**, which stands in the shadow of an ancient Indian earthwork. This former ceremonial and burial site of the Apalachee Indians (see pp44–5) dates from about AD 1400. The museum exhibits artifacts recovered from the mound and other Indian sites nearby, while well-illustrated displays trace more than 10,000 years of human habitation in the Choctawhatchee Bay area.

Three miles (5 km) north of town at Shalimar is the Eglin Air Force Base, the largest air force base in the world. Here, the **US Air Force Armament Museum** displays aircraft, missiles, and bombs dating from World War II to the present day. There is a SR-71 "Blackbird" spy plane as well as high-tech laser equipment. Tours of the 720-sq mile (1,865-sq km) base are available.

Indian pot, Temple Mound Museum

Gulfarium
1010 Miracle Strip Parkway.
Tel (850) 244-5169. **Open** daily.
Closed Thanksgiving, Dec 24, Dec 25.
limited. **W** gulfarium.com

Indian Temple Mound Museum
139 SE Miracle Strip Parkway.
Tel (850) 833-9595. **Open** Mon–Sat.
Closed Jan 1, Thanksgiving, Dec 25.
limited. **W** fwb.org

US Air Force Armament Museum
100 Museum Drive (Route 85).
Tel (850) 651-1808. **Open** daily.
Closed public hols.

People strolling along the Gulf of Mexico's white powder sands at Fort Walton Beach

❽ Destin

Road map: A1. Okaloosa Co.
🏙 12,000. ✈ 🚌 Fort Walton Beach.
ℹ 4484 Legendary Dr, Suite A, (850)
837-6241. 🌐 destinchamber.com

Situated between the Gulf of Mexico and Choctawhatchee Bay, Destin is a narrow strip of a town that runs parallel to the coastal highway, US 98. It started out in 1845 as a fishing camp but the town has since grown into what is claimed to be the "most prolific fishing

Fisherman at work on his catches at the harbor in Destin

village" in the United States. Deep-sea fishing is the big draw and charter boats come and go full of hopeful fishermen. The waters near Destin are particularly rich in fish because of a 100-ft (30-m) drop in the continental shelf only 10 miles (16 km) from the shore. The prime catches include amberjack, tarpon, and blue marlin. There is a busy calendar of fishing tournaments in Destin, the most notable being October's month-long Fishing Rodeo. Another important date is early October, when people flock to Destin for the annual Seafood Festival. Cockles, mussels, shrimp, and crab tempt the crowds.

With its stunning beaches and the clear waters so typical of the Emerald Coast, Destin has also become a very popular seaside resort. There are plenty of good opportunities for diving, and for snorkeling too.

🎪 **Destin Seafood Festival**
Destin (Early Oct).

A wooden tower characteristic of Seaside's gulfshore homes

❾ Seaside

Road map: B1. Walton Co. 🏙 200.
ℹ (850) 231-4224. 🌐 seasidefl.com

When Robert Davis decided to develop Seaside in the mid-1980s, the vanished resorts of his childhood provided his inspiration. Davis's vision was of a nostalgic vacation town of traditional northwest Florida-style wooden cottages, with wraparound verandas, steeply pitched roofs, and white picket fences. The original style was

The Beaches of the Panhandle

Between Perdido Key and Panama City Beach lie some of the most beautiful beaches in Florida. The finely ground sand – 90 percent quartz, washed down from the Appalachian mountains – sweeps into broad beaches and can be nearly blinding in the sunlight. The hordes descend in June and July, but the Gulf waters are still pleasantly warm as late as November. You can choose between quiet, undeveloped beaches and the more dynamic resorts; there is also plenty of opportunity for diving and other water sports.

③ **Pensacola Beach** has miles of pristine sand overlooked by a string of shops, hotels, and bars. A large crowd gathers on weekends (see p238).

① **Perdido Key** Some of the state's most westerly shores, on Perdido Key, are inaccessible by car and are therefore quieter than most (see p235).

② **Gulf Islands National Seashore** offers camping, a superb beach for popular coastal activities, and historical fortifications to explore.

④ **Navarre Beach** is one of the quieter of the island's beaches. It has good facilities, including a pier for fishing (see p238).

0 kilometers   15
0 miles   10

rapidly hijacked, however, by quaint gingerbread detailing, turrets, and towers *(see p35)*.

The town's pastel-painted, Neo-Victorian charms have an unreal, Disneyesque quality, and if you're driving along US 98 it's hard to resist stopping for a quick peek. And then, of course, there is the additional appeal of the beach.

Environs

1 mile (1.5 km) west of Seaside, the **Grayton Beach State Park** boasts another fine stretch of Panhandle shoreline, and one that regularly features high in the rankings of the nation's top beaches. In addition to its broad strand of pristine quartz-white sand, the park offers good surf fishing, boating facilities, a nature trail, and also a campground. During the summer, families can take part in ranger-led programs.

Grayton Beach State Park
County Rd 30A, off US 98, (1 mile) 1.5 km W of Seaside. **Tel** (850) 231-4210.
Open daily.
W floridastateparks.org

Statue amid the lush surroundings of the Eden State Gardens

⓾ Eden Gardens State Park

Road map: B1. Walton Co. Point Wash-ington. **Tel** (850) 231-4214.
Fort Walton Beach. Gardens: **Open** daily. House: **Open** Thu–Mon.
10am–2pm.
W floridastateparks.org

Lumber baron William H. Wesley built this fine Greek Revival mansion overlooking the Choctawhatchee River in 1897. The gracious two-story wooden building, styled after an antebellum mansion, with high-ceilinged rooms and broad verandas, is furnished with antiques. The gardens, planted with camellias and azaleas, and shaded by southern magnolia trees and live oaks; these lead to picnic tables by the river, near where the old lumber mill once stood. Whole trees were once floated from inland forests downriver to the mill, where they were sawed into logs, then sent by barge along the Intracoastal Waterway to Pensacola.

⑦ Santa Rosa Beach
This undeveloped sandy beach is backed by dunes and marshlands teeming with birds and other wildlife.

⑨ Panama City Beach
Condos, hotels, and amusement and water parks line buzzing Panama City Beach. Diving and water sports are popular pastimes *(see p242)*.

Valparaiso
Fort Walton Beach
Choctawhatchee Bay

Seaside

Panama City

⑥ Destin
attracts bathers to its gorgeous beach, as well as a macho deep-sea fishing crowd.

⑧ Grayton
provides boardwalks across the dunes to one of the finest beaches in the country.

⑤ Fort Walton Beach
is a relaxed, family-oriented resort and one of the best for water sports *(see p239)*.

⓾ St. Andrews
has a superb beach that, unlike Panama City Beach, is protected against developers *(see pp242–3)*.

Panama City Beach, the liveliest seaside resort in the Panhandle

⓫ Panama City Beach

Road map: B1. Bay Co. 🚌 14,500.
✈️ 🚌 ℹ️ 17001 Panama City Beach
Pkwy, (850) 233-5070. Captain
Anderson's: **Tel** (850) 234-3435.
Treasure Island Marina: **Tel** (850)
234-8944.
w **visitpanamacity beach.com**

A brash postcard sort of a
place, Panama City Beach is a
27-mile (43-km) "Miracle Strip"
of hotels, amusement parks,
and arcades, bordered by a
gleaming quartz sand beach.
The Panhandle's biggest resort,
it caters both to the young
crowds at Spring Break *(see
p38)* and to families, who
dominate in summer. The
sports facilities are excellent.
   Panama City Beach, nicknamed the "wreck capital of the
south," is a famous diving
destination. Besides natural
coral reefs, it has more than 50
artificial diving sites created by
wrecked boats – providing
some of the best diving in the
Gulf. Dive operators offer scuba
and snorkeling trips and lessons.
For the less energetic, Captain
Anderson's and Treasure Island
Marina offer dolphin feeding
trips and glass-bottomed
boat tours.

🐬 Gulf World Marine Park

15412 Front Beach Rd. ℹ️ (850) 234-
5271. **Open** daily. **Closed** Thanksgiving, Dec 25. 🅿️ 🚻
w **gulfworldmarinepark.com**

Dolphin and sea lion shows
are the highlights here. The
aquariums and a walk-
through shark tank are set
in lush tropical gardens
with a resident troupe of
performing parrots.

🏛️ Museum of Man in the Sea

17314 Panama City Beach Parkway.
Tel (850) 235-4101. **Open** daily.
Closed Jan 1, Thanksgiving, Dec 25.
🅿️ 🚻 w **maninthesea.org**

The Museum of Man in the Sea
provides a homespun but
educational look at the history
of diving and marine salvage.
It has exhibits ranging from
ancient diving helmets to
salvaged treasures from the
17th-century Spanish galleon
Atocha (see p32), and there is a
parking lot full of submarines.
A favorite exhibit is Moby
Dick, a whale rescue vessel
resembling a killer whale.

🦓 ZooWorld

9008 Front Beach Rd.
Tel (850) 230-1243. **Open** daily.
Closed Dec 25. 🅿️ 🚻
w **zooworldpcb.net**

ZooWorld is home to more than
350 animals, including bears, big
cats, alligators, camels, giraffes,
and orangutans, as well as more
than 15 endangered species.
   The Gentle Jungle Petting
Zoo, which offers plenty of
opportunity to interact with the
wildlife, is particularly popular
with young children.

An orangutan, one of ZooWorld's more
entertaining residents

🎢 Shipwreck Island Water Park

12201 Hutchison Blvd. **Tel** (850) 234-
3333. **Open** Apr–May: Sat, Sun; Jun–
Aug: daily (subject to change). 🅿️
🚻 limited. w **shipwreckisland.com**

This water park will have no
trouble keeping the family
entertained for the entire day.
The 1,600-ft (490-m) Lazy River
tube ride is great and there are
higher-energy options for the
more adventurous: try the
35-mph (55-km/h) Speed
Slide, the Raging Rapids, or the
370-ft (110-m) White Knuckle
Rapids. There are gentler rides
for youngsters, as well as a
kids' pool. Other attractions
include a wave pool and
sunbathing areas.

Fun on the Lazy River ride at Shipwreck
Island Water Park

🎢 Coconut Creek Family Fun Park

9807 Front Beach Rd. **Tel** (850) 234-
2625, (888) 764-2199. **Open** 9am–
11:30pm daily. **Closed** Dec 24, 25.
🅿️ Children under 6 play free. 🚻
w **coconutcreekfun.com**

This park has two 18-hole mini-
golf courses, featuring an
African safari theme. There is
also a giant maze the size of a
football field, which has as its
theme voyaging from one
South Pacific island to another,
and is the largest of its kind in
the country.

Environs
An easy 3-mile (5-km) hop
southeast of the main Strip,
St. Andrews State Park is a
good antidote to Panama City

A replica of a turpentine still in St. Andrews State Park

Beach, though it can get very busy in summer. The preserve has a white sand beach – named the best beach in the US in 1995. The swimming is good, and there is excellent snorkeling around the rock jetties. Behind the dunes, lagoons and marshland are home to alligators and wading birds. Also within the park, not far from the fishing pier, is a modern re-creation of an early turpentine still, like those found throughout the state in the early 1900s *(see p235)*.

⚓🏕 St. Andrews State Park
4607 State Park Ln. **Tel** (850) 233-5140.
Open daily. 🅿️ ♿ limited. ⛺
🌐 **floridastateparks.org**

⑫ Florida Caverns State Park

Road map: B1. Jackson Co. 3345 Caverns Rd, off Route 166, 3 miles (5 km) N of Marianna. 🚌 Marianna; **Tel** (850) 482-9598. **Open** daily. 🅿️ ♿ 🍴 ⛺ 🌐 **floridastateparks.org**

The limestone that underpins Florida is laid bare in this series of underground caves hollowed out of the soft rock and drained by the Chipola River. The filtering of rainwater through the limestone rock over thousands of years has created a breathtaking subterranean cavescape of stalactites, stalagmites, columns, and glittering rivulets of crystals. Wrap up warm for the guided tours, since the caverns maintain a cool 61–66 °F (16–19 °C).

The park also offers hiking trails and horseback riding, and you can swim and fish in the Chipola River. A 52-mile (84-km) canoe trail slips through the high limestone cliffs along the river's route south to Dead Lake, just west of Apalachicola National Forest *(see p244)*.

⑬ Torreya State Park

Road map: C1. Liberty Co. Route CR 1641, 13 miles (21 km) N of Bristol. 🚌 Blountstown. **Tel** (850) 643-2674. **Open** daily. ♿ 🅿️ limited. 🌐 **floridastateparks.org**

More off the beaten track than most other parks in Florida, Torreya State Park is well worth seeking out. Named after the torreya, a rare type of yew tree that once grew here in abundance, the park abuts a beautiful forested bend in the Apalachicola River. High limestone bluffs, into which Confederate soldiers dug gun pits to repel Union gunboats during the Civil War, flank the river, offering one of the few high natural vantage points in Florida.

Gregory House, a fine 19th-century Classical Revival mansion, stands on top of the 150-ft (45-m) bluff. In 1935 it was moved here from its first site downriver by conservationists and has since been restored.

It is a 25-minute walk from Gregory House down to the river and back, or you can take the 7-mile (11-km) Weeping Ridge Trail. Both paths run through woodland and offer a chance to spot all kinds of birds, deer, beaver, and the unusual Barbours map turtle (so-called for the maplike lines etched on its shell).

⑭ St. Joseph Peninsula State Park

Road map: B1. Gulf Co. Route 30E. 🚌 Blountstown. **Tel** (850) 227-1327. **Open** daily. 🅿️ ♿ limited. ⛺ open all year. 🌐 **floridastateparks.org**

At the tip of the slender sand spit that extends north from Cape San Blas to enclose St. Joseph's Bay, this beautifully unspoiled beach park is ideal for those in search of a little peace and quiet. The swimming is excellent, and snorkeling and surf fishing are also popular activities. Bird-watchers should pack their binoculars, since the bird life is prolific along the shoreline: over 200 species of birds have been recorded here. You can stay in cabins overlooking the bay, and there are basic camping facilities, too.

Venture from the beach and explore the saw palmetto and pine woodlands, where you may see deer, raccoons, bobcats, and even coyotes.

The forested course of the Apalachicola River in Torreya State Park

Restored houses on the water's edge in Water Street, Apalachicola

⓯ Apalachicola

Road map: B1. Franklin Co.
🏙 3000. 🚌 Tallahassee. ℹ️ 122
Commerce St, (850) 653-9419.
🆆 apalachicolabay.org

A riverside customs station established in 1823, Apalachicola saw its finest days during the first 100 years of its existence. It boomed first with the cotton trade, then sponge divers and lumber barons made their fortunes here. Today, a swath of pines and hardwoods still stands as the Apalachicola National Forest, extending from 12 miles (19 km) north of Apalachicola to the outskirts of Tallahassee.

At the end of the lumber boom in the 1920s, the town turned to oystering and fishing in the waters at the mouth of the Apalachicola River. Oyster and other fishing boats still pull up at the dockside, which is lined with refrigerated sea-food houses and old brick-built cotton warehouses. Among the seafood houses on Water Street there are several places to sample fresh oysters.

The old town is laid out in a neat grid with many fine historic buildings dating from the cotton boom era. A walking map, available from the chamber of commerce, takes in such privately owned treasures as the 1838 Greek Revival Raney House.

Devoted to the town's most notable resident, the **John Gorrie Museum State Park** has a model of Gorrie's patent ice-making machine. Designed to cool the sickrooms of yellow fever sufferers, Dr. Gorrie's 1851 invention was the vanguard of modern refrigeration and air conditioning.

🏛 John Gorrie Museum State Park
46 6th Street (Gorrie Square). **Tel** (850) 653-9347. **Open** Thu–Mon. **Closed** Jan 1, Thanksgiving, Dec 25. 🦽

⓰ St. Vincent, St. George, and Dog Islands

Road map: B2, C2, C1. Franklin Co.
🚌 Tallahassee. ℹ️ 122 Commerce St, Apalachicola, (850) 653-9419. Jeannie's Journeys: **Tel** (850) 927-3259.
🆆 sgislandjourneys.com

This string of barrier islands separates Apalachicola Bay from the Gulf of Mexico. St. George is linked by a bridge to Apalachicola. However, a 9-mile (14-km) stretch of dunes at its eastern end is preserved as the **St. George Island State Park**; the main expanse of beach is on the gulf side. The beaches on St. George are consistently named among the best nationally.

To the west, the **St. Vincent National Wildlife Refuge** is uninhabited and accessible only by boat: Jeannie's Journeys, on East Gorey Drive, runs tours.

Surf fishing, a popular activity on the quiet sands of St. George Island

Kayak tours to the island's interior are available between May and October. Visitors can see nesting ospreys in spring, sea turtles laying their eggs in summer, and migrating waterfowl in winter.

To the east, little Dog Island must be reached by boat from Carrabelle on the mainland. It has a small inn, big dunes, and excellent shell hunting.

🏞 St. George Island State Park
Tel (850) 927-2111. **Open** daily.

🏞 St. Vincent National Wildlife Refuge
Tel (850) 653-8808. **Open** Mon–Fri.

Fun in the pool at Wakulla Springs

⓱ Wakulla Springs State Park

Road map: C1. Wakulla Co. 550. Wakulla Park Drive, Wakulla Springs. **Tel** (850) 926-0700. 🚌 Tallahassee. **Open** daily. 🦽 ♿
🆆 floridastateparks.org

One of the world's largest freshwater springs, the Wakulla pumps 700,000 gal (2.6 million liters) of water a minute into the large pool which is the big appeal of this park.

You can swim or snorkel in the clear, limestone-filtered water, or take a ride in a glass-bottomed boat. There are also trips on the Wakulla River – look out for alligators, ospreys, and wading birds – and you can follow woodland trails.

Do not leave without visiting the Spanish-style Wakulla Springs Lodge hotel and restaurant, built in the 1930s.

Fishing for Shellfish in Apalachicola Bay

Apalachicola Bay is one of the most productive estuarine systems in the world. Fed by the nutrient-rich Apalachicola River, the bay is a valuable nursery, breeding, and feeding ground for many marine species. The warm, shallow waters of the salt marshes between Apalachicola Bay and Cedar Key *(see p249)* are important feeding grounds too, and the fishing tradition extends all along the coast. Oysters, blue crab, shrimp, and other crustaceans, as well as a large variety of fish, all contribute to the local fishing industry, which is worth about $15 million a year. Apalachicola Bay is most famous for its oysters, which account for 90 percent of the state's total catch. The oysters grow rapidly in the bay's ideal conditions and reach a marketable size of 3 inches (8 cm) in under two years.

"Tongs," a pair of rakes joined like scissors, are used to lift the oysters from the sea.

A **"culler"** separates the oysters by size, throwing back any that are too small.

Oyster Fishing

Oystermen, known locally as "tongers" after the tools they use, fish from small wooden boats, primarily in public grounds called oyster bars. The oysters can be harvested all year, but there is usually a lull in the summer and autumn, when fishermen focus on other species.

Fishing for oysters in Apalachicola Bay

Fresh oysters, best served on ice

Fresh seafood is sold throughout the year around Apalachicola. On the first weekend of November, seafood lovers converge on the town for the annual Florida Seafood Festival.

White, brown, and pink shrimps are fished both from small boats in the bay, and off-shore in the Gulf of Mexico from larger vessels, which may be out for a week or more. The catch is brought back to seafood houses on land for sorting and distribution.

Blue crabs, both the hard-shell and soft-shell varieties (the latter known as "peelers"), are caught in baited wire traps, which are dropped and collected by small boats. The crabs appear in warm weather, sometimes as early as February.

⑱ Tallahassee

Just 14 miles (23 km) from the Georgia border, encircled by rolling hills and canopy roads, Tallahassee is the epitome of "The Other Florida" – gracious, hospitable, and uncompromisingly Southern. The former site of an Apalachee Indian settlement and a Franciscan mission, this remote spot was an unlikely place to found the new capital of Territorial Florida in 1824 *(see p229)*. However, from its simple beginnings, Tallahassee grew dramatically during the plantation era and after Florida's elevation to full statehood in 1845. The elegant town houses built by politicians, plantation owners, and businessmen during that period can still be enjoyed today.

Exploring Tallahassee

The historic district, where you'll find the city's fine 19th-century homes, is focused around Park Avenue and Calhoun Street, both quiet, shady streets planted with century-old live oak trees and southern magnolias. The Brokaw-McDougall House on Meridian Street is a splendid Classical Revival building. Similar influences are evident in The Columns, an 1830 mansion on Duval Street, and the city's oldest building. The Capitol Complex is at the very heart of downtown Tallahassee. Here, the venerable Old Capitol building has been beautifully restored to its 1902 state, with a pristine white dome and striped awnings. Inside, you can visit the Supreme Court chamber, the old cabinet meeting room, and also the Senate. The 22-floor New Capitol building behind, where the March–May legislative sessions take place, casts a shadow over its predecessor. But although it is a grim 1970s structure, it does at least offer a lovely view of Tallahassee from its top floor. The Visitor Center on Jefferson street has walking-tour maps.

Wood carving in the Old Capitol Senate

🏛 Knott House Museum

301 East Park Ave. **Tel** (850) 922-2459. **Open** Wed–Sat. 🅿 ♿
W museumoffloridahistory.com

This house is unusual in that it was built by a free black in 1843 – 20 years prior to the emancipation of Florida's slaves. Now one of the most beautifully restored Victorian homes in Tallahassee, it is named after the Knotts, who moved here in 1928 and completely

Tallahassee City Center

① Museum of Florida History
② Old Capitol
③ New Capitol
④ The Columns
⑤ Knott House Museum
⑥ Brokaw-McDougall House

Key to Symbols *see back flap*

refurbished the house. The lovely interior is evocative of the former owners. Poems that Luella Knott composed for and tied to her antique furnishings are still in place today.

🏛 Museum of Florida History

500 S Bronough St. **Tel** (850) 488-1484. **Open** daily. **Closed** Thanksgiving, Dec 25. &

W museumoffloridahistory.com

The museum tackles 12,000 years of the region's history in entertaining style. Varied dioramas feature elements of paleo-Indian culture, massive armadillos, and a mastodon skeleton made of bones found in Wakulla Springs *(see p244)*. Numerous artifacts and succinct storyboards provide an excellent history from the colonial era up to the "tin can" tourists of the 1920s *(see p55)*.

Environs

Three miles (5 km) southwest of the city, Lake Bradford Road leads to the **Tallahassee Museum of History and Natural Science**, which is very popular with children. The centerpiece is Big Bend Farm – a superb recreation of late 19th-century rural life; employees dressed as farmhands tend goats and geese among authentic 1880s farm buildings. Bellevue, a small plantation home built in the 1830s, is among the other attractions. There is also an interactive discovery center and a zoo. On the shores of Lake Bradford, this woodland area provides natural habitat enclosures for black bears and

Boardwalk in the Museum of History and Natural Science

AB Maclay Gardens State Park near Tallahassee, at their best in the spring

bobcats, while alligators lurk amid the water lilies and cypress swamp areas. **Goodwood Museum and Gardens**, on the northeastern edge of Tallahassee, was a major producer of cotton and corn in the 19th century *(see pp50–51)*. The main house, built in the 1830s, retains many original features, including a mahogany staircase. After years of neglect, the plantation buildings are being restored.

🏛 Tallahassee Museum of History and Natural Science

3945 Museum Drive. **Tel** (850) 576-1636. **Open** daily. **Closed** Jan 1, Thanksgiving, Dec 24–25. 🐾 &

W tallahasseemuseum.org

🏛 Goodwood Museum and Gardens

1600 Miccosukee Rd. **Tel** (850) 877-4202. **Open** Mon–Fri. 🐾 Mon–Sat

W goodwoodmuseum.org

⓳ AB Maclay Gardens State Park

Road map: C1. 3540 Thomasville Rd, Leon Co. **Tel** (850) 487-4556. 🚍 Tallahassee. 🚌 Tallahassee. **Open** Mon–Sat. **Closed** Sun. 🐾 & (limited). **W** floridastateparks.org

These gorgeous gardens, 4 miles (6 km) north of Tallahassee, were originally laid out around Killearn, the 1930s winter home of New York financier Alfred B. Maclay. More than 200 varieties of plants are featured in the landscaped gardens that surround the shores of Lake Hall.

They remain eye-catching even in winter, when the camellias and azaleas are in full bloom (from January to April). Visitors can also swim, fish, go boating, or stroll along the Big Pine Nature Trail.

⓴ Monticello

Road map: C1. Jefferson Co. 🚗 2,800. 🚍 Tallahassee. 🚌 Tallahassee. 🛈 420 W Washington St, (850) 997-5552. **W** monticellojeffersonfl.com

Founded in 1827, Monticello (pronounced "Montisello") was named after the Virginia home of former President Thomas Jefferson. Lying at the heart of northern Florida's cotton-growing country, the town prospered and funded the building of elegant homes. Some of these are now bed-and-breakfasts, making the town a good base for exploring the Tallahassee area.

Monticello radiates from the imposing courthouse on US 90. The historic district lies to the north, where you'll find tree-canopied streets and a wealth of lovely old buildings, ranging from 1850s antebellum mansions to Queen Anne homes with decorative woodwork and Gothic features. Every year at the end of June, the town hosts its Watermelon Festival to celebrate a mainstay of the local agricultural economy. Pageants, dancing, rodeos, and the traditional watermelon seed spitting contest are among the festival's many attractions.

Unadorned Presbyterian church, Monticello

㉒ Suwannee River State Park

Road map: D2. Suwannee Co.
13 miles (21 km) W of Live Oak.
🚌 Live Oak. **Tel** (386) 362–2746.
Open daily. 🅿️ ♿ limited. ⛺
W **floridastateparks.org**

Made famous the world over by the song *Old Folks at Home*, written by Stephen Foster in 1851, the Suwannee's sources are in Georgia and it runs 265 miles (425 km) to the Gulf of Mexico.

The Park offers some of the best back-country canoeing in Florida. The river is easy flowing here with low banks, and canoeists have a good chance of seeing a range of wildlife, including herons, American coots, and turtles. Canoe rental is available, and there is a boat ramp and a shady campground.

The nearby **Stephen Foster Folk Culture Center State Park** is the oldest park on the river, and offers similar sporting activities.

Enjoying the sun at a wharf in Suwannee River State Park

🏛 **Stephen Foster Folk Culture Center State Park**
11016 Lillian Saunders Drive.
Tel (386) 397-4331. **Open** daily. 🅿️
W **floridastateparks.org**

㉓ Steinhatchee

Road map: D2. Taylor Co. 🚶 1,000.
🚌 Chiefland. 🅸 428 N Jefferson, Perry, (850) 584-5366.
W **taylorcountychamber.com**

Set back from the mouth of the Steinhatchee River, this is a sleepy old fishing town along the riverbank. To get a flavor of the place, ignore the trailer parks and stroll among the fish camps, bait shops, and boats tied up to the cypress wood docks. Trout fishing is big here, and people go crabbing along the coast.

About 26 miles (42 km) northwest is **Keaton Beach**, a tiny but popular coastal resort.

㉔ Cedar Key

Road map: D2. Levy Co. 🚶 950.
🚌 Chiefland. 🅸 525 2nd Street, (352) 543-5600. W **cedarkey.org**

At the foot of a chain of little bridge-linked keys jutting out into the Gulf of Mexico, Cedar Key is a picturesque, weathered Victorian fishing village. In the 19th century it flourished as the gulf terminal of Florida's first cross-state railroad and from the burgeoning lumber trade. However, within a few decades its namesake stands of cedar

㉑ Cotton Trail Tour

In the 1820s and '30s, the area around Tallahassee was the most important cotton-growing region in Florida. From the outlying plantations, horse-drawn wagons creaked along red clay roads to market in the capital. Today, these old roads pass through one of the last corners of unspoiled rural Florida.

This tour follows the old Cotton Trail, along canopied roads and past cattle pastures and paddocks carved out of deep green woodlands. It takes about 3.5 hours, or it could be done en route between Tallahassee and Monticello *(see p247).For*

④ **Bradley's Country Store**
Famous for its homemade sausages, this traditional country store is still run by the Bradleys, who established the business in 1927.

③ **Old Pisgah United Methodist Church**
This unadorned Greek Revival church, built in 1858, is the oldest Methodist building in Leon County.

② **Miccosukee Road**
Originally an Indian trail, this canopy road was used by 30 local plantations in the 1850s.

① **Goodwood Plantation**
This former cotton plantation *(see p247)* retains its lovely 1840s mansion shaded by live oak trees.

Key

 Tour route

Other road

forest had been transformed into pencils, and the logging boom ended. A few of the old lumber warehouses have been turned into shops and restaurants, but the Cedar Key of today is blissfully quiet.

You can take a boat from the docks to an offshore island beach in the Cedar Keys National Wildlife Refuge, or take a bird-watching trip along the salt-marsh coast. Various boats run trips from the docks.

Alternatively, visit the entertaining **Cedar Key Historical Society Museum**, in which eclectic exhibits include some fossilized tapir teeth, Indian pottery shards, and crab traps. You can also pick up a map of the town's historic buildings.

🏛 Cedar Key Historical Society Museum

Corner of D and 2nd Streets.
Tel (352) 543-5549. **Open** 1–4pm Sun–Fri, 11am–5pm Sat. **Closed** Jan 1, Thanksgiving, Dec 25. 🚫 ♿

Environs

Thirty miles (50 km) to the north of Cedar Key is **Manatee Springs State Park**, where a spring gushes from a cave mouth 30 ft (9 m) below the surface of an azure pool. The spring water feeds the Suwannee River, is as clear as glass and popular with divers and snorkelers. Sightings of manatees, which occasionally winter here, are unreliable, but it is easy to spot dozens of turtles, fish, and egrets feeding in the shallows, and the turkey vultures hovering overhead. You can also swim, rent a canoe, take a boat tour, or follow one of the hiking trails; you may be lucky enough to see an armadillo in the undergrowth.

🏞 Manatee Springs State Park

Route 320, 6 miles (10 km) W of Chiefland. **Tel** (352) 493-6072.
Open daily. 🚫 ♨
W floridastateparks.org

Weather-beaten hut on stilts off the coast of Cedar Key

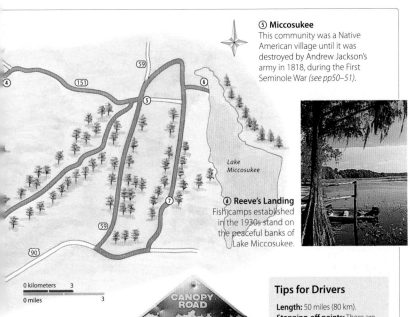

⑤ Miccosukee

This community was a Native American village until it was destroyed by Andrew Jackson's army in 1818, during the First Seminole War (*see pp50–51*).

Lake Miccosukee

④ Reeve's Landing

Fish camps established in the 1930s stand on the peaceful banks of Lake Miccosukee.

0 kilometers 3
0 miles 3

⑦ Magnolia Road

One of Florida's last unpaved canopy roads, this track led to the now-vanished port of Magnolia, from which cotton was shipped to New York.

Tips for Drivers

Length: 50 miles (80 km).
Stopping-off points: There are no restaurants along the route, so take your own provisions or buy a snack at Bradley's Country Store, and enjoy a picnic on the banks of Lake Miccosukee.

THE GULF COAST

For many visitors the Gulf Coast begins and ends with its fabulous beaches, bathed by the warm, calm waters of the Gulf of Mexico, and their accompanying resorts. However, with only a little effort you can kick the sand from your shoes and visit some of Florida's most interesting cities or explore wilderness areas that have been left virtually untouched by the vagaries of time.

Ever since the Spanish colonization, the focus of activity along the Gulf Coast has been around Tampa Bay, the large inlet in Florida's west coast. Pánfilo de Narváez anchored in the bay in 1528, and Hernando de Soto *(see p47)* landed nearby in 1539. The bay was a perfect natural port and became a magnet to pioneers in the 19th century. The favorable climate even drew the odd sugargrower: Gamble Plantation near Bradenton is the southernmost plantation house in the US *(see p270)*.

After the Civil War, the Gulf Coast became a significant center for trade between the US and the Caribbean. This was due in part to Henry Plant, whose rail line from Virginia, laid in the 1880s, helped to fuel both Tampa's and the region's greatest period of prosperity. Pioneers flooded in, from ethnic groups such as the Greek sponge fishermen who settled in Tarpon Springs, to wealthier American immigrants – chief among whom was circus king John Ringling, whose splendid Italianate home and impressive European art collection is the city of Sarasota's top attraction. Henry Plant, like Flagler in eastern Florida *(see pp52–3)*, used the promise of winter sunshine to lure wealthy travelers from the north. The west coast's much-advertised average of 361 days of sunshine a year still helps attract great hordes of package tourists to the generous scattering of beaches. Lively beach scenes are the norm around St. Petersburg and Clearwater, but you can easily escape the cosmopolitan vacation atmosphere: only a short distance inland are quirky cattle towns, rivers perfect for canoeing, and swamps and forests where wild animals reside undisturbed.

A beautiful clear morning at Clearwater Beach

◄ The Tampa skyline is reflected in Tampa Bay at dusk

Exploring the Gulf Coast

The beaches that run in an almost continuous line along the Gulf Coast, interrupted only by a series of bays and inlets, are hard to resist. But the joy of this region is that it is easy to spice up a Gulf Coast vacation with some sight-seeing. The abundant accommodations by the water, from quaint cottages to no-expense-spared resorts, makes this the natural place to base yourself, and all the main cities and inland sights are within easy reach. You'll find some of Florida's best museums in St. Petersburg, Tampa, and Sarasota, as well as high-profile attractions like Busch Gardens and The Florida Aquarium in Tampa. There are also other interesting sights: from the world's largest concentration of Frank Lloyd Wright buildings at Florida Southern College to the weird and wonderful mermaids of Weeki Wachee Spring.

The glistening towers and dome of the old Tampa Bay Hotel *(see p248)*

Exploring the pristine landscapes of Myakka River State Park

For hotels and restaurants in this region see pp314–25 and pp329–49

Getting Around

The region is easy to get around by car. US 19 runs along the coast north of Tampa Bay, crossing the mouth of the bay over the magnificent Sunshine Skyway Bridge, while US 41 links the coastal communities south of Tampa. If speed is of the essence you'll want to use I-75, which runs farther inland.

As in every other region of Florida, life is hard without a car. Greyhound buses link the main towns, but rail services are more limited; Amtrak trains run only as far as Tampa, but its connecting "Thruway" buses *(see p384)* provide a link to St. Petersburg and south along the coast as far as Fort Myers.

Deserted Clearwater Beach at sunset

Key

=== Highway

=== Major road

▬▬ Secondary road

=== Minor road

— Scenic route

--- Main railway

0 kilometers 30
0 miles 25

The old-fashioned pier on Anna Maria Island, a well-known local landmark west of Bradenton

Sights at a Glance

For additional map symbols *see back flap*

❶ Crystal River

Road map: D2. Citrus Co. 🏛 5,000.
🚌 🚹 28 NW US 19, (352) 795-3149.
🌐 **crystalriverfl.org**

Crystal River has two main attractions. In winter people come to watch the manatees, which gather in herds of up to 300 to bask in the warm local springs, between January and March. You need to make a reservation with one of the boat operators in the area for an early morning trip around the **Crystal River National Wildlife Refuge**, which was set up specifically to protect the manatees. Manatees are active only in the very early morning hours, and the clear water makes spotting them easy.

A year-round attraction is the **Crystal River Archaeological State Park**, a complex of six Indian mounds 2 miles (3 km) west of the town. The site is thought to have been occupied for 1,600 years, from 200 BC to AD 1400, one of the longest continually occupied sites in Florida. An estimated 7,500 Native Americans visited the complex every year for ceremonial purposes, frequently traveling large distances to do so. Excavation of 400 of the possible 1,000 graves at the site has also revealed that local tribes had trade links with peoples north of Florida.

Climb up to the observation deck for a bird's-eye view of the site. Just below is the main temple mound, built in around AD 600. Beyond, two stelae or

Pottery at Crystal River

carved ceremonial stones, erected in around AD 440 can be seen flanking two of the site's three burial mounds. This stone is typical of the pre-Columbian cultures of Mesoamerica, but no evidence exists to link them with Crystal River. On the western edge of the site is a large village area marked by two midden mounds *(see p44)* on a midden ridge. A model of the site in the visitor center has examples of the pottery found.

🏛 Crystal River National Wildlife Refuge
1502 SE Kings Bay Drive. **Tel** (352) 563-2088. **Open** daily (Apr–mid-Nov: Mon–Fri). 🌐 **fws.gov/crystalriver**

🏛 Crystal River Archaeological State Park
3400 N Museum Point. **Tel** (352) 795-3817. **Open** daily. 🅿 ♿ limited.

The Manatee in Florida

You cannot go far in Florida without hearing about the sea cow, or manatee, an animal in serious risk of extinction. It is believed that there are only about 2,500 manatees left in the US, concentrated in the warm waters of Florida. Once plentiful, the animals were extensively hunted for meat and sport until the beginning of the 20th century, since when habitat destruction and boat accidents have done most of the damage.

The manatee, which grows to an average length of 10 ft (3 m), is a huge but gentle creature. It lives in shallow coastal waters, rivers, and springs, spending about five hours a day feeding; sea-grass is its favorite food.

The manatee, an inhabitant of both salt and fresh water

❷ Homosassa Springs Wildlife State Park

Road map: D2. Citrus Co. 4150 South Suncoast Blvd, Homosassa. 🚌 Crystal River. **Tel** (352) 628-5343. **Open** daily. 🅿 ♿ 🌐 **floridastateparks.org**

One of the best places to see manatees is at Homosassa Springs Wildlife State Park, where a floating observatory enables visitors to get close up to the animals.

Injured manatees, usually the victims of boat propellers, are treated and rehabilitated here before being released into the wild. There are often half a dozen in the recovery pool, and more outside the park fence in winter: in cold weather manatees are attracted by the warm spring water.

❸ Weeki Wachee Springs

Road map: D2. 6131 Commercial Way, Spring Hill, Hernando Co. Junction of US 19 & SR 50. **Tel** (352) 592-5656. 🚌 Brooksville. **Open** daily. 🅿 ♿ 🌐 **weekiwachee.com**

This long-standing theme park is built on one of Florida's largest freshwater springs. In the 1940s, ex-Navy frogman Newton Perry hit on the idea of using women swimmers to take the part of "live mermaids" performing a kind of

A performing "mermaid" at Weeki Wachee Springs

underwater ballet. A theater was built 15 ft (5 m) underwater with strategically placed air pipes for the swimmers to take in air.

Other attractions include a water park, a Misunderstood Creatures show, and a popular wilderness river cruise.

❹ Tarpon Springs

Road map: D3. Pinellas Co. 🚇 24,000. 🚌 Clearwater. ℹ️ 11 E Orange St, (727) 937-6109.
🌐 tarponspringschamber.com

This lively town on the Anclote River is most famous as a center of Greek culture – the legacy of the immigrant fishermen lured here at the start of the 20th century by the prolific local sponge beds. You'll find restaurants specializing in Greek food, an Athens Street, and a Poseidon gift shop, as well as a Parthenon bakery.

Alongside Dodecanese Boulevard are the Sponge Docks, which are busy once more – thanks to the recovery of the nearby sponge beds, decimated by bacterial blight in the 1940s. Boat trips organized by local sponge fishermen include a demonstration of sponge diving by a diver fitted out in a traditional suit.

The **Spongeorama** museum and shopping village is housed in former dockside sheds, and the Sponge Exchange, now refurbished, is an upscale complex with galleries, boutiques, and quaint restaurants. Two miles (3 km)

Trimming natural sponges before sale in Tarpon Springs

The nature trail through unspoiled woodland on Caladesi Island

south rises **St. Nicholas Greek Orthodox Cathedral**, a symbol of Tarpon Springs' Greek heritage. The Byzantine Revival church, a replica of St. Sophia in Istanbul, was erected in 1943 using marble transported from Greece. It is the starting point for the Epiphany Festival *(see p41)*.

📷 **Spongeorama**
510 Dodecanese Blvd.
Tel (727) 943-2164. **Open** daily.
🌐 spongeorama.com

🏛️ 📷 **St. Nicholas Greek Orthodox Cathedral**
36 N Pinellas Ave at Orange St.
Tel (727) 937-3540. **Open** daily. ♿

❺ Dunedin

Road map: D3. Pinellas Co. 🚇 38,000. 🚌 Clearwater. ℹ️ 301 Main St, (727) 733-3197. 🌐 dunedin-fl.com

Dunedin was founded by a Scotsman, John L Branch, who in 1870 opened a store to supply ships on their way down the Gulf Coast to Key West. Passing sea and rail routes brought trade and prosperity, and this soon attracted a number of his compatriots. Dunedin's Scottish heritage is still expressed in its annual Highland Games festival held in late March or early April.

The renovated properties on and around Main Street impart the authentic flavor of early 20th-century small-town Florida. The **Historical Museum**, which occupies Dunedin's former railroad station, has a fine collection of photographs

and artifacts from the town's early days. Nearby Railroad Avenue is now part of the Pinellas Trail, a paved walking and cycling path running for 47 miles (76 km) from Tarpon Springs to St. Petersburg, along the route of the former railroad.

🏛️ **Historical Museum**
349 Main St. **Tel** (727) 736-1176.
Open Tue–Sat. **Closed** public hols. ♿

Environs
Three miles (5 km) north of Dunedin, a causeway crosses to **Honeymoon Island State Park**. You can swim and fish there, but this barrier island is largely undeveloped, in order to preserve its status as an important osprey nesting site. It is also the departure point for the passenger ferry to the even more alluring **Caladesi Island State Park**, which can also be reached from Clearwater Beach *(see p256)*.

Caladesi's 3-mile (5-km) beach, fronting the Gulf of Mexico, was rated in 1995 as the second best in the country. The beach gives way to dunes fringed by sea oats and there is a 3-mile (5-km) nature trail through cypress and mangrove woods.

🏞️ **Honeymoon Island State Park**
Route 586, 3 miles (5 km) NW of Dunedin. **Tel** (727) 469-5942.
Open daily. 🚗 ♿ limited.

🏞️ **Caladesi Island State Park**
1 Causeway Blvd. **Tel** (727) 469-5918. **Open** daily. 🚗 ♿
🌐 floridastateparks.org

Interior of the McMullen Log House, Pinellas County Heritage Village

❻ Clearwater Beach

Road map: D3. Pinellas Co. 🚗 23,000.
✈ 🚌 Clearwater. 🚌 tourist trolley
from Cleveland St. ℹ 1130 Cleveland
St, (727) 461-0011.
ⓦ **clearwaterflorida.org**

The satellite of Clearwater city,
this lively resort marks the start
of the vacation strip that
extends as far as Tampa
Bay. Hotels and bars,
often filled with
European tourists,
dominate the
waterfront, but
Clearwater Beach
manages to retain
some character. If the
Gulf side is expensive,
there are cheaper hotels
by the Intracoastal
Waterway.

The broad sandy beach
is very impressive, and the
water sports facilities are
excellent. Boat trips of all kinds
depart from the marina, from
diving to fishing expeditions.

Environs
Across Clearwater Pass is
Sand Key, which runs south
for 12 miles (19 km). **Sand Key
Park**, near the top, has a
popular palm-fringed beach
ranked in the top 20 in the
country, and offers a more
down-to-earth scene than in
throbbing Clearwater Beach.

About 7 miles (11 km) to the
south – beyond the chic
residential district of Belleair,
complete with a hotel built by
Henry Plant *(see pp52–3)* – is the
Suncoast Seabird Sanctuary.
Up to 500 injured birds live at
this sanctuary.

Screech owls in
the Suncoast
Sanctuary

Pelicans, owls, herons, egrets,
and other species are all on
view, while Ralph Heath, who
runs the sanctuary, and his
helpers offer guided tours.

It is well worth making the
diversion inland to Largo, 8 miles
(12 km) southeast of Clearwater
Beach, to visit the **Pinellas
County Heritage Village**. This
consists of 16 historic buildings,
brought here from various
sites, such as the
McMullen Log House
(see p34) and the
Seven Gables Home
(1907), which offers a
taste of the lifestyle of a
wealthy Victorian
family. Spinning,
weaving, and other
skills are demonstrated
in the museum.

🐦 **Suncoast Seabird Sanctuary**
18323 Sunset Blvd, Redington
Shores. **Tel** (727) 391-2473.
Open 9am–sunset daily. ♿

🏛 **Pinellas County
Heritage Village**
11909 125th Street N. **Tel** (727)
582-2123. **Open** Tue–Sun. **Closed**
public hols. ♿ limited.
ⓦ **pinellascounty.org/heritage**

❼ St. Petersburg Beaches

Road map: D3. Pinellas Co.
✈ 🚉 Tampa. 🚌 St. Petersburg.
🚌 many services from St. Petersburg.
ℹ Tampa Bay Beaches Chamber of
Commerce, 6990 Gulf Blvd, (727)
360-6957. ⓦ **tampabaybeaches.com**

South of Clearwater you enter
the orbit of the St. Petersburg
Beaches. Until you reach
Madeira Beach the waterfront
scenes are rather disappointing.
Madeira Beach, however, is a
good place to stay if you prefer
a laid-back atmosphere to the
buzzing scenes of the bigger
resorts. Johns Pass Village, a
re-created fishing village nearby,
also offers a quirkier-than-
average choice of restaurants
and shops. There is also a fishing
pier and a marina.

Farther south, monotonous
ranks of hotels characterize
Treasure Island. Next in line, **St.
Pete Beach** (St. Petersburg was
officially shortened to St. Pete
because it was considered more
evocative of a fun-filled resort)
has a 7-mile (11-km) strip of
white sand and a buzzing scene
along the waterfront. At its
southern end towers the Don
CeSar Resort. Built in the 1920s,
the hotel's scale and roll call of
celebrity guests are typical of the
grand hotels of that era.

At the southern tip of the
barrier island group, **Pass-a-
Grille** is a breath of fresh air after
crowded St. Pete Beach. Skirted
by the main coastal road, this
sleepy community has some
lovely homes from the early
1900s and beaches still in their
natural state. A word of warning:
take lots of change for the
parking meters.

The extravagant Don CeSar Resort overlooking St. Pete Beach

Gulf Coast Beaches

With an average of 361 days of sunshine a year and just two hours' drive from Orlando, the coast between St. Petersburg and Clearwater is the busiest resort area along the Gulf Coast, attracting hordes of overseas visitors. Known variously as the Holiday Isles, the Pinellas Coast, or the Suncoast, the strip encompasses 28 miles (45 km) of superb barrier island beaches. Due to the high quality of the sand and water, plus the relative scarcity of pests, litter, and crime, the Suncoast regularly appears in lists of the nation's top beaches. Farther south, Sarasota's barrier island beaches are of an equally high standard: they attract more Floridians than package tourists. Wherever you are, expect a more laid-back mood than on the east coast.

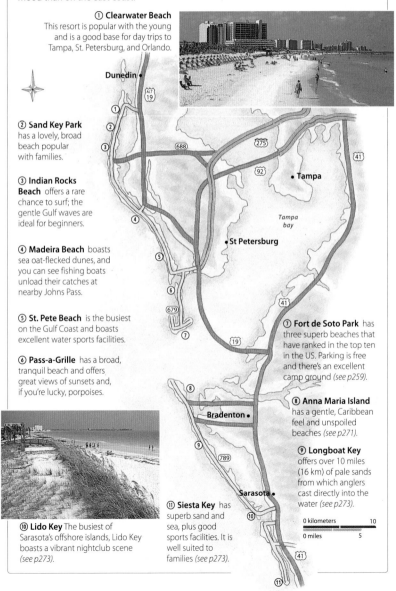

① **Clearwater Beach**
This resort is popular with the young and is a good base for day trips to Tampa, St. Petersburg, and Orlando.

② **Sand Key Park**
has a lovely, broad beach popular with families.

③ **Indian Rocks Beach** offers a rare chance to surf; the gentle Gulf waves are ideal for beginners.

④ **Madeira Beach** boasts sea oat-flecked dunes, and you can see fishing boats unload their catches at nearby Johns Pass.

⑤ **St. Pete Beach** is the busiest on the Gulf Coast and boasts excellent water sports facilities.

⑥ **Pass-a-Grille** has a broad, tranquil beach and offers great views of sunsets and, if you're lucky, porpoises.

⑩ **Lido Key** The busiest of Sarasota's offshore islands, Lido Key boasts a vibrant nightclub scene *(see p273)*.

⑦ **Fort de Soto Park** has three superb beaches that have ranked in the top ten in the US. Parking is free and there's an excellent camp ground *(see p259)*.

⑧ **Anna Maria Island** has a gentle, Caribbean feel and unspoiled beaches *(see p271)*.

⑨ **Longboat Key** offers over 10 miles (16 km) of pale sands from which anglers cast directly into the water *(see p273)*.

⑪ **Siesta Key** has superb sand and sea, plus good sports facilities. It is well suited to families *(see p273)*.

Dunedin

Tampa

Tampa bay

St Petersburg

Bradenton

Sarasota

0 kilometers 10
0 miles 5

❽ St. Petersburg

This city of broad avenues grew up in the great era of 19th-century land speculation. In 1875, Michigan farmer John Williams bought a plot of land beside Tampa Bay, with a dream of building a great city. An exiled Russian nobleman called Peter Demens soon provided St. Petersburg with both a railroad and its name – the latter in honor of his birthplace.

"St. Pete," as it is often called, used to be best known for its aging population. But times have changed, and the city now has a much more vibrant image. Extensive renovation has brought new life to the waterfront area downtown, and St. Petersburg's claim to be a lively cultural center is greatly boosted by the presence of the prestigious Salvador Dalí Museum *(see pp260–61).*

St. Petersburg's eye-catching Pier, its best known landmark

Exploring St. Petersburg

The landmark that appears in every tourist brochure about the city is **The Pier**. Its distinctive upside-down pyramid contains shops, restaurants, a disco, an aquarium, and an observation deck, and acts as a magnet for visitors heading for the downtown area. A tourist trolley service runs from the pier and stops at all the major attractions.

Looking north from the pier, the handsome **Renaissance Vinoy Resort** *(see p322),* built in the 1920s as the Vinoy Hotel and much modernized, dominates the downtown skyline. Away from the waterfront is the massive **Tropicana Field**, St. Petersburg's other main landmark. This is a popular place for large-scale activities ranging from rock concerts to sports events *(see p361).*

🏛 St. Petersburg Museum of History

335 2nd Ave NE. **Tel** (727) 894-1052. **Open** Wed–Sun. **Closed** Thanksgiving, Dec 25, Jan 1. 🅿 ♿ 🆆 spmoh.org

This museum tells the story of St. Petersburg from prehistoric times to the present. Exhibits range from mastodon bones, fossils, and native pottery to an entertaining mirror gallery, which gives visitors a comic taste of how they would have looked in Victorian fashions.

A special pavilion houses a replica of a sea plane called the *Benoist*, which marks St. Petersburg as the birthplace of commercial aviation. This aircraft made the first flight with a paying passenger across Tampa Bay in 1914.

St. Petersburg City Center

① Tropicana Field
② Mahaffey Theater
③ Museum of Fine Arts
④ St. Petersburg Museum of History
⑤ The Pier
⑥ Salvador Dali Museum
⑦ Florida Holocaust Museum

Key to Symbols *see back flap*

Poppy, one of Georgia O'Keeffe's acclaimed flower paintings, in the Museum of Fine Arts

🏛 Great Explorations

1925 4th Street N. **Tel** (727) 821-8992.
Open daily. 🚻 🚹 📶 **greatex.org**

"Hands on" is the ethos of this museum, which is aimed at children but is equally fascinating to adults.

You can have a great time exploring any of the unique exhibits that are waiting for the right level of creativity and curiosity to bring them to life. Youngsters are encouraged to crawl, climb, touch, and smack everything. For example, the popular Orange Grove has kids picking, packing, and shipping oranges from a mock grove, making pizza, or creating animated videos. The emphasis here is on teamwork.

🏛 Florida Holocaust Museum

55 Fifth St S, St. Petersburg **Tel** (727) 820-0100 or (800) 960-7448.
Open daily. **Closed** Thanksgiving, Dec 25, Jan 1, Jewish hols. 🚻 🚹
📶 **flholocaustmuseum.org**

This museum, located in downtown St. Petersburg, honors the millions of people who suffered or died during the Holocaust.

There are no displays depicting the atrocities that took place; instead the exhibits focus on tolerance, education, and the history of anti-Semitism. There are many exhibits illustrating Jewish life as it was before the Holocaust and after *Kristallnacht* (the Night of Broken Glass), November 9–10, 1938. There is an introductory film, an interactive Tolerance and Learning Center, and an impressive memorial area.

🏛 Museum of Fine Arts

255 Beach Dr NE.
Tel (727) 896-2667.
Open daily. **Closed** Jan 1, Martin Luther King Day, Thanksgiving, Dec 25. 🚻
🚹 📷 📶 **fine-arts.org**

Housed in a striking Palladian-style building overlooking the bay, the Museum of Fine Arts is renowned for its wide-ranging collection of European, American, pre-Columbian, and Asian works. Supreme among the French Impressionist paintings are *A Corner of the Woods* (1877) by Cézanne and Monet's classic *Parliament, Effect of Fog, London* (1904). Other prominent works are the vivid *Poppy* (1927) by Georgia O'Keeffe, *La Lecture* (1888) by Berthe Morisot, and Auguste Rodin's *Invocation* (1886), which stands in the sculpture garden.

A large collection of photographs, dating from the early 1900s to the present, rounds off the collection.

🏛 Mahaffey Theater

400 1st St S. **Tel** (727) 982-5767.
Open daily. 🚻 🚹
📶 **mahaffeytheater.com**

This modern, glass-enclosed building on the waterfront provides spectacular views across Tampa Bay. It contains a 2,031-seat, state-of-the-art theater that features box-style seating, along with a ballroom area. Named for the St. Petersburg family who contributed significantly to the capital campaign, the theater hosts Broadway roadshows, music and dance events, celebrity entertainers, special exhibitions, and children's theater. The theater is also home to the classical music concerts of the Florida Orchestra.

🌿 Sunken Gardens

1825 4th Street N. **Tel** (727) 551-3102.
Open daily. 🚻 🚻 🚹 📶 **stpete.org/sunken**

Thousands of tropical plants and flowers flourish in this large walled garden, which descends to 10 ft (3 m) below the street outside. The site was once a

VISITORS' CHECKLIST

Practical Information
Road map: D3. Pinellas Co. 🅿 265,000. ℹ 100 2nd Ave N, (727) 821-4715. 🎪 Festival of the States. 📶 **festivalofstates.com**

Transport
✈ St. Petersburg/Clearwater International Airport, 10 miles (16 km) N of Down-town. 🚌 180 9th St North, (727) 898-1496; also Amtrak bus to Pinellas Square Mall, Pinellas Park, (800) 872-7245.

water-filled sinkhole *(see p26)*; its soil is kept dry by a network of hidden pipes.

Wander among the bougainvillea and hibiscus, and visit the extensive orchid garden. Other features include a walk-through butterfly encounter and horticulture program.

Lush tropical plants flanking a stream at the Sunken Gardens

Environs

Five islands in Boca Ciega Bay south of St. Petersburg make up **Fort De Soto Park**. The park offers great views of the Sunshine Skyway Bridge and superb beaches, especially along the southern and western coasts. The islands are thick with vegetation and bird colonies.

History fans should head for the chief island, Mullet Key, where massive gun emplacements concealed by high concrete walls mark the remains of Fort De Soto. The fort was begun during the Spanish-American War *(see p53)* but was never finished.

🏰 Fort De Soto Park

3500 Pinellas Bayway South, Tierra Verde. **Tel** (727) 582-2267.
Open daily. 🚹 📶 **fortdesoto.com**

Salvador Dalí Museum

Although far from the native country of Spanish artist Salvador Dalí (1904–89), this museum boasts the most comprehensive collection of his work outside of Spain, spanning the years 1914–76. The first museum opened in 1982, 40 years after Ohio businessman Reynolds Morse first met Dalí and began collecting his works. The museum moved to a spectacular waterfront location in 2011. In addition to 96 original oil paintings, the museum has more than 100 watercolors and drawings, along with 1,300 graphics, sculptures, and other objects. The works range from Dalí's early figurative paintings to his first experiments in Surrealism and the mature, large-scale compositions described as his "masterworks."

The Building
Crawling along the building's con-crete walls is the impressive *Enigma*. Named after one of Dalí's paintings, this large geodesic bubble contains more than 900 triangular pieces of glass.

Nature Morte Vivante
This 1956 work is an example of Salvador Dalí's use of a mathematical grid and the DNA spiral (as shown in the cauliflower) as the basis of a composition.

Museum Shop

Theatre

Main Entrance

First floor

Classroom

View of Cadaqués
Impressionist influences are evident in this view, painted in 1921, of the shadow of Mount Pani stretching toward Dalí's family home and other houses around the bay.

The Discovery of America
Inspired by a "cosmic dream," this work (1958–9) pays homage to the Spanish painter Velázquez while predicting man's first step on the moon.

The helical spiral staircase represents Dalí's interest in science.

For hotels and restaurants in this region see pp314–25 and pp329–49

Don Quixote and Sancho
This 1968 etching is just one of over 1,000 drawings and other illustrations produced during Dalí's Classic Period. Examples appear in the museum's special exhibitions.

Education Gallery

VISITORS' CHECKLIST

Practical Information
1 Dalí Boulevard, St. Petersburg.
Tel (727) 823–3767.
Open 10am–5:30pm Mon–Sat
(8pm Thu), noon–5:30pm Sun.
Closed Thanksgiving, Dec 25. ✍
✉ ♿ 🎥 🎧 🌐 thedali.org

Transport
🚌 4, 32, trolley from the Pier.

The Sick Child
This early painting was composed in 1914, when Dalí was just ten years old and already showing huge talent.

Daddy Longlegs of the Evening–Hope!
This bizarre image was the foundation stone of the collection. Painted in 1940, it shows a daddy long-legs crawling over the face of a hideously distorted violinist.

Gallery Guide

The collection of Dalí's paintings is displayed on the third floor. The theater, on the first floor, shows a short film about the museum, and the second floor houses the library, which is used by researchers and scholars.

Third floor

Key to Floor Plan

🟦 Introduction
🟦 Early Works
🟦 Anti-Art
🟦 Surrealism
🟦 Nuclear Mysticism
🟦 Collection Galleries
🟦 Special exhibitions
🟦 Nonexhibition space

How Dali's Art Came to St. Petersburg

Reynolds Morse and his fiancée Eleanor were fascinated by Salvador Dalí from the time they saw an exhibition of his art in 1941. They bought their first Dalí work, *Daddy Longlegs of the Evening–Hope!*, two years later and met the artist soon after. Thus began the Morses' life-long friendship with Dalí and his wife, Gala. Over the next 40 years the Morses amassed the largest private collection of Dalí's art in the world. After a nationwide search, Morse chose the previous waterfront site for the collection because of its resemblance to the artist's home town of Cadaqués. The museum was rehoused in a hurricane-proof building, six blocks to the north, in 2011.

❾ Tampa

Tampa is one of the fastest-growing cities in Florida. Modern skyscrapers have replaced many original buildings, but vestiges of a colorful history remain – mainly in the historic Latin quarter, Ybor City *(see pp264–5)*, where Tampa's famous cigar industry took root in the 1880s, and in some quirky architecture downtown. The Spanish arrived here in 1539, but Tampa was just a small town until the late 1800s, when Henry Plant *(see pp52–3)* extended his railroad here. Today, Tampa's big attraction is Busch Gardens *(see pp268–9)*, one of the top theme parks in the US, but the sleek Florida Aquarium in the Channel District is drawing more and more people into the heart of Tampa.

Sunrise over downtown Tampa's office buildings and bridge

Exploring Downtown

You can easily explore Tampa's compact downtown area on foot. Here, you'll find the historic Tampa Theatre and several examples of the public art on which the city justifiably prides itself.

Situated at the mouth of the Hillsborough River, Tampa can also be enjoyed from the water. *Starlite Cruises* and *Yacht Star Ship (see p361)* run lunch and dinner cruises around Tampa Bay. Water taxis also provide good views of the city's chief sights, including the old Tampa Bay Hotel, now the University of Tampa, and the Museum of Art.

For another view of the city, ride the uptown–downtown connector free of charge. This is a rubber-wheeled trolley that travels from Harbour Island north to Tampa Street, stopping on every block to pick up passengers.

Another way of traveling through downtown is to ride one of the streetcars of the TECO Line Streetcar System, which runs from downtown through the Channel District and into Ybor City. The streetcars are replicas of the Birney Safety Cars that ran on Tampa's streets until 1946. Running seven days a week, they are air-conditioned and take around 22 minutes to complete the route. The uptown–downtown connector trolley meets with the TECO Line Streetcar.

🚇 Henry B. Plant Museum

401 W Kennedy Blvd. **Tel** (813) 254-1891. **Open** Tue–Sun. **Closed** Jan 1, Thanksgiving, Dec 25. Donation requested. 🚹
w plantmuseum.com

The luxurious Tampa Bay Hotel, now home to the University of Tampa, houses the Henry B. Plant Museum. The famous landmark has Moorish minarets that are visible from all over the city.

Henry Plant commissioned the building in 1891 as a hotel for the well-to-do passengers of his newly built railroad. The construction alone cost $3 million, with an additional $500,000 spent on furnishings. The hotel was not a success, however, and it fell into disrepair soon after Plant's death in 1899. The hotel was bought by the city in 1905 and became part of the University of Tampa in 1933. The south wing of the ground floor was set aside and preserved as a museum.

Complete with a solarium, the museum is splendidly furnished and equipped, with 90 percent of the exhibits on display original to the hotel. Wedgwood china, Venetian mirrors, and 18th-century French furniture effortlessly evoke the sense of a lost age. Visitors are welcome to walk around what is now the university campus to appreciate the sheer size of the building.

🏛 Tampa Museum of Art

120 W Gasparilla Plaza. **Tel** (813) 274-8130. **Open** daily. **Closed** Easter, Thanksgiving, Dec 25, Jan 1. 🎟 🚹
w tampamuseum.org

The Tampa Museum of Art houses a growing collection of

The elegant solarium at the Henry B. Plant Museum

The Sunshine Skyway Bridge, which spans the mouth of Tampa Bay

world-class art ranging from Classical Greek, Roman, and Etruscan antiquities to contemporary American, Cuban, and European works and world-class traveling exhibitions. The museum houses both permanent and temporary collections of photography, sculpture, paintings, and sketches. The museum itself is considered a work of art, made with aluminum, glass, and fiber-optic lights. Part of Tampa's scenic Riverwalk, it also hosts outdoor events.

Tampa Theatre
711 N Franklin St. **Tel** (813) 274-8981.
Open daily. **Closed** Dec 25.
tampatheatre.org

In its day, the Tampa Theatre was one of the most elaborate movie theaters in America. The building was designed in 1926 by the architect John Eberson in an architectural style known as Florida-Mediterranean. The lavish result was described by the historian Ben Hall as an "Andalusian bonbon."

In an attempt to create the illusion of an outdoor location, Eberson fitted the ceiling with lights designed to twinkle like stars. Other effects included artificial clouds, produced by a smoke machine, and lighting to simulate the rising sun.

The easiest way to visit the beautifully restored theater, is to see a movie here (see p361). Movie festivals, plays, and special events are all held here. Guided tours, which take place twice a month, include a 20-minute movie about the theater and a mini-concert on a traditional 1,000-pipe theater organ.

Tampa City Center

① Henry B. Plant Museum
② Tampa Museum of Art
③ Tampa Theater
④ Florida Aquarium
⑤ Harbour Island

Street-by-Street: Ybor City

A Spaniard named Don Vicente Martinez Ybor moved his cigar business from Key West to Tampa in 1886. About 20,000 migrant workers, mostly from Cuba and Spain, eventually joined him. The legacy of the cigar boom of the late 1800s and early 1900s is still visible in Ybor City. Its main street, 7th Avenue, with its Spanish-style tiles and wrought-iron balconies, looks much as it did then. Today the district is enjoying a new lease on life. What were once cigar factories and workers' cottages now house shops, restaurants, and clubs. Quiet during the day, Ybor City comes to life in the evening.

Cigar Museum and Visitor Center
Housed in the world's largest cigar box, the Visitor Center provides information about accommodation and events in the city.

Historic Clubs
Built 1917–18, the landmark Tampa Cuban Club (El Circulo Cubano de Tampa) is one of several cultural societies in Ybor City.

Don Vicente De Ybor Historic Inn
is a 16-suite luxury boutique hotel and restaurant located in the Gonzalez Clinic building.

9TH AVENUE

13TH STREET

AVENIDA REPUBLICA DE CUBA

8TH AVENUE

15TH STREET

7TH AVENUE

The Ritz, a stunning 1917 movie theater, now houses one of Ybor's top nightclubs.

José Martí Park
A statue commemorates José Martí, the Cuban freedom fighter who made several visits to Ybor City to rally support for Cuba's inde-pendence campaign (see p52).

Key

— Suggested route

0 meters	100
0 yards	100

★ Cigar Worker's House
This tiny house (attached to Ybor City State Museum) is furnished to look like a cigar worker's home. "La Casita" is a fine example of the shotgun houses (see p305) built for the flood of immigrants who came to work in Ybor city in the late 1800s.

Centennial Park, has an open-air market selling fresh produce.

Ybor City State Museum, housed in a former bakery, explores the history of Ybor City and also organizes walking tours of the district. There is a small ornamental garden attached.

9TH AVENUE

19TH STREET

18TH STREET

17TH STREET

LA SEPTIMA

← Columbia Restaurant

La Tropicana serves traditional Cuban fare to its crowd of regulars.

Columbia Restaurant
Florida's oldest restaurant takes up a whole block on 7th Avenue. The Spanish-Cuban food and lively flamenco make it popular with tourists (see p341).

The Cigar Industry in Tampa

With ships able to bring a regular supply of tobacco from Cuba to its port, Tampa was ideally located for cigar-making. Several huge cigar factories sprang up soon after V.M. Ybor moved here, and by 1900 Ybor City was producing over 111 million cigars annually. Each cigar was skillfully rolled by hand by workers who were often entertained by a lector reading aloud to them. Automation and the growing popularity of cigarettes changed all this. Cigars are still made in Tampa (mostly with leaves grown in Honduras), but now usually by machine. The Gonzalez y Martínez Cigar Company is one of the few companies to hand roll cigars.

El Sol Cigars
Although Ybor's oldest cigar store (opened in 1929) no longer rolls its cigars by hand, it is a good place to buy them.

Workers in an Ybor City cigar factory, 1929

A diver amid reefs and exotic fish at the Florida Aquarium

🐠 The Florida Aquarium

701 Channelside Drive. **Tel** (813) 273-4000. **Open** daily. **Closed** Thanksgiving, Dec 25. 🅿 ♿
W flaquarium.org

This enormous aquarium is located on the waterfront, and unmistakable with its blue, shell-shaped dome, it is a state-of-the-art interpretation of a modern aquarium. Inside, visitors will not only find tanks of fish but will also come face to face with baby alligators, birds, otters, and all kinds of other creatures living in their authentic habitats. The aquarium also offers a 90-minute cruise around the bay.

The purpose of the Florida Aquarium is to enable visitors to follow the passage of a drop of water from its first appearance in an underground spring to its arrival in the sea, passing through various habitats along the way.

The conditions of each habitat are re-created in separate galleries. The Florida Coral Reefs Gallery, for instance, takes visitors underwater for a panoramic view of a coral colony and its schools of colorful tropical fish. You can rent recorded commentaries by experts at different stages of the tour, and there are regular hands-on labs, with special projects and activities, and biologists and botanists standing by to explain them.

🏛 Hyde Park

Across the river, southwest of Downtown off Bayshore Boulevard, Hyde Park is a rare historic area in Tampa. Dating from the late 19th century, its houses display a striking mix of architectural styles from Colonial to Gothic Revival. The quiet residential streets of Hyde Park are best explored by car. The one part to tempt people out of their vehicles is Hyde Park Village, off Snow Avenue, where you'll find several upscale shops and restaurants. On some days, musicians come out to entertain the shoppers.

An open-air concert for visitors to Old Hyde Park Village

🏛 Museum of Science and Industry

4801 E Fowler Ave. **Tel** (813) 987-6100. **Open** daily. 🅿 ♿ **W** mosi.org

This excellent museum is another distinctive addition to the Tampa skyline; its Art Nouveau-style dome houses an IMAX® cinema, and the museum features all kinds of interactive displays. The Amazing You is an exploration of the human body and how it works, and in the hurricane room visitors can create their own tropical storm. The GTE Challenger Learning Center is a living memorial to the crew of the space shuttle Challenger, with space station simulators and an impressive mission control room. Another major attraction is the Focus Gallery, which houses visiting exhibits.

MOSI is also home to the Saunders Planetarium, which hosts regular astronomical shows. On every Friday and Saturday evening, there are special star-viewing sessions at which, weather permitting, telescopes are set up in the parking lot so that visitors can observe the night sky.

🐾 Lowry Park Zoo

1101 West Sligh Ave. **Tel** (813) 935-8552. **Open** daily. **Closed** Thanksgiving, Dec 25. 🅿 ♿
W lowryparkzoo.com

This zoo, 6 miles (10 km) north of downtown Tampa, is one of the best in North America. One of the main attractions is the manatee center, which has up to 20 animals in residence at any one time and a rehabilitation pool. You can learn more about this endangered species by taking part in the "Manatee Sleepover," a special program that offers the chance to explore the zoo after closing time, learn about the rehabilitation program, and spend the night at the manatee center.

The zoo's Florida Wildlife Center, a special sanctuary for native animals such as alligators and the Florida panther, is another highlight. Other areas to visit are Primate

The eye-catching dome of the Museum of Science and Industry

The Legend of Gaspar

José Gaspar was a legendary pirate who preyed on ships and communities between Tampa and Fort Myers in the 19th century. His stronghold was among the isles of the Lee Island Coast *(see pp282–3)*, many of whose modern names recall the association – including Gasparilla and Captiva, where Gaspar is said to have kept his female captives. The story goes that the pirate was eventually cornered by a US warship, and that he drowned himself in anchor chains rather than be taken prisoner.

Tampa suffered from several of Gaspar's raids, and now holds a Gasparilla Festival each January *(see p41)*. The highlight of this celebration is a mock invasion of the city by hundreds of rowdy villains aboard the world's only fully-rigged "pirate ship."

"Pirates" celebrating Tampa's Gasparilla Festival in the 1950s

A Sumatran tiger lounges at Asian Domain, Lowry Park Zoo

World, the Asian Domain, home to Sumatran tigers and an extremely rare Indian rhino, and a free-flight aviary. There is also a children's museum, an amusement center, and a pleasant picnic area.

⑩ Busch Gardens

See pp268–9.

⑪ Hillsborough River

Road map: D3. Hillsborough Co.
🚉 Tampa. 🚌 Tampa.

Extending through the countryside northeast of Tampa, the Hillsborough River provides a pleasant respite from the hustle and bustle of the city. It is flanked on both sides by dense backwoods of live oak, cypress, magnolia, and mangrove trees, which once covered great swathes of Florida's terrain

One of the best ways to experience the Hillsborough River is by canoe: **Canoe Escape** organizes trips along a stretch of the river about 15 minutes' drive from downtown Tampa. Located just beyond the city line, the area is surprisingly wild, and you have a good chance of spotting a great variety of wildlife, including herons, egrets, alligators, turtles, and otters. Canoeing conditions are ideal for beginners. You can choose from three main itineraries, each of which covers about 5 miles (8 km) – involving roughly two hours' paddling and allowing you plenty of time to absorb the surroundings; longer day trips are also available.

A section of the river is protected as **Hillsborough River State Park**. Canoeing is a popular way to explore here too; there are also walking trails, and you can swim and fish. The park has a large and popular campground, which is open all year round, and there are picnic sites.

Developed in 1936, the Hillsborough River State Park became one of Florida's earliest state parks partly due to the historic significance of Fort Foster, built during the Second Seminole War *(see p50)* to guard a bridge at the confluence of the Hillsborough River and Blackwater Creek. The fort and bridge have been reconstructed, and a battle is re-enacted here annually in March. Tours visit the fort every weekend and on holidays; a shuttle bus runs to it from the park's entrance.

Canoe Escape
12702 US 301, Thonotosassa, 12 miles (19 km) NE of Tampa. **Tel** (813) 986-2067. **Open** daily. **Closed** Thanksgiving, Dec 24 & 25. ♿

🛶 **Hillsborough River State Park**
15402 US 301 N, 12 miles (19 km) NE of Tampa. **Tel** (813) 987-6771.
Open daily. ♿ 🅱 limited. ⛺
🌐 floridastateparks.org

Re-created buildings at Fort Foster in Hillsborough River State Park

⑩ Busch Gardens

Busch Gardens is one-of-a-kind – a theme park that incorporates one of America's top zoos. To fulfill its unusual aim of re-creating life in colonial-era Africa, the park supports over 2,000 animals, with giraffes and zebras roaming freely over the "Serengeti Plain"; lions gorillas, and other African animals can be seen from a safari ride. Bird Gardens features macaws, cockatoos, and birds of prey. Animals are the main attraction, but there are thrill rides too which are great for visitors of all ages. SheiKra, North America's first and only dive coaster is Florida's tallest roller coaster. Adventure Island, adjacent to Busch Gardens, is a 30-acre (12-ha) Key West-themed water park.

Congo River Rapids
Rapids, geysers, waterfalls, and a dark cave await rafters set adrift on a swift river current.

Kumba
Participants on this roller coaster plunge 135 ft (41 m) at more than 60 mph (100 km/h) while spiraling 360°, and tearing through one of the world's largest vertical loops.

★ **Jungala**
Explore a three-story play land of climbing nets and mazes, and then connect up close with exotic jungle animals.

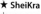

★ **SheiKra**
This dive coaster sends you on a breathtaking 3-minute journey through a loop and into a water feature finale.

KEY

① Bird Gardens

② Gwazi

③ Stanleyville

④ Timbuktu

⑤ 4-D movie theater

⑥ Serengeti Plain

⑦ **A train** can be taken around all the major areas within the park.

⑧ Guest Relations

| 0 meters | | 100 |
| 0 yards | | 100 |

Edge of Africa
This safari experience, on the southern edge of the Serengeti Plain, offers visitors a chance to have a close-up view of lions, hippos, hyenas, and other African animals.

VISITORS' CHECKLIST

Practical Information
Road map 3D. 10165 N McKinley Dr. Tampa. **Tel** (813) 987 5082.
w buschgardens.com
w adventureisland.com.
Open 10am–6pm daily, extended hours for summer and holidays.

Transport
Tampa. Tampa. 5 from Marion St, downtown Tampa, 39 from Netpark Transfer Center.

Egypt
The hair-raising ride, Montu, is found here, as well as a replica of Tutankhamun's tomb, a museum, and a bazaar.

Entrance

Myombe Reserve
This simulated rainforest is the habitat of western lowland gorillas and chimpanzees, both of which are endangered species.

★ Cheetah Hunt
A high-speed roller coaster that climbs high above the African landscape before racing across the plains above the heads of visitors. It can reach speeds of up to 60 mph (97 kph).

⓬ Florida Southern College

Road map: E3. Polk Co. 111 Lake Hollingsworth Drive, Lakeland. **Tel** (863) 680-4111. 🚉 Lakeland. 🚌 Lakeland. **Open** daily. **Closed** Jul 4, Thanksgiving, Dec 25, Jan 1. Visitor Center: **Open** until 2pm Mon–Sat. **Closed** Sun. 🚻 🌐 flsouthern.edu

This small college has the world's largest collection of buildings designed by Frank Lloyd Wright. Amazingly, the college president persuaded Wright (one of the most eminent architects of his day) to design the campus at Lakeland with the promise of little more than the opportunity to express his ideas – and payment when the money could be raised. Work began in 1938

The light and spacious interior of the Annie Pfeiffer Chapel

on what Wright, already famous as the founder of organic architecture, termed his "child of the sun." His aim of blending buildings with their natural surroundings made special use of glass to bring the outdoor light to the interiors. The original plan was for 18 buildings, but only seven had been completed by the time Wright died in 1959; five were finished or added later.

The Annie Pfeiffer Chapel is a particularly fine expression of his ideas. Windows of stained glass break the monotony of the building blocks, and the entire edifice is topped by a spectacular tower in place of the traditional steeple; Wright called it a "jewel box."

As a whole, the campus has the light and airy feel that Wright sought to achieve. The buildings are linked to each other by the Esplanades – a covered walkway, stretching for 1.5-miles (2 km), in which light, shade, and variations in height draw attention from one building to the next.

You can wander around the campus at any time, but the interiors can be explored only during the week. The Thad Buckner Building, complete with clerestory windows, now houses a visitor center, where you can see drawings and furniture by Wright and photographs of the building work.

The antebellum Gamble Mansion

⓭ Gamble Plantation Historic State Park

Road map: D3. Manatee Co. 3708 Patten Ave, Ellenton (Highway 301, 1.5 miles west of I-75). **Tel** (941) 723-4536. 🚉 Tampa. 🚌 Bradenton. **Open** daily. **Closed** Thanksgiving, Dec 25, Jan 1. 🅿️ 🚻 limited. 🎦 🌐 floridastate parks.org/gambleplantation

The only Antebellum home left in southern Florida, this whitewashed mansion is on the main road into Bradenton.

It was built in 1845–50 by Major Robert Gamble, who settled along the fertile Manatee River after the Second Seminole War *(see p50)*. Today only a fraction of the plantation's 3,500 acres (1,416 ha) remains. The site

Florida Southern College

① Emile Watson Building
② Benjamin Fine Building
③ J. Edgar Wall Waterdome
④ Raulerson Building
⑤ Thad Buckner Building
⑥ Annie Pfeiffer Chapel
⑦ William Danforth Chapel
⑧ Polk County Science Buildings
⑨ Lucius Pond Ordway Building

Key

▭▭ Esplanade

0 meters 100
0 yards 100

For map symbols *see back flap*

of the old slave quarters, for instance, is now a school. The house is furnished just as it was in its heyday, and the garden, flourishing with live oak trees draped with Spanish moss, is pure Deep South.

However, romantic notions about Gamble's life are swept away in the small museum in the visitor center. Gamble got into financial difficulties and was forced to sell the house to pay his debts; among the artifacts on display in the museum is a document showing that the plantation, along with the grounds and 191 slaves, was sold in 1856 for the sum of $190,000.

⑭ Bradenton

Road map: D3. Manatee Co. 🅰 48,000. ✈ 🚌 including Amtrak Thruway bus. 🛈 222 10th St W, (941) 748–3411.

The seat of Manatee County, Bradenton is best known as the home of the Nick Bollettieri Tennis Academy *(see p367)*, the school that has nurtured the early promise of such world tennis stars as Andre Agassi and Pete Sampras.

The local beaches are a big attraction, but a couple of sights deserve a visit before you head off to the beach. **Manatee Village Historical Park** recounts the story of the Florida frontier a century ago through a fascinating collection of restored buildings. These include a boat house, a general store, and an early settler's house, and all have been furnished as they would have looked originally.

The **South Florida Museum** is both educational and fun. "Florida from Stone Age to Space Age" is the theme, with exhibits ranging from dinosaur dioramas to life-size replicas of 16th-century Spanish-style buildings and early cars. Laser shows add excitement to the Bishop Planetarium program, while the Parker

The kitchen of an early settler's house at Manatee Village Historical Park

Aquarium gives a lively overview of local marine life.

🚼 Manatee Village Historical Park
1404 Manatee Ave E. **Tel** (941) 749–7165. **Open** Mon–Fri (Winter: Sun pm). **Closed** public hols. ♿

🏛 South Florida Museum
201 10th St W. **Tel** (941) 746–4131. **Open** daily. **Closed** Apr–May & Aug–Dec: Mon; 1st Sat Nov; Thanksgiving, Dec 25, Jan1. 📷 ♿ 🌐 **south floridamuseum.org**

Stone monument to explorer De Soto

Environs
Five miles (8 km) west of central Bradenton, the **De Soto National Memorial** commemorates the landing near here in 1539 of Hernando de Soto *(see pp46–7)*. He and his 600 men set out on an epic four-year 4,000-mile (6,500-km) trek into the southeastern US in search of gold. They discovered the Mississippi, but the trek was disastrous and de Soto and half his army died. A monument recalls the luckless

explorers and marks the start of the De Soto Trail, which follows part of the route they took. The park also has a replica of de Soto's base camp; this is staffed by costumed volunteers, who give a memorable insight into the daily routines of the Spanish conquistadors. A visitor center has a museum, a bookstore, and exhibits of 16th-century weapons and armor. There is also a half-mile (1-km) nature trail through mangroves.

Two bridges link Bradenton to **Anna Maria Island**, whose sandy shoreline, backed by dunes, is largely undeveloped but is washed by breakers big enough to attract a handful of surfers. There is a scattering of small resorts based around the three main communities of Anna Maria, Holmes Beach, and Bradenton Beach. In the north stands the picturesque Anna Maria Pier, which was built in 1910.

🏞 De Soto National Memorial
8300 DeSoto Memorial Hwy. **Tel** (941) 792–0458. **Open** daily. **Closed** Thanksgiving, Dec 25, Jan 1. ♿ 🌐 **nps.gov/deso**

Sunset on Anna Maria Island's beautiful, unspoiled beach

⓯ Sarasota

This city is known as Florida's cultural center, a fact often credited to John Ringling *(see p274)*, who was one of many influential people attracted to the up-and-coming town in the early 1900s. Ringling poured money into the area, and his legacy is all around, nowhere more so than in his house and fine art collection, the city's biggest attraction *(see pp274–7)*. Sarasota's other great asset is that it seems to have escaped the worst excesses of the state's other cities. Promoted as "Florida's Mild Side," Sarasota is an attractive and clean community, with the bonus of a waterfront setting. You can join its affluent and conservative inhabitants browsing around its stylish shops or lying on the beach. Fabulous barrier island beaches are just a short drive from downtown Sarasota and are the best places to stay.

Flamingos gather at a small lake at Sarasota Jungle Gardens

Exploring Sarasota

The most pleasant area of downtown Sarasota focuses on Palm Avenue and Main Street, where restored storefronts dating from the early 20th century house antique shops, bars, and restaurants. Shopping and eating are also the main activities at nearby Sarasota Quay, and you can sign up for dinner cruises and other boat trips at the adjacent marina.

Dominating the waterfront to the north is the striking Van Wezel Performing Arts Hall *(see p35)*. Opened in 1970, this distinctive pink and lavender building is worth both to admire its sweeping, seashell-inspired lines, and to attend one of the many events, including concerts and Broadway shows, which are staged here *(see p361)*.

🏛 Sarasota Classic Car Museum

5500 N Tamiami Trail. **Tel** (941) 355-6228. **Open** daily. **Closed** Dec 25. 🅿️ 🚻 🎫 **W** sarasotacarmuseum.org

One of the oldest of its kind in the world, Sarasota Classic Car Museum opened its doors to the public in 1953. It is now home to 120 classic cars acquired either through exchanges with other car museums, or as donations from collectors.

An 1890s carousel organ at the museum

Highlights of the collection are a rare 1954 Packard Model 120 convertible, a 1955 Rolls-Royce Silver Wraith, a 1981 De Lorean in mint condition, and a Cadillac station wagon – one of only five ever made. John Lennon's Mercedes Roadster is also on show here, as is Paul McCartney's beloved Mini Cooper.

🌴 Sarasota Jungle Gardens

3701 Bay Shore Rd. **Tel** (941) 355-1112. **Open** daily. **Closed** Dec 25. 🅿️ 🚻 **W** sarasotajunglegardens.com

Originally developed as a botanical garden, this 10-acre (4-ha) former banana grove offers an oasis of tropical plants, trees, and flowers from around the world, with palm forests and gardens of hibiscus, ferns, roses, gardenias, and bougainvillea. The flamingo lagoon is a big attraction.

Other attractions, including a children's petting zoo and butterfly garden, place an emphasis on education and conservation. Simple entertainment is offered by the exotic bird shows and a reptile show. There are also a café and a gift shop.

🌴 Marie Selby Botanical Gardens

811 S Palm Ave. **Tel** (941) 366-5731. **Open** daily. **Closed** Dec 25. 🅿️ 🚻 🚻 **W** selby.org

You needn't be a gardener to appreciate the former home of wealthy Sarasota residents William and Marie Selby. Set among laurel and banyan trees overlooking Sarasota Bay, the estate was designed by Marie during the early 1920s as an escape from the modern world: you can still see the bamboo curtain she had planted to obscure the growing Sarasota skyline.

The gardens have more than 20,000 tropical plants and are particularly famous for their collection of orchids and

Christy Payne House in the Marie Selby Botanical Gardens

For hotels and restaurants in this region see pp314–25 and pp329–49

epiphytes *(see p294)*. There are also areas devoted to all kinds of exotic plants, from tropical foods and herbs to colorful hibiscus plants. The Tropical Display House has an impressive array of jungle vegetation.

The Spanish-style house, now a gift shop, is of less interest than the 1930s Christy Payne House. This delightful plantation-style mansion holds a Museum of Botany and Arts.

St. Armands Circle

This upscale shopping and dining complex on St. Armands Key was one of John Ringling's creations. He purchased the island in 1917 and produced an adventurous plan for a housing development, which centered on a circular shopping mall featuring gardens and classical statues. The area flourished briefly before being caught up in the Depression but was revived in the 1950s. It now looks much as Ringling planned, with shady avenues radiating from a central point.

St. Armands Circle, well placed between Downtown and the beaches, is popular both during the day and at night. The shops are mostly expensive, but anyone can enjoy the street entertainers who often congregate here.

Mote Aquarium and Mote Marine Laboratory

1600 Ken Thompson Parkway. **Tel** (941) 388-4441. **Open** daily. **mote.org**

This aquarium is located on City Island, between Lido and Longboat Keys. It has a bay walk with an excellent view of the

Tropical fish at the Mote Aquarium and Mote Marine Laboratory

Sarasota skyline, but the real attractions can be found inside. Among the most popular exhibits is a huge shark tank, complete with underwater observation windows, and a "touch tank," where you can come to grips with all kinds of marine creatures, from horseshoe crabs and whelks to stingrays. More than 30 other aquariums are stocked with local fish and plants; there is a display on the rivers, bays, and estuaries of the surrounding area.

Explanatory leaflets provide a useful insight into every exhibit, while guides explain how the aquarium ties in with the work of the attached laboratory, prominent in the study of sharks and pollution.

Asolo Repertory Theatre

5555 North Tamiami Tr. **Tel** (941) 351-8000. **Open** Sep–Jul. **asolorep.org**

For more than 50 years, the Asolo has been Florida's premier professional theater, and one of the most important cultural forces in the Sarasota's rich arts scene and the southeastern US. It stages up to 15 productions

every season, a diverse repertoire of newly commissioned plays, reinterpretations, and musical theater. Asolo Rep is the creative home of more than 100 artists and technical craftsmen, and its resident acting company is complemented by award-winning directors, designers, and guest artists.

Asolo Repertory Theatre – an important cultural center of Sarasota

Sarasota Beaches

The nearby barrier islands, Longboat Key, Lido Key, and Siesta Key, boast superb sandy beaches facing the Gulf of Mexico, and they are understandably popular *(see p257)*. Development has been intense, with condos along the shore in places, but there are several quieter areas too. The beach in South Lido Park, on Lido Key, is peaceful during the week and has a pleasant woodland trail too.

On Siesta Key the main residential area is in the north, focused around a network of canals. The broad Siesta Key Beach nearby is lively at any time. You'll find a quieter scene at Turtle Beach, which also has the only campground on these Keys. Longboat Key is well known for its golf courses. Wherever you are, the water sports are excellent.

South Lido Park beach, with a view south of nearby Siesta Key

Ringling Museum of Art

John Ringling was an Iowa-born circus owner whose phenomenally successful show *(see p276)* made him a multimillionaire. In 1925, he decided to build an art collection and a museum to house it, both as a memorial for himself and his wife, Mable, and as a gift to Sarasota. He and his wife had a particular affection for Italy, and their magnificent Italian Baroque paintings are the cornerstone of the collection. Their estate, which includes the palatial Cà d'Zan *(see pp276–7)*, was bequeathed to the state following John Ringling's death in 1936.

Statuary
The courtyard is dotted with bronze casts of Classical sculpture, such as this chariot.

The James Turrell "Skyspace" is in the Selby courtyard

A replica of Michelangelo's David

Closed for renovation
Future site of the Wall-Apelt Asian Art Wing.

12

13

14

15

16

17

18

Spanish Gallery
This gallery contains Spanish works of the 17th century, including paintings by El Greco and Velázquez, such as this magnificent portrait of Philip IV of Spain (1625–28), possibly Velázquez's earliest military portrait of Philip.

★ **Astor Rooms**
These lavish 19th-century interiors came from a New York mansion.

Gallery Guide

The galleries are arranged around a sculpture garden. Starting with the galleries to the right of the entrance hall, the rooms roughly follow a chronological order counterclockwise, ranging from late medieval painting to 20th-century European art; 16th- and 17th-century Italian painting is well represented. Modern art and special exhibitions are displayed in the Searing Wing. The Visitors' Pavilion is home to the Historic Asolo Theater.

Plan of Ringling Museum

Cà d'Zan

Circus Museum

Tibbals Learning Center

The Historic Asolo Theater Entrance

Visitors' Pavilion

P

Sarasota Bay

Rose Garden

Museum of Art

P

41

The ULLAR and Arthur F. Searing Wing is used for temporary exhibitions.

★ Courtyard
A gallery of 91 antique columns of various styles surrounds the courtyard. Some of them date from the 11th century.

Fountain of Oceanus

The Building of a Palace
This Italian Renaissance painting by Piero di Cosimo is one of the gallery's proudest possessions. Painted in oil on a wooden panel, it dates from around 1515.

★ Rubens Gallery
This gallery has great treasures, including *The Gathering of the Manna*, painted in 1625.

Entrance

Statue of Apollo

Fountain of the Tortoises

Key to Floor Plan

- Dutch and Flemish 1600–1700
- Rubens Gallery
- Medieval and Renaissance
- Italian 1500–1700
- Spanish 1600–1700
- European 1700–1800
- Astor Rooms
- French 1600–1700
- Flemish 1600–1700
- Ringling Master Plan
- European and North American 1850–1940

Ringling Museum: Cà' d'Zan

The Ringlings' winter residence, Cà' d'Zan, was the first part of the Ringling estate to be completed, providing a spectacular foretaste of what was to come. The Ringlings' love of Italy, nurtured during frequent visits to Europe, was displayed for all to see in the building's design as well as in its Venetian name, meaning "House of John." The property, which overlooks Sarasota Bay, was modeled after a Venetian palace, but there are also features drawn from French and Italian Renaissance architecture.

★ **Ceramic Decoration**
The exterior of Cà' d'Zan boasts some of the finest examples of ceramic work in the country.

Entranc

Set off by a 200-ft (60-m) marble terrace and crowned by a distinctive tower, Cà' d'Zan took two years to build and was finished in 1926. The ballroom, court, formal dining room, and bedrooms all provide glimpses of the life of the American super-rich of the period, and most of the original furniture is still in place.

★ **Ballroom**
The dominant feature of the ballroom is the extraordinary ceiling painting *Dancers of the Nations*. Depicting a variety of national dance costumes, it was painted by Willy Pogany, a 1920s' Hollywood set and costume designer.

KEY

① **The court**, with its marble floors and onyx columns, was the Ringlings' living room and is the focal point of the house.

② **Solarium**

③ **The tower**, was lit up when the Ringlings were at home.

④ **Mable Ringling's bedroom**, features an elegant 1920s Louis XV-style suite and pillowcases she made herself.

⑤ **Servants' rooms**

⑥ **Kitchen**

⑦ **John Ringling's Office**

⑧ **Exercise room**

The Ringling Circus

What started as a traveling wagon show, founded in 1884 by the five Ringling brothers, developed into one the most successful circuses of the era. The Ringlings' varied bill of entertainment proved more enduring than their rivals' offerings, and the brothers gradually bought up their competitors. In 1907, they formed a partnership with Phineas T. Barnum, whose taste for Siamese twins and exotic animals gave the circus a new slant from its more traditional origins.

The Circus Museum, opened in 1948, was not Ringling's idea, but with its models, carved circus wagons, and other rare items it gives a colorful insight into circus life.

Barnum's *Five Graces* circus wagon, 1878

Taproom
With its vaulted ceiling and stained-glass windows, the Taproom illustrates Ringling's love of collecting objects from far afield; he bought the bar from Cicardi's Restaurant in St. Louis, Missouri.

John Ringling's Bedroom
The handsome 19th-century mahogany furniture, lends an austere air to this room. Jacob de *Wit's Dawn Driving Away the Darkness* (1735) adorns the ceiling.

Breakfast Room
This simply decorated room was used mainly for informal family occasions. The Venetian blinds are original.

Bathroom
John Ringlings' attention to detail extended even to his bathroom, which has walls faced with Siena marble and a tub carved from a single block of stone.

Lush vegetation overhanging the river in Myakka River State Park

⑯ Myakka River State Park

Road map: D3 Sarasota Co. 13207 SR 72, 9 miles (14 km) E of Sarasota. 🚌 Sarasota. **Tel** (941) 361-6511. **Open** daily. 🐾 ♿ limited. 🛒 ⛺ 🌐 myakkariver.org

In spite of its proximity to the city of Sarasota, in the Myakka River State Park you can enjoy a taste of how the region must have looked to its first settlers. Dense oak, palm thickets, pine flatwoods, and an expanse of dry prairie are interspersed with marshland, swamps, and lakes.

The parkland's 28,000 acres (11,300 ha), which stretch along the Myakka River and around Upper Myakka Lake, form an outstanding wildlife sanctuary. More than 200 species of birds have been recorded here, including egrets, blue herons, vultures, and ibis, all of which are plentiful, as well as much rarer ospreys, bald eagles, and wild turkeys. Alligators and deer can usually be seen, though other denizens such as foxes are glimpsed only rarely. Observation platforms, from which you can view the wildlife, are dotted throughout the park.

Ambitious explorers can take to the park's 39 miles (63 km) of marked hiking trails or 15 miles (24 km) of bridle trails; alternatively, there are guided tours by tram between December and May, the best time to visit, and narrated river tours by airboat all year

⑰ Venice

Road map: D4. Sarasota Co. 👥 20,000. 🚌 ℹ️ 597 Tamiami Trail S, (941) 488-2236. 🌐 **venicechamber.com**

Venice is a sleepy seaside town, situated slightly off the beaten track and awash with flowers and palm trees, which line the center of the main shopping street, Venice Avenue. The town has a fine collection of carefully restored historic buildings, including the Venice Little Theater on Tampa Avenue, which dates from 1927.

Caspersen Beach, fringed by sea oats and palmettos, lies at the southern end of Harbor Drive. It is a popular place to swim and fish, and to collect shells,

Fossil hunting, Caspersen Beach

although the main shelling beaches are further south (*see pp282–3*). The area is famous for the fossilized sharks' teeth brought in by the tide. Brohard Paw Park on Harbor Drive South is a haven for dog lovers.

⑱ Gasparilla Island

Road map: D4. Lee Co, Charlotte Co. 🚌 Venice. ℹ️ 5800 Gasparilla Rd, Boca Grande, (941) 964-0568. 🌐 bocagrandechamber.org

Discovered originally by fishermen, and later by the wealthy fleeing northern winters, Gasparilla is a perfect island hideaway midway between Sarasota and Fort Myers.

Activity is centered around the community of Boca Grande, which is joined by a causeway to the mainland. The restored former railroad station, the San Marco Theater, and the grand Gasparilla Inn are eloquent reminders of times past. Many old wooden buildings have been saved and given a fresh coat of paint, giving the place a pleasant, tropical feel. Fishing has been big business here for a long time – Boca Grande is known as the "tarpon capital of the world" – and there are a number of marinas where you can arrange boat trips, some of which go to nearby barrier islands (*see*

The Range Light, which warns off ships from Gasparilla Island's coast

pp282–3). Another way to explore is to follow the bike trail that runs down the island.

At the island's southern tip, the **Gasparilla Island State Park** has quiet beaches where you can fish and swim as well as hunt for shells. A squat late 19th-century lighthouse overlooks Boca Grande Pass, but its function is fulfilled by the more modern Range Light.

Gasparilla Island State Park
880 Belcher Rd, Boca Grande. **Tel** (941) 964-0375. **Open** daily.

The colorful 1920s Schlossberg-Camp Building in Arcadia

⑲ Arcadia

Road map: E3. De Soto Co. 6,000.
16 S Volusia Ave, (863) 494-4033. **desotochamber.net**

It is a pleasure to stroll around the old cattle ranching town of Arcadia. Local cowboys are more likely to ride around in a pickup truck than on horseback, but the horse is still very much part of the local culture. Cowboy fever reaches a peak twice a year, in March and July, when competitors and devotees from all over the US converge for the All-Florida Championship Rodeo, the oldest rodeo in the state.

Arcadia's flamboyant and sometimes colorful architecture recalls the prosperity and confidence of the 1920s. The best examples are the Florida Mediterranean-style Koch Arcade Building, on West Oak Street, and the Schlossberg-Camp Building, on West Magnolia Street.

Many earlier buildings were destroyed by a fire in 1905; the striking J.J. Heard Opera House on Oak Street was constructed the following year. Only a few buildings from the late 1800s survive; these can be seen by arrangement with the Chamber of Commerce.

⑳ Babcock Wilderness Adventures

Road map: E4. Charlotte Co. 8000 SR 31. **Tel** (800) 500-5583. Punta Gorda. **Open** daily. **Closed** Dec 25. compulsory. **babcockwilderness.com**

The huge Crescent B Ranch was originally owned by lumber baron, E.V. Babcock, who bled the cypress swamp for timber in the 1930s. It is still run by the phenomenally rich Babcock family, and part of the 90,000-acre (36,420-ha) working ranch is open as the Babcock Wilderness Adventures.

Swamp buggy exploring Babcock Wilderness Adventures

During 90-minute trips led by trained naturalists, swamp buggies take visitors through deep woods and a dense patch of cypress swamp, with plenty of opportunities to see wildlife. Panthers, which are bred successfully here, are in a specially designed paddock; alligators cruise just a short distance away. The ranch's herds of horses and Cracker cattle are also on view. Babcock's tours are very popular and must be booked well in advance.

Rodeos in Florida

Much of Florida's interior scrubland is ranching country, focused around cattle towns such as Arcadia, Kissimmee (see p195), and Davie (see p141), where rodeos are a feature of everyday life. Speed is the key during competitions. In events such as calf roping and steer wrestling (in which the cowboy must force the animal to the ground), the winner is the one with the fastest time – usually well under ten seconds. In bareback or saddle bronco riding the cowboys must stay on the bucking horse for at least eight seconds, but they are also judged on their overall skill and technique. During the competition a commentator keeps the audience informed of the cowboys' current form, giving details of any titles held.

Steer wrestling at Arcadia's All-Florida Championship Rodeo

㉑ Fort Myers

The approach to Fort Myers across the Caloosahatchee River is stunning, a fine introduction to a city that still has an air of old-time Florida. Following the sweep of the river is McGregor Boulevard, lined with ranks of royal palms; the first of these were planted by the inventor Thomas Edison, who put Fort Myers on the map in the 1880s, when it was just a small fishing village.

In addition to Edison's home and a few other sights, the old downtown area around First Street, with its many shops and restaurants, is worth exploring; a trolley service runs regularly through the downtown area linking the main sights. When you have had your fill of the city, there are beaches only a short distance away.

VISITORS' CHECKLIST

Practical Information
Road map: E4. Lee Co.
🏙 62,000. 🛈 2310 Edwards Drive, (239) 332–3624, (800) 366–3622. 🎪 Edison Festival of Lights (Feb). 🌐 fortmyers.org

Transportation
✈ 7 miles (11 km) SE. 🚌 2275 Cleveland Avenue, (800) 231–2222; also Amtrak Thruway bus, (800) 872-7245.

The original equipment on show in Thomas Edison's laboratory

🏛 Edison and Ford Winter Estate

2350 McGregor Blvd.**Tel** (239) 334-7419. **Open** daily. **Closed** Thanksgiving, Dec 25. 🅿 📷 ♿
🌐 edisonfordwinterestates.org

The waterfront retreat of one of America's most famous inventors, the Edison Winter Home is Fort Myers' most enduring attraction. Thomas Edison (1847–1931) built the estate in 1886, and the house, laboratory, and botanical gardens are much as he left them.

The two-story house and adjoining guesthouse were among the first prefabricated buildings in the US, built in sections to Edison's specifications in Maine and shipped to Fort Myers by schooner. This precluded extravagance, but the house is large and comfortable, and spacious overhanging porches around the ground floor kept the buildings cool. Many of the original furnishings are inside.

Edison was the holder of more than 1,000 patents, and his interests ranged from the light bulb to the phonograph, which recorded on wax cylinders. His laboratory, on the opposite side of McGregor Boulevard from the house, contains the original equipment he used in his later experiments in synthetic rubber production. The museum displays samples of Edison's work as an inventor, including the telegraph, telephone, and X-ray machine, personal items, dozens of phonographs, and a 1916 Model T car that was given to him by Henry Ford.

Thomas Edison was also an enthusiastic horticulturalist, and the gardens around the house and laboratory contain a great variety of exotic plants. The giant banyan tree, which was given to Edison by the tire magnate Harvey Firestone in 1925, boasts a circumference in excess of 400 ft (120 m).

Edison was a popular man locally, and tours of the home are notable for the breadth of knowledge and enthusiasm shown by the guides.

🏛 Ford Winter Home

2350 McGregor Blvd. **Tel** (239) 334-3614. **Open** daily. **Closed** Thanksgiving, Dec 25. 🅿 📷 ♿

Next to the Edison home (and viewable on the same ticket) is Mangoes, the small estate bought in 1916 by the car manufacturer Henry Ford. The Fords were great friends of the Edisons, and following Thomas Edison's death in 1931 they never returned here.

The rooms have been faithfully re-created with period furnishings and still have the homey air favored by Clara Ford. Some early Ford cars are displayed in the garage.

🏛 Imaginarium Hands-On Museum and Aquarium

2000 Cranford Ave. **Tel** (239) 321-7420. **Open** 10am–5pm Mon–Sat, noon–5pm Sun. **Closed** Thanksgiving, Dec 25. 🅿 ♿ 🏠
🌐 imaginariumfortmyers.com

The Imaginarium Hands-On Museum and Aquarium has something to offer the entire family. It has over 60 exciting interactive exhibits which are designed for all ages, where visitors can touch a cloud, feel

One of the several beautiful beaches to be found at Fort Myers

Young visitors on the boardwalk at the Calusa Nature Center

the huge force of a hurricane or run through a thunderstorm. There is a movie theater, dinosaur dig, and children can also become a TV weatherman in a mini-studio as part of a daily program of shows and interactive presentations. The aquarium houses a variety of different fish, including sharks and moray eels, as well as other animals, such as turtles, swans, and iguanas.

Southwest Florida Museum of History

2031 Jackson St. **Tel** (239) 321-7430. **Open** 10am–5pm Tue–Sat (Feb–Apr: also Sun). 🅿️ 🅰️
W swflmuseumofhistory.com

Housed in the former railroad station, this museum recalls Fort Myers' heyday as a cattle town and delves into the area's early history as represented by the Calusa Indians and Spanish explorers. Highlights include a scale model of Fort Myers in 1900 and a refurbished 1930 private railroad car – the type used to bring northerners to the area for the winter sunshine. There is also an exhibit of pre-historic art and artifacts.

Calusa Nature Center and Planetarium

3450 Ortiz Ave. **Tel** (239) 275-3435. **Open** daily. **Closed** Jan 1, Thanksgiving, Dec 25. 🅿️ 🅰️ 🅲️ by request. **W** calusanature.com

This 105-acre (42-ha) patch of wilderness is an excellent introduction to the flora and fauna of southwest Florida. There is a large aviary, and you can follow wooden walkways past ferns and mangrove, where it is often possible to spot herons, egrets, and the occasional ibis. The museum provides illustrated talks on snakes and alligators, and there are also regular guided nature walks and tours of the aviary.

The center also boasts a butterfly aviary and butterfly plant nursery where you can buy plants to start your own butterfly garden.

The planetarium features star and laser shows, for which there is a separate charge.

Environs

A souvenir shop on a massive scale, **The Shell Factory** lies 4 miles (6 km) north of Fort Myers. On sale are shell ornaments and jewelry, but most impressive is the collection of shells and coral, claimed to be the largest in the world. The shop also stocks sponges, sculpted driftwood, posters, books, and other gift items. There is also a zoo and waltzing water show.

The Shell Factory

2787 N Tamiami Trail. **Tel** (239) 995-2141. **Open** 10am–9pm Mon–Sat, 10am–8pm Sun. 🅰️
W shellfactory.com

㉒ Koreshan State Historic Site

Road map: E4. Lee Co. Estero, 14 miles (23 km) S of Fort Myers. **Tel** (239) 992-0311. 🚌 Fort Myers. **Open** daily. 🅿️ 🅰️ 🅲️ 🅰️
W floridastateparks.org

Those interested in obscure religions mix with nature lovers at the Koreshan State Historic Site, the former home of the Koreshan Unity sect.

In 1894 the sect's founder, Dr. Cyrus Teed, had a vision telling him to change his name to Koresh (Hebrew for Cyrus) and to move to southwest Florida, where he was to establish a great utopian city with streets 400 ft (122 m) wide. He chose this beautiful location on the Estero River, where members pursued a communal lifestyle, with equal rights for women and shared ownership of property.

Far from the city of ten million people that Teed had envisaged, the Koreshan Unity sect had a mere 250 followers at its peak, and membership dwindled after his death in 1908. The last four members donated the site to Florida in 1961. Twelve of the sect's 60 buildings and their gardens survive; they include Cyrus Teed's home, which has been completely restored.

The park has canoe and nature trails, camping facilities, opportunities for fresh and saltwater fishing, and also arranges guided tours.

Cyrus Teed's restored home at the Koreshan State Historic Site

㉓ Lee Island Coast

The Lee Island Coast offers an irresistible combination of sandy beaches (famous for their shells), exotic wild-life, lush vegetation, and stupendous sunsets. Most people head for Sanibel and Captiva islands, with their chic resorts, marinas, and golf courses. However, other less developed islands – where there are few distractions from the beaches and natural beauty – are just a short boat trip away. Boat tours and charters can be picked up at many places, and there are also some regular boat services, whose routes are marked on the map below.

Tranquil beachfront cottages on Sanibel island

VISITORS' CHECKLIST

Practical Information
Road map: D4, E4. Lee Co.
🛈 1159 Causeway Rd, Sanibel, (239) 472-1080. Boat services: Tropic Star (239) 283-0015; Captiva Cruises (239) 472-5300; North Captiva Island Club Resort (239) 395-1001.

Transportation
✈ SW Florida International Airport, 15 miles (24 km) E. 🚌 2275 Cleveland Ave, Fort Myers, (800) 231-2222.

by avid shell hunters. Sanibel may not be most people's idea of an island retreat – with its manicured gardens and rows of shops and restaurants along Periwinkle Way, the hub of Sanibel town – but there are no condos, and two areas are protected as preserves. Most of the beaches with public access are along Gulf Drive, the best being Turner and Bowman's beaches.

Captiva is less developed than Sanibel, but you'll still find the odd resort, including the South Seas Plantation Resort (see p312), with its busy marina – a starting point for boat trips to Cayo Costa.

Sanibel and Captiva Islands

Despite being more accessible than the other islands, Sanibel and Captiva have a laid-back, Caribbean air. They are famous both as havens for lovers of the good life and for their shells. Most visitors soon get drawn into the shell-collecting culture, which has given rise to the expressions "Sanibel Stoop" and "Captiva Crouch" the posture adopted

🖂 Sanibel Captiva Conservation Foundation

Mile Marker 1, Sanibel-Captiva Rd. **Tel** (239) 472-2329. **Open** May–Nov: Mon–Fri; Dec–Apr: Mon–Sat. 🅿 🔲 🔲 sccf.org

This private foundation oversees the protection of a chunk of Sanibel's interior wetland. Its 4 miles (6 km) of boardwalk trails are much quieter than those in the better known "Ding" Darling refuge nearby. An observation tower provides a perfect vantage point.

Key
-- Boat service
▬ Road

For map symbols see back flap

🏛 Bailey-Matthews Shell Museum

3075 Sanibel-Captiva Rd. **Tel** (239) 395-2233. **Open** daily. 🅿 🔲 🔲 shellmuseum.org

Even if you aren't interested in shelling, this museum is well worth a visit. The centerpiece Great Hall of Shells includes displays grouped according to habitat, from barrier islands to the Everglades. It claims to have one-third of the world's 10,000 shell varieties.

⬛ JN "Ding" Darling National Wildlife Refuge

Mile Marker 2, Sanibel Captiva Rd. **Tel** (239) 472-1100. **Open** daily. **Closed** public hols. 🅿️ 🅲 **w** fws.gov/dingdarling

This refuge occupies two-thirds of Sanibel. Resident wildlife, including raccoons, alligators, and birds such as roseate spoonbills, bald eagles, and ospreys, are surprisingly easy to spot. The popular 5-mile (8-km) scenic "Wildlife Drive" can be covered by bike as well as by car, and there are tram tours too. Paths and canoe trails are lined with sea grape, red mangrove, and cabbage palm. Canoes, fishing boats, and bikes can be rented.

Roseate spoonbills in the JN "Ding" Darling National Wildlife Refuge

⬛ Cayo Costa Island State Park

Cayo Costa Island. **Tel** (941) 964-0375. **Open** daily. 🅿️ 🅱️ 🅰️ **w** floridastateparks.org

Cayo Costa Island is one of the state's most unspoiled barrier islands. Much of it is planted with non-native Australian pine and Brazilian pepper trees. These were originally imported during the 1950s for their shade and wood, but are now gradually being cleared to let domestic species take over.

There are 9 miles (14 km) of dune-backed beach and, on the eastern side, several mangrove swamps. Inland, there is a mix of pine flatwoods, grassy areas, and hammocks. The whole island offers plenty of bird-watching opportunities and excellent shelling, especially in winter.

Yachts at anchor in the peaceful marina of Cabbage Key

Boat trips take visitors to Cayo Costa all year round; Tropic Star, from Bokeelia on Pine Island, offers the most frequent service. A tram links the bayside dock to the gulf side. Cayo Costa has a basic campground with 12 cabins.

Cabbage Key

This island was chosen by the novelist Mary Roberts Rhinehart for her home in 1938. Her house, built in the shade of two 18th-century Cuban laurel trees, is now the Cabbage Key Inn. This is best known for its restaurant, which is deco-rated with around 30,000 autographed one-dollar bills. The first bill was left by a fisherman anxious to make sure he had funds to buy drinks on his next visit. When he returned, he had money to spare and left the bill where it was. Other visitors then took up the idea.

A 40-ft (12-m) water tower nearby provides a lovely view of the small island, and there is also a short nature trail. Tropic Star from Pine Island and Captiva Cruises from Captiva Island run the most regular trips to the island.

Pine Island

This island, fringed with man-grove rather than beaches, is useful mainly as an access point to nearby islands. You can arrange all kinds of boat trips at the marina in Bokeelia; allow time to enjoy its fine collection of fishing piers.

Shells and Shelling

The beaches of Sanibel and Captiva are among the best in the US for shelling. The Gulf of Mexico has no offshore reef to smash the shells, and the waters are relatively shallow and warm, with a flat bed – all factors that **Junonia** encourage growth. The wide plateau off the southern tip of Sanibel also acts as a ramp, helping to roll the shells ashore. Live shelling is a federal offense on Sanibel and subject to restrictions elsewhere, so collect only empty shells.

The best advice is to go early, and look just beneath the surface of the sand where the surf breaks. Seabirds feeding along the shore are a good indication of a good crop of shells. Shelling is best in winter or directly following a storm. The junonia and the lion's paw scallop are particularly sought after.

Florida fighting conch

Common fig shell — Lion's paw scallop — Janthina

For hotels and restaurants in this region see pp314–25 and pp329–49

THE EVERGLADES AND THE KEYS

Southwest Florida is mostly occupied by the world-famous Everglades – low-lying wetlands of huge ecological importance. Resorts and towns pepper the Keys, where Floridians and visitors alike come to enjoy the region's other natural wonder, the coral reef.

Before the arrival of the Europeans, south Florida was home to tribes like the Calusa and the Matecumbe *(see pp44–5)*. From the 1500s on, the Keys were visited by a succession of settlers, pirates, and wreckers *(see p307)*, but the mosquito-infested mainland was not settled until the mid-19th century, with the establishment of what is now the thriving coastal resort of Naples.

The first road to open up the area by linking the Atlantic and Gulf coasts was the Tamiami Trail, built in 1928. Pioneer camps located off it, such as Everglades City and Chokoloskee, have barely changed since the late 1800s and today seem caught in a time warp. They mark the western entrance of the Everglades National Park. This broad river of sawgrass, dotted with tree islands, possesses a peculiar beauty and is a paradise for its thrilling and prolific wildlife. Running southwest off the tip of the peninsula are the Keys, a chain of jewel-like islands protected by North America's only coral reef. Henry Flagler's Overseas Railroad once crossed the Keys; it has since disappeared and been replaced by the Overseas Highway – the route of one of the country's classic road trips. The farther south you go, the easier it is to agree with the saying that the Keys are more about a state of mind than a geographical location. At the end of the road is legendary Key West, where there is plenty to see and do, but where the relaxed Keys approach to life reigns supreme.

A vibrant mural in Key West's Bahama Village, reflecting the Caribbean origins of its inhabitants

◄ A warm summer's day in a Florida swamp

Exploring the Everglades and the Keys

Naples and Marco Island in the northwest are the best bases for enjoying the Gulfshore beaches, and they boast some superb golf courses too. They also offer easy access to the wild and expansive scenery of Big Cypress Swamp and Everglades National Park, which together take up a great proportion of the region. The Florida Keys are justifiably famous for their activities focused on the nearby coral reef, such as fishing, diving and snorkeling. Islamorada and Key Largo in the Upper Keys both have plenty of accommodations to choose from, while bustling Marathon and colorful Key West, with its picturesque bed-and-breakfast inns, are excellent bases for exploring the more laid-back Lower Keys.

The Overseas Highway, the main artery through the Florida Keys

Sights at a Glance

1. Naples
2. Big Cypress Swamp
3. Ah-Tah-Thi-Ki Museum
4. Miccosukee Indian Village
5. *Everglades National Park pp290–95*
6. Biscayne National Park
7. Key Largo
8. John Pennekamp Coral Reef State Park
9. Tavernier
10. Theater of the Sea
11. Islamorada
12. Indian and Lignumvitae Keys
13. Dolphin Research Center
14. Marathon
15. Pigeon Key
16. Lower Keys
17. *Key West pp302–7*
18. Dry Tortugas National Park

0 kilometers   25

0 miles   25

The untouched wilderness of Big Cypress Swamp

Key

▭▭ Highway

▭▭ Major road

▬▬ Secondary road

┅┅ Minor railway

━━ Scenic route

H-TAH-THI-KI MUSEUM ③

Big Cypress Seminole Indian Reservation

Fort Lauderdale

846

833

75

G

CYPRESS SWAMP

② Florida State Miccosukee Indian Reservation

Big Cypress National Preserve

41 Monroe Station

Miccosukee Indian Reservation

MICCOSUKEE INDIAN VILLAGE ④

41 Miami

Shark Valley

EVERGLADES

997

⑤

NATIONAL PARK

BISCAYNE NATIONAL PARK ⑥

'and 'oint

Homestead Miami

Pa-hay-okee Overlook

Florida City

Elliot Key

Shark Point

Old Rhodes Key

Whitewater Bay

Mahogany Hammock

'thwest Cape

Cape Sable

Key Largo

'le Cape

Flamingo

East Cape

JOHN PENNEKAMP ⑧ CORAL REEF STATE PARK

KEY LARGO ⑦

Florida Bay

⑨ TAVERNIER

Plantation Key

⑩ THEATER OF THE SEA

ISLAMORADA ⑪

INDIAN AND ⑫ LIGNUMVITAE KEYS

Long Key

DOLPHIN RESEARCH ⑬ CENTRE

Marathon Shores

Keys

⑤ ⑭ MARATHON

PIGEON KEY

'ia Honda 'te Park

Florida

Getting Around

There are no rail services in the region, but Key West, Marathon, and Naples all have airports, and long-distance buses link Miami to Naples and Key West. The Tamiami Trail (US 41) and I-75 connect Miami and Fort Lauderdale with Naples. The Overseas Highway (US 1) begins at Florida City, but the Card Sound Road (Route 997), which has less traffic and better views, offers an alternative approach to the Keys. The Overseas Highway is most scenic after the 7-Mile Bridge, where the islands are less built up and the views more panoramic. Directions and addresses in the Keys are often given in Mile Markers, which refer to the small green and white signs at the roadside indicating the distance from Key West.

For map symbols *see back flap*

❶ Naples

Road map: E4. Collier Co. 🏞 21,000.
🚉 ✈ 🚌 2390 Tamiami Trail N, (239)
262-6141. **w** napleschamber.org

A conservative and affluent
beach city, Naples prides itself on
its manicured appearance and
on its golf courses; with 55 of
them, it has the greatest per
capita concentration of courses
in the state.

Downtown, most of what is
called "historic" Naples dates
from the early 20th century, and
with its pastel-colored buildings
is a pleasant area to explore.
Many of the 19th-century
houses were destroyed by
hurricane Donna in 1960, which
also claimed the original 1887
pier. Rebuilt in 1961, this is now a
popular spot for both anglers
and pelicans; the latter are a
common sight perched upon
the railings.

A beautiful white sandy beach
stretching for 10 miles (16 km) is
flanked mostly by condos, but it
offers easy public access and safe
swimming in warm Gulf waters.

The informative **Collier County
Museum** focuses on local history
and includes a re-created
Seminole village. Exhibits range
from ancient indigenous Indian
artifacts to those connected
with the region's pioneering past
and the building of the Tamiami
Trail (US 41), on which the
museum stands.

The popular gulf shore beach alongside Naples pier

🏛 Collier County Museum

3331 Tamiami Trail E. **Tel** (239) 252-
8476. **Open** 9am–5pm Mon–Fri.
Closed public hols. ♿
w colliermuseums.com

Environs

Developed as a resort since the
1960s, **Marco Island** is the most
northerly of the Ten Thousand
Islands chain and a good base for
exploring the western fringe of
the Everglades (see p290).
Outstanding archaeological items,
some 3,500 years old, were found
here. These are now kept in
museums elsewhere, but here
and there you can still see the
remains of midden mounds –
discarded shells and bones giving
clues to the lifestyle of the ancient
Calusa Indians (see pp44–5).

❷ Big Cypress Swamp

Road map: E4. Collier Co, Monroe Co.
Tel (239) 695-1201.

Home to several hundred
species such as the
endangered Florida panther
(see p131), this vast, shallow
wetland basin is not, in fact, a
true swamp. It features a range
of habitats, determined by
only slight differences in
elevation, which include sandy
islands of slash pine, wet and
dry prairies, and hardwood
hammocks (see p291). One-
third of the swamp is covered
by cypress trees, growing in
belts and long narrow forests
("strands"). It is the scale of
these strands as opposed to
the size of the trees that gives
the area its name.

The swamp functions as a
wet season water storage area
for the greater Everglades
system and as a buffer zone
for the Everglades National
Park (see pp290–91). Finished
in 1928, the Tamiami Trail, also
known as US 41, cuts through
the swamp and has opened
up the area. The road skirts
the Everglades and stretches
from Tampa to Miami, hence
its name. Today, such
engineering feats are
environmentally questionable,
as they block the natural
movement of water and
wildlife essential to the fragile
balance of southern Florida's
unique ecosystem.

Boardwalk winding through Fakahatchee Strand, Big Cypress Swamp

The Seminoles of Florida

"Seminole" (meaning "wanderer" or "runaway") was first used in the 1700s for several Creek Indian tribes, forced to flee south to Florida by land-hungry Europeans and later retreated into the Everglades *(see p51)*. Today, the Seminole tribe is officially distinct from the other main grouping, the Miccosukee tribe, but members of both are known as Seminoles.

Historic land disputes led the US Government to allocate reservation lands to the Florida Indians in 1911. Here, Seminoles maintain their traditions but also incorporate elements of modern American life. Since then, bingo halls and gambling casinos have significantly increased tribal wealth *(see p141)*. Billie Swamp Safaris offers tours of Seminole tribe backcountry.

Seminole dress in the late 1800s, showing European influence

Wood storks nesting in the trees of Corkscrew Swamp Sanctuary

Big Cypress National Preserve is the largest of the protected areas. Most visitors here enjoy the views from US 41 and stop at the Oasis Visitor Center for information.

On the western edge of the swamp is the **Fakahatchee Strand Preserve State Park**, one of Florida's wildest areas. A huge natural drainage ditch or slough (pronounced "slew"), it is 20 miles (32 km) long and 3–5 miles (5–8 km) wide.

Logging ceased here in the 1950s, having destroyed 99 per-cent of old growth cypresses; the Preserve's only remaining examples, some dating from the 15th century, are found at Big Cypress Bend. Here, a short trail passes through a mosaic of plant com- munities, including magnificent orchids and nestlike epiphytes *(see p294)*. Here too is the US's largest stand of native royal palms. Route 846, running northeast from Naples, takes you

to the popular **Audubon of Florida's Corkscrew Swamp Sanctuary**. A 2-mile (3-km) boardwalk traverses various habitats, including Florida's largest stand of old growth cypress trees. The sanctuary is famous for its many birds and is an important nesting area for endangered wood storks, which visit during the winter.

🦅 **Big Cypress National Preserve**
Oasis Visitor Center, US 41. **Tel** (239) 695-1201. **Open** daily. **Closed** Dec 25.
💺 🌐 nps.gov/bicy

🦅 **Fakahatchee Strand Preserve State Park**
Big Cypress Bend, US 41. **Tel** (239) 695-4593. **Open** daily. 💺

🦅 **Audubon of Florida's Corkscrew Swamp Sanctuary**
375 Sanctuary Rd W, off Route 846.
Tel (239) 348-9151. **Open** daily. 🏛
💺 🌐 corkscrew.audubon.org

❸ Ah-Tah-Thi-Ki Museum

Road map: F4. Hendry Co. Snake Rd, 17 miles (27 km) N of Exit 14 off I-75. **Tel** (863) 902-1113. **Open** 9am–5pm daily. **Closed** public hols. 🏛 🎦 2:30pm daily. 💺 🌐 ahtathiki.com

This museum is located on 64 acres (26 ha) of the Big Cypress Seminole Indian Reservation. On site is a traditional village where Seminole tribal members tell stories and demonstrate crafts.

The museum is dedicated to the understanding of Seminole culture and history; Ah-Tah-Thi-Ki means "a place to learn." There is an impressive 180-degree, five-screen film.

❹ Miccosukee Indian Village

Road map: F5. Dade Co. US 41, 25 miles (40 km) W of Florida Turnpike. **Tel** (305) 552-8365. **Open** daily. 🏛 💺 🌐 miccosukee.com

Most of the Miccosukee tribe live in small settlements along US 41. The best way to find out more about them is to visit the Miccosukee Indian Village near Shark Valley *(see p291)*.

Here, visitors can see traditional *chickees (see p34)* and crafts like basket-weaving, doll-making, and beadwork. Native artifacts, clothing, paintings, and cooking utensils are displayed at the Miccosukee Museum. There is also a luxurious resort and gaming facility, which offers spa facilities, golf course, and country club.

Palmetto dolls and beadwork for sale in the Miccosukee Indian Village

⑤ Everglades National Park

Covering 1.5 million acres (566,580 ha), this huge park still makes up only one-fifth of the entire Everglades area. The main entrance on its eastern boundary is 10 miles (16 km) west of Florida City. The park's walking trails are mostly elevated boardwalks, about half a mile (1 km) long and clearly marked; some are suitable for bicycles. Boats and canoes can be rented, and there's a variety of boat trips to choose from. Lodgings consist of campgrounds, including more primitive sites where visitors stay in chickees *(see p34)*, most of which are accessible only by canoe. There's a small charge for backcountry camping permits which must be obtained in person at ranger stations in Everglades City or Flamingo; reservations can be made only in the 24 hours prior to departure.

Everglades City
The Ten Thousand Islands archipelago and the national park's west coast are accessible from Everglades City.

Whitewater Bay
Only where the sheet river of the Everglades meets the Gulf of Mexico and Florida Bay does open water, in the form of rivers, tidal creeks, and shallow lakes like Whitewater Bay, appear.

Naples

Everglades City (29)

Chokoloskee

Tamiami Trail (41)

Ten Thousand Islands

BIG CYPRESS NATIONAL PRESERVE

GULF OF MEXICO

Safety Tips

Protection against biting insects is vital, especially during the summer months. Follow the advice given by rangers and on information boards, and respect all wildlife: alligators can jump and move quickly on land; some trees and shrubs like the Brazilian pepper tree are poisonous, as are some caterpillars and snakes. If planning to go off the beaten path, let someone know your itinerary. Always drive slowly: much wild-life can be seen from the road – and may also venture onto it.

Coral snake

0 kilometers   15
0 miles   10

Canoeing in the Everglades
Along the western coast and around Florida Bay are countless opportunities to explore the park's watery trails. These range from short routes to the week-long adventure of the challenging and remote Wilderness Waterway.

Shark Valley

Take a narrated tram ride or cycle along this 15-mile (25-km) loop road. At its end is a 60-ft (18-m) tower that offers great views.

Anhinga Trail

Starting at the Royal Palm Visitor Center, this is one of the most popular trails in the park. Its namesake, the anhinga bird, is often seen drying its distinctive plumage in the sun after diving for fish.

VISITORS' CHECKLIST

Practical Information
Road map: E4, E5, F5. Monroe Co, Dade Co, Collier Co. **Open** daily. 🛈 all visitor centers open Dec–Apr daily; during rest of year, call in advance to check. Main Visitor Center: **Tel** (305) 242-7700. **Open** 8am–5pm. Gulf Coast Visitor Center: (in Everglades City) **Tel** (239) 695-3311; for boat tours and canoe rental call (239) 695-2591. **Open** 9am–4:30pm. Shark Valley Information Center: **Tel** (305) 221-8776; for tram tour reservations and bicycle rental (305) 221-8455. **Open** 8:30am–5:15pm. Royal Palm Visitor Center: **Tel** (305) 242-7700. **Open** 8am–4:15pm. Flamingo Visitor Center: **Tel** (239) 695-2945; for canoe, boat, or bicycle rental, boat tours, marina, call (239) 695-3101. **Open** 8:30am–5:30pm. ♿ most park boardwalks are accessible. Call (305) 242-7700. 🏕 call (800) 365-2267 to book. Excellent interactive map: Ⓦ nps.gov/ever

Key

▨	Mangrove
▨	Saltwater prairie
▨	Cypress trees
▨	Freshwater prairie
▨	Freshwater slough
▨	Pinelands
▨	Hammock
– –	Wilderness Waterway
– –	Park boundary
▬▬	Paved road
═══	Road closed to private vehicles

Flamingo has the park's largest campground. Several hiking and canoe trails are in its vicinity.

Mahogany Hammock Boardwalk

This trail meanders through a large, dense tropical hardwood hammock. It is noted for its colorful tree snails (see p295) and epiphytes (see p294) and for being the home of the largest mahogany tree in the country.

For additional map symbols see back flap

The Wildlife of the Everglades

The Everglades is a vast sheet river system – the overspill from Lake Okeechobee *(see p132)* that moves slowly across a flat bed of peat-covered limestone. Some 200 miles (322 km) long and up to 50 miles (80 km) wide, its depth rarely exceeds 3 ft (1 m).

Tropical air and sea currents act on this temperate zone to create combinations of flora that are unique in North America. Clumps of vegetation, such as cypress domes *(see p29)*, tropical hardwood hammocks, and bayheads, break the expanse of sawgrass prairie. And there are hundreds of animal species – some 350 species of birds, for which the Everglades is particularly renowned. This unique ecosystem, with its rich vegetation and associated wildlife, can only be sustained by the cycle of dry (winter) and wet (summer) seasons – the Everglades' life force.

Osprey
This fish-eating bird is seen around the park's coast, bays, and ponds. Its large nests are easily recognizable.

The strangler fig
starts life as a seed carried in bird droppings to a crevice of another tree. In time, it completely engulfs the host tree.

Green Tree Frog
This endearing amphibian has a resonant call that can be heard throughout the Everglades.

Snowy Egret
Beautiful breeding plumage, yellow feet, and a black bill identify this bird.

Bromeliad
(see p294)

Bayheads
are hammocks dominated by bay trees, that thrive on rich organic soil.

Sweet bay

Wax myrtle

Sawgrass

Cattail

Tree Islands

Hammocks or tree islands are areas of elevated land found in freshwater prairies. They support a fantastic variety of flora and fauna.

Alligator flag

Bladderwort

Water Lily

'Gator holes are made by alligators hollowing out ponds and depressions during the dry season to reach the water below. The water-filled holes sustain many species during the winter.

American Alligator
With its rough hide and toothy grin, the alligator is one of the park's best known (and most feared) residents.

Royal palm

Great Blue Heron
Found all over Florida, this wading bird has a 6-ft (2-m) wingspan. In south Florida its plumage can sometimes be completely white.

Roseate Spoonbill
These striking birds winter in the park and use their spatulate bills to fish for food in shallow water.

The mahogany is just one of the West Indian species that predominates in tropical hardwood hammocks.

The gumbo-limbo's bark is red and peeling, hence its nickname the "tourist tree."

Saw palmetto

Peat

Red mangrove trees are easily recognized by their distinctive roots. Salt-tolerant, they play a crucial role in protecting the shoreline and act as a nursery for marine animals.

Tree Snail
There are 58 varieties of the colorful tree snail, which live in hammocks and move around only during the wet season.

Otter
Related to the weasel, this delightful animal is often seen frolicking in freshwater ponds.

Exploring Everglades National Park

Most visitors come to Everglades National Park on a day trip, which can easily be spent exploring just one or two of the trails. However, a popular excursion involves stopping at the different boardwalk trails along the Main Park Road (Route 9336); it is an easy drive down and back to Flamingo on Florida Bay. Try to include at least one of the less-visited trails and ponds located off the southern part of the road between Mahogany Hammock and Flamingo. Information boards abound to help you identify the flora and fauna. Remember to bring insect repellent and protection against the sun.

Long Pine Key, which boasts a lovely campsite and shady trails

Rangers and visitors examining wildlife on a "slough-slog"

Around the Royal Palm Visitor Center

The highly informative Royal Palm Visitor Center and two nearby boardwalk trails are located on the site of Florida's first state park, created in 1916. The popular **Anhinga Trail**, passing over Taylor Slough, contains slightly deeper water than the surrounding terrain; in the dry winter months it attracts wildlife to drink. Its open site means

there are better photo opportunities and fewer insects, but the intense sun can be hazardous. Alligators congregate at the 'gator hole (see p292) at the beginning of the trail, and a wide range of fauna, including deer, raccoons, and the splendid anhinga bird, can be spotted.

The shady **Gumbo Limbo Trail**, on the other hand, is mosquito paradise in summer. However, it is an easy walk, and, if your visit is confined to the park's eastern half, it offers the best chance to explore a tropical hardwood hammock. Watch for bromeliads, members of the pineapple family and a type of epiphyte. This nonparasitic plant grows on other plants but gets its nourishment from the air and rainwater. There are also many types of orchids and the trail's namesake, the gumbo-limbo tree (see p293).

Bromeliads on a mahogany tree

Long Pine Key

This area takes its name from a large stand of slash pines that are unique to southern Florida. Insect- and rot-proof, they have long been a popular building material. Pinelands need fire for survival; without it, they progress to hardwoods. As roads and canals act as fire breaks, park rangers set controlled fires to encourage the pinelands' regeneration and that of associated species like the saw palmetto.

The campsite here occupies a stunning position and is one of the main reasons for people to stop at Long Pine Key. Several shady trails lead off from it, and there's a half-mile (1-km) loop of the Pineland Trail, located 2 miles (3 km) to the west. Don't stray from the path: the limestone bedrock contains "solution holes" created by rain eroding away the rock. These can be quite deep and difficult to spot.

Trails Around Flamingo

As a general rule, canoe trails through open water are a good way to escape the summer's insects, while the hiking trails are undoubtedly most agreeable during the winter months.

Key

–– Hiking trail

— Canoe trail

━ Paved road

═ Unpaved road

From Pa-hay-okee to Flamingo

The open expanse of sawgrass prairie that can be viewed from the elevated **Pa-hay-okee Overlook** is the epitome of the Everglades. The observation tower here is a perfect spot to watch the fluid light changes dancing across this sea of grass, especially in the late afternoon. Tree islands or hammocks break the horizon, and you will see a multitude of wading birds, hawks, and snail kites, whose only food, the apple snail, lives on the sawgrass. This prairie is also home to cattails and other wetland plants.

The **Mahogany Hammock Trail** *(see p291)*, by contrast, leads through one of the park's largest hammocks. This area is home to a wide variety of fauna and flora; the bromeliads here are very impressive, and the junglelike vegetation is especially dense during the wet summer months.

The various trails and ponds between Mahogany Hammock and Flamingo tend to attract fewer people but are no less rewarding, especially for the bird life. Try exploring West Lake Trail or Snake Bight Trail, which ends on Florida Bay.

The settlement of **Flamingo** lies 38 miles (60 km) from the main park entrance. In the late 1800s, it was a remote outpost and hideaway for hunters and fishermen; today, a few park rangers are the only long-term residents. Its position on

The sawgrass prairie stretching away from the Pa-hay-okee Overlook

Florida Bay gives visitors a wide choice of activities such as hiking, fishing, boating, and watching wildlife. An over-night stay at the campsite is recommended especially for bird-watching, which is most rewarding in the early morning and late afternoon.

Apart from countless species of birds and animals, the bay and creeks around Flamingo contain manatees *(see p254)* and the endangered American crocodile. This is easily distinguished from the alligator by its gray-green color and the fact that the teeth of both jaws show when its mouth is shut. You may spot one in this area.

Flamingo's visitor center has wildlife guides and information about local ranger-led activities. These include evening slideshows and talks, and day-time "slough-slogs" – intrepid walks through the swamp.

6 Biscayne National Park

Road map: F5. Dade Co. 9700 SW 328th St, Convoy Point. 🚉 Miami. 🚌 Homestead. **Tel** (305) 230-7275. **Open** daily. **Closed** Dec 25. Visitor Center: **Open** 9am–5pm. Boat tours: **Tel** (305) 230-1100. 🚻 limited. ⚠ 🅦 nps.gov/bisc

Dense mangrove swamp protects the shoreline of Biscayne National Park, which incorporates the northernmost islands of the Florida Keys. Its shallow waters hold the park's greatest draw – a living coral reef with myriad forms and around 200 types of tropical fish. The barrier islands are untouched, so the coral here is healthier and the water even clearer than in the more pop-ular underwater parks farther south around Key Largo.

You can take glass-bottomed boat tours, and there are also diving and snorkeling trips; these all leave from the visitor center, and it is advisable to reserve in advance.

The Everglades Under Threat

Everglades National Park enjoys good protection within its boundaries, but threats from outside are more difficult to control. Since it was created in 1947, the park's greatest problems have been water related. The Everglades ecosystem and Florida's human population are in direct competition for this priceless commodity: irrigation canals and roads disrupt the natural through-flow of water from Lake Okeechobee *(see p132)*, and the drainage of land for development has also had detrimental effects on wildlife. Agriculture in central Florida uses vast amounts of water, and high levels of chemical fertilizers promote the unnatural growth of swamp vegetation. The state and federal governments are studying how best to protect the area and return water flow to its natural state.

Agriculture near the Everglades uses great quantities of water

Elkhorn coral and tropical fish in Biscayne National Park

❼ Key Largo

Road map: F5. Monroe Co. 🚗 16,000.
🚌 ℹ️ MM 106, (305) 451-1414, (800)
822-1088. African Queen: **Tel** (305)
451-4655. 🌐 **keylargochamber.org**

The first of the inhabited Keys,
this is the largest island in the
chain and was named "long
island" by Spanish explorers.
Its proximity to Miami
makes it also the
liveliest, especially
on weekends when
it is crowded.

The island's great-
est draws are the
diving and
snorkeling
opportunities along the
coral reef found just
offshore, in the John
Pennekamp Coral
Reef State Park and
the National Marine Sanctuary.

Another Key Largo attraction
is the *African Queen*, the boat
used in the 1951 film of the same
name. This makes short pleasure
trips (between extensive

periods of restoration). It is
moored at MM 100, which is
also the base for a casino ship
offering a different kind of
trip – one that provides a rare
chance to gamble *(see p360)*.

Local legend tells of a
mysterious and secretive former
government official who lives
in the hammocks and returns
to civilization only when
an ecological need
arises. His various
exploits over the
years have resulted
in land, once slated
for development,
being returned
to pristine wilderness.
Much of Florida's
wetlands, hammocks,
and beaches
have gone under
the bulldozer for
apartments, resorts, and
shopping malls, but with
the help of concerned
citizens, there is hope for
keeping Florida's delicate
ecosystem intact.

**Gold ornament from
a treasure ship**

❽ John Pennekamp Coral Reef State Park

Road map: F5. Monroe Co. MM 102.5.
🚌 Key Largo. **Tel** (305) 451-1202.
Open daily. 🅿️ ♿ limited.
🌐 **floridastateparks.org**

Just under five percent of this
park is on dry land, and its
facilities include a visitor's center,
a small museum on the ecology
of the reef, swimming areas, and
woodland trails. The park is best
known for its fabulous
underwater reaches, which
extend 3 miles (5 km) east from
Key Largo and provide an
unforgettable glimpse of the
vivid colors and extraordinary
forms of coral reef life.

There are canoes, dinghies, or
motorboats for rent, as well as
snorkeling and scuba gear.
Snorkeling and diving trips can
easily be arranged, and there's a
diving school that offers certified
courses. Those who are less
inclined to get wet can take a

Florida's Coral Reef

North America's only live coral reef system extends
200 miles (320 km) along the length of the Keys, from
Miami to the Dry Tortugas. A complex and extremely
delicate ecosystem, it protects these low-lying islands
from storms and heavy wave action emanating from the
Atlantic Ocean. Coral reefs are created over thousands
of years by billions of tiny marine organisms known as
polyps. Lying 10–60 ft (3–18 m) under the surface, the
reef is an intricate web of countless cracks and cavities
and is home to a multitude of plants and diverse sea
creatures, including more than
500 species of fish.

The scaleless green moray, fearsome in looks but
generally harmless to humans

Sea fans, "soft" corals
that have no skeleton

A large-eyed squirrelfish, best suited to
a nocturnal existence

Key to Corals

① Smooth starlet coral
② Sea fan
③ Flower coral
④ Elliptical star coral
⑤ Sea rod
⑥ Pillar coral

⑦ Orange tube coral
⑧ Elkhorn coral
⑨ Brain coral
⑩ Staghorn coral
⑪ Large flower coral
⑫ Sea plume

Diver and spiny lobster, John Pennekamp Coral Reef State Park

glass-bottomed boat trip. Most tours go to destinations that are actually located in the neighboring section of the Florida Keys National Marine Sanctuary, known as the Key Largo National Marine Sanctuary, which extends 3 miles (5 km) farther out to sea.

Some parts of the reef here are favored by snorkelers, such as the shallow waters of White Bank Dry Rocks, with its impressive array of corals and colorful tropical fish. Nearby Molasses Reef offers areas for both snorkelers and divers, who may encounter a myriad fish such as snapper and angelfish. Farther north, French Reef has various swim-through caves where divers can find darting shoals of glassy sweepers. At Key Largo Dry Rocks, the *Christ of the Deep* statue lies submerged at 20 ft (6 m) and is a popular underwater photo stop.

❾ Tavernier

Road map: F5. Monroe Co. 🚗 2,500.
ℹ MM 106 (305) 451-1414.

Henry Flagler's railroad *(see pp52–3)* reached this part of the Keys around 1910. Today, a number of buildings, constructed in the 1920s and '30s as the settlement grew, are located around MM 92; of these only the Tavernier Hotel is open to the public.

Tavernier's most notable attraction is the **Florida Keys Wild Bird Rehabilitation Center**. Here, sanctuary is offered to injured birds, most of whom have been harmed by humans, involving cars or fishing tackle. They recuperate in spacious cages set in tranquil surroundings, contrasting with the bustle of the rest of the island.

🦅 Florida Keys Wild Bird Rehabilitation Center

MM 93.6, Overseas Highway
Tel (305) 852-4486. **Open** daily.
♿ Ⓦ fkwbc.org

A hard coral polyp secretes a limescale skeleton to protect its fleshy body. Coral heads and branches are eventually formed by the growth cycles of countless polyps. Microscopic plants, which live in the polyps' tissues, determine the coral's color.

Mouth · Fleshy tentacles · Stony base · Stomach

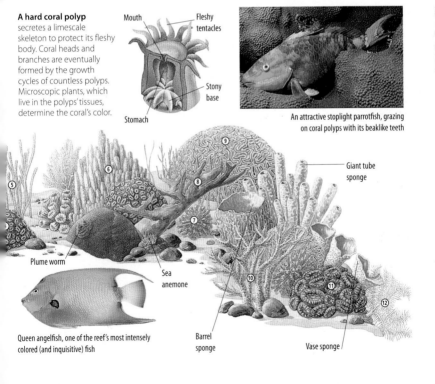

An attractive stoplight parrotfish, grazing on coral polyps with its beaklike teeth

Giant tube sponge

Plume worm

Sea anemone

Queen angelfish, one of the reef's most intensely colored (and inquisitive) fish

Barrel sponge

Vase sponge

⑩ Theater of the Sea

Road map: F5. Monroe Co. MM 84.5.
Tel (305) 664-2431. **Open** daily. ♿
♿ Ⓦ theaterofthesea.com

Windley Key is home to the Theater of the Sea, which opened in 1946 and is Florida's second oldest marine park. Situated in a former quarry created during the construction of Flagler's railroad (see pp52–3), the attraction is famous for its traditional sea lion and dolphin shows. It is also possible to take boat trips to investigate wildlife in the local lagoons, and to enroll in sessions such as the "Trainer for a Day" program.

The Dolphin Adventure package includes a swim with the dolphins and two hours of continuous shows, and should be reserved well in advance.

Triumphant fishermen in Whale Harbor Marina, Islamorada

⑪ Islamorada

Road map: F5. Monroe Co. 🚗 8,500.
🚌 ℹ️ MM 82.5, (305) 644-4503.
Ⓦ islamoradachamber.com

Proudly declaring itself "The Sport fishing Capwital of the World," Islamorada, pronounced "Eye-luh-mo-rada," encompasses seven islands and is best known for its outstanding big game fishing.

Whale Harbor Marina in the town of Islamorada, on Upper Matecumbe Key, bristles with impressive deep-sea charter craft used to catch blue-water fish. Fishing party boats based here take people of all levels of experience, so even if you are not a dedicated angler, these trips can be a great way to spend half a day out at sea. Back

in town at MM 82, the Art Deco Hurricane Monument marks the grave of 500 people killed by a tidal surge in the hurricane of 1935 (see p30).

⑫ Indian and Lignumvitae Keys

Road map: F5. Monroe Co.
🚤 Islamorada. 🚤 Lower Matecumbe Key. ℹ️ Islamorada, (305) 664-4503.

These uninhabited islands, on opposite sides of the Ocean Highway, are accessible only by boat.

Tiny Indian Key has a surprising amount of history for its size. An early Indian site, it was settled in 1831 by Captain J. Houseman, an opportunistic wrecker (see p307). A small community flourished under his autocratic rule, but in 1840 Seminole Indians attacked, killing these settlers. The key was abandoned and today only the outlines of the village and its cisterns remain, amid vegetation impressive for both its variety and rampant growth. An observation tower provides splendid views of the island.

Larger Lignumvitae Key, which can be explored only on a guided tour, is of even greater botanical interest. It boasts 133 native tree species, including its namesake, a blue-flowering tree that can live for 1,000 years. Scientists believe that other vegetation here is as much as 10,000 years old. Notable wildlife includes some colorful tree snails (see p293) and impressively large spiders. Be prepared for mosquitoes.

Dolphins playing in protected waters, Dolphin Research Center

⑬ Dolphin Research Center

Road map: E5. Monroe Co. MM 59.
Tel (305) 289-1121. **Open** daily.
Closed public hols. ♿ ♿
Ⓦ dolphins.org

A nonprofit-making concern, the Dolphin Research Center on Grassy Key is a serious establishment whose main function is to research dolphin behavior. The Center also acts as a rest home for sick and injured dolphins, or those just worn out from the stresses of a busy life as a theme park attraction.

There are exhibits, regularly scheduled lagoon-side walking tours, and special programs like the college-credit Dolphin Lab and the "Dolphin Encounter," which allows you to swim with these amazing marine mammals. All events are very popular; reservations must be made only from the first day of the month preceding your intended visit.

The observation tower and original ruined water cisterns on Indian Key

Fishing in the Florida Keys

There are three main fishing zones in South Florida, each offering its own type of experience and rewards. Near the warm Gulf Stream, offshore gamefish such as marlin abound in conditions excellent for deep-sea (or blue-water) angling. The Atlantic coastal waters up to and including the coral reef itself contain tropical species like snapper and grouper. And to the north of the Keys, the shallow backcountry flats of the Gulf are home to game fish such as tarpon. Islamorada, Marathon, and Key West are the area's major fishing centers, and small marinas throughout the region have boats for rent. There are enough options to suit most tastes, budgets, and abilities, but you might have a greater chance of success if you book a place on a fishing party boat or hire an experienced guide. Weather conditions and seasonal variations determine the available species, but you can fish the waters of the Florida Keys all year round.

Deep-Sea Versus Backcountry

Deep-sea fishing, one of the most exhilarating options available, appeals to the Hemingway spirit of the trophy angler. Renting your own sports boat, however, is expensive. Skiffs fish the tranquil and scenic backcountry reaches, where cunning and stealth help secure a catch.

Flat-bottomed skiffs are poled through inshore waters; motors can get snarled up in the seagrass.

Fishermen in sports boats fitted with fighting chairs wear harnesses to battle deep-sea fish.

Bait and tackle shops are found along the Overseas Highway and in marinas. They not only rent and sell equipment and licenses (*see p365*) but are often the best places to find out about guides and fishing trips offered locally.

Big game fish are the ultimate trophy. Local restaurants can clean and cook your catch for you, but for a long-lasting memento, let a taxidermist prepare and mount your fish (*see p365*).

Fishing party boats are a popular and economical way to fish around the reef. The per-person price usually includes a fishing license, tackle, and bait, as well as the crew's expertise.

Marathon's Boot Key Harbor, with the 7-Mile Bridge in the distance

⑭ Marathon

Road map: E5. Monroe Co. 🏠 13,000.
✈️ ℹ️ MM 53.5, (305) 743-6555.
🌐 floridakeysmarathon.com

Marathon was originally named Vaca ("cow") Key by the Spanish settlers, probably for the herds of manatees or sea cows (see p254) once found offshore. It was renamed in the early 1900s by the men who had the grueling task of laying the Overseas Railroad (see p285).

Door detail, Crane Point Hammock

The main center of the Middle Keys, this island is rather heavily developed and at first glance appears to be an uninviting strip of shopping plazas and gas stations. Marathon's principal appeal lies in the surrounding fishing grounds; those located under the bridges where the Atlantic Ocean and the Gulf of Mexico meet are considered to be particularly fertile.

Devotees can choose from a broad range of angling techniques (see p299). These include spear-fishing (illegal in the Upper Keys but allowed here) and line-fishing off what may be the longest pier in the world – a 2-mile (3-km) stretch of the old 7-Mile Bridge. There are several pleasing waterfront resorts with small beaches, created artificially from imported sand; turn south off the Overseas Highway for these.

Definitely worth a visit is **Crane Point Hammock**, consisting of 64 acres (26 ha) of tropical hardwood forest and wild mangrove wetlands. There are nature trails and a traditional conch-style house (see p305) built out of tabby – a type of local homemade concrete, made of burned seashells and coral rock. The entrance to the hammock is via the **Crane Point Museum**, opened on Earth Day in 1991. The interesting collection explains the history and geology as well as the ecology of the islands, and is designed to appeal in particular to younger visitors.

🏛 **Crane Point Museum**
MM 50.5. **Tel** (305) 743-9100.
Open daily. **Closed** Dec 25. 🎟 ♿
🌐 cranepoint.net

⑮ Pigeon Key

Road map: E5. Monroe Co. MM 47.5, via the old 7-Mile Bridge. **Tel** (305) 289-0025. **Open** daily. 🎟 ♿
🌐 pigeonkey.net

This tiny Key was once the construction base for Henry Flagler's 7-Mile Bridge, described by some as the eighth wonder of the world when it was eventually completed in 1912. Seven wooden structures, originally used by building and maintenance crews, are today part of a marine research and educational foundation and form one of the last intact railroad villages from the Flagler era.

There's a historical museum in the Bridge Tender's House, but many people visit simply to enjoy the island's tranquil surroundings. The old bridge, running parallel to the "new" 7-Mile Bridge built in 1982, marches across the Key on concrete piles and provides a stunning backdrop to the island. It is also the only way to reach the Key. No cars are allowed on the Key, so go by foot or by bicycle, or take the shuttle bus from the foundation's headquarters at MM 48.

⑯ Lower Keys

Road map: E5. Monroe Co. 🚌 Key West. ℹ️ MM 31, (305) 872-2411.
🌐 lowerkeyschamber.com

Once beyond the 7-Mile Bridge, the Keys appear to change. The land is rugged and less developed than in the Upper

The Negro Quarters, an example of Pigeon Key's original dwellings

Bahia Honda's beautiful beach, one of the few natural sand beaches in the Florida Keys

Keys, and the vegetation more wooded, supporting different flora and fauna. The pace of life slows right down, upholding the local claim that the Lower Keys are more about a state of mind than a geographical location.

Just 37 miles (60 km) from Key West is **Bahia Honda State Park**, a protected area of 524 acres (212 hectares) that boasts the finest beach in all the Keys. Brilliantly white sand is backed by a dense, tropical forest crossed by a number of trails. If you follow these you will find various unusual species of tree, such as silver palm and yellow satinwood, and there are lots of birds. The usual water sports equipment is available to rent, but visitors should remember that the current here can be very strong.

Trips out to the **Looe Key National Marine Sanctuary** are also available from the park. This 5-mile (8-km) section of the reef is a spectacular dive location, with unique coral formations and abundant marine life.

From Bahia Honda, the highway swings north and reaches the next major point of interest, and second largest island in the chain, **Big Pine Key**. This island

Perky's Bat Tower

is the Lower Keys' main residential community and the best place to see the diminutive Key Deer, most often spotted at dusk or in the early morning. Take the turning for Key Deer Boulevard near MM 30 to reach the **Blue Hole**, a flooded quarry set in woodlands. The viewing platform here is ideal for watching the deer and other wildlife that come to drink. Nearby, the one-mile (two-km) looped path of the Jack Watson Nature Trail has markers to help in identifying the trees and plants.

Continuing on down the Overseas Highway, as you cross Cudjoe Key keep a lookout for **"Fat Albert"**, a large white surveillance blimp. Tethered at a height of 1,400 ft (427 m), Fat Albert's job is to monitor anything from drug smugglers to political activities in Cuba.

Neighboring Sugarloaf Key, once the location of a sponge-farming enterprise, is now famous for its **Bat Tower**, reached by turning north off the Overseas Highway just after MM 17. It was built in 1929 by Richter C. Perky, a property speculator, for the purpose of attracting the bats that he believed would rid the island of its ferocious mosquitos, allowing him to develop it as a resort. Unfortunately, not a single bat came and the tower remains as a testament to his plan's resounding failure.

🏖 **Bahia Honda State Park**
MM 37. **Tel** (305) 872-2353.
Open daily. 🅿 ♿ limited.
🌐 **floridastateparks.org**

Key Deer

Related to the white-tailed deer, Florida's endangered Key Deer are found only on Big Pine Key and the surrounding islands. They swim between these keys, but are more often sighted as they roam around the slash pine woodlands. Despite the enforcement of strict speed restrictions, and the establishment of a refuge on Big Pine Key, around 50 deer are killed in road accidents each year. The number of deer has stabilized at around 300. It is strictly forbidden to feed them.

A fully grown Key Deer, no bigger than a large dog

⓱ Street-by-Street: Key West

The southernmost settlement in the continental US, Key West is a city like no other and a magnet for people who want to leave the rest of Florida, and even America, behind. This is a place to join in with locals busy dropping out and to indulge in the laid-back, tropical lifestyle.

First recorded in 1513, the island soon became a haven first for pirates and then for "wreckers" *(see p307)*, both of whom preyed on passing merchant ships and their precious cargos. Key West grew to be the most prosperous city in Florida, and the opportunistic lifestyle on offer lured a steady stream of settlers from the Americas, the Caribbean, and Europe; you'll find their legacy in the island's unique architecture, cuisine, and spirit. A large gay community, writers, and new-agers are among the more recent arrivals who have added to Key West's cultural cocktail.

The Curry Mansion
This opulent 19th-century home's interior reflects the wealth of Key West's wreck captains *(see p306)*.

Sloppy Joe's was Ernest Hemingway's favorite haunt. The bar moved here from its former site on Greene Street in 1935.

Pier House Resort
Just off Mallory Square, this resort has a popular terrace where people gather to watch the famous Key West sunsets.

Mallory Square

★ Mel Fisher Maritime Museum
All kinds of shipwreck treasures, and the gear used to find them, are displayed in this excellent museum *(see p306)*.

Audubon House, built in the 1840s, contains period pieces and ornithological prints by John James Audubon *(see p50)*.

The Wreckers' Museum *(see p306)*

Key

— Suggested route

0 metres 100
0 yards 100

Duval Street
Key West's main thoroughfare, Duval Street is lined with souvenir shops and is often busy with tourists. Several of the Old Town's sights are located here.

Fleming Street
Typical of the quiet, shady residential roads of the Old Town, Fleming Street boasts many beautiful wooden houses. These are fine examples of traditional Key West architecture *(see p305)*.

St. Paul's Episcopal Church
This 1912 church is dedicated to the patron saint of shipwrecked sailors. Some of its 49 stained-glass windows feature nautical imagery.

VISITORS' CHECKLIST

Practical Information
Road map: E5. Monroe Co. 🚉 28,000. 🛈 402 Wall Street, (305) 294-2587. 🖳 **keywestchamber. org** Audubon House: **Tel** (305) 294-2116. **Open** daily. 🎏 Conch Republic Independence Celebration (Apr), Hemingway Days Festival (Jul), Fantasy Fest (mid-Oct).

Transportation
✈ 2 miles (3 km) E of Duval St. 🚌 Simonton and Virginia sts, (305) 296-9072. 🚢 Mallory Sq, (305) 292-8158.

Margaritaville
Jimmy Buffet, the Floridian singer, owns this café and adjoining shop, where T-shirts and memorabilia are on sale *(see p349)*.

The San Carlos Institute
was founded by Cubans in 1871. Today it occupies a beautiful Baroque-style building, which dates from 1924 and functions as a Cuban heritage center.

EATON STREET

WHITEHEAD STREET

FLEMING STREET

SOUTHARD STREET

THOMAS STREET

Bahama Village

★ Bahama Village
As yet relatively undeveloped, this old Key West neighborhood is filled with brightly painted clapboard buildings.

Exploring Key West

Most of the sights are either on or within two or three blocks of Duval Street, which links the Gulf of Mexico with the Atlantic and is the main axis of Old Key West. Focused between Whitehead and White streets, this district boasts the largest concentration of 19th-century wooden buildings in Florida. Simple shotgun houses, which were erected to house Cuban cigar-workers, contrast with the whimsically Romantic style of the homes of wealthier citizens. To get your bearings, take the Conch Train or Old Town Trolley tour, rent a bicycle, or just wander around the back streets. In the south of the island, you'll find lovely sandy beaches.

Shady palms lining a subtropical beach in southern Key West

A Tour of Key West

On the northern edge of the old town, **Mallory Square** is the famous place to watch the sunset, when performance artists vie with each other to amuse the crowds. During the day, to get the feel of the city, head down Duval Street and take side streets at random. These pretty streets are lined with Key West's distinctive gingerbread houses, set among shady tropical trees and drooping bougainvillea.

Even more rewarding, and named after Key West's earliest settlers, is **Bahama Village**. This historic neighborhood on the western fringe of the old town is bordered by Fort, Virginia, Petronia, and Whitehead streets. Life here is lived outside, with animated domino games on street corners and chickens wandering freely – a taste of the Caribbean in North America. The typical shotgun houses have largely escaped the enthusiastic renovations found elsewhere.

🏛 Fort East Martello Museum and Gallery

3501 S Roosevelt Blvd. **Tel** (305) 296-3913. **Open** daily. **Closed** Dec 25. 🅿 ♿ limited. 🆆 **kwahs.com**

Located in the east of the island, the East Martello tower was begun in 1861 to protect Fort Zachary's defensive position (*see p306*). It was never completed, as its design quickly became outmoded.

Today, the squat tower is an informative museum that gives the visitor an excellent introduction to Key West and its checkered past. Everything is included here, from stories about Key West's many literary connections to the island's changing commercial history. You can also see one of the unbelievably flimsy rafts used by Cubans to flee Castro's regime (*see pp56–7*).

The tower itself offers fine views and houses works of art by a number of local artists.

🏠 Hemingway Home

907 Whitehead St. **Tel** (305) 294-1136. **Open** daily. 🅿 ♿ limited. 🆆 **hemingwayhome.com**

Probably the town's major (and most hyped) attraction, this Spanish colonial-style house built of coral rock is where Ernest Hemingway lived from 1931 to 1940. Above the carriage house is the room where the novelist penned several works; *To Have and Have Not* was the only book set in Key West. His library and mementos from his travels are displayed, as are memorabilia such as the cigar-maker's chair upon which he sat and wrote. Guides describe the hard-living writer's nonliterary passions of fishing and hell-raising in Sloppy Joe's (*see p302*).

Descendants of his six-toed cats still prowl around the house and its luxuriant garden.

🏛 Lighthouse Museum

938 Whitehead St. **Tel** (305) 294-0012. **Open** daily. **Closed** Dec 25. 🅿 🆆 **kwahs.com**

Across the road from Hemingway House stands the town's lighthouse, built in 1848. The clapboard keeper's cottage at its foot houses a modest museum containing lighthouse and other historical artifacts.

Original Lighthouse flag

The greatest attraction is the tower itself. Make the 88-step climb for panoramic views and the chance to step inside and look through the old lens, once capable of beaming light some 25 miles (40 km) out to sea.

Boza's Comparsa (1975), Duval Street by M Sanchez, East Martello Museum

Key West Style

The architecture of Key West is striking above all for its simplicity, a response to the hot climate and the limited materials available – principally wood, which was either salvaged or imported. Early "conch" houses, built at the beginning of the 19th century, were often built by ships' carpenters who introduced elements they had seen on their travels. From the Bahamas came various devices to increase shade and ventilation against the Florida sun. Later, Classical Revivalism filtered in from the north, while the Victorian style of the late 1800s introduced a highly decorative influence. Key West's prosperous inhabitants favored often extravagant gingerbread details, but carvings also adorn humbler dwellings. Since the 1970s, when the town's architectural legacy was first properly acknowledged, many houses have been renovated, especially inside. But their essential flavor remains.

Shutters keep out the sun and give protection during storms; originally some windows had no glass.

Large sash windows admit cooling breezes.

Wide verandas provide much needed shade.

Gingerbread-style fretwork often decorates balustrades; rarely do you find two houses with identical styles of carving.

Three Bay House

The most common type of Key West house, the three bay, is only a little more refined than the "shotgun" style, named for the fact that a bullet fired through the front door would exit cleanly out the back. Orienting the gable toward the street maximized the number of houses that could be fitted on one block.

A foundation of sunken pillars supports the house, leaving room for cooling air to circulate under the floor.

Doorways often display the most obvious Classical Revival influences.

The "eyebrow" virtually obscures the upper windows from view.

Roof hatches, inspired by a similar device found on ships, bring extra ventilation to the building's top floor.

Colored paintwork is popular today, although the more traditional whitewash remains the most common.

Five Bay "Eyebrow" House

Classic Key West symmetry is much in evidence in this five-bay house. Unique to the island is the "eyebrow" feature or roof overhang, which shades the top-floor rooms from the heat of the sun.

The impressive brick vaulting of Fort Zachary Taylor

🏛 Fort Zazchary Taylor Historic State Site

End of Southard St. **Tel** (305) 292-6713.
Open daily. 🅿 🏛 🅰 limited.
🔲 **floridastateparks.org**

Part of the national coastal defense system begun in the mid-19th century, this brick fort was completed in 1866. During the Civil War, Union troops were stationed here to keep the island loyal to the north. Originally, the fort was three stories high and had toilets that were flushed by the tides. It was remodeled in the 1890s.

Today, it houses a museum which contains a fine collection of Civil War artifacts. Visitors can also explore the grounds and enjoy the view from an observation deck. Nearby is Key West's best public beach, which has shady picnic areas.

🏛 The Mel Fisher Maritime Museum

200 Greene St. **Tel** (305) 294-2633.
Open 9:30am–5pm daily. 🅿 🅰
🔲 **melfisher.com**

A plain stone exterior belies the opulence of some of the treasures this museum holds. The late Mr. Fisher grabbed the headlines in 1985 when he discovered the wrecks of the Spanish galleons *Nuestra Señora de Atocha (see p32)* and *Santa Margarita*, about 40 miles (64 km) west of Key West; inside were 47 tons of gold and silver bars and 70 lbs (32 kg) of raw emeralds that sank with them in 1622.

Items on display include jewelry, coins, and crucifixes. The story of the salvage operation is also told, but check the awesome website.

🏛 The Wreckers' Museum

322 Duval St. **Tel** (305) 294-9502.
Open daily. 🅿 🅰 limited.
🔲 **oirf.org**

Originally the home of wreck captain, Francis B. Watlington, this is thought to be the oldest house in Key West. Built in 1829, its design reveals some rather idiosyncratic maritime influences, such as the hatch used for ventilation in the roof. The house is stuffed full of nautical bric-a-brac, ships' models and paintings, and an array of documents concerning wrecking – the industry that first made Key West (and Captain Watlington) rich. Visitors are greeted by volunteer staff, whose anecdotes make the history of the house come alive.

Don't miss the separate kitchen house in the backyard, the oldest of the few examples that still remain in the Keys. Located away from the main building, it minimized the risk of fire and in addition helped to keep the temperature down in the rest of the house.

The ship-style hatch in the attic of the Wreckers' Museum

🏛 The Curry Mansion

511 Caroline St. **Tel** (305) 294-5349.
Open daily. 🅿 🅰
🔲 **currymansion.com**

This grand and embellished mansion was begun in 1855 by William Curry, a Bahamian wreck captain who became Key West's first millionaire. His son Milton completed the work 44 years later.

In addition to its sweeping verandas, the house boasts many original features, including wood-paneled rooms and electrical fittings. The rooms are furnished with Victorian and later objects, from Tiffany-stained glass to a rifle once owned by Ernest Hemingway – all collected by the present owner. It is said that key lime pie *(see p328)* was first made here by Aunt Sally, the cook, using canned condensed milk (first available in 1895). The Curry Mansion is also a guest house *(see p324)*.

The charming Robert Frost Cottage in the garden of Heritage House

🏛 Heritage House Museum and Robert Frost Cottage

410 Caroline St. **Tel** (305) 296-3573.
Open Mon–Sat. **Closed** Thanksgiving, Dec 25, Jan 1. 🅿 🅰

Built in 1834 and originally the home of a British captain, this house is one of Key West's oldest buildings. It is in near-original condition and contains period furnishings and travel curios that belonged to the Porters, a wealthy Key West family. The garden contains an outdoor kitchen house and, beneath a fine banyan tree, the Robert Frost cottage; this is named after the American poet who stayed here during his many visits to Key West between 1945 and 1960.

🪦 Key West Cemetery

701 Passover Lane. **Tel** (305) 292-8177.
Open daily. ℹ️ Tue & Thu only. ♿

Due to the proximity of the limestone bedrock and water table, most of the tombs here are above ground. Laid out on a grid system, the cemetery holds the remains of many of Key West's earliest residents. Within the compound there are separate areas for Jews and Roman Catholics, while many of the Cuban crypts are crowned with a statue of a chicken, probably associated with the Santería religion *(see p81)*. There is even a special burial area devoted to pets.

A statue of a single sailor commemorates the loss of 252 crewmen on the battleship USS *Maine*, which was sunk in Havana's harbor at the onset of the Spanish-American War in 1898 *(see p53)*. Stroll around to read the often amusing inscriptions and epitaphs, "I told you I was sick" among others. Many of the town's early settlers were known simply by their first or nicknames, and this Key West informality followed them to their graves. There are references to Bunny, Shorty, Bean, and so forth. Dismissive of this tradition, Ernest Hemingway is reported to have said "I'd rather eat monkey manure than die in Key West."

Statue of the Lone Sailor

The Business of Wrecking

In the late 1700s, the waters off the Keys were fished mainly by Bahamians of British descent, who patrolled the reef in order to salvage shipwrecks. Lookouts, or "Wreckers," at their vantage points would shout "Wreck ashore!" to send salvage vessels racing toward the reef to be the first to claim a grounded ship. In this way, goods from around the world ended up in the Keys; these ranged from basics such as timber to luxury goods like lace, wine, and silver. This opportunistic scavenging came to be known as "wrecking." It grew so popular that in 1825 an act of the US Congress legislated for much tighter control and decreed that only US residents could have such salvage rights. Key West boomed, and in the years that followed, it became the richest city in Florida.

Facsimile of a wrecker's license

⓲ Dry Tortugas National Park

Road map: D5. Monroe Co. 🚌 Key West. ℹ️ 1601 N Roosevelt Blvd, (305) 292-5000. 🌐 **keywestinfo.com**

The Dry Tortugas consist of seven reef islands lying 68 miles (109 km) west of Key West. Of these, Garden Key is the most visited, being the site of **Fort Jefferson**, the largest brick fortification in the US. The hexagonal design included a moat 70 ft (21 m) wide, and walls up to 8 ft (2.5 m) thick and 50 ft (15 m) high.

It was originally envisaged that the fort would control the Florida Straits with a garrison of 1,500 men and 450 cannons. Beginning in 1845, construction continued for the next 30 years, but the fort was never completed or involved in any battle. During the Civil War, after being occupied by Union forces, it was downgraded to a prison for captured deserters.

The only access is by boat or seaplane. Most people come on organized trips from Key West, which often include an opportunity to snorkel in the crystal-clear water. The bird-watching is especially good between March and October, when the islands are home to migrant and nesting birds, such as boobies, sooty terns, and magnificent frigatebirds with their 7-ft (2-m) wingspan.

Remote Garden Key in Dry Tortugas National Park, occupied by the imposing 19th-century Fort Jefferson

TRAVELERS' NEEDS

WHERE TO STAY

Florida has a huge variety accommodations suitable for all budgets and tastes – from rustic cabins with minimal facilities to luxurious resorts that can cater to every need and whim. In between, guests can choose from hotels, charming bed and breakfasts, intimate inns, motels, fully equipped apartments, cabins, and campsites where campers can pitch a tent or hook up an RV or mobile home. Prices tend to fluctuate greatly according to the season, location, and even the day of the week. Local tourist offices can help provide more detailed information about options in their particular areas.

Lobby of the Eden Roc Renaissance Resort and Spa in Miami (see p314)

Hotels and Resorts

Hotels range from historic Spanish and stylish Art Deco to the ultra modern. Chain hotels are popular, and have the advantage of being familiar, though prices vary depending upon the location. They range from the upscale Ritz-Carlton and W Hotels through the mid-range Marriott and Hilton.

Several hotels are large complexes often set in immaculately kept grounds; the best ones come with their own private beach. Prices at these are high, but larger properties provide all types of amenities, from swimming pools – sometimes Olympic-sized – to shops and usually a choice of restaurants. Many resorts have excellent sports facilities, including golf courses and tennis courts, and may also provide instructors for individual lessons. Spas and health clubs are increasingly popular, some with services designed to pamper and some offering daily fitness classes. With their well-equipped games rooms, special children's programs, and other facilities, these resorts can be good options for families.

Bed and Breakfasts

Anyone in search of a more traditional sense of hospitality might choose to stay in a bed and breakfast (B&B). These are often private homes where the owner is the host. Breakfast is usually excellent, with home-made breads and coffee, and guests often eat together in an informal atmosphere.

Any place called an inn tends to be slightly larger and pricier than a B&B and may even have a restaurant. However, it is likely to be friendlier and more intimate than a standard hotel.

The drawbacks with B&Bs are that they may have restrictions with regards to children, or may not have provide extra room or beds for them. They may also require a minimum stay during the tourist season. Moreover, since most have just a few rooms, an advance booking is essential.

Several agencies specialize in arranging B&B accommodation. These include **Florida B&B Inns**, which specializes in historic establishments across the state, and the **Key West Innkeepers Association**. Regional publications and local tourism guides offered by the **AAA** are useful sources as well.

How to Reserve

While it is relatively easy to book a room at short notice in a hotel of your choice off season, securing a room in season, particularly in Orlando or Miami, may require making a reservation several months in advance. However, given the many options at one's disposal, it is possible to find a room any time of the year, as long as your choice is not limited to the high-end resorts and luxury hotels only.

Bookings can be made online or by phone with a credit card; note that a deposit is usually required. To avoid losing a reservation, give advance notice if arriving after 5pm.

Dhady gardens and pool typify many plush Florida resorts

◄ Golfers take on one of the many challenging courses in the region

Facilities

Competition in Florida's hotel trade is fierce so facilities are generally good. Rooms without a TV, private bath, and air conditioning are extremely rare, even in B&Bs. Most have a refrigerator and desk; some hotels also provide microwaves or kitchenettes. Bedrooms usually have two queen-sized beds and can accommodate up to four people.

People with disabilities will be best provided for in a modern, conventional hotel or resort. In addition to elevators and ramps, a few hotels have rooms especially designed for people in wheelchairs. In case of any special needs, inform the hotel when reserving a room.

Prices

Room rates vary enormously depending on the time of year, with prices in tourist season often 30–50 percent more than in off season. In south Florida, the high season runs from mid-November to Easter, while in the Panhandle and the Northeast, where it is cooler in winter, hotels charge their highest rates in spring and summer. Wherever you are, however, expect to pay peak rates at Christmas, Easter, February school holiday periods, and Thanksgiving. At any time of the year, a room facing the water may cost 25 percent more, so it's worth asking for the full range of prices.

Winter rates are considerably lower in January after the holidays. Another way to save would be to stay mid-week rather than weekends; even Sunday nights are often less expensive, since many weekenders tend to check out on Sunday.

It is difficult to find even a motel room these days for less than $150 in popular beach locations during the season. Rates are usually calculated per room rather than per person. This means that only a small reduction is made on the cost of a double room when calculating the price of a single guest.

Many hotels offer special deals on their own websites, such as discounts for stays over three or four nights and package deals including breakfast. A number of hotels also offer discounts for senior citizens and families.

Hidden Extras

Room rates are generally quoted exclusive of both sales tax *(see p350)* and the so-called resort tax, which is 2–5 percent of the price of the room (depending on the area). So taxes can add as much as 15 percent to the rate quoted.

The cost of making phone calls from a hotel room is usually exorbitant. A few places offer free local calls from rooms, but as a general rule using your own cell phone is far cheaper. Do consider using free Wi-Fi instead. There are often charges for receiving faxes as well.

Many hotels charge for valet parking: a fee of anything from $10 to $30 a day, not counting the optional tip for the attendant.

The fashionable Delano Hotel in South Beach, Miami *(see p315)*

One of the most outrageous practices is a resort fee, a charge that covers amenities such as beach chairs and towels, as well as Wi-Fi access. This is an automatic charge, not an option, and can add $20 a day to the bill in some resorts. Be sure to ask before booking.

Given the hugely inflated price of most hotel breakfasts, guests would do well to go out to a nearby café or diner instead. Be warned too that there are charges for watching certain in-room movies: read the screen before pressing the remote control button.

Motels

Motels lack charm but are a good budget or last-minute option, particularly during the tourist season. City or town outskirts are classic motel territory. Parking is free and located conveniently near the rooms.

Offerings range from the more upscale Hampton Inns to the budget Days Inn chain. Larger chains may offer free breakfast and amenities including pools, rooms with a microwave and refrigerator. Feel free to inspect rooms before checking in.

Local tourist offices have lists of available motels, and the AAA regional guides give ratings in their motel listings.

A sumptuous bedroom at the Casa Monica Hotel, St Augustine *(see p319)*

Cabins for rent by the ocean at Bahia Honda in the Keys *(see p297)*

Accommodations in Orlando

For anyone planning to visit the theme parks, proximity is a major consideration: arriving early is the best way to avoid the worst lines. Waiting in traffic for an hour or more just to get to the park only reduces quality time. Furthermore, staying nearby means that the option to return to the hotel for a break during the day, or when the lines are too long, is available.

Universal Orlando® has on-site hotels, and Walt Disney World® Resorts offers a host of on-site and adjacent options. Rooms at these mega-resorts are costlier, but convenient, and may offer great package deals. However, both Universal and Disney have "good neighbor hotels," which are conveniently located, less expensive, and also offer admission packages to guests.

Lodgings are in big demand at these hotels near the parks and must be booked six months to a year in advance, especially if visiting at Easter or Christmas. There are so many hotels in Greater Orlando, though, that you need never worry about finding a room. When choosing where to stay, ask how long it takes to get to the parks, whether shuttle buses are available, and how often they run.

Apartment Rentals

Being a much sought-after big family destination, apartment accommodations are quite popular among those visiting Florida. Condominiums (condos), consisting of complete apartments, are available for rent and are found mainly on beach resorts. They may seem expensive ($1,200 per week is on the low side), but can be good value especially for large families. **Villas of the World** and **Vacation Rentals by Owner (VRBO)** are among the many agencies that arrange condo rentals and may even organize rentals of a private apartment or a house.

Rooms with cooking facilities are known as efficiencies, and are available in some hotels and motels. These may cost more than standard rooms but enable families to avoid expensive restaurant meals. In rural areas efficiency cabins can be found attached to campgrounds.

Visitors can also choose to stay in a private home for free by doing a house swap. To arrange this, enroll as a member of a home-exchange organization; **HomeAway**, for example, has members worldwide.

Camping

Florida has a huge number of campsites. These range from the basic, where there may be no running water, to the luxurious, with swimming pools, shops, restaurants, and boat rentals. RV parks have space for tent campers as well, and some rent out trailers and cabins too.

Florida has dozens of state parks with camping sites. In addition, some 20 parks also offer comfortable cabin accommodations that are among the state's most reasonable lodgings, often costing less than $100 for cabins that can accommodate a family of four. These range from rustic with shared bath lodges to fully equipped modern facilities. The **Florida State Parks** has a complete roster with pictures on its website.

State parks charge $10–25 per site, while charges at a private campground go up to about $40 per night. Most sites take advance bookings, but state parks hold back some spaces for people who arrive on the day.

The **Florida Association of RV Parks and Campgrounds (ARVC)** produces the annual *Florida Camping Directory*, listing its licensed members; copies can be ordered online directly from the ARVC website. Additionally, **Kampgrounds of**

One of the luxurious rooms at the Sandestin Resort, Destin *(see p320)*

America (KOA) runs a number of good quality sites in Florida and issues its own directory.

Youth Hostels

Florida has several youth hostels, some in South Beach and Orlando as well. The Florida chapter of **Hostelling International** can also provide useful information.

Facilities can be excellent, sometimes with swimming pools and game rooms, and rates are very low: around $15–$25 per night. Book ahead in tourist season to avoid disappointment.

The Honeymoon Cottage at The Moorings Village, Islamorada *(see p323)*

Traveling with Children

Most hotels provide basic facilities such as cribs (cots) for families; a babysitting service may be available too. Some places, however, particularly in Orlando and popular beach

A trailer in a tranquil spot in a Panhandle park

locations, put children higher on their list of priorities and provide kids' swimming pools and play areas. Some have children's programs, with organized activities too, though these may cost extra.

Most hotels do not charge for children under 12 sharing the room with their parents; in some cases this could be extended to those under 18. Some rooms have a sofa that folds out into a bed; otherwise an extra bed may be set up for a small additional fee.

Recommended Hotels

The hotels listed in the following pages are a sampling of the many available, chosen for their special value, facilities, and location. From five-star luxury resorts to boutique hotels, humble B&Bs and inns to the standard modern hotels,

they are all characterful and usually in great locations. Entries are listed by region, beginning with Miami.

The large number of motels means only a few could be included; see local tourism guides for a comprehensive list. While many beachfront hotels call themselves resorts, those listed here as resorts have extensive tennis facilities and/or golf in addition to a beach and pool. Spas and exercise facilities are available in even moderately priced hotels these days. Rates are for a standard room for two during high season, and will be less the rest of the year. Taxes will add 13 percent to all rates.

The entries marked as DK Choice are those that are find exceptional within their categories. The majority of these are quite popular, so be sure to reserve well ahead.

DIRECTORY

Bed and Breakfasts

AAA Auto Club South
Ⓦ aaasouth.com

Florida B&B Inns
Tel (561) 223-9550.
Ⓦ florida-inns.com

Key West Innkeepers Association
316A Simonton St,
Key West, FL 33040.
Tel (305) 295-9500.
Ⓦ keywestinns.com

Apartment Rentals

HomeAway
Tel (877) 228-3145.
Ⓦ homeaway.com

Villas of the World
PO Box 1800, Sag Harbor,
NY 11963.
Tel (631) 324-8455.
Ⓦ villasoftheworld.com

VRBO
Ⓦ vrbo.com

Camping

ARVC
1340 Vickers Dr,
Tallahassee, FL 32303.
Tel (800) 395-2267.
Ⓦ arvc.org

Florida State Parks
3900 Commonwealth
Blvd, Tallahassee,
FL 32399.
Tel (850) 245-2118.
Ⓦ myflorida.com

KOA

PO Box 30558, Billings,
MT 59114.
Tel (406) 248-7444.
Ⓦ koa.com/where/fl

Youth Hostels

Hostelling International
8401 Colesville Rd, Suite
600, Silverspring, MD
20910.
Tel (240) 650-2100.
Ⓦ hiusa.org

Where to Stay

Miami

Miami Beach

Aqua $$
Modern **Map** 2 F2
1530 Collins Ave, 33139
Tel *(305) 538-4361*
W aquamiami.com
Well-equipped modern rooms in an Art Deco building. Fabulous terrace and tropical garden.

Clay Hotel $$
Historic **Map** 2 E3
1438 Washington Ave, 33139
Tel *(305) 534-2988*
W clayhotel.com
Built in the 1930s, this atmospheric hotel has bright rooms with modern decor, some with balconies.

Cadet Hotel $$$
Historic **Map** 2 F2
1701 James Ave, 33139
Tel *(305) 672-6688*
W cadethotel.com
Once home to Captain Clark Gable's cadets, this hotel has comfortable rooms, luxurious suites and a spa.

Clinton Hotel $$$
Boutique **Map** 2 E4
825 Washington Ave, 33139
Tel *(305) 538-1471*
W clintonsouthbeach.com
Modernist building with con-temporary interior design. Some suites have balconies with a spa.

Eden Roc Miami Beach $$$
Boutique **Road Map** F5
4525 Collins Ave, 33140
Tel *(305) 531-0000*
W edenrocmiami.com
Elegant Art Deco landmark with spacious rooms, a lavish pool, and beach. Wonderful ocean views.

Relaxing terrace with pool at Clinton Hotel, Miami Beach

Fontainebleau Hotel $$$
Resort **Road Map** F5
4441 Collins Ave, 33140
Tel *(305) 538-2000*
W fontainebleau.com
Fabulously retro, this hotel features Las Vegas-style glitzy decor. Spectacular pool and spa.

Freehand Miami $$$
Hostel **Road Map** F5
2727 Indian Creek Dr, 33140
Tel *(305) 531-2727*
W thefreehand.com
A block away from the beach, this stylish hostel offers double and dorm rooms. Pool and bar on site.

Hotel Astor $$$
Luxury **Map** 2 E3
956 Washington Ave, 33139
Tel *(305) 531-8081*
W hotelastor.com
The sleek Astor has large suites with warm decor and top-end linen. Popular restaurant, too.

Hotel St. Augustine $$$
Boutique **Map** 2 E4
347 Washington Ave, 33139
Tel *(305) 532-0570*
W hotelstaugustine.com
A chic hotel and spa with loft-style rooms and steam baths.

Impala Hotel $$$
Boutique **Map** 2 F3
1228 Collins Ave, 33139
Tel *(305) 673-2021*
W impala-miami.com
Mediterranean-style intimate boutique hotel with Murano glass fixtures and custom furnishings.

Lord Balfour $$$
Luxury **Map** 2 E4
350 Ocean Dr, 33139
Tel *(305) 673-0401*
W lordbalfourmiami.com
Lord Balfour offers accommodation with British-inspired, modern decor and contemporary art.

Nassau Suite Hotel $$$
Historic **Map** 2 F3
1414 Collins Ave, 33139
Tel *(305) 532-0043*
W nassausuite.com
Built in 1937, this landmark hotel provides a full-service experience. Suites are equipped with kitchens.

National Hotel $$$
Historic **Map** 2 F2
1677 Collins Ave, 33139
Tel *(305) 532-2311*
W nationalhotel.com
Quiet Art Deco classic with an authentic 1940s vibe, and a luxurious swimming pool.

Price Guide

Prices are based on one night's stay in high season for a standard double room, inclusive of service charges and taxes.

$	up to $100
$$	$100 to $200
$$$	over $200

Park Central Hotel $$$
Historic **Map** 2 E4
640 Ocean Dr, 33139
Tel *(305) 538-1611*
W theparkcentral.com
Modern amenities matched with 1940s ambience in this Art Deco hotel with a rooftop sun deck.

Pelican Hotel $$$
Boutique **Map** 2 F4
826 Ocean Dr, 33139
Tel *(305) 673-3373*
W pelicanhotel.com
Quirky hotel with themed rooms including a Viva Las Vegas and a Tarzan Jungle Room.

Ritz-Carlton South Beach $$$
Luxury **Map** 2 F2
1 Lincoln Rd, 33139
Tel *(786) 276-4000*
W ritzcarlton.com
Experience utter indulgence at the Ritz-Carlton. Some rooms have sea views, and there are two opulently large swimming pools.

The Albion $$$
Historic **Map** 2 F2
1650 James Ave, 33139
Tel *(305) 913-1000*
W rubellhotels.com
This beautiful 1939 building has been decorated in minimalist tones and trendy furnishings.

DK Choice

The Angler's $$$
Luxury **Map** 2 E4
660 Washington Ave, 33139
Tel *(305) 534-9600*
W theanglersresort.com
Stay in either a spacious suite, studio or villa in one of the four majestic buildings that make up this Mediterranean Revival complex. Relax in the private gardens, Jacuzzis, or rooftop terraces. Indulgent spa treatments are also available.

The Beach Plaza Hotel $$$
Boutique **Map** 2 F3
1401 Collins Ave, 33139
Tel *(305) 531-6421*
W beachplazahotel.com
Art Deco hotel with large, tropically themed rooms, a courtyard bar, and evening wine reception.

The Delano $$$
Luxury Map 2 F2
1685 Collins Ave, 33139
Tel *(305) 672-2000*
W delano-hotel.com
This Phillippe Starck-inspired hotel is famous for its decor and celebrity clientele. Crisp all-white rooms, and a great pool and bar.

The Hotel of South Beach $$$
Luxury Map 2 E4
801 Collins Ave, 33139
Tel *(305) 531-2222*
W thehotelofsouthbeach.com
Decorated by fashion designer Todd Oldham. All accommodation has fantastic balcony views.

The Kent $$$
Modern Map 2 F3
1131 Collins Ave, 33139
Tel *(305) 604-5068*
W thekenthotel.com
With a fabulous Art Deco exterior, this hotel offers comfortable rooms with contemporary decor.

The Mondrian $$$
Boutique Map 2 D3
1100 West Ave, 33139
Tel *(305) 514-1500*
W mondrian-miami.com
Architect Ian Shrager's glamorously designed hotel is the ultimate in comfort and stunning views.

The Palms Hotel & Spa $$$
Luxury Road Map F5
3025 Collins Ave, 33140
Tel *(305) 534-0505*
W thepalmshotel.com
With private gardens leading to the beach, The Palms offers guests a quiet, relaxed ambience.

The Sagamore $$$
Luxury Map 2 F2
1671 Collins Ave, 33139
Tel *(305) 535-8088*
W sagamorehotel.com
Indulgent hotel famed for its stunning art collection. All rooms have a kitchenette and spa bath.

The Sanctuary $$$
Luxury Map 2 F2
1745 James Ave, 33139
Tel *(305) 673-5455*
W sanctuarysobe.com
The Sanctuary's contemporary suites and rooftop pool make for an intimate retreat. Each room has a fully-equipped kitchen.

The Setai $$$
Luxury Map 2 F1
2001 Collins Ave, 33139
Tel *(305) 520-6000*
W thesetaihotel.com
This oceanfront hotel has gorgeous accommodation as well as world-class dining and spa facilities.

The Spanish-style exterior of Biltmore Hotel in Coral Gables

Townhouse Hotel $$$
Modern Map 2 F1
150 20th St, 33139
Tel *(305) 534-3800*
W townhousehotel.com
Chic hotel offering simple rooms with modern decor, a rooftop bar, and sushi restaurant.

Villa Paradiso $$$
Modern Map 2 F3
1415 Collins Ave, 33139
Tel *(305) 532-0616*
W villaparadisohotel
Former apartment building with bright, airy suites and studios, as well as a tranquil garden.

DK Choice

W South Beach $$$
Luxury Map 2 F1
2201 Collins Ave, 33139
Tel *(305) 938-2000*
W wsouthbeach.com
This stunning flagship of W Hotels has spacious rooms with balconies, kitchenettes, and ocean vistas. Guests are spoiled for choice between the private beach, swimming pool, rooftop tennis, basketball courts, and many dining options.

Whitelaw Hotel $$$
Boutique Map 2 E4
808 Collins Ave, 33139
Tel *(305) 398-7000*
W whitelawhotel.com
Whitelaw's snug, quirky rooms have a lively vibe to match its motto of "clean sheets, hot water, stiff drinks".

Downtown and Little Havana

Conrad Hotel $$$
Modern Map 4 E3
1395 Brickell Ave, 33131
Tel *(305) 503-6500*
W conradmiami.com
This 36-story tower building offers fantastic views from most of its comfortably furnished rooms.

Mandarin Oriental $$$
Luxury Map 4 F2
500 Brickell Key Dr, 33131
Tel *(305) 913-8288*
W mandarinoriental.com
Frequented by celebrities, this extravagant hotel boasts lavish rooms, spa and five-star dining.

The Four Seasons $$$
Luxury Map 4 E3
1435 Brickell Ave, 33131
Tel *(305) 358-3535*
W fourseasons.com/miami
Business-oriented skyscraper favored by jet-setters. Fantastic accommodation and skyline views.

Coral Gables and Coconut Grove

Courtyard by Marriott $$
Modern Map 5 C1
2051 LeJeune Rd, 33134
Tel *(305) 443-2301*
W marriott
This contemporary building has comfortable rooms with traditional decor and a rooftop pool.

Hotel St. Michel $$
Boutique Map 5 C1
162 Alcazar Ave, 33134
Tel *(305) 444-1666*
W hotelstmichel.com
No two rooms are alike at this hotel with an old-world ambience and traditional furnishings.

DK Choice

Biltmore Hotel $$$
Resort Map 5 A2
1200 Anastasia Ave, 33134
Tel *(305) 445-1926*
W biltmorehotel.com
Large rooms and fabulous suites match the élan of this luxurious Spanish-style 1920s landmark, complete with a Giralda-inspired bell tower. Facilities include a golf course, 10 tennis courts, and a gigantic pool, as well as four highly-regarded restaurants.

For more information on types of hotels *see page 313*

Grove Isle Hotel & Spa $$$
Resort   Off map
4 Grove Isle Dr, 33133
Tel *(305) 858-8300*
🅦 groveisle.com
Tropical private island hideaway featuring warmly furnished suites with bay views and spa facilities.

Mayfair Hotel and Spa $$$
Boutique   Map 6 F4
3000 Florida Ave, 33133
Tel *(305) 441-0000*
🅦 mayfairhotelandspa.com
With gorgeous Art Nouveau detailing, the Mayfair has bright, tastefully furnished rooms with private balconies. Pets welcome.

Ritz-Carlton Coconut Grove $$$
Luxury   Map 6 F4
3300 SW 27th Ave, 33133
Tel *(305) 644-4680*
🅦 ritzcarlton.com
Expect stunning accommodation at this intimate tropical retreat that over-looks the bay.

Farther Afield

Ritz-Carlton Key Biscayne $$$
Resort   Road Map F5
455 Grand Bay Dr, Key Biscayne, 33149
Tel *(305) 365-4500*
🅦 ritzcarlton.com
This luxurious hotel has a private beach and excellent spa facilities.

Trump International $$$
Resort   Road Map F5
18001 Collins Ave, Sunny Isles 33160
Tel *(305) 692-5600*
🅦 trumpmiami.com
Contemporary beach front tower building offers stylish accommodation. Each room has a balcony and kitchenette.

Turnberry Isle Resort $$$
Resort   Road Map F5
19999 W Country Club Dr, Aventura, 33180
Tel *(305) 932-6200*
🅦 turnberryislemiami.com
This expansive holiday escape has a spa, a private beach, and tennis and golf courses.

The Gold and Treasure Coasts

BOCA RATON:
Boca Raton Resort $$$
Resort   Road Map F4
501 E Camino Readl, 33432
Tel *(561) 447-3000*
🅦 bocaresort.com
Exquisite historic building designed by architect Addison Mizner, this retreat has kids' camp facilities.

BOCA RATON: Ocean Lodge $$$
Motel   Road Map F4
531 N Ocean Blvd, 33432
Tel *(561) 395-7772*
🅦 oceanlodgeflorida.com
Two-story upscale motel located across from a beach, featuring large rooms with kitchenettes.

CLEWISTON: Clewiston Inn $$
Inn   Road Map F4
108 Royal Palm Ave, 33440
Tel *(863) 983-8151*
🅦 clewistoninn.com
Reasonably priced rooms with simple decor and good dining.

DELRAY BEACH:
Sundy House $$$
Boutique   Road Map F4
106 S Swinton Ave, 33444
Tel *(561) 272-5678*
🅦 sundyhouse.com
Beautiful historic cottages in a garden setting, with homely decor and a freshwater swimming pond.

FORT LAUDERDALE:
The Hotel Deauville $
Hostel   Road Map F4
2916 N Ocean Blvd, 33308
Tel *(954) 568-5000*
🅦 thedeauvillehotel.com
Clean dorms and private rooms with communal kitchen and pool. Located close to beach.

FORT LAUDERDALE: Harbor Beach Marriott Resort & Spa $$$
Luxury   Road Map F4
3030 Holiday Dr, 33316
Tel *(954) 525-4000*
🅦 marriottharborbeach.com
Located on a secluded beach, this Marriott hotel has attractive rooms, a large pool, and spa.

DK Choice

FORT LAUDERDALE: Lago Mar Resort $$$
Resort   Road Map F4
1700 S Ocean Ln, 33316
Tel *(954) 523-6511*
🅦 lagomar.com
There may be more lavish resorts but few as gracious or unpretentious than this family-run charming retreat. Amenities include a private beach, lagoon-style pool, tennis courts, golf putting course, and a giant outdoor chessboard.

FORT LAUDERDALE:
Riverside Hotel $$$
Historic   Road Map F4
620 E Las Olas Blvd, 33301
Tel *(954) 467-0671*
🅦 riversidehotel.com
Downtown 1930s landmark with great rooms, a pool, and terrace.

FORT LAUDERDALE:
The Atlantic $$$
Luxury   Road Map F4
601 Fort Lauderdale Beach Blvd, 33304
Tel *(954) 567-8020*
🅦 atlantichotelfl.com
Beachfront hotel that boasts large rooms with kitchenettes and balconies. There is also a pool and spa.

FORT LAUDERDALE:
The Pillars Hotel $$$
Luxury   Road Map F4
111 N Birch Rd, 33304
Tel *(954) 467-9639*
🅦 pillarshotel.com
Richly furnished hideaway on the Intracoastal Waterway. Gorgeous pool and an extensive library.

FORT LAUDERDALE:
W Fort Lauderdale $$$
Luxury   Road Map F4
401 N Fort Lauderdale Beach Blvd, 33304
Tel *(954) 414-8200*
🅦 whotels.com/fortlauderdale
Trendy beachfront hotel with stylish rooms and a popular bar.

HOBE SOUND: Jonathan Dickinson State Park $
Lodge   Road Map F4
16450 SE Federal Hwy, 33455
Tel *(772) 546-2771*
🅦 floridastateparks.com
Located near Loxahatchee River. Cabins with kitchens and other modern amenities, accommodating up to six people.

HOLLYWOOD: Seminole Hard Rock Hotel and Casino $$$
Luxury   Road Map F4
1 Seminole Way, 33314
Tel *(954) 327-7625*
🅦 seminolehardrockhollywood.com
Spacious rooms and a lavish pool, though the casino is the main attraction for choosing this hotel.

The exterior of Seminole Hard Rock Hotel and Casino and its lagoon-style pool

Key to Price Guide *see page 314*

The playful interior of Hotel Biba in West Palm Beach

**HOLLYWOOD: Westin
Diplomat Resort** $$$
Resort **Road Map** F4
3555 S Ocean Dr, 33019
Tel *(954) 602-6000*
W diplomatresort.com
Large, glitzy hotel with a glass-
bottom pool and a private beach.

JUPITER: La Quinta Inn $$
Motel **Road Map** F4
34 Fisherman's Wharf, 33477
Tel *(561) 575-7201*
W laquintainn.com
Traditionally furnished rooms and
modern facilities, including a
gym and pool.

**LAUDERDALE BY THE SEA:
A Little Inn by the Sea** $$
Inn **Road Map** F4
4546 El Mar Dr, 33308
Tel *(954) 772-2450*
W alittleinnhotel.com
Charming guest house with
tropical themed decor. Most
rooms have a sea view.

**NORTH HUTCHINSON ISLAND:
The Mellon Patch Inn** $$
B&B **Road Map** F3
3601 N Hwy A1A, Fort Pierce, 34949
Tel *(772) 462-6699*
W themellonpatchinn.com
Small, welcoming cottage-style
B&B operating since 1949. Simple
furnishings and good breakfast.

**PALM BEACH: Palm Beach
Historic Inn** $$
Inn **Road Map** F4
365 S County Rd, 33480
Tel *(561) 832-4009*
W palmbeachhistoricinn.com
This antique-filled historic inn
offers comfortable rooms within
walking distance from the beach.

**PALM BEACH:
Chesterfield Hotel** $$$
Historic **Road Map** F4
363 Coconut Row, 33480
Tel *(561) 659-5800*
W chesterfieldpb.com
A landmark hotel with gorgeous
rooms and a shaded courtyard.
Don't miss the elaborate high tea.

**PALM BEACH: Four
Seasons Palm Beach** $$$
Resort **Road Map** F4
2800 S Ocean Blvd, 33480
Tel *(561) 582-2800*
W fourseasons.com
Elegant beach haven with sleek
furnishings, fine dining, a bar and
lounge, as well as sports facilities.

PALM BEACH: The Colony $$$
Luxury **Road Map** F4
156 Hammon Ave, 33480
Tel *(561) 655-5430*
W thecolonypalmbeach.com
Elegant rooms with British-colonial
decor. English breakfast included.

**PALM BEACH GARDENS:
PGA National Resort** $$$
Resort **Road Map** F4
400 Ave of the Champions, 33418
Tel *(561) 627-2000*
W pgaresort.com
Famed championship golf courses,
19 tennis courts, and a lavish spa
are the highlights of this resort.

**PORT ST. LUCIE:
Club Med Sandpiper** $$$
Resort **Road Map** F3
4500 SE Pine Valley, 34952
Tel *(772) 398-5100*
W clubmed.com
Family-oriented all-inclusive resort
with golf and tennis academies.

**SEBASTIAN: Floridana
Beach Motel** $
Motel **Road Map** F3
*6580 S Hwy A1A, Melbourne Beach,
32951*
Tel *(321) 726-6560*
W motelfloridana.com
Budget lodging, some with
kitchenettes. The owner can show
those keen on fishing the best
local spots.

**SINGER ISLAND: Hilton
Singer Island Resort** $$$
Resort **Road Map** F3
3700 N Ocean Dr, 33404
Tel *(561) 848-3888*
W hilton.com
This elegant establishment offers
comfortable rooms with sea views.

**SOUTH HUTCHINSON ISLAND:
Dockside Harborlight Inn** $$
Inn **Road Map** F3
1160 Seaway Dr, 34949
Tel *(772) 468-3555*
W docksideinn.com
Lovely inn with nautically themed
rooms and waterfront balconies.

**VERO BEACH:
The Driftwood Resort** $$
Resort **Road Map** F3
3150 Ocean Dr, 32963
Tel *(772) 231-0550*
W thedriftwood.com
Rustic-chic accommodation in
nine cabins with balconies and
all the modern amenities.

VERO BEACH: Islander Inn $$
Motel **Road Map** F3
3101 Ocean Dr, 32963
Tel *(772) 231-4431*
W islanderinnverobeach.com
This inn – with its ceiling fans,
wicker furniture, courtyard, and
pool – exudes an old-Florida feel.

**VERO BEACH: Disney's Vero
Beach Resort** $$$
Resort **Road Map** F3
9250 Island Grove Terrace, 32963
Tel *(772) 234-2000*
W disneybeachresorts.com
Family resort with studios and
villas, a Mickey-shaped pool, mini-
golf, and lots of kids' activities.

**WEST PALM BEACH:
Hotel Biba** $$
Boutique **Road Map** F4
320 Belvedere Rd, 33407
Tel *(561) 832-0094*
W hotelbiba.com
A 1940s motor lodge re-imagined
with flair. The rooms are comfort-
able and have colorful decor.

Orlando and the
Space Coast

**CELEBRATION:
Bohemian Hotel** $$
Inn **Road Map** E3
700 Bloom St, 34747
Tel *(407) 566-6000*
W celebrationhotel.com
Elegantly furnished inn located at
a lakeside setting. Great option
away from the Disney crowds.

**COCOA BEACH:
Doubletree Hotel** $$
Modern **Road Map** F3
2080 Atlantic Ave, 32931
Tel *(321) 783-9222*
W cocoabeachdoubletree.com
Comfortable oceanfront spot
with snug rooms and freshly
baked cookies on arrival.

For more information on types of hotels *see page 313*

COCOA BEACH:
The Inn at Cocoa Beach $$
Inn   **Road Map** F3
4300 Ocean Blvd, 32931
Tel *(321) 799-3460*
ⓦ theinnatcocoabeach.com
Located by the beach, with each
room individually styled. Fantastic
wine and cheese evenings.

KISSIMMEE: Quality Inn & Suites $
Motel   **Road Map** E3
2945 Entry Point Blvd, 34747
Tel *(407) 390-1254*
ⓦ qualityinn.com
Budget choice near the Disney
parks. Clean rooms, with free
breakfast and guest laundry.

KISSIMMEE: Gaylord
Palms Resort $$$
Resort   **Road Map** E3
6000 W Osceola Pkwy, 34747
Tel *(407) 586-0000*
ⓦ gaylordpalms.com
Big, lavish resort and convention
center with its own water park.
Rooms are tastefully decorated.

NEW SMYRNA BEACH:
Riverview Hotel $
Historic   **Road Map** E2
103 Flager Ave, 32169
Tel *(386) 428-5858*
ⓦ riverviewhotel.com
Overlooking the Indian River,
this charming Victorian hotel
has comfortable rooms, a pool,
and a spa.

ORLANDO: Grand Bohemian $$$
Luxury   **Road Map** E3
325 S Orange Ave, 32801
Tel *(407) 313-9000*
ⓦ grandbohemianhotel.com
Top choice in downtown Orlando.
Featuring great rooms, fine art, a
pool, and a jazz-themed bar.

UNIVERSAL ORLANDO®:
Hyatt Place Universal $$
Modern   **Road Map** E3
5895 Caravan Court, 32819
Tel *(407) 351-0627*
ⓦ orlandouniversal.place.hyatt.com
Located near three major theme
parks. The large suites are tastefully
decorated and have kitchenettes.

DK Choice

ORLANDO: Villas of
Grand Cypress $$$
Resort   **Road Map** E3
1 N Jacaranda, 32836
Tel *(407) 239-4700*
ⓦ grandcypress.com
This lush, beautifully landscaped
complex has extravagant villas
with kitchens, patios, and
bathrooms with Roman tubs.
Choose from four golf courses, a
racquet club, climbing wall, and
pools with waterfalls and slides.
Free shuttle to the theme parks.

UNIVERSAL ORLANDO®:
Hard Rock Hotel $$$
Luxury   **Road Map** E3
5800 Universal Blvd, 32819
Tel *(407) 503-2000*
ⓦ hardrockhotelorlando.com
This Hard Rock flagship has, as
expected, a fun rock and roll theme.
Spacious rooms and spa facilities.

DK Choice

UNIVERSAL ORLANDO®:
Loews Portofino
Bay Hotel $$$
Luxury   **Road Map** E3
5601 Universal Blvd, 32819
Tel *(407) 503-1000*
ⓦ loewshotels.com
A beautifully re-created Italian
village, complete with canals and
festive piazza, this extravagant
complex has spacious rooms
and suites as well as three pools
and spa facilities. Enjoy the
hotel's exclusive theme park
benefits such as early admission
and skipping the regular lines.

WALT DISNEY WORLD®:
Disney's All Star Resorts $$
Hotel   **Road Map** E3
*World Dr & Osceola Pkwy, Lake
Buena Vista, 32830*
Tel *(407) 934-7639*
ⓦ disneyworld.com
Disney's least expensive lodgings.
Small rooms with three themed
towers and lots of fun activities.

WALT DISNEY WORLD®:
Animal Kingdom Lodge $$$
Luxury   **Road Map** E3
*2901 Osceola Pkwy, Lake Buena
Vista, 32830*
Tel *(407) 938-3000*
ⓦ disneyworld.com
Luxury safari lodge with African-
style decor and views of zebras
and giraffes from picture windows.

WALT DISNEY WORLD®: Disney's
Caribbean Beach Resort $$$
Resort   **Road Map** E3
*900 Cayman Way, Lake Buena Vista,
32830*
Tel *(407) 934-3400*
ⓦ disneyworld.com
Five island "villages" set around a
huge lake, with pirate boats and
mini-golf. Fantastic experience.

WALT DISNEY WORLD®: Disney's
Coronado Springs Resort $$$
Resort   **Road Map** E3
1000 W Buena Vista Dr, 32830
Tel *(407) 939-1000*
ⓦ disneyworld.com
A luxury haven, with a Mayan
pyramid pool and evening camp-
fires. Mini-golf and fitness center.

WALT DISNEY WORLD®: Disney's
Port Orleans Resort $$$
Resort   **Road Map** E3
*2201 Orleans Dr, Lake Buena Vista,
32830*
Tel *(407) 934-5000*
ⓦ disneyworld.com
With wrought-iron balconies,
horse-drawn carriages, and a
lagoon lake, this resort has a
fantastic New Orleans ambience.

The Northeast

DK Choice

AMELIA ISLAND: Omni
Amelia Island Plantation $$$
Resort   **Road Map** E1
6800 First Coast Hwy, 32035
Tel *(904) 261-6161*
ⓦ omnihotels.com
This sprawling 2 sq-mile (5 sq-
km) this retreat has everything
needed for an active vacation:
a beach, indoor and outdoor
pools, golf courses, tennis
center, and nature trails. The
rooms are comfortable, too.

DAYTONA BEACH:
Shoreline All Suites Inn $$
B&B/Inn   **Road Map** E2
2435 S Atlantic Ave, 32118
Tel *(386) 252-1692*
ⓦ daytonashoreline.com
Lining the foreshore of the

The large swimming pool and opulent terrace at Grand Bohemian in Orlando beach, these simple motel suites are equipped with kitchens. Breakfast is included.

DAYTONA BEACH:
The Villa Inn $$
B&B Road Map E2
801 N Peninsula Dr, 32118
Tel *(386) 248-2020*
W thevillabb.com
Spanish-style mansion with elegant European furnishings, antiques, and a walled garden. Guest must be 16 or older.

DAYTONA BEACH:
Hilton Daytona Beach $$$
Luxury Road Map E2
100 N Atlantic Ave, 32118
Tel *(386) 254-8200*
W daytonahilton.com
Oceanfront high-rise with attractive rooms and great views. There is also a kids' pool and activities.

DAYTONA BEACH:
The Plaza Resort & Spa $$$
Historic Road Map E2
600 N Atlantic Ave, 32118
Tel *(386) 255-4471*
W plazaresortandspa.com
Well-refurbished beachfront hotel featuring traditionally furnished rooms with kitchenettes.

DAYTONA BEACH:
The Shores Resort & Spa $$$
Resort Road Map E2
2637 S Atlantic Ave, 32118
Tel *(386) 767-7350*
W shoresresort.com
Fantastic resort with Atlantic or Intracoastal views from rooms. Free shuttle to attractions.

FERNANDINA BEACH:
Hampton Inn & Suites $$
Motel Road Map E1
19 S 2nd St, 32034
Tel *(904) 491-4911*
W hamptoninn3.hilton.com
Spacious, elegantly furnished rooms and suites. Pets are welcome and breakfast is included in room cost.

DK Choice

FERNANDINA BEACH:
Elizabeth Pointe Lodge $$$
B&B Road Map E1
98 S Fletcher Ave, 32034
Tel *(904) 277-4851*
W elizabethpintelodge.com
Elizabeth Pointe is an award-winning Nantucket-style shingled beach house with gorgeous ocean views from the wide porch and windows. Offers elegantly decorated rooms, scrumptious breakfasts and evening wine and *hors d'oeuvres*.

Stylish Spanish decor at Casa Monica Hotel, St Augustine

JACKSONVILLE: Hyatt Regency Riverfront $$
Modern Road Map E1
225 E Coastline Dr, 32202
Tel *(904) 588-1234*
W jacksonville.hyatt.com
Modern high-rise by the Riverwalk with comfortable rooms, a rooftop pool, and spa.

JACKSONVILLE: The House on Cherry Street $$
B&B Road Map E1
1844 Cherry St, 32205
Tel *(904) 384-1999*
W geocities.com/houseoncherrystreet
Colonial-style B&B with by the St. Johns River, with antiques, four-poster beds, and great porch views.

NEPTUNE BEACH: Seahorse Oceanfront Inn $$
Motel Road Map E1
120 Atlantic Blvd, 32266
Tel *(904) 246-2175*
W jacksonvilleoceanfronthotel.com
Old-fashioned motel with oceanfront balconies and patios. Complimentary breakfast.

PONTE VEDRA BEACH:
Ponte Vedra Inn $$$
Resort Road Map E1
200 Ponte Vedra Blvd, 32082
Tel *(904) 285-1111*
W pontevedra.com
A landmark since 1928, this 5-star resort has Spanish-style decor, beautifully presented rooms and suites, as well as a golf course.

ST AUGUSTINE: Best Western Bayfront Inn $$
Inn Road Map E1
16 Avenida Menedez, 32087
Tel *(904) 824-4482*
W bestwesternbayfront staugustine.com
This hotel has comfortable rooms with modern amenities and a pool overlooking Matanzas Bay.

ST AUGUSTINE:
Casa de Solana $$
Inn Road Map E1
24 Aviles St, 32094
Tel *(904) 824-3316*
W casadesolana.com
This inn has homely rooms with British-colonial decor and fireplaces. Lavish breakfasts.

ST AUGUSTINE:
The Pirate House Inn $$
B&B Road Map E1
32 Treasury St, 32084
Tel *(904) 808-1999*
W piratehaus.com
This popular B&B offers doubles, family rooms, bunk dorms, and an unlimited pancake breakfast.

ST AUGUSTINE:
Victorian House $$
Historic Road Map E1
11 Cadiz St, 32084
Tel *(904) 824-5214*
W victorianhousebnb.com
This 1897 charming Victorian hotel has eclectic decor and generous breakfast.

DK Choice

ST AUGUSTINE:
Casa Monica Hotel $$$
Historic Road Map E1
95 Cordova St, 32084
Tel *(904) 827-1888*
W casamonica.com
Old Spanish charm pervades this restored 1888 beauty, from the frescoed lobby to the atmospheric guest rooms and the acoustic guitar music in the Cobalt lounge. Rooms have all modern conveniences and the pool deck is a welcome private haven. A great experience.

The Panhandle

APALACHICOLA:
Coombs House Inn $$$
Inn Road Map B1
80 6th St, 32320
Tel *(850) 653-9199*
W coombshouseinn.com
Charming inn located within three beautiful Victorian houses. Rooms are furnished with antiques and four poster beds.

APALACHICOLA: Gibson Inn $$$
Inn Road Map B1
51 Ave C, 32320
Tel *(850) 653-2191*
W gibsoninn.com
Built in 1907, this stunning inn is a local landmark. Wraparound porches and great period furnishings. Free breakfast.

For more information on types of hotels *see page 313*

Spectacularly large pool and magnificent beach house at Watercolor Inn, Santa Rosa Beach

DESTIN: Summer Place Inn $$
Inn   Road Map A1
14047 Emerald Coast Pkwy, 32541
Tel *(850) 650-8003*
W summerplaceinn.com
Well-appointed rooms with
modern amenities. Enjoy a selec-
tion of pools and free breakfast.

DESTIN: Sandestin Resort $$$
Resort   Road Map A1
9300 Emerald Coast Pkwy, 32541
Tel *(850) 267-1816*
W sandestin.cm
Range of lodgings from cottages
to high-rise accommodation. Golf,
tennis, pools, beach, and zip line.

FORT WALTON BEACH:
Aunt Martha's B&B $$
B&B   Road Map A1
315 Shell Ave, 32548
Tel *(850) 243-6702*
W auntmartasbedandbreakfast
Resembling an old Florida beach
house. Charming rooms with
views and big Southern breakfast.

FORT WALTON BEACH:
Ramada Plaza Beach Resort $$
Modern   Road Map A1
1500 E Miracle Strip Pkwy, 32548
Tel *(850) 243-9161*
W ramadafwb.com
Comfortable well-equipped
rooms. A beach, waterfall, grotto
pool, and playground facilities.

FORT WALTON BEACH:
Holiday Inn Sunspree $$$
Luxury   Road Map A1
573 Santa Rosa Blvd, 32548
Tel *(800) 238-8686*
W hifwb.com
This beachfront high-rise offers
family suites with kitchen facilities.
Waterfall pool and kids' activities.

FORT WALTON BEACH:
Islander Beach Resort $$$
Luxury   Road Map A1
790 Santa Rosa Blvd, 32548
Tel *(850) 244-4237*
W emeraldcoastrentals.com
Comfortable condos, studios, and
three-bedroom apartments with
kitchenettes, balconies, and a pool.

GRAYTON BEACH:
Grayton Beach State Park $$
Lodge   Road Map B1
357 Main Park Rd, 32459
Tel *(900) 326-3521*
W floridastateparks.com
Get back to nature at this cabin site
located near the park's expansive
beach. There is a no phone and TV
policy. Two-day minimum stay.

PANAMA CITY BEACH:
Beachcomber by the Sea $$
Modern   Road Map B1
17101 Front Beach Rd, 32413
Tel *(850) 233-3600*
W beachcomberbythesea.com
Seven-story hotel by the beach.
Rooms with kitchenettes and
Continental breakfast.

PANAMA CITY BEACH:
Flamingo Motel $$
Motel   Road Map B1
15525 Front Beach Rd, 34213
Tel *(850) 324-2232*
W flamingomotel.com
Family-owned beachfront motel.
Basic but comfortable rooms
with kitchens. Good value.

PANAMA CITY BEACH:
Sunset Inn $$
Inn   Road Map B1
8109 Surf Dr, 32408
Tel *(850) 234-7370*
W sunsetinnfl.com
Sunset Inn has comfortable
self-contained units and suites
as well as a fabulous sundeck.

PANAMA CITY BEACH:
Wyndham Bay Point Resort $$
Resort   Road Map B1
4114 Jan Cooley Dr, 32408
Tel *(850) 236-6000*
W wyndham.com
Luxury resort with golf courses, spa
pools, and a shuttle to the beach.

PENSACOLA: Lee House $$$
B&B   Road Map A1
400 Bayfront Pkwy, 32502
Tel *(850) 912-8770*
W leehousepensacola.com
Spacious, modern B&B with lovely
bay and Seville Square views.

PENSACOLA BEACH:
Portofino Island Resort $$$
Resort   Road Map A1
10 Portofino Dr, 32561
Tel *(877) 484-3405*
W portofinoisland.com
Apartments in five Mediterranean-
style condos with kitchens, spa,
pools, golf, and kids' activities.

DK Choice

SANTA ROSA BEACH:
Watercolor Inn $$$
Inn   Road Map B1
34 Goldenrod Circle, 32459
Tel *(850) 534-5000*
W watercolorresort.com
Watercolor is a luxurious but
relaxed beach house with
spacious rooms, king-sized
beds, walk-in showers, and
balconies. Complimentary bikes,
canoes and kayaks are available.

TALLAHASSEE:
Governors Inn $$$
Historic   Road Map C1
209 S Adams St, 32301
Tel *(850) 681-6855*
W thegovinn.com
Convenient downtown choice
with old-fashioned warmth and
rooms named after past governors.
Free Continental breakfast.

The Gulf Coast

CAPTIVA ISLAND:
Captiva Island Inn $$$
Inn   Road Map E4
11508 Andy Rosse Ln, 33924
Tel *(239) 395-0882*
W captivaislandinn.com
Delightful complex near the
beach with cottages including
kitchenettes. Complimentary
breakfast at nearby restaurants.

CAPTIVA ISLAND:
South Seas Resort $$$
Resort   Road Map E4
5400 Plantation Rd, 33924
Tel *(239) 472-5111*
W southseas.com
Expansive retreat with golf and
tennis facilities and a 2.5-mile
(4-km) private beach. Luxurious
rooms with all amenities.

CAPTIVA ISLAND:
Tween Waters Inn $$$
Resort   Road Map E4
15951 Captiva Rd, 33924
Tel *(239) 472-5161*
W tween-waters.com
Rooms and cottages spread over
a huge private area between Gulf
and Bay Beach. Spa, tennis, and
golf facilities. Continental breakfast.

CLEARWATER:
Amber Tides Motel $
Motel **Road Map** D3
420 Hamden Dr, 33767
Tel *(727) 445-1145*
W ambertides-motel.com
Old-fashioned motel close to the
beach. Clean, basic rooms with
microwaves and refrigerators.

CLEARWATER BEACH:
Clearwater Beach Marriott $$$
Luxury **Road Map** D3
1201 Gulf Blvd, 33767
Tel *(727) 596-1100*
W marriott.com
Pleasant hotel located on the
beautiful Sand Key. All suites have
cooking facilities and balconies.

CLEARWATER BEACH: Hyatt
Regency Clearwater $$$
Luxury **Road Map** D3
301 S Gulfview Blvd, 33767
Tel *(727) 373-1234*
W clearwaterbeach.hyatt.com
This beachfront hotel has
extravagant suites with balconies
and kitchens. Camp for kids.

FORT MYERS BEACH:
Palm Terrace Aparments $$
Modern **Road Map** E4
3333 Estero Blvd, 33931
Tel *(239) 765-5783*
W palm-terrace.com
Modestly furnished self-contained
apartments set around an enticing
pool. Most suites have balconies.

FORT MYERS BEACH:
Diamond Head Resort $$$
Luxury **Road Map** E4
2000 Estero Blvd, 33931
Tel *(239) 765-7654*
W diamondheadfl.com
All-suite hotel by the beach
with screened balconies, a pool,
outdoor whirlpools and a spa.

A spacious villa with beach views at Pink
Shell Beach Resort, Fort Myers Beach

DK Choice
FORT MYERS BEACH:
Edison Beach House $$$
Inn **Road Map** E4
830 Estero Blvd, 33931
Tel *(239) 463-1530*
W edisonbeachhouse.com
This beachside hotel cannot be
beat for its space and amenities.
Airy suites for two to six people
are furnished with beach-style
wicker and have ceiling fans,
balconies, kitchens, and laundry
facilities. There is a heated pool
and children's playhouse as well.

FORT MYERS BEACH:
Outrigger Beach Resort $$$
Luxury **Road Map** E4
6200 Estero Blvd, 33931
Tel *(239) 463-3131*
W outriggerfmb.com
Choose between self-contained
suites or motel-style rooms, some
with beach views. Large pool.

FORT MYERS BEACH:
Pink Shell Beach Resort $$$
Luxury **Road Map** E4
275 Estero Blvd, 33931
Tel *(239) 463-6181*
W pinkshell.com
Expansive luxury hotel by a
white-sand beach. Studios and
villas with cooking facilities.

LONGBOAT KEY: The Resort
at Longboat Key Club $$$
Resort **Road Map** D3
220 Sands Point Rd, 34228
Tel *(941) 383-8821*
W longboatkeyclub.com
Spacious, upmarket lodgings
with self-catering, golf and tennis.

PALM HARBOR:
Innisbrook Golf Resort $$
Resort **Road Map** D3
36057 US Hwy 19N, 34684
Tel *(727) 942-2000*
W innisbrookgolfresort.com
This resort is renowned for its
four championship golf courses.
Deluxe rooms and kids' club.

SAFETY HARBOR:
Safety Harbor Resort & Spa $$
Resort **Road Map** D3
105 N Bayshore Dr, 34695
Tel *(727) 726-1161*
W safetyharborspa.com
Choose from the many fitness and
spa packages at this bayside resort.
Beautifully presented rooms.

SANIBEL ISLAND: Casa Ybel $$$
Resort **Road Map** E4
2255 W Gulf Dr, 33957
Tel *(239) 472-3145*
W casaybelresort.com
Upscale condo beachfront retreat.

Suites have great balcony views
and fully-equipped kitchens.
Many children's activities.

SANIBEL ISLAND: Island Inn $$$
Inn **Road Map** E4
3111 W Gulf Dr, 33957
Tel *(239) 472-1561*
W islandinnsanibel.com
Vintage cottages and modern
lodges set in expansive grounds
near a beach. Tennis, lawn games,
and Continental breakfast.

SANIBEL ISLAND:
Sanibel Inn $$$
Inn **Road Map** E4
937 E Gulf Dr, 33957
Tel *(239) 472-3181*
W sanibelinn.com
Spacious and well-equipped
rooms and condos. Great beach,
plus tennis and biking facilities.

SANIBEL ISLAND:
Seaside Inn $$$
Inn **Road Map** E4
541 E Gulf Dr, 33957
Tel *(239) 472-1400*
W sanibelinn.com
Pleasant 1960s beachside inn.
Golf and tennis club privileges
and complimentary breakfast.

SANIBEL ISLAND:
Sundial Resort $$$
Resort **Road Map** E4
1451 Middle Gulf Dr, 33957
Tel *(239) 395-6031*
W sundialresort.com
Studio to three-bedroom condos
by the beach with tennis-golf
club privileges, pools and spa.

SANIBEL ISLAND:
Tarpon Tale Inn $$$
Inn **Road Map** E4
367 Periwinkle Way, 33957
Tel *(239) 472-0939*
W tarpontale.com
This friendly place features bright,
airy studios and cottages. Each has
a kitchenette, is individually styled,
and surrounded by lush gardens.

SARASOTA: Holiday Inn
Sarasota Airport $$
Motel **Road Map** D3
8009 15th St E, 34243
Tel *(941) 355-9000*
W holidayinn.com
Ultra-modern six-story motel
with excellent rooms and an
indoor pool. A short drive to town.

SARASOTA:
La Quinta Inn & Suites $$
Modern **Road Map** D3
1803 N Tamiami Trail, 34234
Tel *(941) 366-5128*
W lq.com
Tastefully decorated and furnished
budget hotel. Free breakfast.

For more information on types of hotels *see page 313*

SARASOTA:
Captiva Beach Resort $$$
Resort   Road Map D3
6772 Sara Sea Circle, Siesta Key,
34242
Tel *(941) 349-4131*
w captivabeachresort.com
Near Sonesta Key's white-sand
beach, this resort is a complex of
clean, modern units with kitchens.

SARASOTA:
Helmsley Sandcastle Hotel $$$
Luxury   Road Map D3
1540 Ben Franklin Dr, Lido Key, 34236
Tel *(941) 388-2181*
w helmsleyhotels.com
Located by Lido Beach, this hotel
offers beach game facilities, pools
and outdoor dining. Some rooms
have beach views and balconies.

SARASOTA: The Cypress $$$
B&B   Road Map D3
621 Gulfstream Ave, 34236
Tel *(941) 955-4683*
w cypressbb.com
A great find tucked amid mango
and palm trees overlooking the
bay. Lovely antiques and Oriental
rugs in rooms. Excellent breakfast.

SARASOTA: The Ritz-Carlton $$$
Resort   Road Map D3
1111 Ritz-Carlton Dr, 34236
Tel *(941) 309-2000*
w ritzcarlton.com
Relax in typical Ritz-style luxury.
Spa and tennis facilities, private
golf club, and Lido Key beach club.

DK Choice

SARASOTA:
Turtle Beach Resort $$$
Resort   Road Map D3
9049 Midnight Pass Rd, Siesta Key,
34242
Tel *(941) 349-4554*
w turtlebeachresort.com
This private bayside cottage
complex, tucked away on the
quiet southern end of Siesta
Key, has an Old Florida charm.
It offers individually-styled
studios and suites with private

Tranquil lounge beside the pool at Turtle Beach Resort, Sarasota

patios and hot tubs. Amenities
include a pool, shaded
hammocks and complimentary
kayaks and bikes.

ST PETE BEACH: Beach Haven $$
Motel   Road Map D3
4980 Gulf Blvd, 33706
Tel *(727) 367-8642*
w beachhavenvillas.com
Located on the beachfront, these
simple motel-style units offer
excellent value. The one-
bedroom units have kitchens.

ST PETE BEACH:
Loews Don CeSar Hotel $$$
Historic   Road Map D3
3400 Gulf Blvd, 33706
Tel *(727) 360-1881*
w loewshotels.com
Beautifully restored 1928 palatial
hotel by the beach. Offers vintage
charm with modern amenities,
including a pool and spa.

ST PETE BEACH:
Tradewinds Island Grand $$$
Resort   Road Map D3
5500 Gulf Blvd, 33706
Tel *(727) 367-6461*
w tradewindsresort.com
This luxurious beachfront
resort has five huge pools and
waterways with paddleboats.
Some rooms have kitchenettes.

ST PETERSBURG:
Dickens House $$
B&B   Road Map D3
335 8th Ave NE, 33701
Tel *(727) 822-8622*
w dickenshouse.com
A stunning 1912 Arts and Crafts
house with five beautiful rooms,
some with whirlpools. Enjoy the
fantastic gourmet breakfast.

ST PETERSBURG: Hotel Indigo $$
Modern   Road Map D3
234 3rd Ave NE, 33706
Tel *(727) 822-4814*
w hotelindigo.com
Comfortable hotel with modern
rooms. Facilities include 24-hour
fitness center, pool and whirlpool.

DK Choice

ST PETERSBURG:
Renaissance Vinoy Resort $$$
Historic   Road Map D3
501 5th Ave NE, 33701
Tel *(727) 894-1000*
w marriott.com
This beautifully restored building
has retained the grandeur of the
past while adding top resort
amenities including a lavish pool,
tennis, golf, spa facilities and a
highly regarded restaurant. Worth
the expense to experience Florida
as it was in its 1920s heyday.

ST PETERSBURG: Watergarden
Inn at the Bay $$$
Inn   Road Map D3
126 4th Ave NE, 33701
Tel *(727) 822-1700*
w innatthebay.com
Tastefully restored period homes
with luxuriously comfortable beds.
Delicious buffet breakfast.

TAMPA: Baymont Inn & Suites $
Motel   Road Map D3
3001 University Dr, 33612
Tel *(813) 971-8930*
w baymontinns.com
Excellently priced rooms and
suites with kitchenettes. Free
shuttle to nearby Busch Gardens.

TAMPA: Hilton Garden Inn $$
Inn   Road Map D3
1700 E 9th Ave, 33602
Tel *(813) 769-9267*
w hiltongardeninn.com
Tastefully decorated rooms and
suites. Facilities include a pool, spa,
fitness center, and kid's activities.

TAMPA: Embassy Suites
Westshore $$$
Luxury   Road Map D3
555 N Westshore Blvd, 33609
Tel *(813) 875-1555*
w embassysuites.com
Good option for families, with
two-room suites and cooking
facilities. Free breakfast.

TAMPA: Marriott Waterside $$$
Luxury   Road Map D3
700 S Florida Ave, 33602
Tel *(813) 221-4900*
w marriott.com
Centrally located 22-story opulent
hotel with comfortable rooms,
rooftop pool, and good views.

TAMPA: Sheraton
Riverwalk Hotel $$$
Luxury   Road Map D3
200 N Ashley Dr, 33602
Tel *(813) 223-2222*
w sheratontampariverwalk.com
The Sheraton Riverwalk is a
comfortable downtown hotel

A cottage porch overlooking lush gardens and the ocean at The Moorings Village, Islamorada

with access to pleasant riverside walks and an outdoor pool. Good restaurant with patio seating.

TAMPA:
Westin Harbour Island $$$
Luxury **Road Map** D3
725 S Harbour Island Blvd, 33602
Tel (813) 229-5000
W westintampaharbourisland.com
This contemporary hotel with modern rooms are located on a private island. Great water views.

VENICE: Inn at the Beach $$$
Luxury **Road Map** D4
725 W Venice Ave, 34285
Tel (941) 484-8471
W innatthebeach.com
Comfortable motel-style lodgings by the beach. Cooking facilities and free Continental breakfast.

The Everglades and the Keys

EVERGLADES CITY:
Ivey House $$
B&B **Road Map** E5
107 Camelia St, 34139
Tel (239) 695-3299
W iveyhouse.com
Choose to stay in either a comfortable, modern B&B or an inexpensive 1920s-era lodge with shared bathrooms. The hosts also run Everglades Adventures outings.

EVERGLADES CITY:
Rod & Gun Club $$
Inn **Road Map** E5
Riverside Dr and Broadway, 34139
Tel (239) 695-2101
W evergladesrodandgun.com
Riverside sportsman's lodge with a luxurious pool in a screened veranda. Complimentary breakfast.

FLORIDA CITY: Best Western Gateway $$
Motel **Road Map** F5
411 S Krome Ave, 33034
Tel (305) 246-5100
W bestwestern.com

Conveniently located for the Keys or Everglades, this motel has a pool and offers free breakfast.

FLORIDA CITY: Everglades International Hostel $$
Hostel **Road Map** F5
20 SW 2nd Ave, 33034
Tel (305) 248-1122
W evergladeshostel.com
Great for backpackers and budget travelers. Dorms as well as family rooms, with communal kitchen and a pancake breakfast.

ISLAMORADA:
Ragged Edge Resort $$
Resort **Road Map** F5
243 Treasure Harbor Rd, 33036
Tel (305) 852-5389
W ragged-edge.com
Choose between comfortable rooms and cottages in this quiet, spacious oceanfront resort. There is a large pool and free bike hire.

ISLAMORADA: Casa Morada $$$
Luxury **Road Map** F5
136 Madeira Rd, 33036
Tel (305) 664-0044
W casamorada.com
This upscale Caribbean-style hideaway features suites, some with Jacuzzis, and great views. Continental breakfast included.

ISLAMORADA: Cheeca Lodge & Spa $$$
Resort **Road Map** F5
81801 Overseas Hwy, US 1 at MM 82, 33036
Tel (305) 664-4651
W cheeca.com
Relaxed luxurious retreat. Spacious rooms with West Indian decor and marble baths. Snorkeling, nature trails, and a fun kids' camp.

ISLAMORADA: Postcard Inn at Holiday Isle $$$
Inn **Road Map** F5
84001 Overseas Hwy, US1 at MM 84, 33036
Tel (305) 664-2321
W holidayisle.com
With its lively ambience and legendary Tiki bar, Postcard Inn is

a reliable favorite. Panoramic views from some rooms. Beach, pool and water sports on site.

DK Choice

ISLAMORADA:
The Moorings Village $$$
Luxury **Road Map** F5
123 Beach Rd, 33036
Tel (305) 664-4708
W themooringsvillage.com
Eighteen beautifully furnished cottages with porches and balconies spread over an expansive area, including one of the best beaches in the Keys. Excellent spa offers yoga classes and outdoor massages. There is also a lap pool, tennis court, and hammocks under the palms.

KEY LARGO:
Jules' Undersea Lodge $$$
Luxury **Road Map** F5
51 Shoreland Dr, 33037
Tel (305) 451-2353
W jul.com
Amazing underwater lodge for diving-enthusiasts, with fish swimming past windows. Rates include breakfast and dinner.

DK Choice

KEY LARGO: Kona Kai Resort & Gallery $$$
Resort **Road Map** F5
97802 Overseas Hwy, 33037
Tel (305) 852-7200
W konakairesort.com
Kona Kai is a retreat with tropically themed cottage suites set in a botanical garden home to over 250 rare plants. Amenities include garden tours, beach game facilities, kayaks, paddle-boats, freshwater pool, and a Jacuzzi. There is also a great art gallery on site. Resort is reserved for adult guests only.

KEY LARGO:
Ocean Pointe Suites $$$
Luxury **Road Map** F5
500 Burton Dr, Tavernier, 33070
Tel (305) 853-3000
W providentresorts.com
Comfortable suites spread out over an extensive area with a private marina and beach.

KEY WEST: Key West Hostel & Seashell Motel $
Motel **Road Map** E5
718 South St, 33040
Tel (305) 296-5719
W keywesthostel.com
Basic rooms with en suites as well as bunk-bed dorms. Laundry and common kitchen facilities.

For more information on types of hotels see page 313

Tastefully decorated suite at Marquesa Hotel, Key West

KEY WEST:
Angelina Guest House **$$**
Inn **Road Map** E5
302 Angela St, 33040
Tel *(305) 294-4480*
W angelinaguesthouse.com
Once a bordello, Angelina is now a popular guesthouse. Continental breakfast. No children.

KEY WEST: Southernmost
Point Guest House **$$**
Inn **Road Map** E5
1327 Duval St, 33040
Tel *(305) 294-0715*
W southernmostpoint.com
Airy Victorian guesthouse on a quiet street. With porches, a pool, Jacuzzi, and shaded hammocks.

KEY WEST:
Ambrosia Key West **$$$**
Hotel **Road Map** E5
622 Fleming St, 33040
Tel *(305) 296-9838*
W ambrosiakeywest.com
Popular hotel in a spacious garden, with themed rooms and suites, three pools and hot breakfast.

KEY WEST:
Curry Mansion Inn **$$$**
Historic **Road Map** E5
511 Caroline St, 33040
Tel *(305) 294-5349*
W currymansion.com
Lovely Victorian inn with wide porches, wicker furnishings, and antique fixtures. Fantastic breakfast and evening cocktail hour.

KEY WEST: Doubletree by Hilton
Hotel Grand Key Resort **$$$**
Luxury **Road Map** E5
3990 Roosevelt Blvd, 33040
Tel *(305) 293-1818*
W doubletreekeywest.com
Comfortable rooms in this island-styled hotel with amazing waterfall pool. Pet friendly and free shuttle.

KEY WEST: Duval House **$$$**
B&B **Road Map** E5
815 Duval St, 33040
Tel *(305) 924-1666*
W theduvalhouse.com
Attractive cottage complex around a courtyard with a pool and gardens. Continental breakfast.

KEY WEST:
Island City House Hotel **$$$**
Historic **Road Map** E5
411 William St, 33040
Tel *(305) 294-5702*
W islandcityhouse.com
Housed in three historic buildings sharing a patio and pool, the suites here have old-fashioned decor and kitchens.

KEY WEST: La Pensione **$$$**
Historic **Road Map** E5
809 Truman Ave, 33040
Tel *(305) 292-9923*
W lapensione.com
Victorian hotel in historic Old Town dating back to 1891. Rooms have king-sized beds and balconies. Continental breakfast.

DK Choice

KEY WEST:
Marquesa Hotel **$$$**
Historic **Road Map** E5
600 Fleming St, 33040
Tel *(305) 292-1919*
W marquesa.com
Three beautifully restored 1880s homes and a contemporary unit form an oasis within walking distance from town center. Light, airy rooms with ceiling fans. On-site Café Marquesa is one of the town's best.

KEY WEST: Ocean Key Resort **$$$**
Luxury **Road Map** E5
Zero Duval St, 33040
Tel *(305) 296-7701*
W oceankey.com
Located near the busy Mallory Square. Spacious rooms with balconies and a gorgeous seafront pool.

KEY WEST: Reach Resort **$$$**
Resort **Road Map** E5
1435 Simonton St, 33040
Tel *(305) 296-5000*
W reachresort.com
Attractive rooms with balconies in a quiet area. Lavish spa and access to the town's only natural beach.

KEY WEST:
Sunset Key Cottages **$$$**
Luxury **Road Map** E5
245 Front St, 33040
Tel *(305) 292-5300*
W westinsunsetkeycottages.com
Set on a private island just

offshore, this lavish cottage colony offers kitchen facilities and a free shuttle to town.

DK Choice

KEY WEST:
The Gardens Hotel **$$$**
Luxury **Road Map** E5
526 Angela St, 33040
Tel *(305) 294-2661*
W gardenshotel.com
Located in a secluded botanical garden estate, The Gardens has handsome rooms with island-style furnishings, marble baths, and Jacuzzis. Enjoy the Continental breakfast on a porch overlooking the lush gardens. For ages 16 and older.

KEY WEST: The Grand **$$$**
B&B **Road Map** E5
1116 Grinnell St, 33040
Tel *(305) 294-0590*
W thegrandguesthouse.com
Friendly guesthouse offering snug rooms and self-catering suites. The free Continental breakfast is very hearty.

KEY WEST:
Weatherstation Inn **$$$**
Inn **Road Map** E5
57 Front St, 33040
Tel *(305) 294-7277*
W weatherstationinn.com
Located in a gated community, this restored weather station offers airy rooms with breakfast baskets at the door. Ages 15 and up only.

KEY WEST: Westwinds Inn **$$$**
Historic **Road Map** E5
914 Eaton St, 33040
Tel *(305) 296-4440*
W westwindskeywest.com
Stay in a unique 1900s clapboard home. Rooms with modern amenities, plus a pool and library. Continental breakfast.

LITTLE TORCH KEY:
Little Palm Island **$$$**
Luxury **Road Map** E5
28500 Overseas Hwy, US 1 at MM 28.5, 33042
Tel *(305) 515-4004*
W littlepalmisland.com
Experience paradise on this private island with thatched villas and all the amenities one can think of. Ages 16 and up.

LITTLE TORCH KEY:
Parmer's Resort **$$$**
Hotel **Road Map** E5
565 Barry Ave, 33043
Tel *(305) 872-2157*
W parmersresort.com
Waterfront resort with elegant rooms, some with kitchens, and

a Lagoon Cottage that offers total privacy. Mini-golf, a bocce court and Continental breakfast.

LONG KEY:
Lime Tree Bay Motel $$
Motel Road Map F5
68500 Overseas Hwy, US 1 at MM 68.5, 33001
Tel *(305) 664-4740*
W limetreebayresort.com
This quiet Gulfside getaway has pleasant rooms. Also has a pool, beach access and free kayak hire.

MARATHON: Banana Bay
Resort and Marina $$
Resort Road Map E5
4590 Overseas Hwy, US 1 at MM 49.5, 33050
Tel *(305) 743-3500*
W bananabay.com
Well-located by the bay, this romantic getaway has attractive rooms, a pool, bocce court, and tennis and snorkeling facilities.

MARATHON:
Conch Key Cottages $$$
Luxury Road Map E5
US 1 at MM 62/3, 33050
Tel *(305) 289-1377*
W conchkeycottages.com
A great option on a tiny private island with a small beach. Guests stay in tin-roofed cottages built from old Florida pine.

MARATHON:
Hawk's Cay Resort $$$
Luxury Road Map E5
61 Hawk's Cay Blvd, 33050
Tel *(305) 743-7000*
W hawkscay.com
Swim with dolphins at the on-site research center of this stylish resort. Rooms feature West Indies-style decor. Also has a fishing dock and kids' programs.

MARATHON: Holiday Inn
Express & Suites $$$
Modern Road Map E5
13201 Overseas Hwy, 33050
Tel *(305) 289-0222*
W holidayinnkeys.com
Comfortable modern hotel in the

Keys. Offers top-class fitness and business facilities, and a pleasant pool. Free hot breakfast.

MARCO ISLAND:
The Boat House Motel $$
Motel Road Map E5
1180 Edlington Pl, 3414
Tel *(239) 642-2400*
W theboathousemotel.com
Family-owned motel on Marco River. Clean rooms, kitchenettes, pool, and a fishing dock.

MARCO ISLAND:
Hilton Marco Beach Resort $$$
Luxury Road Map E5
560 s Collier Blvd, 34145
Tel *(239) 394-5000*
W hiltonmarcoisland.com
Spacious, well-furnished rooms with balconies in this beachfront hotel. Spa and tennis courts.

MARCO ISLAND:
Marco Beach Ocean Resort $$$
Luxury Road Map E5
480 S Collier Blvd, 34145
Tel *(239) 393-1400*
W marcoresort.com
Stay in this luxury high-rise located by a 4-mile (6.5-km) beach. Suites with balconies, a rooftop pool, and a stunning sundeck.

MARCO ISLAND:
Marco Island Marriott $$$
Resort Road Map E5
400 S Collier Blvd, 34145
Tel *(239) 394-2511*
W marcoislandmarriott.com
A huge resort with everything one could ask for: a 3-mile (5-km) beach, two golf courses, tennis courts, and several pools.

MARCO ISLAND:
Olde Marco Inn & Suites $$$
Historic Road Map E5
100 Palm St, 34145
Tel *(239) 394-3131*
W oldemarcoinn.com
Dating to 1883, this historic building houses modern rooms and condo suites with lanais and kitchenettes. Beautiful garden and a fantastic French restaurant.

NAPLES: Sea Shell Motel $
Motel Road Map E4
82 9th St S, 34102
Tel *(239) 262-5129*
This no-frills budget motel has simply furnished rooms and some self-catering units.

NAPLES: Lighthouse Inn Motel $$
Motel Road Map E4
9140 Gulf Shore Dr, 34108
Tel *(239) 597-3345*
Old-fashioned motel. Spotless and simple efficiencies and suites with small kitchens. Great value.

NAPLES: Staybridge Suites $$
Modern Road Map E4
4805 N Tamiami Trail, 34103
Tel *(239) 643-8002*
W igh.com
Full-service suites with on-site laundry and fully-equipped kitchens. Free buffet breakfast.

NAPLES: Hotel Escalante $$$
Hotel Road Map E4
290 5th Ave S, 34102
Tel *(239) 659-3466*
W hotelescalante.com
Small boutique hotel in a secluded area but close to the beach. Attractive rooms and garden, plus many spa services.

NAPLES: Inn on Fifth $$$
Inn Road Map E4
699 Fifth Ave S, 34102
Tel *(239) 403-8777*
W innonfifth.com
Elegant rooms and special golf and tennis club privileges makes Inn on Fifth a good choice.

NAPLES: La Playa Resort $$$
Resort Road Map E4
9891 Gulf Shore Dr, 34108
Tel *(239) 597-3123*
W laplayaresort.com
Popular resort with a prime beachfront location, huge rooms, and an exclusive golf club.

NAPLES:
Naples Beach Hotel $$$
Resort Road Map E4
851 Gulf Shore Blvd, 34102
Tel *(239) 261-2222*
W naplesbeachotel.com
Golf course, tennis courts, on-site beach, and an excellent kids' program make this family-owned resort a perennial favorite.

NAPLES:
Waldorf Astoria Naples $$$
Resort Road Map E4
475 Seagate Dr, 34103
Tel *(239) 597-3232*
W waldorfastoria.com
Luxurious resort with lavish rooms, a pool with slides, and sports facilities.

The bright interior of a suite at Hawk's Cay Resort, Marathon

WHERE TO EAT AND DRINK

While fast food is a staple in Florida as anywhere in the US, the real joy of dining here comes from abundant fresh produce – from tropical fruits to seafood – all used to great effect by restaurants across the state. Waterfront views add to the pleasure of dining in the many eateries located along the bountiful coastline. Restaurants in Florida, from the trendiest establishments that set or follow the latest culinary fashions to more homely and traditional places, cater to every palate and budget. Wherever you travel, it is possible to find unique locally owned restaurants along with the familiar chains.

Miami Beach's famous Escopazzo restaurant *(see p330)*

Types of Restaurants

Florida's elite restaurants tend to have European-style (often French) menus, while still making the most of local fare. "New American" is another name for more creative takes on familiar dishes, using imaginative combinations and sauces. A breed of innovative chefs has combined Florida's fine produce with zesty Caribbean flavors to create a unique cuisine that people call New Florida or "Floribbean". Menus often change daily or weekly to ensure using the freshest of ingredients.

Fine dining can be found throughout the state, but Miami and the cities of the Gold and Gulf coasts have a special reputation for their restaurants. Some of the most famous chefs from across America have established outposts here, as well as in eateries of Walt Disney World® and Universal® in Orlando.

Florida boasts a large concentration of Caribbean and South American-inspired restaurants and cafés. There is also a special emphasis on Cuban food, especially in Miami and Tampa where the Cuban population is large. Southern dishes such as shrimp and grits and New Orleans-style blackened fish are popular as well.

Restaurants of every size and shape serve seafood, with coastal areas offering delectable freshly caught fish. One popular institution, the raw bar, offers fresh raw oysters or clams as well as steamed shrimp.

Vegetarians need not have any concern as almost every restaurant will have a choice of vegetarian dishes on the menu. Cafés and bars, for drinking and more informal eating, are listed on pages 348–9.

Eating Hours

Breakfast usually can be found anytime from 7am to 11am. Sunday brunch is an especially popular tradition served from around 10am to 2pm. Some establishments offer lavish brunch buffets.

Lunch is generally available from 11:30am to 2:30pm and the most popular dinner hours are between 6pm and 9pm. Many places stay open till later on Friday and Saturday evenings. The early-bird special, generally offered before 6pm at special rates, is intended for those who like to eat early. Eating hours can always change, so it would be wise to check.

Reservations

To avoid disappointment it is always wise to reserve a table, especially on weekends or at the more upscale or popular eateries. At some places, such as Joe's Stone Crab in Miami Beach *(see p330)*, diners cannot book ahead and instead must wait in line for a table. In such cases, it is always wise to dine early or late to minimize the waiting time. Reservations are a good idea during peak season.

Tips on Eating Out

Dining out in Florida is mostly an informal affair. There are very few restaurants that require a jacket or tie, and those that do will provide these for diners to wear. "Casual but neat" is the general rule.

Old-world Spanish decor at the Columbia Restaurant, Tampa *(see p345)*

All eateries in Florida are non-smoking establishments so smokers should be prepared to step outside if they want to light up.

Tips range from 15 to 20 percent. At sophisticated places, guests frequently tip a generous amount if the service has been good. The state sales tax of 6 percent is added automatically to all checks, but the tip should be calculated on the food amount alone.

Travelers' checks and credit cards are readily accepted at almost all eateries.

Outside dining at Aunt Catfish's in Daytona Beach *(see p339)*

Dining on a Budget

There are several ways to cut the food budget. Helpings in restaurants tend to be large, so an appetizer is often enough for a light meal. Patrons may also share dishes, but there could be a small charge for this. Some restaurants offer small plates or a choice of small servings of entrées. Most restaurants now have menus on their websites, making it easier to choose wisely.

All-you-can-eat buffets are a bargain, and some restaurants have cheaper meals on a prix fixe menu. It may be wise to call the restaurant ahead for such details as the times and conditions may vary.

Smaller restaurants sometimes advertise BYOB meaning you are welcome to bring your own bottle of wine and openers and glasses will be provided. This option, when available, can be a welcome saving.

If keen to eat in a chic place, remember that lunches are usually cheaper than dinners. Breakfast in hotels, however, can be woefully over-priced. Instead, join the locals at a nearby deli or diner. Choosing a hotel with Continental breakfast included is a real money-saver.

Some bars also serve reasonably priced food. Many offer free or half-priced hors d'oeuvres during happy hours. Sports bars have TVs for watching games, and also have inexpensive snacks on their menus.

Delis and supermarkets are good for picnic provisions; the former also often provide cooked dishes and sandwiches to be eaten on or off the premises. Many state parks have barbecue grills where you can grill your catch or whatever food you care to bring along. Many restaurants in the Keys will also grill your catch for a reduced price.

Menus

Menus throughout the state rely heavily on fresh fish and other seafood items such as clams, lobsters, shrimp, crab, and conch. You can also find crawfish, blackened fish (coated with Cajun spices and cooked quickly in a smoking hot pan), and gumbos. Beef, chicken, and pork are also readily available. Surf 'n' Turf is a popular combination of seafood and beef, usually steak and lobster. If "dolphin" appears on a Florida menu, it refers to mahi mahi. If guests are unsure about menu items or require a special menu, the staff will be pleased to help.

Children

Most restaurants are happy to accommodate the needs of younger diners. Many offer special menus with child-sized meals of dishes children like such as pasta, pizza, burgers, hot dogs, and fries. Most also provide high chairs or booster chairs; call ahead to check what is available.

Kids are not allowed in bars, but if food is served on the premises they can accompany adults and have a meal in an area away from the bar. Other than this, almost all places will welcome well-behaved youngsters.

Recommended Restaurants

A tourist mecca, Florida has thousands of restaurants to choose from. Serving diner food to fancy cuisine, the establishments listed on pages 329–47 are some of the best and have been selected for their quality of food and service. The listings also reflect factors such as authentic cuisine, outdoor dining, or live music. DK Choices represent the best of the best – be it value for money, a celebrity chef, unusual features, great ambience, or exceptional food. Within each price category, the entries are alphabetically listed by location.

Cheap eats at a picnic site in one of Florida's state parks

The Flavors of Florida

With an ideal climate, Florida is blessed with a profusion of tropical fruits, bountiful vegetables year-round, and fresh seafood from both ocean and gulf, and these are the major elements found in the state's cuisine. In the cities of central and south Florida, the large Cuban and Caribbean populations have made a strong culinary impact, and Latin America contributes dishes such as *ceviche*. In the north, food show the influence of neighboring southern states. But, in order to please the thousands of tourists who visit the "sunshine state," almost every type of international cuisine is available.

Giant shrimp

Fish straight from the ocean, ready for sale to local restaurateurs

Florida Seafood

Among the best of the local catch to watch for on Florida menus are amberjack, mahi-mahi, pompano, snapper, tuna, and wahoo. Grouper, part of the sea bass family, is especially popular. The fillets appear both as main dishes and in delicious sandwiches. Florida gulf shrimp, another favorite, is large, sweet, and tender. They may be boiled, peeled and served cold with cocktail sauce, cooked in a spicy sauce and served in the shell, or used in numerous other main courses.

Cuban Cuisine

In cities with large Cuban populations, like Tampa and Miami, many dining places serve dishes that show a strong Spanish influence. Roast pork, *arroz con pollo* (chicken with spiced rice), and paella are mainstays. Cuban sandwiches, and flan for dessert, are also typical.

Tropical Treats

Florida's tropical climate produces much of the exotic fruit found in America, from kumquats and papaya to lychees and star fruit. The variety grown means that a bountiful supply of top-quality produce is always in season. Weekly local farmers' markets, found in almost every community, are fun to visit.

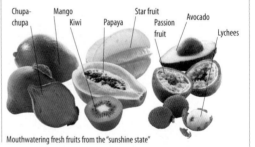

Chupa-chupa Mango Kiwi Papaya Star fruit Passion fruit Avocado Lychees

Mouthwatering fresh fruits from the "sunshine state"

Regional Dishes and Specialties

Stone crabs, rich, sweet, and firm in texture, are the most prized of Florida seafoods, perhaps partly because they are available only from mid-October to mid-May. The meat is always cooked, but is usually served chilled, with melted butter and mustard sauce. Conch (a giant sea snail), another important shellfish, may be served as an appetizer, in salads, or as the base for chowder. Shrimp comes in two varieties – large and pink-hued from the Gulf, or white and delicate from the Atlantic. The state's signature dessert is Key Lime Pie, truly authentic only when its tangy filling is made with the small, round, yellow-green, aromatic limes grown in the Florida Keys. Fish dishes may be grilled, sautéed, or pan-seared; but are often marinated with lime juice and served with sauces or side dishes made with local fruits.

Limes

Stone crab claws The claws are the only part of this local delicacy to be eaten, delicious dipped in butter and sauce.

Where to Eat and Drink

Miami
Miami Beach

11th Street Diner $
American **Map** 2 F3
1065 Washington Ave, 33139
Tel *(305) 534-6373*
Classic old-time diner with a
fun ambience. Serves favorites
such as meatloaf, fried chicken,
sandwiches, and burgers.

Big Pink $
American **Map** 2 E5
157 Collins Ave, 33139
Tel *(305) 532-4700*
Popular waterside café known
for its diner-type menu and big
portions. Good sandwiches and
salads, and all-day breakfast.

Café Charlotte $
Argentinian/Italian **Map** 2 F3
1497 Washington Ave, 33139
Tel *(305) 535-1522*
No-frills setting and delicious
Argentinian specialties including
skirt steak, *empanadas* (pastry
filled with meat, vegetables and
cheese), and lime chicken..

Lime Fresh $
Mexican **Map** 2 D3
1439 Alton Rd, 33139
Tel *(305) 532-5463*
Part of a reliable chain, with
reasonably priced Mexican
favorites including tacos, burritos,
quesadillas, and fajitas.

Puerto Sagua $
Cuban **Map** 2 E4
700 Collins Ave, 33139
Tel *(305) 673-1115*
A favorite since 1962 with a
good Cuban menu as well as
American turkey and grilled
cheese sandwiches.

Roasters 'n Toasters $
Deli **Map** F4
525 Arthur Godfrey Rd, 33140
Tel *(305) 531-7691*
New York-style deli with
everything from corned beef,
pastrami, and bagels to wraps,
sandwiches, and soups.

Rosinella $
Italian **Map** 2 E2
525 Lincoln Rd, 33139
Tel *(305) 672-8777*
Comfortable family-style dining
with home-made pastas and
budget-priced pizzas. Selection
of Italian and American wines.

Shake Shack $
American **Map** 2 D2
1111 Lincoln Rd, 33139
Tel *(305) 434-7787*
Come to Shake Shack for quality
burgers at bargain prices, plus
great fries and shakes worth
standing in line for.

DK Choice

Tap Tap Haitian $
Haitian **Map** 2 E4
819 5th St, 33139
Tel *(305) 672-2898*
Since 1994, this restaurant, art
gallery, and cultural center all
rolled into one has attracted a
vibrant, multi-cultural crowd.
Known for its authentic Haitian
dishes such as steamed whole
fish in lime sauce, shrimp in
Creole sauce, goat stew, sweet
potato pie, and banana fritters.

Balans $$
International **Map** 2 D2
1022 Lincoln Rd, 33139
Tel *(305) 534-9191*
With jambalaya, crab linguine,

Price Guide
Prices are based on a three-course meal
for one with glass of house wine, and all
unavoidable extra charges including tax.

$	up to $35
$$	$35 to 50
$$$	over $50

Thai curry, and burgers, this
British import has something
for everyone. Good brunch and
a busy bar.

Fratelli la Bufala $$
Italian **Road Map** F4
437 Washington Ave, 33139
Tel *(305) 532-0700*
Enjoy scrumptious pizza and
pasta at this Neapolitan chain
outlet. Good choice for a
reasonably priced meal.

Front Porch Café $$
American **Map** 2 F3
1458 Ocean Dr, 33139
Tel *(305) 531-8300*
An excellent choice for breakfast
and brunch, Front Porch also
serves dinner, with dishes
ranging from grilled chicken to
braised short ribs and steak.

News Café $$
American **Map** 2 F4
800 Ocean Dr, 33139
Tel *(305) 538-6397*
Large crowds flock this to round-
the-clock café serving crab cakes,
grilled salmon, pizza, and pasta.

Nexxt Café $$
International **Map** 2 E2
700 Lincoln Rd, 33139
Tel *(305) 532-6643*
Nexxt has a range of choices,
from small plates and tapas
to mains including Cajun
chicken and Miso salmon.
Good cocktail menu.

The colorful exterior of Big Pink

For more information on types of restaurants *see page 327*

DK Choice

1500 Degrees $$$
American   **Road Map** F4
4525 Collins Ave, 33140
Tel *(305) 674-5594*
Named for the temperature the chef prefers to cook the juicy steaks at, 1500 Degrees is a stylish restaurant at the Eden Roc Hotel. The daily changing creative menu features fresh farm-to-table fresh fare. The prix fixe three-course dinner is a treat not to be missed.

A Fish Called Avalon $$$
Seafood   **Map** 2 E4
700 Ocean Dr, 33139
Tel *(305) 532-1727*
Fresh seafood on offer, with some surprises such as orzo paella and crab-crusted grouper. Enjoy live music on the veranda.

Barton G. The Restaurant $$$
American   **Map** 2 D3
1427 West Ave, 33139
Tel *(305) 672-8881*
Glitzy spot, with whimsical decor and a focus on extravagant presentation and enticing fragrances. Try the king salmon and samurai tuna.

Casa Tua $$$
Italian   **Map** 2 E2
1700 James Ave, 33139
Tel *(305) 673-1010*
Dine on exquisite cuisine in Casa Tua's romantic dining room or garden. The honey-glazed duck breast and almond-crusted black cod are two delicious options.

Escopazzo $$$
Italian   **Map** 2 F3
1311 Washington Ave, 33139
Tel *(305) 674-9450*   **Closed** Mon
Escopazzo's chef serves up creative Italian dishes made with the freshest organic ingredients. Great service and decor reminiscent of a Tuscan courtyard.

Grillfish $$$
Seafood   **Map** 2 F2
1444 Collins Ave, 33139
Tel *(305) 538-9908*
A local favorite for its absolutely fresh seafood served with tasty sauces. There are also lots of seafood pasta combinations.

Joe's Stone Crab $$$
Seafood   **Map** 2 E5
11 Washington Ave, 33139
Tel *(305) 673-0365*   **Closed** Aug–Oct
Despite the long lines, Joe's is not be missed. On offer is fresh seafood and, of course, absolutely wonderful stone crabs.

Las Vacas Gordas $$$
Argentinian   **Road Map** F4
933 Normandy Dr, 33141
Tel *(305) 867-1717*
Enjoy big portions of juicy steak and well-priced Argentinian fare in a lively, contemporary setting.

Nobu Miami Beach $$$
Japanese   **Map** 2 F1
1901 Collins Ave, 33139
Tel *(305) 695-3232*
An international brand, with fantastic sushi and other Japanese specialties. Extremely popular spot, so book in advance.

Ola $$$
Latin American   **Map** 2 E2
1745 James Ave, 33139
Tel *(305) 695-9125*
One of Miami's best, Ola offers wonderful *seviche* (seafood cooked using citrus juice) and beef *churrasco (grilled steak)*. For dessert, try the chocolate cigar.

Osteria del Teatro $$$
Italian   **Map** 2 F3
1443 Washington Ave, 33139
Tel *(305) 538-7850*
An intimate oasis renowned for its excellent traditional North Italian veal and pasta dishes.

Prime One Twelve $$$
Steakhouse   **Map** 2 E5
112 Ocean Dr, 33139
Tel *(305) 532-8112*
Join Prime One Twelve's celebrity clientele and enjoy luscious steaks, dry-aged beef, and seafood.

Sardinia Enoteca Ristorante $$$
Italian   **Map** 2 D2
1801 Purdy Ave, 33139
Tel *(305) 531-2228*
Choose from dozens of Italian wines by the glass or bottle to be paired with delicious pastas and entrées.

The sophisticated bar at Azul, with ice-cold champagne nestled in the bar top

Spiga $$$
Italian   **Map** 2 E3
1228 Collins Ave, 33139
Tel *(305) 534-0079*
Handmade pastas are the specialty at this quiet, romantic restaurant. Try the green veal ravioli with mushrooms, or fettucine with shrimp and asparagus.

Tantra $$$
International   **Map** 2 E2
1445 Pennsylvania Ave, 33139
Tel *(305) 672-4765*   **Closed** Sun
Tantra's sensuous Asian decor complements the adventurous menu blending Asian, Caribbean, and European cuisine. There is also a popular lounge with a DJ.

Yuca $$$
Cuban   **Map** 2 E2
501 Lincoln Rd, 33139
Tel *(305) 532-9822*
Serves contemporary Cuban cuisine including guava baby-back ribs and plantain-coated mahi mahi. Also offers salsa classes.

Striking decor at Joe's Stone Crab

Downtown and Little Havana

Hy Vong $
Vietnamese **Road Map** F4
3458 SW 8th St, 33135
Tel *(305) 446-3674* **Closed** *Mon*
A reliable favorite for over 30 years, this tiny restaurant offers exquisite Vietnamese fare worth waiting in line for. They also offer cooking lessons.

Islas Canarias $
Cuban **Road Map** F4
285 NW 27th Ave, 33135
Tel *(305) 649-0440*
Decent Cuban favorites including sandwiches, pork, and chicken dishes. Great value.

La Casita $
Cuban/Mexican **Road Map** F4
3805 SW 8th St, 33134
Tel *(305) 448-8224*
Cuban café that also offers Mexican standards such as tacos, burritos, and enchiladas all at great prices.

People's Bar-B-Que $
Southern **Road Map** F4
360 NW 8th St, 33136
Tel *(305) 373-8080*
Quick and reliable soul food with ribs, pulled pork, mac 'n' cheese, and collard greens. Basic decor.

S&S Restaurant $
Diner **Map** 4 E1
1757 NE 2nd Ave, 33132
Tel *(305) 373-4291*
An old-time corner diner with counter seating. Delicious sandwiches and salads at remarkably low prices.

Versaille $
Cuban **Map** 4 E2
3335 8th St, 33135
Tel *(305) 444-0240*
Choose from two sampler plates for a delicious introduction to Cuban cuisine at Little Havana's best-known restaurant.

Azul $$$
American/Asian **Map** 4 F2
500 Brickell Key Dr, 33131
Tel *(305) 913-8288*
Closed *Sun & Mon*
Sophisticated dining in a gorgeous waterside setting. Fantastic menu of American dishes and Asian specialties. Go for the lobster pot pie or Berkshire pork loin.

DB Bistro Moderne $$$
French **Map** 4 F1
255 Biscayne Blvd, 33131
Tel *(305) 421-8800* **Closed** *Sun*
Run by celebrity chef Daniel Boulouds, this chic bistro is known for its *escargot* (snails), duck confit, and the extravagant but delectable sirloin burger.

Il Gabbiano $$$
Italian **Map** 4 F1
One Miami Tower, 335 S Biscaye Blvd, 33131
Tel *(305) 373-0063* **Closed** *Sun*
Enjoy inspired Italian cuisine in a sublime bayside setting. Delicious pastas and fantastic veal dishes.

Michael's Genuine Food & Drink $$$
American **Road Map** F4
33 NE 40th St, 33137
Tel *(305) 573-5550*
Trendy spot where all the ingredients are sourced fresh from the sea or nearby farms. Serves a range of dishes, from small to extra-large helpings.

Michy's $$$
American **Road Map** F4
6927 Biscayne Blvd, 33138
Tel *(305) 759-2001*
Upscale bistro run by a celebrity chef. Known for its luxurious comfort food that puts a new twist on family dishes.

Naoe $$$
Japanese **Map** 4 F2
661 Brickell Key Dr, 33131
Tel *(305) 947-6263* **Closed** *Mon*
For an extraordinary dining experience head to Naoe. Divine Japanese cuisine is served in a multi-course format priced by number of courses ordered.

The River Seafood and Oyster Bar $$$
Seafood **Map** 4 E2
650 S Miami Ave, 33130
Tel *(305) 530-1915*
Enjoy seafood of all kinds prepared in every way imaginable. Grand, sophisticated setting. The crab fried brown rice is a must-try.

DK Choice

Tuyo $$$
American **Map** 4 E1
415 NE 2nd Ave, 33132
Tel *(305) 337-3200* **Closed** *Sun & Mon*
The highly creative chef at Tuyo prepares delicious "Floribbean" cuisine by blending fresh local ingredients with Latin spices. Romantic setting atop the Miami Culinary Institute, with fantastic city-bay views. Some standouts from the daily changing menu include marinated duck breast, Keys yellowtail with citrus butter, *foie gras* and cornbread-stuffed quail.

Coral Gables and Coconut Grove

Jaguar $$
Latin American **Road Map** F5
3067 Grand Ave, 33133
Tel *(305) 444-0216*
Artfully seasoned Latin dishes and many grilled items feature in Jaguar's colorful tropical menu. Seafood taster platters available.

DK Choice

Seasons 52 $$
American **Road Map** F4
321 Miracle Mile, 33134
Tel *(305) 442-8552*
Choose from a range of fresh, healthy food, with no entrée over 475 calories, and dishes such as cedar plank roasted salmon and grilled T-bone lamb chops. Also sample from an extensive wine and drinks list that features pomegranate margarita martini and mandarin orange cosmopolitan. Live piano music in the bar adds to the charm.

The elegant lounge and bar at DB Bistro Moderne

For more information on types of restaurants *see page 327*

Caffe Abbracci $$$
Italian **Map** 5 C1
318 Aragon Ave, 33134
Tel *(305) 441-0700*
This is where Miami's elite go for authentic Italian. The owner is very welcoming, ensuring that diners feel relaxed and at home. Wide choice of American and European wines.

Calamari $$$
Italian **Road Map** F5
3540 Main Hwy, 33133
Tel *(305) 441-0219*
Courtyard diner known for its bountiful Sunday brunch buffet. Also serves delicious seafood specialities, pizza, and pasta.

George's in the Grove $$$
French **Road Map** F5
3145 Commodor Plaza, 33133
Tel *(305) 444-7878*
French bistro with lively ambience. Everything from mussels and steak frite to burgers and pizza. Free glass of champagne on arrival.

Gibraltar $$$
Mediterranean **Road Map** F5
4 Grove Island Dr, 33133
Tel *(305) 857-5007*
Gibraltar promises spectacular views and an appealing menu with signature dishes including seafood risotto, seafood *parrillada* (mixed grill) and secret spice chicken tagine.

La Palme d'Or $$$
French **Map** 5 A2
1200 Anastasia Ave, 33134
Tel *(305) 913-3201* **Closed** *Sun & Mon*
A great choice for formal dining and special occasions. Exquisite surroundings and traditional

French food including venison, rack of lamb, and lemon sole.

Le Bouchon du Grove $$$
French **Map** 6 F4
3430 Main Hwy, 33133
Tel *(305) 448-6060*
With delightful French posters on the walls, this chef-owned casual bistro serves award-winning French cuisine.

Ortanique on the Mile $$$
Caribbean **Map** 5 C1
278 Miracle Mile, 33134
Tel *(305) 446-7710*
Trendy Caribbean restaurant in the heart of historic Coral Gables. With lots of seafood and fresh fruits on the menu. Try one of their notable and delicious Bacardi mojitos.

Pascal on Ponce $$$
French **Map** 5 C2
2611 Ponce de Leon Blvd, 33134
Tel *(305) 444-2024* **Closed** *Sun*
This small, classy café covered with beautiful art pieces has a big reputation for fine food and a bargain prix fixe bistro menu.

Red Fish Grill $$$
Seafood **Road Map** F5
9610 Old Cutler Rd, 33156
Tel *(305) 668-8788* **Closed** *Mon*
Enjoy fine seafood in a romantic seaside setting in Matheson Hammock Park. Excellent wines.

Farther Afield

Mario the Baker $
Italian **Road Map** F4
14691 Biscayne Blvd, North Miami Beach, 33181
Tel *(305) 891-7641*
For a quick pizza and pasta fix, Mario does not disappoint. Try

the white sauce Alfredo pizza or over-stuffed nine-inch subs. Dine-in, takeout, and delivery.

Shorty's BBQ $
Southern **Road Map** F5
9200 Dixie Hwy, South Miami, 33156
Tel *(305) 670-7732*
Shorty's is well-known for its delectable Southern ribs, barbecued brisket, pulled pork sandwiches, and chicken. Good bargain lunch platters.

Sushi House $$
Asian **Road Map** F4
15911 Biscayne Blvd, North Miami Beach, 33160
Tel *(305) 947-6002* **Closed** *Mon*
Along with its specialty sushi, this chic Asian eatery offers a wide-ranging menu including Szechwan cuisine and dishes cooked on a *hibachi* (Japanese grill).

Cantina Beach $$$
Mexican **Road Map** F4
Ritz Carlton, 455 Grand Bay Dr, 33149
Tel *(305) 365-4622*
Great oceanside restaurant under a thatched roof. Enjoy Mexican favorites prepared with the usual Ritz pizzazz and choose from over 85 kinds of tequila. Also try the table-made guacamole.

Gourmet Diner $$$
Diner **Road Map** F4
13951 Biscayne Blvd, North Miami Beach, 33181
Tel *(305) 947-2255*
This retro diner has a quirky menu featuring everything from *escargot* (snails) and *filet mignon* to burgers and roasted chicken. The daily specials are also great.

Kitchen 305 $$$
American **Road Map** F4
16701 Collins Ave, Sunny Isles, 33160
Tel *(305) 749-2110*
Located in the lobby of the Newport Beachside Resort, Kitchen 305 is a trendy restaurant with an eclectic menu including paella, crab cakes, and *osso buco* (veal shank stew). Enjoy the all-you-can-eat lobster Wednesdays.

DK Choice

Rusty Pelican $$$
American **Road Map** F4
3201 Rickenbacker Causeway, 33149
Tel *(305) 361-3818*
With a creative chef at the helm and spectacular bay and city views from the dining room, Rusty Pelican is a great choice. Offers sushi, land or sea entrées, a bargain prix fixe menu and

The sun-soaked courtyard of Calamari in Coconut Grove

Key to Price Guide *see page 329*

The facade of Mexican restaurant Casa Maya Grill in Deerfield Beach

small plates for sharing. Try their signature dishes including bouilabaisse of lobster, seafood en papillote, and shrimp, clams, and mussels in lobster broth. There is a raw seafood bar as well.

Timo $$$
Mediterranean **Road Map** F4
17624 Collins Ave, Sunny Isles, 33160
Tel *(305) 936-1008*
An upscale eatery highly rated for its seasonal Italian-Mediterranean dishes. Try the *zuppa di pesce* (lobster, shellfish, and Sardinian couscous).

The Gold and Treasure Coasts

BOCA RATON: Ben's Kosher Deli
Deli **Road Map** F4 $
9942 Clint Moore Rd, 33496
Tel *(561) 470-9963*
Ben's is a busy New York-style deli with an extensive menu featuring corned beef, pastrami, potato pancakes, and stuffed cabbage. There is an inventive kid's menu available.

BOCA RATON: Tin Muffin Café $
American **Road Map** F4
364 E Palmetto Park Rd, 33432
Tel *(561) 392-9446*　**Closed** *Sun*
This appealing bakery and café offers delicious sandwiches, salads, and home-made soups. Popular lunch spot. Credit cards not accepted.

BOCA RATON: Abe & Louie's $$$
Steakhouse **Road Map** F4
2200 Glades Rd, 33431
Tel *(561) 447-0024*
An upscale Steakhouse with top-

quality meats, and an impressive wine list. Fun club ambience with leather seats and spacious booths. The bone-in filet mignon is a must try.

BOCA RATON: Kathy's Gazebo $$$
Continental **Road Map** F4
4199 N Federal Hwy, 33431
Tel *(561) 395-6033*　**Closed** *Sun*
An old-fashioned café known for Contentinental specialties such as rack of lamb, veal medallions, scampi, and Dover sole. Excellent wine and champagnes available.

BOCA RATON: Legal Seafoods $$$
Seafood **Road Map** F4
6000 W Glades Rd, 33431
Tel *(561) 447-2112*
Though part of a chain, this is still a great choice for fresh seafood – try the signature crab cakes, and delicious clam chowder.

BOCA RATON: Max's Grille $$$
American **Road Map** F4
404 Plaza Real, 33432
Tel *(561) 368-0080*
Diners are spoilt for choice at this popular, lively bistro with everything from chicken wings and salads to grilled meat and fish on the menu. Good brunches.

DK Choice

BOCA RATON: Sapori $$$
Italian **Road Map** F4
301 via de Palmas, 33432
Tel *(561) 367-9779*
The Italian word for 'flavors', Sapori is a small, unpretentious restaurant rightly known for its flavorful fish dishes and some of the city's best pasta. Expect surprises such as short

rib ravioli or sweet-and-sour salmon filet. Go on one of their pasta Thursdays when chef Marco Pindo explains ingredients and shows how each dish is made.

DANIA BEACH: Jaxson's $
Ice Cream Parlor **Road Map** F4
128 S Federal Hwy, 33004
Tel *(954) 923-4445*
Jaxson's serves fine sandwiches and salads, but its delicious and huge ice creams are the big draw. Good ambience with colorful memorabilia on the walls.

DANIA BEACH: Le Petit Café De Dania $$
French **Road Map** F4
3308 Griffin Rd, 33312
Tel *(954) 967-9912*　**Closed** *Mon*
Authentic French favorites prepared by chefs from Brittany in a welcoming, intimate bistro setting. Try the specialty crêpes.

DAVIE: Buca di Beppo $
Italian **Road Map** F4
3355 S University Dr, 33328
Tel *(954) 577-3287*
Enjoy big portions of tomato sauce based Italian perennials at the lively Buca di Beppo. Family-style portions at affordable prices. Delicious desserts as well.

DEERFIELD BEACH: Casa Maya Grill $
Mexican **Road Map** F4
301 SE 15th Terrace, Cove Shopping Ctr, 33441
Tel *(954) 570-6101*
Authentic Mexican dishes such as tacos, enchiladas and burritos served at reasonable prices in a pleasing setting with lots of Mayan artwork. Try the refreshing margaritas and sangrias.

For more information on types of restaurants *see page 327*

DEERFIELD BEACH:
Little Havana $
Cuban **Road Map** F4
721 S Federal Hwy, 33441
Tel *(954) 427-6000*
Family-owned place serving
authentic Cuban fare and home-
made bread. Good daily dinner
specials. Music on weekends.

DELRAY BEACH:
Caffe Luna Rosa $$
Italian **Road Map** F4
34 S Ocean Blvd, 33483
Tel *(561) 274-9404*
Serving a varied menu during
the day and exclusively Italian
cuisine in the evening, Caffe Luna
Rosa guarantees a great meal in a
beautiful beach-side setting.

DELRAY BEACH:
Sundy House Restaurant $$$
American **Road Map** F4
106 S Swinton Ave, 33444
Tel *(561) 272-5678* **Closed** *Mon*
Savor well-prepared American
fare in a romantic garden setting
with an outdoor bar. Great Sunday
brunch with lots of seafood and
Mediterranean dishes.

FORT LAUDERDALE:
The Floridian $
Diner **Road Map** F4
1410 E Las Olas Blvd, 33301
Tel *(954) 463-4041*
An old-time diner open round
the clock. Serves big portions of
hearty fare at great prices.

FORT LAUDERDALE:
By Word of Mouth $$
American **Road Map** F4
3200 NE 12th Ave, 33334
Tel *(954) 564-3663* **Closed** *Sun*
Sample fine American entrées
and delectable desserts at this
suburban restaurant. Choose from
the day's offerings shown off in
the display case.

FORT LAUDERDALE:
Tarpon Bend $$
American **Road Map** F4
200 SW 2nd Ave, 33301
Tel *(954) 523-3233*
A lively sports bar known for its
happy hour and young clientele.
Decent grilled fish, burgers, and
beer on tap.

FORT LAUDERDALE: 15h Street
Fisheries & Dockside Café $$$
Seafood **Road Map** F4
1900 SE 15th St, 33316
Tel *(954) 763-2777*
Watch the boats and feed
the tarpons at this café by the
marina. Delicious seafood on
offer, along with a more casual
menu for light snacking. Good
bar. Arrival by boat or car.

The dining room of The Floridian in Fort Lauderdale

FORT LAUDERDALE:
Blue Moon Fish Co. $$$
Seafood **Road Map** F4
44405 Tradewinds Ave, 33308
Tel *(954) 267-9888*
Dine on fresh seafood while
watching yachts sail along the
Intracoastal. Good two-for-one
lunches. Reserve ahead and
ask for alfresco seating.

FORT LAUDERDALE:
Café Seville $$$
Spanish **Road Map** F4
2768 Oakland Park Blvd, 33306
Tel *(954) 565-1148* **Closed** *Sun*
Plentiful tapas, gazpacho and
paella among the many Spanish
favorites at Café Sevile. Extensive
list of Spanish wines.

FORT LAUDERDALE: Canyon $$$
American **Road Map** F4
1818 E Sunrise Blvd, 33304
Tel *(954) 475-1950*
Trendy and highly popular spot
known for big portions made
from locally sourced produce,
and its prickly pear margaritas.
No reservations taken so expect
long lines.

FORT LAUDERDALE:
Casablanca Café $$$
American **Road Map** F4
3049 Alhambra St, 33304
Tel *(954) 764-3500*
Casablanca has a beautiful,
romantic setting with ocean
views and live music. The
extensive menu features chili-
dusted sea scallops, walnut
chicken, and Atlantic swordfish.

FORT LAUDERDALE:
Eduardo de San Angel $$$
Mexican **Road Map** F4
2822 E Commercial Blvd, 33308
Tel *(954) 772-4731* **Closed** *Sun*
Great Mexican fine-dining
experience. The chef-owner
serves truly gourmet food in a
warm hacienda-style setting.

FORT LAUDERDALE:
Greek Islands Taverna $$$
Greek **Road Map** F4
3300 N Ocean Blvd, 33308
Tel *(954) 568-0008*
Excellent Greek place where
loyal patrons line up to sample
the *meze*, fresh fish, and lamb.
A range of Greek and other
international wines on offer.

FORT LAUDERDALE:
Le Café de Paris $$$
French **Road Map** F4
715 E Las Olas Blvd, 33301
Tel *(954) 467-2900*
A local institution since 1962,
this upscale and elegant French
restaurant has *escargot* (snails)
and ducklings on the menu,
along with delicious dinner
crêpes for the thrifty.

FORT LAUDERDALE:
Lobster Bar Sea Grille $$$
Seafood/Steakhouse **Road Map** F4
450 E Las Olas, 33301
Tel *(954) 772-2675*
Delectable fresh seafood,
live lobsters, and prime steaks
served in an upscale yet casual
atmosphere. Try their home-
made ice creams and sorbets.

DK Choice

FORT LAUDERDALE:
Market 17 $$$
American **Road Map** F4
1850 SE 17th St, 33316
Tel *(954) 835-5507* **Closed** *May–*
Oct: Mon
The elegant food at Market 17
is prepared using fresh farm-to-
table organic produce. Choose
from petite and large entrées,
including pan-roasted free
range chicken and sautéed Key
West red shrimp. Over 350 wines
to choose from. Great happy
hour from 4:30 to 7pm with
half-priced drinks and appetizers.

Key to Price Guide *see page 329*

FORT LAUDERDALE:
Sette Bello $$$
Italian **Road Map** F4
6241 N Federal Hwy, 33308
Tel *(954) 351-0505* **Closed** *Sun*
Decorated with traditional Italian flare, this restaurant is run by an attentive chef known for his well-prepared classics and ricotta cheesecake. Good daily specials.

FORT LAUDERDALE: Valentino's
Cucina Italiana $$$
Italian **Road Map** F4
620 S Federal Hwy, 33301
Tel *(954) 523-5767* **Closed** *Sun*
Innovative Italian cuisine and superb service are hallmarks of this chef-owned sophisti-cated restaurant. Fine dining at its best.

HOLLYWOOD:
Las Vegas Cuban Cuisine $
Cuban **Road Map** F4
1212 N State Rd 7, 33021
Tel *(954) 961-1001*
Part of a small chain that promises big portions of tasty Cuban fare at low prices. Good lunch specials and a kids' menu.

HOLLYWOOD: Le Tub Saloon $
American **Road Map** F4
1100 N Ocean Dr, 33019
Tel *(954) 921-9425*
A busy outdoor seating saloon in a trendy gas station setting. Serves legendary burgers and brews, and delicious Key Lime pie.

HOLLYWOOD: Taverna Opa $$
Greek **Road Map** F4
410 N Ocean Dr, 33019
Tel *(954) 929-4010*
A fun place with belly dancers and Intracoastal views. Choose from delicious *meze*, grilled fish, lamb, and souvlaki platters, accompanied by Greek wines.

JENSEN BEACH:
11 Maple Street $$$
American **Road Map** F4
3224 NE Maple Ave, 34957
Tel *(772) 334-7714* **Closed** *Sun*
Quaint homely eatery with a sophisticated menu. Artful small plates for sharing with octopus, quail, ribs, and steak on offer.

PALM BEACH: Pizza Al Fresco $$
Italian **Road Map** F4
14 Via Mizner, 33480
Tel *(561) 832-0032* **Closed** *Sun*
Savor delicious thin-crust pizza straight from a wood-burning oven plus a range of entrées in a lovely garden setting. Great choice for breakfast.

PALM BEACH:
Bice Ristorante $$$
Italian **Road Map** F4
313 1/2 Worth Ave, 33480
Tel *(561) 835-1600*
Upscale, high-quality Italian cuisine served in a swanky setting. Fantastic landscaped patio and attentive service.

PALM BEACH: Bonefish Grill $$$
Seafood **Road Map** F4
11658 US Hwy 1, 33408
Tel *(561) 799-2965*
This chain outlet near Palm Beach serves reliably fresh fish, oysters, lobsters and more. Good martinis. Lively spot, though a bit noisy.

DK Choice

PALM BEACH: Buccan $$$
American **Road Map** F4
350 S County Rd, 33480
Tel *(561) 833-3450*
With a highly renowned chef, an energetic vibe and a creative menu featuring many small plates to share, Buccan stands out from the rest. The menu

---

goes beyond steak and swordfish to offer a range of meals from short rib *empanadas* (stuffed pastry), hot dog paninis to wood-fired pizza with quail or lamb chop toppings.

PALM BEACH: Café Boulud $$$
French **Road Map** F4
301 Australian Ave, 33480
Tel *(561) 655-6060*
New York's star chef Daniel Boulud brings elegant French cuisine to the south. The prix fixe lunch here is a great bargain.

PALM BEACH:
Chez Jean Pierre $$$
French **Road Map** F4
132 N County Rd, 33480
Tel *(561) 833-1171* **Closed** *Sun*
With arty surroundings and elegant cuisine, Chez Jean Pierre is worth the splurge. Specialities include dover sole and profiteroles.

PALM BEACH: Echo $$$
Asian **Road Map** F4
230A Sunrise Ave, 33480
Tel *(868) 918-1719* **Closed** *Mon*
Sample excellent sushi and delicious entrées like Thai roast duck and lemon chicken. Sleek environs with a lively bar.

PALM BEACH:
Palm Beach Grill $$$
American **Road Map** F4
340 Royal Poinciana Way, 33480
Tel *(561) 835-1077*
Lively restaurant serving reliably delicious ribs and snappers among other American favorites. Key lime pie and burgers for the thrifty.

POMPANO BEACH: Calypso $$
Caribbean **Road Map** F4
460 S Cypress Rd, 33060
Tel *(954) 942-1633* **Closed** *Sat & Sun*
Relish island favorites such as Jamaican jerk chicken, West Indian curries, and conch chowder in Calypso's no-frills setting.

DK Choice

POMPANO BEACH:
Café Maxx $$$
American **Road Map** F4
2601 E Atlantic Blvd, 33062
Tel *(954) 782-0606*
Lovers of fine cuisine have been making pilgrimage to Café Maxx since 1984. An impressive wine list augments the chef's innovative offerings that include jerk-spiced scallops, pine nut-crusted rack of lamb, and pumpkin bisque.

The interior of Italian restaurant Sette Bello in Fort Lauderdale

For more information on types of restaurants *see page 327*

The entrance and terrace of French bistro Pistache in West Palm Beach

VERO BEACH: Ocean Grill $$$
American   Road Map F3
1050 Sexton Plaza, 32963
Tel *(772) 231-5409*
Enjoy fine dining on a sand dune with beautiful ocean views. There is a varied menu with many seafood options. Kids' menu available.

WEST PALM BEACH: Agora $
Turkish   Road Map F4
2505 North Dixie Hwy, 33407
Tel *(561) 651-7474*   **Closed** *Sun*
Agora offers a combination of traditional Turkish classics and modern interpretations of Mediterranean dishes paired with unusual Turkish wines.

WEST PALM BEACH:
Hot Pie Pizza $
Pizza   Road Map F4
123 S Olive Ave, 33401
Tel *(561) 655-2511*
Thin-crust pizzas, burgers, and pastas on offer at this eatery. The authentic New York-style coal oven adds to the exposed brick-walls and wooden-booth ambience.

WEST PALM BEACH:
Pistache $$$
French   Road Map F4
101 N Clematis St, 33401
Tel *(561) 833-5090*
The menu at this French bistro features mussels, coq au vin, and crêpes. Terrace seating overlooking the Intracoastal Waterway.

WEST PALM BEACH:
Rhythm Café $$$
American   Road Map F4
3800A S Dixie Hwy, 33405
Tel *(561) 833-3406*   **Closed** *Mon*
Located in a converted gas station, this quirky café in the antique district offers tapas and the catch of the day cooked many ways.

Orlando and the Space Coast

COCOA: Café Margaux $$$
French   Road Map F3
220 Brevard Ave, 32922
Tel *(321) 639-8343*   **Closed** *Sun*
French fine dining with creative choices such as filo-encased Norwegian salmon, and pear, brie, and walnut-stuffed pork loin. Exceptional wines.

COCOA BEACH: Oh Shucks $
Seafood   Road Map F3
401 Meade Ave, 32931
Tel *(321) 783-7549*
Casual open-air dining located on a pier. Menu includes oysters, coconut beer shrimp, and crab legs. Home-made Key lime pie.

COCOA BEACH:
Pompano Grill $$
Seafood   Road Map F3
110 N Brevard Ave, 32931
Tel *(321) 784-9005*   **Closed** *Sun & Mon*
Extremely popular café offering fresh local catch and excellent seafood crêpes. A small place, so reserve ahead.

COCOA BEACH: The Fat Snook $$
Seafood   Road Map F3
2464 Atlantic Ave, 32931
Tel *(321) 784-1190*
Family-owned restaurant offering creative seafood specialties, as well as beef, chicken, and Caribbean-inspired dishes. A relaxed, casual atmosphere.

INTERNATIONAL DRIVE:
Bahama Breeze $$
Caribbean   Road Map E2
8849 International Dr, 32819
Tel *(407) 248-2499*
Part of the top-quality chain popular for its great Caribbean menu and tropical drinks. Try the coconut shrimp and pulled pork sliders. Great island ambience.

INTERNATIONAL DRIVE:
Cuba Libre $$$
Cuban   Road Map E2
9101 International Dr, 32819
Tel *(407) 226-1600*
Decent Cuban fare offered in a festive ambience reminiscent of Havana, complete with refreshing mojitos, sangrias, and salsa dancing on Saturdays.

INTERNATIONAL DRIVE:
Everglades $$$
Steakhouse   Road Map E2
Rosen Center Hotel, 9840 International Dr, 32819
Tel *(407) 996-9840*
This restaurant celebrates "everything Florida" including fresh Florida grouper, rock shrimp, venison steak, and their specialty dish – gator chowder soup. Also try the Key lime pie.

INTERNATIONAL DRIVE:
Napa at the Peabody $$$
American   Road Map E2
9801 International Dr, 32819
Tel *(407) 352-4000*
Upscale restaurant facing a grotto pool. Serves organic and fresh Californian cuisine, albeit with a Floridian take on it. Don't miss the signature dish, *cioppino* (fish stew).

INTERNATIONAL DRIVE:
The Capital Grille $$$
Steakhouse   Road Map E2
9101 International Dr, 32819
Tel *(407) 370-4392*
This high-end restaurant chain serves only the choicest of steaks and delicious side dishes. Try the chef's daily seafood platter. Expensive but worth it.

INTERNATIONAL DRIVE:
The Oceanaire $$$
Seafood   Road Map E2
9101 International Dr, 32819
Tel *(407) 363-4801*
Perfectly prepared seafood and attentive service. Sleek setting with ocean liner decor. Opt for the quieter patio seating.

KISSIMMEE: Pacino's Italian
Ristorante $$$
Italian   Road Map E3
5795 W Hwy 192, 34746
Tel *(407) 396-8022*
Elegant, traditional Italian restaurant serving wood-fired brick-oven pizzas, grilled steaks and chops, pastas, and seafood. Congenial ambience.

LAKE BUENA VISTA:
Hemingway's $$$
Seafood   Road Map E2
Hyatt Regency Resort, 1 Grand Cypress Blvd, 32836
Tel *(407) 239-3854*
Inspired by Ernest Hemingway's fishing exploits, this restaurant offers fantastic seafood including local swordfish, Florida rock shrimp, mahi mahi, and Cayo Huesto crab cakes. Ask for their signature drink Papa's Doble, concoted by Hemingway himself.

ORLANDO: Little Saigon $
Vietnamese   Road Map F2
1106 Colonial Dr, 32803
Tel *(407) 423-8539*
A neighborhood favorite, Little Saigon offers well-priced, authentic Vietnamese fare. Delicious appetizers and noodle and rice dishes.

ORLANDO: Pine Twenty 2 $
American   Road Map E2
22 E Pine St, 32801
Tel *(407) 574-2160*
Choose from excellent build-it-yourself burgers, barbecue dishes, and sweet potato fries. The emphasis here is on organic, hormone-free meats. Good wine and beer options.

ORLANDO: Seasons 52 $$
American   Road Map E2
7700 Sand Lake Rd, 32819
Tel *(407) 354-5212*
Seasons 52 is proof that healthy, low-calorie meals can still be utterly delicious. Good happy-hour 'Flights and Flatbreads', with exceptional hand-selected wines and flatbreads.

ORLANDO: Smokey Bones $$
American   Road Map F2
3400 E Colonial Dr, 32803
Tel *(407) 894-1511*
Part of a chain, this popular

sports bar offers a hearty menu of generous wings, baby-back ribs, pulled pork, brisket, and burgers.

DK Choice

ORLANDO: Christini's
Ristorante $$$
Italian   Road Map E2
7600 Dr. Phillips Blvd, 32819
Tel *(407) 583-4472*
Having received several awards for both its food and wine, this bastion of fine dining has been a favorite for over 25 years. Beautiful wood paneling, celebrity photographs, and paintings add to Christini's warm ambience. Those who find the meat dishes prohibitively expensive can choose from the equally delicious and more affordable chicken or pasta dishes on the menu.

ORLANDO: FishBones $$$
Steakhouse/Seafood Road Map E2
6707 Sand Lake Rd, 32819
Tel *(407) 352-0135*
Savor steak, prime ribs, chops and chicken prepared in an open pit grill. Extensive menu of fresh seafood as well. Attentive staff assist in pairing of the food with the perfect wine.

ORLANDO: Le Coq au Vin $$$
French   Road Map F2
4800 S Orange Ave, 32806
Tel *(407) 851-6980*   **Closed** *Mon*
Quality French café renowned for bronzed fish with roasted pecans and citrus *beurre blanc* (butter sauce) cooked in cast-iron skillet.

ORLANDO: The Boheme $$$
American   Road Map F2
325 S Orange Ave, 32801
Tel *(407) 248-2499*
Fine dining in a gorgeous setting

replete with elegant art, stately columns, and music and cocktails in the piano lounge. Renowned Jazz brunch on Sundays.

UNIVERSAL ORLANDO®:
Bubba Gump Shrimp $$
Seafood   Road Map E3
6000 Universal Blvd, 32819
Tel *(407) 903-0044*
Shrimp mac 'n' cheese and popcorn shrimp are favorites at this familiar chain outlet with lots of options on the extensive menu. Fun atmosphere and a kids' menu.

UNIVERSAL ORLANDO®:
Emeril's Orlando $$$
Creole   Road Map E3
6000 Universal Blvd, 32819
Tel *(407) 224-2424*
New Orlean's Creole favorites re-created in a lofty, modern setting with an open kitchen. Kids' menu also available.

UNIVERSAL ORLANDO®:
Emeril's Tchoup Chop $$$
Asian   Road Map E3
6300 Hollywood Way, 32819
Tel *(407) 503-2467*
Choose from an interesting Asian menu featuring banana leaf-wrapped pork, Chinese spiced lamb shank, grilled garlic tiger shrimp and more. Serene surroundings. Fantastic tiki classics and signature cocktails.

WALT DISNEY WORLD®:
Chef Mickey's $
American   Road Map E3
Contemporary Resort, 4600 N World Dr, 32830
Tel *(407) 824-1000*
A great treat for the whole family. Gorge on the bountiful American buffet and get to meet Mickey, Minnie, Donald and other Disney friends. The sundae bar is especially popular with children.

The warmly decorated dining room with exceptional views at Seasons 52 in Orlando

For more information on types of restaurants *see page 327*

The well-stocked bar at Flying Fish Café in Walt Disney World®

DK Choice

WALT DISNEY WORLD®:
Boma-Flavors of Africa $$
African **Road Map** E3
*Animal Kingdom Lodge, 2901
Osceola Pkwy, 32830*
Tel *(407) 938-4722*
Boma features all the color and
flavor of an African market–
with a thatched roof, tree trunk
tabletops, and an amazing array
of serving stations offering
delicately spiced meats and
fish, along with curries, and mac
'n' cheese. For dessert, go for
the Zebra Dome, a chocolate
mousse striped with dark and
white chocolate.

WALT DISNEY WORLD®:
Bongos Cuban Café $$
Cuban **Road Map** E3
*Downtown Disney, 1498 E Buena
Vista Dr, 32830*
Tel *(407) 828-0999*
Cuban specials like shrimp criolla,
shredded beef, and fried rice.
Good kids' menu and fun late-
night dancing for adults.
Gorgeous setting in a re-created
1950s Havana nightclub.

WALT DISNEY WORLD®:
Cape May Café $$
Seafood **Road Map** E3
*Beach Club Resort, 1800 Epcot
Resorts Blvd, 32836*
Tel *(407) 939-3463*
Admiral Goofy presides over
breakfast, while evenings bring
traditional New England seafood
in Cape May Café's relaxed
beach-like setting.

WALT DISNEY WORLD®:
Ohana $$
Polynesian **Road Map** E3
*Polynesian Resort, 1600 Seven
Seas Dr, 32836*
Tel *(407) 824-1334*
Amidst storytellers, coconut

races and other festive fun,
Ohana serves up excellent
Polynesian food cooked in an
open pit and served on
skewers.

WALT DISNEY WORLD®:
Whispering Canyon Café $$
American **Road Map** E3
*Wilderness Lodge Resort, 901
Timberline Dr, 32830*
Tel *(407) 939-3463*
A log cabin feast complete with
sing-alongs and hobby horse
races. Try the bottomless shakes,
and 'smores cheesecakes.

WALT DISNEY WORLD®:
California Grill $$$
American/Japanese **Road Map** E3
*Contemporary Resort, 4600
N World Dr, 32830*
Tel *(407) 939-3463*
California Grill serves superb
sushi along with creative takes
on Florida snapper, oak-fired
beef, and organic chicken.
Choose from a list of excellent
wines and enjoy great views.

WALT DISNEY WORLD®:
Cinderella's Royal Table $$$
American **Road Map** E3
*Fantasyland, Magic Kingdom Dr,
32830*
Tel *(407) 939-3463*
Experience fairytale dining in a
grand hall with Cinderella and
her prince. Souvenir photo is
included in the tab.

WALT DISNEY WORLD®:
Flying Fish Café $$$
Seafood **Road Map** E3
*Boardwalk Inn, 2101 Epcot Resorts
Blvd, 32830*
Tel *(407) 939-2359*
Upscale dining amid a
whimsical seaside setting.
Sample from an extensive
seafood menu, including oak-
grilled mahi mahi and potato-
wrapped snapper.

DK Choice

WALT DISNEY WORLD®:
Les Chefs de France $$$
French **Road Map** E3
Epcot World Showcase, 32830
Tel *(407) 827-8709*
Located in Epcot's France
Pavilion, Les Chefs de France
promises a great dining
experience. The brasserie menu
created by famous French chefs,
with dishes such as Coquille St.
Jacques and duckling with
cherries, appeals to the adults.
Kids get their own menu and
visits from Ratatouille's Chef
Remy. The signature dessert,
profiterole, is a must-try. The prix
fixe menu is unbeatable value.

WALT DISNEY WORLD®:
Portobellow $$$
Italian **Road Map** E3
*Downtown Disney, 1650 E Buena
Vista Dr, 32830*
Tel *(407) 934-8888*
The terrace of this gourmet
eatery overlooks a lagoon.
Serves Italian favorites as well
as steak and seafood. Good
kids' menu.

WALT DISNEY WORLD®:
Todd English's Bluezoo $$$
Seafood **Road Map** E3
*Swan and Dolphin, 1500 Epcot
Resorts Blvd, 32830*
Tel *(407) 934-1111*
Bluezoo features a stunning
"undersea" setting for celebrity
chef Todd English's out-
standing seafood creations.
Kids' menu available.

WALT DISNEY WORLD®:
T-REX $$$
American **Road Map** E3
1676 E Buena Vista Dr, 32830
Tel *(407) 828-8739*
Dinosaurs abound at T-REX.
The quirky menu offers paleo

shrimp, bronto burgers, fossil fish and chips, chocolate extinction and more.

WALT DISNEY WORLD®:
Victoria & Albert's $$$
American   Road Map E3
Grand Floridian Resort, 4401 Floridian Way, 32830
Tel *(407) 939-7707*
Where Victorian elegance meets haute American cuisine. One of the top fine-dining choices in the area with an elegant multi-course prix fixe menu. Excellent wine list.

WALT DISNEY WORLD®:
Wolfgang Puck Grand Café $$$
American/Japanese   Road Map E3
Downtown Disney, 1482 E Buena Vista Dr, 32830
Tel *(407) 938-9653*
This café plus formal restaurant has a wide menu ranging from pizza to sushi to Puck's signature fine-dining cuisine.

WINTER PARK:
Café de France $$$
French   Road Map E2
526 Park Ave S, 32789
Tel *(407) 647-1869*   **Closed** *Sun & Mon*
Reliable favorites at this chic French café include duckling, *coq au vin*, and grilled salmon. Range of French and other European wines on offer.

WINTER PARK: Park
Plaza Gardens $$$
European   Road Map E2
319 Park Ave S, 32789
Tel *(407) 645-2475*
This romantic café features excellent entrées such as rack of lamb, pork tenderloin, and lobster tail *francaise* in its extensive Continental menu. Great value happy hour.

WINTER PARK:
Ravenous Pig $$$
Gastropub   Road Map E2
1234 N Orange Ave, 32789
Tel *(407) 628-2333*   **Closed** *Sun & Mon*
The chef-owner has put an emphasis on comfort food with a sophisticated gastronomic twist, such as tea-smoked salmon and pork porterhouse.

The Northeast

DAYTONA BEACH:
Hog Heaven $
American   Road Map E2
37 N Atlantic Ave, 32118
Tel *(386) 257-1212*
Standard barbecue joint with all the fixings: ribs, pulled pork, chicken, and four kinds of sauce. Good kids' baskets.

DK Choice

DAYTONA BEACH: Aunt Catfish's On the River $$$
American   Road Map E2
4009 Halifax Dr, Port Orange, 32127
Tel *(386) 767-4768*
A laid-back Old South outpost by the river, well known for its buffet bar. Feast on grilled or fried catfish, fried alligator, ribs, coconut shrimp, and great salads served with hush puppies (deep-fried cornmeal) and the restaurant's famous cinnamon rolls. Big, delicious brunch on Sunday and music every night.

DAYTONA BEACH: Azure $$$
American   Road Map E2
2637 S Atlantic Ave, 32118
Tel *(386) 767-7356*
One of Daytona Beach's best restaurants, Azure has an elegant dining room with an oceanfront terrace. Specialties include *étouffée* (seafood and rice covered in thick sauce), and house-cured steak.

DAYTONA BEACH:
Down the Hatch $$$
Seafood   Road Map E2
4894 Front St, 32127
Tel *(386) 761-4831*
This informal eatery overlooking Ponce Inlet offers big portions of fresh seafood, as well as steaks and pasta. Interesting daily specials.

FERNANDINA BEACH:
29 South $$$
American   Road Map E1
29 S 3rd St, 32034
Tel *(904) 799-7919*
An eclectic menu with small plates and creative entrées such shrimp and grits (cornmeal), wild salmon, and short ribs. Large salads and pizzas available too.

FERNANDINA BEACH:
Joe's 2nd Street Bistro $$$
American   Road Map E1
14 S 2nd St, 32034
Tel *(904) 321-2558*
Set in a restored early 20th-century home with a pleasant courtyard, this elegant eatery offers a varied menu featuring almond-crusted tilapia, leg of lamb, pork schnitzel, and pastas.

FERNANDINA BEACH: Salt $$$
American   Road Map E1
2750 Amelia Island Pkwy, 32034
Tel *(904) 277-1100*   **Closed** *Mon*
Sophisticated, award-winning dining with wood-burning grilled dishes and a unique menu of salted meats. Great for special occasions. Decadent soufflés provide the perfect ending.

GAINESVILLE:
Harry's Seafood Bar & Grill $$
Seafood/Creole   Road Map D2
110 SE 1st St, 32601
Tel *(352) 372-1555*
Sample from a range of New Orleans favorites such as jambalaya, crawfish, and shrimp creole, along with crab cakes, fried platters, and large salads.

GAINESVILLE:
Paramount Grill $$
American   Road Map D2
12 SW 1st Ave, 32605
Tel *(352) 378-3398*
An appealing downtown restaurant, whose innovative owner-chef uses the freshest of ingredients to create brilliant combinations. Pair the dishes with one of many excellent American and international wines.

Beautifully presented dish from the menu at Café de France in Winter Park

For more information on types of restaurants *see page 327*

Local art adorns the walls at Florida Cracker Café in St. Augustine

JACKSONVILLE:
Clark's Fish Camp   **$$**
American   **Road Map** E1
12903 Hood Landing Rd, 32258
Tel *(904) 268-3474*
Featuring standard seafood along with alligator, kangaroo, and ostrich dishes, Clark's is a rustic and quirky place also known for its taxidermy collection.

JACKSONVILLE: bb's   **$$$**
American   **Road Map** E1
1019 Hendricks Ave, 32207
Tel *(904) 306-0100*   **Closed** *Sun*
This popular restaurant and bar offers light fare as well as fine cuisine featuring specialty seafood. Bargain prix fixe on weeknights.

JACKSONVILLE: Biscottis   **$$$**
American   **Road Map** E1
3556 St. Johns Ave, 32205
Tel *(904) 387-2060*
An elegant place with local art and exposed brick. On offer are big salads, nightly entrée specials, great desserts, and a kids' menu.

JACKSONVILLE: Bistro Aix   **$$$**
American   **Road Map** E1
1440 San Marco Blvd, 32207
Tel *(904) 398-1949*
This hip bistro in Jacksonville's historic area offers small plates as well as pizzas and French treats such as mussels and steak frites.

DK Choice

JACKSONVILLE:
Matthew's Restaurant $$$
American   **Road Map** E1
2107 Hendricks Ave, 32207
Tel *(904) 396-9922*   **Closed** *Sun*
This is a great fine-dining choice with sleek and elegant

surroundings and a 2,000-bottle wine cellar. Matthew Meure's beautifully presented fare is well-priced, given the high quality. Excellent entrées including pistachio-crusted Arctic char, steak with portobello mushrooms, and Gorgonzola cheese. Choose from great desserts like flourless chocolate cake and ricotta cheesecake. Music on weekends.

JACKSONVILLE: Orsay   **$$$**
French   **Road Map** E1
3630 Park St, 32205
Tel *(904) 381-0909*
Charming restaurant with a classic brasserie menu featuring dover sole, *duck a l'orange*, and *coq au vin*. Good weekday prix fixe bargains.

JACKSONVILLE BEACH: Mojo   **$**
American   **Road Map** E1
1500 Beach Blvd, 32250
Tel *(904) 247-6636*
A smokehouse, barbecue pit and blues bar rolled into one. Promises good old Southern barbecue with great sides. Check the schedule for fantastic blues music nights.

JACKSONVILLE BEACH:
Marker 32   **$$$**
Seafood/American   **Road Map** E1
14549 Beach Blvd, 32250
Tel *(904) 223-1534*   **Closed** *Sun*
Enjoy choice specialties like Florida pompano and thick pork chops while watching the sun set over the Intracoastal Waterway.

OCALA: Sonny's Real
American
Barbecue   **$**
4102 E Silver Springs Blvd, 34470
Tel *(352) 236-1012*
Sonny's may be an ubiquitous chain, but with reliably great barbecue at fantastic prices.

OCALA: Arthur's Bistro   **$$$**
Southern   **Road Map** E2
3600 SW 36 Ave, 34474
Tel *(352) 390-1515*
Sample Southern treats such as rib eye, bayou shrimp, and char-grilled grouper. Sandwiches and other lighter fare available too.

ORMOND BEACH:
Frappe's North   **$$$**
American   **Road Map** E2
123 W Granada Blvd, 32174
Tel *(386) 386-4888*
Come to Frappe's for tasty, eclectic, and often organic choices such as pork *saltimbocca* (marinated meat topped with prosciutto and sage), Cajun chicken, shrimp, and yellowfin tuna.

ORMOND BEACH:
Stonewood Grill & Tavern   **$$$**
Steakhouse   **Road Map** E2
100 S Atlantic Ave, 32176
Tel *(386) 671-1200*
Comfortable tavern with specialty grilled steaks and chops. The varied menu also has amazing seafood, burgers, and sandwiches.

PONTE VEDRA BEACH:
Palm Valley Fish Camp   **$$**
Seafood   **Road Map** E1
299 N Roscoe Blvd, 32082
Tel *(904) 285-3200*
Offering a wide choice of delectable fresh fish, oysters and other seafood, this small place has a loyal clientele. Best to reserve ahead. Take-out available.

ST. AUGUSTINE:
Florida Cracker Café   **$$**
American   **Road Map** E1
81 St George St, 32084
Tel *(904) 829-0397*
This pleasant café features local art and has an eclectic menu of shrimp and grits (cornmeal), meat loaf, and sandwiches, along with the famous Key lime pie. Good selection of beers.

The stylish interior of Orsay in Jacksonville

Atmospheric dining at 95 Cordoba in St. Augustine

ST. AUGUSTINE:
Gypsy Cab Company $$
Seafood   **Road Map** E1
838 Anastasia Blvd, 32808
Tel *(904) 824-8244*
A renowned restaurant with
creative combinations such as
salmon and scallop Provençale,
and steak and shrimp carbonara
on the menu. Sunday brunch.

ST. AUGUSTINE: The Floridian $$
American   **Road Map** E1
39 Cordova St, 32084
Tel *(904) 829-9655* **Closed** *Tue: lunch*
Head to the Floridian for
Southern comfort – shrimp mac
'n' cheese, chicken, and waffles –
along with sandwiches, salad
bowls, and vegetarian choices.

DK Choice

ST. AUGUSTINE:
95 Cordoba $$$
International   **Road Map** E1
95 Cordoba St, 32084
Tel *(904) 824-0402*
Come to 95 Cordoba to get
a taste of Old Spain in St.
Augustine. Settle into high-back
tapestry chairs amid columns,
arches, and wrought-iron
chandeliers and sample skillfully
blended cuisines. Appetizers
such as *escargot* (snails) and
fried green tomatoes, and a
range of entrées including veal
stew, Bohemian lobster, and wild
bass with black-eyed pea mash.

ST. AUGUSTINE:
Bistro de Leon $$$
French   **Road Map** E1
12 Cathedral Pl, 32084
Tel *(904) 810-2100* **Closed** *Wed*
The chef-owner from Lyon
prepares authentic French fare in
an informal bakery-café setting.
Great early-bird and children's
menus, and afternoon tea with
French cheese platters.

ST. AUGUSTINE: Raintree $$$
American   **Road Map** E1
102 San Marco Ave, 32084
Tel *(904) 824-7211*
This popular restaurant, set in a
romantic Victorian home with a
courtyard, serves up delectable
traditional steak, beef Wellington,
and the choicest of seafood.

ST. AUGUSTINE: Columbia $$$
Spanish   **Road Map** E1
98 St. George St, 32084
Tel *(904) 824-3341*
A branch of the famed Tampa
restaurant, this festive restaurant
features hacienda-style decor
and a well-prepared Spanish-
Cuban menu. Take out available.

The Panhandle

APALACHICOLA:
Up the Creek Raw Bar $
Seafood   **Road Map** B2
313 Water St, 32320
Tel *(850) 653-2525*
This casual spot with a waterfront
deck is the place to find out why
Apalachicola oysters are as
famous as they are. Also try the
chef's house specialties.

APALACHICOLA: Owl Café $$
Seafood/American **Road Map** B2
15 Ave D, 32320
Tel *(850) 653-9888*
Pleasant café and taproom.
Offers local oysters, grouper,
pastas, and crab cakes. A good
spot for Sunday brunch.

APALACHICOLA:
Tamara's Café Floridita $$
Spanish   **Road Map** B2
71 Market St, 32320
Tel *(850) 653-4111* **Closed** *Mon*
This pleasant upstairs café offers
decent Spanish fare including
tapas, paella, pecan-crusted
grouper, and margarita chicken.

DESTIN: Donut Hole $
American   **Road Map** A1
635 Hwy 98 E, 32541
Tel *(850) 837-8824*
Great choice for all-day breakfast
food with corned beef hash,
omelets, eggs Benedict,
sandwiches, burgers, and salads.
Wide range of fresh doughnuts.

DESTIN: The Back Porch $$
Seafood   **Road Map** A1
1740 Old Hwy 98, 32541
Tel *(850) 837-8824*
Informal seafood shack with its
porch facing the beach and the
Gulf. Specials on the menu
include oysters and grilled
amberjack. Good lunch deals.

DESTIN: Marina Café $$$
American/Seafood **Road Map** A1
404 Hwy 98 E, 32541
Tel *(850) 837-7960*
Elegant nautical dining room
with outdoor deck seating and
great harbor views. Formal
cuisine such as steaks and
seafood paired with delicious
wines. Also offers wood-fired
pizza, pasta, and sushi.

FORT WALTON BEACH:
Pandora's Steakhouse $$$
Steakhouse   **Road Map** A1
1120B Santa Rosa Blvd, 32548
Tel *(850) 244-8669* **Closed** *Mon*
This family-owned Steakhouse
is famous for its steak grilled over
a wood-burning open pit. There
are also seafood options as well
as a children's menu.

FORT WALTON BEACH:
Staff's Seafood Restaurant $$$
Seafood   **Road Map** A1
24 Miracle Strip Pkwy, 32548
Tel *(850) 243-3482*
Family-owned traditional
restaurant with fresh local
seafood, combination shrimp
and fish platters, steak, delicious
sides, and gumbo.

For more information on types of restaurants *see page 327*

GRAYTON BEACH: Picolo's Restaurant and the Red Bar $$
Seafood   Road Map B1
70 Hotz Ave, 32459
Tel *(850) 231-1008*
This restaurant, with its laid-back vibe and live jazz music, offers a small but excellent seafood menu. No credit cards.

PANAMA CITY BEACH: Hunt's Oyster Bar $$
Seafood   Road Map B1
1150 Beck Ave, 32401
Tel *(850) 763-9645*   **Closed** *Sun*
Family-owned no-frills restaurant offering some of the freshest Apalachicola oysters – both raw and cooked. Well-priced weekday lunch specials.

PANAMA CITY BEACH: Schooners $$
Seafood   Road Map B1
5121 Gulf Dr, 32408
Tel *(850) 235-3555*
With a fantastic location near the beach, this restaurant serves decent seafood and often has live music. Good early bird specials.

PANAMA CITY BEACH: Capt. Anderson's $$$
Seafood   Road Map B1
5551 N Lagoon Dr, 32408
Tel *(850) 234-2225*   **Closed** *Sun*
Watch the boats unload the day's catch at this seafood standout, a marina fixture since 1953. Try the specialty grilled shrimp and South African lobster tails. Expect long queues in season.

DK Choice

PANAMA CITY BEACH: Firefly $$$
American   Road Map B1
535 Richard Jackson Blvd, 32407
Tel *(850) 303-0962*
Firefly provides a fantastic dining experience beneath a giant oak tree with twinkling lights, and is a great choice for a romantic meal. The sophisticated menu on offer features she-crab soups, rack of lamb, double-cut pork chops, andouille-crusted red snapper, and lobster tail. Great martini menu in the Library Lounge, a sushi happy hour, and a menu for children.

PENSACOLA: Cactus Flower Café $$
Mexican   Road Map A1
1425 M 12th Ave, 32502
Tel *(850) 912-4856*   **Closed** *Sun*
Popular for its mahi mahi fish tacos, tortilla soup, freshly made salsa, and traditional favorites such as quesadillas and burritos.

PENSACOLA: Five Sisters Blues Café $$
American   Road Map A1
421 W Belmont St, 32501
Tel *(850) 912-4856*
Enjoy live music and relish Southern specials including gumbo, fried chicken, crab cakes, pulled pork, and pot roast. Excellent Sunday brunch.

DK Choice

PENSACOLA: Dharma Blue $$$
American   Road Map A1
300 S Alcaniz St, 32502
Tel *(850) 433-1275*   **Closed** *Sun*
Dharma Blue is located in a lovely Victorian home overlooking the historic Seville Square. Sample exquisite cuisine such as blackened fish with sautéed shrimp, grilled duck breast, beef filet, and thick pork chops. Great lunch specials including portobello focaccia, fish tacos, or quiche of the day.

PENSACOLA: McGuire's Irish Pub $$$
Steakhouse   Road Map A1
600 E Gregory St, 32502
Tel *(850) 433-6789*
Steakhouse, pub, brewery, and wine cellar all rolled into one. Offers excellent Irish stew, meats, corned beef and cabbage, and seafood. Their huge burgers are highly recommended.

SANTA ROSA: Fish Out of Water $$$
Seafood   Road Map B1
Watercolor Inn, 34 Goldenrod Circle, 32459
Tel *(850) 534-5050*
Located between Grayton Beach and Seaside, this award-winning restaurant has a relaxed setting. The Southern-inspired kitchen

uses some of the freshest ingredients to deliver outstanding results. Delicious sunset cocktails.

SEAGROVE BEACH: Café 30A $$$
American   Road Map B1
3899 E County Hwy 30A, 32459
Tel *(850) 231-2166*
Café 30A has a striking multi-level dining room and a choice of wood-oven roasted seafood, grilled meats, and pizzas on the menu.

SEASIDE: Bud & Alley's $$$
American   Road Map B1
2236 E County Rd 30A, 32459
Tel *(850) 231-5900*
With a menu emphasizing fresh seafood, this lively waterfront restaurant also serves taco and pizza, and has a kids' menu.

SEASIDE: Great Southern Café $$$
American   Road Map B1
83 Central Square, 32459
Tel *(850) 231-7327*
True to its name, this restaurant serves great Southern favorites all through the day. Don't miss the grits a ya ya.

TALLAHASSEE: Dog et Al $
American   Road Map C1
1456 Monroe St, 32301
Tel *(850) 222-4099*   **Closed** *Sun*
A classic joint, with hot dogs every which way possible: big ones, little ones, footlongs, corn dogs, and turkey dogs. Served with chili, cheese, and kraut.

TALLAHASSEE: Mom & Dad's $$
Italian   Road Map C1
4175 Apalachee Pkwy, 32311
Tel *(850) 877-4518*   **Closed** *Sun & Mon*
Family-owned eatery that has been serving exquisite old-fashioned Italian fare for over 50 years. Good wine list.

Enjoy the fantastic vista at Schooners in Panama City Beach

TALLAHASSEE: Azu $$$
Asian   **Road Map** C1
3220 Apalachee Pkwy, 32311
Tel *(850) 893-4112*
Savor some of the city's best Chinese fare along with delicious Japanese teriyaki, sushi, tempura, and fusion dishes. The mango beef and honey pineapple shrimp are favorites.

TALLAHASSEE:
Cypress Restaurant $$$
American   **Road Map** C1
320 E Tennessee St, 32301
Tel *(850) 513-1100*   **Closed** *Sun & Mon*
This chef-owned restaurant boasts of a sophisticated menu featuring kumquat glazed duck breast, pecan-crusted grouper, and some of the best shrimp and grits (cornmeal) in town.

TALLAHASSEE:
Kool Beanz Café $$$
Caribbean   **Road Map** C1
921 Thomasville Rd, 32303
Tel *(850) 224-2466*
This trendy and noisy café serves terrific fare: try the jerk spiced scallops and lime basil shrimp. Excellent brunch.

The Gulf Coast

DK Choice

ANNA MARIA ISLAND:
Beach Bistro $$$
American   **Road Map** D3
6600 Gulf Dr, Holmes Beach, 34217
Tel *(941) 778-6444*
One of Florida's top-rated restaurants, Beach Bistro is a great spot for a romantic meal, with beautiful sunset views over the sea. Some of the delicacies on offer include Floridian grouper with cashew-toasted coconut crust, *boullabaise* filled with lobster tail, sinful sliders of sirloin, *foie gras*, and *bearnaise* sauce on a sweet roll.

ANNA MARIA ISLAND:
Sign of the Mermaid $$$
American/European   **Road Map** D3
9707 Gulf Dr, 34216
Tel *(941) 778-9399*
Wonderfully decorated restaurant in a restored 1912 cottage. Sample from an unusual and extensive variety of formal Floridian and European cuisine. Luscious desserts, and a range of wines, both American and international.

The romantic setting of Beach Bistro, Anna Maria Island

CAPTIVA ISLAND:
Bubble Room $$$
American   **Road Map** E4
15001 Captiva Rd, 33924
Tel *(239) 472-5558*
Enjoy steaks and seafood in kitschy surrounds with toys, trains, juke boxes, old records, and Christmas lights.

CAPTIVA ISLAND:
Mucky Duck $$$
American/Seafood   **Road Map** E4
11546 Andy Rosse Ln, 33924
Tel *(239) 472-3434*
Informal beachfront café serving grouper, coconut shrimp, roast duckling, and chicken marsala. Lovely sunset views.

CAPTIVA ISLAND:
Old Captiva House $$$
American/Seafood   **Road Map** E4
15951 Captiva Dr, 33924
Tel *(239) 472-5161*
Fine dining in a charming 1931 home. Choose from a varied menu and enjoy piano music and sunset views.

CLEARWATER BEACH:
Frenchy's South Beach Café $$
American   **Road Map** D3
351 S Gulfview Dr, 33767
Tel *(727) 441-9991*
Casual beach café whose specialty grouper sandwiches are very popular. Also serves she-crab soup, salads, ribs, seafood platters, and pasta.

CLEARWATER BEACH:
The Lobster Pot Bistro $$$
Seafood   **Road Map** D3
478 Mandalay Ave, 33767
Tel *(727) 446-8809*
Offers fantastic Maine lobster and steak along with an affordable lunch menu featuring lobster bisque. Jazz music on the patio Thursdays through to Sundays. Children's menu available.

DUNEDIN: Bon Appetit $$$
American   **Road Map** D3
150 Marina Plaza, 34698
Tel *(727) 733-2151*
Upscale dining on the waterfront with indoors and alfresco seating. There is a formal menu as well a choice of comfort foods. Good prix fixe dinner bargains.

FORT MYERS: The Veranda $$$
American   **Road Map** E4
2122 2nd St, 33901
Tel *(239) 332-2065*   **Closed** *Sun*
Located in a charming historic home, the Veranda offers Southern-style fine dining. Try the grouper on grits (cornmeal), chicken with bay shrimp, and crawfish-topped snapper.

DK Choice

LONGBOAT KEY:
Euphemia Haye $$$
European   **Road Map** D3
5540 Gulf of Mexico Dr, 34228
Tel *(941) 383-3633*
Located in a cottage amid tropical greenery, this restaurant addresses two distinct needs. Find romantic fine dining downstairs, with dishes such as pistachio-crusted snapper, lamb shank, and the signature duckling. The Haye Loft upstairs has live music, drinks, pizza, and a dazzling dessert bar with apple walnut crumble pie and banana foster treats.

LONGBOAT KEY:
Pattigeorge's $$$
Asian   **Road Map** D3
4120 Gulf of Mexico Dr, 34228
Tel *(941) 383-5111*
This sophisticated eatery with great bay views and Asian influences has delectable stir-frys, wok dishes, as well as dim sum and sushi.

For more information on types of restaurants *see page 327*

SANIBEL ISLAND: Island Cow $$
American   Road Map E4
2163 Periwinkle Way, 33957
Tel *(239) 472-0606*
Very well-priced breakfast,
burgers, sandwiches, and fish
done nine ways. Kids love the
nightly mooing contest.

SANIBEL ISLAND:
Mad Hatter $$$
American   Road Map E4
6467 Sanibel-Captiva Rd, 33957
Tel *(239) 472-0033*   **Closed** *Mon*
This romantic waterfront café
has creative seasonal menus
featuring shrimp wrapped in
filo, black truffle scallops, and
duckling with berry sauce.

SANIBEL ISLAND: Timbers
Restaurant and Fish Market $$$
Seafood   Road Map E4
703 Tarpon Bay Rd, 33957
Tel *(239) 395-2722*
Big, busy place with fresh
seafood, a raw bar, chowder, and
platters. Try the specialty crunchy
grouper and delicious steaks.

SARASOTA: Nancy's Bar-B-Q $
America   Road Map D3
301 S Pineapple Ave, 34236
Tel *(941) 366-2271*   **Closed** *Sun*
Worth waiting in line at the
counter for some great barbecue,
including pulled pork, brisket,
chicken, ribs, and salmon, along
with scrumptious sides.

SARASOTA: Yoders $
American   Road Map D3
3434 Bahia Vista St, 34239
Tel *(941) 955-7771*   **Closed** *Sun*
Serving Amish treats since 1975.
Big breakfasts, delicious fried
chicken, and famous pies such
as the peanut butter cream pie.
No alcohol.

SARASOTA: Café L'Europe $$$
French   Road Map D3
431 St. Armands Circle, 34236
Tel *(941) 388-4415*
Long-established bastion of fine
dining with great ambience. This
café counts Dover sole and
chateaubriand (particular cut of
steak) among its specialties. Prix
fixe early bird dinner.

SARASOTA:
Derek's Culinary Casual $$$
American   Road Map D3
514 Central Ave, 34231
Tel *(941) 366-6565*   **Closed** *Sun*
& *Mon*
The innovative owner-chef has
won national praise for dishes
such as cilantro (coriander) and
wine-braised lamb shank and
crispy duck. Exquisite soups and
superb small plates.

Key to Price Guide *see page 329*

SARASOTA: Michaels on East $$$
American   Road Map D3
1212 E Ave S, 34239
Tel *(941) 366-0007*   **Closed** *Sun*
This sophisticated restaurant offers
terrific "Epicurean Adventures"
menus focusing on particular
world cuisines, as well as prix fixe
dinners. Over 350 exceptional
wines to choose from.

ST. PETE BEACH: Madfish $$$
American   Road Map D3
5200 Gulf Blvd, 33706
Tel *(727) 360-9300*
Casual yet upscale retrofit diner
with great breakfast as well as
late night menus. Delicious prime
rib. Early bird specials.

ST. PETE BEACH:
Maritana Grille $$$
European   Road Map D3
*Don Cesar Hotel, 3400 Gulf Blvd,
33706*
Tel *(727) 360-1881*
Upscale restaurant an airy
dining room. Try their specialty
griddled seafood or choose from
top-notch steak, venison, and
wood grilled rack of lamb.

ST. PETERSBURG:
Red Mesa Cantina $$
Mexican   Road Map D3
128 3rd St S, 33701
Tel *(727) 896-8286*
Excellent Mexican fare including
tortillas and *seviche* (seafood
cooked using citrus juice) in the
colorful interiors or beautiful court-
yard. Live music in the tequila bar.

ST. PETERSBURG:
The Moon Under Water $$
Gastropub   Road Map D3
332 Beach Dr NE, 33701
Tel *(727) 896-6160*
Trendy pub with British and
Indian influences. Seventeen

traditional and craft beers on
tap. Serves fish and chips,
along with curries, burgers,
and pot pies.

ST. PETERSBURG: Cassis
American Brasserie $$$
French/American   Road Map D3
170 Beach Dr NE, 33701
Tel *(727) 827-2927*
This elegantly decorated, trendy
brasserie serves great seafood,
and offers pleasant sidewalk
seating. Has a separate menu
for pet dogs.

TAMPA: Benjarong Thai $
Thai   Road Map D3
14402 N Dale Mabry Hwy, 33618
Tel *(813) 265-2667*   **Closed** *Sun*
Small, family-owned restaurant
with authentic pad Thai, duck
dishes, and excellent curries on
the menu. Well-priced lunch.

TAMPA: Mel's Hot Dogs $
American   Road Map D3
4136 Busch Blvd, 33617
Tel *(813) 986-8000*   **Closed** *Sun*
This local legend near Busch
Gardens has been a favorite since
the early 1970s. Serves hot dogs
plus great burgers.

TAMPA: Bella's Italian Café $$
Italian   Road Map D3
1413 S Howard Ave, 33606
Tel *(813) 254-3355*
A local favorite for over 25 years,
this warm and informal café has
a wood-burning pizza oven and
serves traditional Italian fare.
Excellent late-night happy hour.

TAMPA: Bern's Steakhouse $$$
Steakhouse   Road Map D3
1208 S Howard Ave, 33606
Tel *(813) 251-2421*
Known for its opulent decor,
prime steaks, and delicious

The cheerful and colourful dining area of Island Cow, Sanibel Island desserts, this Steakhouse also offers amazing wine cellar tours. Has a decadent dessert room.

TAMPA: Ceviche Tapas Bar and Restaurant $$$
Spanish **Road Map** D3
2500 W Azeele St, 33609
Tel *(813) 250-0203*
Trendy restaurant with live music and flamenco dance shows. Offers over a hundred kinds of tapas for sharing, plus paella and *seviche* (seafood cooked using citrus juice).

DK Choice

TAMPA:
Columbia Restaurant $$$
Spanish **Road Map** D3
2117 E 7th Ave, Ybor City, 33605
Tel *(813) 248-4961*
Filled with old-world Spanish atmosphere, Florida's oldest restaurant has now grown to fill a city block. But despite its size and the crowds who flock here, this family-owned institution has maintained the quality of their Spanish-Cuban menu and signature dishes such as paella and snapper Alicante. Flamenco dancers nightly, except Sunday, add to the atmosphere.

TAMPA: Mise en Place $$$
American **Road Map** D3
442 W Kennedy Blvd, 33606
Tel *(813) 254-5373* **Closed** *Sun & Mon*
Elegant restaurant perfect for a special occasion. The Kobe beef and rack of lamb are highly recommended. Prix fixe options too.

DK Choice

TAMPA: Restaurant BT $$$
French **Road Map** D3
2507 S MacDill Ave, 33629
Tel *(813) 258-1916* **Closed** *Sun*
Food lovers come from afar to savor the subtle blend of French and Vietnamese techniques and seasonings by the talented chef of this stylish café. Some of the chef's most memorable creations include snapper Saigon with lemongrass and curry, Viet bouillabaisse, Cote Basque prawns, and ducking with mango sauce.

TAMPA: The Refinery $$$
American **Road Map** D3
5137 N Florida Ave, 33603
Tel *(813) 237-2000*
Using fresh ingredients and creative seasonings, the weekly

The creative drinks menu at The Refinery, Tampa

changing menu at the Refinery features the likes of grilled amberjack with fennel and cilantro (coriander), and chicken with tarragon Dijon butter.

VENICE: Sharky's on the Pier $$
Seafood **Road Map** D4
1600 S Harbor Dr, 34285
Tel *(941) 488-1456*
Located right on the beach, this restaurant and tiki bar serves delightful snacks, sandwiches, and full meals. Live music Wednesdays through Saturdays.

The Everglades and the Keys

EVERGLADES:
Coopertown Restaurant $
Seafood **Road Map** E5
22700 SW 8 St, 33194
Tel *(305) 226-6048*
Grab a paper plate and devour swamp specialties such as alligator tail, frog legs, and catfish. Delicious sandwiches and great breakfasts too.

EVERGLADES:
City Seafood and Market $
Seafood **Road Map** E5
702 Begonia St, 34139
Tel *(239) 695-4700*
This riverside café offers sandwiches and freshly-caught seafood such as stone crabs and shrimp as well as alligator tail and frog legs. For dessert, opt for homemade Key lime pie and ice creams.

ISLAMORADA: Marker 88 $$$
Seafood **Road Map** F5
88000 Overseas Hwy, 33070
Tel *(305) 852-9315*
Enjoy upscale dining in a casual beachside setting. A range of fresh seafood on the menu as well as excellent meat choices. Extensive wine list.

ISLAMORADA: Pierre's $$$
French **Road Map** F5
81600 Overseas Hwy, MM 81.6, 33036
Tel *(305) 664-3225*
Perfect for special occasions, Pierre's promises exquisite fine dining with gorgeous views from the verandas. Savor elegant gourmet seafood and steaks.

ISLAMORADA:
Wahoo's Bar and Grill $$$
Seafood **Road Map** F5
83413 Overseas Hwy, MM 83.5, 33036
Tel *(305) 664-9888* **Closed** *Sun*
Watch the fishing fleet come in while feasting on freshly-caught snapper, grouper, tuna and more. For the thrifty, a range of sandwiches are available.

KEY LARGO:
Mrs. Mac's Kitchen $$
Seafood **Road Map** F5
99336 Overseas Hwy, MM 99.4, 33037
Tel *(305) 451-3722* **Closed** *Sun*
Head to Mrs. Mac's for some good old down-South cooking. Chili, conch chowder, crab cakes, fresh fish of the day, and homemade pies on the menu.

KEY LARGO: Fish House Restaurant and Market $$$
Seafood **Road Map** F5
102401 Overseas Hwy, MM 102.4, 33037
Tel *(305) 451-4665*
Have the catch of the day cooked to your liking: broiled, fried, grilled, or blackened. Along with shrimp, crab and other seafood. There are meats and pasta on offer as well.

KEY WEST: Banana Café $$
French **Road Map** E5
1215 Duval St, 33040
Tel *(305) 294-7227*
Small bistro with specialty seafood crêpes as well as fantastic ribeye and sauteed local snapper. Good breakfast selections.

For more information on types of restaurants *see page 327*

KEY WEST: Camille's $$
American   Road Map E5
1202 Simonton St, 33040
Tel *(305) 296-4811*
This family-friendly restaurant has quirky decor and serves great breakfast (crab Benedict) and has reasonable dinner options (stone crab meat cake).

KEY WEST: El Siboney $$
Cuban   Road Map E5
900 Catherine St, 33040
Tel *(305) 296-4184*
Savor home-cooked Cuban fare at excellent prices. To order their paella, call in an hour ahead. Good daily specials.

KEY WEST:
La Trattoria Restaurant $$
Italian   Road Map E5
3593 S Roosevelt Blvd, 33040
Tel *(305) 296-1075*
Enjoy traditional Italian favorites in a relaxed setting with fantastic ocean views. Excellent martinis.

KEY WEST: Mangia Mangia
Pasta Café $$
Italian/Seafood   Road Map E5
900 Southard St, 33040
Tel *(305) 294-2469*
Home-made pastas reign at Mangia Mangia, both as mains or as a side dish with scampi, mahi mahi, or chicken. The lobster linguini is a must-try.

KEY WEST: Mangoes $$
American   Road Map E5
700 Duval St, 33040
Tel *(305) 292-4606*
Has a varied menu with many seafood choices and, true to its name, signature drinks including mangorita and mango colada. Great patio seating, ideal for people-watching.

KEY WEST: Sarabeth's Kitchen $$
American   Road Map E5
530 Simonton St, 33040
Tel *(305) 293-8181* **Closed** *Mon & Tue*
Florida import of the New York favorite, known for its brunch and lunch menus. Excellent soups, salads, and dinner choices ranging from meat loaf to snapper.

DK Choice

KEY WEST: Seven Fish $$
American   Road Map E5
632 Olivia St, 33040
Tel *(305) 296-2777*   **Closed** *Tue*
Step away from the tourist crowds to discover this locals' favorite: a corner bistro where mahi mahi and meatloaf share the menu with surprises such as banana chicken and crab

The exterior of Mangia Mangia Pasta Café in Key West

and shitake mushroom pasta. Everything is prepared expertly and well priced. Small space, so reserve well ahead.

KEY WEST: Sloppy Joe's Bar $$
American   Road Map E5
201 Duval St, 33040
Tel *(305) 294-5717*
Ernest Hemingway's famous haunt, this friendly pub features live music and standard but delicious pub grub. Beer on tap and an extensive drinks menu.

KEY WEST:
A&B Lobster House $$$
Seafood   Road Map E5
700 Front St, 33040
Tel *(305) 294-5880*
Occupying a prime spot on the harbor, this restaurant offers freshly caught seafood, excellent lobster tail with coconut pecan rice, and great steaks.

KEY WEST:
Antonia's Restaurant $$$
Italian   Road Map E5
615 Duval St, 33040
Tel *(305) 294-6565*
Upscale and intimate, this highly rated Italian restaurant has an extensive menu and wine list. Reservations essential.

KEY WEST: Blue Heaven $$$
American   Road Map E5
729 Thomas St, 33040
Tel *(305) 296-8666*
Trendy spot with live music and mismatched decor. Terrific seafood including lobster, stone crab, and seared sea scallops. Excellent brunch options.

KEY WEST: Café Marquesa $$$
American   Road Map E5
600 Fleming St, 33040
Tel *(305) 292-1244*
Sophisticated and intimate restaurant with a highly rated

menu that features interesting dishes such as duck breast with chicken and apple sausage.

DK Choice

KEY WEST: Café Sole $$$
French/American   Road Map E5
1029 Southard St, 33040
Tel *(305) 294-0230*
This small café with a romantic garden has at its helm a talented chef whose fantastic menus combine the best of Provence and Florida. Think lobster bisque and French onion soup, conch *carpaccio* and *duckling a l'orange*. Try the specialty hog snapper, a delicate white meat fish served with roasted red pepper sauce.

KEY WEST:
HarbourView Café $$$
Seafood   Road Map E5
Pier House Resort, 1 Duval St, 33040
Tel *(305) 296-4600*
Lovely waterfront restaurant serving fresh local seafood and old favorites all day, with a more formal dinner. Dine on the deck with gorgeous views and live music at the piano bar.

KEY WEST: La Te Da $$$
American   Road Map E5
1125 Duval St, 33040
Tel *(305) 296-6706*
Upscale but laid-back restaurant. Offers a varied menu with meat loaf, scampi, snapper, and Tahitian roasted chicken.

KEY WEST: Louie's Backyard $$$
American   Road Map E5
700 Waddell Ave, 33040
Tel *(305) 294-1061*
With the ocean as its backyard, Louie's promises dazzling views and the food is as worthy as the setting. Relish fantastic fare with just a touch of Caribbean spices. Popular, so reserve well ahead.

KEY WEST:
Michael's Key West $$$
American **Road Map** E5
532 Margaret St, 33040
Tel *(305) 295-1300*
A local favorite, Michael's
has three gorgeous settings to
enjoy the gourmet cuisine: a
formal dining room, a romantic
patio, and a garden bar serving
fantastic fondue.

KEY WEST: Pisces $$$
Seafood **Road Map** E5
1007 Simonton St, 33040
Tel *(305) 294-7100*
With interesting contemporary
decor, including artwork by Andy
Warhol, Pisces dishes up superb
seafood such as lobster tango
mango and yellowtail atocha.

KEY WEST:
Square One Restaurant $$$
American **Road Map** E5
1975 Duval St, 33040
Tel *(305) 296-4300*
Well-established upmarket
restaurant with warm ambience
and live piano. The chefs use
fresh, regional herbs and seasonal
produce in traditional dishes.
Try the rack of lamb or snapper.

MARATHON: Butterfly Café $$
American/Caribbean **Road Map** E5
2600 Overseas Hwy, 33050
Tel *(305) 289-7177*
Attractive dining room at the
Tranquility Bay resort, serving up
delicious conch chowder, coconut
shrimp, burgers, and meals for
kids, all with a Caribbean touch.

MARATHON:
Herbie's Restaurant $$
Seafood **Road Map** E5
6350 Overseas Hwy, 33050
Tel *(305) 743-6373* **Closed** *Sun*
& Mon
Justifiably popular for its conch
fritters and fresh seafood, offered
at fair prices and served in a low-
key Old Florida setting.

MARATHON:
Lazy Days South $$$
American **Road Map** E5
725 11th St Ocean, 33050
Tel *(305) 289-0839*
Very popular oceanfront
restaurant. Varied menu with
seafood, steaks, pasta, and
sandwiches. Great sunset views.

MARCO ISLAND: Arturo's $$$
American **Road Map** E5
844 Bald Eagle Dr, 34145
Tel *(239) 642-0550*
Elegant restaurant that offers a
wide choice, from frog legs to
chicken Parmesan to its specialty,
stuffed pork chops. Popular bar.

MARCO ISLAND: Old Marco
Lodge Crab House $$$
Seafood **Road Map** E5
401 Papaya St, Goodland, 34140
Tel *(239) 642-7227*
Picturesque lodge restaurant
with a big outdoor deck and
water views. Serves fresh seafood,
as well as soups, salads, and
sandwiches. Kids' menu too.

MARCO ISLAND: Sale e Pepe $$$
Italian **Road Map** E5
480 S Collier Blvd, 34145
Tel *(239) 393-1600*
Elegant resort dining with
Gulf views and sophisticated
preparation of home-made pastas,
fresh seafood, and prime meats.

MARCO ISLAND: Snook Inn $$$
Seafood/American **Road Map** E5
1215 Bald Eagle Dr, 34145
Tel *(239) 394-3313*
Casual waterfront dining at the
Snook Inn, where the menu
ranges from sandwiches to
formal entrées. Specialties
include stuffed shrimp and
Carribean-style barbecue ribs.

NAPLES: First Watch $$
Café **Road Map** E4
225 Banyan Blvd, 34102
Tel *(239) 434-0005*
Head to First Watch for hearty
and healthy breakfasts with
multi-grain pancakes and skillet
hashes. The lunch sandwiches
come with a soup or salad.

NAPLES: Noodles Italian Café
and Sushi Bar $$
Italian/Japanese **Road Map** E4
1585 Pine Ridge Rd, 34109
Tel *(239) 592-0050*
Traditional Italian and sushi bar
coexist happily here. Choose

Stylish decor with Italian flare at Sea Salt
in Naples

from the low-carb menu that
features gourmet pizzas and
specialties such as beef Oscar
and salmon florentine.

NAPLES: Barbatella Spirited
Italian Trattoria $$$
Italian **Road Map** E4
1290 3rd St, 34102
Tel *(239) 263-1955*
With a trendy dining room and
courtyard seating, this gourmet
Italian restaurant offers excellent
rotisserie and grill specialties,
along with wood-fired pizzas,
home-made pastas, and gelati.

NAPLES: Bistro 821 $$$
International **Road Map** E4
821 5th Ave, 34102
Tel *(239) 261-5821*
With a distinctly South Beach
vibe, this upscale bistro has a
varied menu featuring pot pie,
paella, risotto, trademark miso-
sake, and roasted sea bass.
Excellent wine list.

NAPLES: Café Lurcat $$$
American **Road Map** E4
494 5th Ave, 34102
Tel *(239) 213-3357*
A trendy and popular hangout
that serves lovely tapas and small
plates at the bar. Upstairs and
outside, savor American fine
dining, with creative cuisine and
several low-calorie choices.

NAPLES: Cote d'Azur $$$
French **Road Map** E4
11224 Tamiami Trail N (US41), 34110
Tel *(239) 597-8867* **Closed** *Mon*
This top-rated intimate bistro
features fantastic provincial
French cuisine. Try its specialty
roasted seafood, boned and
filleted at the table.

NAPLES: Sea Salt $$$
Italian **Road Map** E4
1186 3rd St S, 34102
Tel *(239) 434-7258*
A stylish, modern setting and
a talented Venetian-born chef
make Sea Salt one of Naples's
top restaurants. Start with raw
oysters, hand-cut carpaccio,
or cured meats selections and
move on to swordfish on
Parmesan polenta, halibut with
beluga lentil ragu or venison
tenderloin. Excellent wines .

NAPLES: USS Nemo $$$
Seafood **Road Map** E4
3745 Tamiami Trail (US 41), 34103
Tel *(239) 261-6366*
Sample superb seafood
with Asian influences amidst
whimsical undersea decor. Try
the signature dish miso-broiled
bass with citrus-ginger butter.

For more information on types of restaurants *see page 327*

Bars and Cafés

Florida's easy-going lifestyle helps to ensure an abundance of bars and cafés. The term café often denotes an informal, bistro-style restaurant but can also refer to a coffee house or, indeed, a bar. Sports bars are very popular and usually have several television sets, each tuned to a different station – but often the sound is turned off while loud music plays in the background. Many bars and cafés have a happy hour, generally from 4 to 7pm, when drinks are less expensive and snacks are served free of charge; those included here are good for just a drink as well as a meal, or a coffee and a snack.

Miami

Miami Beach: News Café
800 Ocean Drive. **Map** 2 F4.
Tel *(305) 538-6397.*

With ample sidewalk tables, this laid-back café is the top meeting place in South Beach and is open 24 hours a day. People gather to drink, eat, and take in the Ocean Drive scene. The eclectic menu features good breakfasts and huge bowls of pasta as well as light, healthy meals. There are a dozen kinds of coffee, and the pastry list is equally long. 🌐 🔲 *AE DC MC V*

Miami Beach: Van Dyke Café
846 Lincoln Rd. **Map** 2 E2.
Tel *(305) 534-3600.*

This popular SoBe hangout, with tables inside and out, occupies a lovely restored Mediterranean-style building. House specialties are bread pudding and *zabaglione* with fresh berries. There is a good choice of coffees and herbal teas, and a jazz trio performs in the evenings. 🔲 🌐 *AE DC MC V*

Downtown: Hard Rock Café
401 Biscayne Blvd. **Map** 4 F1.
Tel *(305) 377-3110.*

Tourists and locals alike fill the Hard Rock Café, which is festooned with rock memorabilia and throbs with loud music. There's a bar for those intent on drinking and soaking up the atmosphere, but reserve ahead if you want to eat. The food is American, from juicy burgers to hot, tasty apple pie, and the portions are generous. 🌐 *AE DC MC V*

Coral Gables: Café Books & Books
265 Aragon Ave. **Map** 5 C1.
Tel *(305) 448-9599.*

Located in the courtyard of Books & Books, this European-style deli serves soup, sandwiches, and fantastic desserts, all made by Lyon & Lyon

Caterers. There's a coffee bar open 9am–7pm daily. 🌐 🔲 *AE MC V*

Coconut Grove: Monty's in the Grove
2550 S. Bayshore Dr. **Map** 6 E4.
Tel *(305) 856-3992.*

With stunning water views, island music, and a wide variety of seasonal seafood, Monty's is a popular weekend spot. It's kid-friendly on weekends. 🔲 *AE DC MC V*

Coconut Grove: Fat Tuesday's
Coco Walk, 3015 Grand Ave. **Map** 6 E4.
Tel *(305) 441-2992.*

This former sports bar has three satellite dishes, 51 TVs, and five pool tables. It is now one of the Fat Tuesday's chain bar/cafés, which serves as a meeting place for the young at heart. US and imported beer are available, and the menu offers light meals and snacks, such as buffalo wings, veggie pizza, giant burgers, and Mississippi mud pie. 🌐 *AE DC MC V*

The Gold and Treasure Coasts

Boca Raton: Tin Muffin Café
364 East Palmetto Park Rd.
Road map F4. **Tel** *(561) 392-9446.*

This tiny café offers delightful sandwiches and quiches, plus the homemade desserts are a treat. Try the shrimp salad or a piece of banana cake while you sit outside and watch the world go by. Tin Café is not a destination restaurant, but worth a visit if you're in the neighborhood. 🌐 🔲

Fort Lauderdale: Shooters
3033 NE 32nd Ave. **Road map** F4.
Tel *(954) 566-2855.*

This waterfront bar and restaurant is a people-watcher's paradise, always packed with a casual crowd eating, drinking, and watching the boats sail by. The menu is quite extensive and

reasonably priced. You can nibble on shrimp and crab cakes, or tuck into more substantial food like a Florida grouper sandwich. 🌐 🔲 *AE DC MC V*

Palm Beach: The Leopard Lounge
363 Cocoanut Row. **Road map** F4.
Tel *(561) 659-5800.*

Located in the Chesterfield Hotel, the Leopard Lounge is strikingly decorated with scarlet and black drapes, and the leopard theme is picked out in the plush carpeting and tablecloths. On weekends the place is jammed with locals who dance to the sounds of the "big band" era, performed live. A full menu is served. 🌐 *AE DC MC V*

Orlando and The Space Coast

Orlando: Bongos Cuban Café
1498 E Buena Vista Drive.
Road map E3. **Tel** *(407) 828-0999.*

This hip café in the middle of Downtown Disney® is owned by Gloria Estefan and husband Emilio, and features outstanding Cuban cuisine and hot dance music. Try the *arroz con pollo* and black bean soup. There are two floors of indoor and outdoor tables – the upstairs balcony is a great place to people watch. 🌐 🔲 *AE DC MC V*

Orlando: NASCAR Café
Universal Orlando City Walk.
Road map E3. **Tel** *(407) 224-7223.*

If you love racing cars then this place is for you. Several authentic race cars are on display and a huge variety of racing memorabilia. There are 40 televisions showing racing highlights, a shop, and racing simulators. The food is typical American fare, with steaks and burgers. 🌐 🔲 *AE DC MC V*

The Northeast

Jacksonville: River City Brewing Company
835 Museum Circle. **Road map** E1.
Tel *(904) 398-2299.*

Home-brewed beer and a varied selection of food at reasonable prices make this a popular spot with the locals. On Friday there's a live band, and Saturday nights offers a local DJ. There is no cover charge. 🌐 🔲 *AE DC MC V*

St. Augustine: A1A Ale Works
1 King St. **Road map** E1.
Tel *(904) 829-2977.*

Situated at the foot of the Bridge of Lions, this friendly pub and restaurant has a microbrewery on site. Ale aficionados come for the seven varieties of home-brewed ale that are available. Live bands play at weekends. 🍽 🖽 *AE DC MC V*

St. Augustine: OC White's Seafood and Spirits
118 Avenida Menendez.
Road map E1. **Tel** *(904) 824-0808.*

In an 18th-century building found across the street from St. Augustine's marina, OC White's offers a great view and live entertainment nightly. The interior is decorated with wax figures of pirates, and a full menu of seafood, steaks, and burgers is served. 🍽 🖽 *AE D MC V*

Daytona Beach: Oyster Pub
555 Seabreeze Blvd. **Road map** E2.
Tel *(386) 255-6348.*

Just one block from the beach, this pub has a raw bar serving fresh oysters, shrimp, and other seafood. During happy hour, prices are cut for drinks and seafood. There is sports coverage on 27 TVs, a pool room, and a disc jockey on weekends. 🍽 *AE MC V*

Gainesville: 2 Bits Lounge
1714 SW 34th Street. **Road map** D2.
Tel *(352) 371-3600.*

Located in the Hilton Hotel near the University of Florida campus, this popular bar is dedicated to sports, and shows all the favorite games. Snacks are also available. *AE DC MC V*

The Panhandle

Panama City Beach: Shuckum's Oyster Pub
15614 Front Beach Rd. **Road map** B1.
Tel *(850) 235-3214.*

The bar at this unpretentious and popular watering hole is covered with signed dollar bills left by satisfied customers. Shuckum's is best known for its local oysters, which are served raw, baked, steamed, or fried in a sandwich. Other seafood dishes are also available. 🍽 🖽 *MC V*

Pensacola Beach: Sidelines Sports Bar and Restaurant
2 Via de Luna Drive. **Road map** A1.
Tel *(850) 934-3660.*

This informal meeting place in Pensacola Beach has a different special for each night of the week; on "Cajun Night," for example, they serve up Cajun Bloody Marys. There's seating in booths, and the ubiquitous sports memorabilia and giant-screen televisions adorn the walls. 🍽 *AE MC V*

Tallahassee: Tomahawk Sports Bar
609 West Tennessee St. **Road map** C1.
Tel *(850) 298-4295.*

The go-to bar for watching Florida State University football, basketball games, and just about any other sports event. A fun, loud, crowded, and sometimes rowdy bar, which serves over 100 different beers. The kitchen is open until 3am and serves surprisingly good food – fried gator tail included. A generous Sunday brunch is also available. 🍽 *AE DC MC V*

The Gulf Coast

Lee Island Coast: The Mucky Duck
11546 Andy Rosse Lane, Captiva Island.
Road map E4. **Tel** *(239) 472-3434.*

This British-style pub occupies a charming 1930s building in Captiva town. Its creator, a former British policeman, named it after his favorite pub back home. You can play darts, enjoy a beer, and watch the sunset. The eclectic menu has English meals such as fish and chips and vegetarian platters. 🍽 🖽 *AE DC MC V*

Tampa: Elmer's Sports Café
2003 E 7th Ave, Ybor City. **Road map** D3. **Tel** *(813) 248-5855.*

Ybor City's original sports bar is renowned for its thick and chewy pizzas, great wings, and good beers. Elmer's has giant-screen TVs scattered all around the café, and there's also a pool table. This place is far from fancy, but the homemade food is tasty and the atmosphere pleasant. 🍽 *AE MC V*

St. Petersburg: Ferg's Sports Bar & Grill
1320 Central Ave. **Road map** D3.
Tel *(727) 822-4562.*

This former gas station, located across the street from Tropicana Stadium, has been converted into a two-story bar with a large covered patio and sidewalk café seating. The menu features chicken wings, burgers, sandwiches, and steaks.

There are over 40 televisions, and big games draw throngs of locals and visitors. 🍽 🖽 *AE DC MC V*

The Everglades and The Keys

Naples: HB's On The Gulf
851 Gulf Shore Blvd N. **Road map** E4.
Tel *(239) 435-4347.*

Sophisticated HB's On The Gulf, opened in 1946, is located in the Naples Beach Hotel on Naples Pier. It is a fine place for watching the sun go down, although you need to arrive early to get a seat. After sunset, the huge outside bar is packed with people, and a live band provides musical entertainment. HB's serves a full menu, but the food is not the highlight here. 🍽 🖽 *AE DC MC V*

Key West: Hog's Breath Saloon
400 Front St. **Road map** E5.
Tel *(305) 296-4222.*

The original Hog's Breath Saloon was established by an Alabama expatriate in Fort Walton Beach in 1976, but it moved down to Key West in 1988. It is now a local favorite, offering a raw bar, local seafood dishes, and tasty desserts (including a fine version of the famous Key Lime Pie). There is live music every day from 1pm until 2am. 🍽 🖽 *AE MC V*

Key West: Jimmy Buffet's Margaritaville Café
500 Duval St. **Road map** E5.
Tel *(305) 292-1435.*

There are plenty of Jimmy Buffet trinkets here, both on display and for sale (see p303), though the local singer-songwriter is rarely seen. Frosty Margaritas are the house specialty, and light meals, sandwiches, burgers, and local seafood such as conch fritters are also available. 🍽 *AE MC V*

Key West: Sloppy Joe's
201 Duval St. **Road map** E5.
Tel *(305) 294-5717.*

Formerly Ernest Hemingway's favorite drinking place *(see p302),* Sloppy Joe's is more commercial than in the novelist's day, attracting mainly tourists. However, it retains its Key West character, and when bands play it can be hard to get a seat. The menu includes typical bar fare, with jalapeño or conch fritters, chicken fingers and fries, and the renowned "original Sloppy Joe" burger. 🍽 *MC V*

SHOPPING IN FLORIDA

Shopping is probably the most popular pastime in Florida, and many use it as an enjoyable way of escaping the heat for a few hours. Orlando and Miami in particular, attract many overseas shoppers. The state is known for its discount stores, but at the other end of the scale, it also boasts some extraordinarily upmarket shops, usually clustered in fashionable shopping districts or malls. For first-time visitors to Florida, the shopping culture might require some getting used to. Rather than doing their shopping in town or city centers, Floridians generally gravitate towards huge shopping malls, where department stores and other shops sell everything from clothes to computers. For souvenirs and gifts *(see pp352–3)*, however, the small specialty shops are your best bet. If you're looking for something specific, local tourist offices can provide listings of stores in their area. Shops in Miami are described on pages 98–9.

Mizner Park in Boca Raton, with shops as elegant as its architecture

When to Shop

Most stores open from 10am to 6pm Monday to Saturday, often staying open late once a week. Shopping mall shops, and many department stores, stay open up to 9pm. Some stores, including those in the shopping malls, open Sundays, typically from 10am to 6pm, while others (mostly in the larger cities) never close.

During the festive month of December, many stores extend their opening and closing times by one or two hours, to allow ample time for people to do their holiday shopping.

Sales Tax

Florida levies a six percent sales tax (may vary in different counties) on all goods except drugs, groceries, and children's clothes. Tax is not included in displayed prices, but is automatically added to the bill. It's worth noting that every year, usually in the last week of July or the first week of August, the state allows for a "tax-free shopping week" for the benefit of families who need to shop for the upcoming school year. Avail of this opportunity and take advantage of the tax-free status on most clothing and book purchases up to $50. This way, you will be able to save a rather considerable six percent off your total bill.

Department Stores

Most shopping malls include at least one department store. These are often huge affairs, offering an amazing range of products and services, from complimentary gift-wrapping to assistants who help you with your shopping.

Most of the department stores can be found all over the US, and all of them have a particular reputation for the quality of their merchandise. For example, Bloomingdale's has a good name for its stock of new fashions, as well as its gourmet food. Some stores specialize only in designer fashion such as the elegant, Saks Fifth Avenue, Neiman Marcus, and the conservatively classy Lord & Taylor. The well-known national department store Macy's also has several branches throughout the state. Shopping stalwarts Sears and JCPenney offer everything from clothing and cosmetics to appliances and power tools.

For essentials, from pencils to toothpaste, as well as grocery and electronics, you need look no further than the no-frills superstores such as Target, Kmart, and Walmart, all of which can be found in many locations throughout the state. You can also find basic necessities and sundries, along with snacks and one-hour photo developing at stores such as Walgreens and CVS Pharmacy. Many of

A stylish fashion boutique in Bal Harbour Shops in Miami

these stores remain open around the clock, especially in larger cities.

Shopping for Bargains

For some people, the chief appeal of Florida's shops are their cut-price goods. Discount stores carry all kinds of general merchandise, but electronic equipment, household goods, and clothes are the biggest draw. Some stores specialize in inexpensive fashion, chief among them being Ross, TJ Maxx, and Marshalls, all of which have branches in all the major cities. Best Buy is a great store for discounts on CDs, DVDs, computers, and electronics.

Factory outlet malls are particularly popular among bargain hunters. In these stores, you can buy slightly imperfect or discontinued merchandise at 50 to 75 percent below the retail price. Most factory outlet malls also contain brand-name stores selling household items and all types of clothing, such as Benetton sweaters and Levi's jeans at throwaway prices.

Orlando's International Drive (see p186) is lined with a multitude of discount and factory outlet stores. You can even find cheaper Disney souvenirs here, but be warned that the quality is usually not as good as those available in the theme parks themselves. You're better off visiting the Character Warehouse stores in several of the city's factory outlet malls, as these sell the previous season's official theme park merchandise at a discount of up to 75 percent.

The famous Orange World fruit stand in Kissimmee, selling top-quality Florida fruit

Flea markets, usually large, lively affairs that function on weekends, are popular territory for bargains. Used goods may not interest you, but at most markets you'll find crafts, antiques, and other things you may consider taking home. The food stands are an added bonus. Some markets are equally good for their enter-tainment value, such as the Fort Lauderdale Swap Shop (see p138) and Flea World in Orlando, which combines a flea market with a mini-circus and amusement park. Both venues claim to be the state's largest flea market and both are equally suited for a fun-filled afternoon.

Sponges for sale in Key West

Gifts and Souvenirs

Fresh oranges are a popular buy for Florida's visitors. The best-quality fruit is grown by the Indian River (see p119), where oranges are sold by the sackful. Another popular citrus is the key lime, which can be found statewide in a variety of food products, from sauces to pies. Shops usually deliver the fruit home for you if you live within the US.

Seashells also have wide appeal, but check their origins. The Lee Island Coast (see pp282–3) is most famous for its shells. You can buy harvested specimens in the Shell Factory near Fort Myers (see p281). The shells and corals touted by roadside stalls along US 1 in the Keys are often imported. Such stalls also sell natural sponges, but Tarpon Springs (see p255) is the classic place for them.

Native Americans sell crafts made on their reservations in Miccosukee Indian Village (see p289) and Hollywood (see p140), but Florida is not the best place for crafts. However, many towns are known for antiques, such as Dania (see p140), Micanopy (see p226), and Mount Dora (see p224).

Disney has honed merchan-dising into an art. Shopping is a major activity at Walt Disney World® and other theme parks. Museum stores also sell souvenirs, from repro-duction artifacts to educational games.

One of Florida's many factory outlets, advertising its bargain prices

What to Buy in Florida

People will probably tell you that you can buy just about anything you could ever want in Florida, from a designer bikini to a state-of-the art CD player – or even a new home. Indeed some overseas visitors go to Florida specifically to shop. Even if you are searching for more humble souvenirs or gifts, you will have your choice in the state's theme parks and seaside tourist centers. You may have to search around if you want to avoid kitsch memorabilia – though, in fact, this is what Florida probably does best and is what evokes more than anything else the flavor of the Sunshine State.

Miami Dolphins cap

Unmistakably Florida

All over Florida you can buy fun (and tacky) souvenirs from towels to ashtrays, often at reasonable prices. They are frequently emblazoned with "Florida," a palm tree, alligator, or some other characteristic image.

Keyring

Dried meal from the Kennedy Space Center

Theme Park Fare

All the theme parks, from Universal Studios® to Busch Gardens, produce their own merchandise, designed to appeal to all ages.

Fake Oscar from Universal Studios®

Tile with flamingos – a favorite motif

Alligator money bank

Seminole Crafts

Crafts made by Florida's Seminole Indians are available in a few places (see p351). You can pick up dolls and jewelry for just a few dollars, and brightly colored clothes, bags, and blankets can be a good buy, too.

Hand-Rolled Cigars

The Cuban tradition of hand-rolling cigars survives in Ybor City in Tampa (see pp264–5) and in Miami's Little Havana (see p99), though many are now made by machine. They make a fine gift for cigar-smoking friends.

Books

Books about Miami's Art Deco district often feature superb photos and make a lasting souvenir of the city. Or take home the flavors of Florida in the form of a cookbook.

Latin Music

If you get a taste for the Latin rhythms of Miami's Hispanic community, there is plenty of locally produced music to buy.

Inexpensive Goods

Many overseas visitors to the US will find that because of lower taxes, a whole range of goods are cheaper than they are at home, including jeans, sunglasses, running shoes, CDs, cameras, books, and so on. Florida also has many discount stores (see p351) that offer lower prices still; small electrical appliances are often a good buy. Downtown Miami is famous for its bargain shops (see pp98–9), which sell primarily low-cost gold, jewelry, and electronic equipment. Feel free to bargain if you have the nerve. Note that if you buy electronic equipment you will need to get a transformer for it to work outside the US. Most shops are used to foreign visitors and can send bulky purchases back home for you.

T-Shirts
Sold everywhere from gift shops to ordinary discount stores, T-shirts can be very cheap – but you should check the quality before buying.

Western Gear
The leather goods sold in stores such as JW Cooper are not necessarily made in Florida, and may not appeal to visitors from Texas. However, they are often a good value by international standards.

Authentic cowboy boots

Leather belt

The Flavors of Florida

Florida is famous worldwide for its citrus fruits, which you can buy either fresh (all year round in the case of some varieties) or preserved – as colorful candies, jams, or jellies, or as tasty marinades and oils for cooking. For those with a sweet tooth there are all sorts of sugary goodies, from sticky coconut patties to chewy sweets like salt water taffy. Locally made chocolate is not of great quality, but often comes in fun shapes.

Coconut patties

A basket of jellied citrus fruit, a favorite edible souvenir

Florida-grown oranges, sold by the sack

Colorful salt water taffy, popular among visitors

Lime marmalade

Tangerine jelly or "butter"

Hot jalapeño pepper jelly

Mango marinade

Key lime oil for cooking

Florida Shopping Malls and Districts

Shopping malls in Florida offer the very best in retail therapy, with a wide variety of stores, restaurants, and entertainment, all located in one complex. Many malls are anchored by two or more department stores (see p350), and include an array of shops covering everything from clothing, health, and beauty to books, music, and DVDs. While most malls are fully enclosed, there are some open-air structures as well. There are also several factory outlet malls (see p351), which sell branded goods at dramatically reduced prices. Parking is easily available and most shopping centers are accessible by the city's public transportation system.

Shoppers who want to enjoy Florida's sunny weather as they stroll from store to store may prefer the state's numerous outdoor shopping districts. These fashionable areas are mainly home to chic and exclusive boutiques, as well as some down-to-earth stores.

Shopping Districts

For those who dislike the idea of shopping malls, Florida's open-air shopping districts are a fine alternative, offering a selection of shops over a five or six block radius, rather than a cluster of shops operating in one complex.

These shopping areas have breathed new life into historic districts, and the stores here are predominantly upscale.

Miami Area

Miami's largest mall, **Aventura Mall**, has more than 250 stores, followed closely by **Dadeland Mall** and **Dolphin Mall**. The smaller **Bal Harbour Shops** in Miami Beach caters to upscale shoppers, with its chic designer boutique. Downtown, the **Bayside Marketplace** offers waterfront shops, restaurants, and entertainment.

The best shopping districts in the Miami area (see pp98–9) include Coral Gables' **Village of Merrick Park** and **Downtown Coral Gables and Miracle Mile**. Downtown Coconut Grove is also superb, with malls such as **CocoWalk** and **Streets of Mayfair**. Other leading districts include South Beach's chic, eight-block-long **Lincoln Road Mall**, and **Cauley Square Historic Village**, which is closer to the Everglades than to downtown Miami.

Gold & Treasure Coasts

Travelers looking to cut costs will adore **Sawgrass Mills** in Fort Lauderdale. With over 300 budget department stores and outlet shops, this place could occupy an entire day of your trip. For more upmarket shopping, visit **The Galleria**.

Palm Beach's **Worth Avenue**, fashionable since the 1920s, is now one of the world's most exclusive shopping streets. Just down the coast in Boca Raton, **Mizner Park**, named after the famous architect who designed it, also indulges the rich and famous. Not far away in Boca Raton, the large, upscale **Town Center Mall** in Glades Road is a convenient place to shop.

Orlando & the Space Coast

Orlando has the highest number of outlet malls in Florida. International Drive is home to **Premier Outlets**, as well as **Festival Bay Mall**. **Orlando Premium Outlets** and **Lake Buena Vista Factory Stores** are near Walt Disney World®.

A shopping tradition for Orlando visitors, **The Florida Mall** has many budget shops, while **Pointe Orlando** and **Mall at Millenia** are more upscale. **Park Avenue** in Winter Park (see p193) is full of boutiques and gourmet restaurants.

The Northeast

Shoppers in Jacksonville can see the beautiful St. Johns River from The **Jacksonville Landing** complex, while **The Avenues** offers a slightly more traditional mall experience.

Further down the coast, bargain shoppers should visit **St. Augustine Premium Outlets**. No visit to Daytona Beach is complete without a stop at **Ocean Walk Shoppes**, which true to its name, faces the sea.

The Panhandle

Visitors to Destin can choose between the open-air **Destin Commons** mall or **Silver Sands Premium Outlets**, which specializes in budget designer clothes.

In Tallahassee, the state capital of Florida, **Governor's Square Mall** offers the widest selection of stores.

The Gulf Coast

Bargain shoppers will find three outlet malls along the Gulf Coast's I-75 corridor. From north to south, you can do your discount shopping at **Ellenton Premium Outlets** near Sarasota, **Tanger Outlets** in Fort Myers, and **Miromar Outlets** in Estero.

For more upscale shopping, go to **International Plaza and Bay Street** near Tampa airport, or **Centro Ybor**, situated in Ybor City, Tampa's Latin Quarter district.

Shopping districts of note include Sarasota's **St. Armands Circle**, a haven for gourmets, **Hyde Park Village** in Tampa, and **Johns Pass Village** near Madeira Beach, which is modeled after a late 19th-century fishing village.

The Everglades & The Keys

Cost cutters will enjoy the **Outlets** in both Naples and in Florida City.

The upmarket district of **Fifth Avenue South** in Naples has a variety of boutiques. Any trip to Key West has to include the artsy **Mallory Square**, with its gift shops, boutiques, and street vendors.

DIRECTORY

Miami Area

Aventura Mall
19501 Biscayne Blvd,
Aventura.
Tel (305) 935-1110.
W aventuramall.com

Bal Harbour Shops
9700 Collins Ave, Bal
Harbour.
Tel (305) 866-0311.
W balharbourshops.
com

Bayside Marketplace
401 Biscayne Blvd, Miami.
Map 4 F1.
Tel (305) 577-3344.
W baysidemarketplace.
com

**Cauley Square
Historic Village**
22400 Old Dixie Hwy (US
1), Miami. **Road Map** F5.
Tel (305) 258-3543.
W cauleysquare.com

CocoWalk
3015 Grand Ave, Coconut
Grove. **Map** 6 E4.
Tel (305) 444-0777.
W cocowalk.net

Dadeland Mall
7535 N Kendall Drive,
Kendall.
Tel (305) 665-6226.

Dolphin Mall
11401 NW 12th St, Miami.
Tel (305) 365-7466.
W shopdolphinmall.
com

**Downtown Coral
Gables and Miracle
Mile**
224 Miracle Mile, Coral
Gables. **Map** 5 C1.
Tel (305) 569-0311.
W shopcoralgables.com

Lincoln Road Mall
Lincoln Rd at Meridian
Ave., Miami Beach.
Map 2 E2.
Tel (305) 531-3442.

Streets of Mayfair
3390 Mary St., Coconut
Grove. **Map** 6 E4.
Tel (305) 448-1700.
W mayfairinthegrove.
com

**Village of Merrick
Park**
358 San Lorenzo Ave,
Coral Gables. **Map** 5 C4.

Tel (305) 529-0200.
W villageofmerrick
park.com

Gold & Treasure Coast

The Galleria
2414 E Sunrise Blvd, Fort
Lauderdale.
Tel (954) 564-1015.
W galleriamall-fl.com

Mizner Park
327 Plaza Real,
Boca Raton.
Tel (561) 362-0606.
W miznerpark.com

Sawgrass Mills
12801 W Sunrise Blvd,
Fort Lauderdale.
Tel (954) 846-2350.
W sawgrassmills.com

Town Center Mall
6000 Glades Road,
Boca Raton.
Tel (561) 368-6000.
W simon.com

Worth Ave
Palm Beach.
Tel (561) 659-6909.
W worth-avenue.com

Orlando and the Space Coast

Festival Bay Mall
5250 International Dr,
Orlando.
Tel (407) 351-7718.
W shopfestival baymall.
com

The Florida Mall
8001 S Orange Blossom
Trail, Orlando.
Tel (407) 851-6255.

**Lake Buena Vista
Factory Stores**
15591 Apopka Vineland Rd,
Orlando.
Tel (407) 238-9301.
W lbvfs.com

Mall at Millenia
4200 Conroy Rd, Orlando.
Tel (407) 363-3555.
W mallatmillenia.com

**Orlando Premium
Outlets**
8200 Vineland Av, Orlando.
Tel (407) 238-7787.
4951 International Drive,
Orlando.
Tel (407) 352-9600.

Park Avenue
Winter Park, Orange Co.
Tel (877) 972-4262.
W wpfl.org

Pointe Orlando
9101 International
Drive, Orlando.
Tel (407) 248-2838.
W pointeorlando.com

The Northeast

The Avenues
10300 Southside Blvd,
Jacksonville.
Tel (904) 363-3060.

Jacksonville Landing
2 Independent Drive,
Jacksonville.
Tel (904) 353-1188.
W jacksonvillelanding.
com

Ocean Walk Shoppes
250 N Atlantic Ave,
Daytona Beach.
Tel (386) 258-9544.
W oceanwalk shoppes.
com

**St. Augustine
Premium Outlets**
2700 State Rd 16, St.
Augustine.
Tel (904) 825-1555.

The Panhandle

Destin Commons
4300 Legendary Drive,
Destin.
Tel (850) 337-8700.
W destincommons.com

Governor's Square Mall
1500 Apalachee Pkwy,
Tallahassee.
Tel (850) 877-8106.
W governorssquare.com

**Silver Sands
Premium Outlets**
10562 Emerald Coast
Pkwy, W Destin.
Tel (850) 654-9771.
W premiumoutlets.com

The Gulf Coast

Centro Ybor
1600 E 8th Ave, Tampa.
Tel (813) 242-4660.
W centroybor.com

**Ellenton
Premium Outlets**
5461 Factory Shops Blvd,
Ellenton.

Tel (941) 723-1150.
W primeoutlets.com

**International Plaza
and Bay Street**
2223 N Westshore Blvd,
Tampa.
Tel (813) 342-3790.
W shopinternational
plaza.com

Johns Pass Village
12901 Gulf Blvd, Madeira
Beach.
Tel (727) 394-0756.
W johnspass.com

Miromar Outlets
10801 Corkscrew Rd,
Estero.
Tel (239) 948-3766.
W miromaroutlets.com

Hyde Park Village
1509 W Snow Ave, Tampa.
Tel (813) 251-3500.
W hydeparkvillage.net

St. Armands Circle
300 Madison Drive,
Sarasota.
Tel (941) 388-1554.
W starmandscircle
assoc.com

Tanger Outlets
20350 Summerlin Rd,
Fort Myers.
Tel (888) 471-3939.
W tangeroutlet.com/
fortmyers

The Everglades & The Keys

Fifth Avenue South
649 5th Ave S, Naples.
Tel (239) 692-8436.
W fifthavenue south.
com

**Florida Keys
Outlet Center**
250 E Palm Drive, Florida
City. **Tel** (305) 248-4727.

Mallory Square
400 Wall St, Key West.
Tel (305) 809-3700.
W mallorysquare.com

Naples Outlet Center
6060 Collier Blvd, Naples.
Tel (239) 775-8083 .

Specialty Shops in Florida

Shopping is as natural as breathing in Florida, and there are a plethora of stores specializing in all kinds of merchandise statewide. From antiques to outdoor gear to music, there is a store to fulfil every shopping need.

Most specialty stores are not found in major shopping areas, so public or private transportation is needed to access them. However, the vast selection of goods available, and the opportunity to interact with knowledgeable sales staff, makes these shops well worth a visit.

Antiques

Just northwest of Orlando, Mount Dora (see p224) is the self-proclaimed antiques capital of Florida. **Renninger's Twin Markets** is one of the largest antiques markets in this haven for collectors. Micanopy (see p226), another hub for vintage goods, has more than 18 antiques stores.

Other notable destinations for antiques shopping include **Waldo's Antique Village**, a flea market in the tiny town of Waldo near Starke, and the **Hillsboro Antique Mall** in Pompano Beach. For sheer volume, visit the **Historic Antique District** in Dania (see p140). It offers over 100 shops within a one-block radius.

Arts and Craft Galleries

The Florida Keys are a great place to shop for locally-made arts and crafts. In Key Largo (see p296), drop into **Happy Feathers** for unique Florida crafts that also make fantastic gifts. Further down the road in Key West, Duvall Street has a multitude of local craft and art galleries, including **Alan S. Maltz Gallery**, which features the photog-apher's award-winning works.

In the resort town of Seaside (see p240), **Ruskin Place Artists' Colony** is a joy for art lovers, with its multitude of galleries and shops offering works by local artists-in-residence.

Farmers' Markets

Farmers' Markets are excellent places to pick up fresh Florida citrus fruits and other produce that come straight from local farms and orchards. Many markets also offer a variety of crafts and other attractive and interesting merchandise from street vendors.

Downtown Farmer's Market in Orlando opens for business every Sunday morning, and offers baked goods, farm produce, and flowers. **Lincoln Road Mall**, which opens on Sunday, is very popular with South Beach locals, while in the Panhandle, **Tallahassee Downtown Marketplace** opens on Tuesday, Thursday, and Saturday. In the Gulf Coast, explore **Clearwater Downtown Farmer's Market**, which opens Wednesday and Saturday, from mid-October to mid-April. **Ybor City Fresh Market** is held year-round, every Saturday.

Gifts and Souvenirs

Not surprisingly, Miami, with its Little Havana neighborhood, has many treats in store for cigar aficio-nados. **El Crédito Cigar Factory,** has an excellent collection of hand-rolled cigars, while downtown, you will find the highly-regarded **Puros Indios Cigars**. **Sosa Family Cigars** at Walt Disney World® also stocks quality cigars and cigar accessories. For a less smoky experience, try **Little Havana To Go,** which touts itself as the official souvenir store for Cuban art, music, books, and more.

Items from **Key West Aloe**, with its vast range of Aloe-based beauty products, have a distinct Floridian touch. Their frangipani soaps are a fragrant reminder of the Keys.

Get your motor running with a visit to **Orlando Harley-Davidson**, Florida's largest motorcycle dealership. Their logo merchandise is guaranteed to delight the motorcycle enthusiast back home.

Gourmet Food and Drink

Key West has a wide variety of tasty gourmet offerings. Try the fiery flavorings of **Peppers of Key West**, the fresh-baked artisan breads of **Cole's Peace**, and the incredibly fresh fish sold by the **Conch Republic Seafood Company**.

Florida Orange Groves Winery eschews grapes in favor of citrus fruit to create exotic vintages, but **Lakeridge Winery** offers a range of reds, whites, and rosés made from Florida's Muscadine grape.

For desserts, try **Peterbrooke** for delicious custom-made chocolate treats, and take their fascinating factory tour.

International Food Club sells a vast range of foods from all over the world, from bangers and mash to Indian teas and Chinese spices.

Music and DVDs

Carrying a wide range of music and movies, the **F.Y.E.** chain has several locations throughout Florida, including Miami and Orlando.

For more genre-specific options, try an independent store. The **Park Ave CDs** specialize in indie rock. **Uncle Sam's** in Miami offers a similar selection.

Outdoor and Water Sports

With its perennial sunshine, Florida is a great place for outdoor and water sports. Happily, it also has the stores to outfit you for any activity.

Soccer enthusiasts will find everything they desire at **Soccer Locker** in Miami. Further up the coast, Cocoa Beach is home to **Ron Jon Surf Shop**. This legendary water sports store is open 24 hours for all your sun, sea, and sand needs. If you're into camping and fishing, **Bass Pro Shops** has several locations in Florida, with its newest, and possibly largest branch located at Festival Bay in Orlando.

DIRECTORY

Antiques

Hillsboro Antique Mall and Café
2900 W. Sample Rd, Pompano Beach.
Tel (954) 571-9988.
w hillsboroantiquemall.com

Historic Antique District
Federal Hwy, Dania Beach Blvd, Dania.
Tel (954) 925-6935.

Renninger's Twin Markets
20651 US Hwy 441, Mount Dora.
Tel (352) 383-8393.
w renningers.com/dora

Waldo's Antique Village
17805 NE US Hwy 301, Waldo.
Tel (407) 877-5921.
w waldosfleamarket.com

Arts and Crafts Galleries

Alan S. Maltz Gallery
1210 Duval St, Key West.
Tel (305) 295-0005.
w alanmaltz.com

Happy Feathers
99150 Overseas Hwy, Key Largo.
Tel (305) 453-1800.

Ruskin Place Artists' Colony
Ruskin Place, Seaside.
Tel (888) 732-7433.

Farmers' Markets

Clearwater Downtown Farmer's Market
112, S Osceola, Clearwater.
Tel (727) 461-7674.
w clearwaterfarmersmarket.com (Open 8am–1pm)

Downtown Farmer's Market
Lake Eola Park, Orlando.
Tel (321) 202-5855.
w orlandofarmersmarket.com
(Open 10am–4pm)

Lincoln Road Mall
Lincoln Rd at 16th St, Miami Beach.
Map 2 E2.
Tel (305) 531-3442.
w lincolnroad.org

Tallahassee Downtown Marketplace
1415 Timberlane Rd at Market Sq, Tallahassee.
Tel (850) 224-3252.
w downtownmarket.com (Open 8am–2pm)

Ybor City Fresh Market
8th Ave and 19th St, Ybor City.
Tel (813) 241-2442.
w ybormarket.com

Gifts and Souvenirs

El Crédito Cigar Factory
1106 SW 8th St, Miami.
Map 3 B2.
Tel (305) 858-3810.

Key West Aloe
540 Greene St, Key West.
Tel (800) 445-2563.
w keywestaloe.com

Little Havana To Go
1442 SW 8th St, Miami.
Map 3 B2.
Tel (305) 857-9720.

Orlando Harley-Davidson
3770 37th St, Orlando.
Tel (407) 423-0346.
w orlandoharley.com

Puros Indios Cigars
114 NW 22nd Ave, Miami.
Map 3 A1.
Tel (305) 644-1116.
w purosindioscigars.com

Sosa Family Cigars
1502 E Buena Vista Drive, Lake Buena Vista.
Tel (407) 827-0114.
w sosacigars.com

Gourmet Food and Drink

Cole's Peace
1111 Eaton St, Key West.
Tel (305) 292-0703.
w colespeace.com

Conch Republic Seafood Company
631 Greene St, Key West.
Tel (305) 294-4403.
w conchrepublicseafood.com

Florida Orange Groves Winery
1500 Pasadena Ave S, St. Petersburg.
Tel (800) 338-7923.
w floridawine.com

International Food Club
4300 LB McLeod Rd, Orlando.
Tel (321) 281-4300.

Lakeridge Winery
19239 US 27 N, Clermont.
Tel (800) 768-9463.
w lakeridgewinery.com

Peppers of Key West
602 Greene St, Key West.
Tel (800) 597-2823.
w peppersofkeywest.com

Peterbrooke
1470 San Marco Blvd, Jacksonville.
Tel (800) 771-0019.
w peterbrooke.com

Music and DVDs

F.Y.E.
Coral Square, 9009 W Atlantic Blvd, Coral Springs.
Tel (954) 755-8052.
Altamonte Mall, 451 E Altamonte Dr, Altamonte Springs.
Tel (407) 332-8851.

Park Ave CDs
2916 Corrine Dr., Orlando.
Tel (407) 447-7275.
w parkavecds.com

Uncle Sam's
939 Washington Ave, Miami Beach.
Map 2 E3.
Tel (305) 532-0973.
w unclesamsmusic.com

Outdoor and Water Sports

Bass Pro Shops
Festival Bay Mall, 5156 International Drive, Orlando.
Tel (407) 563-5200.
w basspro.com

Ron Jon Surf Shop
4151 N Atlantic Ave, Cocoa Beach.
Tel (888) 757-8737.
w ronjons.com

Soccer Locker
9601 S Dixie Hwy, Miami.
Road Map F5.
Tel (866) 957-6223.
w soccerlocker.com

ENTERTAINMENT IN FLORIDA

Whether your preference is for a Broadway drama, a lavish Las Vegas-style floorshow, a night in a disco, or a bit of gambling, Florida has something for everyone. You'll find the greatest range of entertainment in South Florida, particularly along the Gold Coast and in Miami *(see pp100–101)*, but Sarasota and Tampa are also major cultural centers. Walt Disney World® and Orlando offer the best choice of family entertainment, with theme parks galore to thrill the children during the daytime and dinner shows at night. In the

Northeast and the Panhandle the entertainment is more limited, being best in resorts like Panama City Beach and university cities such as Gainesville and Tallahassee.

Wherever you are, in cities with distinct mainland and beach areas, such as Fort Lauderdale, the liveliest nightlife is on the waterfront. As far as the performing arts are concerned, most high-quality shows take place between October and April, although there is a good choice of events all year round.

The Raymond F. Kravis Center for the Performing Arts, West Palm Beach

Sources of Information

Most regional newspapers in Florida have a special weekend section that lists all local attractions and events, as well as details of venues. Local Convention and Visitors' Bureaus and chambers of commerce are also chock-a-block with brochures.

Making Reservations

The easiest way to purchase tickets for a concert, play, football game, or other event is to call the relevant box office and pay by credit card. Some places, however, will require you to make your reservation through **Ticketmaster**. This company runs an extensive pay-by-phone operation and also has outlets in music and discount stores. It charges a commission of $2–8 per ticket above the ticket's face value, depending on the event.

Major Venues

Florida's largest venues, some of which are known as performing arts centers, are used for a whole range of performances, from operas to rock concerts, as well as for special events including, in some cases, sports events. This is where major national touring companies or artists usually perform, though you can sometimes see local productions here too.

Some of the most important venues in Florida: the **Raymond F. Kravis Center for the Performing Arts** in West Palm Beach; Fort Lauderdale's **Broward Center for the Performing Arts**; the **Adrienne Arsht Center for the Performing Arts** in Miami *(see p100)*; the huge **Straz Center**; the **1-800-ASK-GARY Amphitheatre** in Tampa;

Theatre emblem, Pensacola

and the **Van Wezel Performing Arts Hall** in Sarasota. Other major theaters include the **Florida Citrus Bowl** in Orlando, a 70,000-seat arena where stars from Paul McCartney to George Michael perform. The **EverBank Field** in Jacksonville hosts major rock concerts, too.

Theater

Road shows, often lavish productions with extravagant sets and big casts, originate on Broadway and are the highest-quality productions you are likely to see in Florida. The state has several good theater companies of its own, whose shows are performed in smaller, more atmospheric spots such as the **Mann Performing Arts Hall** in Fort Myers or Key West's **Red Barn Theatre**. The **Florida State University Center for the Performing Arts** is home to Sarasota's own Asolo Theater Company. The building, originally the opera house of Dunfermline in Scotland, was brought to Sarasota in the 1980s. The **Players of Sarasota** is the city's longest established theater company, such famous actors as Montgomery Clift launched their careers. Its performances of musicals and plays usually earn widespread praise.

Classical Music, Opera, and Dance

Most major cities have their own symphony orchestra. The **Symphony of the Americas** performs mainly in Fort Lauderdale and in the cities along the Gold Coast, as well as touring internationally. Miami's New World Symphony *(see p100)* also tours internationally. Keep an eye open for performances by the Jacksonville Symphony Orchestra, which is based at the city's **Times-Union Center for the Performing Arts**.

The **Florida Grand Opera**, the state's largest opera company, currently performs at the Adrienne Arsht Center for the Performing Arts. The Broward Center for the Performing Arts is the home of the Gold Coast Opera, a private theatrical company that presents classical operas such as *Carmen* and *The Barber of Seville*. For a more intimate experience, visit the small **Monticello Opera House**, which hosts opera between September and May.

The best ballet company is the Miami City Ballet *(see p100)*, whose choreographer is Edward Villela, a protegé of the late George Balanchine.

Movies

For arts movies you'll do better in New York or Los Angeles, but Florida has plenty of multiscreen cinemas showing blockbuster films. The state's most famous cinema is the historic **Tampa Theatre** *(see p263)*, which hosts a variety of live acts but serves up mainly a mixture of classic and foreign films.

Also watch out for annual film festivals: Sarasota has one in November, and the Miami International Film Festival is in February, when films are shown at the Gusman Center for the Performing Arts *(see p100)*. Orlando hosts the Florida Film Festival in the spring.

Dinner Shows

Dinner shows are a popular form of family entertainment in Florida, especially in Orlando *(see p195)*. Here, diners sit at communal tables and are served huge meals that are generally themed to the show that you are watching. Audience participation is normally *de rigueur*.

Outside Orlando, the dinner shows tend to be less raucous but still provide varied entertainment, from conventional plays to comedies and musicals, and even murder-mystery dinners. The **Mai Kai** in Fort Lauderdale, a long-running and superbly tacky Polynesian revue, entertains with dancers dressed in grass skirts, fire eaters, and the like. Jacksonville's **Alhambra Dinner Theater** puts on ambitious musicals of the *Oklahoma* and *South Pacific* school.

A singer entertains at Miami's Latin Carnival *(see p38)*

Live Music and Nightclubs

Some of the most entertaining places to dance are clubs where you can dance to live instead of canned music. The best are often clubs where the music is provided by a big band or orchestra; "supper clubs" offer food as well as a band. The music can be varied: the **Coliseum Ballroom**, a Moorish-style gem in St. Petersburg, draws a crowd for both ballroom and country dancing. South Beach has the greatest choice of conventional discos *(see p101)*, but you'll find good clubs in popular vacation spots. **Razzles** in Daytona Beach offers high-energy music, and **Cheers** in Fort Lauderdale showcases current rock bands and has a busy dance floor. **Cowboys Orlando** is a popular country music dance club. Nightclubs require you to show ID to prove that you are over 18 or, in some cases, 21.

Festivals are fertile territory for live music, and there are also countless spots where dancing to the music isn't compulsory. Key West has several well-established places, like the Hog's Breath Saloon *(see p349)*. Tampa's **Skipper's Smokehouse** offers reggae and blues. Country and western music is popular, for which Pace's **Farmers' Opry House** is a major venue. Some of the bars listed on pages 348–9 also offer live entertainment.

Sign for Hog's Breath Saloon in Key West

The lavish interior of the Tampa Theatre, an historic cinema

Street performers in Mallory Square in Key West, providing nightly entertainment at sunset

Cruise and Boat Trips

Florida is the world's leading departure point for cruises to the Caribbean, and ships set off regularly from Miami, Port Everglades, and other ports. Companies offering cruises for several days or more include **Disney, Royal Caribbean**, and the **Carnival Cruise Line**.

You can also go on mini-cruises, for a day or just an evening – the cost of which starts at around $40. Evening cruises usually entail dinner and dancing, and sometimes on-board gambling. The proximity of Freeport, Grand Bahama, allows one-day mini-cruises on lines such as Balearia Bahamas Express in Fort Lauderdale.

Pleasure boat trips are available all over Florida. The Jungle Queen in Fort Lauderdale *(see p139)*, the **Manatee Queen** in Jupiter *(see p121)*, and St. Petersburg's **Starlite Cruises** are popular boats. The **St. Johns Rivership Company** offers trips on the St. Johns River starting from Sanford *(see p224)*.

Gambling

Gambling on cruise ships is popular because conventional casinos are illegal on most of the mainland: once a ship is in international waters, about 3 miles (5 km) from shore, the law

no longer applies. But you can visit one of the state's six **Seminole Indian Casinos**: two are in Hollywood *(see p141)*, one in Coconut Creek, another in Immokalee near Naples, one near Tampa, and one in Okechobee. The Miccosukee tribe own a casino near Miami. Gulfstream Park Racetrack and Mardi Gras at Hollywood Racetrack, both in Hallandale, and Pompano Park Harness Track in Pompano Beach all have casinos.

Children's Entertainment

Kids are catered to all over Florida, not just at the theme parks. Museums often have excellent hands-on exhibits, and in many zoos and some parks you find "petting zoos," where children can enjoy direct contact with the animals. Kids can also

The Rivership Romance on the St. Johns River

have great fun at the water parks *(see p365)*, found all over the state. With **Walt Disney World® Resort, Universal Orlando®, SeaWorld®**, and other big attractions, Orlando has no shortage of family entertainment; keep an eye out for what's on at the **Amway Center**, which hosts everything from ice-skating shows to circuses and NBA games.

There is also plenty of free entertainment. Kids often enjoy street entertainers, and

there are festivals to choose from all year round *(see pp38–41)*.

Gay Entertainment

South Beach in Miami is well known for its vibrant gay scene *(see p101)* that is attracting more and more gay visitors from home and abroad each year. Key West has been a gay mecca for a number of years, as has Fort Lauderdale, where **Scandal's Saloon** offers music and drinks along with cowboy cool and tongue-in-cheek humor.

For additional information, go online and visit **Gay Guide to Florida**; a very useful web resource for a variety of gay entertainment and lifestyle options in Florida, including information on popular nightlife venues, restaurants, accommodation, local activities, and businesses.

Festivities during the Gay Pride celebration in Fort Lauderdale

DIRECTORY

Making Reservations

Ticketmaster
Tel (800) 745-3000.
w ticketmaster.com

Major Venues

1-800-ASK-GARY Amphitheatre
4802 US 301 North,
Tampa.
Tel (866) 614-4183.

Adrienne Arsht Center for the Performing Arts
1300 Biscayne Blvd,
Miami.
Tel (786) 468-2000.

Broward Center for the Performing Arts
201 SW Fifth Ave, Fort
Lauderdale.
Tel (954) 522-5334.

EverBank Field
1 Stadium Blvd,
Jackson-ville.
Tel (904) 633-6100.

Florida Citrus Bowl
1 Citrus Bowl Place,
Orlando.
Tel (407) 423-2476.

Raymond F. Kravis Center for the Performing Arts
701 Okeechobee Blvd,
West Palm Beach.
Tel (561) 832-7469.

Straz Center
1010 N MacInnes Place,
Tampa.
Tel (813) 229-7827.

Van Wezel Performing Arts Hall
777 N Tamiami Trail,
Sarasota.
Tel (941) 955-7676.
w vanwezel.org

Theater

Florida State University Center for the Performing Arts
5555 N Tamiami Trail,
Sarasota.
Tel (941) 351-8000.

Mahaffey Theater
400 First St South, St
Petersburg.
Tel (727) 892-5798.

Mann Performing Arts Hall
8099 College Parkway,
Fort Myers.
Tel (239) 481-4849.

Players of Sarasota
838 N Tamiami Trail,
Sarasota.
Tel (941) 365-2494.

Red Barn Theatre
319 Duval St, Key West.
Tel (305) 296-9911.

Classical Music, Opera, and Dance

Florida Grand Opera
8390 NW 25th St, Miami.
Tel (305) 854-7890.

Monticello Opera House
West Washington St,
Monticello.
Tel (850) 997-4242.

Symphony of the Americas
2425 E Commercial Blvd,
Fort Lauderdale.
Tel (954) 335-7002.

Times-Union Center for the Performing Arts
300 W Water St,
Jacksonville.
Tel (904) 633-6110.

Movies

Tampa Theatre
711 N Franklin St, Tampa.
Tel (813) 274-8981.
w tampatheatre.org

Dinner Shows

Alhambra Dinner Theater
12000 Beach Blvd,
Jacksonville.
Tel (904) 641-1212.

Mai Kai
3599 N Federal Highway,
Fort Lauderdale.
Tel (954) 563-3272 or
(800) 262-4524.

Live Music and Nightclubs

Cheers
941 E Cypress Creek Rd,
Fort Lauderdale.
Tel (954) 771-6337.

Coliseum Ballroom
535 4th Ave North, St.
Petersburg.
Tel (727) 892-5202.

Cowboys Orlando
1108 S Orange Blossom
Trail, Orlando.
Tel (407) 422-7115.

Farmers' Opry House
8897 Byron Campbell Rd,
Pace, Florida.
Tel (850) 994-6000.

Razzles
611 Seabreeze Blvd,
Daytona Beach.
Tel (386) 257-6236.

Skipper's Smokehouse
910 Skipper Rd, Tampa.
Tel (813) 971-0666.

Cruise and Boat Trips

Balearia Bahamas Express
Terminal 1, Port Everglades,
Fort Lauderdale.
Tel (866) 699 6988 .

Carnival Cruise Line
3655 NW 87th Ave, Miami.
Tel (800) 764-7419.

Royal Caribbean Cruise Line
Miami, Fort Lauderdale,
Port Canaveral.
Tel (800) 561-7225.

St. Johns Rivership Company
433 N Palmetto Ave, Sanford.
Tel (321) 441-3030.

Starlite Cruises
3400 Pasadena Ave
South, St. Petersburg.
Tel (727) 462-2628.

Manatee Queen
1065 N Ocean Blvd,
Jupiter.
Tel (561) 744-2191.

Yacht Star Ship
601 Channelside Drive,
Tampa.
Tel (813) 223-7999.

Gambling

Seminole Hard Rock Hotel and Casino
5223 N Orient Rd, I-4 Exit
5, Tampa.

Tel (866) 502-7529.
506 South 1st St,
Immokalee.
Tel (800) 218-0007.
5550 NW 40th St,
Coconut Creek.
Tel (866) 222-7466.

Children's Entertainment

Amway Center
400 W Church St, Orlando.
Tel (407) 440-7000.

SeaWorld®/Busch Gardens
Tel (407) 363-2613.
w buschgardens.com

Universal Orlando®
Tel (407) 363-8000.
w universalorlando.com

Walt Disney World®
Tel (407) 934-7639.
w disneyworld.com

Gay Entertainment

Gay Guide to Florida
w gay-guide.com
Scandal's Saloon 1373 NE
6th Ave, Wilton Manors.
Tel (954) 567-2432.

SPORTS AND OUTDOOR ACTIVITIES

Thanks to Florida's climate, you can take part in many sports and outdoor activities all year round, making the state a top destination for all sports enthusiasts, from golfers and tennis players to canoeists and deep-sea divers; some people even base their entire vacation around the sports opportunities available. Water sports of all kinds are well represented, with wonderful beaches on both the Atlantic and Gulf coasts. Florida also boasts approximately 10 million acres (4 million ha) of protected land, which can be explored on foot, horseback, bicycle, or boat. For those who prefer to watch rather than take part, Florida has a wide range of spectator sports to offer; these are described on pages 36–7.

A seaside golf course at Boca Raton on the Gold Coast

Source of Information

The two best sources of general information are the **Florida Sports Foundation** and the **Department of Environmental Protection (DEP)**, which can provide information on most outdoor activities. The *Florida Vacation Guide*, available from Florida tourist board offices abroad, gives useful addresses, or you can contact local tourist offices for information about specific areas. Further sources are given in individual sections.

Golf

Florida is a golfer's paradise; with over 1,100 courses, it is the country's top golfing destination. Palm Beach offers so many courses (150 total) it claims to be the "golfing capital of the world," even though Naples boasts the greatest concentration.

Courses in Florida are flat by most standards, but landscaping provides some relief. Many of the most challenging courses are attached to resort hotels along the coast (some offer vacation packages); you'll find courses inland too, including at Walt Disney World® *(see p179)*. About two-thirds of courses are open to the public.

Golf is a year-round sport, but winter is the busiest season. If you play in summer, start early in the day to avoid late afternoon thunderstorms and lightning. Greens fees vary from under $20 to over $75 per person and are highest in the peak winter season.

The *PLAY FLA GOLF* guide, from the Florida Sports Foundation, lists all public and private courses.

Tennis

Tennis, like golf, is very popular in Florida. Many hotels have courts, and some resorts offer vacation packages that include lessons. Contact the **United States Tennis Association (Florida Section)** for information on coaching, clubs, and competitions. The state's most famous tennis school is the **Nick Bollettieri Tennis Academy** *(see p271)*, which offers weekly training programs for $800 and up, as well as one-day sessions.

Diving and Snorkeling

Florida is superb diving and snorkeling territory. The country's only living coral reef skirts the state's southeast coast, stretching the length of the Keys, where there is a magnificent variety of coral and fish *(see pp296–7)*. The reef lies 3–5 miles (5–8 km) offshore and is easily accessible to amateur snorkelers. Guided snorkeling trips are available throughout the Keys and are generally excellent.

The state's estimated 4,000 diving sites have increased, thanks to the artificial reefs program. All over Florida, everything from bridge spans to freighters have been used to create a habitat for coral and colorful fish; there is even a Rolls Royce off Palm Beach. Sunken Spanish galleons also provide fascinating dive sites, mainly in south Florida.

If you don't have a Certified Divers Card you'll need to take a course. Recognized NAUI or PADI courses are widely available, and

Freshwater swimming at Wakulla Springs near Tallahassee

Colorful jet ski and boat rental outlet in the Panhandle

novices can learn in just four days for $300–400.

For more information, the Florida Sports Foundation's *Florida Boating and Diving Guide* is helpful, or you can call the **Keys Association of Dive Operators (KADO)**.

Swimming and Water Sports

Swimming is as natural as breathing to most Floridians. Many hotels have pools, but the joy of Florida is the chance to swim in the ocean or in the many lakes, springs, and rivers.

The Atlantic provides the best waves and Florida's only surfing beaches, including Cocoa Beach *(see p199)*. The warm, gentle swells of the Gulf of Mexico are better for kids. These western beaches are beautiful, with white sands and dunes in the Panhandle. Coastal erosion means that the southeastern beaches are often quite narrow, while there are only a couple of sandy beaches in the Keys.

Beach access is sometimes controlled: many lie within parks, which charge admission. Some hotels like to give the impression that their beach is for guests only, but they can't stop public access. Lifeguards monitor the most popular beaches in high season.

Many inland parks have freshwater swimming areas, including some beautifully clear spring water holes, such as in Blue Spring State Park *(see p224)*. Another alternative are the water parks, with all kinds of rides and pools, found throughout the state.

The full range of water sports, from windsurfing to jet skiing, is offered at Florida's resorts; waterskiing can also be enjoyed on freshwater lakes and inland waterways. Avoid swimming in the interior lakes during summer, as algae growth can pose danger.

Fishing

Florida's numerous lakes and rivers are overflowing with fish, and fishing is not so much a sport as a way of life for a great many Floridians. The opportunities are endless both inland and all along the coast.

The Atlantic and Gulf shores are dotted with dedicated fishermen. Fishing right off the pier is popular at many coastal spots, but for those who enjoy angling on a different scale there is plenty of sport fishing for which the state is probably best known.

Deep-sea fishing boats can be chartered at many seaside resorts. The biggest fleets are in the Panhandle, especially around Fort Walton Beach and Destin, and in the Keys. With the Gulf Stream nearby, the waters off the Keys offer the most varied fishing in the state *(see p299)*. Organized group excursions are an excellent option for novices. If you want to take your big fish home, a taxidermist will preserve it for you; the more eco-conscious alternative these days is to have a model made of your catch. Bait and tackle shops or the charter boat operator can give you the names of local taxidermists.

Florida has thousands of lakes, as well as rivers and canals, for freshwater fishing. Boat rentals and fishing guides are available along the larger rivers, such as the Anclote and the St. Johns, and in other popular fishing areas like Lake Okeechobee *(see p132)*. Fishing is also permitted in many state and other parks. In rural parts, fish camps offer simple accommodations and basic supplies, though some are open only during the summer.

Licenses, costing from $12 to $30, are required for fresh-water and saltwater fishing. The *Fishing Handbook*, available from the **Florida Fish and Wildlife Conservation Commission**, gives information on locations and licensing. It also gives details of the entry dates, fees, regulations, and prizes of Florida's fishing tournaments; one of the best known is Destin's Fishing Rodeo *(see p40)*.

For more information on fishing or hunting, contact the Department of Environmental Protection, or the Florida Fish and Wildlife Conservation Commission *(see p365)*.

Pelicans observing anglers on a pier on Cedar Key

The Intracoastal Waterway at Boca Raton, on the Gold Coast

Boating

Florida's waterways attract boats of every description, from state-of-the-art yachts to wooden skiffs. With over 8,000 miles (12,870 km) of tidal coastline and 4,500 sq miles (11,655 sq km) of inland waters, the state is a paradise for boaters. Having a boat is as normal as having a car for some Floridians; the state has over 700,000 registered boats, and this doesn't include the 300,000 brought in annually from outside Florida.

The Intracoastal Waterway, extending 500 miles (800 km) down the east coast to the tip of the Keys (see pp26–7), is very popular. Often sheltered from the Atlantic Ocean by barrier islands, the route runs through rivers, creeks, and dredged canals. Although most of the west coast is open, the most interesting territory for boaters is where the Intracoastal Waterway resumes among the islands of the Lee Island Coast (see pp282–3).

The 135-mile (217-km) Okeechobee Waterway, which cuts through the state, is another popular route, becoming positively busy during the summer. It runs along the St. Lucie Canal from Stuart, across Lake Okeechobee and then on to Sanibel Island via the Caloosahatchee River.

These inland waterways, like many of the state's 166 rivers, are suitable for small boats or houseboats. Many of the latter are more like floating apartments, often being equipped with air-conditioning, microwave ovens, and even television. Houseboats

can be rented from several marinas, in Sanford on the St. Johns River, for example (see p224), while small to medium-sized boats are available at many fish camps or marinas.

Florida has an astonishing 1,250 marinas. Those along the coast usually have excellent facilities, with accommodations and rental outlets for boats and fishing tackle; inland marinas tend to be more basic. *Florida Boating and Diving*, a brochure available from the **Florida Sports Foundation**, lists most marinas in the state, with details of their facilities.

Florida State Park emblem

Backcountry Pursuits

Florida's protected areas vary from popular beaches to much wilder areas like the Everglades. The provision of facilities varies too, but most parks have some kind of visitors' center, dispensing maps and other information.

Some also organize guided tours. Winter is the best time to explore, when the summer rains and mosquitos are over.

Over 110 areas are protected by the state, classified variously as State Parks and State Preserves. They all charge admission and usually open from 8am to sunset daily. The Department of Environmental Protection (DEP) has a free guide, *Florida State Parks*, which lists them all plus their facilities, or visit www.floridastateparks.org

Information on the fewer federally run national parks is available from the **National Park Service** in Georgia. Many other parks are private, including sanctuaries run by the **Florida Audubon Society**; these are particularly good for bird life. The *Florida Trails* guide, issued by the national tourist board (see p371), has a complete list of private, state, and national parks. As a result of the Florida Rails-to-Trails Program, old train tracks have been turned into trails, suitable for hiking, biking, in-line skat- ing, and riding. Best are the 16-mile (26-km) Tallahassee–St. Marks Historic Railroad State Trail, south of Tallahassee, and the Gainesville–Hawthorne State Trail (see p227) in the Northeast. The DEP's Office of Greenways and Trails has information on these and many other trails.

Outdoor adventure tours are organized by a few companies. One is **Build a Field Trip**, which arranges trips all over the state.

Visitors on a boardwalk in the Everglades National Park

Biking

There is plenty of opportunity for both on-road and off-road biking in Florida, where the flatness of the landscape makes for easy cycling territory – though avid bikers may find it rather dull. The rolling countryside of the Panhandle is by far the most rewarding area to explore, while the Northeast has some good trails too, for example in Paynes Prairie *(see p227)*.

If you don't bring your own, bicycles can usually be rented on site or from a local source. For general biking information, visit the **Florida Trails and Greenways** website.

Canoeing in the Blackwater River State Park

Walking

Florida might not seem ideal walking country, but the variety of habitats makes up for the flat landscape. Most state parks have hiking trails, and there is a project currently underway to create the National Scenic Trail – starting at the Big Cypress National Preserve *(see p288)* in south Florida and ending near Pensacola. So far, 1,000 miles (1609 km) of the planned 1,292-mile (2,079-km) route have been completed.

The **Florida Trail Association** is the best place to get information on hiking trails.

Canoeing

There is ample opportunity for canoeing in Florida; the Florida Canoe Trail System is made up of 36 routes along creeks and rivers totaling 950 miles (1,520 km). A number of parks are known for their canoe runs, the most famous being the exhilarating, 99-mile (160-km) Wilderness Waterway in the Everglades National Park *(see pp290–95)*. Some of the best rivers, such as the Blackwater River *(see p238)*, can be found in the North, while the Hillsborough River on the Gulf Coast is also

Enjoying the countryside near Ocala on horseback

popular *(see p267)*. Always check the water level before setting off, as both high and low levels can be dangerous.

Horseback Riding

The Ocala National Forest in the Northeast *(see p225)* has over 100 miles (160 km) of trails suited to horseback riding. There are 15 state parks with riding trails, including Myakka River *(see p278)*, Jonathan Dickinson *(see p121)*, and the Florida Caverns *(see p243)*; about half the parks have facilities for overnight stays.

Information is available from the *Florida Horse Trail Directory*, issued by the **Department of Agriculture and Consumer Services**, or from the DEP.

DIRECTORY

Sources of Information

Department of Environmental Protection (DEP)
3900 Commonwealth Blvd, Tallahassee, FL 32399. **Tel** (850) 245-2052.

Florida Sports Foundation
Tallahassee, FL 32308.
Tel (850) 488-8347.
w flasports.com

Tennis

Nick Bollettieri Tennis Academy
5500 34th St West, Bradenton, FL 34210.
Tel (800) 872-6425.
w imgacademies.com

United States Tennis Association (Florida Section)
Deuce Court, Daytona Beach, FL 32124.
Tel (386) 671-8949.
w florida.usta.com

Diving and Snorkeling

Keys Association of Dive Operators (KADO)
3128 N Roosevelt Blvd, Key West, FL 33040.
w divekeys.com

Fishing

Florida Fish and Wildlife Conservation Commission
Tel (850) 488-4676.

Tel (888) 347-4356. (fishing licenses).
Tel (888) 486-8356 (hunting licenses).
w myfwc.com

Backcountry Pursuits

Florida Audubon Society
Tel (407) 539-5700.
Tel (305) 371-6399.
w fl.audubon.org

Build a Field Trip
1925 NE 45th St, Suite 132, Fort Lauderdale, FL 33308.
Tel (954) 772-7800.

National Park Service (Southeast)
100 Alabama St SW, Atlanta, GA 30303.
Tel (404) 507-5600.

Biking

Florida Trails and Greenways
w visitflorida.com/trails

Walking

Florida Trail Association
PO Box 13708, Gainesville, FL 32604.
Tel (352) 378-8823 or (800) 343-1882.

Horseback Riding

Department of Agriculture and Consumer Services
Tel (850) 487-3867.
w doacs.state.fl.us

WEDDINGS IN FLORIDA

Apart from its fame as an immensely popular vacation spot, Florida is now widely recognized as one of the most sought-after wedding and honeymoon destinations. The state's picture-perfect weather is ideal for wedding ceremonies that range from inexpensive backyard affairs to theme park extravaganzas that cost thousands of dollars. Themed weddings are extremely popular and organizers can create anything the bride and groom desires, even tying the knot near Cinderella's castle. Florida is also famous for its unusual weddings. Couples can exchange vows while golfing, fishing, on the beach, or in a hot-air balloon. Many local planners offer ceremonies to fulfill every fantasy, and honeymoon packages to suit all budgets.

Romantic ceremony at the beach

Wedding Packages

Most resorts and hotels in Florida offer a wide range of wedding and vacation combination packages to those getting married in the state.

The **Grand Bohemian Hotel** in Orlando offers a Bohemian-themed wedding, with the ceremony conducted at their rooftop garden. Prices, including a one-night stay in the Art Deco-inspired hotel, range from $1,600 to more than $3,000. **The Inn on Fifth** in Naples is housed in a renovated 1930s bank, and retains most of the original architecture and decor, including crystal chandeliers, stairs lined with burgundy carpeting, and wrought-iron railings. The hotel's rooftop pool area, complete with water-falls, also makes a scenic setting for a wedding. The legendary **Biltmore Hotel** in Coral Gables offers a variety of stunning locations to exchange vows,

from a lovely rose-strewn pool gazebo to the spacious ballroom, with packages starting at $3000.

Key West sunsets are absolutely gorgeous, and getting married in front of one can make the ceremony even more romantic. The **Westin Key West Resort & Marina** and its sister resort, **Westin Sunset Key Guest Cottages**, allow you to do just that. Tie the knot on the Hilton Pier with the setting sun in the background, or on the beach at Sunset Key, which is a separate island, a three-minute boat ride away from the Hilton. For the ultimate tropical wedding, **Little Palm Island Resort & Spa**, just off Little Torch Key, offers an unmatched island ambience. Packages start at $1500, barring accommodation, but come with a guarantee that yours will be the only wedding held on the island that day.

Theme Parks

Call it romantic, child-like, or corny, a **Walt Disney World®️ Resort** wedding is always special. More than 2,000 couples take the plunge every year, and the wedding packages start at around $3,000, while custom arrangements begin at about $7,500 and can cost upwards of $20,000 for large gatherings. You could opt for a fairytale wedding at Magic Kingdom®️ where the bride arrives in Cinderella's glass coach, a safari-themed affair in Animal Kingdom®️, star in your own movie at Disney's Hollywood Studios®️, or marvel at dazzling shows in a country pavilion of your choice at Epcot®️. There are lots of other options too – check their official website for details.

If giraffes and gazelles are your thing, **Busch Gardens** will host your ceremony in one of its exotic habitats while providing unique tailor-made live entertainment.

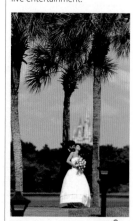

Bride and groom at Walt Disney World®️

Outdoor Extravaganzas

Located close to downtown Orlando, **Harry P. Leu Gardens** *(see p192)* is a lush 50 acres (20 ha) of horticultural splendor. It offers several garden settings for weddings amid masses of roses and camellias. The Rose Garden, the Floral Clock, and the Butterfly Garden here are very popular wedding venues.

Historic Bok Sanctuary *(see p197)* in Lake Wales is one of the highest points in Florida, and is a National Historic Landmark. Exchange marriage vows in a romantic setting of palm trees, flowering plants, and a 57-bell carillon.

The Unusual

Couples who wish to have a truly unique wedding have a range of options. **Orlando Balloon Rides** offers hot-air balloon weddings, including transport to the flight site, a ground-based ceremony, an hour long balloon flight for two, and a champagne toast. The **Medieval Times Dinner & Tournament** allows you to wed against a backdrop of 11th-century England, while

Orange Blossom Balloons, which offers hot-air balloon weddings

biker couples can rev it up at **Orlando Harley-Davidson®**. The bride and groom ride on Harleys, followed by a cavalcade of bikes. At **Daytona International Speedway** the ceremony is performed in the winner's circle and includes a victory lap. Highfliers will love the **Fantasy of Flight**, where the wedding ceremony is held in an aircraftladen hangar. **Brevard Zoo** offers its Serengeti Pavilion, Flamingo Pond, and Australian Aviary for weddings and receptions.

Wedding Details

There are entire books filled with lists of wedding planners, caterers, and photographers. The free publications, **Perfect Wedding Guide** and **The Knot**, are great starting points. Order invitations from print stores and office supply shops. Flowers can be bought from budget dealers or boutique florists. Haute couture shops and stores in high-end shopping malls supply wedding gowns. Wedding planners can take care of all these details.

Legalities

Marriage licenses are available at any courthouse in the state. The **State of Florida Official Marriage Guide** lists all their addresses. The bride and groom need to present proper identification such as a driver's license or a passport. The license will be issued at the time of application and is effective immediately; it must be used within 60 days. No blood test or waiting period is needed for out-of-state residents. If previously married, the date of divorce or date of spouse's death is required.

DIRECTORY

Wedding Packages

Biltmore Hotel
1200 Anastasia Ave, Coral Gables.
Tel (305) 445-1926.

Grand Bohemian Hotel
325 S Orange Ave, Orlando.
Tel (407) 313-9000.

Little Palm Island Resort & Spa
28500 Overseas Hwy, Little Torch Key.
Tel (800) 343-8567.

The Inn on Fifth
699 5th Avenue S, Naples.
Tel (888) 403-8778.

Westin Key West Resort & Marina
245 Front St, Key West.
Tel (305) 294-4000.
w starwoodhotels.com

Westin Sunset Key Guest Cottages
245 Front St, Key West.
Tel (305) 294-5300.
w westinsunset keycottages.com

Theme Parks

Busch Gardens
w buschgardens groupevents.com/fla

Walt Disney World® Resort
w disneyweddings. com

Outdoor Extravaganzas

Harry P. Leu Gardens
w leugardens.org

Historic Bok Sanctuary
w boksanctuary.org

The Unusual

Brevard Zoo
8225 N. Wickham Rd, Melbourne. **Tel** (321) 254-9453. w brevardzoo.org

Daytona International Speedway
1801 W International Speedway Blvd, Daytona Beach.**Tel** (386) 253-7223.
w daytona internationalspeedway. com

Fantasy of Flight
1400 Broadway Blvd SE, Polk City.
Tel (863) 984-3500.
w fantasyofflight.com

Medieval Times Dinner & Tournament
4510 W Irlo Bronson Hwy, Kissimmee.
Tel (407) 396-1518.
w medievaltimes.com

Orlando Balloon Rides
7769 W. Irlo Bronson Hwy, Kissimmee. **Tel** (407) 894-5040. w orlandoballoon rides.com

Orlando Harley-Davidson®
3770, 37th St, Orlando.
Tel (877) 740-3770.
w orlandoharley.com

Wedding Details

The Knot
w theknot.com

Perfect Wedding Guide
w perfectwedding guide.com

Legalities

State of Florida Official Marriage Guide
w stateofflorida.com

SURVIVAL GUIDE

PRACTICAL INFORMATION

With more than 40 million visitors a year, Florida is very well geared to catering to tourists' needs. It is the ultimate family vacation destination. A strong emphasis is placed on entertaining children, and the informal lifestyle and excellent facilities make traveling with youngsters a real pleasure. The only complaint a child is likely to have is if the lines at

Walt Disney World®, or the other theme parks, are too long (which is likely in peak season) or the sun too hot. Given its warm climate, for most visitors Florida is a winter destination. The peak season runs from December to April, when rates for flights and hotels are at their height, and the beaches and attractions are at their busiest.

Tourist information center, Florida

Visas and Passports

British citizens, members of EU countries, citizens of Australia and New Zealand do not need a visa provided they have a return ticket and their stay in the US does not exceed 90 days. However, they must register online with the Electronic System for Travel Authorization (ESTA) at least 72 hours before (and preferably well in advance of) departure (www.cbp.gov). Note that a fee is charged.

Canadians need only a valid passport, while other citizens must apply for a nonimmigrant visa from a US consulate.

Before travel, it is advisable to check the latest information at www.uscis.gov.

Customs Allowances

Customs allowances for visitors over 21 years of age are: 0.95 liter (1 quart) of alcohol, gifts worth up to $100, and 200 cigarettes, 50 cigars (not Cuban ones), or 4.4 pounds (2 kg) of tobacco. Prohibited goods include cheese, fresh fruit, meat products, and illegal drugs.

Tourist Information

Most large cities in Florida have a Convention and Visitors' Bureau (CVB), where you will find a huge array of brochures. The majority of hotels have free "WHERE" magazines that list entertainment, museums, shopping, and restaurants. Also, there is usually a brochure rack in the hotel lobby.

For information before you leave home, contact **Visit Florida** for a vacation pack.

Admission Charges

Museums, parks, and other attractions generally charge an admission fee. This can vary enormously, from $2 at a small museum to close to $100 for a day pass into Walt Disney World®'s Magic Kingdom®.

Children, card-carrying students, and senior citizens can often claim a discount, and anyone can use the coupons found in brochures available at tourist offices. These can significantly cut the price of

admission fees and also buy budget meals in local restaurants. Coupons from the information center on International Drive in Orlando *(see p194)* can save you hundreds of dollars.

Opening Times

State parks are usually open every day from sunrise to sunset, though attached visitor centers may close earlier. The theme parks extend their opening hours during summer months and holiday periods. Most sights close on major national holidays: typically New Year, Thanksgiving, and Christmas *(see p41)*.

Etiquette

Dress in Florida is casual, except in a few top restaurants *(see p326)*. On the beach itself it is illegal for women to go topless, except in a few places, such as Haulover Beach near Miami, and Playalinda Beach near Cape Canaveral. Drinking alcohol on beaches and in other public places is also illegal.

It is against the law to smoke in buses, trains, taxis, restaurants, and in most public buildings.

In restaurants unless a tip is already added to the bill (usually for parties of six or more people) you should tip 15–20 percent of the bill. Taxi drivers expect a similar tip. For hotel porters, $1 per bag is usual.

ISIC student discount card

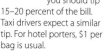

◀ One of the many lifeguard towers used to supervise swimmers and spot potential danger on Florida's beaches

Travelers with Special Needs

US federal law demands that all public buildings be accessible to people in wheelchairs, although some old buildings are exempt. This guide specifies whether or not a sight is accessible, but you are advised to call ahead for details.

A few rental companies have cars adapted for people with disabilities, and some buses have "kneeling" wheelchair access – watch for a sticker on the windshield or by the door. Amtrak and Greyhound offer reduced fares.

Mobility International gives general advice for travelers with disabilities. Visit Florida, the state-run tourism board, issues a useful services directory, and Walt Disney World® has its own special guide both online and in print form.

Traveling with Children

As a top family destination, Florida places the needs of children high on its list of priorities *(see p360)*. You can rent strollers or small wagons at the major theme parks; car rental firms must supply children's seats; and many restaurants offer special menus *(see p327)*. On planes, buses, and trains, children under 12 usually pay only half the standard fare, less if they are very young. For information on hotel facilities, *see page 313*.

The main concern is the sun. Just a few minutes' exposure to the midday sun can burn young skin; use sunblock and hats, and carry or buy water.

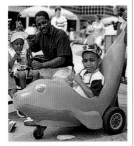

Boy enjoying a ride in a dolphin stroller, SeaWorld®

Senior Travelers

Florida is a Mecca for senior citizens, both to visit and to settle. Anyone over 65 (less in some instances) is eligible for all kinds of discounts – at attractions, hotels, restaurants, and on public transit. The **National Parks Service** offers lifetime entrance to its sites for a one-time, $10 fee.

The **American Association of Retired Persons** can help members plan their vacation and offers discounts on air fares, car rental, and rooms.

Traveling on a Budget

Traveling off peak is a good way to reduce costs. Check online booking and hotel websites for special deals. Hotels near theme parks are usually cheaper than those in the parks. Many restaurants offer cheap deals and happy hour specials before 6pm.

Electricity

You will need a voltage converter and an adapter to use the American 110–120 volts AC system; adapters for the two-prong plugs used in the US can be bought abroad or locally. Many hotels, however, have plugs that power both 110- and 220-volt electric shavers, and often supply wall-mounted hair dryers.

Responsible Tourism

As one of the country's great natural wonderlands, Florida offers prime ecotourism opportunities. The multitude of natural parks, from the Panhandle to the sprawling Everglades to the Florida Keys, is second to none. Guide-led river cruises through ancient Florida woodlands are available at Wakulla Springs State Park in the northwest, and you can rent a houseboat to tour along the unspoiled Suwannee River that flows across the state to the Gulf of Mexico. Local tour companies offer guided excursions through pristine nature preserves, some with overnight stays available,

Florida Green Lodging Program

and several former cattle ranches have been converted into resorts for horse trails and nature preserve touring. If you're not eager to camp out, the **Florida Green Lodging Program** provides a list of nearly 700 designated properties that conserve energy, reduce water usage, and protect air quality.

DIRECTORY

Consulates

Australia
1601 Massachusetts Ave.,
Washington, DC 20036-2273.
Tel (202) 797-3000.

Canada
200 S Biscayne Blvd, Suite 1600,
Miami, FL 33131.
Tel (305) 579-1600.

UK
1001 Brickell Bay Drive, Suite 2800, Miami, FL 33131.
Tel (305) 374-3500.
Suntrust Center, Suite 2110, 200 S Orange Ave, Orlando 32801.
Tel (407) 254-3300.

Tourist Information

Visit Florida
W visitflorida.com

Other numbers

American Association of Retired Persons
601 E St, NW, Washington, DC 20049.
Tel (202) 434-2277.
W aarp.org

Florida Green Lodging Program
W dep.state.fl.us/greenlodging/

Mobility International
132 E Broadway, Eugene, OR 97401.
Tel (541) 343-1284. W miusa.org

National Parks Service
W nps.gov

Personal Security and Health

As in any city, there are parts of Miami, Orlando, Jacksonville, and other Florida towns that are not tourist-friendly. You should be alert in urban areas, but anyone who takes precautions should enjoy a trouble-free trip. Police officers are friendly and helpful to tourists, and staff at hotel front desks can offer recommendations.

Police officers on patrol, Florida-style, in St. Augustine

Law Enforcement

Enforcement of the law is shared by three agencies: the city police forces, county sheriffs, and the Florida Highway Patrol, which deals with traffic accidents and offenses outside the cities. Major tourist centers are well policed, and Miami and Orlando also have Tourist Oriented Police (TOP) units.

Given Florida's eagerness to both attract and protect tourists, police officers are friendly and helpful to visitors.

What to be aware of

Most cities in Florida, like elsewhere in the world, have "no-go" areas that should be avoided. The staff at the local tourist office or in your hotel should be able to advise. Some downtown areas are first and foremost business districts, which are dead at night and often unsafe, but the past few years have seen an upsurge in locals living and dining downtown, and Fort Lauderdale, Jacksonville, and Orlando downtowns have blossomed. If in doubt, take a taxi rather than walk.

Burglaries within hotels are not unheard of. Leave your best jewellery at home and lock valuables in the safe in your room, or hand them in at the reception desk; few hotels will guarantee the security of items kept in your room.

If someone knocks on your door claiming to be hotel staff, you may want to check with reception before letting the person in.

Carry as little money as possible, keep your passport separate from your traveler's checks, and leave your duplicate room key with the desk clerk. If you are unlucky enough to be attacked, hand over your wallet immediately. Do not try to resist.

Staying safe in Miami

Although visitors are rarely victims, Miami has one of the highest crime rates in the US. Certain districts are to be avoided at all costs. These include Liberty City and Opa-Locka, both located between the airport and Downtown. Farther north, Little Haiti is an interesting area, but should be treated with caution (see p95). Avoid all deserted areas at night, including the transit terminals and Downtown. Lively night spots such as Coconut Grove and South Beach are the safest areas after dark, but avoid quiet back streets (such as south of 5th Street in South Beach).

Miami's Tourist Oriented Police provide extra cover at the airport, especially around car rental outlets.

In an emergency dial 911, or contact **Miami-Dade Police Information** if you don't need immediate help.

In an Emergency

In an emergency, the police, ambulance, and fire services can be reached by dialing 911. On expressways there are emergency call boxes roughly every half-mile (1 km). If you are robbed in the street, go directly to the closest police station – dial 911 should you need help in locating it.

If you need emergency cash, check if your credit card offers emergency cash access; ask someone to transfer funds from your bank at home to your hotel or a specified bank in Florida; or use the **Moneygram** service, a more tourist-friendly option offered by American Express.

Lost Property

Even though you have only a slim chance of retrieving stolen property, you should report all lost or stolen items to the police. Keep a copy of the police report if you are planning to make an insurance claim.

Most credit card companies have toll-free numbers for reporting a loss, as do **Thomas Cook** and **American Express** for lost cash cards. If you lose your passport, contact your embassy or consulate immediately (see p371).

Hospitals and Pharmacies

Larger cities in the state, and some smaller towns, have 24-hour walk-in medical and dental clinics, where minor

A county sheriff, in the regulation dark uniform, and his patrol car

Emergency ambulance

Fire engine

Orange County sheriff patrol car

casualties and ailments can be treated. For less serious complaints, many drugstores such as Walgreens and CVS (some of which stay open late or for 24 hours), have registered clinics.

If you have a serious accident or illness, you can rely on high-quality treatment at a hospital. Stories of medics making accident victims wait while they haggle over money are largely apocryphal; even so, take great care of your insurance documents. Nothing comes for free: a straightforward visit to the doctor can cost more than $50. Hospitals accept the majority of credit cards, as do most doctors and dentists. Those without insurance may need to pay in advance.

Anyone on prescribed medication should take a supply with them and ask their doctor to provide a copy of the prescription in case of loss or the need for more.

Natural Hazards

Hurricanes are infrequent but devastating (see pp30–31). If the worst should happen, follow the announcements on local television and radio. You can call the **National Hurricane Center** in Miami, which gives out information on impending hurricanes.

The climatic hazard to affect most visitors is the sun. Use sun screen or sun block, and try to wear a hat; make sure that your children are well protected, too. Drink plenty of fluids to prevent dehydration.

As for the animal world, alligators are a thrilling sight, but they can and do kill – so treat them with respect, and keep in mind that any large body of water probably has one or two. There are also several venomous snakes native to Florida, including the water moccasin, whose bite can be fatal. Do not touch unfamiliar vegetation, and steer clear of Spanish moss; it houses the red mite, which causes skin irritation. Wear insect repellent to fend off biting and stinging insects, particularly in areas close to fresh water, and from June to November.

Beaches are usually well supervised by lifeguards, but keep a close eye on young children. Riptides are a danger in some places.

Travel Insurance

Travel insurance coverage of a minimum of $1 million is highly recommended, mainly because of the high cost of medical care.

A lifeguard keeps watch over a beach in the Panhandle

Prices depend on the length of your trip, but make sure the policy covers accidental death, emergency medical care, trip cancellation, and baggage or document loss. Your insurance company or travel agent should be able to recommend a suitable policy, but it's worth shopping around for the optimum deal.

DIRECTORY

In an Emergency

All Emergencies
Tel 911 to alert police, fire, or medical services.

Miami-Dade Police Information
Tel (305) 595-6263.

Moneygram
Tel (800) 926-9400.

Lost Property

American Express
Tel (800) 528-4800 (cards).

Diners Club
Tel (800) 234-6377.

MasterCard
Tel (800) 826-2181.

Thomas Cook
Tel (888) 713-3424 (cash passports).

VISA
Tel (800) 336-8472.

Hospitals and Pharmacies

Baptist Hospital of Miami
8900 North Kendall Drive Miami, FL 33176.
Tel (786) 596-1960.
W baptisthealth.net

Dental Care
W dentists.com/florida_dentists.php

Florida Hospital
601 E Rollins St, Orlando, FL 32803.
Tel (407) 303-2800.
W floridahospital.com

Natural Hazards

National Hurricane Center
Tel (305) 229-4470 recorded message with hurricane details.

Banking and Currency

Foreign currency exchange is available at the main branches of any large city bank. In addition, most of the major airports have exchange desks. For the convenience of residents and visitors alike, automated cash machines (ATMs) throughout the state allow transactions 24 hours a day. Keep your credit cards ready because they can be used to pay for most things.

Banking

Banks are generally open from 9am to 3 or 4pm on weekdays, but some keep slightly longer hours. Banks include Regions Bank, **Bank of America**, Chase, **Fifth Third Bank**, SunTrust, and Wells Fargo, all of which have a number of branches throughout the state. The majority of banks have drive-through banking with live tellers and ATM machines.

Automatic teller machine (ATM)

ATMs

Most banks and supermarkets in Florida have ATMs (Automatic Teller Machines) in their lobbies or in an external wall. These machines enable you to withdraw US bills, usually in $20s, from your bank or credit card account at home, and tend to offer a better exchange rate than a bank or currency exchange.

Before leaving home, ask your credit card company or bank which American ATM systems or banks will accept your bank card, and check the cost of each transaction; often there is a conversion charge. Inform your bank that you will be traveling to avoid the inconvenience of delays or declined charges. Make sure that you know your PIN number.

Credit and Debit Cards

Credit cards are a part of everyday life in Florida. The most widely accepted credit cards are **VISA**, **American Express**, **MasterCard**, and Discover. Debit cards, which draw funds directly from your bank account, are the easiest way to get cash, with better exchange rates than banks or currency exchanges. Thomas Cook offers a prepaid currency card, thus protecting your bank information. It can be purchased online or in person before you leave.

Credit cards can be used to pay for everything from admission fees to hotel bills to emergency medical care. To make a payment, your card will be swiped and then a signature will be required.

It is standard practice for car rental companies (which generally do not accept debit cards) to take an imprint of your card as security; often the only alternative is to pay a hefty deposit in cash. Some hotels adopt the same practice: a "phantom" sum of $200–300 may be debited for one night in a hotel. This should be automatically restored to your credit when you check out, but it's a good idea to remind the clerk when you leave. Traveler's checks, while accepted at larger locations, have become an unrecognized curiosity at most stores or restaurants.

Currency Exchange

Currency exchanges can be found in a surprising number of places in Florida. In Orlando, **Currency Exchange International** has locations at the Mall at Millenia and Florida Mall. Branches can also be found at the Dolphin, Dadeland, and Aventura Malls in Miami, and two at the Sawgrass Mills Mall in Fort Lauderdale. **Interchange** has four locations at Orlando International Airport.

Disney offers currency exchange at Epcot® and Magic Kingdom® Guest Services, and major hotels on Disney property will exchange currency in limited amounts. This is also true for the main hotels at other theme parks.

Banks, though not all, exchange money, and you usually have to make arrangements in advance. Changing money at a bank is usually a cheap option, but you might feel it is worth paying more for the convenience of changing money at your hotel or a currency exchange.

Currency

American dollar bills are all the same size and color, so check the number before paying. The $1 coin is still legal but is rarely seen in circulation.

Always carry cash for giving tips, and to pay public transportation and taxi fares.

Branch of the Fifth Third Bank

Coins

American coins (actual size shown) come in 1-dollar, 50-, 25-, 10-, 5-, and 1-cent pieces. Also in circulation are State quarters, which feature an historical scene on one side. Each coin has a popular name: 1-cent pieces are called pennies, 5-cent pieces are nickels, 10-cent pieces are dimes, and 25-cent pieces are quarters.

25-cent coin
(a quarter)

10-cent coin
(a dime)

5-cent coin
(a nickel)

1-cent coin
(a penny)

Bank Notes (Bills)

Units of currency in the United States are dollars and cents. There are 100 cents to a dollar. Notes come in $1, $5, $10, $20, $50, and $100 denominations and have slight variations in color. The $10, $20, and $50 bills with extra security features are now in circulation. Paper bills were first issued in 1862, when coins were in short supply and the Civil War needed financing.

1-dollar bill ($1)

5-dollar bill ($5)

10-dollar bill ($10)

20-dollar bill ($20)

50-dollar bill ($50)

100-dollar bill ($100)

DIRECTORY

Banking

Bank of America
Tel (800) 732-9194.
W bankofamerica.com

Fifth Third Bank
Tel (800) 972-3030. W 53.com

Credit and Debit cards

American Express
Tel (800) 528-4800.
W americanexpress.com

Mastercard/Cirrus
Tel (800) 627-8372.
W mastercard.us

Thomas Cook Cash Passport
W cashpassport.com

VISA
Tel (800) 847-2911 (information).

Currency Exchange

Currency Exchange International
Tel (305) 937-4999. W ceifx.com

Interchange
Orlando International Airport.
Tel (407) 825-4563.

Communications and Media

Communicating with people both within and outside Florida, whether by mail or telephone, rarely causes problems – though no one claims that the United States' postal system is the world's fastest (at least as far as domestic mail is concerned). Cell phones and Wi-Fi-connected computers have almost completely taken the place of public pay telephones, which can be found at airports if you do a careful search, but few other places. A prudent way to save money is to avoid making telephone calls from your hotel room, for which often exorbitant surcharges are usually imposed.

International and Local Telephone calls

Toll free numbers (which are prefixed by 800, 866, 888, or 877) are common in the US. Note, however, that they are not toll free if calling from outside the US, and be aware that some hotels may impose an access charge for these calls.

For those using a home phone service, long-distance domestic calls are at their lowest rate during evening and weekend hours. Phone services at hotels generally do not reflect that discount, and invariably will include an additional and exorbitant service charge.

Most telephone calls are possible without the aid of an operator (whose intervention raises the price of a normal call). Collect calls can be made only by the operator and so can be very expensive.

Cell phones have largely replaced public payphones

Cell Phones

Inexpensive no-contract cell phones, using prepaid minutes, can be found at supermarkets, convenience stores (such as **7-Eleven**), and big-box electronic and discount department stores including **Target**, **Walmart**, and Best Buy. The differences in American and European phone systems mean that removable SIM cards are not generally used in the US, and European phones may not work during your visit to Florida. It is worth checking this with your provider before you set off.

Public Telephones

Public telephones are extremely rare and have almost completely disappeared from the streets. However, they can sometimes be found at airports.

Most public telephones take coins – you'll need at least $8 worth of quarters to make an international call. There are also phonecard-operated telephones that take special prepaid debit cards, which involve dialing a toll-free number to gain access to your required number. Alternatively, you can use your credit card from both the coin- and phonecard-operated phones. To do this you must simply dial (800) CALLATT, key in your credit card number, and wait to be connected; you will be charged at normal rates.

Telephone directories are supplied at most public phones and give details of rates.

Internet and Wi-Fi

Many hotels in Florida offer guests wireless Internet access (Wi-Fi) in their rooms. Some hotels, usually the more expensive ones, charge by the day for in-room Internet access, but have free access in public areas; value-priced hotels, paradoxically, often include full wired or wireless access in the room rate. Coffee shops, restaurants, libraries, and some city parks offer free Wi-Fi hotspots (search the Internet for locations or look for a sign in the window). Combining free Internet access with a voice-over-IP service such as Skype is a great way to save money and stay in touch with home.

Useful Dialing Codes

- Direct-dial calls to another area code: dial **1** followed by the area code and the 7-digit number. Calls within Florida require dialling the full ten-digit number, even if you're calling across the street.
- International direct-dial calls: dial **011**, then the code of the country (Australia 61, New Zealand 64, UK 44), followed by the local area/city code (minus the first 0) and the number.
- International operator assistance: dial **01**.
- International directory inquiries: dial **00**.
- Local operator assistance: dial **0**.
- Local directory inquiries: dial **411**.
- Long-distance information: dial **1**, then the appropriate area code, followed by **555-1212**.
- An **800, 866, 888**, or **877** ("toll-free") prefix means the call will be free; **900** numbers are not.
- For the police, fire, or ambulance service, dial **911**.

Postal Services

Post office opening hours vary but are usually 9am to 5pm on weekdays, with some offices opening on Saturday mornings too. There are 24-hour Automated Postal Centers inside post office lobbies, which dispense stamps and postage for larger packages. Drugstores, supermarkets, and hotels often sell stamps, but stamps not bought from a post office can cost more.

Surface mail sent overseas from the US takes weeks, so you'd do better to send letters by air mail, which is much quicker.

All domestic mail goes first class and takes one to five days – longer if you forget to include the zip code. You can pay extra for Priority Mail, for a delivery in two to three days, or Express Mail, which offers next-day delivery in the US and within two to three days to many countries. Be sure to use the right mailbox. Mailboxes are painted blue; Express and Priority mailboxes are silver and blue and are clearly marked.

Many Americans use private courier services, such as **UPS** and **Federal Express**, for both domestic and international mail, or **DHL** for overseas packages; they can offer next-day delivery to most places.

Many shops can mail purchases home for you; mailing a parcel yourself involves the use of approved materials available from post offices.

A rank of newspaper-dispensing machines in Palm Beach

Newspapers and Magazines

Most large cities have their own daily newspaper. Among the most widely read are the *Miami Herald, Tampa Bay Times, Orlando Sentinel*, and *Tampa Tribune*. The *Miami Herald* also has a widely read Spanish-language edition, *El Nuevo Herald*. Free weekly newspapers are the best source for local events and entertainment listings; glossy city monthlies (*Orlando Magazine, Miami Monthly, Jacksonville Magazine*) give a look into the upscale local lifestyle and are great for restaurant recommendations.

You can usually pick up a national paper such as *USA Today* from street dispensers, but most of these are given over to local papers. For other national US dailies, such as the *New York Times*, and foreign newspapers, you will normally have to rely on bookstores, convenience stores, and good newsstands.

Television and Radio

Television in Florida, much like anywhere else in the US, tends to to be dominated by daytime talk shows and primetime cop shows. The cable channels offer more variety: ESPN is devoted to sports, CNN to news, for example. Hotel rooms usually have cable TV, but you may have to pay to see a movie *(see p311)*.

Most radio stations pump out pop and easy listening music, but if you hunt around (especially on the FM band) you can

Standard mailbox

often pick up entertaining local stations, including Spanish-language ones in south Florida.

More serious broadcasting is left to the likes of PBS-TV (Public Broadcasting System) and NPR (National Public Radio), which offer jazz and classical music, along with documentaries, talk shows, and dramas – including rebroadcasts of BBC series.

TRAVEL INFORMATION

Florida is the top holiday destination in the US, and is well served by flights from all over the world. The state's chief gateways are Miami, Orlando, and Tampa, and the growing number of charter flights is raising the profile of other airports. Flying is also worth considering if you plan to travel any distance within Florida. The hop between Miami and Key West, for example, takes 40 minutes, compared with four hours by car. However, when it comes to getting around the state, the car reigns supreme, with fast interstates, major highways, and quieter county roads to choose from. Trains and buses are an alternative if you plan your routes carefully.

Miami International Airport, bustling with travelers

Arriving by Air

All the major US carriers, including **Southwest**, **JetBlue**, **American Airlines**, **United Airlines**, and **Delta Air Lines** have hundreds of scheduled domestic services to Orlando and Miami. Many offer direct flights from abroad too, but this normally entails a stop at a US airport en route.

From the UK, **British Airways** and **Virgin Atlantic** have scheduled direct flights to Miami and Orlando; British Airways also has a service between London and Tampa. American Airlines runs daily flights to Miami from London's Gatwick and Heathrow airports. Delta Air Lines flies to Florida from Ireland via Atlanta, Georgia, or New York.

European carriers such as Air France, KLM, and Iberia also offer a range of flights, and Icelandair flies into Orlando from Manchester and Glasgow in the summer months. Qantas and several US airlines offer one- or two-stop flights from Australia and New Zealand.

Charter flights are less popular these days, but still offer direct and relatively inexpensive access to Florida. Most charter flights emanate from Canada, the Caribbean, and Latin America, but there are some from Europe, serving Fort Lauderdale and Orlando via Sanford from Gatwick, Manchester, and Prestwick in the UK.

Increased security measures means that any arrival into a US airport can be long and confusing. Plan time into your vacation for this.

Air Fares

The cheapest round-trip fares to Florida are generally economy on a scheduled flight (which must be booked in advance). The competition between travel agencies and between the numerous airlines serving Florida means that it is worth shopping around. Check online booking services for promotional fares. Some specialty operators offer good deals on charter flights.

Fares can be surprisingly cheap in the off season, and you'll often get a better deal if you are able to fly midweek. During vacation periods, seats

Airport	Information	Distance from City	Taxi Fare to City (Approxtaxi Fare)	Shuttle Bus Fare to City (Approx)
Miami	(305) 876-7000 miami-airport. com	Miami Beach 10 miles (16 km)	$32 to Miami Beach	$14–20 to Miami Beach
Orlando	(407) 825-2001 orlandoairports. net	Walt Disney World® 18 miles (28 km)	$55–60 to Walt Disney World®	$20 per person to Walt Disney World®, or $ 4 by Lynx bus
Sanford	(407) 585-4000 orlandosan fordairport.com	Walt Disney World® 40 miles (64 km)	$90–110 to Walt Disney World®	$20–50 to Walt Disney World®
Tampa	(813) 870-8700 tampaairport. com	Downtown 9 miles (14 km)	$15–25 to Downtown	$12–32 to Downtown
Fort Lauderdale	(954) 359-1200 broward.org/ airport	Fort Lauderdale 8 miles (13 km), Miami 30 miles (48 km)	$20 to Fort Lauderdale, $100 to Miam	$10 to Fort Lauderdale, $15 to Miami

are in big demand and air fares can rocket to more than double their normal rates, being highest during December.

Note that US airlines sometimes offer discounted seats on domestic flights if you buy an inbound ticket from them.

Domestic Flights

Small and medium-sized airlines fly within the state and are a quick way to get additional time in the Florida sun. Several airlines fly between Orlando and the Panhandle; Spirit flies from Fort Lauderdale to Tampa; Atlantic Airlines links Central Florida with both coasts, Key West to the south and Pensacola to the north. Larger airlines fly from Orlando or Miami to every major city in the US, but it may take one or two connections to complete the journey.

Florida Airports

Florida's top international airports are well equipped with information desks, banks, car rental desks, and other facilities. If you're collecting a rental car, you may be taken by bus to a pick-up point nearby. If you are heading into town, check out the shuttle buses (or "limos"), which offer a door-to-door service to and from the airport; they operate like shared taxis but are cheaper than regular cabs. Major hotels usually offer a courtesy bus service to their guests. Ask about this when you make your reservation.

Miami Airport

Miami International Airport is one of the busiest in the world, which can mean long lines at immigration. The walk between concourses and gates is often long too.

Tourist information desks are found outside all customs exits, and car rental counters, taxis, private limos, and shuttle buses are on the lower level concourse. Companies such as **SuperShuttle** run 24- hour

The People Mover monorail at Orlando International Airport

shuttle bus services to all the main districts of Miami. City buses in theory serve the airport, but these services should not be relied upon.

Orlando and Sanford Airports

Orlando International Airport, the country's 13th busiest airport, welcomes 40 million passengers a year and is continually expanding. It offers excellent overall customer convenience. Moving walkways and the automated monorail system (utilizing the same announcement voice as the Disney World monorail) make getting around the two terminals easy. Multilingual tourist information centers by the security checkpoints are open from 7am to 11pm.

Many hotels have their own courtesy buses, but there are also shuttle buses; the **Mears Transportation Group** serves most destinations in the area. A less expensive way to travel to International Drive or downtown Orlando is by Lynx bus *(see p387)*. Services leave from outside the "A Side" terminal every half hour. Both trips take about 50 minutes.

Serving just over one million passengers a year, the Orlando Sanford International Airport, 30 miles (48 km) north of downtown Orlando, is much quieter than the main Orlando airport and is a hub for charter flights. Taxi ranks and several car rental outlets are conveniently located right outside the terminal building.

Package Deals

The cheapest vacation deal to Florida is a package that throws in car rental and/or accommodation with the cost of the flight. Fly-drive deals offer a rental car "free" or at a vast discount, but be warned: there are heavy surcharges to pay *(see pp382–3)*.

Double deals are popular – combining, for example, a week in Orlando with a week at a Gulf Coast resort. Package deals to all the major theme parks are worth considering if you're spending the whole time there; information is available from travel agencies and theme park websites.

DIRECTORY

Airline Numbers

American Airlines
Tel (800) 433-7300.

British Airways
Tel (800) 247-9297.

Delta Air Lines
Tel (800) 221-1212.

JetBlue
Tel (800) 538-2583.

Southwest
Tel (800) 435-9792.

United Airlines
Tel (800) 864-8331.

Virgin Atlantic
Tel (800) 862-8621.

Shuttle Buses

Mears Transportation Group
Tel (407) 423-5566.

SuperShuttle
Tel (305) 871-2000.

Driving in Florida

Driving in Florida is a delight. Most highways are well-paved, and Floridians are generally courteous and considerate drivers. Gasoline is relatively inexpensive and car rental rates are the lowest in the United States *(see pp382–3)*.

You can get by without a car in Orlando *(see p139)*, but wherever you are life is much easier with one. Many rest areas on interstate highways are covered by 24-hour armed security patrols, and direction signs have been improved in Miami *(see p386)*.

The toll plaza on Florida's Turnpike at Boca Raton

What you Need

You must have a valid driver's license in order to drive a car in Florida. When renting a car, stated rates do not include accidental or liability insurance. Remember that when you rent a car, you are the liable party if there is an accident. Check with your credit card or auto insurance company as to their insurance coverage for when you use rental vehicles. The state of Florida requires that you carry a copy of the rental agreement in the car – store it safely out of sight.

While there are many state and federal regulations on the equipment requirements of cars, there are very few that pertain to occupants. Unlike some European countries, there is no requirement to carry warning triangles or safety flares in a car. Drivers and passengers can be fined for not wearing seatbelts, and at certain times of the year state-wide campaigns make it particularly expensive to not buckle up; fines of as much as $116 can be levied at checkpoints on major roads by the Florida Highway Patrol.

If you want to explore off-road trails on a motorbike, be aware that riders under 16 years are required to wear eye protection, over-the-ankle boots, and a safety helmet.

Roads and Tolls

Florida has an excellent road network. The fastest and smoothest routes are the interstate highways, referred to as I-10, I-75, and so on. These usually have at least six lanes with rest areas generally located about 45 minutes' traveling time apart. Major highways may be fast at the best of times, but slow to an interminable crawl near downtown areas such as Miami, Orlando, and Jacksonville, especially during rush hours before and after work.

Interstates form part of the expressway system of roads (sometimes called "freeways"), to which access is permitted only at specified junctions or exits. Among other expressways are turnpikes and toll roads. Chief among the latter are the BeachLine Expressway (between Orlando and the Space Coast) and the Florida Turnpike, which runs from I-75, northwest of Orlando, to Florida City south of Miami. The toll you have to pay is dependent, logically, on the distance covered; if you travel the entire 329 miles (530 km) of the Turnpike, for example, the trip will cost around $20. Tolls can be paid to a collector in a booth or, if you have the right change and don't need a receipt, dropped into a collecting bin, where the money is counted automatically. Certain sections of the Turnpike near Miami have been converted to an electronic collection system and cash is no

Highway Patrol insignia

Tips for Drivers

- Traffic travels on the right-hand side of the road.
- Seat belts are compulsory for both drivers and passengers, and children under three must sit in a child seat.
- You can turn right on a red light unless there are signs to the contrary, but you must come to a stop first.
- A flashing amber light at intersections means slow down, look for oncoming traffic, and then proceed with caution.
- Passing is allowed on both sides on any multilane road, including interstate highways.
- It is illegal to change lanes across a double yellow or double white solid line.
- If a school bus stops on a two-way road to drop off or pick up children, traffic traveling in both directions must stop. On a divided highway, only traffic traveling in the same direction need stop.
- Don't drink even one beer. Driving under the influence (DUI) is very serious; you can be fined hundreds of dollars, have your driver's license suspended, or even be imprisoned.

longer accepted. Tolls are collected via Sunpass transponders or from having your license plate photographed at each toll booth; your rental car agency can provide information on this.

Be warned that local drivers change lanes frequently on expressways. Stick to the right to stay out of trouble and take care when approaching exits, which can be on both sides of the highway; most accidents occur during left turns.

Other routes include the US highways, which are usually, but not always, multilaned. These are also slower than expressways and often less scenic, since they are lined with motels and gas stations. State Roads and County Roads are smaller and better for touring. Unpaved routes exist in some of Florida's more rural areas; note that some car rental companies may not permit you to drive on these.

Navigating

A recent, good road map is vital for touring Florida by car. The *Florida Transportation Map*, available free from most Convention and Visitor's Bureaus and Florida tourist offices abroad, is adequate for general purposes; it gives the location of rest areas on interstate highways and includes maps of the main cities. If you plan to spend any length of time in a city, however, you should try to pick up a local detailed map. The city maps in tourist offices are often inadequate for driving – in

Road Signs

Most road signs are clear and self-explanatory. If you are caught disregarding instructions you might be fined.

Generally, road numbers or names rather than destinations are marked, and different types of roads are indicated by signs of different shapes and colors. Directional signs are usually green. Traffic signals often have cameras.

| City parking restrictions | Mile marker in the Keys | Interstate Highway 4 | US Highway 1, heading south |

| Overhead signs at the junction of two routes | Speed limit (in mph) | Rest area, indicated off an interstate |

which case a good bookstore would be the best source. Check with your car rental company about the availability of GPS rental.

Navigating your way around Florida is comparatively easy. Major east–west routes have even numbers and north–south routes odd numbers. Signs on the roadside, including mile markers in the Keys *(see p287)*, tell you which road you are on; while the name hanging over intersections is not the road you are on but the one you are crossing. Junctions have two

numbers – when through routes follow the same course for a time.

Speed Limits

Speed limits in the US are set by individual states. The limits in Florida are as follows:
• 55–70 mph (90–105 km/h) on highways.
• 20–30 mph (32–48 km/h) in residential areas.
• 15–20 mph (24–32 km/h) near schools.

Speed limits can vary every few miles, so keep a close eye out for the signs. On an interstate you can be fined for driving slower than 40 mph (64 km/h). Speed limits are rigorously enforced by the Florida Highway Patrol, whose representatives issue tickets on the spot. A fine can set you back as much as $300.

Florida's "Move Over Act" requires highway and interstate road drivers to move over to the next lane or slow down to at least 20 miles below the posted speed limit when approaching stopped emergency vehicles.

A typical Florida road intersection, in Tallahassee

Mobile gas station, International Drive, Orlando

Gasoline

Unleaded gasoline is used by most modern cars and vans and comes in three grades – regular, super, and premium. Diesel is usually also available.

Gasoline is less expensive in the US than many other countries, but the price varies according to the location and service. Almost all gas stations are self-service; it is rare to find one that has an attendant to fill the tank. Gas prices are marked inclusive of tax per gallon – the US gallon, that is, which is 3.8 liters, about a liter less than an Imperial gallon. At most gas stations you can pay with cash (in advance) or credit card, and can pay by card at the pump without going inside the station.

Safety for Drivers

Take care wherever you are. Various measures have been introduced to safeguard foreign drivers. For example, the license plate code identifying rental cars was dropped and an orange sunburst sign guides drivers along the main routes to and from the airport. Here are a few tips to help you stay safe:

- If arriving in Florida by air at night, you could arrange to pick up your rental car the next morning in order to avoid driving in unfamiliar territory after dark.
- Avoid having handbags or other valuable items visible inside the car; pack them out of sight in the trunk.
- Keep car doors locked, especially in urban areas.
- Ignore any attempt by a pedestrian or motorist to stop you, e.g., by pointing out some alleged fault on your car or, less subtly, by ramming you from behind. Another ruse is to stand by a "broken-down" vehicle, signaling for help.
- If you need to refer to a map in a city, don't stop until you are in a well-lit and preferably busy area.
- Avoid sleeping in the car off the highway, although some rest areas on expressways have security patrols.
- Avoid taking short cuts in urban areas. Stick to the main highways if possible.
- Keep in mind that while Florida highways are in reasonable repair, they have been rated by the National Highway Traffic Safety Administration as the most dangerous thoroughfares in the country, particularly Interstate 95 (#1) and Interstate 4 (#3).

Highway sign in Miami

Breakdowns

If your car breaks down, pull off the road, turn on the emergency flashers, and wait for the police. On expressways you can make use of one of the Motorist Aid Call Boxes (see p372). It is worth considering renting a cell phone – offered at a small cost by most car rental firms – or buying one at a convenience or electronics store (see also p376).

If you have rented a car, you will find an emergency number on the rental agreement, so try that first; in the event of a serious breakdown, the rental agency will provide a new vehicle. The **American Automobile Association** (AAA) will assist its members. Or, call the Florida Highway Patrol (511 on a mobile phone) or the free Road Ranger service (*347).

Parking

Finding a parking space is rarely a problem at theme parks and other major tourist attractions, shopping malls, or in most downtown districts. Parking near city beaches is more difficult (see p386).

You'll find small and multi-level parking lots in cities, but usually you'll have to use parking meters. Feed the meter generously: the fee varies from 25c to $1 per hour. Overstay and you risk a fine or the possibility of your car being clamped or towed away. Be sure to read parking signs carefully. Restrictions may be posted on telephone poles, street lights, or roadside walls or curbs. Cars parked within 10 ft (3 m) of a fire hydrant will be towed away.

Car Rental

Car rental costs in Florida are already cheap by most standards, and you can save more by booking and paying before leaving home. Fly-drive deals can knock more than 50 percent off the cost, but don't be fooled by offers of "free" car rental. State tax and insurance will not be included in these offers.

If you wait until you arrive to organize your car rental, it is usually cheaper to rent a vehicle at the airport rather than from a downtown outlet.

All you need to rent a car is your driver's license, passport, and a credit card. If you present a debit card, you may be required to allow a large deposit to be charged. The minimum age for car rental is 21, but drivers under 25 may need to pay a surcharge.

Make sure your car rental agreement includes Collision Damage Waiver (CDW) – also known as Loss Damage Waiver (LDW) – or you'll be liable for any damage to the car, even if it was not your fault. Rental agreements include third-party insurance, but this is rarely adequate. It is advisable to buy additional or supplementary Liability Insurance, which should provide coverage of up to $1 million. These extras, plus taxes, can add $35–40 to each day's rental.

Most companies add a premium if you want to drop the car off in another city, and all charge a lot for gas: if you return the car with less fuel than it had initially, the difference can cost you as much as $9 per gallon. Gas stations near airports are notoriously expensive.

Motorcycle Rental

If cruising the streets and highways on a Harley-Davidson is your dream, you may want to visit **Harley-Davidson** or **Eagle Rider** (both in several cities). Charges exceed $100 for 24

hours plus a substantial deposit, and the minimum age is 21. You may get a discount for advance booking.

RV Rental

Recreational vehicles (RVs) or mobile homes are great for groups or families. It costs $500 and up to rent one for a week. RV rental outlets are surprisingly scarce. The largest in the United States is **Cruise America**, which also has agents in other countries.

Rental conditions are usually similar to those for car rental. Size and facilities vary greatly, but most RVs have every imaginable convenience.

Great Drives

Great natural beauty, stretches of pristine and ancient woodlands and coastline, and an almost completely flat terrain – the highest part of Florida is only 345 ft (105 m) above sea level – means that there are some incredibly beautiful places for driving.

One of the most scenic and exciting drives is from Miami to the Florida Keys, spanning 160 miles (257 km), changing from big city to rustic scrub woods, and crossing Seven Mile Bridge to the majestic turquoise waters surrounding the Keys. If you're of an adventurous nature, heading west from Fort Lauderdale across the Everglades offers a thrilling look at ancient Florida, and the drive around Apalachicola Bay on US 98 takes in unspoiled wildlife

and the sight of shrimp boats and oystermen plying their trade. The A1A coastal drive from Daytona to Jacksonville offers views of historical Spanish castles, unspoiled state parks, and a mostly unobstructed landscape of white sand beaches and the Atlantic Ocean.

DIRECTORY

Breakdowns

AAA General Breakdown Assistance
Tel (800) 222-4357.
NOTE: Rental companies provide 24-hour roadside assistance.

American Automobile Association (AAA)
1000 AAA Drive, Heathrow, FL 32746. **Tel** (800) 222-1134.
W aaasouth.com

Car Rental

Alamo
Tel (877) 222-9075.
W goalamo.com

Avis
Tel (800) 331-1212.
W avis.com

Budget
Tel (800) 527-0700.
W budget.com

Dollar
Tel (800) 800-4000.
W dollarcar.com

Enterprise
Tel (800) 261-7331 (US).

Hertz
Tel (800) 654-3131.
W hertz.com

National
Tel (877) 222-9058 (US).
W nationalcar.com

Thrifty
Tel (800) 847-4389.
W thrifty.com

Motorcycle Rental

Eagle Rider
Tel (888) 900-9901.

Harley-Davidson
Tel (407) 944-3700 (Orlando);
(239) 275-4647 (Fort Myers).

RV Rental

Cruise America
Tel (800) 671-8042.
W cruiseamerica.com

Channel Five Bridge, Florida Keys

Traveling Around Florida

Visitors to Florida who rely on public transportation will find their horizons rather restricted. The rail network is limited, leaving buses – which link most sizable towns – as the main form of long-distance land transportation. Places outside the main urban areas will often elude those without cars. Some local bus services are good, but you'll need time and flexibility to make use of these. Public transportation within cities is more useful. Here, the emphasis is on serving commuters rather than visitors, but the main tourist centers have some services that cater to sightseers.

Green Travel

As small towns are swallowed up by the ever-expanding mass of cities, it becomes increasingly harder to get from one end of Orlando or Miami to the other without a car. However, there are several green travel options available.

While public transportation isn't a high priority in Florida in general, some cities are aware of its ecological impact. In Fort Lauderdale's downtown area, **Sun Trolley** runs environmentally friendly bio-diesel vehicles that offer air-conditioned comfort, while Orlando's **Lynx** operates a number of bio-diesel buses on its routes. For theme park visitors, the Lynx system also offers other incentives to not travel by car as it is the best and cheapest way to get to Disney and Universal, and also eliminates parking fees. Buses leave from either downtown Orlando or the International Drive hotel district. The Jacksonville's Skyway system runs elevated tracks across the St. John's River and connects downtown hotels, restaurants, and the Convention Center with the free trolley service that runs along the riverside.

For those concerned about their carbon footprint from air travel or driving, carbon offsets can be bought through companies such as TerraPass, www.terrapass.com.

Arriving by Train

Amtrak, the national passenger rail company, serves Florida from the east coast. There are three daily services from New York City. This Silver Service takes about 25 hours (with sleepers and meals available) and runs via Washington D.C., down through Jacksonville and Orlando, terminating in Miami or Tampa. The Palmetto serves the same route but offers a business-class service.

If you want to travel by train but take your own car, there is Amtrak's Auto Train, which runs daily from Lorton in Virginia to Sanford, 30 miles north of Orlando, taking about 18 hours.

Exploring by Train

Amtrak trains serve only a limited number of towns and cities in Florida *(see the map on pages 16–17)*. Other than Tampa, the Gulf Coast is linked only by Amtrak buses, known as "Thruway" buses. These run from Winter Haven, near Orlando, to Fort Myers via St. Petersburg and Sarasota, with guaranteed connections with Amtrak rail services.

Rail fares do not compete well with those of buses, but trips are obviously more relaxing. When traveling overnight, you can choose between the ordinary (but reclining) seats of "coach class" and a cabin. Both options have surprisingly good meal services available on longer stretches.

Anyone planning to do more than a couple of trips by train might consider buying a rail pass, which gives unlimited travel on Amtrak's network during a set period of time. The pass must be bought before you arrive – either online with Amtrak or through a travel agent that deals with Amtrak.

Another train service is the south Florida regional **Tri-Rail**, which links 15 stations between Miami airport and West Palm Beach, including Fort Lauderdale and Boca Raton. Primarily for commuters, these trains can also be useful for tourists. One-way fares range from about $2.50 to $7, depending on the number of zones you pass through, with discounts for weekends and holidays. Transfers to Miami's Metrorail and Metromover services *(see p394)* are free. Transfers are also available on **SunRail** for Orlando's Lynx Bus service and Volusia County's Votran Bus service.

Spanish Revival-style Tri-Rail station in West Palm Beach

Long-distance Buses

Whether you are traveling from other parts of the country or within Florida, **Greyhound** buses offer the cheapest way to get around. Some services are "express," with few stops en route, while others serve a greater number of destinations.

A few routes have "flag stops," where a bus may stop to deposit or collect passengers in places without a bus station. Pay the driver direct, or, if you want to reserve in advance, visit the website or go to the nearest Greyhound agent – usually in a local store or post office.

Passes provide unlimited travel for set periods of time (from between four and sixty days), but are useful only if you have a very full itinerary. Overseas visitors should also note that passes are cheaper if bought from a Greyhound agent outside the United States. Timetables, information about the different types of ticket, and details of baggage limits are available on the Greyhound website.

Red Coach runs smaller, premium buses, with movies, Wi-Fi Internet, and reclining seats, from Miami to Orlando, Jacksonville, Tampa, Tallahassee, and Gainesville.

Taxis

Taxis are easily found at airports, transit terminals, and major hotels. Taxi stands are rare elsewhere, and since taxis aren't generally licensed to pick people up from the curb, it is best to order one by phone: numbers are listed in the *Yellow Pages*. Alternatively, ask someone at your hotel to call a taxi for you – the concierge or bellman will be happy to do this and will not expect a tip.

If you are traveling off the beaten track in a city, it will help to have your destination marked on a map. Don't trust that the driver will know the way. All taxi fares should be metered according to the distance traveled, unless stated as a fixed fare. Many cabs accept credit cards, but you should check in advance.

Horse and carriage, a pleasant way to go sightseeing in St. Augustine

Water Taxis

In several cities water taxis add a new dimension to urban travel. You'll find them in Jacksonville, Tampa, Fort Lauderdale, and the islands around Fort Myers. Routes are generally geared to tourists, and as a result they are fairly limited in scope – linking hotels, restaurants, and shops, for example. However, they are great for sightseeing and often offer special fares.

Some operate as regular shuttle services, as is the case across the St. Johns River in Jacksonville, while others, such as those in Tampa, can be summoned only by phone. Fares are usually $3–10, which you pay on board.

A yellow water taxi in Fort Lauderdale

Transportation for Tourists

Most popular tourist centers provide special transportation for visitors. This often comes in the form of old-fashioned trolley buses: Tallahassee has a replica streetcar with wooden seats and brass handrails. In Daytona Beach (from mid-January to September) and Fort Lauderdale, trolleys are a useful link between downtown and the beach, and Orlando has a trolley that runs along the International Drive hotel district.

A familiar sight in Key West is the Conch Train, which consists of open-sided cars towed by a butane-powered jeep disguised as an old locomotive. St. Augustine has a similar train, as well as horse-drawn carriages through its narrow streets.

DIRECTORY

Rail Information

Amtrak
Tel (800) 872-7245. W amtrak.com

SunRail
Tel (407) 487-4035. W sunrail.com

Tri-Rail
Tel (800) 874-7245. W tri-rail.com

Bus Information

Greyhound
Tel (800) 229-9424.
W greyhound.com

Jacksonville Transportation Authority
Tel (904) 630-3181.
W jtafla.com

Lynx
Tel (407) 841-2279.
W golynx.com

Metrobus Miami
Tel (305) 891-3131.
W miamidade.gov/transit

Red Coach
Tel (877) 733-0724.
W redcoachusa.com

Sun Trolley
Tel (954) 761-3543.
W suntrolley.com

Traveling Around Miami

Public transportation in Miami is run by **Miami-Dade County Transit**, which operates the buses, the Metrorail commuter train network, and Downtown's elevated Metromover. It is hard to make the most of Miami without a car unless you're happy to stay in South Beach. Taxis are reliable and widely available.

Arriving in Miami

For information on getting away from Miami airport, *see page 379*. If you arrive at the **Amtrak** station, or at one of the **Greyhound** terminals, there are no car rental outlets but plenty of taxis and stops for buses going to Downtown and Miami Beach.

Arriving in Miami by car is direct but not hassle-free. Interstate 95 (I-95), the main road from the north is one of the busiest – and most dangerous – highways in the country. It heads straight through Downtown before joining US 1. The Airport Expressway, or State Road 112, is a toll road that connects Miami International with I-95, and costs around $1.25. Avoid the very hectic Palmetto and Dolphin Expressways. Route A1A is a slower way in from the north that takes you directly into South Beach, and is a far more scenic route. From the west, US 41 runs through Little Havana to the coast, where it links up with the main north–south routes.

Metrorail, Metromover, and Metrobus

Metrorail, a 25-mile (40-km) rail line between the northern and southern suburbs of Miami, provides a useful link between Coral Gables or Coconut Grove, and the downtown area. Services run daily every 10 minutes or so from 6am until midnight, and cost $2 per ride. Purchase an Easy card or Easy ticket at any of the 22 Metrorail stations. This can be used throughout the Metro system, which does not accept cash. All Metrorail stations have elevators, escalators, and/or stairs. You can transfer free from Metrorail to the Tri-Rail line *(see p384)* in Hialeah, and also to the

The Metromover, looping around downtown Miami

Metromover system at Government Center and Brickell stations.

The free Metromover monorail has three loops, connecting the heart of Downtown with the Omni entertainment and Brickell financial districts on separate elevated lines, with 20 stations in total. The Inner Loop provides a quick way to see the downtown area *(see pp76–7)*. Cars operate from 5am to midnight daily, arriving every 90 seconds during rush hours and every 3 minutes during off-peak hours.

Metrobus runs throughout Miami-Dade County, from Miami Beach and Key Biscayne to West Miami-Dade, north to Broward County and south to Homestead, Florida City, and the Middle Keys. A single ride costs $2 and transfers are free. A 24-hour unlimited pass costs $5, while a seven-day pass is $26. There is a fee to transfer between bus and rail services.

Taxis

Taxis charge approximately $3 per mile; the trip from South Beach to Coconut Grove, for example, will cost around $35.

Don't try to hail a passing cab from the curb; it is best to order one by phone *(see p385)*. **Central Cab** and Yellow Taxi are both reliable.

Traveling By Car

Driving in Miami is not as intimidating as you might think. Biscayne Bay is a useful reference point, and you can't go far wrong if you stick to the main through streets. Navigation inside the Miami grid is relatively straightforward; streets run from east to west, while everything else runs north to south.

Parking can be a nightmare in South Beach. On weekends avoid it; at other times bring change for the meters, which operate from 9am to 9pm, and pay heed to the signs threatening to tow away your vehicle. Contact the **Miami Parking Authority** for directions to specific parking lots.

Bicycling

Miami is becoming increasingly bicycle friendly. The network of cycle lanes is expanding, making it safer for bikers to get around the city. With its seafront trail, South Beach is one of the best places to explore by bike. **Bike and Roll** rents bikes, provides maps, and offers daily tours across the city.

Traveling Around Orlando

If you are in Orlando for the theme parks, driving is pretty straightforward, and public transportation offered by the Lynx bus system will take you where you want to go. Getting around outside the prime tourist areas is a bit trickier, as Orlando is very spread out, so usually a car or taxi is needed if you want to explore. For the devoted walker or bicyclist, a connected system of hiking and biking trails is a pleasure.

A Lymmo bus, serving downtown Orlando

Arriving in Orlando

Taxis service Orlando International Airport and are the easiest way to debark. A taxi to Disney will cost around $50. The express **Lynx** bus leaves Orlando Airport from level one of the A Terminal, and is a bargain at $2–4, but can take an hour to arrive downtown. Most hotels offer free shuttle buses from the airport. Driving into Orlando takes you along Interstate 4, running east–west across the state from Daytona to Tampa, which is quick and convenient if you remember to avoid early morning and afternoon commuters, and late-night theme park devotees. The Florida 528 toll road (called the Beachline) runs directly from the airport to the Disney World gates, and costs around $1.75 – have coins ready.

Orlando's Lynx buses logo

Rail

Built in 1926, Orlando's picturesque main **Amtrak** station is minutes from downtown and has taxi stands just outside. Its waiting room is open 7:30am–8:15pm. A cab ride to International Drive costs around $35. The SunRail system runs from Sand Lake Road in south Orlando to Deltona in Volusia County. A one-way fare is $3–4.

Buses

You can survive in Orlando without a car thanks to the Lynx buses. While some residential areas have few or no bus routes, the main tourist areas of the airport, downtown Orlando, International Drive (including Universal Studios® and Sea-World®), and Walt Disney World® are quite well served. A one-way fare costs $2, while a single-day unlimited pass is $4.50, and a seven-day pass is $16. If you will need to use a different route to complete your journey, ask for a free transfer when you board the first bus. Have the exact fare, as drivers don't give change. The free Lymmo service (run by Lynx) travels within downtown Orlando and offers rides to and from the Amway Center sports arena, as well as through the dining and nightlife area.

Taxis

Taxis from **Mears Transportation Group** (Yellow Cab – not always yellow – City Cab, and Checker Cab) blanket the city and offer efficient service. A phone call is necessary to get a cab unless you're at one of the few taxi stands at some hotels and the airport.

Traveling by Car

There are close to two dozen rental car agencies at Orlando Airport, so cars are popular here. On-street parking is free outside of downtown Orlando, where meters and ticketed garages are generally the only places to park. Many downtown restaurants will validate parking. Avoiding the often-jammed Interstate 4 highway is recommended when traveling locally. While street level roads in Orlando are generally in good repair, the multitude of lakes means very few of them run in a straight line; ask your rental car agent for a map.

Bicycling and Walking

Orlando's old and unused railway tracks have undergone conversion to bicycling and walking trails, with plans for a 200-mile loop of trails around Central Florida. The connected South Lake and West Orange Trails run for 29 miles (47 km) from Clermont, just north of Disney, to Apopka, near Wekiva State Park (with 13 miles/21 km of trails), featuring paved walking and cycling paths. **West Orange Trail Bikes and Blades** rents bicycles for use on the trail hourly or by the day and will deliver bikes to your hotel. The delightful Cady Way Trail runs 4 miles (6 km) right through downtown Orlando, taking bikers, joggers, and skaters through some lovely areas. For more information visit the **Rails-to-Trails** website.

DIRECTORY

Amtrak
1400 Sligh Blvd, Orlando.
Tel (407) 843-7611.

Lynx
Tel (407) 841-5969.
W golynx.com

SunRail
Tel (407) 487-4035.
W sunrail.com

Mears Transportation Group
Tel (407) 422-2222.

Rails-to-Trails
W railstotrails.org

West Orange Trail Bikes and Blades
W orlandobikerental.com

General Index

Acknowledgments

Dorling Kindersley would like to thank the following people whose contributions and assistance have made the preparation of this book possible.

Main Contributors
Richard Cawthorne is a freelance travel writer who specializes in the United States.

David Dick is a postgraduate at University College London, specializing in US history.

Guy Mansell writes travel articles for British magazines and newspapers, including *The Sunday Telegraph*, as well as guidebooks.

Fred Mawer is a travel journalist who contributes regularly to the *Daily Telegraph* and the *Mail on Sunday*. He is also the author of half a dozen guidebooks and has contributed to various Eyewitness guides.

Emma Stanford has traveled extensively in Florida and has written several books and articles about the state. She has written guidebooks for Berlitz, the AAA, and Fodor's.

Phyllis Steinberg lives in Florida. She writes about food, travel, and lifestyle for various Florida and US magazines and newspapers.

Other Contributors and Consultants
Frances and Fred Brown, Monique Damiano, Todd Jay Jonas, Marlena Spieler, David Stone.

Additional Photography
Dave King, Ian O'Leary, Magnus Rew, Rough Guides/Angus Oborn, Tony Souter, Arvin Steinberg, Clive Streeter, James Stevenson, Stephen Whitehorn, Peter Wilson.

Additional Illustrations
Julian Baker, Joanna Cameron, Stephen Conlin, Gary Cross, Chris Forsey, Paul Guest, Stephen Gyapay, Ruth Lindsay, Maltings Partnership, Paul Weston.

Design and Editorial
Researcher Fred Brown
Managing Editor Vivien Crump
Managing Art Editor Jane Ewart
Deputy Editorial Director Douglas Amrine
Deputy Art Director Gillian Allan
Production David Proffit
Picture Research Monica Allende
Revisions Team Lesley Abravanel, Umesh Aggarwal, Shahnaaz Bakshi, Claire Baranowski, Vandana Bhagra, Hilary Bird, Louise Boulton, Sherry Collins, Cathy Day, Surya Deogun, Caroline Elliker, Niki Foreman, Emer FitzGerald, Fay Franklin, Jo Gardner, Jennifer Greenhill-Taylor, Donald Greig, Emily Green, Vinod Harish, Joseph Hayes, Leanne Hogbin, Laura Jones, Kim Kemp, Sumita Khatwani, Desiree Kirke, Maite Lantaron, Jude Ledger, Carly Madden, Hayley Maher, Nicola Malone, Alison McGill, Sam Merrell, Ella Milroy, Sonal Modha, Claire Naylor, George Nimmo, Mary Ormandy, Helen Partington, Sangita Patel, Susie Peachey, Rada Radojicic, Mani Ramaswamy, Lee Redmond, Lucy Richards, Rockit Design, Harvey de Roemer, Ellen Root, Michael Sasser, Shailesh Sharma, Jonathan Shultz, Azeem Siddiqui, Asavari Singh, Susana Smith, Michelle Snow, Arvin Steinberg, Phyllis Steinberg, Paul Steiner, Lia Sussman, Alka Thakur, Conrad Van Dyk, Deepika Verma, Ingrid Vienings, Ros Walford, Marian Virginia Warder, Michael Wise, Ed Wright, Sophie Wright.

Cartography
Malcolm Porter, David Swain, Holly Syer and Neil Wilson at EMS Ltd. (Digital Cartography Dept), East Grinstead, UK; Alok Pathak, Kunal Singh.
Map Co-ordinators Emily Green, David Pugh.

Proof Reader Stewart Wild

Indexer Hilary Bird

Special Assistance
Dorling Kindersley would like to thank all the regional and local tourist offices in Florida for their valuable help. Particular thanks also to: Rachel Bell, Busch Gardens; Alison Sanders, Cedar Key Area Chamber of Commerce; Marie Mayer, Collier County Historical Museum, Naples; Mr. and Mrs. Charlie Shubert, Coombs House Inn, Apalachicola; Nick Robbins, Crystal River State Archaeological Site; Emily Hickey, Dali Museum, St. Petersburg; Gary B. van Voorhuis, Daytona International Speedway; James Laray, Everglades National Park; Sandra Barghini, Flagler Museum, Palm Beach; Ed Lane, Florida Geological Survey, Florida Department of Environmental Protection, Tallahassee; Dr. James Miller, Archaeological Research, Florida Department of State, Tallahassee; Florida Keys National Marine Sanctuary; Jody Norman, Florida State Archives; Damian O'Grady and Tanya Nigro, Florida Tourism Corporation, London; Larry Paarlberg, Goodwood Plantation, Tallahassee; Dawn Hugh, Historical Museum of Southern Florida; Ellen Donovan, Historical Society of Palm Beach County; Melissa Tomasso, Kennedy Space Center; Valerie Rivers, Marjorie Kinnan Rawlings State Historic Site, Cross Creek; Carmen Smythe, Micanopy County Historian; Bob McNeil and Philip Pollack, Museum of Florida History, Tallahassee; Frank Lepore and Ed Rappaport, National Hurricane Center, Miami; Colonel Denis J. Kiely, National Museum of Naval Aviation, Pensacola; Richard Brosnaham and Tom Muir, Historic Pensacola Preservation Board; Ringling Museum of Art, Sarasota; Ardythe Bromley-Rousseau, Salvors Inc., Sebastian; Arvin Steinberg; Wit Tuttell, Universal Studios; Holly Blount, Vizcaya, Miami; Melinda Crowther, Margaret Melia and Joyce Taylor, Walt Disney Attractions, London.

Photography Permissions
Dorling Kindersley would like to thank the following for their assistance and kind permission to photograph at their establishments:
The Barnacle Historic Site; © 1996 FL Cypress Gardens, Inc.;

all rights reserved, reproduced by permission; © Disney Enterprises, Inc.; Dreher Park Zoo: The Zoo of the Palm Beaches; Fish and Wildlife Service, Department of the Interior; Florida Park Service; Harry P. Leu Gardens, Orlando, FL; Key West Art and Historical Society: Lighthouse Museum and East Martello Museum; Metro-Dade Culture Center, Historical Museum of Southern Florida; Monkey Jungle Inc., Miami, FL; National Park Service, Department of Interior; Pinellas County Park Department; National Society of the Colonial Dames of America in the State of Florida; Suncoast Seabird Sanctuary Inc., Indian Shores, FL; and all other museums, churches, hotels, restaurants, stores, galleries, and sights too numerous to thank individually.

Picture Credits

a-above; b-below/bottom; c-center; f-far; l-left; r-right; t-top.

Works of art have been reproduced with the permission of the following copyright holders:

Courtesy of General Services Administration, Public Building Services, Fine Arts Collection: Denman Fink, *Law Guides Florida's Progress* (1940) at US Federal Courthouse, Miami 76cl.

Dorling Kindersley would like to thank the following individuals, companies, and picture libraries for their kind permission to reproduce their photographs:

Aisa, Barcelona: 211bc; Museo de America 48cl; Vidler 117br, 130t; **Alamy Images**: America 351tr; Pat & Chuck Blackley 15br; Pat Canova 340tl; Ian Dagnall 280br, 382tl; Dylan Garcia Photography 273cr; Jeff Greenburg 123bl, 123br; NASA Photo 56-7; PF-(space1) 205tr; Peter Titmuss 370cla; ZUMA Press, Inc 36br, 317tl; **Allsport/Getty Images**: Brian Bahr 37cr; Steve Swope 37bc; **Appleton Museum of Art, Ocala**: *Jeune Bergere (Young Shepherdess)*, William Adolphe Bouguereau (1825–1905), French. Oil on canvas 226tl; **Archive Photos, New York**: 53ca, 56clb; Bert & Richard Morgan 122br; **Archivo de Indias, Seville**: 46cb; **Tony Arruza**: 27cb, 30clb, 42, 132tl, 144bl, 294c, 301br, 359tr; **Aunt Catfish Restaurant, Daytona Beach**: Gerald Sprankel 327tr; **Avalon Hotel, Miami**: 65tl; **Azul**: 331tr.

www.barefootweddings.net: 366cla; **Beach Bistro**: 343tr; Larry Benvenuti: 297cr; **Biblioteca Nacional, Madrid**: *Codice Osuna* 47cb; **Big Pink**: 329b; **The Biltmore Hotel**: 315tr; **British Museum**: 45tl, 49cr; **The Bridgeman Art Library, London**: *The Agony in the Garden (Christ in the Garden of Olives)*, 1889 by Gauguin, Paul (1848–1903), Norton Gallery, Palm Beach 131tc; **Busch Gardens Tampa Bay**. All Rights Reserved.: 112bl, 268b, 268clb, 269tl, 269br. All Rights Reserved, **Discovery Cove**: 187c, 187b. **Café de France**: 339bl; **Calamari**: 332bl; **Camera Press**: Steve Benbow 170bl; John Carter: 25bl; **Casa Maya Grill**: 333t; **Courtesy of Carnival Center for the Performing Arts**: 100bl; Robin Hill 101tl; **Courtesy of The Charleston Museum, Charleston, South Carolina**: Osceola portrait 50cla; **Robert Clayton**: 58–9, 382clb; **Clinton Hotel**: 314bl; **Pat Clyne**: 118tr; **Bruce Coleman, London**: Atlantide SDF 298tr; Erwin & Peggy Bauer 293bc; Raimund Cramm GDT 198cla; Jeff Foott Productions 29bl; © John Shaw 29cl; George McCarthy 29t;

Library of Congress, LC-USF33-30491-M3 55cr; **Columbia Restaurant**: 326br; **Corbis**: 47tl, 48–9c; Morton Beebe 328cla; Jonathan Blair 150t; Fotog/Tetra Images 114; **Cuban Club**: © Burget Brothers, photo courtesy of the Tampa Hillsborough County Public Library 264tr; **Culver Pictures, Inc., New York**: 52cla, 55tl. **Salvador Dali Museum, St. Petersburg**: 260tr; All works of art by Salvador Dali © Kingdom of Spain, Gala - Salvador Dali Foundation, DACS, London 2011, *Nature Morte Vivante* 260ca, *The Sick Child* 261cra, *Cadaques* 260clb, *Don Quixote y Sancho Panza* 261t, *Discovery* 260bc, *Daddy Longlegs of the Evening–Hope* (1940) 261crb; Salvador Dali by Marc Lacroix 261br; © **International Speedway Corporation, Daytona**: 222tr, 223cl, 223bl; Nascar 223crb; **DB Bistro Moderne**: 331br; **The Charles Deering Estate**: 96tr; © **Disney Inc.**: 146br, 147tl, 147br, 156cl, 156cl, 157b, 158b, 164–5, 166tr, 172–3 all, 174–75 all, 176br, 177tl, 366br; "The Twilight Zone™ is a registered trademark of CBS, Inc. and is pursuant to a license from CBS, Inc." 147br; © LEGO 173br; *La Nouba*™ by Cirque du Soleil® 177c; **Dreamstime.com**: Walter Arce 10cl; Benkrut 206tr; Ivan Cholakov 368-9; Songquan Deng 74; Fotoluminate 92; Gary718 308-9; Jorg Hackemann 62, 284; Judy Kennamer 262cl; Daniel Korzeniewski 13tl; Lunamarina 58-9; Luvemak 251b; Glenn Nagel 110-11; Offaxisproductions 11br; Ruth Peterkin 290tr; Craig Sims 14tr; Typhoonski 82; Edwin Verin 203tr; Brian Winshell 2-3; Michael Wood 22; **David Dye, University of Memphis**: South Florida Museum 44crb, 47cla.

Eden Roc Renaissance Resort And Spa: Jon Moe 310cla; **Escopazzo Restaurant**: 326cla; **ET Archive**: Natural History Museum 49ca. **Fairchild Tropical Garden**: 96b; **Fifth Third Bank**: 374br; © **Henry Morrison Flagler Museum, Palm Beach**: 53tl, 126tr, 128cl, 128bc, 129tr, 129cra, 129crb; Archives 128tr, 129bl; **Florida Department of Environmental Protection**: 371tr; **The Floridian**: 334tr; **Fontainebleau Hilton, Miami**: 73bl; **Sandra Friend**: 12bl, 15tr. **Pet Gallagher**: 24bl; **Genesis Space Photo Library**: NASA 204cla, 204tl; **Getty Images**: Steve Bly 383bl; CBS Photo Archive 57tc; John Coletti 14br; Sir John Lavery/The Bridgeman Art Library 8-9; David Rojas /FilmMagic 376c; Bruce Weaver/Stringer 202clb; **Giraudon, Paris**: Bridgeman Sir Francis Drake portrait, Olivier Isaac (1540–1596) 47cr; Laurus 43b; **Grand Bohemian**: 318bl; **The Granger Collection, New York**: 50clb, 50prb, 53cr; 54cl; **Gulfstream Park Racetrack**: 100cr; G.WIZ. **Hawk's Cay Resort**: 325bl; © **The Miami Herald**: © Al Diaz 37cl, 130bc; © Guzy 57cla; © Charlie Trainor 81cr; **Division Historical Resources, State Department, Tallahassee**: 45crb, 118cla; **Courtesy of Hibel Museum of Art, Palm Beach, FL**: *Brittany and Child*, oil, gesso, and gold leaf on silk, Edna Hibel 24½" x 20½" (1994) 125cl; **Historical Museum of Southern Florida, Miami**: 54clb, 55clb, 56c, 67tr, 289tc; **IGFA (International Game Fish Association)**: 140tl; **The Image Bank, London**: 25c, V. Chapman 54–5c; **Images Colour Library**: 21tl, 55cra, 61crb, 290br, 303br; **Index Stock Photography, Inc., New York**: 27br, 38cra, 40ca, 40bl, 41cra, 52t, 125br, 188c, 267tr, 358c; © Bill Bachmann 28cl; © James Blank 21br, 286cla; J. Christopher 31cr; © Henry Fichner 29cr; © Warren Flagler 57cra; Scott Kerrigan 299cr; Larry Lipsky 181bc, 295br; Wendell Metzen 36cla, 198cra, 292tr; Jim Schwabel 275tl,